UNIVERSITY OF GLASGOW
PRESS

THE UNIVERSITY OF GLASGOW
1451–1577

The mace of the University of Glasgow, of fifteenth-century workmanship, in silver gilt and enamel.

THE UNIVERSITY OF GLASGOW 1451-1577

by

John Durkan

and

James Kirk

UNIVERSITY OF GLASGOW
PRESS
1977

ISBN 0 85261 137 4

Printed in Great Britain by
T. & A. Constable Ltd., Edinburgh

Contents

Illustrations

Foreword

THE HISTORY of the University of Glasgow, spanning as it does more than five centuries of an ascendant western culture, abounds with notable advances in scholarship and research. Changes in the conduct of University business, the teaching of students and the structure of curricula were much rarer and are less well known. If one disregards those incremental revisions of ordinances and syllabuses reflecting the gradual emancipation of Society and the expansion of Knowledge, the University Charter has undergone only two basic revisions since its institution in 1451. These were brought about by the *Nova Erectio* of 1577 and the Universities (Scotland) Act of 1858.

Of the two revisions, the superseded *Nova Erectio* has undoubtedly received less attention in the official histories of the University by James Coutts and J. D. Mackie. Yet numerous records of the development of the University from its foundation up to the end of the sixteenth century are extant, and John Durkan and James Kirk were afforded an opportunity to undertake a thorough study of them when, in the spring of 1975, they were invited by the University Court to commemorate the fourth centenary of the *Nova Erectio* by preparing for publication a detailed work tracing the development of the University in the first century and a half of its existence.

Invited works of such complexity are normally accident-prone, so that Dr Durkan and Dr Kirk are all the more to be congratulated for completing a major piece of historical research of such high quality on time. There has been a division of labour with Dr Durkan describing the first foundation in the medieval period and its initial success followed by a threat of near collapse and Dr Kirk in a second section examining the impact of the Reformation and the *Nova Erectio* on the nature and organisation of the University. But continuity from one section to the other is maintained because both have been written in the light of modern knowledge of the scholastic and intellectual trends of fifteenth- and sixteenth-century Europe.

ALWYN WILLIAMS
Principal and Vice-Chancellor

September 1976

Acknowledgments

We would record our gratitude to the University Court for the honour of its invitation to prepare this book, and to Professor A. A. M. Duncan, whose idea it was to commemorate in this volume the fourth centenary of the *Nova Erectio*.

To those who read the typescript in whole or in part and gave us good counsel we are particularly indebted; here we would thank our colleagues in Glasgow, Professor Duncan, Professor A. L. Brown and Dr I. B. Cowan, and in St Andrews, Professor J. K. Cameron and Mr R. G. Cant.

To Mr M. S. Moss and Mrs Anne Ross in our University archives, to all archivists and librarians from whom we have received assistance, and to Wing Commander R. F. Pemberton who compiled the index, we acknowledge our debt.

The University Court has generously made available a sum from the Hunter Marshall Fund to help cover the cost of the illustrations.

JOHN DURKAN
Research Fellow in Scottish History
JAMES KIRK

The University   *Lecturer in Scottish History*
Glasgow   *September* 1976

Abbreviations

The following are the most commonly used abbreviations:

ACSB   *The Apostolic Camera and Scottish Benefices, 1418–88*, ed. A. I. Cameron (Oxford, 1934)

AFA   *Acta Facultatis Artium Universitatis Sanctiandree*, ed. A. I. Dunlop (SHS, and St Andrews University Publications, no. 56, Edinburgh, 1964)

ALHT   *Accounts of the Lord High Treasurer*, edd. T. Dickson and J. B. Paul (Edinburgh, 1877–1916)

APS   *Acts of the Parliaments of Scotland*, edd. T. Thomson and C. Innes, 12 vols. (Edinburgh, 1814–75)

Auctarium   *Auctarium Chartularii Universitatis Parisiensis*, vols. 1–2, edd. H. Denifle and E. Chatelain; vols. 3–5, edd. C. Samaran and E. van Moé; vol. 6, edd. A. L. Gabriel and G. C. Boyce (Paris, 1894–1964)

BUK   *The Booke of the Universall Kirk of Scotland: Acts and Proceedings of the General Assemblies of the Kirk of Scotland*, 3 vols. and appendix vol. (Maitland Club, Edinburgh, 1839–45).

CPL   *Calendar of Entries in the Papal Registers: Papal Letters*, edd. W. Bliss *et al.* (London, 1893–)

CSP Scot   *Calendar of State Papers relating to Scotland and Mary, Queen of Scots, 1547–1603*, edd. J. Bain *et al.*, 13 vols. (Edinburgh, 1898–1969)

CSSR   *Calendar of Scottish Supplications to Rome*, vol. 1 (edd. E. R. Lindsay and A. I. Cameron (SHS, Edinburgh, 1934); vol. 2, ed. A. I. Dunlop (1956); vol. 3, edd. I. B. Cowan and A. I. Dunlop (1970)

CUP   *Chartularium Universitatis Parisiensis*, edd. H. Denifle and E. Chatelain, 4 vols. (Paris, 1889–97)

ER	*Rotuli Scaccarii Regum Scotorum. The Exchequer Rolls of Scotland*, edd. J. Stuart *et al.* (Edinburgh, 1897–1908)
Evidence	*Evidence, oral and documentary, taken by the Commissioners appointed by King George IV, for visiting the Universities of Scotland*, 4 vols. (London, 1837).
GCA	Strathclyde Regional Archives incorporating Glasgow City Archives
Glas. Mun.	*Munimenta Alme Universitatis Glasguensis*, ed. C. Innes 4 vols. (Maitland Club, Glasgow, 1854)
Glas. Reg.	*Registrum Episcopatus Glasguensis*, ed. C. Innes, 2 vols. (Bannatyne and Maitland Clubs, Edinburgh and Glasgow, 1843)
GUA	Glasgow University Archives
GUL	Glasgow University Library
HMC	*Historical Manuscripts Commission*
IR	*Innes Review*
Liber Decani	Liber Decani Facultatis Artium (Annales Collegii Facultatis Artium in Universitate Glasguensi), GUA 26614, Clerk's Press no. 2
Liber Rectoris	Liber Rectoris Universitatis Glasguensis (Annales Universitatis Glasguensis), GUA 26613, Clerk's Press no. 1
NLS	National Library of Scotland
OPS	*Origines Parochiales Scotiae* (Bannatyne Club, Edinburgh, 1851-5)
PRO	Public Record Office
PSAS	*Proceedings of the Society of Antiquaries in Scotland*
Reg. Supp.	Registra Supplicationum, Vatican Archives
RMS	*Registrum Magni Sigilli Regum Scotorum: Register of the Great Seal of Scotland*, edd. J. M. Thomson *et al.*, vols. 1–7 (Edinburgh, 1882–1912)
RPC	*Register of the Privy Council of Scotland*, edd. J. H. Burton and D. Masson, 14 vols. (Edinburgh, 1877–98)

RSS   *Registrum Secreti Sigilli Regum Scotorum. Register of the Privy Seal of Scotland*, ed. M. Livingstone *et al.*, 7 vols. (Edinburgh, 1908–66)

SHR   *Scottish Historical Review*

SHS   Scottish History Society

SRO   Scottish Record Office

SRS   Scottish Record Society

STS   Scottish Text Society

TCD   Trinity College, Dublin.

Note: Unless specifically stated to be £ Sterling, all references are to £ Scots.

For convenience, all dates between 1 January and 25 March are given in modern form.

I
THE OLD FOUNDATION

1. Founder and Foundation

'In the year of our Lord 1451, Glasgow university was firmly
founded on a firm rock . . . so that the first products of the said
university might from the beginning pass on to posterity a doctrine
pure and sound . . . by acceptance of the privileges of our mother the
university of Bologna, freest of all universities. . . .'

Prologue: University and Arts Statutes

SUNNY Italy and the wind from the south that would still our native
northern blasts are evoked in one of Glasgow University's first foundation documents drawn up by an enthusiastic contemporary hand. The
south wind blew from Bologna, 'freest of universities', of whose
constitution a few years afterwards a Glasgow papal supplication was to
claim relative ignorance, a paradox requiring explanation.[1]

Throughout the fifteenth century individual Scots were to be found
in European universities, even as far off as Cracow.[2] There were other
student wanderers at Vienna,[3] Heidelberg[4] and Caen,[5] many of them
doubtless undistinguished; some reached high office like Alan Lennox,
'Ecossois', in 1479 Rector of Bourges,[6] and Andrew de Hawick, in 1424
Rector of Siena.[7] The outbreak of the Anglo-French Burgundian War
in 1415 and the end of the Great Schism in 1418 had changed the
pattern of university going, but the occasional Scot would still venture
to Oxford and Cambridge.[8] There was a steady trickle as always to
Paris and increasingly also to the newer institutions of Cologne (1388)
and Louvain (1426). Since the foundation of St Andrews, it is true,
some of these Continental wanderers had returned to teach there,
sometimes with bracing effect.[9] The reasons for multiplying small
foundations at home were, partly, Parliament's wish to stem this brain
and money drain; partly the new nationalism exemplified by our
spokesmen at General Councils of the Church[10]; and partly also the
urgent need in Church and State for a better educated clerical class.
The answer of the ruling powers of that time seemed to lie in inventing
new, rather than in buttressing old, institutions: but to found a new
university you first had to find your founding bishop and obtain your
papal bull.

William Turnbull, bishop of Glasgow, with a long scholastic career
behind him and a good slice of his life spent abroad, seemed the
obvious choice.[11] He was born on the borders of the diocese and the
kingdom, at remote Bedrule in Black Douglas country, probably about

1400: his mother may have been a Stewart.[12] He began his university studies at St Andrews in exciting days. It was a new university, dominated by Laurence of Lindores, inquisitor, whose inflexible orthodoxy exercised against the early Lollard heretics of Ayrshire and elsewhere he would have upheld, but against whose philosophical nominalism ('the fallacies of Aristotle and his misleading sophisms', as Robert Gardiner, his contemporary, had harangued[13]) he, with others at St Andrews, had reacted.[14] The new philosophical fashion of Turnbull's generation was Albertism, a new school of realist philosophers following Albertus Magnus, who up to 1400 had no following that could be called a school.[15] Looking for a firm basis for their thinking, they found his Aristotelianism had a strong neo-platonic colouring that was more acceptable than traditional realism, such as that of Aquinas, to these opponents of Wyclif (himself a philosophical realist).[16] He was a medieval polymath as *Ratis Raving* details at some length:

> Albert, the subtyll clerk and wyss
> That in his tyme seruit gret price.[17]

The Great Schism of the west was coming to an end as Turnbull finished his arts course and Christendom once more had one pope instead of several: Robert Harding, an English Franciscan, argued that Scotland should stay with the antipope, but Turnbull would have disagreed with his nominalist 'super-logic'.[18] Concord had replaced discord, but conciliar theory remained very much alive among Scots and, as a student of canon law (or decreets) in St Andrews, Turnbull became familiar with it. He had perhaps a too pragmatic, or too authoritarian, cast of mind to be an ardent conciliarist.

He was described as a licentiate in decreets in 1430,[19] somewhat prematurely, as next year he went on to Louvain and remained there for a time as a bachelor. Here again there was a prevailing Albertism (we have proof that it affected one Scot there) and one Louvain Albertist, Heimeric de Campo, combined a moderate papalism with a moderate conciliarism, suggestive of the later Nicholas of Cusa.[20] Such a position might have made Turnbull the most tactful envoy to send to the Council of Basle in 1435.[21] He was in Italy for at least five years, partly as student, but partly also a busy agent for the Scots king and a passionate adherent of Pope Eugenius. Finally he went to Pavia and took his doctorate in canon law there in 1439; he had the company of Thomas Kent, an Englishman, later to lecture there in the Collegio Castiglioni.[22] How much influence the Barzizzas, Lorenzo Valla, Francesco Filelfo, Maffeo Vegio and similar humanist luminaries of the Pavia of the period may have had on him is quite conjectural.[23] There was tyranny as well as lay initiative in the Italian cities: but Turnbull had at least known a wider world than the provincial circles of his old patrons, the Douglases.

His service in the court of James II as keeper of the privy seal and principal secretary brought him face to face daily with problems of authority. In the eyes of Popes Eugenius and Nicholas, the papacy's problems were not too dissimilar to those of kings forced to measure their powers against unreliable magnates or not too docile councils of state. The purely political elements in the arguments forged for a new theology of the papacy compelled them to encourage a royal absolutism that won temporary victories but would in due course come near to destroying the Roman see.[24]

Turnbull must have seemed to James II and Nicholas V, both of them cordially attached to him, well fitted to manage a new university. He had been the recipient of continuous patronage, as a university man of those days needed to be, since his first appointment as vicar of East Calder. He had been a protégé of Wardlaw, the bishop-founder of St Andrews, was knowledgeable about the problems of a learned society, was a pope's man and a king's man. James Bruce, his predecessor as bishop in Dunkeld and Glasgow, appeared to have divided loyalties as between Eugenius and the Livingstones, of whom both pope and king were distrustful. Thomas Livingstone, prominent Scots conciliarist, hoped to get him, as an ally of his family and as one of the Bruces of Clackmannan, to rally Glasgow to the cause of yet a fresh antipope, Felix V.[25] Episcopal policies would be reversed with Turnbull's coming to Glasgow.

It was a small town with, it is conjectured, fewer than two thousand inhabitants. Its markets at this time were mainly local and it is unlikely that, like Ayr, it had ships trading as far off as La Rochelle.[26] (Ayr itself could not compete with the North Sea ports and was thus unlike Perth to which James I had once contemplated transferring the university of St Andrews.) The noble cathedral of Glasgow was one of the more solemn in Scotland in spite of the calamitous fire of 1406.[27] To its square central tower a spire reminiscent a little of Salisbury's had recently been added and its episcopal keep had been strengthened by Bishop Cameron. Besides St Kentigern, 665 saints were piously believed to be buried there.[28] Its ecclesiastical population had swollen and had overspilled its ancient precinct between the Girth Cross and the Girth Burn running north of Rottenrow. In the High Street a thin ribbon of houses ran past the Dominican priory to the riverside trading nucleus clustered round the Fishergate and Walkergate. As yet there was no collegiate church. New collegiate churches with their team ministries springing up in lowland towns may be seen as threatening moves on the ecclesiastical chessboard. A particularly sumptuous one was being planned by the Black Douglases at Douglas itself,[29] a plan that like the contemporary Livingstone project at Falkirk, collapsed with the downfall of their families.[30] The Hamiltons proposed one at Hamilton, the Lennox family at Dumbarton. A new collegiate foundation at Glasgow, with a more all-embracing educational programme, may well have been part of Turnbull's original dream.

Glasgow had a learned nucleus in its 'canons in residence'—when they were in residence. There was a small library, mostly legal and theological, for their use, containing in 1433 the *De Vita Solitaria* of Petrarch, and, as far as its philosophical orientation went, already with a clear realist bias; there was nothing, for instance, of Lindores.[31] There were few feeder grammar schools in the diocese: Glasgow itself, Ayr, Irvine, Dumbarton, Paisley, Lanark, Peebles, Kelso.[32] There was at least one ambitious teacher in Kyle, John Kendal at Ayr, to be involved later in the university story. It may have been a Lollard trend or threat that urged the Ayr council in 1442 to give Kendal wide powers not only in the town but in all Ayrshire, powers that, even if they had existed in earlier generations, had been allowed to lapse.[33] He was to have the rectorship of all schools in the burgh 'of whatever faculty' (probably, that is, whether song or grammar), with power to receive 'scolage' fees from his pupils, to distrain them to pay if needed, punish wrongdoers, expel the rebellious and incorrigible, appoint in his absence a substitute, but, rather more surprisingly, to 'skail' or disperse the county schools which have not full grammar schools ('partial schools') and prosecute their rectors.[34] The attempt by Kendal, a 1438 St Andrews graduate,[35] to reassume such wide powers was bound to fail. His absence was real enough, mostly at the Roman court, as he tried to fortify by papal authority his acquisition of other benefices, none of which he felt himself able to hold.

The new bishop meant to use his considerable influence with pope and king to build up the city and see. He moved against whatever threat to the town's trade came from other Clyde ports, Rutherglen and Renfrew, in both of which Paisley abbey had some interest[36]; but not against Dumbarton, where George Lauder, bishop of Argyll, was forced to retreat from highland inhospitality at Lismore.[37] Turnbull had some understanding with the Lauders, because of ties of kinship.[38] Trade in Glasgow's farming hinterland in milk foods and butter was encouraged at least in Lent by obtaining papal exemption from an ancient ban.[39] There was the need to resist the growing prestige of St Andrews, in which a great new collegiate church had just been created by Bishop Kennedy. Glasgow claimed second place among Scots cathedrals and this claim was used in furthering an attempt by Turnbull, against a resistant laird of Kilmaurs, to annexe Glencairn to the canons' commons and so help 'the growth of Glasgow university'.[40] There was the need to proceed with repairs on the church begun by Bishop William Lauder and his successor Cameron and finish the upper chapter house: Turnbull's coat of arms is on its western external wall. To ensure final royal backing, it may not have taken great persuasion to induce James II to become a cathedral canon.[41] Kirk and king had identical interests, as did king and pope: unlike his immediate predecessors who were bishops 'by God's blessing', Turnbull was so by 'favour of God and the apostolic see'. He uses the older formula only when he is copying a Bishop Wardlaw charter.[42]

The chroniclers' attitude to Turnbull perhaps reflects the Lollard distrust of prelates felt in some areas of south-west Scotland. The so-called 'Auchinleck' chronicle in the Asloan Manuscript is discreet, but in its account of the fall of the Livingstones in 1449, it links Turnbull's first appearance, or at least his first mass, in Glasgow with their arrest on the Kelvin not far north of the town. The Livingstones were not great landlords but they were powers in the land who held great offices of state of which they were promptly stripped.[43] Since Turnbull inherited the Livingstone lodging in Stirling,[44] contemporaries would see justification for linking him with the royal move. The indirect accusation in the chronicle reflects concern in the south west with new schemes for Glasgow's aggrandisement.

The John Law chronicle goes further. Its author wrote as canon of St Andrews, but originally he was one of Kendal's successors at Ayr grammar school.[45] He openly accuses Turnbull of conspiring in the fall of the Black Douglases and, along with the powerful Crichton family, in the death of Earl William who had been his patron. Law inserts this record of the university's foundation into his recital of the Douglas collapse,[46] thereby suggesting that not only was the bishop the king's man but the king's creature.

'Auchinleck' records the university foundation as follows:

> That samyn ȝere the privilege of the universite of glasqw come to glasqw throw the instance of king James the secund and throw instigacioun of master willame turnbull that tyme bischop of glasqw and was proclamit at the croce of glasqw on the trinite sonday the xxti day of Iune. And on the morne thair was cryit ane gret indulgence gevin to glasqw at the request of thaim forsaid be pap nycholas as it war the ȝere of grace and with all indulgens that thai mycht haf in rome contenand iiii monethis begynnand the ix day of Iuly and durand to the x day of november.[47]

The word 'instigation' is usually found in the context of sinister events and the entry is preceded by the note of the murder of Patrick

Corntoun, a member of the new university.[48] Law's account is more summary.[49] The reason for postponement of the announcement of the indulgence (granted at Rome on 22 November 1450) and the foundation (dated 7 January 1451, the feast of St Kentigerna, said to be related to St Mungo) was probably that it would first be announced at the Whitsunday chapter to the canons.

Founding a university was an expensive business. Expenses had to be recouped not merely by minor concessions in indulgences. The original petition to the pope is missing, so that we cannot be sure that the king's part is not being overstressed at the expense of the 'instigation' of the bishop and the Estates.[50] The pope's part may be in the choice of Bologna as model: Nicholas V was, so to speak, a humanist by metier with personal associations with the see and university there. The ambiguous phrase styling the bishops 'Rectors called chancellors' reflects less the position in that 'freest of universities' than Turnbull's determination to be master in hostile territory. The bull authorises university officers but appoints no conservators; it authorises also the setting up of the various faculties (left open at the maximum) and includes the usual requirement that graduates were to be accepted without further examination elsewhere: an experience Turnbull did not personally, as we have seen, always have. James is said to want the university not only for his own subjects but for those of neighbouring lands, and Glasgow is represented as an important centre with mild air and plenty of the necessities of life. Orthodoxy and loyalty to Rome are, of course, emphasised.

The 'very great indulgences' which Law mentioned were listed in the other bull.[51] The king had represented to Nicholas that he, members of the royal household and other Scots (unlike the earl of Douglas, we may note) could not for reasons of state and other causes visit Rome in the previous jubilee year (1450). The pope appointed four confessors (Turnbull, Andrew de Durisdeer, Andrew Hunter, abbot of Melrose and Robert de Essy, theologian) or their deputies, with extraordinary powers, similar to those granted in Rome for the jubilee year, for penitents making contributions to the cathedral between the dates given above by the 'Auchinleck' chronicler: one-third portion would be for the cathedral's repair and use; one-third for Rome; and a third for other churches and holy places in Scotland. In January 1452, however, the dean, chanter and chancellor were to deliver the money to Simon Dalgleish, his official, for transmission to the bishop in Edinburgh.[52] A little more than a month later James killed the earl of Douglas and had to meet the expenses of a civil war.[53] Under strong guarantees of repayment 800 merks were lent from these jubilee funds to the royal exchequer on the security of some rents in Bute, Arran and Cowal, and the great customs of Ayr, Irvine and Dumbarton. This strongly royalist attitude of the bishop would not be appreciated by James's victims. The Exchequer Rolls show that some of this money was recovered, but Douglas and the highland rebels made impossible the return of the revenues from Arran. Ayr, in particular, probably resented these payments: the Rolls noted, 'And (Ayr) is not to be further burdened, as the lord king granted to the lord bishop of Glasgow the great customs of the burgh for ten years from the said 1 May (1452)'.[54] Thus funds that might have been used for a proper university endowment were lost at least in part.

The opening 'general chapter' of the university, of 37 members, met at an unstated date in 1451 in the Dominican chapter-house before these unsettling events, and while skies still seemed relatively untroubled.[55] This first gathering, apart from three monks of Kilwinning and the Augustinian prior of Blantyre, seems to have been made up almost exclusively of cathedral canons and vicars choral. It included John Mouswald, chaplain to lord Hamilton, who had accompanied the Douglas party to Rome in 1450,[56] and Gilbert Park, former secretary to Douglas of Leswalt.[57] Patrick Corntoun, chaplain to Isabella, duchess of Albany and countess of Lennox, himself a warrior and man of violence, was murdered by the porter of Dumbarton castle in August of that very year.[58] Some Maxwells, including the laird of Caerlaverock's son, followed in mid-August and next month, on 23 September, the first arts regents.

The first mention of a Rector in this first year was, as is argued below, on 29 July. He was David Cadzow, chanter of Glasgow, whose name and connections do not suggest an enemy of the Hamiltons;[59] he was elected or appointed, it would seem in his absence, in the first general congregation. The evidence hardly indicates that Turnbull was using his university as a sword of division rather than as an instrument of reconciliation. On 19 November, a congregation took place in the cathedral chapter-house 'with the consent of the masters of the faculties' (no students, it seems, were involved), to appoint deputies to hold counsel on matters of university concern, that is, among other things, to draw up statutes. This university committee included some canon lawyers—Cadzow himself, Patrick Leitch (chancellor of the diocese), John Arrous (archdeacon), David Nairn, Simon Dalgleish (official), Gilbert Park; some theologians—Alexander Geddes (monk of Melrose), Robert de Essy; some civil lawyers—William Lennox, William Elphinstone; some arts graduates—Andrew de Durisdeer (subdean), Alexander McAlon, William Semple and possibly, John Dundoff.[60] They were to meet meantime every Thursday in the Rector's house, presumably the chanter's manse to the north of the cathedral. This statutes committee

represented former alumni of several universities, St Andrews, Paris'
Rome, Louvain, Cologne and probably Orleans.[61] Durisdeer had been
in the household of Cardinal d'Estouteville who was responsible for
Paris university reforms.[62] Cadzow may have been at Bologna, though
the evidence is indirect.[63] He looks like a genuine choice by the university body. There is no reason indeed for doubting his genuine devotion
to the city and the see,[64] but, unlike Turnbull, he was a late convert to
the cause of Pope Eugenius.

The official incorporation of members of the arts faculty staff took
place on 23 September (before the fixing of the statutory opening of 19
October). A university bedellus or beadle, John Moffat, was the first of
all members to be incorporated: he perhaps stayed to study as he was
soon replaced by another beadle. A receiver or bursar was not mentioned at this stage: and the four keys of the university chest (*archa*)
were at this point in the hands of the four procurators of the 'nations' of
Clydesdale, Teviotdale, Albany and Rothesay. The Rector and his
assessors had drawn up some statutes and these were entered in a paper
book, from which they were in 1490 copied into the surviving parchment book.[65] How far these were based on Bologna usage, as specified
in the papal bull, is conjectural. Yet it would be an exaggeration to
assert that Scots were unacquainted with Bologna at this date.

Some Scots were apparently present at Bologna at the time of
Glasgow's foundation and immediately after; Neil Cormac, for
instance, clerk of Sodor diocese, claimed by May 1455 to have studied
there for a long time.[66] John Steel of Scotland, who described himself
as bachelor of decreets in 1451, was witness to an Englishman's doctorate
of theology at Bologna in 1453.[67] There is mention in 1457 and subsequently of George Kinninmonth, clerk of St Andrews, continual
commensal member of the household of Filippo Calandrini, Cardinal of
Bologna, half-brother of Pope Nicholas V, and a fine manuscript of
Cyprian written in a good humanistic hand shows that he was Calandrini's scribe in the previous year.[68] The particular section of the later
Glasgow petition which claims ignorance of conditions at Bologna
seems, therefore, to be special pleading: its purpose, however, is real
enough, as, it is hoped, will be evident.

If Turnbull was suspected of intimate involvement in the Livingstone
downfall, some reconciliation may have taken place, for by September
1451 Alexander Livingstone, rector of Ayr and Duns, had become a
university member and remained for some time in the arts faculty.[69]
John Ralston as rector of Ayr was received burgess there in June 1447
and Livingstone probably succeeded when Ralston was provided to the
see of Dunkeld in October. The family of Callendar in Ayr were
related to Livingstone, though they do not seem important in forming

the burgh's policies.[70] Yet in October 1451 there is a startling entry in the Ayr records:

> Quo die it is accordit betwix the Alderman the balȝeis and communite on the ta part And maister John Kendale notar on the toyer part that is to say the said maister John has giffin our the sang skule to the said Alderman balzeis and communite, the said maister John ramaynand with the grammer skule with al profetis in al thingis efter the tenour of our letter, exceppand gif thar haldis within us ane universite. . . .[71]

This is the first and last mention of a university project in the Ayr records. It could have been merely the creature of Kendal's ambitious dreams, of course, and perhaps was given its quietus, at least as far as he was concerned when at some uncertain date Turnbull settled a suit between him and another concerning offerings made at the chapel of St Mary of Grace (Ladykirk) in Kendal's own favour.[72] It could reflect temporary pique on the part of the Ayr civic powers at Glasgow's stealing a march on them, but, if the rector of Ayr had been persuaded to join Glasgow University, the council would not be encouraged to continue. It seems unlikely that the king was involved or that, in imitation of his father, he already considered transferring the university to Ayr out of the immediate area of Douglas hostility, as the Kennedies, the dominant family there, may well themselves have been coldly disposed to rival projects on Glasgow's part. The combined Donald Balloch and Douglas force that soon devastated the offshore islands and nearby Inverkip, where there was a royal chapel, destroyed any illusions there might have been about the security of this south-western coastline.

The names of the university nations show that Ayr and Galloway were included in Rothesay nation, which may signify something more than geographical proximity. It was intended to draw students, if possible, from all Scotland and from neighbouring Ireland which did not have a university in the pre-Reformation period.[73] After the 1452 raid on Turnbull's rents in the isles, it is interesting to see three rectors of parish churches in Islay incorporated in the university in 1453, possibly the rectors of Kildalton, Kilarrow and Kilchoman: the 1490 scribe has had difficulty with the names and dedications.[74] The presence of the rector of Dunoon is explicable since Turnbull shared the keepership of the castle with Lauder, bishop of Argyll.[75]

From the beginning students from Glasgow diocese naturally predominated. Some were at the grammar school and this seems to be the meaning of 'scolaris'; at this time the scholars may have shared quarters with the students.[76] In 1478 a house in Rottenrow is described as having formerly been called the Pedagogy, and it may be for a short time two pedagogies were in use, partly inhabited by grammar boys.[77] This house was acquired by a John Dalgleish, vicar choral, in 1410, who turned it over to the vicars to establish an obit.[78] With the consent of another Dalgleish (Simon, then presiding over the chapter as official), the vicars feued it to the archdeacon in February 1466.[79] This is the first building connected with the university of whose existence in its first years we can be fairly sure. In 1466 it needed reconstruction and repair to its frontage and its eastern wing; it had two courts, inner and outer, as the feu was witnessed in its fore court (*in parte anteriori*), though there is no indication that anything more than a yard existed in the inner area.

Of the High Street pedagogy in Turnbull's time we can be less sure. The site belonged to the provost of Bothwell collegiate church, Gavin Hamilton, brother of James, lord Hamilton. He seems to have been much out of the country.[80] Although his mother was a Livingstone, this did not prevent his son, Robert, from enrolling at Glasgow, though he completed his course at St Andrews.[81] The university could have hired the building, or part of it, from the Dominicans who held it by outright donation: in 1453 there is mention of internal decoration ('repair') of the school in the Blackfriars. Growing alienation of the Douglas faction from Turnbull seems to have induced Hamilton to threaten to cancel this 'plane gift'[82] in February 1455, when the see was vacant and he felt more able to insist on a reversion. There are other indications in the records of examinations being brought forward by the arts faculty because of considerable difficulties.[83] Nevertheless, the Blackfriars themselves were prepared to be hospitable to the university from the start: like the Ayr Blackfriars, who had a grammar school, they had a school for the liberal arts, a house *studium*, within their precincts.[84] Civil war and violence told against a settled life. Not only did Robert Hamilton leave Glasgow, but Alexander Livingstone, rector of Ayr, is last recorded in April 1454 and did not complete his mastership till 1468.[85] The second revolt of Hamiltons and Douglases was still in the making, but dearth and plague existed in these years.[86]

In September 1451 at least three theologians were incorporated: two monks, one a Cistercian of Melrose, and the other of Newbattle[87]; and the inquisitor, Robert de Essy, of whose orthodoxy there can hardly be doubt. All were at Cologne, though Essy and Hardgate were also at St Andrews.[88] Other religious incorporands may have come as theological students: three Benedictines from Kilwinning, though none from the Cluniac house of Paisley. Apart from the beadle, abbot Boyd heads the list of early university members and was perhaps a close associate of the founder: among those involved with James II in the Douglas murder was Sir Alexander Boyd, the kind of circumstance that must have given credit to rumours that Turnbull and the Boyds were enemies of the Douglases.[89] Another monk was an unidentified 'Reginaldus monachus' and another possibly John Middlemast, if he can be identified with the subprior of Melrose, formed bachelor in theology in 1453.[90] There is also a Trinitarian from Failford, possibly also a theologian.[91] When Turnbull was at Pavia, there were many law lecturers but only one theologian.[92] The Glasgow Blackfriars do not seem able to offer the services of a theologian as yet, and it is probable, as is argued below, that the principal was intended by Turnbull to be qualified in theology and combine its study with arts teaching. No recorded proceedings have descended to us of faculties of theology and law. What information we have about theology comes from the university statutes, foundation bull and Rector's book, or from external evidence.

The bull likewise authorised the teaching of law, and it was obviously one of the four faculties mentioned in the university statutes, for a few statutes in canon law survive and its schools are mentioned in passing. In this context the Bologna model, moreover, need not have been so very theoretical after all. Indeed, considerations will be offered below in support of the contention that not only did Turnbull envisage a law school as part of a long-term programme (about which, assuredly, there might be general agreement) but that he at once began to implement his intention in 1451 and that the initial lectures in the laws did in fact take place in that same year.

For the date when teaching began we have to rely on the following entry as printed in the Maitland Club edition of the university muniments:

> Memorandum that on 29 July, 1460, the venerable man, Master David Cadzow, chanter of the church of Glasgow, and Rector of the mother university, at nine o'clock in the morning in the chapterhouse of the Friars Preachers, read to all the clerics and masters therein congregated, the title or rubric of the third book, that is 'Of the life and good estate of clerics' and continued at the will of his hearers; and Master William de Levenax on the same day read the rubric of the civil law in the same chapter house.[93]

This passage is both crucial and misleading. It seems incredible, if Turnbull meant his university to be a school of law, that effective teaching should have been postponed till after his death. The date 1460 can certainly be confirmed in the manuscript. But it has to be remembered that the manuscript here is a transcript, certainly from earlier manuscripts now lost, yet made, not by a contemporary, but forty years after the earliest entries. It can be established from other external evidence that, in reading 1460, this later scribe has misread 'lx' for 'li'. These lectures, in fact, took place in the first year of the university's existence.

In the first place, as chapter seven shows, several canon lawyers were unquestionably among those incorporated in the late summer of 1451. Secondly, relatively few of the incorporated members for these opening months are traceable in the arts faculty. Thirdly, while Cadzow was Rector in 1460, he was likewise Rector in 1451. Fourthly, the place of meeting would support either 1451 or 1460 since the initial incorporations took place in the Blackfriars chapter-house.

Suspicion of the printed record here is deepened when we discover that those it shows as allegedly joining the university in 1460 had quite certainly graduated or left by then: one determined in 1451 itself, four in 1452.[94] On four the arts records are silent, and one was the university beadle.[95] On re-examining the manuscript, we find that these incorporations have been rearranged by the editor. Indeed, the entry following the memorandum above should read, not *Item eodem die*, but *Item eodem die xxiii*. They belong in fact to 23 September 1451, on which day several arts regents were also incorporated, the record of which almost immediately precedes in the manuscript.[96] The memorandum cited above has been interpolated, inserted as a memorandum because a little out of its place, but still belonging in fact to 1451. The editor of the Maitland Club edition, misled by the undoubted reading 1460, has transposed the whole section from its place among 1451 entries to 1460 without explanation.

There are other indications that help to confirm the earlier date. If we accept the identification proposed for the above William Lennox, there is no problem.[97] There were two men of this name, one the 'bachelor' of 1451, later William Lennox of Cally in the public records. The William Lennox in the above memorandum on law teaching is the elder, already a licentiate in laws and bachelor in decreets in 1435, and licensed in both laws by 1453.[98] To the biographical evidence adduced by Burns can be added the information that *Master* William Lennox (presumably the same man) was a witness to a David Cadzow deed in Glasgow in 1446.[99] He may have studied at Orleans, was at the Council of Basle, and was on the university's statutes committee.

The other indications regarding Cadzow are equally conclusive. In the memorandum he is described as Rector, which applies both in 1451 and 1460. He was also described as 'chanter', but in 1460 was no longer so, having resigned the post because of old age some years before. On his return to the university in 1459, he is styled simply Rector, but from 1460 'canon of Glasgow'. References to him as 'former chanter' after his resignation or after his death are quite understandable.[100] The memorandum, therefore, relates to a time when Cadzow was still chanter and so must precede 1460 in date, and 1451 is the date to which other converging lines of evidence point.[101]

In the face of this evidence, and other evidence to be cited below, it seems clear that Turnbull did have an ambitious project for a school of law at Glasgow, for which there is earlier evidence than for a school of arts of which our records are fortunately much fuller.

There are, nevertheless, problems even in the arts faculty as a few arts students existed before the date in 1451 when arts regents were incorporated, 23 September.[102] Three regents in arts were mentioned and there is no certainty that a single pedagogy, such as Turnbull on the basis of his St Andrews experience might have hoped for, existed from the beginning, though it did exist by 1457.[103]

In the Dean's book a distinction is drawn between the actual beginnings of teaching (*exordium*) and the formal inauguration (*formale inicium*) of the faculty. The masters of the faculty met in 1451 on an unstated date (perhaps left indefinite because it preceded the actual arrival of Pope Nicholas's bull) and elected as dean William Elphinstone, senior, a graduate in arts of St Andrews and in laws of Louvain,[104] the father of the founder of King's College, Aberdeen. Some statutes already existed in November, but it was not till 28 July 1452 that the statutes committee had a body of statutes ready, while a co-regent, William Arthurlie, took instruments.[105] The masters who confirmed these statutes are listed, doubtless all from the committee that drew them up and representing between them the universities of St Andrews, Louvain, Cologne and Paris.[106]

The general impression is of an ambitious and purposeful founder, starting off with something of a flourish, to found a little university on the firm basis of approval from a re-established papacy (*super firmam petram*) at a time when orthodoxy might seem to have had a second spring. It was stronger as yet in the 'higher' faculty of law than in arts, and perhaps he projected a college not too unlike St Salvator's in St Andrews, with a lesser theological bias. He had strong royal support, which never extended as far as endowment, and some of the king's friends were early members.[107] James also gave exemptions and privileges, though these in fact echo word for word what his father, James I, had already granted to St Andrews.[108] There is some evidence that Turnbull attempted to draw hostile factions together into some circle of reconciliation, though we can scarcely doubt the chroniclers that he wanted the downfall of Douglas as a threat to royal absolutism as well as firm episcopal control of the University by himself and his successors, 'Rectors called chancellors'. Yet some reconciling of conflicting interests is evident even when he was personally present at the 1452 Rectorial election and, 'with the consent of university members', Cadzow, a probable Hamilton partisan, was re-elected.[109] The cold blasts that Turnbull had hoped to turn to make way for more conciliatory breezes began to blow very vigorously once more. The king became more of a drain than a support as the university got under way; there was a hint of defiance if not of heresy in the hinterland; and to civil turmoil in 1455 was added food scarcity and eventually plague. Referring to his early death in September 1454, the Book of Pluscarden said of Turnbull that he did not last long, and remarked, with only a little exaggeration, that between them the sees of Dunkeld and Glasgow had ten bishops in as many years.[110] The 'labours and expenses' of its founder would not, however, be utterly lost, nor the 'liberties' of Bologna, as they were set out 'most evidently in the bull of erection and foundation', altogether forgotten.[111]

NOTES

1. *Glas. Mun.*, ii, 3–5, 20–22 (the latter is the earlier version); I. B. Cowan, 'The Vatican Archives', *Glasgow University Gazette*, no. 74, 2–4.
2. Joseph Muczkowski, *Statuta et Liber Promotionum Philosophorum Ordinis in Universitate Studiorum Jagellonica* (Cracow, 1849), 69–70.
3. *Essays on the Scottish Reformation*, ed. David McRoberts (Glasgow, 1962), 319.
4. Gustav Toepke, *Die Matrikel der Universität Heidelberg* (1884), i, 161.
5. *Archives Départmentales, Calvados, series D* (Caen, 1894), ii, 17.
6. Nicolas Catherinot, *Annales Académiques de Bourges* (n.p., 1684).
7. Walter Brandmuller, *Das Konzil von Pavia-Siena 1423-4:* ii, Quellen (Munster, 1974), 357, 359, 392, 394, 397–8.
8. See s.v. Fergus Makdouell in A. B. Emden, *A Biographical Register of the University of Cambridge to 1500* (Cambridge, 1963), 385; and s.v. Alexander Cornwell, Emden, *Biographical Register of the University of Oxford*, i, 491. Additional details of Scots students abroad in A. I. Dunlop, *Scots Abroad in the Fifteenth Century*, Historical Association Pamphlet no. 124 (London, 1942), 13–19.
9. R. Swanson, 'The University of St Andrews and the Great Schism' in *Journal of Ecclesiastical History* (Cambridge, 1975), xxvi, 223–245.
10. J. Durkan, 'Scots National Feeling at Constance and Siena', *IR*, xvii, 63–5.
11. For what follows see J. Durkan, *William Turnbull, bishop of Glasgow* (Glasgow, 1951), Ch. 1.
12. He appointed the first provost in the city, John Stewart: *Liber Collegii Nostre Domini*, ed. J. Robertson (Maitland Club, Glasgow, 1846), 176.
13. *Acta Facultatis Artium Universitatis Sanctiandree 1433-1588* ed. A. I. Dunlop (SHS and St Andrews University Publications no. 56) (Edinburgh, 1964), 39–41 and n. (Hereafter referred to as *AFA*.)
14. *AFA*, xxi, xxv. For Laurence of Lindores and his reputation, note the European scatter of his manuscripts as listed by C. H. Lohr, 'Medieval Latin Aristotle Commentaries' in *Traditio*, xxvii (1971), 313–15; for an additional one at Poznan, *Classica et Mediaevalia*, xxvii (1966), 374.

15. G. Meersseman, 'Les origines parisiennes de l'albertisme colonais', *Archives d'histoire doctrinale et littéraire du Moyen Age*, vii (1932).
16. F. Ehrle, *Der Sentenzenkommentar Peters von Candia* (Munster, 1925), 153; *Turnbull*, 34–5.
17. *Ratis Raving*, ed. R. Girvan (STS, Edinburgh, 1937), 48.
18. A contemporary called Harding, with whom Lindores seems privately to have sympathised, *perlogista*: J. H. Baxter, *Copiale Prioratus Sanctiandree*, 3.
19. *AFA*, 25.
20. Antony Black, 'Heimericus de Campo: The Council and History' in *Annuarium Historiae Conciliorum* (Amsterdam, 1970), ii, 78–86.
21. J. H. Burns, *Scottish Churchmen and the Council of Basle* (Glasgow, 1962), 38.
22. *Codice Diplomatico dell' Università di Pavia*, ed. R. Maiocchi (Pavia, 1915), ii, 393 (Società Pavese di Storia Patria). For Kent, see Emden, *Biog. Dict. Oxford*, ii, 1037.
23. On these, Pietro Vaccari, *Storia della Università di Pavia* (Pavia, 1948), 61ff. There cannot be much doubt that our William Turnbull is the doctoral candidate at Pavia, for his younger contemporary of the same name who acted as his chamberlain, was a nephew, as the chamberlain's brother, John of Bedrule, secured his lands in Stablegreen to his son George and so later to Sir Patrick Colquhoun of Glen: GUL, Murray MS 645, p. 425 (Dillon transcripts). These lands were in part Barony lands and they were held by him as canon of Glasgow *secundo* (vicar of Glasgow).
24. Antony Black, *Monarchy and Community: Political Ideas in the Later Conciliar Controversy, 1430–1450* (Cambridge, 1970), 80ff.
25. *Copiale*, 345–6; Ranald Nicholson, *Scotland: The Later Middle Ages* (Edinburgh History of Scotland, 2), (Edinburgh, 1974), 340, 343, 351.
26. SRO, Ayr Burgh Court Book, i, f. 62.
27. Reg. Supp. 433, f. 43v; John Durkan, 'The Great Fire at Glasgow Cathedral', *IR*, xxvi (1975), 89–92.
28. Reg. Supp. 433, 43v. Alexander P. Forbes, *Lives of St. Ninian and St. Kentigern* (Edinburgh, 1874), 118.
29. *Calendar of Papal Letters*, x, 84 ('miro et sumptuoso opere de nouo construi fecerit'), 86, 429.
30. A. I. Dunlop, *Life and Times of James Kennedy, Bishop of St Andrews* (Edinburgh, 1950), 405.
31. *Glas. Reg.*, ii, 336.
32. *Essays on the Scottish Reformation*, ed. McRoberts, 168. For Kelso, see *Liber S. Marie de Calchou* (Bannatyne Club, 1846), i, 142. Hamilton had a 'fundacioune to ye sang scole., SRO, GD 237/202/4 (Hamilton rentals).
33. SRO, Ayr Burgh Court Book, i, f. 151v. Copied into it in Kendal's hand, beside which an unfriendly hand writes, 'Quod falsum est'.
34. *CPL*, ix, 542, 548, 568; the vicarage of Terregles, the preceptory of Ladykirk, the ministry of Failford. Mr John Boyle, minister of Failford, was received burgess in 1455: Ayr Burgh Ct. Bk, i, f. 70.
35. *AFA*, 48 (entry unindexed). He is not recorded as determining in St Andrews and was perhaps an Englishman.
36. I. B. Cowan, *The Parishes of Medieval Scotland*, SRS (Edinburgh, 1967), 175. Renfrew was Paisley's neighbour.
37. *Asloan MS*, ed. W. A. Craigie (STS, Edinburgh, 1923-4), i, 222. The bishop, a Lowlander, was accompanied by John McArthur, a former Bologna student: *CSSR*, ii, 140.

38. David Lauder was (1461) cousin of John Turnbull of Bedrule: GUL, Murray MS, 645, p. 425.
39. *Glas. Reg.*, ii, 389.
40. *Ibid.*, ii, 377, 404.
41. *Ibid.*, ii, 375.
42. See below, Chapter 10.
43. *Asloan MS*, i, 235.
44. *Glas. Reg.*, ii, 374.
45. John Durkan, 'St Andrews in the John Law Chronicle', *IR*, xxv, 49.
46. Edinburgh University Library, MS Dc.7.63, f. 128v.
47. *Asloan MS*, i, 225.
48. *Ibid.*
49. 'Venerunt privilegia universitatis glasguensis et cum indulgentiis maximis concessis a papa Nicola ex requestu regis et Willelmi trumbyl eiusdem episcopi' entered after 'Sed paulo post secundis afflatibus' which refers to Douglas (f. 128v). Law's reference to the short-lived concord between James II and the earl echoes 'Auchinleck' verbally, 'De hac concordia tota scocia letata est' (f. 129).
50. *Glas. Reg.*, ii, 385–7; *Glas. Mun.*, i, 4, 22 (the latter the earlier version).
51. *Glas. Reg.*, ii, 380–5.
52. *Ibid.*, ii, 391.
53. Durkan, *Turnbull*, 48–9.
54. *ER*, v, 491.
55. *Glas. Mun.*, ii, 55.
56. He was unsuccessful in his attempt to become canon of Glasgow, Reg. Supp. 447, f. 290v.
57. Durkan, *Turnbull*, 49n.
58. *Asloan MS*, i, 225; *Stirlings of Craigbernard and Glorat*, ed. J. Bain (Edinburgh, 1883), 64 (witness in 1442 at Inchmurrin); *CPL*, x, 493, 547.
59. *RMS*, ii, 511; *Glas. Mun.*, i, 15.
60. For details, see below. Dundoff may be the John 'Dundas', bachelor of decreets in 1444: Reg. Supp., 398, f. 258.
61. See below, Chapter 3; also Durkan, *Turnbull*, chapter 7.
62. Durkan, *Turnbull*, 40–1.
63. *ACSB*, 115; when collated afresh to his precentorship, he was in Bologna.
64. At his stall in choir was a life of Sts Serf and Kentigern and he founded an altar to the former: *Glas. Reg.*, ii, 335, 364.
65. *Glas. Mun.*, ii, table of contents, vi.
66. Reg. Supp., 480, f. 124.
67. Reg. Supp., 448, f. 42v; *Archivum Franciscanum Historicum*, liiii (1960), 424.
68. Reg. Supp., 502, f. 102; Rome, Vatican Library, Vat. Lat. MS 200, f. 258, completed by him on 5 June. He determined at St Andrews in 1450/1 and stated in 1462 that he had been eleven years at the curia; *AFA*, 86; Reg. Supp., 582, f. 246.
69. *Glas. Mun.*, ii, 57, 179, 184.
70. SRO, Ayr Burgh Court Book, i, 48v, 72 (Robert of Callendar to pay for the rector).
71. *Ibid.*, i, f. 59.
72. Reg. Supp., 551, f. 227.
73. *Glas. Mun.*, i, 6.
74. *Ibid.*, ii, 61. Kildalton is given as St John 'Baptist' for 'Evangelist'; Kilarrow's dedication has been left blank, but it was St Maelrubha; Dominicus Donaldi's name left unfinished, but cf. *ACSB*, 146.

75. *Glas. Mun.*, ii, 60 (*Master* David Rede in *OPS*, ii, 63); *ER*, vi, 48.
76. *Glas. Mun.*, ii, 85.
77. *Glas. Reg.*, ii, 437–8.
78. *Liber Collegii Nostre Domine*, 237.
79. GUA 16375 (Blackhouse 76); a subsequent endorsement refers to the site as 'ye auld pedagog'.
80. He was at Paris in 1448 and presumably again in 1462 when once more in a university: Reg. Supp. 429, f. 35; 549, f. 199v. George Hamilton, *A History of the House of Hamilton* (Edinburgh, 1933), 636.
81. Durkan, *Turnbull*, 48.
82. *Glas. Mun.*, i, 14; ii, 182. It is not clear if 'in loco predicto' refers to 'in vico' or to 'in loco fratrum predicatorum' in the same paragraph.
83. *Ibid.*, ii, 183–4.
84. Durkan, *Turnbull*, 60; *CPL*, viii, 553.
85. *Glas. Mun.*, ii, 184, 209.
86. Nicholson, *Scotland: The Later Middle Ages*, 364, 367, 375. The chroniclers date the plague in 1455, and the university records confirm this: *Glas. Mun.*, ii, 188. But perhaps there was a wave of pestilence, at its worst in that year.
87. Durkan, *Turnbull*, 36.
88. H. Keussen, *Die Matrikel der Universität Köln*, i, 312; *AFA*, 50, 54, 94, 106.
89. *Glas. Mun.*, ii, 55; *Asloan MS*, i, 241.
90. *Glas. Mun.*, ii, 58, 60. *Liber Sancte Marie de Melros*, Bannatyne Club (Edinburgh, 1837), ii, 560. There was a bachelor of decreets, however, of the same name in 1440, Reg. Supp. 364, f. 234v.
91. Friar John Blenk, later minister at Peebles: *Glas. Mun.*, ii, 62; *Extracts from the Records of Peebles* (Scottish Burgh Records Society, 1872), 162.
92. Vaccari, *Pavia*, 63.
93. *Glas. Mun.*, ii, 67.
94. *Ibid.*, ii, 55, 57, 179, 181.
95. The old beadle, John Moffat, may have taken up study. A person of that name, priest, Dunkeld diocese, bachelor in decreets, was notary in Dumbarton in 1468: GUL, Murray MS 643, f. 473.
96. *Glas. Mun.*, ii, 57; in the MS *Liber Rectoris*, pp. 39–40.
97. Burns, *Scottish Churchmen and the Council of Basle*, 41.
98. *Glas. Mun.*, ii, 62.
99. GUA, 12412 (Blackhouse 61).
100. *CPL*, xii, 49. In 1451, the printed record qualifies him as 'subdean', but this describes the following name, Andrew de Durisdeer, as is clear in the manuscript: *Glas. Mun.*, ii, 57, 68–72. References to his successor, Simon Dalgleish, as chanter from 1456, are common; e.g. *Miscellany of the Scottish History Society*, v, 44.
101. *Glas. Reg.*, ii, 414, gives a summarised document, the date of which (1465) mystifies, as Cadzow, according to the university records, was alive in 1466: *Glas. Mun.*, ii, 72 (where he is described as 'canon of Glasgow'). In the document from which the editor of *Glas. Reg.* took his summary there is no mention of 'precentor' in connection with Cadzow, GUL MS 199 ('Cartulary of Glasgow', Paris transcripts), f. 653. He is 'canon' there too, of Durisdeer, according to *CPL*, xii, 49.
102. *Glas. Mun.*, ii, 57.
103. *Ibid.*, ii, 191.
104. *Ibid.*, ii, 178, Reg. Supp. 396, f. 279 (i.e., not 'canon law' as in *Turnbull*, 11).
105. *Glas. Mun.*, ii, 179.

B

106. Durkan, *Turnbull*, 39.
107. Alexander de MacKalon was at St Andrews in 1445 when the king joined Bishop Kennedy in a petition to Rome on his behalf: Dunlop, *Kennedy*, 292.
108. *Glas. Mun.*, i, 6.
109. *Ibid.*, ii, 59–60.
110. *The Book of Pluscarden* (Historians of Scotland) ed. F. J. H. Skene (1877), i, 381.
111. *Glas. Mun.*, ii, 178.

2. Endowments and Buildings

'We came to the city of Glasgoaw . . . an ancient university, one only college . . . wherein are four schools. . . . Here the library is a very little room, not twice so large as my old closet; that part of it which is now standing is old, strong, plain building.'

Sir William Brereton (*c.* 1636)

'Next than from Ayre unto Glasgow go,
A goodly cytee and universitee,
Where plentifull is the countree also,
Replenished well with all commoditee.'

John Hardyng, *Chronicle*

THE university's founder had died within three years of its foundation and most of the time he had been, as his commission for the foundation of the collegiate church of Hamilton expresses it, 'occupied daily about the king in arduous and necessary business of the realm'.[1] He had already been at considerable expense in procuring the foundation.[2] He proceeded to give exemption from customs and ensure that the university as well as the townsmen would have a say in the cost of hiring university buildings,[3] although he seems to have been prepared to go no further than suggesting a united pedagogy, a building in which teaching would be concentrated on a single site, but without permanent collegiate endowment and even that proposal ran into difficulties. He obtained the usual tax exemption for university members from James II, but the latter was in no position to establish or assist in founding a royal college.[4]

His successor was Andrew de Durisdeer and great things might have been expected of one who had been a close friend of Turnbull and a familiar of Cardinal d'Estouteville. But there was in the beginning much local opposition to his appointment to the see. The Douglas party may have hoped that someone more favourable to themselves might succeed.[5] He did not expect to obtain peaceable possession of his diocese and events justified his expectations.[6] It says something not only for his diplomacy, but also for the advantages arising from certain ties of kinship, that the opposition was won over in due course. The Douglases did indeed take a prominent part in the university's survival, leaving the bishop free for other designs close to this heart, the establishment of a hospital of St Nicholas within the cathedral and chanonry area, the erection of the vicars choral into a 'college' and the provision

21

of a vicar's hall and close to the north of his cathedral with the establishment of a resident subchanter.[7]

Other sources of income might have been the town, the episcopal chapter and others in whom the gift of chaplainries and other church revenues was vested, and, in the event, most fruitful of all, the local lairds. The town of Glasgow was in no position to make any permanent grant in 1451; nor initially did it control any benefices as did some university towns elsewhere in Europe. The earliest regents must have been funded from some source, presumably the episcopal purse, though Duncan Bunch was vicar of Wiston (a benefice in the gift of Kelso abbey) by 1456, of Dundonald (in the gift of Paisley abbey) by 1460 and later he was to join the Glasgow chapter of canons.[8] But all this was after some years of service; and the danger of such a course of advancement was that it could act as a dissuasive rather than persuasive force to continuance in the labour of university teaching, since the benefices were not tied to the post. A similar progress is found with another regent, William Arthurlie.[9]

Before estimating the university endowments, which in any event can hardly have been substantial, it is necessary to note that we lack totally any original deeds or sealed documents for the first century of its history, and that the same was true when the first surviving inventory was drawn up in 1582.[10] The only deeds that survived with the university were those registered in the Rector's book or in the two Dean's books (one a register of faculty meetings, the other a small book of faculty statutes), and the Rector's book was not then available, for it was removed at the Reformation and was not returned till 1625.[11]

The first site may have been the Old Pedagogy in Rottenrow: or the first regents may have had two pedagogies, partly accommodating grammar students, one hired from Sir James Hamilton or his assignees in High Street,[12] and another from the vicars choral in Rottenrow, in which event the scarcity of scholars may have caused the abandonment of the Rottenrow site. Strained relations with the Hamiltons may, however, have interrupted the tenancy of the High Street site, except for the occupancy of the schools of canon law under Hamilton's protégé, David Cadzow. With inadequate documentation, discussion is necessarily speculative.

The original site on Rottenrow was acquired by John Dalgleish in 1410. At that time its frontage was given as four ploughgates, presumably four roods, burghal measure, that is about twenty or so yards.[13] The tenement was partly built up by Dalgleish, himself a vicar choral, before he donated it to them. How long this Old Pedagogy was occupied by the university is not clear: probably only briefly, for on 8 February 1466, John Smyth, vicar choral, as procurator for his fellow vicars, feued it to Gilbert Rerik, archdeacon. This was done with the express consent of another Dalgleish, Simon, then chanter and, in the dean's absence, chapter president. The archdeacon promised to construct, repair and improve the site in its east and front parts. The deed, completed partly in the cathedral chapter and partly on the forepart of the site, was witnessed, among others, by William Elphinstone, rector of Kirkmichael, the future founder of Aberdeen university.[14] Although there is no mention of the name Pedagogy in the document itself, it is endorsed, 'Copy of the feu charter of the tenement called the auld Petagog made to the former venerable man master Gilbert Rerik, once archdeacon of Glasgow, by the vicars choral'. This same Rottenrow tenement was, on 19 December 1478, made over by the archdeacon to his chaplainry of St Michael, at which date it was designed 'the tenement . . . formerly called the Pedagogy' (*quod alias Petigogium vocabatur*).[15] The likelihood is that it had ceased to be used as a pedagogy many years before 1478.

A later reference in 1485 to John Smyth and the archdeacon may be cited here. The principal of the time had borrowed sums from Smyth to spend 'on the repair of the stonework' (*super reparacione lapicidii*),[16] and had given a receipt to David Gray, then faculty bursar as well as chaplain to the archdeacon. Smyth wanted the money returned, but the principal was unable and unwilling. In the end the faculty appointed Gray to receive it and expend it on pedagogy repairs and hoped to get the archdeacon's advice on how it should be spent.[17] These proceedings must be understood, however, not as referring to the pedagogy on the Rottenrow, already abandoned, but to that on the High Street site.

The problem of accommodation for the infant university was solved by the acquisition of a nobleman's—lord Hamilton's—town house. Even as late as 1636, that part of it still standing could be described by an English traveller as an 'old, strong, plain building'.[18] The negotiation of this valuable gift was clearly an exercise in university diplomacy of some complexity, especially as a gift of this sort by a lay magnate is unparalleled in Scottish university history till the foundation by the Earl Marischal at Aberdeen late in the next century.

William, eighth earl of Douglas, was murdered in February 1452 by the King. The Hamiltons, furious, must have withdrawn their patronage, whatever it was, from Turnbull's schemes. A few straws in the wind are there to indicate their initial patronage: Sir James Hamilton's chaplain, John Mouswald, was an incorporated member in 1451[19] as was Robert Hamilton on 16 March of the following year,[20] the day before the angry Hamiltons laid waste the King's town of Stirling. As we have seen, moreover, the indulgence money which

Turnbull had set aside for the uses of his see had, in the event, to be surrendered to James II to conduct his war against the Hamiltons along with the rest of the Douglas adherents. If the faculty of arts or the university already had use of the Glasgow Hamilton property before 1460 and the legal transaction of that year, then it is reasonable to believe that the use of it was discontinued for part of the period. The year 1453 was certainly a critical one. In 1455 one of the reasons given for annexing the revenues of Glencairn to the city's cathedral was 'the growth of the university' (*universitatis Glasguensis augmentum*).[21] The situation was not to change dramatically in that year, though debts for 'the hire (*firma*) of the pedagogy' in 1457 may already indicate re-use of the Hamilton building.[22]

James, lord Hamilton, as he had now become, and Euphemia Douglas, his wife (widow of the fifth earl of Douglas, daughter of a family obnoxious to the royal house, two of whose sons had been the victim of a judicial murder),[23] had made their peace with James II, acquired a barony and inherited some of the former Douglas lands. The way was thus open for reconciliation with the bishop of Glasgow, whose see and university had suffered most from the Black Douglas rebellion. Progress could be eased by an act of restitution, if not to Turnbull's memory, at least to the see as such.

A reconciliation could, however, scarcely have happened without mediation. One mediator was surely William Herries, who may have been specially invited for he is not recorded as having been in the university previously but who was now elected Rector.[24] He was patently a person of influence, acceptable to all parties, who had known Turnbull as his dean of faculty at St Andrews.[25] He had the gift of eloquent persuasion, and it is not too hard to guess why the university was so grateful to him. One must suspect that, among other things, he had solved the university's building problem, at least temporarily. He can be confidently identified with a perpetual chaplain of the parish kirk of Douglas in 1431 who was also a bachelor of decreets.[26] In 1453, Herries had claimed to be a kinsman of James II and also of James, master of Douglas, later ninth earl, when the latter petitioned the pope on his behalf.[27] Against the fact of these strong pro-Douglas connections must, however, be set the story of the Black Douglas's hanging of John Herries of Terregles, which if factual, might have served to help rather than hinder Herries as mediator.[28] In 1458, Herries was succeeded as Rector by David Cadzow.[29] If Herries was closer to the Douglas members of the Hamilton family, Cadzow had been known to lord Hamilton himself for many years: at Cadzow (the older name of Hamilton) he witnessed a charter of his in 1444.[30] Another link with the founder was the new bishop, whose kinswoman, a Muirhead of

Lauchope, was married to the Gavin Hamilton, in fact lord Hamilton's son by a daughter of Livingstone of Callendar, who occupied the town house in Glasgow which the university acquired.[31]

The house, a tenement in the High Street, was given by lord Hamilton in a charter of 6 January 1460 founding the College of Arts, the original document bearing his seal. It was an act of restitution made in favour of 'all those souls' from whom he had received 'anything good, either directly or indirectly'. Although the gift was made for students in the arts faculty, there is no evidence of other faculties occupying another site. The tenement was bounded on the north by another tenement of Thomas Arthurlie, chaplain, and on the south by the place of the Dominicans. To the east, beyond the Molendinar burn, were four acres of land on Dovehill. The terminology of the royal charter of privileges is echoed almost word for word in the opening phrases of Hamilton's deed of foundation.[32] In it, at one point, he associates his wife, countess of Douglas and lady Bothwell, with him as co-founder. The gift was made to Duncan Bunch, described as principal regent, not in the university or pedagogy, but 'in the faculty of arts', as long as he was in personal residence, and also to monitors and regents properly instituted by the principal. The mention of monitors makes it pretty certain that grammar scholars were at first accommodated in the new college. The first on record in Glasgow (though a cathedral school must have long preceded this mention) appear in December 1458 when six scholars of the grammar school witnessed a foundation by the cathedral chancellor.[33] Monitors are never mentioned thereafter, because the grammar school was in 1461 provided with a home almost directly opposite the university by Simon Dalgleish, chanter and official.[34]

In return for this gift by lord Hamilton, the faculty assumed certain obligations.[35] On appointment, each principal regent was to take an oath to the bishop to fulfil certain terms of the foundation. These were of a religious nature, but nothing on the scale of such services as would exist in a normal collegiate foundation, such as King's College, Aberdeen. Nor was there as yet any chapel or oratory as there had been in St Andrews at St John's College, so that meantime the singing of the 'Ave Gloriosa' was replaced by a mere low-voiced recitation in the neighbouring Blackfriars kirk. There was to be a common table in hall, with commemoration during grace of the founders. While it was not envisaged that all regents would be ordained, those who were priests were required to commend the founders' souls to the prayers of the congregation at the gospel, as were all priest students. Their anniversary was to be celebrated in the cathedral, all priests, clerics and students being bound to certain masses and prayers. Finally, as was common also in later times, all regents were obliged to give faithful advice (normally, one suspects, legal advice) when desired by the family of the founder.

The only charges to the faculty were certain annual rents and the burgh ferme due to the bishop, which he, on the patronal feast a week later, remitted.[36] The tenement was then handed over by the rector of Monyabroch (Kilsyth), Robert Hamilton, his grandson and son of Gavin, former occupier of the site, as procurator for the donor.[37] Bunch accepted in the faculty's name and took instrument.

The scribe who copied these documents into the Dean's book also copied the friars' letter of reversion of five years earlier, but that adds nothing to our knowledge, except that the tenement is said to be on 'the north syde of the Freris Kyrk'. While in the text of the Hamilton foundation document the building is described as a college, the headings provided by the scribe call it a pedagogy, thus tending to confirm the belief that it was the rented pedagogy of a few years before of which Hamilton was now making outright donation, or at least that the rented building was absorbed in the new foundation.[38]

With these important deeds, the scribe also registered one concerning a chaplainry of St Thomas the Martyr, which raises the question whether the tenement to the north of the College of Arts was part of the original endowment of the chaplainry with that dedication founded by an earlier generation of Hamiltons.[39] This was possessed by David Cadzow in 1449, but united shortly afterwards by the future lord Hamilton to his new collegiate church in Hamilton.[40] It was clearly at the north end of the city; in 1462 Cadzow arranged that an annual university procession should start from a chapel of St Thomas the Martyr at the north end of the city.[41] Clearly this was the same 'Cadzow chapel' yet it was not to this Cadzow chaplainry that the tenement to the north belonged, nor do we know from what revenues it was supported. The chapel of St Thomas the Martyr given to the arts faculty by a university member of 1452, Sir Thomas Arthurlie,[42] had other patrons and it was sited at a totally different end of the town, beyond the West Port and possibly in the Fishergate (the older name of the Stockwell).[43] As will become clear, it already existed before the division in 1439 or 1440 of the Steward's lands of Arthurlie between Ross of Hawkhead and Stewart of Castlemilk's son (later Walter Stewart of Arthurlie): at that date John de Pollok occupied both halves (and the name of the chapel reappears in the university's accounts much later). Since the foundation was made before the division, it is not improbable, in view of the dedication, that here we have a twelfth-century chapel, founded not long after Becket's death, by the Steward of Scotland himself.[44]

Thomas Arthurlie's gift of this south-western chapel of St Thomas was made on 24 February 1467.[45] Unfortunately what we have, once again, is not the original foundation, but we gather that 'priestly service mentioned and laid down in the said foundation' was to be done during the donor's lifetime and after his death by William Arthurlie, regent, or his deputy, and sasine was given to William and not to the principal. Moreover, William was to keep the house for life as a convenient residence adjacent to the university with a tail extending to the burn and parallel to the Hamilton lands. After William's death, the house and land were to be placed at the disposal of regents in the arts faculty 'and in other respects according to the tenor of the foundation'. This new house gave Arthurlie a privileged position in comparison with the principal regent.

But there were stubborn problems in ensuring that what was acquired in theory was also acquired in fact. The revenue supporting this chaplainry included ten merks from the lands of Arthurlie in Renfrewshire, as was stated in a papal petition of 20 May 1474.[46] In this the chapel near the city was said to be decayed in walls and roof. The petitioners, Sir John Ross and the heirs of Walter Stewart, layman, contributed to its support from their Renfrewshire lands, yet, they claimed, divine service was rarely celebrated in the chapel. If, however, on the death or resignation of the present chaplain, the chaplainry were to be removed and united instead to the chaplainry at the altar of St Thomas Martyr in Renfrew parish kirk (which, they averred, was very near the Glasgow chapel, and where the parents of Ross were buried—that is, in the Ross aisle),[47] these religious services could be transferred from the ruinous chapel near Glasgow to the chaplain serving the altar in Renfrew.

In November 1475, the arts faculty decided that the protocol instruments regarding the union to the pedagogy of Arthurlie's Place, then held by William Arthurlie, should be copied out in duplicate, one copy to be retained by the faculty.[48] But by the beginning of February 1477, four university representatives had to ride to Ayr to appear before papal judges delegate, the abbots of Crossraguel and Paisley, in an apostolic commission obtained by Sir John Ross and the heir of Sir Walter Stewart.[49] Ayr hardly seems the place best calculated to serve the university's interest and not surprisingly the matter did not end there. The bishop tried to bring the case back to Glasgow and his own courts. Some years dragged on and, in January 1480, the dispute had reached national level.

In that year the Lords of Council summoned the university on behalf of the owners of Arthurlie, the laird of Hawkhead and Sir Thomas Stewart of Minto. They insisted that the matter was one for the civil courts, not the Church courts. The university, however, proved tenacious. To counter one objection that had been placed before the Roman authorities, they turned their attention to the preservation of the chapel and its use. In 1481, it was agreed that a chaplain would celebrate yearly for Sir Thomas Arthurlie at the principal's expense. In 1483 money was authorised from the university purse to be expended on the chapel's reconstruction and, again later (though the revenues due from Ross were as yet unpaid), for repair of the altar and vestments.[50] By 1490 this reconstruction had taken place, but there was still a problem regarding the Renfrewshire income.[51] It was, however, eventually acquired and the St Thomas 'kirk and kirk yaird' are mentioned in post-Reformation records.[52]

Arthurlie House or Place, adjacent to the university with a tail extending to the burn, was easier to retain. It consisted of a single court, with a vaulted forehouse and 'inner houses', the latter presumably older buildings, whose roofs were to be repaired in 1490 at the principal's expense.[53] As the main building was flush with the street,[54] it was presumably in better condition, though by 20 June 1522 the whole house was described as of little benefit and nearly ruinous.[55] The Glasgow earth tremor of 1521, which left no place unaffected and set the nearby Blackfriars steeple on fire, was perhaps a contributory cause to its ruin.[56] It was, therefore, decided to feu it to some powerful person (who would, of course, restore and maintain it) for an annual payment, though, with the expected arrival of a new archbishop (Gavin Dunbar), there was talk also of postponement.[57] In fact, it was most probably at this time that it was first leased to Lindsay of Dunrod for a yearly return of £6 6s 8d from the lands of Wester Rogerton near East Kilbride, though we have only a post-Reformation reference for this.[58] The university authorities obviously just did not have the resources to meet inevitable maintenance expenses from their own funds.

David Cadzow, first Rector, is said to have been a great benefactor to the early university: we are told he had done 'several notable and memorable deeds to the utility and exaltation of the said university and the faculty of arts'.[59] He left ten merks annually in return for certain religious services, the value of which was considerably reduced a century later.[60] He also in 1463 assigned an annual rent of twelve merks to support a lecturer in canon law[61]: the rents supporting this are listed in 1517, and a few are identifiable in a miscellaneous list of rents of the pre-Reformation foundation given in 1575.[62] The source of other minor items in this list is untraced. One, however, 'ane lytle yaird apperteining to the Beddell', was in St Tenew's Gait (later Trongate).[63] Another, the Regents's annual, was a small sum left by the vicar of Cadder, Archibald Calderwood, for his obit, from whom perhaps a Bredisholme annual also originated,[64] and who showed a readiness to demit his vicarage in the university's favour.[65]

Other small items, whose worth is hard to assess, not included in the 1575 list, include the chaplainry of St Michael founded in the high kirk by John Reston, vicar of Dunlop, in the presentation and under the annual supervision of the Rector and his assessors: it may have been intended as a burse for students.[66] Likewise, there is the chaplainry at the high altar in the Blackfriars kirk, founded in 1487 by William Stewart, canon-prebendary of Killearn and rector of Glassford, of which the Rector, arts regents and town authorities were conservators, whose benefits might conceivably be restricted to the friars' goodwill.[67] In 1501, Cuthbert Simson was presented by Archbishop Blackadder as perpetual chaplain of St Nicholas in the hospital of that name for personal residence in the Pedagogy as a lecturer in grammar.[68] In March 1530, Thomas Lees, subdean of Dunblane and perpetual vicar of Dreghorn, also gave three tenements and £3 7s to found another chaplainry of St Michael in the archdeacon's aisle of the cathedral kirk, of which the Rector and Dean of faculty were constituted patrons: and while a relative of the founder's was to be instituted as first chaplain, nevertheless the principal held it at the Reformation.[69]

In the circumstances of the period, the only way to make the college fully collegiate seemed the annexation of benefices. Hence the proposal of Blackadder on 8 June 1506, to incorporate in his college the vicarages of Cadder, Stobo, Linton, Kilbirnie, and the rectories of Kirkmichael (later cancelled) and Garvald.[70] The chapter resisted the ratifying of this move and merely 'allowed' it subject to papal authorisation, as Kilbirnie was in any case already in the patronage of Kilwinning abbey. Another attempt was made in the dean's absence on 26 June 1507, at the Whitsunday chapter, this time adding the vicarage of Girvan in the patronage of the abbey of Crossraguel.[71] A similar attempt, this time in the presence of the dean and that of some powerful lay neighbours, was made in February 1508.[72] Patently Archbishop Blackadder was using strong-arm methods as the expression 'according to the dictates (*dictamen*) and lengthy disquisition (*dilatacionem*)' of the archbishop indicates. He had rid the town of the earl of Lennox as provost and replaced him by a juvenile Blackadder and simultaneously had made Henry Burrell bailie, for acceptance of which the latter was killed by the earl's servants at the 'blak freir yett'.[73] The archbishop's overbearing personality probably nullified his unexceptionable aim, namely to favour within the university's bounds 'a varied and richer teaching programme (*doctrinam*) and the existence of a company of contemporary men of learning'. The chapter continued to be obstructive and papal confirmation of appropriations of benefices was never obtained. Some years later, at a time when the moribund Pedagogy at St Andrews was being transformed into St Mary's College, a similar attempt at Glasgow was made by Archbishop Dunbar on 15 August 1537, a feastday when the chapter might well be in a generous mood. He set out to annexe the vicarages of Erskine and Cadder (with Monkland) in his own patronage, Colmonell in the chapter's patronage, with the two St Michael chaplainries of Reston and Lees, and Cadzow's St Mary chaplainry. This was to be a new erection of the college, but already there was dissent from Gilbert Binning, rector of Ayr and chaplain of the Reston foundation. The Rector of the university took instruments,[74] hopeful that the archbishop's scheme would succeed. Nevertheless, the annexations of vicarages were still obstructed; Colmonell, for instance, on the grounds that the Kennedies of Bargany had contributed great sums to the rebuilding of the pedagogy.[75] It was 1557, twenty years later, before Colmonell was safely annexed,[76] by which time Dunbar's paper project had collapsed.

The foundation about 1539 of the new collegiate church of St Mary of Loreto and St Anne in the city could well have been seized on as a chance to strengthen the bonds between town and gown. But here the townsmen again may have proved resistant. The archbishop had fortified himself behind a strong castle wall; the vicars choral lived in the protection of the vicars' close[77]; the university must have seemed just another closed society and, in a new approach to the townsmen's goodwill, it was perhaps necessary to found a collegiate kirk near the market place as a token of civic pride. In so doing, an opportunity to follow the pattern of such collegiate churches as those attached to the academic colleges of Aberdeen and St Andrews was unfortunately missed. Nevertheless, the Rector and Dean were to enjoy certain small sums in return for keeping a watchful eye over the college, in Lent, December and May.[78] It is possible that the two prebends of archpriest and major sacrist (based on the two halves of the vicarage of Maybole and not directly in the town's patronage but in the archbishop's) did indeed go to maintaining university personnel.[79] They do form part of the university's revenue in post-Reformation days, but may only have come with other Church revenues then.[80]

There was never any danger of the pre-Reformation institution becoming a town's college. It is true that £20 annually was paid out of the customs of the Tron of Glasgow. Here, however, we must see again the strong arm of Archbishop Blackadder, for part of the Tron customs (not enjoyed by the bishops until Blackadder's time) was also payable to two of his chaplainry foundations.[81] Archbishop Dunbar, when farming out these customs to the parish clerk of Cadder in 1547, mentioned that payment had been made by himself and his predecessors in times gone by.[82]

While it is possible that some of the university's revenues have, in the absence of documentation, escaped notice, there can be little doubt that, in this first century of existence, the university's story is one of realistic withdrawal and contraction from Turnbull's project rather than of imaginative expansion of it. Turnbull might have been satisfied with a university such as existed at St Andrews in his youth, one serving little beyond the immediate hinterland, with scarcely any endowment and only a very shadowy collegiate structure in the shape of the college of St John, yet at the same time with ambitions to provide not only teaching in arts but also some law and theology. There was therefore something of an irony in the fact that at Glasgow the law faculty's resources should have been absorbed in a subsequent remodelling into nothing more than a college of arts on a pattern set less by Turnbull than by the former enemies of Turnbull of the Hamilton and Douglas faction, and that it should have been re-established as such a century later on the basis of a genuine misunderstanding of its founder's original purpose.

To reconstruct a medieval building from documentary evidence alone is a hazardous business, but where the documents afford at least some clear clues, it is worth the effort. The nobleman's town house that the university acquired in 1460 presumably had a longer frontage than the alternative Rottenrow accommodation. Judging from Slezer's print of the building that succeeded it on the site, it was probably originally flush with the west gable of the Blackfriars but with an ample foreland and this may have been old thirteenth-century work to which a 'forefront' (the 'frons anterior' of 1460) provided a fifteenth-century frontage, the 'forework' that was demolished two centuries later to make room for the fine façade shown in the print by Captain Slezer.

If we start at the western end of the Outer Court (or Close), that is at the High Street end, we find there, as in the later building (demolished in Victorian times), the Foreschools. In 1636 when the medieval building still stood intact, apart from the north quarter of the Inner Court, there were four schools.[83] If I interpret the building accounts correctly,[84] the three large windows of the foreschools, mentioned in 1608–1609, were for three schools; that is, the separate classrooms for undergraduates and bachelors in arts and a larger common faculty school for the combined groups, the last possibly that known as the 'lang Skuile' (1582), furnished with a master's desk.[85] Dividing them would be the porter's lodge at the foregate.[86]

Above one of the schools at the north end and extending into the

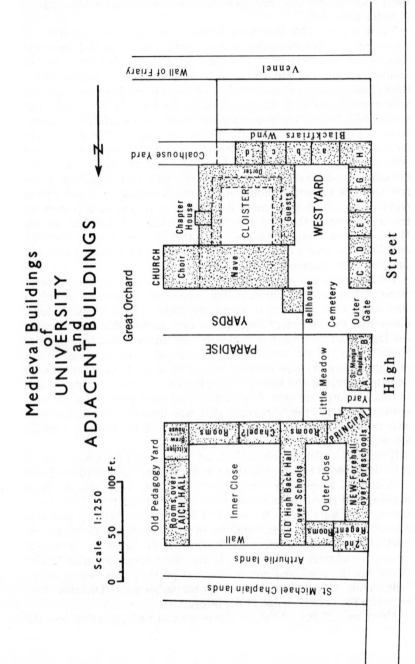

Medieval Buildings
of
UNIVERSITY
and
ADJACENT BUILDINGS

Scale 1:1250

N

Wall of Friary

Vennel

Blackfriars Wynd

Coalhouse Yard

Great Orchard

CHURCH

Chapter House

CLOISTER

Dorter

Guests

WEST YARD

Choir

Nave

Bellhouse

Cemetery

Outer Gate

PARADISE

YARDS

Little Meadow

St. Mungo Chaplain

Old Pedagogy Yard

Kitchen Brew house

Rooms

Chapel?

Rooms

PRINCIPAL

Rooms over LAICH HALL

Inner Close

Wall

OLD High Back Hall over Schools

Outer Close

NEW Forehall over Foreschools

Regent Rooms

2nd

Arthurlie lands

St. Michael Chaplain lands

High Street

C D E F G H

a b c d

north quarter seems to have been one of the larger rooms for the use of a regent.[87] Adjacent to it in the centre was the Forehall or High Forehall ('high' here seems to mean 'in the fore or outer court') mentioned in 1608–1615 when it was extensively repaired.[88] Since, as we shall see, an Old Hall is mentioned, this Forehall was clearly the New Hall mentioned in 1497[89]—'new' because it was in the newer part of the building. It is unlikely to have been a completely new hall although the period between 1480 and 1497 was one of considerable structural repair and even of alteration, first mooted in 1480.[90]

The north quarter probably extended on its inside face for forty or so feet. Nothing is known of it, except that there were rooms there. 'Tua studie durris on ye north syd of ye clois' were repaired in 1608.[91] Non-regents may occasionally have taken rooms here. The south quarter of the Outer Close included what may be called Bunch House, a principal's house with a principal's room in the western part of the main structure, but with a separate Principal's House at right angles to it facing the street (similar to the small house adjacent to the south end of the main front in Slezer's print). This house 'on the south of the college of the faculty of arts' was mooted at the same time as the Arthurlie gift of a house to the north of the main building and Bunch was responsible for its building.[92] Also on the south was the Library where it could catch the light. It was clearly near the principal's room[93] and this would explain why the principal occasionally confused his private collection with the university's. There was a library here towards the street even as late as 1704 (that is, in the post-medieval building).[94] Midway along this south quarter were rooms extending east,[95] perhaps originally for important officials.[96]

After the Reformation, the University acquired the large tenement attached to the chaplainry of St Mungo in the lower church of the cathedral and a tablet recalling this fact and the chaplainry patrons, the Blackadders of Tulliallan, disappeared only with the final demolition of the principal's house in 1870.[97] This history of this large tenement is fairly continuous and its replacement can be seen just north of the old College Open in the Slezer print: it was 'next to our outer gate' according to the Blackfriars endorsement on an early deed.[98] The principal took over the 'little meadow yard' at its rear and afterwards the Bellhouse of the Blackfriars adjacent to the friars' west gable at the north corner (not shown by Slezer).[99] The point of this digression is that 'the bigging of the Bak House at the bak of the Principallis hous quhair he duellis' mentioned in 1610 could refer to a new back house, but also to an old one to which additions were made because of recent encroachment on to former Blackfriars' land.[100]

The east quarter of the Outer Court was the west quarter of the

Inner Court. It contained the High Back Hall,[101] and in the early seventeenth-century factor's accounts it can clearly be identified with the 'auld hall' when its floors were relaid (1602–3), and, later, windows and adjacent chambers were repaired (1607–8).[102] The term 'high' here still refers to the Outer Court from which it would normally be entered. This hall would be the common hall of the university.[103] Unfortunately the earliest inventory (of 1582) is not a list of rooms, being concerned principally with muniments and furnishings, so that in it only two halls are mentioned, one a dining hall with tables and forms and another a hall for solemn university or faculty functions with a 'pulpet'.[104]

Below this hall would be the university schools, whose existence in this back area seems implied in the term foreschools (which were faculty schools). Here, it would appear, were the Schools of Canon Law, first mentioned as 'the public schools' in 1463.[105] That they were in the older part of the building seems evident for they were ruinous in 1483.[106] Though we are told that they served the whole university, the cost of their repair was to be raised from graduates in canon law[107]; because the hall was above, the university met the cost of roof repairs.[108] A new gable window was placed in these schools in 1502, perhaps to allow the room to be partitioned to give an extra chamber.[109] Three beams of oak lay in these common schools in 1582.[110] They are also 'our greater schools' (1507) where the act of a bachelorship in theology was carried out.[111] The Blackstone examination would take place on this site as it did in later centuries. There were chambers also in this middle quarter, but there does not appear to have been a steeple in the original building.[112] The bell is, however, mentioned.[113] The proportions of this Outer Court were irregular and, as such, dictated the proportions of the Outer Court in the new seventeenth-century edifice.

There is nothing to indicate how far back the Inner Court went or how extensive was the garden area for kitchen fowl and vegetables to its rear, behind the Low or Laich Hall at its far eastern end.[114] It could not have been a complete quadrangle, as one of the aims of its rebuilders was to add 'a good fair and college-like structure to be built quadrangular'.[115] It was approached by a pend from the Outer Court to be 'calsayed' (paved)[116] in 1628. The Inner Close is mentioned as such in 1611–1612.[117] In the post-medieval rebuilding, its north quarter was remodelled first (1632), and previously there may have been only a wall there. Its east quarter was a low building, including a Laich Hall with some attics above. Behind it stood a kitchen yard, part of the tail of the Hamilton building, 'the awld College yaird' (1575) or 'auld Pegagog yaird' (1608) south of an alleyway ('Ala') beyond which was another College yard presumably that of Arthurlie.[118] This kitchen yard is referred to in 1490 when a mudwall dyke was built in the 'pedacok yard'.[119] The Laich Hall was used more or less exclusively as a dining hall: it is the hall with three 'burdis . . . with thare binkis and furmis' of 1582.[120] The statutes required abiding at table and the college founder required all students along with the principal and regent masters to use it.[121] This quarter of the building was vaulted; two vaults were used as cellars[122] by the steward and above these, flanking the Laich Hall, stood a kitchen, brewhouse and other kitchen offices. The kitchen was thoroughly renovated and is referred to as a 'new kitchen' in 1496, but an earlier reference to 'the mending' of its chimney suggests it was not rebuilt as such.[123] There are casual mentions of a cook (1463), a provisor (food contractor) or steward (1476).[124] It had a brewhouse and pantry (1492), a larder (1502) and its list of utensils gives the impression that the 1582 inventory has several omissions.[125] A limehouse, wellhouse and coalhouse are mentioned in 1604 to 1615,[126] and presumably there were stabling quarters, but these may have stood adjacent in the south quarter.

The south quarter of this Inner Court is harder to reconstitute. Presumably it consisted mainly of students' rooms: the larger and more private rooms would be given to priests as part of the favours extended to them in the Hamilton foundation.[127] Each room, at least when accommodation was tight, would normally serve three or four students. Most rooms would have two beds and since there were in 1582 twenty-five students' studies, there were possibly fifteen students' chambers at the maximum.[128] However, this quarter is evidently that which is ruinous in 1641.[129]

It is possible that part of the north or south quarters of this Inner Court was occupied by a university chapel. If so, it could have been from this building that in 1582 were salvaged sixteen song and mass books.[130] Lord Hamilton had not himself provided a chapel but had ordained that until a chapel or oratory was built stµdents were to remember him with a recited antiphon and collect on Saturdays at vespers in the Blackfriars Kirk, to be sung, however, when they had an oratory of their own. A room may have been fitted up temporarily as an oratory.[131] Finally, in 1508, Archbishop Blackadder in his will left £60 to constructing 'a church in the college of Glasgow in honour of the most holy name (sic) of Jesus and Mary'.[132] We have no further record of this; it seems like the crown of his scheme for what might have been a Jesus College, the endowments for which he was doomed to fail to acquire. The idea was again taken up, unsuccessfully on the whole, by Archbishop Dunbar for a refoundation of the 'college of the university of masters and scholars in Glasgow'.[133] The most enduring, however, of these foundations was paradoxically lord Hamilton's which till the nineteenth century remained the core of university life in Glasgow.

NOTES

1. *Historical Manuscripts Commission, Hamilton*, i, 48.
2. *Glas. Mun.*, ii, 21.
3. *Ibid.*, i, 7–9.
4. *Ibid.*, i, 6.
5. Durkan, *Turnbull*, 53.
6. *CPL*, xi, 1–2, 270.
7. R. Renwick and Sir J. Lindsay, *History of Glasgow* (Glasgow, 1921), i, 225ff. For the subchantership, *CPL*, xiii, 628.
8. *Glas. Mun.*, ii, 189, 193 (Wiston); 68, 73 (Dundonald); 207, 79 (his canonries were the vicarage of Glasgow or Glasgow *secundo*, and Renfrew). Lord Hamilton, whom Kelso made bailie of Lesmahagow in 1456, may have influenced Bunch's Wiston appointment.
9. In 1469 stallar of Bothwell (in Lord Hamilton's gift) and vicar of Kilbirnie (Kilwinning was patron); and rector of Hutton before that (1462), *Glas. Mun.*, ii, 74, 196.
10. *Ibid.*, iii, 517.
11. Liber Rectoris, 151, 'This buik is delyuerit be me Ja. balfour of tarrie in anno 1625'.
12. The tail of Lord Hamilton's lands over the Molendinar in Dovehill is mentioned in a vicars choral deed of 17 August 1447: GUA 12419. But perhaps he was there much longer.
13. *Liber Collegii Nostre Domine*, 237.
14. GUA 16375.
15. *Glas. Reg.*, ii, 437.
16. 'Lapicidium', literally 'quarry', which cannot be right. The defective stonework of the pedagogy, 'le riggin stanis', seems to be referred to, *Glas. Mun.*, ii, 242, 246.
17. *Ibid.*, ii, 251: 'cum consilio dicti Archidiaconi super cuius summe exposicione' (omitted from printed text).
18. Sir William Brereton in P. H. Brown, *Early Travellers in Scotland* (Edinburgh, 1891), 153.
19. *Glas. Mun.*, ii, 56; *CPL*, x, 97.
20. *Glas. Mun.*, ii, 57; and even in mid-1453, Hamilton's grandson, *ibid.*, ii, 61.
21. *Glas. Reg.*, ii, 404.
22. *Glas. Mun.*, ii, 191.
23. Dunlop, *Kennedy*, 4, 33, 146.
24. *Glas. Mun.*, ii, 64. Elected in 1457.
25. Durkan, *Turnbull*, 54. A Hamilton and a brother of James II were incorporated on the same day.
26. The name is given as 'Hert' in Reg. Supp. 387, f. 236.
27. *CPL*, xi, 261, 498.
28. Nicholson, *Scotland; The Later Middle Ages*, 357.
29. This election is not recorded: but see *Glas. Mun.*, ii, 66.
30. Durkan, *Turnbull*, 49; *RMS*, ii, 511.

31. G. Hamilton, *House of Hamilton* (Edinburgh, 1891), 636.
32. *Glas. Mun.*, i, 9–14.
33. SRO, Glasgow Registrum MS (Liber Ruber), iv–v. They were 'scolaribus tunc temporis scole grammaticalis glasguensis'.
34. *Glas. Chrs.*, i (2), 436; cf. ii, 557.
35. There is a scriptural echo here which has been mistranscribed. It should read, 'ad locum unde exierunt flumina ut iterum fluant', not 'et interim fluant'.
36. *Glas. Mun.*, i, 12–13.
37. *House of Hamilton*, 636–7.
38. Liber Decani, 102–3 (Hamilton gift), 104–7 (conveyance), 108–9 (second copy), 107 (friars' reversion). The charter of gift is in David Gray's hand, entered in the book *c.* 1490.
39. *Glas. Reg.*, i, 227–8 (it existed by 1320).
40. *Glas. Mun.*, i, 15; *CPL*, x, 75–6; *HMC Hamilton*, i, 47–8.
41. *Glas. Mun.*, ii, 39. For this procession, see Chapter 11.
42. *Ibid.*, ii, 59.
43. *Liber Collegii Nostre Domine*, 244, 258.
44. *RMS*, ii, 213, 214.
45. *Glas. Mun.*, i, 18–19. Arthurlie held this land at least from 1454: *Liber Collegii Nostre Domine*, 175, with the house of John Carnis to the north.
46. Reg. Supp. 705, f. 172v. Five merks were due from the Lord Ross side of Arthurlie, the rest from the Stewart half. Isabella Stewart was heiress: *RMS*, ii, 1856.
47. *PSAS*, xxix, 368–74.
48. *Glas. Mun.*, ii, 220; the tenement of Arthurlie was in the faculty's possession at least by 1478: *Glas. Reg.*, ii, 438.
49. *Glas. Mun.*, i, 27, citing the *Acta Dominorum Concilii* (1839), 48.
50. *Ibid.*, ii, 93, 96.
51. *Ibid.*, i, 254; in MS Liber Decani, after 'structura eiusdem' add 'ac capellanie quondam domini thome Arthurlie'.
52. *Ibid.*, i, 93.
53. *Ibid.*, iii, 558 (forehouse); ii, 254–5. The forehouse may have had an upper storey and attics, cf. *ibid.*, i, 91; iii, 557.
54. R. Baillie, *Letters and Journals*, ed. D. Laing (Bannatyne Club, Edinburgh, 1841–2), ii, 432.
55. *Glas. Mun.*, ii, 145.
56. *IR*, v, 91.
57. *Glas. Mun.*, ii, 145.
58. *Ibid.*, i, 70; *Glas. Prots.*, ii, 683; v, 1500.
59. *Glas. Mun.*, i, 20.
60. *Ibid.*, i, 21, 93.
61. *Ibid.*, i, 17.
62. *Ibid.*, ii, 131; i, 92. The rent collected from James Houston is probably due from the same property as that collected from the later George Elphinstone; from Alexander Gilchriston, that from the former Arthur of the same name; from Gavin Graham, that from the former grammar school lodging of Alan Stewart.
63. *Glas. Mun.*, i, 93; *Glas. Prots.*, x, 3144.
64. *Glas. Mun.*, i, 43–4, 91, 93.
65. *Liber Protocollorum M. Cuthberti Simonis*, Grampian Club (1875), hereafter referred to as *Prot. Bk. Simon*, 119.
66. *Glas. Mun.*, i, 28–32; 'for the sustentatioun of bursaris' in 1569, *ibid.*, i, 77.

67. *Glas. Mun.*, i, 33.
68. *Ibid.*, i, 39.
69. *Ibid.*, i, 49-53, 65; *Glas. Prots.*, v, 1368.
70. *Prot. Bk. Simon*, 132.
71. *Ibid.*, 198–9.
72. *Ibid.*, 252.
73. SRO, Glasgow Regality Papers, RH.11.32/1. The juvenile was ten or twelve (evidence given in 1557 before deputies of the Justice Clerk).
74. *Glas. Mun.*, i, 493–5 (this gives 1527 in error). 'Jershin' may be a misreading, as some contemporary extracts from these protocols give 'Irskin': SRO, NP1/195, f. 12 (Protocol Book of Cuthbert Simson).
75. *Glas. Mun.*, i, 56.
76. *Ibid.*, i, 62.
77. The formulas used in Andrew de Durisdeer's deed of 1459 about 'church ministers innocent and holy, and separated from sinners', typify what seems a prevalent attitude: *Glas. Reg.*, ii, 409.
78. *Glas. Mun.*, i, 54–5; *Liber Collegii Nostre Domine*, 48–50.
79. *Ibid.*, 23–6.
80. *Glas. Mun.*, i, 173.
81. *Glas. Reg.*, ii, 464–9, 519.
82. *Glas. Chrs.*, i (2), 119–121.
83. Brown, *Early Travellers*, 150.
84. The three windows of the 'Foirscooleis' required 'fyve scoir xii fut of glas and wyre': *Glas. Mun.*, iii, 562. These three windows are twice mentioned in the MS of these accounts, from which extracts merely were printed in *Glas. Mun.*, that is GUA 26620 (Clerk's Press 8), p. 81.
85. *Glas. Mun.*, iii, 518.
86. Mentioned 1582, *ibid.*, iii, 518.
87. This at least was the arrangement in the later building.
88. The 'Heich Foirhall' (1609–10), *ibid.*, iii, 562. 'Losanis' for its windows are frequently mentioned in GUA 26620, Clerk's Press 8, pp. 90 (twice), 116, 133. (This manuscript is paged.)
89. *Glas. Mun.*, ii, 272 ('pro reparacione nove aule').
90. *Ibid.*, ii, 232. 'Super reparacione collegii arcium in suis structuris' and 'ad reformacionem dicti collegii'.
91. GUA Clerk's Press 8, p. 72.
92. Mentioned in 1467 and 1469, *Glas. Mun.*, ii, 203, 210.
93. Principal's room mentioned 1491 (Patrick Coventry, principal), *ibid.*, ii, 259. Early gifts of books were to the Pedagogy.
94. 'In the ffront of this college, towards the streete, is a good library . . .' (Anonymous): *North of England and Scotland in MDCCIV* (Edinburgh, 1818), 49. For its situation near the principal's room before the rebuilding, cf. *Glas. Mun.*, iii, 538, 545.
95. *Glas. Mun.*, iii, 522.
96. A Dean's room and a Rector's room, for example. Cf. *Glas. Mun.*, ii, 8, 281.
97. John C. Gibson, *Diary of Sir Michael Connal* (Glasgow, 1895), 151, 268.
98. *Liber Collegii Nostre Domine*, 190, and see Appendix B.
99. See Appendix B.
100. *Glas. Mun.*, iii, 562.
101. 'Chalmir windois in ye heich bak hall', GUA Clerk's Press 8, p. 63.
102. 'For xx daillis to fluir ye auld hall', GUA Clerk's Press 8, p. 12. Also p. 62 (windows), p. 63 (storm window in high chamber of old hall).

103. In 1626, there was a meeting of the university authorities in the 'public hall of the university': *Glas. Mun.*, ii, 301 (i.e. not a faculty meeting).
104. *Ibid.*, iii, 518.
105. *Ibid.*, i, 17.
106. *Ibid.*, ii, 93–4.
107. *Ibid.*, ii, 95.
108. *Ibid.*, ii, 107.
109. *Ibid.*, ii, 116.
110. 'Three cuitis of unsawyng aik lyand in ye commone skuilis', Liber Decani, 168 (scored through, and omitted in printed *Glas. Mun.*, iii, 518).
111. *Glas. Mun.*, ii, 121.
112. GUA Clerk's Press 8, pp. 62, 64, 81.
113. Presumably not just a handbell as its 'stokkyn' was relatively expensive in 1490: *Glas. Mun.*, ii, 256.
114. *Ibid.*, i, 91; iii, 521.
115. Brown, *Early Travellers*, 152.
116. GUA Clerk's Press 8, p. 252.
117. The 'long stair' and a 'laich chalmer' were repaired in this close (1611), *ibid.*, pp. 97–8.
118. *Glas. Mun.*, i, 91; iii, 521.
119. *Ibid.*, ii, 256.
120. *Ibid.*, iii, 518.
121. *Glas. Mun.*, ii, 30; i, 11.
122. *Ibid.*, iii, 521.
123. *Ibid.*, ii, 256, 259.
124. *Ibid.*, ii, 70, 86.
125. See Appendix E.
126. Clerk's Press 8, pp. 22, 125.
127. *Glas. Mun.*, i, 11.
128. *Ibid.*, iii, 518.
129. *Ibid.*, ii, 461.
130. *Ibid.*, iii, 518.
131. *Ibid.*, i, 11.
132. *IR*, xxiii, 139, 147.
133. *Glas. Mun.*, i, 493.

3. The Government of the University

'We make known to all men that we take and specially reserve under our firm peace, guardianship, defence and maintenance all Rectors for the time, Deans of faculty, procurators of nations, regents, masters and scholars present and to come, studying in the aforesaid university. And also by these presents we freely exempt the same Rectors, Deans, procurators, regents, masters, beadles, scribes, booksellers, parchment-sellers and scholars in continuous study from all tributes . . . henceforward within our realm.'
Letter of Protection of James II

WHEN one first turns to the statutes of a medieval university one is immediately struck by two things: on the one hand, that, while contemporary society was very conscious of hierarchical divisions, members of the university are concerned to stress throughout their basic equality as well as their reciprocal obligations, that nobody is 'anybody's man'[1] and, on the other hand, that everybody becomes 'everybody else's man' by virtue of a network of oaths. A university was a sworn society, and any further advancement within that society, whether by promotion to degrees or appointment to offices, was safeguarded by oath-taking, to protect the community's collective personality, its capacity to own property and acquire authority, to ensure support against outside agencies and lifelong support from its transitory student population.[2]

This development was assisted in different ways in Bologna and Paris, by which the liberties and immunities of students and masters were 'licensed' and the licence was at length granted freely. Partly the model is to be sought in the early medieval confraternities and other spontaneous groupings, but partly also in cathedral chapters whose recruitment was by way of co-option, but all of which had the same characteristics of mutual dependence and shared ceremonies and meals, by which the members could acquire a more intense community feeling.[3] The individual was a necessary member of the university; but he affirmed his own individual nature as a group member by integrating himself as fully as possible into its collective legal and moral personality.

The main sources for a constitutional account of Glasgow university, to which these early developments are the background, are the bull of foundation, the university statutes, the statutes of the faculty of arts and some excerpts of statutes from the original faculty of canon law. But the statutes by themselves are meaningless without reference to the medieval Rector's book for university business and the Dean's book for arts faculty business. Even so, these skeleton minutes yield a very meagre quota of solid fact for the history of teaching as such and have to be supplemented, where this is possible, from external historical sources.

The bull of foundation of a university is its official charter of incorporation. At every stage from his initial inscription to graduation, and on his assuming office, the member had to swear to keep the privileges, statutes and liberties of the university.[4] Nicholas V's bull to Glasgow granted 'the privileges, liberties, honours, exemptions and immunities granted by the apostolic see or otherwise given' to Bologna. The word privilege, 'private law', means a specific arrangement, as distinct from a public enactment, and originated in the pre-university agreements protecting the persons and property of strangers and scholars in the Italian cities. 'Liberties' here refers not to what is now understood by 'academic freedom' so much as to freedom from civil jurisdiction. The 'exemptions' were tax exemptions, the 'immunities' were from civil obligations, and, as a body, also from military service and ecclesiastical excommunication. The word 'honours' refers to degrees as can be seen from 'magisterii . . . honorem' later used in the same bull.

The university also exacted obedience to statutes.[5] It was clearly impracticable for all the 'university of masters' to frame such statutes: the masters therefore deputed some of their number to legislate regarding academic dress, the order of lectures and disputations, and funerals.[6]

To administer its statutes the university required officers. Canonists found universities difficult entities to envisage. They were unlike cathedral chapters, though at Glasgow the first congregation refers to the 'general chapter' of the university.[7] The methods and studies of the constituent faculties differ greatly, yet they cohere together and have interdisciplinary bonds. At Paris the arts faculty, a corporation within a corporation, gradually came to act on behalf of other faculties. The university itself required a procurator in law to defend its interests at the Roman court and elsewhere, a genuine representative chosen by the members, and hence the need for general assemblies or congregations of university members. At Paris, too, the arts faculty constituted the four nations with separate procurators for each, and this pattern was copied in most universities, though elsewhere, and in the Scottish universities, they are a pale shadow of their Parisian originals.

At Bologna the nations were parts of the double university there, the cismontane and ultramontane universities, both of which acquired common policies. In Paris they were societies of masters; in Bologna of students. To adopt the Paris system was often awkward, especially if the arts faculty was numerically weak. Heidelberg, Erfurt and Cologne had no nations at all.[8] The first book of 'Acts of the Rector' (*Acta Rectorum*) has not survived at St Andrews and the university statutes only exist in a defective sixteenth-century transcript, but the bishop's supplication of 1413 stated that the Rector was to be 'assumed' or elected by the faculties (*per hujusmodi facultates assumendus seu eligendus*).[9] Scots students at Avignon would have found no nations there, though perhaps the adoption of a process of electing rather than 'assuming' a Rector to office may have forced a change of mind on Bishop Wardlaw.[10]

The Glasgow nations, as fixed by statute and ordinance 'with the consent of all' in Turnbull's presence in 1452 were Clydesdale, Teviotdale, Albany and Rothesay.[11] Albany, chosen perhaps as at St Andrews for its recent royal associations, described all land north of the Forth, a province with a character of its own. Rothesay, chosen probably for similar reasons, included Ayr (with its three deaneries), all Galloway west of the Urr Water (the boundary of the Desnes deanery), Argyle (a bishopric), the Isles (a bishopric whose see was moved from Snizort,[12] probably to Rothesay), Lennox (a deanery) and Ireland (which had no university). All were Celtic areas or in close touch with Celtic areas, though the northern highlands as such are excluded. Even at Aberdeen, where there is a problem about the original division of these provinces, the highlands as such seem to be overlooked.[13]

Clydesdale, a geographical unit, included Erickstanebrae ('Arykstane'), Dumbarton, the whole barony of Renfrew and the parish of Old Kilpatrick, that is the Clyde valley from the mouth of the river up to its headwaters: in other words, incorporating Paisley, Rutherglen, Hamilton and Lanark. Teviotdale corresponded in the main to the Lothian nation at St Andrews: it included Lothian, Stirling (whose 'provincial' sympathies may have approximated more closely to those of the Albany nation), and all towns east of the Urr Water (i.e. Dumfries and the Border towns).

These nations do not merely represent the sees of Glasgow, Lismore and the Isles.[14] They are regions of Scotland (with Ireland added, appropriately) and not nations in the sense of Bologna and Paris. This arrangement was not unique to Scottish universities. The later university foundations had become less cosmopolitan and, at least, Glasgow was prepared to look overseas to Ireland. Nations were student groups gathering together students of homogeneous outlook, and were representative, not of the student's domicile, but his birthplace.[15] At Glasgow in 1530, as there were no representatives of Albany and Teviotdale, these nations were non-existent for that year.[16]

To vote—and every student had a vote in the Rector's election—the student had to become a member of the university corporation. After incorporation he was a 'suppost', one 'placed under' the rule of the Rector, and so became involved in the cycle of oath-taking. He swore that he would obey the Rectorial commands, no matter what his future station in life; that he would keep the university's secrets (matters discussed in congregation) and not reveal them to the university's prejudice, and that he would maintain its 'privileges, statutes and liberties'.[17] A St Andrews statute laid down that no new student (*nouicius scolarum*, that is novice, bejant) should be admitted by any master to ordinary and extraordinary lectures in any faculty without having taken oath to the Rector and university in his first fortnight in the *studium*; nor would his time spent in any faculty beforehand count towards promotion. Graduates or students were exempted only if under fourteen—to comply with canonical requirements regarding the age for legal oath-taking. The oath at St Andrews was taken on the gospels and included the promise that, after summons to attend congregation, he would give loyally of his advice and help.[18]

How far this rule that the oath be taken on entry was kept is another matter altogether. For instance, there is evidence that some students did not become incorporated till they were already bachelors[19]; Robert Penven is recorded in the arts faculty a year before his incorporation in the university[20]; a number of incorporations were not entered at all[21]; in some instances the date is doubtful (though this may be due to re-arrangement by the 1490 scribe of earlier paper records)[22]; and at others the full name is omitted.[23] Sometimes the place of origin is fully given, as with 'Robert Bunch, son of John Bunch of St Johnston' (Perth); more often we are left to guess.[24]

The origin of the Rector's office is obscure. At Paris initially there were officers who were essentially procurators for the corporation of masters and at Oxford for a time both terms were interchangeable. At Bologna he was Rector of the mature law students, who began by combining for the hire of a lecturer and who ended by dominating the *studium*.[25] How far this 'student power' phenomenon really meant that Bologna was in fact 'the freest of universities', as the Glasgow founders clearly believed,[26] is a controverted matter. If the Glasgow foundation, as has been suggested here, was intended in the first place for such mature students who were mostly graduates already, the freedom guaranteed to undergraduates must have been more in the matter of tax and other immunities granted by the pope, the King and the town than in the possibility of an undergraduate Rector (which never happened) or undergraduate presence in the central committees controlling university and faculty. The Rector, however, and not the chancellor was the head of the university; he had to be a cleric as clerics were under his rule.

The election of the Rector followed the pattern laid down in canon law, and that can be clearly discerned at Glasgow where the complete statutes are available. The law prescribed that nobody could put himself in possession of an office, but must be designated for it, and that by competent authority; that is, whether nominated by an authority with competence to nominate, presented by a patron, postulated or elected by a collective body. In the last instance, the elect was merely 'designate' until the election was confirmed, or in the matter of a Rectorial election, where confirmation was unnecessary, ratified by the elect's acceptance of office.[27] The first Rector at Glasgow, David Cadzow, was probably 'assumed' to office at Turnbull's suggestion, and the bishop presumably had his way again by turning up for the congregation in 1452 when Cadzow was continued in office although the decision is said to have been accepted amicably enough.[28] Another Rector is said to have accepted not at the wish of members but of the 'lords of the university', but this may have been because he needed persuasion to accept.[29] In 1498 Patrick Elphinstone was absent when he was elected; he may have been embarrassed because his bishop relative was founding a rival university in Aberdeen, but his initial reluctance to serve was overcome by the members' insistence and he took office.[30]

It is well known that in the Glasgow bull the bishops are described as 'Rectors, called chancellors', with the same power over doctors, masters and students as had the Rectors of the two universities of Bologna.[31] The provision may have been meant to avoid appeals beyond the diocese or the habit of stormy Rectorials as at Pavia,[32] where Turnbull studied. The former seems the more likely motive, especially to safeguard against the potential intrusion into Glasgow's affairs of the conservators of the university of St Andrews.

The Glasgow statute ruled that election of the Rector should take place annually on the feast of Sts Crispin and Crispinian (25 October), shortly after the session began and not, as at St Andrews, in mid-course.[33] The retiring Rector, as chief of the electoral college, convoked, in consultation with his 'deputies', the congregation, a general one of all university members. He first fixed the date, if other than the statutory one, as well as the place, usually a church, as being secure from lay interference, especially the cathedral chapter-house, the door of which could be locked. The method used was probably proposed by the outgoing Rector, but by statute it was to be decided upon by members in their nations, who informed the retiring office-holder through their procurators.[34] The general electoral principles applied: certain voters were disqualified for various reasons such as notoriety (*infamia juris*), excommunication or deprivation of active voice in university government by judicial sentence of the university. The voter's freedom of choice had to be guaranteed: freedom from coercion and entitlement to secrecy.

The usual preliminary in ecclesiastical elections was a mass of the Holy Spirit. This was provided for by statute and was re-introduced by William Elphinstone, apparently a stickler for canonical procedure, perhaps because of negligence due to a change in the day of election from the middle to the beginning of October.[35] The students robed for the occasion, gathered outside the outgoing Rector's house, at eight or thereabouts and formed a processional company, led by the beadle, probably as the first bell rang for the service. Once the electoral congregation had assembled, nobody was authorised to leave till all was over.[36] The old Rector and his retiring council would then preside, asking that all the acts of his period of office be ratified or at least be not opposed, and then followed preliminary deliberations among the nations, the nations going to other parts of the lower church (or chapterhouse, if it could hold everybody) for this. The impression is given that the special electors alone may have followed this procedure.[37] By statute new procurators were first elected, but this is not clearly so till after 1482 and sometimes they appear to be elected after the Rector's election.[38] As at all general congregations the scribe called the roll, in which event it is hard to see how students entered in the faculty's but not in the university's books could have voted unless the student vote was not too highly prized.[39] When all was ready, the invocation to the Holy Spirit (*Veni Creator*) was recited, and the retiring Rector probably divested himself of the Rectorial cope.

There were three possible electoral methods: scrutiny, which involved the election of tellers, compromise and quasi-inspiration (*via Spiritus Sancti*). In the first the 'scrutators' gathered votes expressed by written ballot or by oral or other sign, noted in writing by the teller. The first two scrutinies were counts; after a further recount, the elect who had a majority of any kind was proclaimed, and the electoral papers then burnt. Procurators may have been elected in this way;[40] but our Rectorial elections (though, exceptionally, election without intrants was envisaged) show no trace of this method.[41] The method of compromise was advised by the Glasgow statutes,[42] but could not be compulsory, as in law the electors must be free to choose it and give it their written consent. The members by this method left the choice to one or more special electors acting in their names: such 'fit persons' had to be able to represent their mostly clerical constituency and this would tend to rule out undergraduate electors. The electors had to ratify such an election as if it were direct election. Compromise ended when the special electors revoked it, or if they postponed the choice too long (inevitable postponements occurred when the elect was absent) or did not observe the prescribed forms or take due time or chose an ineligible candidate. If the elect refused, the compromisers could proceed to repeat the election.

These special electors had no particular name at Bologna; at Paris and elsewhere they were called intrants, minor intrants for procuratorial, major for Rectorial, elections. Very seldom was a procurator himself an intrant, as with the procurator for Teviotdale in 1456; and at Paris the intrants were elected before, the Rector after, the religious service.[43] The time-limit given to the intrants to take counsel was usually fixed by the burning of a small candle.[44] The Glasgow students vacated the chapter-house to allow the intrants to be locked inside or the intrants themselves may have removed to another secure place.[45] At Paris nobody had the right of entry as long as the candle burned. There also the intrant, from whose nation the Rector had been elected, was allowed to emerge first from the conclave, a usage followed at St Andrews.[46] The Rector was still only Rector designate, and in the sixteenth century the intrants, are often called 'designators of the moderator'. For instance, at Paris in October, 1551, Mr John Stewart, was so appointed.[47] At St Andrews in 1517, the intrants were at cross purposes and a new congregation had to be publicly notified for new intrants to be chosen.[48]

The third method of election was via Spiritus Sancti where the result was technically 'an inspired choice', an election by acclamation. But the inspired choice was the work of the intrants.[49]

The new Rector designate had still to be proclaimed, and this the retiring Rector who presided over the electoral assembly proceeded to do; the intrants thanked him and ratified his acts on behalf of the university.[50] If there was a delay in awaiting the new Rector's acceptance, the law allowed a thirty-day interval. A few days elapsed in the 1466 election of Patrick Leitch and if an absentee was elected (absentem tamquam presentem), the delay could be longer.[51] The masters added their persuasion, but usually the university's will prevailed. The new Rector then took the oath in the hands of his predecessor to stand by the 'statutes, liberties and privileges' and compel others to do likewise; not to incorporate anybody who had not taken the usual loyalty oaths to the Lord Rector; to defend university members in their persons, servants and property; only to call general congregations when so required by the procurators or a majority of them (which effectively inhibited his absolute power) and then to follow faithfully the majority will; to have all acts and conclusions of the university during his period of office inserted in the university book; and not to give testimonials to anyone on his own authority alone.[52] This oath was taken publicly before the assembled members (*in facie universitatis*). He then received from the outgoing Rector the symbols of his office, the university seal and the Rectorial copes: at Aberdeen the great scarlet and the smaller cope.[53] Theoretically the university should then have rendered obedience individually, but this was probably covered by the oath taken at inscription. The scribe proceeded to record the election and a public thanksgiving, the *Te Deum*, was rendered. The Rector might give his blessing. The company then went in procession to the Rector's house, where, if Paris procedure was followed, wine and fruits were consumed.[54]

A post-Reformation St Andrews statute (which must have repeated an earlier one) laid down in the time of Laurence of Lindores, that subsequent Rectors should be chosen by four sworn electors from each nation, each to be given full elective power, and, in the event of a tie, the outgoing Rector could give his casting vote.[55] The statute is valuable as indicating the existence of an intrants' oath, not on record at Glasgow. The regulation did not obviate discord: the St Andrews intrants of 1518 seem to have come to blows when the Albany nation could not bring itself to agree on its choice of intrant, so that the retiring Rector decided that the election would have to be completed by the three who remained.[56] At St Andrews originally all members were involved and there survives a brief memorandum that students must proceed to congregation two by two, but the university decided to end the 'pointless uproar' of student elections in 1475 by confining the active say in them to doctors, masters, licentiates and bachelors in all the faculties, along with priests and priest religious.[57] At Aberdeen the ornaments of the Rector were kept in King's College Chapel; it is probable that there he merely received the Rector's bonnet on acceptance, but was then brought to the Rector's seat in chapel and installed and instituted with the copes and maces.[58]

The Rector's authority was, like a bishop's, not unconditional; just as a bishop was procurator for his canons and could not alienate or transact without their consent,[59] likewise the Rector was expected to protect and not alienate university property and defend the persons who had elected him. He could well be tempted to call to congregation only those in agreement with him, but once again such personal and secret arrangements were provided against at St Andrews.[60]

In cases before his tribunal the Rector was obliged by the Glasgow statutes to make use of the counsel of lawyers and especially of his four deputies—hence their other name, 'assessors'. These deputies looked after the interests of the nations. In his absence he must likewise choose as vice-Rector someone who could command authority: the statutes recommended a senior master in the arts faculty (reminiscent again of the domination by Paris of this faculty), a beneficed person who could receive obedience as Rector till the latter's return. That members might not plead ignorance of the law and that the Rector might show himself a constitutional ruler, the Glasgow Rector was expected to read the statutes twice annually, at least once in general congregation.[61] Such congregations have gone unrecorded, but at St Andrews one was held shortly after the election in a place fixed by him.[62]

What is the precise distinction in the Scottish universities of the period between decree (statute) and ordinance? It looks as though an ordinance meant the work of the Rector or Dean's advisory councils, whereas, statutes had only statutory force when confirmed by the university in a congregation of masters (*congregata in suppositis discretis*), which reserved to itself the power of adding to or subtracting from existing statutes and limiting the scope of dispensation, even when sought by the Rector himself.[63] The procedure can be followed in 1483. In January of that year the Rector called a meeting and invited the deliverance of the university on certain articles.[64] The deputies elected the previous October took the matter to their nations and, after debate, certain new deputies, four from each nation except Rothesay, were appointed, all men of experience, to an *ad hoc* committee, sitting with the Rector, but representing the whole university body. After some weeks the deliverance of this committee was published, not for ratification, but for execution, according to the mind and ordinance of the deputies (*ordinacio* here meaning 'order to execute'). Besides these statutes (which are those printed as such),[65] they issued others, *ordinances*, of a temporary nature. A similar *ad hoc* committee appointed on the university's foundation was representative only of the different faculty graduates for the nations were not yet constituted and first took oath to the university.[66] That these deputies of 1483 tampered as little as possible with the original university statutes is apparent from internal evidence: but additions and changes there were, some indicated by the use of the word 'henceforward'.[67] The originals were few in number, we are told.

Ordinances generally met a temporary emergency and concerned matters on which the Rector had power of decision and on which he took the advice of his council (*ut eorum utatur consilio*), to which they in turn brought clarification, and which could be ratified by the whole body at his successor's election.[68] The university also made ordinances on minor matters in general congregation, over which, of course, the Rector presided, but with the duty of concluding according to the majority vote.[69] At Glasgow, the deputies first appear in an *ad hoc* capacity, in 1453 concerning the introduction of a seal and archival chest, in 1465 taxation of the various faculties. By 1468 these Rector's assessors have acquired a permanent status.[70]

A statute of 1483 lays down that from that time on, the Rector must summon university congregations by prior notice ('schedule') on the doors of the cathedral and, if necessary, other churches and the university schools.[71] This notification must mention the time, place and motive of the congregation, presumably indicating an agenda: for instance, in 1453, there were three articles on the agenda, but in 1457 the reason for the congregation, apart from the election, was only intimated at the meeting itself.[72] General congregations, apart from statutory ones, could only be called on working days (lecturing days), and not without urgent need. To limit their abuse, the Rector must consult the procurators and abide by their majority decision. Absenteeism was discouraged by a system of fines, which in St Andrews were scaled from two shillings for prelates absent without reasonable excuse personally proffered, to sixpence for poor people like religious and certain classes of student.[73] Glasgow had no such sliding scale, but through the promotor exacted the maximum fee from all absentees who were to be summoned at once before the Rector to pay. This comparative stringency was at once nullified by remitting the fine to canons, their servants, vicars choral, high dignitaries and, more understandably, to members far gone in years.[74] In all such congregations the Rector must have with him the statutes and books of conclusions or act book, from 1490 bound in a single volume. The latter contained minutes only of general congregations held, written up often in very generalised or allusive form, acts and conclusions of the university body, names of incorporated members and their year of incorporation, but not meetings of his 'chamber of deputies'. There also was a separate Rector's court book recording instances of his jurisdiction which, unfortunately, we also lack.[75]

Some reference has already been made to the conduct of business in congregation. The final business in most instances seems to have been supplications for graces and complaints. The supplicant went outside while the meeting considered his request.[76] Contrary to general belief, the nations were not mere electoral units, but took part in university business as such.[77]

Council meetings were held with the deputies in the Rector's chamber and proceedings were private. They met on the day following the Rector's election to draw up new statutes if need be, or otherwise discuss the future of the university, 'the rule and exaltation of the university for the coming year'. Afterwards meetings were monthly as need arose and on a day fixed by the Rector. They were expected to give discreet advice on appointments to, or removals from, such offices as were reserved to him personally, that is the university beadle and scribe.[78] Their advice the Rector was compelled to take, but not necessarily to accept, and this was true also in the Rector's tribunal for the correction of delinquent members when that jurisdiction was not in abeyance.[79] These members of council were elected just after the Rector, chosen by him in conjunction with the four nations: that is, chosen by the procurators, who would take into consideration personal acceptability to the new Rector.[80]

The procurators of nations are to be sharply distinguished from that other university official, the Procurator, who is not provided for in the surviving statutes, but whose duties were apparently to represent the university in the courts. This official appears regularly from 1516, sometimes combining the office with another, usually that of Promoter.[81]

The four procurators of nations presided at Paris, and John Mair himself is witness to their precedence over other members, but their importance in Scotland was significantly less.[82] They were expected to be fit persons, which seems to mean at least bachelors in arts,[83] and otherwise capable of interpreting their regional group's viewpoint and presenting it convincingly in congregation and, as at St Andrews, in council.[84] St Andrews demanded a graduate or at least a subdeacon or above.[85] On appointment they received the four keys of the kist in which the university archives were placed with the seal. They could not open it, however, without leave either from the university or the Rector and his council. This was an advance on St Andrews procedure and a consequence of a decision made in 1453.[86] It is clear, however, that in 1501 when a newer, bigger kist was made that at first only two of the keepers were procurators, though next year the keys reverted to all four.[87]

While they could not, as at Orleans, force the Rector to call a general congregation, they were expected to cooperate with him in coming to a decision and he could not ignore their majority opinion.[88] At Glasgow, however, they had no say (apart from one recorded instance)[89] in drawing up statutes and at no Scottish university did they have a say in the regulation of examinations, so important a feature at Paris.

The St Andrews procurators were each required to have a book in which all members of their nation were inscribed, but no such procuratorial book has come down to us. An oath was also exacted, to which likewise there is no Glasgow parallel.[90] At St Andrews, the procurator could not leave the *studium* without letters of authorisation from his nation: he would then appoint a suitable substitute and give advance notice to the Rector. They were to be given places of honour in scholastic acts. At Glasgow the appointment of other university officers (deputies, promotors, bursars, and occasionally the scribe) was in their hands. It is easy to underestimate their position by relying for an account of it upon the statutes alone.[91]

The Scribe or Notary acted as secretary to the university. By statute, he was to be chosen by the Rector at the time of his election with the advice of at least the majority of his council.[92] Yet he was elected by the four nations in 1488, probably in fact by the procurators, who certainly continued him in office next year.[93] His duties included the transcription of judicial acts. When, in 1501, Patrick Coventry was substituted as vice-Rector he was given every faculty to hear and definitively terminate cases and pleas concerning members, in the presence of David Dunn, 'notary public and scribe of our court'.[94] In addition, Dunn acted as Promotor in 1493, not surprisingly as, in this respect, the offices were related.[95] It is to him that we owe the present Rector's book, which also incorporates statutes and copies of documents. He also kept lists of absentees from congregation according to nation. The first pages of the Rector's book are written up by John Gray and some of the other scribal hands can be recognised in the rest of the transcript. We have no record of a parchment maker till 1468 when a burgess was sworn in.[96] After that there is no subsequent record, and, of course, he was not strictly a university officer, but elsewhere in 1532 there is mention of seven 'parchement skynnis coft in Glasgu'.[97] The Scribe took oath to exercise this office to the welfare and honour of the university; to honour and obey the Rector of the period as far as he could; and not to reveal the secrets so largely entrusted to his keeping in a way prejudicial to the university. No officer of this name is accounted for at St Andrews or in the Aberdeen foundation documents.[98]

The Promotor, on the other hand, was an office apparently imported from St Andrews, but not till the new statutes were compiled in 1483. By these statutes he was to be elected with the Rector by the four intrants, and this sometimes happened.[99] Often, however, it was the majority vote of the procurators of nations that selected him. On one occasion the procurator for Clydesdale held the office.[100] His name comes from *promotor causarum*, and his job was to prepare cases for the Rector's court. He is given the title of a general syndic *ad negotia*,[101] meaning not a mere *ad hoc* appointment, but that all suits concerning the university were his concern; and the general run of these would naturally concern debt recovery, and the bringing of debtors before the Rector. When the office was in abeyance (1502–9), the Rector's court was also in abeyance.[102] His duties were not limited solely to financial actions. They concerned all university business.

c

A common defaulter was the licentiate who, having taken the oath to principiate within four months, failed to do so. Only a lawful impediment could excuse this negligence. The motive of this regulation, we are reminded, was to bring home to the graduates their obligations, lest 'in treating their oath as of little consequence they seem to enjoy the advantages of the university and to be better off than others adorning their mother with a son's obedience'.

Another common defaulter was the master of arts who failed to comply with the two years' compulsory requirement of post-graduate lecturing. He was to pay the fine fixed in the arts statutes, unless able to show some commutation or relaxation, whether by total remission or partial reduction of the fine or some other dispensation.[103] The invention of printing diminished the utility of such lectures, especially where confined to transmission of texts, and the rule must have become impossible of enforcement, thereby adding to the burden on the few teachers then considered adequate. Other dues to the common purse in other faculties were to be pursued by this officer, who was entitled to his expenses out of the university purse.[104] His oath stressed the fact that he was not to be moved by personal or emotional considerations. At St Andrews there is an early mention of this officer and his authority over faculty transgressors.[105]

The university had a common purse of a strictly limited nature: more like the fund of a guild than the sum of all the financial resources of the *studium*. It was in the hands of a university Bursar or Receiver. There is, in fact, no mention of him till 1482 when the bursar then named was continued in office.[106] One of the Rector's deputies may have handled the monies before that date. The common purse seems to be referred to in 1453, but then there had probably been an on-the-spot collection from the nations. There were two university collectors for the mace fund in 1460, and in 1465 four taxers (one from each nation) were appointed to carry out a collection by faculties.[107] An undated statute, modified in 1483, mentions the bursar's election on the same day as the Rector's.[108] The kind of stress that could rise between university and faculty can be seen at St Andrews in 1416 when an attempt was made to soak the faculty for the Rector's extraordinary expenses without previous faculty assent.[109]

After 1483, the Glasgow bursar was to be elected annually by the intrants at the Rector's election, and this procedure was occasionally followed.[110] But in 1488, we are informed that the custom was to elect him at a second congregation, apparently on the following day.[111] Frequently he was elected by the procurators of nations and at other times the scribe's phrasing is ambiguous.[112] His job was to recover university monies past and future and to summon debtors judicially for them if need be, in which duty the promotor assisted. He had to present a detailed annual account to the 'lords' deputed to hear it. He could not dispose of university property except by order of the Rector and his council. He was to keep a book in which to inscribe the names of graduates from whom university dues were taken and record the payments made. This book he had to make available on presenting his accounts and it was transferred to the new bursar on taking office. This university bursar's book did not survive at any of the Scottish universities, but at Glasgow and St Andrews there are fragmentary entries in the act books.

The university Beadle was not merely a ceremonial officer, but an indispensable public official: in later days he was known as the Arch-beadle, corresponding to the major beadle at Paris and the general beadle at Bologna.[113] A St Andrews statute of uncertain date maintained that beadles were principally servants of the Rector to execute his orders and that no Dean of faculty should presume to use his faculty beadle when required by the Rector for his purposes, nor should the beadle leave town without asking and receiving the Rector's leave to do so.[114]

At Glasgow he was eligible and removable from office at the Rector's will, after prior consultation with his council. It was implied that he was a priest.[115] The first beadle, John de Moffat, headed the list of initial incorporations and was presumably preceded by his master, the first Rector.[116] On statutory days he had to appear (his later name is *apparitor*) at the house of the Rector to do him service and precede him with the mace. He had to act as a conscientious messenger, but his messages were wholly within the university and concerned principally citations to be made at the Rector's mandate and not otherwise, and he had to report these to the university scribe: hence the evident utility when the offices were identical.[117]

Like the beadle in a Scots town, he was also a kind of public herald or announcer. He had to notify all public acts at the cathedral doors on the feast immediately preceding and promulgate the succeeding act in the schools of whatever faculty was celebrating it so as to avoid duplication. Public acts were bachelorship, licence, mastership, doctorate, general disputations of masters, inceptions of books (inaugural lectures), and university sermons in one of the Glasgow churches. He also intimated all university holidays in the calendar at the doors of 'schools' (lecture-rooms) or at least in some public place. As Rector's servant he was something of a maid-of-all-work.

Other duties resembled a sacristan's, adorning the schools and Rector's general congregations 'discreetly and honourably'. Discreet adornments were tapestries, tapers, hangings and cushions.[118] It was his duty to supervise on great occasions the distribution in the schools of gifts of gloves and bonnets with due regard to personal pre-eminence. It was also his duty to carry invitations to the banquets of graduands. This he was expected to do 'modestly and discreetly' on notice given by the president of the act or graduands themselves. He was also required to celebrate or have celebrated a mass of the Holy Spirit on statutory days.

Finally, he was a kind of serjeant acting on the Rector's behalf. Men of those days were exceedingly touchy about precedence and he had to make sure that he placed nobles and graduates in the seating arrangements in a conscientious and impartial way. It has been assumed that there was only one beadle at Glasgow and certainly only one mace has survived. Three maces are in point of fact mentioned: the Rector's staff of silver as it now exists; an earlier wooden mace, first mentioned in 1469; and a part-silver mace presented in 1519.[119] As at St Andrews, the university beadle may also have acted as beadle of the faculty of canon law.[120] Possibly the theologians, as they seem to have done for a time at least at St Andrews, shared the arts mace and beadle.[121] At Aberdeen two silver maces are listed among the Rector's ornaments.[122]

The word Faculty came to mean 'a corporation within a corporation'; the guild meaning is retained in expressions like the Faculty of Advocates. The term Dean was apparently also corporative in origin. Like the Rector he was really a procurator for his fellows.[123] It is possible that originally at St Andrews in the arts faculty the senior master was just 'assumed' to office automatically without the formality of election: but from 1425 at least he was elected.[124] Moreover, there is trace of only two other officers in the faculty of arts at that time, the beadle and the bursar. There seems to be the same paucity of officers in the early days at Glasgow and it is not clear that the Dean from the very start had deputies as such. At Angers the regents were styled the principal members of the faculty.[125] However, the 1452 statutes in Glasgow, in this respect following almost word for word the St Andrews statutes of 1439, clearly laid down that on the day of the Dean's election four deputies of experience were to be assigned to give him advice, put forward suggestions and generally hold a watching brief on the faculty's behalf. On the basis of such consultation he could put forward articles to congregation which the faculty could then accept or reject. He required their consent to call non-statutory congregations.[126] In spite of this undoubtedly early statute, there is no mention of deputies in the memoranda of the Dean's election till 1481 when they are clearly distinguished from those deputed as auditors of the bursar's accounts, deputies found much earlier.[127] Moreover, there are other occasions, admittedly late, when the Dean's deputies do not appear to be elected.[128]

When the faculty met the Dean and his council we can be sure it was not merely to exchange bows and pleasantries.

Student power, if in any sense it existed, did not attach to the Dean's election. He was elected by all the masters of the arts faculty present in the university at the time.[129] Evidence to the contrary, such as in 1543 and 1552 when the election was open to all student members, can only be adduced for years when there was a dearth of faculty masters proper[130]: and the device of continuation in office was employed in several lean years, 1545–1551 and 1553–1555.[131] The electoral method employed is left unstated, except that occasionally it was unanimous.[132] On election he sometimes required to be persuaded to accept and at times a delay ensued if the elect was absent.[133] He was given the books of statutes and conclusions and the faculty seal[134] after taking oath publicly 'in the face of' or 'in presence of' the faculty.[135] At one point he also promised to take office for a year, presumably to evade the need for a new election.[136] His powers were important for it was he, not the principal, who presided over the faculty and had precedence on all faculty occasions such as banquets: when a substitute was appointed, for instance in 1464, he had committed to him full power and jurisdiction: oddly enough this substitution of a vice-Dean took place then on the very day of the Dean's election.[137] In 1495 John Hutcheson ('Hugonis') was appointed on account of his 'enormous merits' in regard to the building operations; he had, however, absented himself on pilgrimage to the shrine of St Duthac at Tain and it was only later that he took office.[138]

It was rather unusual, however, when one Dean claimed that there could be no appeal from his decision to the faculty since he was its head.[139] The Dean's authority in the early days would need artificial bolstering. If, as suggested, he was, despite the statutes, originally without deputies, he stood alone in his authority. There are some traces of early struggles at St Andrews.[140] There in 1426 an oath was drawn up protecting the faculty's rights, renewed with slightly different wording in 1439 and adopted (and added to) at Glasgow in 1452.[141] In this version stress was laid on his acceptance of the faculty's conclusions as well as of its statutes and pressure was put on him to refuse promotion to students disobedient to regents. Moreover, he must impose the statutory penalty and not have emotive reasons for increasing or decreasing it. But even in 1426 he was to be a peacemaker, a 'common person', and, in exercising his privilege of convoking the faculty, not to do so secretly or bypass any master. Glasgow had additional secret regulations aimed at importunate supplicants for graces, supported by men of power exterior to the faculty, whose influence the Dean was expected to resist.

We are not told anything about procedure in congregation. At Caen, the Dean opened discussion and explained the business, listened first to the deliverance of the senior masters and, where necessary, silenced others under pain of perjury—presumably reflecting the feeling of the meeting! He was expected to compose his faculty minutes so as to reflect faithfully these discussions.[142] but our minutes are so brief that we have barely a hint of stormy sessions. The Dean could not alter statutes on his own authority, or dispense with some or all articles in any statute except as presiding over the faculty in congregation; nor could he dispense any statute defined as indispensable nor call a congregation to that end, under pain of expulsion, unless the faculty desired to meet for consultation. There was a liberal power otherwise of dispensation; so much so, that St Andrews referred to such tactics as behaving like a 'reed shaken by every wind'.[143] Supplications for graces had to be approved unanimously, that is only one or two at the maximum out of ten objecting and the suppliant himself excluded, nor would an application for a general dispensation be granted without a four to one majority.[144] In other matters the congregation probably proceeded by majority vote, the Dean having a casting vote.[145] Congregations took place on working days (lecturing days), unless the Dean's council agreed there was an urgent need. To them the Dean was obliged to bring the statutes and the Dean's act book. The close verbal similarity to the St Andrews statutes is noticeable.[146] At Aberdeen there are a few references to Deans of faculty, but little is known about them nor have their acts survived.[147]

The position of the faculty relative to the university depended on their relative numbers at any time. The Glasgow university statutes legislate for the faculties; at St Andrews, it eventually needed three congregations to overturn a faculty decree which the university had confirmed.[148] In one instance at Glasgow the university modified a faculty statute regarding invitations to university banquets, only to revert to the original later. In fact, a number of these statutes show the university at first legislating over the heads of faculties and then, whether spontaneously or moved by subsequent pressure, modifying its laws.[149]

Besides a university Receiver or Bursar there was also a faculty one, and here again the resemblance to St Andrews is noteworthy. He had to render accounts and not to dispose of faculty goods without due authorisation: the statutory date for this at Glasgow was the first lecturing day after midsummer (St John Baptist). Like the procurator he was responsible for 'procuring' debts.[150] The faculty Bursar was not responsible for regents' fees, though in a crisis they might apply for help, as did two regents in 1457.[151] The accounts entered in the Dean's act book seem to have been written up hurriedly in Roman numerals after the Dean's meeting and their arithmetic is not impeccable, but 'the College Comptis maid of all yeiris byroun unto the lxxix yeir' (up to 1579) no longer survive to make possible a more extensive check.[152] One constant factor was expenditure on the fabric. The names Bursar and Receiver are interchangeable, and the former term is found both early and late. At St Andrews in 1555 he became the quaestor, following a Parisian innovation.[153] This officer is not to be confused with the Steward who received money from students and others for their weekly upkeep.

The Faculty Beadle's duties were similar to those of the university Beadle and here again the Glasgow statutes are like those of St Andrews.[154] He took an oath to give prior service to the Rector and only afterwards to the Dean and faculty. As faculty beadle he had, however, to keep an eye more particularly to faculty custom than had his senior. Having access to many faculty and university secrets he might reveal these only to authorised people at authorised times. Like his university equivalent he arranged seating for scholastic functions according to degree, priority and place and personally took charge of the circuit and other summonses to acts or congregations. He supervised the taking of oaths by graduands and had fees paid to him for his services on various occasions to be discussed in connection with the students. He also claimed a portion of the faculty purse, which may have caused some heartburning. It is possible that his duties may have involved some bell-ringing and gate-keeping.[155]

William Hay, sub-principal of King's College, referring to a text of 1 Peter, said of the clerical tonsure or *corona*: 'The crown signifies that ministers of the church must be kings not as reigning (*regnando*) but as ruling (*regendo*)'.[156] The Regents had rule of the schools (*regimen scholarum*). Unfortunately, the only details of the regent's duties are contained in his oath, which merely relates to such matters as the faculty were directly concerned in and these will be detailed at length in a later chapter. He was not to be over-familiar with his scholars at their games or in invitations to meals (and if so, St Andrews added, rarely and not daily) and not to lead them outside the pedagogy (especially at night, added St Andrews) by shady districts or morally dangerous areas.[157] Each regent had to have a copy of the statutes, the contents of which he could only show to those directly concerned or to a trustworthy scribe: the Dean himself had to read or have read the statutes relating to them publicly three times annually to the gathering of students. A senior non-regent master might have his own copy to keep in his room. Obviously the regent would have knowledge of his students' and colleagues' private affairs which it would have been unprofessional to divulge to others, but here there is more than a hint also of the secretiveness of a closed corporation. This is not the whole picture, however, for the internal government of the college must have been their main concern and of that little is known.

The regents were occasionally referred to as 'professors of arts' or 'professors of philosophy' in the sixteenth century, especially at Aberdeen. This only served, however, to distinguish them from 'regents in grammar' or 'grammarians'[158] of whom there was one on the King's College foundation and, although there may occasionally have been some specialisation in logic or physics when the regents selected their texts at the opening of the new session, the upper limit of three arts regents at Glasgow must have inhibited the development of anything resembling a modern chair. The phrase 'second regent', used for instance in 1501, suggests that by then there were only two, apart from any appointment of a regent in grammar.[159]

The Principal Regent acquired status, less from the minor role he occupied in the original statutes,[160] than from the fact that he was in effective possession of the actual building, a single place after the Hamilton foundation; with him students would be involved in constant financial dealings. At St Andrews the 1533 regulations suggest that before the mushrooming of college foundations he was very much a *primus inter pares*.[161]

The Steward (*senescallus*) or 'Provisor' (provider) was not strictly a faculty appointment. He too would loom larger in the students' life than he does in our records. He was appointed by the principal and had charge of the provision of food and kitchen furnishings.[162] Special extra stewards were appointed for faculty feasts, as, for instance, at St Andrews, the stewards for the feast of St John who collected and expended the funds raised for special occasions.[163] Cooks, pantrymen, laundresses would also be in his charge, and he hired such workers as masons and slaters.[164]

The office of Faculty Promotor was first decided on in 1490 and collapsed for good with the temporary effacement of the Rector's court in the first decade of the sixteenth century: obviously he was meant to counter the interference of the university promotor (from whom he is to be distinguished) in faculty business. He was to act as procurator in all actions concerning the faculty, principally debtors arraigned or due to be arraigned before the Rector. It appears that his salary was not yet fixed by 1498. Only a few promotors are named and their election coincided with the Dean's.[165]

A Wardrobe Officer (*custos habituum*) also existed for a time and will be discussed in another context. David Gray was Faculty Notary, but his term of office was brief, unfortunately for the registration of our records.[166]

Non-regent masters are found helping out in faculty and university business, especially as faculty examiners. They may have done some lecturing of a less formal kind, and although some were clearly just former graduates who happened to live in town, others seem to be students in other faculties. They provided something of an external check on the limited possibilities open to a small staff of 'ordinary' teachers, though with the advance of the printed word students would not be fobbed off with merely routine textual exposition.

An interesting appointment (not strictly of an officer) was that of the Quodlibetarius, mentioned in the first Glasgow statutes and probably active from the beginning, though the first one is not named till 1463,[167] an accident of the record which does not at first record meetings for the opening of the session, a reflection of the lack of a tight faculty organisation before the Hamilton foundation.

The quodlibet disputations were general disputations open to all comers, held originally in Advent and Lent before the holiday breaks of Christmas and Easter.[168] They were not 'ordinary', but 'extra-ordinary', disputations. Nevertheless, they were of a solemn nature and attendance was often enforced, especially on the unfortunate master respondents unwilling to face the unexpected turns a disputation might take if a jealous rival intervened in the dispute with an ambiguous or embarrassing question, as happened to David Guild at St Andrews in 1541.[169] Originally none of the questions was notifiable. They could degenerate into sterile and frivolous debates, but their original virtue was to encourage an alert and well-informed mind in the presiding Quodlibetarius and in the responsals taking part. They are not to be confused with the *quodlibetariae ordinariae*, which were general disputa-tions (and not strictly quodlibets at all) which each master undertook according to his seniority in the faculty.[170] In the arts faculty, bachelors of theology are found acting as Quodlibetarius, and the two nominated at Glasgow were both theologians, Duncan Bunch from Cologne and Patrick Coventry from St Andrews where the office was founded under the stimulus of the Glasgow foundation.[171] The model at Glasgow is said to be Bologna[172] or Cologne,[173] the Parisian disputation having fallen into disuse to be revived by Cardinal d'Estouteville.[174] The Glasgow statutes confine themselves to the bare mention of a few details, the election of the Quodlibetarius, the salary, the opening date and the banquet following its close. The Cologne statutes, in conjunction with those of Louvain, fill in the picture.

The Quodlibetarius was chosen at Glasgow on the first lecturing day after St Luke (18 October). The early choice gave him time to prepare, to collect possible questions for airing; books for the purpose were provided in 1460 at St Andrews.[175] It also gave him time to notify masters to act as respondents in the daily sittings; though they might need arm twisting persuasion more than simple notification.

As at Louvain[176] and Cologne, the actual disputation opened in mid-December, on or about the feast of St Lucy. At both places the territory covered was strictly limited to the seven liberal arts and additional subjects in the arts curriculum. At Louvain the size of the auditorium forced a move from the small chapel to the greater schools. At Cologne the senior master was Quodlibetarius. But, if he declined, a fairly senior regent was chosen, relatively young perhaps but not inexperienced. A salary was paid as at Glasgow, where the Faculty Receiver gave one Scots noble. The presiding Quodlibetarius at Cologne entered schools with a bachelor respondent, who responded to an initial 'expectatory' question till a reasonable quota of masters was present, after which the bachelor was dismissed.

At Cologne and Louvain procedure thereafter was identical. The Quodlibetarius proposed to the respondent for that day one question with arguments and then two quodlibets, that is questions not previously notified. The respondent replied to the notifiable questions by three conclusions and three or more corollaries. He responded to the two quodlibets (*causam quesiti assignando*), probably, that is, not in the form of conclusions and corollaries.

When the presiding master had finished his quodlibets, the bachelors were allowed to choose a master to whom to propound a quodlibet; they did this again according to seniority. The scholars followed suit. To make the disputation more colourful for the young, since much of the matter discussed was above their heads—and so as not to dissuade them from returning to their studies after the holidays—a modicum of seasonable entertainment was permitted provided the jokes were not of a shameful or defamatory character in the style of end-of-term fun. This procedure was repeated each day till the end of responsions. At the close the Quodlibetarius was expected to assemble the heterogeneous questions in some intelligible order and reply to them in a separate sitting, the final magisterial determination. This is not mentioned, however, explicitly in the statutes.

After the quodlibet, the masters who responded were called to a common refreshment (*solatium*) or banquet. At Glasgow likewise all the masters met together on the feast of St Thomas, apostle (21 December), in a place fixed by the faculty and had three drinks together, one of wine if obtainable. There the Quodlibetarius was thanked publicly and duly paid.[177] The later evidence of St Andrews shows more organisation and some loss of spontaneity.

The general picture is of very ambitious beginnings and a top-heavy administrative structure which had to be whittled down. The faculty of arts and the university at first tried to live separate lives but eventually both of them had to coalesce into a single administrative unit, the faculty shedding its parallel administration almost, but not quite, entirely, with only two officers (apart from kitchen staff and regents) whose existence is continuously documented, the Bursar and the Dean.

NOTES

1. P. Michaud-Quantin, 'La conscience d'être membre d'une universitas', *Miscellanea Mediaevalia* (Beiträge zum Berufsbewusstein des mittelalterlichen Menschen, ed. P. Wilpert; Berlin, 1964), iii, 1–14.
2. P. Kibre, 'Academic oaths at the university of Paris in the Middle Ages', *Essays in Medieval Life and Thought presented in honour of Austin Patterson Evans*, ed. John H. Mundy, Richard W. Emery, Benjamin N. Nelson (New York, 1955), 123–37.
3. H. Koeppler, 'Frederick Barbarossa and the Schools of Bologna', *English Historical Review*, liv (1939), 577–607; G. Post, 'Alexander III, the *Licentia docendi* and the rise of universities', *Anniversary Essays in Medieval History by Students of Charles Homer Haskins* (Boston, New York, 1929), 255–77; Hastings Rashdall, *The Universities of Europe in the Middle Ages*, second edition, ed. F. M. Powicke and A. B. Emden (Oxford, 1936), i, 282.
4. P. Kibre, *Scholarly Privileges in the Middle Ages* (1961), *passim*.
5. G. Post, 'Parisian Masters as a Corporation', *Speculum*, ix, 426ff. Cf. J. Verger, 'Les universités comme corporations' in *Les Universités au Moyen Age* (Paris, 1973), 47ff.
6. *Glas. Mun.*, ii, 57–8.
7. *Ibid.*, ii, 55.
8. P. Kibre, *The Nations in the Medieval Universities* (Cambridge, Mass., 1948), 177.
9. J. M. Anderson, 'James I of Scotland and the University of St Andrews', *SHR* (1906), iii, 314.
10. The second book of Acta Rectorum may not be altogether accurate in its statement that the nation system at St Andrews was adopted under the first Rector, Laurence of Lindores: this may be no more than late tradition. The lost Title, one of the 1533 St Andrews statutes, contained the division of the nations in its sixth constitution.
11. *Glas. Mun.*, ii, 6, 59–60.
12. D. E. R. Watt, *Fasti Ecclesiae Scoticanae Medii Aevi ad annum 1638* (SRS, Edinburgh, 1969).
13. W. M. Alexander, *The Four Nations of Aberdeen University and their European Background* (Aberdeen University Studies, no. 108, Aberdeen, 1934), 12. Only three procurators are mentioned in 1516 and nations are not specified, *Officers and Graduates of King's College*, ed., P. J. Anderson (Aberdeen, 1893), 7 (but cf. 346).
14. J. D. Mackie, *The University of Glasgow: 1451 to 1951* (Glasgow, 1954), 14. The deaneries in Scotland are not tidy areas, and Dumbarton, though in the Lennox, was geographically in Clydesdale.
15. Kibre, *The Nations*, 4.

16. *Glas. Mun.*, ii, 156.
17. *Ibid.*, ii, 8, 14.
18. *Early Records*, ed. J. M. Anderson, xxiv. St Andrews University Archives, University statutes, titles 3 and 5.
19. *Glas. Mun.*, ii, 85, 220, which shows that both of them determined that year.
20. *Ibid.*, ii, 59, 178.
21. *Ibid.*, ii, 179 (Thomas Macguffock); 183 (George Crichton), etc.
22. *Ibid.*, ii, 60, Robert Pitcairn and Master Thomas Heclis (Eccles); this should either read 'Monday 11 September, 1452' or '12 September, 1457', otherwise the day is wrong.
23. 'Dominus Normannus' (Scot?), *ibid.*, ii, 64.
24. *Ibid.*, ii, 72.
25. Rashdall, *Universities*, i, 313, note 1; Kibre, The *Nations*, 65; Koeppler, *English Historical Review*, liv, 593.
26. *Glas. Mun.*, ii, 4, 22. The first Glasgow Rector was possibly of Bologna. See below.
27. The following draws heavily on *Dictionnaire de Droit Canonique*, s.v. 'Election'.
28. *Glas. Mun.*, ii, 60.
29. *Ibid.*, ii, 64. The 'lords of the university' were probably the Rector's advisory council.
30. The printed edition (*ibid.*, ii, 114) should read after 'absentem': 'qui tandem dictus (Rector) victus precibus suppositorum onus huiusmodi officii in se acceptauit'.
31. *Glas. Mun.*, ii, 45; Mackie, *University*, 8.
32. Kibre, *The Nations*, 127.
33. *Glas. Mun.*, ii, 5.
34. *Ibid.*, ii, 6.
35. *Ibid.*, ii, 5, 84.
36. *Ibid.*, ii, 5, 14. Cf., for elections in sixteenth-century Paris, Du Boulay, *Historia Universitatis Parisiensis* (Paris, 1665–73), vi, 168.
37. In 1452 'habita communicacione' is used only of the intrants, in 1456 'accedentibus singulis ad proprias nationes' before intrants were chosen: *Glas. Mun.*, ii, 60, 64.
38. There was probably a general 'academic musical chairs' resulting from a new Rector's appointment: *ibid.*, ii, 9.
39. *Ibid.*, ii, 8.
40. Cf. Kibre, *The Nations*, 67.
41. *Glas. Mun.*, ii, 9. The election with intrants was cumbersome with small numbers.
42. Kibre, *The Nations*, 36, 106. The four intrants at Cologne were from the faculties.
43. *Glas. Mun.*, ii, 72; Du Boulay, *Hist. Univ. Paris*, vi, 163, 167.
44. Kibre, *The Nations*, 67 (Paris), 149 (Angers); for Louvain, 'Statuts de l'université de Louvain antérieur à l'an 1459', ed. A. van Hove, *Bull. de la Comm. Royale d'Histoire de Belgique*, vol. 76 (1907), 597–662.
45. *Glas. Mun.*, ii, 128, 'magistri suppositi et studentes inibi pro tempore existentes . . . de novo exierunt'; but 'domini intrantes ad partem removentes et certi temporis intervallo communicantes matura deliberatione prehabita unanimi consensu elegerunt', Liber Rectoris, 73.
46. Alexander, *The Four Nations*, 27; Acta Rectorum, i, 101.
47. 'Ad eligendum futuri moderatoris nostre achademie designatorem, ubi . . . magister Ioannes steward . . . electus est', Paris University, Sorbonne, Archives, Reg. 15, f. 551v.
48. Acta Rectorum, i, 65.

49. *Glas. Mun.*, ii, 62.
50. *Ibid.*, ii, 62, 64.
51. *Ibid.*, ii, 66, 72, 109, etc.
52. *Ibid.*, ii, 6.
53. *Ibid.*, ii, 72, 90; F. C. Eeles, *King's College Chapel* (Aberdeen, 1956), 44–5.
54. *Glas. Mun.*, ii, 14.
55. *Evidence*, iii, 233.
56. Acta Rectorum, i, 68, 70.
57. *AFA*, 13, 459; MS St Andrews University Statutes, Title 5, c. 8. Not *all* religious, as J. M. Anderson, *Early Records*, xiv, implies (only *religiosi patres*).
58. Eeles, *King's College Chapel*, 44–5. This seat was hung with rich cloths adorned with the Elphinstone arms: *ibid.*, 40.
59. B. Tierney, *Foundations of the Conciliar Theory* (Cambridge, 1955), 107.
60. *Ibid.*, 117–24. The term *procurabo* and *procurabit* is found in his oaths of office, *Glas. Mun.*, ii, 6. St Andrews University Statutes, Title 2, c. 1.
61. *Glas. Mun.*, ii, 7.
62. St Andrews University Statutes, Title 3, c. 12.
63. *Glas. Mun.*, ii, 8, 83; 20, 116. Cf. *Statuta Antiqua*, ed. Strickland Gibson (Oxford, 1931), xxiff.
64. *Glas. Mun.*, ii, 93–6. The Rector produced a 'certain paper minute' of, it appears, his own proposed additions.
65. *Glas. Mun.*, ii, 3–20.
66. *Ibid.*, ii, 57–8 (*de consensu magistrorum facultatum*).
67. *Ibid.*, ii, 13, *deinceps* (tightening up on religious students in arts and canon law and on the relaxed procedure in incorporation). Cf. the scribe and promotor (9), the bursar and beadle (11), compulsory graduate lectures (14) and the control of principiation gifts (18). Also the alterations in the original calendar (16–17).
68. *Ibid.*, ii, 74, 77, 87, etc.
69. *Ibid.*, ii, 97, etc.
70. *Ibid.*, ii, 63 (use of the term *ordinauit*), 71, 74, 87 (omitted in latter, but cf. Liber Rectoris f. 53).
71. *Ibid.*, ii, 6–7. The printed edition often omits mention of this preliminary summons. Liber Rectoris, 68 after 'octuagesimo nono' read 'pretextu mandati et edicti publici honorabilis et egregii viri magistri thome murehede canonici glasguensis et Rectoris dicte universitatis' (*ibid.*, ii, 102) and Liber Rectoris, 76 (*Glas. Mun.*, ii, 111) add 'citacione preuia per edictum publicum in waluis ecclesie glasguensis affixum'.
72. *Glas. Mun.*, ii, 62, 65.
73. University statutes, Title 3, c. 6.
74. *Glas. Mun.*, ii, 15.
75. Another book for the Rector's tribunal (*ad lites*) was decided on in 1490, presumably replacing an earlier paper minute book; *ibid.*, ii, 105.
76. *Glas. Mun.*, ii, 15.
77. *Ibid.*, ii, 63; Kibre, *The Nations*, 182–3.
78. *Glas. Mun.*, ii, 8.
79. As it was for a time, *ibid.*, ii, 93, 105, 121.
80. *Glas. Mun.*, ii, 8; 103, 112, 131, etc. On one occasion the intrants chose them, *ibid.*, ii, 128 and cf. 156.
81. *Ibid.*, ii, 130, 136, 149, 158, etc.
82. *In Primum Sententiarum* (Paris, 1516), f. iiB.
83. A student in 1493, *Glas. Mun.*, ii, 110.
84. *Ibid.*, ii, 8.

85. *Early Records*, ed. J. M. Anderson, xii. Cf. Kibre, *The Nations*, 148 (Angers).
86. *Glas. Mun.*, ii, 63.
87. *Ibid.*, ii, 116–17.
88. Kibre, *The Nations*, 136; *Glas. Mun.*, ii, 68.
89. *Glas. Mun.*, ii, 93, 'statuta nonnulla de nouo condenda et maxime per Rectorem'.
90. St Andrews University Statutes, Title 3.
91. At King's College they had considerable say in college appointments, Eeles, *King's College Chapel*, 239.
92. *Glas. Mun.*, ii, 9, 114.
93. *Ibid.*, ii, 101, 103.
94. 'Cum omnimoda facultate causas et placita eiusdem uniuersitatis audiendi et diffinitiue terminandi cum ceteris clausulis ad premissa oportunis et hoc in presencia magistri David Dwne notarii publici et nostre curie scribe', Liber Rectoris, 81 (omitted *Glas. Mun.*, ii, 115).
95. *Glas. Mun.*, ii, 110.
96. *Ibid.*, ii, 73.
97. *Accounts of the Lord High Treasurer*, vi, 50, record this purchase.
98. Originally the beadle may have acted as scribe.
99. Mackie, *University*, 15; *Glas. Mun.*, ii, 9, 126, 128, etc.
100. *Ibid.*, ii, 131, 150–1, 154.
101. *Ibid.*, ii, 9. Cf. 104.
102. *Glas. Mun.*, ii, 117–24.
103. *Ibid.*, ii, 10.
104. *Ibid.*, ii, 10, 20. On p. 10 there should be a full stop after 'seipsum'; 'unipotentis' is a misreading for 'verumptamen'; and the stop should be deleted after 'premissorum'.
105. *AFA*, 3.
106. *Glas. Mun.*, ii, 92.
107. *Ibid.*, ii, 63, 68, 71.
108. *Ibid.*, ii, 20.
109. *AFA*, 13.
110. Mackie, *University*, 15–16; *Glas. Mun.*, ii, 101–2, 128.
111. *Ibid.*, ii, 101–2.
112. *Ibid.*, ii, 103, 112, 121.
113. Kibre, *The Nations*, 75, n. 1; 52, n. 2.
114. St Andrews University Statutes, Title 3.
115. *Glas. Mun.*, ii, 11.
116. *Ibid.*, ii, 55.
117. *AFA*, cxxviii (faculty beadle).
118. Cant, *College of St Salvator* (Edinburgh–London, 1950), 156–7 lists some such 'school' ornaments.
119. *Glas. Mun.*, ii, 73, 137.
120. *AFA*, ccxlix; William Boys was also beadle for canon law.
121. *Ibid.*, 16–17. Later the university shared a beadle with the arts faculty.
122. Eeles, *King's College Chapel*, 44.
123. At Louvain, the Dean was originally called Procurator.
124. *AFA*, 20.
125. *Statuts et Privilèges des Universités Françaises*, ed. M. Fournier (Paris, 1890–94), I, 425.
126. *Glas. Mun.*, ii, 37, t. 7, c. 21; *Statutes*, 105.
127. *Glas. Mun.*, ii, 190, 233, 237.
128. *Ibid.*, ii, 257, 264, 266, 295–9.

129. *Ibid.*, ii, 178.
130. *Ibid.*, ii, 293 (even so, in this instance the election was said to be unanimous; Liber Decani, 144, 'unanimi consensu' omitted), 298.
131. *Glas. Mun.*, ii, 296–9. Cf. Fournier, III, 179, 277.
132. *Ibid.*, ii, 178.
133. *Ibid.*, ii, 231.
134. Liber Decani, 67, omitted *Glas. Mun.*, ii, 233 (after 'Glasguensis' add, 'libros statutorum et conclusionum unacum sigillo facultatis recipiendo'). Cf. Liber Decani, 94.
135. Phrases usually omitted by the editor of *Glas. Mun.* Cf. Liber Decani, 21, 52.
136. *Glas. Mun.*, ii, 189, omitted after 'Dregarne' is '. . . et in eodem pro anno integro permansurus', Liber Decani, 14.
137. *Glas. Mun.*, ii, 200.
138. *Ibid.*, ii, 266, after 'arcium' (line 5), add 'ipso peregre profecto usque sanctum duthacum qui postea onus in se suscepit et in eadem congregacione continuati fuerunt deputati', Liber Decani, 116.
139. *Glas. Mun.*, ii, 206. Cf. Dean as 'caput facultatis' at Angers, Fournier, i, 425.
140. *AFA*, xx.
141. *Ibid.*, 21–2; *Statutes of the Faculty of Arts and the Faculty of Theology at the Period of the Reformation*, ed. R. K. Hannay (St Andrews University Publications, no. 7, St Andrews, 1910), 99; *Glas. Mun.*, ii, 33, t.b, c. 7.
142. Fournier, iii, 179, for Caen.
143. Hannay, *Statutes*, 104.
144. *Glas. Mun.*, ii, 36, t. 7, c. 13, 14.
145. Cf. Angers in Fournier, i, 425.
146. *Glas. Mun.*, ii, 36; Hannay, *Statutes*, 104–5.
147. *Fasti Aberdonenses*, 26, 39; Eeles, *King's College Chapel*, 163, etc.
148. St Andrews University Statutes, Title 3, c. 13.
149. *Glas. Mun.*, ii, 17–20. For mention of the Dean's seal, *ibid.*, ii, 37.
150. Hannay, *Statutes*, 98 should read 'de mandato decani *et* facultatis' to conform to *Glas. Mun.*, ii, 32.
151. *Glas. Mun.*, ii, 191.
152. *Ibid.*, iii, 517.
153. *AFA*, 405.
154. *Glas. Mun.*, ii, 32; Hannay, *Statutes*, 99.
155. *Glas. Mun.*, ii, 30, t. 5, c. 1–3, t. 6, c. 1, 2, 3. For the Beadle's quota, *Glas. Mun.*, ii, 183.
156. 'Praelectiones Magistri Gulielmi Hay, Primi Subprimarii Regalis Collegii Aberdonensis Manuscripto Redactae a fratre Gulielmi Sceuan Annis D. 1533–35', MS in King's College Library (a commentary on Marsilius of Inghen, partially edited for the Stair Society), f. 21A.
157. *Glas. Mun.*, ii, 35; Hannay, *Statutes*, 101–2.
158. Compare the 'classicus preceptor' of *c.* 1561 at St Andrews, who, however, treats of logic and ethics, Hannay, *Statutes*, 61.
159. *Glas. Mun.*, ii, 277.
160. *Ibid.*, ii, 18 (a subsequent modification).
161. St Andrews University Statutes, Title 4.
162. For lists of these, *Glas. Mun.*, ii, 256, 279–80.
163. *AFA*, cxxxiii–cxxxiv.
164. The pedagogy cook, *Glas. Mun.*, ii, 70; a mason, *ibid.*, ii, 110.
165. *Ibid.*, ii, 272, 275, 281.
166. *Ibid.*, ii, 254–9.

167. *Glas. Mun.*, ii, 198. Statutes, *ibid.*, ii, 24, t. 3, c. 2–3.
168. P. Glorieux, *La Littérature Quodlibétique* (Bibliothèque Thomiste, ed. P. Mandonnet, xxi) (Paris, 1935), 9ff, on which this account draws heavily.
169. J. Herkless and R. K. Hannay, *The College of St Leonard* (Edinburgh–London, 1905), 220ff.
170. *Glas. Mun.*, ii, 25, t. 3, c. 8.
171. *AFA*, xxiii, cxxvi.
172. C. Malagola, *Statuti*, 262.
173. Bianco, *Die alte Universität Köln: Anlagen* (Cologne, 1855), 59ff.
174. *CUP*, iv, 726.
175. *AFA*, 140.
176. *Bulletin de la Commission Royale d'Histoire* (Brussels, 1867) 3rd ser., ix, 172ff. And *Documents relatifs à l'histoire de l'Université de Louvain*, ed. Reusens, ii (1), 239ff.
177. *Glas. Mun.*, ii, 24, t. 3, c. 2, 3. For a similar use of 'solatium', cf. *ibid.*, ii, 39.

4. Arts: Ways Ancient and Modern

'Sanct thomas sayis that ye space fra ye erd to ye mone is xvm and xi mylis.'

The Cart of the Warld (Asloan MS)

'Albert, the subtyll clerk and wyss
That in his tyme seruit gret price . . .
In-tyll his tyme he opnit out
That war wnknawing and to dowt,
And left sindry experimentis,
That pruvis weil sutht his ententis,
That aristotil intil his days
Na plato twichit be na wais.'

Ratis Raving, ed. R. Girvan

To set the scene for the first beginnings in the arts faculty we must retrace our steps in time.[1] The founding of a medieval university necessarily happened in an ecclesiastical setting and, though the arts faculty was primarily a philosophy department, its rulers were constantly aware of the theologians looking over their shoulders, and this especially since the Paris condemnation of certain Aristotelian theses in 1277. The Platonists, by comparison, got off lightly.[2] The result was in some measure a blow to the autonomy of the arts teaching and even promoted a certain anti-Aristotelianism within the Aristotelian framework of the arts course: an infidelity to the text of the great man where this departed from Christian norms because the universities, though not research institutions, saw themselves as the 'think tanks' of a society that thought of itself as Christian. Hence, the Glasgow arts statutes insist that students should not disturb the peace but maintain concord 'with the four faculties, especially the faculty of theology'.[3] The great thirteenth-century pioneers like Thomas Aquinas and Albert were mainly realists in philosophy for whom general ideas, like goodness, were firmly rooted in reality and not just names attached by the mind. The nominalists of the fourteenth century ('modern', that is, to men of the fifteenth) applied 'Ockham's razor' to these generalities and insisted on the concrete and individual character of everything we know. The resulting embittered factionalism, however, of those who followed 'the ancient way' as against those who favoured 'the modern way', though not entirely unprecedented in the history of ideas, had become exacerbated by the start of the fifteenth century.[4] There is no doubt that the first teachers who arrived from Cologne and elsewhere at Glasgow

67

were enthusiastic partisans of 'the ancient way' who saw themselves as educational missionaries and committed advocates of a return to philosophical and theological sanity.

When St Andrews was founded—four decades earlier than Glasgow— the prevailing doctrine, supported by the Church establishment, was nominalist, based on Jean Buridan, a man of moderation in Church matters and a thinker of distinction. The nominalists had begun to feel especially virtuous as the English heretic, John Wyclif, and his Czech followers, were realists. The leading figure at St Andrews when Bishop Turnbull was an undergraduate was the passionately anti-Lollard inquisitor, Laurence of Lindores, a man of powerful mind—and, it would seem, of iron will—but a convinced adherent of the so-called 'modern way'. That young university, however, was acutely sensitive to intellectual cross-currents and already in 1418 an Albertist (the epithet was contemporary university slang) minority group was campaigning for Buridan to be abandoned in favour of the 'ancient way' of Albert the Great: and this in spite of the fact that simultaneously the Lollard threat (*insultum Lollardorum*) was sufficiently live for the faculty to insist on an oath from its new masters to defend the Church against it and the followers of Wyclif.[5] With the renewal of the English wars in France, Lindores had left for Scotland. There was a great university diaspora from Paris, and a new realist current of thinking had gained ground in the empty university halls. This was not exclusively Albertist, but there was a certain Albertist modishness, perhaps because Albert preceded the 1277 condemnations that had been such a watershed in the history of the faculty. The way of Albert had a polemical champion in Johannes de Novo Domo, a secular master, who refused even to debate with anti-Aristotelians and Epicureans, as he styled the followers of Buridan.[6] The strong language may have been used to cover secret blushes at keeping the company of Wyclif, but in the deserted university the realists had the field to themselves.

It is hard to envisage the stern figure of Lindores as in any way Epicurean, but the anti-Aristotelian charge had an element of truth. The advocates of Ockhamism, even as filtered by Buridan, had so revised and, in certain respects, advanced the world-picture bequeathed by Aristotle that to some contemporaries they might not appear as his friends. Ockham's theory of God's 'absolute power' and his perfect and total freedom in regard to his creation was an attempt to release Christian thinking from the grip of Arab 'kismet' and the iron necessity of the Greeks. Lindores likewise was prepared to extend the area of faith beyond what a modern Christian would think reasonable and yet maintain a naturalistic outlook in philosophy. He comes through to us as a kind of schizophrenic, a naturalist in philosophical matters (even, to Michalski, a radical sceptic), but a pessimist about the role of sweet reason in matters of faith.[7] An attitude such as this must have seemed to his younger contemporaries as no more than a holding operation.

It is likely that Lindores gave more attention to the intricacies of novel theories of supposition and consequences in logic than was given after his death when the swing back to realism began. Later, when nominalism once again took a new lease of life in the universities, it was claimed that they, the exponents of the modern way, constantly triumphed in university disputations, embarrassing their realist opponents with their superior command of sophisticated debating techniques. Unfortunately, the St Andrews faculty records shed no light on this, and the accident of manuscript survival suggests rather that the prime concern of Lindores was with physics. Here again, while we now have some insight into his commentary on 'living being' (the *De anima*), his questions on the *Physics* still await a modern editor.

Because of the presence of some of Laurence's manuscripts at Cracow, the university of Copernicus, there has been some interest in his version of the Buridan theory of 'impetus' as a possible ancestor of later scientific theories of free fall.[8] The language of Lindores, like that of the Oxford Merton school and the fourteenth-century Parisian teachers, shows them confusedly struggling with problems that in future centuries the scientific revolution would illuminate more precisely. The expression 'latitude of forms', for instance, conveys nothing to a modern scientist, but was used to account for changes as traversing a range or distance ('latitude'). That could be calculated and translated into mathematical terms. This early science was, moreover, for the most part and with differences of emphasis, the common possession of the rival schools.[9]

There were two stock reactions to the work of Lindores and his fellows. One was that of a Robert Gardiner, whose harangue attacking the liberal arts may, as has been suggested, be merely a sample of a genre involving odious comparisons of one's own chosen study (in this instance, canon law) and others less favoured.[10] But Gardiner's stance has something in common with that of the man of practical piety, with that of the Brethren of the Common Life and their founder, Geert Groote, who abandoned his juvenile nominalism for the 'ancient way' in later life.[11] Another reaction, that seemed saner and safer, was to go back to the sources and beyond the tired arguments of the previous century, and this approach appealed to the more confident and optimistic generation that began to take over as the convulsions of the Great Schism receded further into past history. It seems likely that King James I in attempting to transfer his university from St Andrews to Perth was doing no more than following a European trend which the brute fact of the triumphant re-emergence of Lindores, for which he had to make a special journey to Perth, should not obscure.[12] The kind of arguments for change that the Albertists presented at St Andrews in 1438, snatching victory out of renewed defeat, can be gauged by the parallel experience at Cologne from which Albertism's most effective Scottish partisan, John Athilmer, had come.[13]

By 1425, Paris was not the only centre where men refused to believe that 'Universalia realia sunt haeresis seminaria'. It had a constant good understanding with the relatively new university of Cologne where the imperial Electors of Mainz, Cologne and Trier presented a memorial to the university authorities in which the princes showed themselves anxious to protect the students from hard thinking. The Cologne teachers were remarkably unabashed. The Electors pointed to the subtleties and lofty principles of Thomas and Albert. These were out of the average student's mental reach, and in consequence youth was trapped in pernicious errors like those exemplified in the men of Prague. The masters countered their submission point by point, maintaining that the Czech heresy had to do with Wyclif and nobody else. There were, of course, perils in the path of philosophical discovery, but none that expert teaching found it impossible to overcome.[14]

Three key figures in the new Glasgow foundation were Andrew de Durisdeer from pre-nominalist Paris, William Elphinstone, senior, from Louvain and Duncan Bunch from Cologne.

Durisdeer was on the university statutes committee.[15] His name follows the Rector's. He was at St Andrews about the time of the Robert Gardiner protest.[16] From there he went to Paris where he studied under a teacher from Zwolle, where the Brethren of the Common Life were installed.[17] Like them he had some interest in works of practical charity, for as bishop he endowed the new hospital of St Nicholas in the cathedral area. But, more importantly from our point of view, he had from 1446 been a member of the household of Cardinal d'Estouteville who produced the Paris university reform of 1452.[18] Some of his relatives, the Muirheads, made their presence felt at Glasgow university. One Mark, incorporated there in 1453,[19] was ultramontane Rector at Bologna in 1457–8, lecturing there in 1455–6 in civil law.[20] His nephew, Thomas, is found studying rhetoric at Bologna in 1460–1 and was active thereafter in university congregations at Glasgow.[21] Durisdeer built the vicars' court as a place apart for the cathedral choral staff, of which a single inscribed stone survives:

> Has pater Andreas antistes condidit edes
> Presbiteris choro Glasgu famulantibus almo.[22]

The arts faculty records draw a distinction between the beginnings of teaching (*exordium*) and its formal inauguration (*formale inicium*). The first aspect of the latter to be mentioned is the Dean's election[23] which we are told took place in the first faculty congregation in the cathedral chapter-house at a certain indeterminate date in 1451. The masters elected, and the vote is said to have been unanimous. Already a common purse of twenty-nine shillings existed, presumably gathered from the three determinants of the same year.[24] The foundation bull was read on Trinity Sunday, 20 June, and the faculty could have been constituted any time in that week, on 25 June, for example, which soon became the statutory date for the Dean's election. As the next election was on 28 July 1452, however, this may have been the anniversary of the first election. In favour of this date is the fact that it fits well the revised dating proposed for the start of law teaching.[25]

The date for the publication of the bull, Trinity Sunday, was an apt one. The Rutherglen horse market, though not so important as their October fair, visited by all 'the lords of renown' in Scotland, would still bring visitors to the west in Trinity week, although neither Rutherglen nor Paisley abbey to which its kirk revenues were annexed, would particularly welcome Glasgow's new status.[26] Two other important west of Scotland occasions also occurred in 1451 in Trinity week—the Midsummer fairs at Ayr and Dumbarton.[27] In a contemporary poem 'the haill pepill of ruglingtoun' complained to the lords that the decay of their town was not due to its enemies or to private conspiracies, but to neglect by the great lords of their horse fair.[28]

The Dean elected was a canon of Glasgow, William Elphinstone, senior, father of the more famous son. He had graduated in arts at St Andrews in 1430 and accompanied Turnbull to Louvain in 1431.[29] From a university still dedicated to 'the modern way' he had proceeded to one dedicated to 'the ancient way'.[30] His personal friendship with the founder was an additional advantage. His initial tenure as Dean was short-lived, however, though he did act as an examiner in 1458 and was re-elected Dean in 1469. At least a man of his background would have scholastic ideals not in disharmony with those of the first teachers.

Duncan Bunch did not have the privilege of knowing Lindores: his heroes were in another camp. There was some irony in the fact that he was a native of Perth, in which town James I had threatened to reconstitute the disintegrating university of St Andrews with its multiple teaching centres and air of indiscipline (and, no doubt, of comparative academic freedom). Perth merchants would know Cologne and Louvain: it was the third town in the realm with some important religious houses there or near by. Its Carthusians could write Latin not unworthy of Erasmus, to judge by a letter to their Solomon, prior Haldenstone of St Andrews, who had sent them a commentary of

Ezekiel.[31] There was also an important Dominican study house there and one of Bunch's relatives, Gilbert, may have been a Dominican.[32] The Bunch family, certainly, figure largely in the Perth Dominican records.[33] He had also come from Cologne by way of St Andrews, where he was received in 1448 when Thomas Leitch was elected Dean,[34] who also came from the Albertist centre in Cologne, the *Bursa Laurentiana*. Leitch may have been the Thomas of Scotland under whom Bunch took his mastership in arts in 1447,[35] but his earlier studies there from September 1443 to 1445 when he determined, were under Archibald of Scotland, that is, Archibald Whitelaw. If Bunch graduated at about twenty, he was still a very young man, when, having been dispensed from the two year post-graduate lectures, he made for home.[36]

Since the days before the Council of Constance the sympathies of the ecclesiastical authorities had swung round from the 'modern' to the 'ancient' way.[37] The Hussites had begun to assume a less threatening shape than the collapse of Christian institutions themselves, the babble of contradictory voices at Basle, the Turk at the gate, the wars and aftermath of schism with the apocalyptic voices heard by many in the storms. A return to security and sanity that an institutionalised philosophy would bring is reflected in much of the language of the time. The Cologne arts students were advised, when faced by knotty problems, to follow the 'sane teachings' of Thomas and Albert and if they had to have recourse to other authorities in order to formulate difficulties, to return to the above teachers in order to dispel the 'darkness of ignorance'.[38] The will o' the wisp of a universally valid methodology that would provide keys to open every door is, therefore, part of the reason for the new enthusiasm for the 'ancient way'. In the rhythmic prose of the proemium to the Glasgow statutes, both for university and arts, we learn of 'the untarnished and sane doctrine' that with its brilliance would put an end to the 'darkness of evil and ignorance'.[39] But this lyrical document, not inappropriate to Trinity Sunday, not only emphasises clear ideas, it stresses the need for the warm espousal of them. To the unsympathetic eye it reads like a clumsy pastiche of Biblical phrases: but many of these are from the Wisdom literature (ascribed at the time to Solomon) and Bunch's gifts to the university library did, after all, include a small manuscript Bible written, we are told, in the finest of hands (*litera optima*).[40] A near contemporary of Bunch at Cologne, Richard Guthrie, had, from the evidence of his library, a similar unusual devotion to the Wisdom books.[41]

It was recognised that there were limits to the devotion to be exacted from Christian teachers towards Aristotle, that lay pagan thinker: but there had to be fidelity to the text of the philosopher, though without demanding the impossible.[42] Cardinal d'Estouteville went even further at Paris, detailing the lecturer's duty to be loyal to the text point by point.[43] Cardinal Bessarion, whom Nicholas V had also expedited to Bologna, was a champion of the harmony of Plato and Aristotle. The new Renaissance reverence for the texts of antiquity was present. But still as studied with the help of Albert (who lived before the *De causis* was recognised as a non-authentic work of Aristotle) it was bound, in spite of Albert's opposition, if not to Plato, at least to some Platonists of his day, to wear a certain Neoplatonist air.[44]

Bunch, at this point, would be in his early twenties, rather young to be a principal, at least of the single pedagogy, in which representatives of other faculties might reside with the arts students who were presided over by a theologian, much as the St Andrews Pedagogy had become about this time and not too dissimilar to King's College, Aberdeen, in its first stage of existence. Of course, there are likely to have been at least two separate centres of teaching, and some living in hostels. If Turnbull wanted a candidate as principal of a future single pedagogy it might have been Alexander Geddes, Cistercian monk of Melrose, licentiate in theology, also of Cologne, where he had begun his student days in 1429, and a somewhat maturer candidate.[45] Melrose had property in Glasgow, and, at any rate, Geddes was incorporated with the rest of the arts staff in September 1451.[46] Geddes, and not Bunch, was a member of the committee which produced the original university constitution.[47] He had a place of honour on 2 November among the three 'first regents' in arts, although the solemn act of determination was presided over by Bunch. As a religious he had studied but not graduated, having thus to supplicate the faculty's grace to lecture formally on Aristotle (that is, for the students' formal requirements), which supplication, as he had already been acting as such, the faculty allowed 'saving its privileges'. Geddes presided at the licence of Patrick Cunningham in 1452, but Bunch at his principiation.[48] The young Livingstone students may have felt more at ease with a monk of the same religious family as their internationally known elder relative, Thomas Livingstone, but they too determined under Bunch.[49] The last mention of him is in 1453 and Turnbull's death shortly afterwards may have meant a change of plan.[50] Another older master in arts, Walter Baird, vicar of Alyth (to which the Cistercians of Coupar Angus had the right of presentation),[51] incorporated with Bunch and Geddes, is otherwise unrecorded. The other regent, William Arthurlie, was a recent graduate of St Andrews, perhaps, if anything, slightly junior to Bunch.[52]

We have two main faculty records, one of which is the Dean's book (Liber Decani); like many such books, it is a purely formal record, with little or no information as to what the faculty was actually teaching. It is less reliable as a record for the period 1451 to 3 July 1477, as up to that point it claims to be a transcript of an earlier book. The records from 1510 to 1535 are missing and any few scraps of information have to be garnered elsewhere. After that date, the entries adopt a Sphinx-like discretion.

The arts statutes book goes back to the very origins of the university and faculty. On the face of it, it appears to be the actual copy on parchment which the faculty ordered Duncan Bunch to inscribe.[53] It thus, in its earliest entries, goes back to 1452. The original statutes, prefaced by a contents list, were certified at the end by Bunch's initials, 'd.b.', before subsequently entered conclusions. The editor's puzzlement at this no doubt excuses his interpretation of what clearly is meant to be 'Duncan Bunch' as the pious exclamation, 'Deus benedicatur'.[54] The only statute that would tell against this conclusion is Title One, which may have deepened the editorial puzzlement. There we are told that the mass of the Holy Spirit would be held 'at the time of resumption of ordinary lectures on the first of October' and that these lectures would last from the feast of St Michael to that of St Giles, abbot (1 September), and that, furthermore, the mass would be held in the cathedral.[55] But these entries prove on examination to have been tampered with. The original entries can be re-established from the university statutes, from which we gather that the statutory date for beginning ordinary lectures was originally the morrow of St Luke (19 October), that they continued till the vigil of the Exaltation of the Holy Cross (13 September); and the original meeting place for this mass can be glimpsed under an erasure in the Bunch manuscript—the 'church of the Friars Preachers'. (It is no more than a glimpse for only the 'f' is clearly visible, even under the ultra-violet lamp.)[56]

Not all congregations are recorded in the Dean's book. Some have been extracted and given permanence in the statutes book. Certain faculty statutes are recorded in the excerpts from the ancient Book of Conclusions.[57] It is clear from the Dean's act book that statutory dates were observed. The first day of the ordinary was the morrow of St Luke, when there was mass in the Blackfriars kirk, followed by a congregation in the same precincts and the senior masters' opening solemn disputation. The meeting for receiving determinants was on 2 November; for electing the Dean 25 June; and for opening the examination for licence 2 July.[58]

The Quodlibetarius, a faculty appointment reflecting the new confidence in open debate, was also elected on 19 October, though his disputation actually opened in December. The regents on that day made their choice of texts to lecture on. After 1468, there is no record of the faculty opening congregation in the Blackfriars kirk; like the rest of the arts congregations, it was held in the cathedral chapter-house.[59] Unfortunately not all inaugural meetings are recorded, but, generally speaking, after 1467 the morrow of St Luke was abandoned for the feast of St Remy, two days after Michaelmas.[60] Other illustrations could be cited serving to confirm the view that the statutes we now have are the originals that Duncan Bunch drew up in 1452.

A faculty seal was decided on in 1455, and was used for letters of quittance in 1457. It showed: Centre: a hand holding a book; Dexter: a salmon; Sinister: a bird; and it bore the legend, 'Seal of the faculty of arts of the university of Glasgow'. No faculty deeds as such, apart from those registered in the surviving act and statutes books, have come down to us from pre-Reformation days, so that we have no sample of this seal.[61] In 1452 a faculty cope, for the Dean presumably since it was financed from the common purse, was authorised. For this the Dean of the time and John Young, vicar of Stobo, were to buy the necessary cloth and students too were encouraged to wear their copes.[62] Obviously the faculty, in spite of plagues spiritual and physical, was now on the way to acquiring a permanent shape.

Of new regents in this period, the most interesting were Alexander Wemyss and James Ogilvie. Wemyss had held various faculty posts at St Andrews where he graduated with two future archbishops in that see, Graham and Scheves.[63] From St Andrews he came directly to Glasgow and for the next few years is found working in the college ('ad infra'), mostly with the logicians (determinants), till his departure in 1472.[64] Presumably he was one of John Athilmer's students at St Andrews. James Ogilvie, 'of baronial race by both parents', perhaps one of the Ogilvies of Inverquharity,[65] was an older and more experienced teacher. His bachelorship in arts is recorded in 1429 when Turnbull and Lindores were both still at St Andrews.[66] At the latest, therefore, his date of birth must be set early in 1414; he would have reached the statutory age for mastership by 1434, in which year he incepted at Cologne.[67] Pope Felix V appointed him to St Andrews as a rival to Bishop Kennedy, the client of the Roman pope, and as such Ogilvie wrote to the officials of St Andrews university in somewhat urgent terms to resist the transfer of the Council from Basle to Ferrara.[68] He was a teacher at Louvain in 1446 and at the university of the 'modern way', Vienna, where he was incorporated as a master of arts and a bachelor of theology in midsummer, 1450.[69] He first appears at St Andrews briefly in 1439 (when the arts statutes which provide a model for so many of the Glasgow ones were confirmed) and thereafter, after a renewed spell abroad, was a founded canon of the new St Salvator's College under Athilmer.[70] At this juncture, the latter's powerful personality was having explosive effects on his scholastic entourage at St Andrews and Ogilvie withdrew to quieter havens. Later, in extreme old age, he was to be one of the founding masters at Aberdeen.[71]

We have no hint as to his philosophical position. He was a conciliarist, but not all conciliarists were nominalists. As vicar of Cupar-Fife, he was incorporated at Glasgow in 1470, but his career as a Glasgow arts regent was brief, confined, as far as the records show, to a single year, 1472.[72] He was soon recalled to St Andrews and there, in 1472, he became the new provost of St Salvator's.[73] During Bunch's principalship, we thus find some cross-fertilisation in university life, even if it is not too certain whether it is accidental or planned.

With the advent in Glasgow of the Hamilton college, grammar was free to move out and leave the philosophers to themselves. The 'monitors' cited in passing in that foundation were, it may be suggested, not deputies of the regents like most of the *repetitores* at Bologna or the *submonitores* at Paris, though the latter place still held on to some preliminary literary training at the university stage. The parallel is more with the 'regents in grammar' found a few decades earlier at St Andrews, and, as such, under faculty control.[74] Shortly after Lord Hamilton's initiative, Simon Dalgleish founded in 1461 the grammar school external to the college, a move whereby the lay elements in the city were given a new influence and status. The diocesan chancellor still had a voice in who was to be appointed, but the town's provost and the town's citizens also had their say as to who should actually occupy the *scholas murales*, the buildings themselves. The ecclesiastical nominee was, henceforth, only a nominee, though a strong-minded diocesan chancellor could always risk confrontation with other strong-minded lay governors.[75] All very good and proper, and even an inevitable development, except for the consequent neglect of literary studies at university level. With grammar, which in its origins, had contributed massively to the development of logic, went rhetoric also, to which companion study humanist philologists, like Lorenzo Valla (who preceded Turnbull at Pavia), were then turning as a quarry for arguments against the whole western logical tradition since Boethius. Already Petrarch had turned his face against the trend towards making logic an end in itself: it was only part, the 'morning part', the necessary preliminary, to higher studies.[76]

Bishop Andrew de Durisdeer had begun to improve the music in the cathedral by appointing the first subchanter and refounding the college of vicars choral in a more compact physical setting.[77] In 1464, one student in the university, Sir John Hutcheson, wishing to cultivate music in greater depth, was dispensed from his two-year lecturing stint in arts in order to go to Edinburgh, which at Holyrood, Trinity College and perhaps already in the parish kirk of St Giles, could offer more varied facilities. Hutcheson was a contemporary of a French student (not merely a Scot called French) whose name has baffled the scribe who wrote down 'a certain John born in France'.[78]

Much can be deduced about intellectual trends from book donations. There is an undated gift of books—about a dozen volumes in all, in parchment or paper—from Duncan Bunch, made when he was canon of Glasgow (that is, after 1467) to the regents' library but not recorded until after his death. Some of these are texts, some more elaborate textual commentaries ('questions'). None, apparently, were printed books or manuscript copies of printed books. The gift includes none of his library's theological holdings which may have found another home.[79]

The binding of only one volume is mentioned, a bulky tome in a fine cover, containing all Aristotle's *Organon* as well as Boethius, Porphyry and Gilbert de la Porrée. There is a gloss or textual commentary on the five little logical treatises of Peter of Spain as used by John Elmer, that is Athilmer; Peter of Spain had been excluded from St Andrews until Athilmer's arrival from Cologne and his work became the most favoured manual of logic down to the seventeenth century.[80] There was also a part of the New Logic in a paper book, but there is no excessive emphasis on logic in the list.[81] Noticeable, however, is the unusual interest of the donor in the *Topics* and the *Metaphysics*. At Paris in 1452, d'Estouteville had called for a revival in the latter and also in ethical teaching.[82] But there is nothing on Aristotle's *Ethics* in the donation. Possibly the Bible, with, in particular, the books assigned to Solomon, is meant as a substitute. Yet Athilmer himself had borrowed from the faculty library at St Andrews the pseudo-Aristotelian Great Ethic (*Magna Moralia*).[83] There was a parchment book with Albert the Great on the *Physics*, which indicated clearly the donor's philosophical affiliations, and other works on the physics section of the curriculum, but exclusive of the *quadrivium* entirely: on this evidence, Bunch had no mathematical bent. The fact that the pool of bachelor lecturers were expected to confine themselves to Peter of Spain suggests that the nominalists of Paris were right in 1474 when they pointed to the lack of interest shown by the realists of their day in suppositions, consequences, ampliations and other parts of the medieval legacy: the bachelors would confine themselves strictly to Peter's text and students might have found the minimum of personal commentary involved an attractive feature of the 'ancient way'. Bunch's donation is exclusively a working library for regents in the faculty; if Archibald Whitelaw had given him any literary interests as a young freshman at Cologne, they find no echo here. None of these early manuscripts, however, are now in the university library. His colleague, William Elphinstone, senior, has had better fortune in the the survival of his books.

The *Organon*, Albert and Athilmer were absent altogether from the gift of Bishop John Laing, made in 1475. It consists exclusively of the scientific texts of Aristotle apart from the Eudemian ethics (*Liber de bona Fortuna*) and the spurious *Rhetorica ad Alexandrum*, all on parchment, and a paper book with questions by various commentators, unnamed unfortunately, on the texts of natural philosophy.[84]

Albertism or even the 'ancient way' as such was not laid down in the 1438 decision, suggested by the Church authorities, at St Andrews[85]: anything acceptable to Catholic theologians was acceptable to the Church. In certain parts of Germany the situation was clearly more rigid.[86] Ogilvie had been at Vienna which was almost wholly 'modern' in this special sense, but there is nothing especially specific to the 'modern way' at his time of writing (1441) in his acknowledging the two approaches of the learned and the unlearned. The St Andrews university masters, Ogilvie wrote, were able to handle the theological complexities and mystical depths of Christianity; ordinary people needed plain comprehensible teaching well within their capacities.[87] The shift away from Albertism is more evident in a donation of 1483. By that time Louis XI had failed in his attempt to expunge the 'modern way' as unsafe and unsound from the Paris curriculum.[88] Even so, there is no change in the realist trend.

The gift of John Brown, canon of Glasgow and former principal, is both more varied and more eclectic. The subtleties of logic were coming into their own again. Porphyry has several mentions and there is a small treatise on Suppositions. Peter of Spain, and not Buridan, was still in use and more prominently so. Six books of the *Nicomachean Ethics* were given and a moral commentary. The only mathematical works were the *Sphere* and *Algorismus* (fractions). The *Physics* was much less to the fore than with Bishop Laing. But, there was a diversity of commentary: Duns Scotus on Porphyry's introduction to logic, the commentary of Thomas Aquinas on certain books of the *Physics*, and an unidentified commentary by John Burley ('Burlaw') presumably the obscure Oxford Carmelite (died 1332), said to have commented on Aristotle, Porphyry and Gilbert de la Porrée, which fits in well enough with the pattern of these donations.[89] Later gifts to the library, small as they may have been, are unhappily not recorded.

One factor in the improved material situation of Bunch in his latter years is likely to have been the advancement to royal secretary of his old Cologne teacher, Archibald Whitelaw, and another the fact that James III in his minority was committed by parliament to the guardianship of, among others, the Bishop of Glasgow.[90] The new archbishop of St

Andrews, Patrick Graham, whether the allegations current about his mental breakdown were true or not, was no friend to Bunch. The motivation behind the royal embassy to Rome in May 1474, of which Bunch was the principal member, does not appear in the records, and, although there are references to his leaving the university in the manuscript of the faculty acts,[91] this must have been contingent on other prospects emerging elsewhere. There is no sign of his actually gaining the deanery of Dunkeld which he sought. The probability is that he left the Roman court (he did not die there) shortly after 13 June when he asked the pope's protection from Graham. He then claimed to have been teaching for twenty-four years,[92] and we know that the first decade at Glasgow, after the euphoric beginnings, was a bleak time of civil dissension and plague infection that tested all Bunch's powers of crisis management. In 1468 the teachers admitted that the prospective examinees were behindhand in their books for there was plague in the land.[93] Plague may have struck again in 1474—it raged in 1475—as some months before mid-December, when the news of it reached Rome, Bunch had certainly died.[94]

Before very long, with the advent of printed books, there would be a torrent of reading matter: but, as yet, the key advantage of the medieval graduate's limited bookshelf was the opportunity it offered of reading in depth. Furthermore, the 'academic obstacle race',[95] which made the university such a forcing house, may have lost some of its terrors as long as the revived 'ancient way' persisted. For a space, prolix personal commentaries were curtailed and attention was more directly focussed on a centrally important text that time had canonised and the authorities in Church and State seemed prepared to validate. Moreover, in Scotland at least, there was some mutual intellectual tolerance such as the St Andrews students had called for since the time of the Council of Constance. The inevitable tension between the desire for a comprehensive world-view that would bring about the dawn both of new enlightenment and inner renewal and, on the other hand, the spirit of critical and even sceptical enquiry, free from any theological or metaphysical contamination, that in some sense universities were also founded to foster, was bound to leave the way open to an ultimate revival of the 'modern way'. The arts faculty in 1451 was still thought of as subordinate. It taught only the 'elements of the word', so that 'God who is the word' should perfect his praise on the lips of the young through the teaching of the Divine Child (ut premia celestis philosophie discere studeamus *et elementa verbi. Proinde infantis magisterio subdenda est nostra infantia si forte verbum Deus ex ore infantium et lactentium dignetur laudem suam perficere*).[96] It was perhaps an impossible aim and the Dean and faculty must often have found their initial manifesto embarrassing and may, in consequence, have settled for more manageable ends.

NOTES

1. The following paragraphs on the history of ideas in the fifteenth century owe much to *Miscellanea Mediaevalia: Kölner Mediävistentagung*, ed. A. Zimmermann, ix: *Antiqui und Moderni* (Berlin/New York, 1974).
2. G. Leff, *Paris and Oxford Universities in the Thirteenth and Fourteenth Centuries: An Institutional and Intellectual History* (New York, 1968), 209.
3. *Glas. Mun.*, ii, 31, t. 6, c. 3.
4. N. W. Gilbert, 'Ockham, Wyclif, and the "via moderna" ', *Misc. Med.*, ix, 85ff. Cf. M. T. Clanchy, '*Moderni* in Education and Government in England', *Speculum*, 1 (1975), 671–88.
5. *AFA*, 11–12; Nicholson, *Scotland: The later Middle Ages*, 239–41.
6. *Misc. Med.*, ix, 97. G. Meersseman, 'Les origines parisiennes de l'albertisme colonais', *Archives d'histoire doctrinale et littéraire du Moyen Age*, vii, (1932), 128–30.
7. Cf. L. Moonan, 'Lawrence of Lindores on Life in the Living Being', *Classica et Mediaevalia*, xxvii (1966), 352. Laurence thought the *De anima* was so closely related to moral and theological matters, that it should be studied after the rest of *Physics*.
8. M. Markowski, 'Studien zu den Krakauer mittelalterlichen Physikkommentaren: die Impetustheorie', *Archives d'histoire doctrinale et littéraire du Moyen Age*, xxxv (1969), 188; K. Michalski, *La Philosophie au XIVe Siècle: Six Etudes*, ed. K. Flasch (Frankfurt, 1969), 29, 269–71.
9. On Lindores, see also J. H. Baxter, 'The Philosopher Laurence of Lindores', *The Philosophical Quarterly* (1955), v, 348–54; D. Shaw, 'Laurence of Lindores', *Records of the Scottish Church History Society*, xii, 47–62.
10. *AFA*, 39–41, note 2.
11. R. R. Post, *The Modern Devotion: Confrontation with Reformation and Humanism. Studies in Medieval Life and Thought* (Leiden, 1968), 164.
12. *AFA*, xviii, Cf., however, the comments of Nicholson, *Scotland: The Later Middle Ages*, 300–301.
13. *Ibid.*, 48–9.
14. F. Ehrle, *Der Sentenzenkommentar Peters von Candia*, 282–5.
15. *Glas. Mun.*, ii, 57, where 'subdecanus' should go with his name.
16. His St Andrews degree is only recorded at Paris. See below, n. 17.
17. *Auctarium*, ii, 501, 504.
18. *CPL*, ix, 554.
19. *Glas. Mun.*, ii, 57. His entry is on pp. 30–1 of the Liber Decani and should follow 'Dunnune', *ibid.*, ii, 60. The reference is to January 1453 and the editor's rearrangement is misleading.
20. A. Sorbelli, *Storia dell' Università di Bologna* (Bologna, 1944), i, 170 (Morer), 247 (Mureth). Reg. Supp. 506, f. 89v (Murhed).
21. Reg. Supp. 535, f. 266v; 538, f. 190v. He was canon of Glasgow (Carstairs).
22. *SHR*, ii, 110–11.
23. *Glas. Mun.*, ii, 178.
24. *Ibid.*, ii, 178–9. Two of them, Alexander and Michael Livingstone, are recorded as university members only from 23 September and 12 November, *ibid.*, ii,

57–8, but were presumably there before those dates. Master Robert Penven was received to the faculty at this meeting, though he was an incorporated member of the university till July 1452, *ibid.*, ii, 59, 178, having graduated at St Andrews in 1448, *AFA*, 73.

25. *Glas. Mun.*, ii, 179. Law teaching began on 29 July.
26. The first mention of the two Rutherglen fairs, St Luke's ('Lowkis day'), and that 'of old called the Trinitie Sunday' fair is in 1617, *RMS*, vi, 1618.
27. *The Royal Burgh of Ayr*, ed. A. I. Dunlop (Edinburgh, 1953), 24, 184; *RMS*, vi, 190.
28. *Maitland Folio Manuscript*, i, ed. W. A. Craigie, STS, ser. 2, 7 (Edinburgh, London, 1919), 437–41.
29. *AFA*, 25, 31; Reusens, *Matricule de l'Université de Louvain*, i, 49 ('Elsomsten', St Andrews diocese).
30. *Glas. Mun.*, ii, 192, 209.
31. This refers to Haldenstone's subjects (the canons of St Andrews priory) 'qui de vestro fecundo pectore archam testamenti misticam Ezechielicum volumenque continente talem sapienciam audiunt doctrinalem, quem admodum audivimus studio indefatigabili auscultando', *Copiale*, 203.
32. In a group of Edinburgh Dominicans of 1479, Anderson, *Laing Charters* (Edinburgh, 1899), no. 177.
33. R. Milne, *The Blackfriars of Perth* (1893), 51 for a Duncan Bunch (1459) signing a Perth Dominican document. Robert Bunch of Perth incorporated at Glasgow University was perhaps his nephew, *Glas. Mun.*, ii, 72.
34. *AFA*, 74–5.
35. Thomas Baron also taught at Cologne in the Laurentiana.
36. H. Keussen, *Die Matrikel der Universität Köln*, i, (1928), 467; and cf. also the asterisked pages, 105 (Athilmer), 107 (Whitelaw, Leitch, Baron).
37. Stefan Swiezawski, 'Le problème de la "via antiqua" et de la "via moderna" au XVe siècle et ses fondements idéologiques', *Misc. Med.*, ix, 484–93.
38. F. J. von Bianco, *Die Alte Universität Köln*, i, 295.
39. *Glas. Mun.*, ii, 3–4, 21. The arts version of this is the earlier.
40. *Ibid.*, iii, 405.
41. J. Durkan, 'An Arbroath book inventory of 1473', *Bibliotheck* (1961), iiii, 144–6.
42. *Glas. Mun.*, ii, 35, t. 6, c. 11.
43. *CUP*, iv, 727.
44. One of Guthrie's books was 'liber de causis alberti'. Regarding Albert and Plato, J. A. Weisheipl, 'Classification of the Sciences in Mediaeval Thought', *Mediaeval Studies*, xxvii (1965).
45. Keussen, i, 314. 'Fr Allex. de Mylros', Cistercian.
46. *Glas. Mun.*, ii, 57.
47. *Ibid.*, ii, 58.
48. *Ibid.*, ii, 180.
49. *Ibid.*, ii, 179. Nicholas Bully's incorporation is out of its proper place, *ibid.*, ii, 67. For Thomas Livingstone, cf. Burns, *Scottish Churchmen and the Council of Basle*, 12–14, 60–4, 82–5.
50. *Glas. Mun.*, ii, 63.
51. *ACSB*, 24, procurator at the curia in 1439 for the Cistercian abbot of Kinloss.
52. *AFA*, 73 (graduated in 1448).
53. *Glas. Mun.*, ii, 179. GUA Clerk's Press 3, described *Glas. Mun.*, ii, ix.
54. *Ibid.*, ii, 37.
55. *Ibid.*, ii, 22–3; the alteration is more obvious with 'sancti Michaelis' than with

primo die mensis Octobris'. Cf. *ibid.*, ii, 24, 182, 198, 201, 206, 208 (omitted words refer to choice of books).

56. *Ibid.*, ii, 16–17.
57. *Ibid.*, ii, 37–42.
58. *Ibid.*, ii, 25, 182; 26, 179 (sometimes there is a few days' variation); 23, 182; 27, 189 (the statutes originally had 2 July, altered to the next day).
59. *Glas. Mun.*, ii, 37, 188, show two exceptions (2 October 1454–5), but it was an exceptional time (plague). The reference (ii, 188) to the examination for licence generally opening on the feast of the Nativity of St John, rather than a week later, is an error (in this paragraph read 'proxime' for 'proximo' and 'dubius' for 'dubium').
60. *Ibid.*, ii, 206, 208. It was the original opening day at St Andrews, at Bologna and many of the French law universities. Cf. *AFA*, 3; *Statuti delle Università e dei Collegi dello Studio Bolognese*, ed. C. Malagola (Bologna, 1888), 267 (cf. 101, 473); Fournier, i, 465; ii, 311.
61. *Ibid.*, ii, 186, 191.
62. *Ibid.*, ii, 180–3. Regulations regarding graduates wearing their own copes had been cancelled by d'Estouteville, but remain here in modified form, *CUP*, iv, 733.
63. *AFA.*, 103–60.
64. *Glas. Mun.*, ii, 73, 208–16.
65. *Copiale*, 302ff.
66. *AFA*, 25.
67. Keussen, i, 355.
68. *Copiale*, 204.
69. *Ibid.*, 494; *Die Matrikel der Universität Wien* (Graz/Cologne, 1954), i, 279 (Publikationen des Instituts für Oesterreichsche Geschichtforschung. VI Reihe).
70. *AFA*, 54ff.
71. *Ibid.*, xxx, li, lxxiv.
72. *Glas. Mun.*, ii, 78, 215–16.
73. *ACSB*, 185; *AFA*, 192.
74. D'Estouteville in 1452 mentions these sub-monitors, *CUP*, iv, 726; *AFA*, 18, 31, 34–5.
75. *Prot. Bk. Simon*, 267. The master and scholars, according to the town's inventory (the original is lost) were responsible for certain religious services and the provost and council to be 'patrons, governors and defenders' of the donation: *Glas. Chrs.*, i (2), 436. The appointment in Turnbull's time of a provost, claimed to be the city's first, seems to reflect Turnbull's desire to give a greater place to laymen.
76. C. Vasoli, *La Dialettica e la Retorica dell'Umanesimo* (Milan, 1968), 11, 28ff. The *Elegantiae* appear to go back to 1439.
77. Cowan, *Parishes*, 56; Watt, *Fasti*, 169; *Glas. Reg.*, ii, 616.
78. *Glas. Mun.*, ii, 202 (twice); the first reading should be 'Johannes quidam natus de Francia', Liber Rectoris, 28.
79. *Glas. Mun.*, iii, 404–5.
80. *AFA*, 48.
81. The statutes give 15 weeks in all to lectures in logic, 18 in physics, 6 in metaphysics.
82. *CUP*, iv, 729.
83. *AFA*, 121.
84. *Glas. Mun.*, ii, 403–4.
85. *AFA*, 49.
86. A. L. Gabriel, in *Misc. Med.*, ix, 457–81.
87. *Copiale*, 207.

ARTS: ANCIENT AND MODERN 83

88. Text in Ehrle, 313. Cologne in 1447 was still associating Wyclif and Ockham, *ibid.*, 292.
89. A. B. Emden, ed. *A Biographical Register of the University of Oxford to A.D. 1500* (Oxford, 1957), i, 311–12.
90. Nicholson, *Scotland: The Later Middle Ages*, 398, 409. Though a student in theology, Whitelaw taught in arts at Cologne.
91. *Glas. Mun.*, ii, 226, the accounts have some omissions. After 'solidos' (line 5) and 'Duncani' (line 7) read 'ut ipse retulit in recessu suo'.
92. Reg. Supp. 705, 230v; 706, 292v.
93. *Charters and Documents relating to the Burgh of Peebles* (Scottish Burgh Records Society, Edinburgh, 1872), 157–8 mentions plague in Edinburgh.
94. Nicholson, *Scotland: The Later Middle Ages*, 423 note. *CPL*, xiii, 42. Bunch is only referred to as principal regent twice, both mentions being post-1460.
95. A. B. Cobban, *The Medieval Universities* (London, 1975), 215.
96. The words in italic are confined to the arts statutes which also add 'Unctio quippe magistra est . . .'. Cf. *Glas. Mun.*, ii, 4–5, 22. There are other slight verbal differences from the text of the university statutes.

D

5. Arts: The Faculty Structure

For 'obiectum' or 'subiectum' alsswa
He war expert couth fynd me termys twa
Quhilkis ar als ryfe amangis clerkis in scuyll
As evir fowlis plungit in laik or puyll.
                    Gavin Douglas, *Aeneid*, Bk. I (Prologue)
'And thus it is your quodlibet and dout
Ye gave to us to reid and gif it out.'
                    Anon., *The Thre Prestis of Peblis*

A MEDIEVAL arts curriculum everywhere was in every way quite unlike the typical curriculum of today, dominated as it then was by only one great name, Aristotle. The Glasgow faculty statutes by themselves give meagre information and have to be understood within the general university context of that time. They provide only the basic skeleton on which faculty procedures were built and have to be used cautiously as evidence for current practice, because, on the one hand, of the faculty's wide dispensing power, and, on the other, of the fact (imperfectly recorded sometimes) of subsequent constitutional development.

The Glasgow arts statutes strikingly resemble the St Andrews statutes, even as revised in 1570, and both of them derive from Paris. The St Andrews framers of 1439, including two later teachers of Bunch at Cologne, Thomas Baron and Archibald Whitelaw, had a copy of the Paris statutes before them.[1] When Bunch with his companions worked on the first text of the statutes at Glasgow, he must have had a copy of these 1439 statutes. He had just come to Glasgow from St Andrews,[2] but he had more experience of Cologne and this must have influenced him, apart altogether from the verbal mentions of that university which we find in the text.

The medieval vocabulary of learning is so strange to modern ears and its academic procedures such a minefield of potential misunderstanding that even eminent scholars tend to pick their way through it decently veiled in a mist of esoteric terminology. Some preliminary words of explanation may, therefore, not be altogether otiose.

The basis of medieval higher learning (technical education being the domain of the craft guilds) was books. They were scarce, expensive to write and beyond the purse of most private readers. Their contents were, therefore, transmitted by public reading, hence the lecture system. For this reason the statutes stress the central place of texts, dictated by the masters, reported by the students. Because of the time-factor, texts were divided into convenient units and more time was given for the more important texts which, as James Melville would phrase it, were 'more exactlie teachit'.[3] The production of printed texts shortly after the Glasgow foundation was a main factor in curtailing university courses and in lessening the importance of routine (called 'cursory') lectures by bachelors. At first the only access to texts was in a small library for the use, in the first place, of the university teachers and, by extension, the masters in the faculty. The texts raised questions requiring authoritative answers and so the senior faculty masters gave the main or 'ordinary' lectures and when the text was written or printed it was often accompanied by the master's questions in the form of a literary commentary.

The Question often, however, took on a separate life of its own as the 'disputed question', a life quite independent of the Lecture (or 'reading') as such. This was because the questions raised could not always be solved authoritatively or 'determined' without mutual dialogue and even mutual confrontation in which there were trials of strength between opposing positions in an intellectual tournament. It could add to the mental suspense if the final instalment, the 'determination', were postponed till another day. Just as the 'faderis of the order' of knight-hood, as Gilbert of the Hay describes[4] them, encouraged the squire bachelor in his knightly apprenticeship, so a master would act as 'father' or moderator to encourage the apprentice master of arts. There must have been some channelling of intellectual aggressiveness in these academic exercises and students were trained to use measured language and an adult manner of speech.[5] The basic aim was proof rather than persuasion, and, used without finesse, the method could narrow rather than broaden the scope of verbal exchange and degenerate into a strident quibbling. But the theoretical aim was the acquisition of poise and a sense of almost physical participation in the learning process. The Disputation is only another face of the disputed Question. 'Legible days' were days for lecturing; 'disputable days' for disputation primarily. Apart from revision and play periods, the student's time-table oscillated between lectures and disputations.

There were traditionally seven liberal arts, but the more strictly literary of these, grammar and rhetoric, had been downgraded to the grammar school. They had a linguistic branch made up of three called the 'trivium', and a numerate or arithmetical branch of four called the 'quadrivium'. John Mair is only echoing the tradition when he says grammar concerned the apt use of words; logic their truth or falsity; and rhetoric, as a technique of persuasion, was verbal ornament (he cites

Terence's 'verbis phaleratis').[6] Of these three, logic—although purely an instrument (*organon*) of knowledge, because of the intense intellectual effort it involved, and because its method was common to all branches of knowledge—came to dominate the medieval curriculum. The rest of arts learning was philosophy: physics, ethics with its related disciplines, metaphysics.[7]

Logic divided itself into the Old Logic (*vetus ars*), so called because it was already part of the medieval heritage long before the first universities appeared: and, after the Arab cultural invasion, the New Logic so called because it was still, in the thirteenth century, a discovery comparatively fresh. Something of the culture shock experienced in this first wrestling with Aristotle as seen through minds unsympathetic to Christian belief was re-experienced in the fifteenth century when fresh rumblings followed the new translations of Aristotle by Bruni and Argyropoulos.

The curriculum at Glasgow started with the Old Logic. Within narrow limits the official teachers were allowed a free choice of books, a choice exercised publicly at Glasgow on the opening day of the session.[8] It has already been shown how this date originally varied.[9] If two masters chose the same book the senior would have preference, unless, as the statutes hopefully observe, there 'was such a crowd of hearers that it was possible to read the same book in different schools and at different hours'. The word 'school' here means classroom and there must have been three schools, one for freshmen or 'sophisters',[10] another for bachelors, and a common faculty school to accommodate all students. The scholar had no choice of books except by dodging lectures. Guidelines for lecturing time-limits were laid down by statute. The winter term in practice lasted a mere two months and the complete Old Logic was expected to be covered in the first six weeks: that is, Porphyry's *Isagoge* or introduction to logic, Aristotle's *Liber Predicamentorum* (or *Categories*) and *Perihermeneias* (*Interpretation*). These were ordinary books, therefore lectured on at 'ordinary' hours, that is, at the most convenient lecturing times, usually in the morning. To this group was added an extraordinary book, Gilbert de la Porrée's *Liber de Sex Principiis*, the reading of which, however, was not indispensable, as well as the text of the *Summulae* of Peter of Spain (later Pope John XXI) with his treatise *de Syncategorematibus*, also lectured on at extraordinary hours. Teaching and learning techniques are said to follow the pattern of Paris and Bologna.[11]

The ordinary books read in this first term would begin ideally by introducing the novice in logic to simple perceptions only, with no complications involving their interpretation and analysis: simple terms and things and classes of things, with no problems as to whether they should be affirmed or denied. The Peter of Spain treatise on syn-categorematics concerns 'logical operators', that is, connecting words linking such simple terms.[12] In addition the *Perihermeneias* would introduce the novice learner to the next stage, the stage of judgment, involving the enunciation of propositions affirming or denying some-thing. Modal propositions—the 'medalles' of James Melville—were based on this book. The different stages in this study were of ascending difficulty and would involve daily periods of memorisation and a weekly one of more extended learning practice or exercise by way of a catecheti-cal exchange between master and pupil. It is not certain that this ideal order was followed, as, with the paucity of teachers the new students must have occasionally shared classes, hearing these books twice, once as undergraduates and once as bachelors, together in the common schools.[13]

There is no time-table given in these medieval statutes, but life started early in the morning and the first lecture was probably regulated by the bell of the neighbouring Blackfriars ringing for prime (7 a.m.), and later exercises or meals by the bells for other religious offices. In addition, a small internal bell would be sounded, presumably in the first instance by the faculty beadle.

The four-year course at Glasgow from incorporation to mastership was clearly an abridgement of what had originally been one of seven years, as it continued to be in the English universities. Clearly, too, an older state of affairs is reflected in fossilised form in our statutes where there can still be found a theoretical gap of five years between the bachelor stage (minimum age, 15) and graduation as master (minimum age, 20).[14] Theoretically it was possible to become a bachelor in one and a half years though this is hard to verify for students at Glasgow, yet it would have been easier before 'regenting' started, the system whereby one teacher took his student through the whole course. It is doubtful if Glasgow could afford the luxury of 'regenting' in quite the way of the better staffed colleges of St Andrews,[15] and the usual Glasgow complement of two or three regents in arts can be paralleled in other small universities elsewhere.[16] In the earlier days of its history it had other ways of augmenting its meagre lecturing staff.

The next stage in the freshman's studies was the New Logic. The first book of the *Prior Analytics* probably took up the first three weeks of the following spring term and the *Posterior Analytics* the next three. These books concern the summit of logic, analysis or resolution. The *Prior Analytics* mostly concern the formal art of syllogistic reasoning and the *Posterior* propositions whose conclusions follow necessarily and lead to strict scientific proof. James Melville refers to these volumes as 'the Demonstrations'. A further three weeks was given to the 'book of commonplaces' or *Topics* and the two books of *De Sophisticis Elenchis*. Only Books One, Two, Six and Eight of the *Topics* were indispensable, and in them dialectic was studied in the special sense of probable reasons useful in the discovery of truth ('invention'), an aspect of logic that would be taken up enthusiastically in the sixteenth century. The other work concerns false propositions and sophistical arguments. These lectures took James Melville at St Andrews well into his second year, but he began with some rhetoric in his first year, which had not infiltrated into the programme laid down in our 1452 statutes.[17] At the end of this study of the *Organon*, the student would be fully equipped to discuss *sophismata* or 'sophisms' in the special sense of arguments concerned with purely logical puzzles or semantic points.[18]

The Disputation or disputed Question was the other half of the teaching programme. Every lecture involved, of course, a question session in the more literary dictated questions arising directly from the text and, as such, part of the master's presentation of the text. The disputation as such took several forms. It could be a general one, in a public act, the public disputation of the regent master, that is the ordinary disputation in the faculty's common schools as laid down by faculty ordinance: 'item, after the feast of Luke the evangelist the senior regent master if he chooses will begin to dispute for the student's formal requirements (*pro forma*) and together with him the others in their turn'.[19] What seems to have happened is that the senior man was privileged to take the first course of disputations.[20] These disputations took place on 'disputable' as distinct from lecture days, that is at least once weekly. The respondents also took turns, but could not fix their own order. If they were junior students they could only respond to 'sophisms' or logical problems, but these would be part of the programme to involve all grades of undergraduate as disputants.[21] 'Sophisms' in public acts were to be carried out with thoroughness (*digeste*) and dignity (*mature*).[22] The first appearance of a junior defending a sophism must have been a testing occasion as few would want to emulate the character in 'The Talis of the Fywe Bestes' of whom the writer observes:

> He was na gret bachillar in sophistry.[23]

The distinction between these purely problematic discussions and the question proper is kept by the poet, John Rolland, when describing the Seven Sages:

> In all wisdom, and Science Liberaill
> Thay are but dout the seid of Salamon
> For to discus Problewm or zit Questioun.[24]

There were other disputations, private class disputations, extraordinary disputations, usually by regent masters, the disputations of bachelors and the evening disputations (*disputationes serotinae*) which appear in Germany and elsewhere. In all school acts Glasgow masters were to follow the example of the university of Paris or of Cologne.[25] When ordinary disputations were held all lectures were suspended, though they probably did not start quite so early in the morning.[26] More than one question could be debated,[27] which meant that the first question might be the most daunting for juvenile disputants, whether as prior respondents or prior opponents.[28] Solemn disputations such as quodlibets will be discussed elsewhere. The fruit of the various disputations was occasionally circulated in manuscript, but, for instance, the questions on physics in part of John Elmer (Athilmer) given by Duncan Bunch to the faculty library in 1475, and some other questions (which may have included his own, or those of his teachers, Whitelaw and Baron),[29] were almost certainly directly related to texts. In some books of questions, exposition of the author's meaning and intention would be the primary consideration and these would reflect procedure in the ordinary lecture; others reflected rather the commentator's personal teaching and these were the product of the analysis the master conducted in the other academic exercises. Disputations may additionally have taken place in a *parvis* (from *paradisus*), an enclosed area near a church porch. The Blackfriars church had a porch which may not have been at the west gable, but to the north, on the site of the later 'paradise yards', and this is a likely site.

With the end of the study of logic, the student was believed to be grounded in a common method applicable in any scientific enquiry. The next stage was the intermediate or mathematical sciences which did not demand experience or require an effort to bypass imagination, but were intermediate in the sense that they called for application to the material of physics: music theory, astronomy, optics. Arithmetic and geometry were not applied mathematics in the same sense.[30] There was, however, no medieval divorce between philosophy and science as in modern mathematical physics: the one looked for its verification in the other. In the Glasgow scheme, however, the quantitative branches of knowledge were relegated to the extraordinary lectures and are left incomplete: only 'perspective, *algorismus* and the principles of geometry if they are read'.[31] Perspective here means optics; *algorismus* involved fractions; the geometry would be Euclid. An indispensable book though read extraordinarily (in this special sense) was the *Sphere*, an astronomical work probably of Joannes de Sacrobosco, as revised and developed by later commentators, upon which Buchanan's didactic poem of that name was partly based.[32] No handbook of musical theory

was listed and of the regents' library by 1482 only a 'treatise of the
Sphere and the *algorismus*' reflects this area of study.[33]

When Robert Gardiner of St Andrews in 1435 pronounced his global
denunciation of the arts course he asked, 'What is there in natural
philosophy but the proportions of elements, the thrusting movements
of clouds and exhalations, the complexions of animals and whatever
human nature can investigate rationally?'[34] Here he was presumably
referring to what Laurence of Lindores, whose commentary on the
eight books of Aristotle's physics were popular in central Europe,
covered in his lectures. The 'proportions' are the varying ratios in the
relationships of things. One of Laurence's questions was, 'Whether any
simple body such as an element has within itself the principle of its
alteration?'[35] The next question referred to natural phenomena like the
cycles of precipitation and evaporation and the 'complexions' of
animals to their composite qualities, 'diverse co-ordinated parts for
exercising diverse functions'.[36] It is unlikely, however, that in the detail
of the argument the early Glasgow school followed Laurence. The
tendency was to go back to Albert the Great, a parchment copy of
whose commentary was presented by Bunch to the library along with
some questions edited by John Athilmer. A later donor gave Aquinas.[37]
These books took up two months of the course, and may have been
covered in the second or third years, as also other ordinary books like
the *De celo et mundo*, *De generatione et corruptione*, the *De Anima* (on
which Lindores commented), *De sensu et sensato*, *De memoria et
reminiscentia* and the *De somno et vigilia*. The first two took four
weeks, the *De anima* and the last three, the *Parva naturalia*,[38] six
weeks.

Of the ten books of the *Nicomachean Ethics* six were read as extraordinary books and these are qualified by the phrase, 'if they are read',
a qualification which seems to go back to the Paris 'if desirable' (*si
placet*) of 1215. The 'old ethics', known to the earlier Middle Ages,
received the addition of the 'new ethics' or part of it from Michael Scot
about 1217. The greatest medieval contribution was made by the
commentary of Albert and the new translations directly from the
Greek, and eventually the Greek text itself, in the fifteenth century won
the enthusiastic adhesion of the humanists and gradually of the university men. A pioneer was the Scot, Gilbert Crab. The hostility to
Aristotle's *Ethics* initially shown by Luther was not shared by John
Mair, who, like Crab, used the translation of Argyropoulos, and
celebrated the concord of the Christian pursuit of eternal happiness and
Aristotle's devotion to the heroic virtues. But thereafter not everybody
thought the advocacy of pagan ideals to the young altogether 'desirable'. In 1553 an excellent translation by a Frenchman, 'gentilhomme de

la maison de Monsieur le comte d'Aran' appeared under Vascosan's imprint at Paris, the first good French translation.[39]

It is doubtful if the young undergraduate would by the time of his first faculty test have encompassed all this reading. The reading of the master-to-be was expected to be more encyclopaedic. But, while the study of logical paradoxes in logic itself could still be pursued in the paradoxes of physics, the subjects of the mathematical group and, even more, those of the moral and physical group, were considered as 'real' sciences and a future bachelor had to be able to cross the threshold to these sciences of reality by disputing a 'question', and even sharing in the master's 'determination' of the question. We have no evidence for Glasgow but it seems most probable that the determiner generally determined a moral question as at St Andrews and in the French universities, sometimes possibly one based on the *Economics* or the *Politics*.[40] This normally took place in the third year of the student's course, and marked a further stage in the student's progress to maturity. But at Paris it was possible to gain admission to determination in the second year of the course and having read only the *De anima* apart from the whole logic, though in 1461 this practice seems to be discouraged.[41] The Glasgow statute does specify one and a half years, but in practice this was an absolute minimum.[42]

There were a number of formalities before the student could pass this 'first gateway' (to cite d'Estouteville) in the student's academic career.[43] The first of these was presentation. The faculty wished to show that it controlled admission to all degrees. In an emergency students could present themselves, but the general practice was for the Dean on the faculty's behalf to notify a general congregation for the purpose on the cathedral doors.[44] The statutory date for this was the nearest 'legible' day to All Saints (1 November), and this date was faithfully adhered to up till 1509 at least, when there is a break in the faculty records.[45] The dean's duty was then to enquire of the regents in general congregation if they had any candidates. This congregation was to be held 'in the place to be appointed by the faculty', generally the lower or upper cathedral chapter-house, but occasionally at adjacent altars.[46] There was the problem of absentee or sick candidates: in 1453, the admission of an absentee was authorised, provided he turned up within three days and in 1495 a sick man (William Lang) is not recorded as having proceeded.[47]

The dean was principally interested in maintaining faculty standards, especially academic standards, as is clear from an entry which described the students as fulfilling the requirements as to knowledge and this is certified by the schedules of the regent masters and their verbal oaths testifying to this.[48] There was therefore oral evidence from the teachers or the teacher (at a later period, one, often the principal regent, alone presents), as well as the schedules (rolls of parchment). There was a time qualification for no academic year counted in which absences exceeded two months, and an age qualification of fifteen, which, for good reasons, could be reduced to fourteen, which certainly suggests that boys matured rather rapidly in earlier centuries.[49] The former consideration may not, however, have applied so strongly as at a later stage. The schedules, to which were affixed their masters' signets, gave details of books heard and disputations attended[50]: unfortunately there are no precise details. The four examiners were then elected, and when (and if) they accepted, took 'bodily oath' in the Dean's hands, that is placed their joined hands inside his.[51] They were usually two regent masters and two non-regent masters who took on this burden, and the Dean could and did sometimes join them.[52] The chancellor had nothing whatever to do with the bachelor degree for the faculty licensed students as bachelors. This elaborate procedure inherited from Paris may have helped Glasgow students to be accepted *ad eundem* (to the same degree) more easily in other larger universities abroad, although they could not claim to have come from a 'solemn *studium*' or 'famous university', if defined as one with the modest number of six arts regents as at Paris and Louvain.[53]

The 'triers' (*temptatores*) usually consisted of four masters, two internal (*ad infra*) or regent examiners, and two external (*ad extra*), not in the modern sense of external examiner, but merely non-regent members of the faculty. The place of the examination is not specified, and its nature not clarified, except that it was to be conducted in such a way as not to dishonour the faculty.[54] It is implied that some appeared for this test who had not been present at the congregation for admission, as nobody was to be admitted by them about whom any master in the faculty had a complaint, especially in disobeying the regents or in unpaid debts, at least until personally or through the faculty he had satisfied such persons. If the master acted from envy, the faculty had to be informed and it would correct the master concerned as it saw fit. The bachelors-to-be had to swear that they had carried out the oaths they had taken publicly, that is in the faculty congregation. But secret oaths are also mentioned. These refer to 'secrets of the test' and were administered before it began.

First of all the student promised that if he were failed, he would not cause the examiners bodily damage or attack their good name or their property either in his own person or less directly through others. In this examination, the procedure was to take each student singly and proceed to question him on the ordinary and extraordinary books one by one. This investigation was not to be too lax or too strict,[55] in other words, not just to avoid favouritism or its opposite, but to examine in the more straightforward and more commonly emphasised items in the course.[56] This explanation is taken from the 1462 Nantes procedure where the oath regarding 'secrets of the test' is explained as not revealing the special questions to those who had still to be examined.[57] At Cologne the examiners expressed their votes by attaching to the schedules little black stones for ignorance and white for knowledge.[58] This rather than the black block of stone on which the examinee sat may be the origin of the term Blackstone for these examinations. The timing of the examination would be by hour-glass, and after it was over the faculty was involved again in the person of the Dean who along with the examiners decided on the pass list and fixed the date for determination.[59] At St Andrews, this test was different. It took place in Lent after determination, and the order of their determination decided the order in which they were examined. There the determinants were collected and proceeded to the schools with their hoods up: each took turns on the stone and the rest sat near by in their hoods.[60]

Before final admission the Glasgow students' names were entered in the Dean's book after various dues were paid and the schedules probably deposited in the faculty archives.[61] Fees paid on this occasion were to the faculty, the beadle and the Rector.[62] The future bachelors also took oath on this occasion to dispute in cope and furred hood three times a week throughout the whole of Lent, and they also promised the Dean not to seek dispensations through non-faculty members.[63]

The next stage was determination which, as we have seen, originally meant the final resolving of some disputed question, and sometimes was postponed and thus became a separate act. It was strictly speaking a magisterial prerogative, and thus the presence of the master, invariably the student's own regent, was necessary to preside over the act as moderator. It was a public act. How far it was purely ceremonial by this time it is hard to judge, but the faculty test certainly seems more important.[64] The determiner before Christmas was only *determinans* and was not considered to have finally determined till his last Lenten responsion. The phrase 'the underwritten bachelors determined' should read the 'underwritten bachelors-to-be determined for their bachelorship'.[65] The term 'determinant' is of university origin, the term bachelor borrowed from the language of chivalry,[66] that is he was like a soldier who had already been engaged in close fighting and raised his hand against an opponent.[67]

The act was notified by the university or faculty beadle on the cathedral doors on the nearest preceding feast and orally in the previous public act to prevent clashing arrangements.[68] On such a day no ordinary lectures were allowed after eight.[69] The university beadle was expected to give a gala nature to the proceedings by adorning—discreetly, with such things as tapestry and cushions—the main schools, especially the president's seat, the bishop's chair, the doctors' and nobles' benches. He also collected gloves and similar gifts from the determinants, preferring university members generally to others, except for distinguished strangers.[70] There is a notable insistence that all must wear ankle-length gowns.[71] One of the beadles, probably the faculty beadle, led the determinants in a circuit. In processional order they visited the schools and were to make not too noisy a circuit of houses in the town convoking at least masters in the faculty, including those the procession met in the street, to the school and the banquet following.[72] The original arrangement in the faculty statutes was that one poor student had to invite twelve masters, along with the Rector and others at the presiding master's will; two poor students (the maximum allowed in a single act) had between them to invite eighteen, with the Rector and those the president named. No limit was laid down for the rich. The university tried to modify this arrangement and insisted only on invitations to the Rector, the Dean, the faculty regents and the four examiners, with others such as canons, beneficed men and friends being left to their and the president's discretion. The faculty insisted, however, on invitations for all faculty masters. The more important seats were at the front, and the duty of the beadle was to avoid scandal by putting the claims of precedence in seating the gathering before his own predilections. The purpose of such invitations was to attract the attention[73] of officials to suitable nominees to benefices or to those bright students who needed financial help in prosecuting their studies. Even so, the purchase of gifts must have caused many an acute strain on their purses. There is no record of this act elsewhere that can be applied with confidence to Glasgow.[74]

Before the president ascended the chair, which probably had two levels to it, from the lower level of which the bachelor could speak,[75] the Dean's advice was sought and the receiver's schedule must certify that the necessary payments had been made.[76] In fourteenth-century Prague, the president propounded a sophism to the bachelor-to-be sitting among the scholars and still in his scholar's mantle, to which he responded but to which the master did not reply. It was only then that the beadle made him rise, put on his bachelor's cope and hood and sit among the bachelors.[77] This may have influenced the Cologne development, which the Glasgow procedure confessedly followed,[78] whereby a youth responded to an expectatory sophism: expectatory, to allow the gathering to settle and the masters to appear. The presiding master moved the questions and in so doing gave direction to the debate by putting forward preliminary considerations pro and con. The determinant took up one of them, transformed it into propositions, argued his viewpoint, was challenged by masters present under the control of the president moderator and finally 'determined' or decided the question.[79] The other determinants followed. The president probably noted defects in grasp of procedure and this might affect the relative order of the new bachelors, already in most respects fixed by the earlier test. The bachelor was here acting as a quasi-master, but the president's own determination need not agree with his. This could have been a long and exhausting procedure if the bachelors-to-be had no natural gift for public debate or felt nervous in such distinguished company. It could be exhilarating for a gifted youth able to parry arguments and return dialectical blow for blow with senior faculty members. The numbers were reduced to seven in one act (five rich and two poor), to make the session less protracted.[80] Copes were hired from the faculty, but there is an oddly worded statute where it is laid down that they were indispensable for rich students unless they were dispensed.[81]

The determiners then took oaths, repeating them after the beadle: to show loyalty, obedience and honour to the Dean; to keep the peace; to show honour to masters and defend faculty privileges; and, if any projected harm to the Dean or to any master came to their ears, to notify it and so prevent its accomplishment. It is not clear when the president pronounced his commendations of the students,[82] but since it is likely that they knelt then,[83] it was probably at the end, as they received a blessing with the words, 'I by the authority of the faculty of arts, my mother, which I enjoy in this matter, pronounce you bachelors, to be so considered here and everywhere in the name of the Father', etc.[84]

Before leaving determination, it should be pointed out that as time proceeded, and possibly as students appeared at university at a younger age, there was some weariness at over-long proceedings. By 1549, the festive element clearly predominates at Aberdeen, when we are told that in future the act of determinants would be very perfunctory, beginning at eight and finishing two hours later, for fear any unsuitable intruders should enter the hall while determination proceeded in the schools. The intruders were said to be 'vile persons and urchins' (*garsiones*) and nobody was to enter either school or hall unless called by name and identified.[85]

The interim between determination and Lent was spent acquiring further experience in disputation, fulfilling a minor role in the senior bachelors' disputations for their formal requirements which continued to St Valentine (14 February).[86] But, as exercise, responsion three times weekly in Lent in their bachelor copes and furred hoods was still necessary. The junior bachelor notified his questions on the doors of the school and he had a quasi-presidential authority as nobody could oppose him without his permission and he could stop anyone arguing. He had to hire his own school and was accompanied by a younger student, and nobody was to leave the disputation without good reason under pain of perjury.[87] These Lenten disputations which the bachelor was on oath required to complete were obviously not ordinary disputations; the pleated cope he wore is sometimes called 'an extraordinary cope' for that reason. The three days laid down were, at Nantes, Mondays, Wednesdays and Fridays.[88] The later arrangement at Cologne was two per week for 'new bachelors', accompanied by their scholars 'for their exercise', that is, for their term's quota of disputations. Each had to complete ten disputations at Cologne (two per week, the last week of Lent being free) with questions in each disputation on natural philosophy, logic and one or two sophisms.[89] This resembles what must have been the Glasgow pattern.

Another symbol of the bachelor's new authority was his authorisation to give cursory lectures on the different treatises of Peter of Spain, again for exercise.[90] But as this was supervised by the regents, his teaching function was limited and he had no say in the books chosen. Still he was recognised by them as a junior collaborator and it was yet another stage in his apprenticeship. The former more ample role assigned to bachelor teaching seems here to be very curtailed. It could have interfered with his personal study and is one reason that bachelors found some difficulty in completing their study of the *Sphere* and the *Metaphysics* in time for the licentiate stage.

In the fourth or final year of his course, the bachelor, now a senior bachelor, had as his first hurdle Great Responsions, which we find named as such in St Andrews in 1570 and as 'major responsions' in Aberdeen in 1549.[91] These were part of the formal requirement for licence, and had a time-factor since they must be over by St Valentine (14 February). They took place in 'general schools', that is at the public disputations of regent masters for the students' formal requirements.[92] They took place, as the phrase went, *in vico*, in the university schools, and, as masters and young students, also took part the senior bachelors involved were obliged to take up questions based on all the books in the course (as such they were similar to the *quodlibet*): they were thus the most exacting test the student had so far met.

As 'general disputations of masters' were public acts,[93] dress was strictly regulated. In 1453 at Glasgow each group of three wishing to 'respond generally' had to have one appropriate academic dress between them and each rich student his own.[94] The order (*vices*) in these disputations was important, and, if St Andrews custom is a guide,

senior bachelors were known to absent themselves once their responsions had been completed.[95] There was a responsions banquet where
expenses were limited to one merk Scots.[96]

Aberdeen also uses the term Little Responsions[97]: and their existence
is implied at St Andrews by the use of Great Responsions. In Aberdeen
they followed Great Responsions, and seem to be equivalent to the
Lenten responsions required of junior bachelors. It is likely that seniors
attended them as part of the term exercises though attendance was not
formally required. They were 'little', because in the charge of bachelors.
At Aberdeen they also involved a feast in hall.

The next stage of difficulty was what had originally been the chancellor's examination. The Dean once again notified the calling of a
general congregation of faculty for 3 July (possibly altered from 2
July), that is the morrow, not the day, of Sts Processus and Martin-
ianus.[98] This late date is not paralleled at St Andrews, and, while it
gave more time for study, it lessened the interval between the two
pre-licence examinations. It suggests automatic copying from some
early source and is not particularly Parisian. The feast of these saints
had been thrown into the shadows by the adoption by Pope Urban VI
during the Great Schism of the same day for the feast of the Visitation,
which along with its morrow is in fact in our earliest university calendar.[99] The countries, like Scotland, outside the Roman obedience did
not generally accept this feast, till authorised once again by the Council
of Basle in 1441, ten years before the university's foundation. The day
following the feast of the two Roman martyrs was adhered to for the
next fifty years.[100]

In the congregation, the Dean, in the presence of the faculty, asked
the Regents about their presentations. The senior bachelors then listing
ordinary and extraordinary books, and bearing their master's signets,
offered their schedules and supplicated for admission. In 1477, John
Brown, regent, presented four bachelors 'who by the schedules of the
said master John and his loyal testimony were found to have the
requisites for knowledge except for the third responsion *in vico* and the
reading of certain books of the *Metaphysics* and the treatise on the
Sphere. The faculty, favourably inclined to their supplications dispensed
them mercifully as to the said third responsion and admitted them to
the examination on condition that, before entering it, the treatise on
the *Sphere* was read through to them and the seven books of the
Metaphysics also first read to them, as to which the faculty would not
dispense'.[101] A similar dispensation in vaguer terms is found in 1476,
but then a half merk was exacted.[102] The rule was that texts formally
required could not be dispensed, at least as regards ordinary lectures,
but that the faculty could dispense a bachelor who had only two

responsions *in vico* to his credit, depending on convenience, necessity, good conduct and the state of his knowledge.[103] The bachelor could not present himself. If he did so without leave of his regent, the Dean could not admit him.[104] He must be nineteen (that is, be in his twentieth year) by the date of his mastership, and have passed four years in the faculty; three and a half were indispensable.[105] The minimum age for a bachelor being what it was, there was an inherent contradiction here, especially as the student must have studied continuously (allowing for a break, at most, of a single year),[106] and one must assume that from the start it would be impossible to adhere to the letter of the law and that, besides inheriting a system of faculty legislation from other universities, the faculty and the Dean inherited also a flexible system of customary interpretation.

Admission to licence was the key to the final, important degree, and the last time the faculty as a body could effectively exercise its power over the student's advancement. There could be various classes of supplicant before it in this congregation: a bachelor from another university; a student, possibly with some support from his seniors, who had a gap in the continuity of his studies; a person claiming to have a qualification because of the chancellor's letters in his favour or even a higher authority such as the pope. The graduate of another university could only be received if he had the formal requirements of that other faculty or university from which he came. The faculty intended to exalt its sons to knowledge, not for vanity's sake to promote them to an unreal (*sophistice*) dignity. Nobody in whatever civil position or ecclesiastical rank, who could point to the evidence of his previous knowledge of which there was, however, no present evidence, was to be received either: the faculty's intention was to judge their qualifications now, not then. This statute stressed the faculty's intention to look after its own good name as a degree-granting body, especially if the candidate had not fulfilled the time requirements. If the chancellor chose to go over the faculty's head and grant degrees on his own authority, the faculty would resist this by expelling any master who lent his presence to such an academic promotion and the candidate himself would be everlastingly excluded from it.[107] These preliminaries having been investigated, the examiners were elected, oaths taken and dues collected. The next formality was inscription. The Dean inscribed their names on a roll which he handed to the newly elected examiners, who, under penalty of perpetual expulsion, were enjoined not to admit anybody else. The regents elected were to be expert and conscientious, the two non-regents merely experienced; in view of the fact that often the faculty only had two regents it added, 'as far as it was possible to judge'.[108]

From the beginning this first test was not individual, but, following Cologne practice, as the statute acknowledged, six or eight of the senior bachelors were tested together. The place was the faculty schools to which the beadle probably brought them, the date as fixed by the faculty, generally within less than a fortnight, in which some defects in textual knowledge might be rectified, although it must have sometimes taken longer.[109] In one instance, it had to be postponed from July to November.[110] The examiners could not accept late arrivals on their own initiative on pain of expulsion.[111] At Glasgow various expressions point to two examinations for licence: on the whole *temptamen*, test or trial, is used for the first of them, *examen*, examination as such, for the second. Theoretically the idea of the first test was as a preliminary trial of the student's acquaintance with the books of the course, which produced a preliminary order of merit, and if there were enough students might place them in broad groups and exclude those unworthy of presentation to the bishop or his vice-chancellor, which now took place at this stage.

There followed a second examination, technically the chancellor's own, but in point of fact there is no record of his ever infringing the faculty's autonomy in the choice of examiner or in the substitution of a vice-chancellor. On the other hand, some of the point of the second examination was removed when the same examiners were continued in office. The bishop or his vice-chancellor was to enjoin the dean and the examiners to carry out this second examination and produce a rigorous order of merit. The Glasgow documents provide only meagre information. At Angers there is a short 'collation' given by one examiner, comforting the failed and urging the others to greater endeavour. At Caen there is an 'oration', before the candidates were called in the first order of merit by the chancellor's authority to enter rooms for the more specialised second examination.[112] At Glasgow these rooms (*camerae*) are never cited, but the expression 'bachelor intrants' indicates that the same process was followed.[113] These rooms were originally in the bishop's manor in the early days of universities and contrast with his hall (*aula*). The term 'audience' is also used of early groups of licentiands,[114] but by now it was not the bishop's but the faculty's audience room. In Glasgow there may have been one room set aside for this with an inner and outer 'chalmer'. It was at this point after the first test, that the students at Angers were forbidden to pass through the town without copes and unaccompanied till duly licensed or rejected.[115] Likewise the Dean at Glasgow, apparently after the first test and after their admission to the second examination, ordered the examinees under oath not to leave their lodging without their examination outfit (*habitus*) until their licence.[116] The purpose of this injunction may have been to induce students to confine themselves to their studies.

This second examination was, as we saw, more specialised than the first. At Caen the second examiners '*in propriis* and on several different days will test and examine them going through each book', which sounds like a separate examination by single examiners. At Bourges, the emphasis is rather on examination 'in their proper persons'.[117] At Paris, in the fourteenth century, a licentiate speaks of himself and his associates paying the chancellor's servants a tip 'together on leaving the room'.[118] What we must visualise is an audience chamber with an ante-room, one student under examination, with the rest on call outside, possibly with recourse to their books; this corresponds to the usual arrangement of regents' rooms.[119] There is no evidence as yet of a special Blackstone room. The Blackstone examination was later changed in nature but there is reason to believe that the timing procedure was already normalised whereby the beadle shouldered his mace until the sand in the upper glass of the sand-glass disappeared into the lower one when he grounded it with the word, 'Fluxit' ('It has passed through') and observed, 'Ad alium, Domine' ('Next, sir!').[120] An earlier reference mentioning a fee 'to the bedall of the college for holding the glass at his *examinatio*' is found at Glasgow in 1683.[121]

At the end of this second examination, presumably the more important, though this appears not to be the case at St Andrews,[122] the names of the successful candidates were duly placed in a letter closed with the Dean's signet and kept sealed by the senior examiner till the day of licence, for presentation to the chancellor on that day.[123] No person was to present himself for licence to the chancellor then unless he had first passed the faculty test; 'to do otherwise (*oppositum*) would be to usurp the degree in an unauthorised fashion'.[124]

The day of licence varied from year to year, but was probably within a month or so after the start of the first test. An early date (23 July) is found in 1461, but thereafter, as long as these original arrangements for licence were adhered to, it was usually in August.[125] 'The questions of licentiands' are listed among public acts and therefore had to be publicly notified.[126] The university was convoked in the customary circuit by the bachelors themselves who then proceeded to the schools with the beadle at their head and accompanied by the vice-chancellor, although already in October 1452, it was decided to confine the notification in the case of licentiands to the notice affixed at the cathedral.[127] It thus was a more private affair. The senior examiner then in the schools presented the letter unopened to the chancellor or vice-chancellor who handed it to the beadle to read out in a loud clear voice.

The students, who were apparently waiting outside or perhaps, if the room had a screen, beyond the screen, entered in order. There is a subsequent reference of 1612 or 1613 to money expended 'quhen ye ordour of ye bairnis was cryit in'.[128] The Rector, Dean, masters and undergraduates were present and the licentiands disputed and determined their questions under the presidency of the vice-chancellor.[129] A short conference (*collatio*) was then given by the chancellor or vice-chancellor and 'other things' were carried out. These 'other things' included the oaths of the licentiands given at the beadle's injunction, this time to the chancellor and Rector as well as the Dean. The other oaths were the usual ones about keeping the privileges, statutes and liberties of the faculty—with, this time, 'and they will advance them'— and that they would not receive their master's insignia elsewhere.[130] The candidates then sank to their knees 'in honour of God and the apostolic see' (in memory of Pope Alexander III who first conferred the universal licence to teach). The revised St Andrews statutes of 1570 omit mention of the apostolic see.[131] The Chancellor then gave the licence with the words, 'I, chancellor (or vice-chancellor) of the university of Glasgow, by the authority of almighty God and the apostles Peter and Paul and the apostolic see which in this regard I enjoy, give you (here he probably named them in order) placed on your knees the degree of licence in the faculty of arts, for lecturing, disputing and exercising all acts (within it *omitted*, but given at St Andrews) as long as you complete whatever is required for their solemnity'. Then followed his blessing.[132] The final phrase cited above obviously assured autonomy even in the licence to the university.

The procedure at licence is described so briefly and possibly elliptically that it is hard to be sure of more than its general lines. The faculty acts clarify matters a little. Students are said to be licensed *under* the vice-chancellor which means that he presided over the disputation. The university statutes themselves show that the episcopal chair in the schools was quite separate from that of the president of the act.[133] On 30 August 1476, certain students were licensed under John Brown, vice-chancellor, though the bishop is declared to have been present and to have granted the licence.[134]

Vesperies or *vesperiae*, that is vespers in arts, are only mentioned once in the records of Scottish universities and that at St Andrews in 1455.[135] Oddly it speaks of the act as happening 'on the night preceding licence', rather than preceding inception. In it, the vesperiand acted as respondent as usual under his president.[136] It took place in the late afternoon, like the liturgical celebration of a great feast called first vespers.

The term 'inception' at Glasgow is confined to the arts statutes which are largely copied from lost statutes of Paris and Cologne and therefore use their terminology. Unlike the other Scottish universities, however, Glasgow's usual terminology, both in the university statutes, and throughout the faculty acts is 'principiation',[137] a word borrowed, it seems, from Bologna.[138] In it the masters formally invested the student in office after his long years of apprenticeship as an undergraduate: in that sense it was a 'principiation', a new beginning.

The usual arrangements for a public act, including the 'circuit', were made on the day of principiation. The university statutes laid down that on the day of the master's *aula* (a name taken from the bishop's hall), if the bishop of Glasgow or some great prelate was present, he should have an expensive bonnet worth ten shillings, with a bonnet half that price for the president, the Rector, the Dean, each regent and each examiner. This original statute was soon modified to exclude the regents and examiners. Expenses were also gathered by one of their number as steward for the inception banquet. In 1304 or thereabouts Robert Bruce had arranged an expensive inception feast for his brother, Alexander, at Cambridge.[139]

At Glasgow, according again to Cologne usage, the proceedings opened with a bachelor responding to the 'expectatory question' and was opposed by masters, a responsion that would count towards one of his three formal or great responsions.[140]

At principiation, the Glasgow inceptor in arts acted, as was general practice, as opponent. As at St Andrews, he may have been restricted to one main argument against the position defended by those masters responding and to two of their counter-arguments. The St Andrews statute is ambiguous, but has to be read in the context of the responsals *a latere* mentioned below.[141] But before the main part of the proceedings began, the new master was given the master's insignia, which may have been given to accompany (although the statute suggests rather, 'to precede') the oath repeated after the beadle. While insignia are regularly mentioned, only the imposition of a bonnet is in fact cited.[142] Examples from elsewhere give us a possible reconstruction of the Glasgow act. There is a reference at St Andrews to the presence at this ceremony of masters acting as respondents *a latere*, possibly forming a crown round the chair, which confirms that the inceptor himself opposed, and a 'sophist'.[143] At Caen the inception of the first of a number of inceptors was carried out with great pomp, his genealogy declared and a 'sophism played' by the youths, which would imply a touch of humour. One of the signs of mastership was when the new masters took off their bachelor's copes and put on great copes and then ascended the chair to share the presidency of the disputation with the presiding regent. Some masters, corresponding to those 'responsals *a latere*', took up the positions below the high chair which had been vacated by the inceptors, and then took turns at arguing with the masters below.[144]

This done, the president thanked all present and all proceeded to the solemn meal in the hall at which as many as twenty masters could be present. These banquets were increasingly convivial and the 1549 visitation at Aberdeen calls them 'bacchanalia'.[145] The maximum number of principators allowed originally was four, two rich and two poor.[146] At the beginning these rules were strictly adhered to, but later the number begins to be exceeded: there were eleven in December 1507.[147] Obviously the ceremonial aspect had begun to assume importance.

At the principiation, which took place in the winter term so that bachelors could formally respond in the act, some oaths were taken.[148] These included one of life-long devotion to the faculty; a promise to respect the seniority in precedence granted in licence; another to keep peace and concord between the four faculties and especially the theological faculty; likewise to give reliable depositions regarding bachelors awaiting promotion; a promise not to repeat the Glasgow degree in another university; and finally, an oath to continue study in the arts faculty for two years (that is during the remainder of the year in which principiation took place), unless duly dispensed. Glasgow tends to confine its use of the word incept to this second inception (*de novo*), which, by statute, took place within eighty days of principiation.[149] These solemn inceptions (*inceptiones librorum*) were public acts at which the beadle was present, really resumptions or inaugural lectures.[150] Stiff fines were imposed for non-fulfilment of this period of readership. As lecturers found it more and more difficult to get an audience because of the advent of the printed book, this statute more and more wore an archaic air, and eventually became quite unenforceable, even though originally only the gravest of reasons excused from it—plague, the ending of study in the university, sickness or the destruction of the place.

Some of these developments will be pursued in other chapters. In intention at least, as far as its constitutional arrangements inform us, the faculty of arts was meant to be ancillary to other faculties. The faculty was small, but medieval faculties and universities were generally smaller than we might expect. The arts faculty calculated on developing in its students a critical mind, although we may think more radical questions were being asked outside than inside the universities. It also intended to give the student a well-stocked mind in the light of the accepted body of knowledge at the time. Thus the faculty at Glasgow struggled to make its own small contribution to creating a more literate public in Scotland.

NOTES

1. *AFA*, 52–4.
2. *Ibid.*, 75 and note.
3. Melville, *Diary* (Wodrow Society, Edinburgh, 1842), 28.
4. *Prose Manuscript*, ii, 2, line 26 ('The Buke of Knychthede').
5. *Glas. Mun.*, ii, 36, 'quod Regentes omni studio et diligentia instruant scolares tractim et mature loqui' (title 7, chapter 8). The title and chapter divisions of Duncan Bunch are given in an appendix. Cf. *Statutes*, 104.
6. *Quaestiones logicales* (1528), f. 1. Cf. J. A. Weisheipl, 'Classification of the Sciences in Mediaeval thought', *Mediaeval Studies*, xxvii (1965), 54–90.
7. This Logic/Philosophy division is found in *Glas. Mun.*, ii, 26, t. 3, c. 13.
8. *Glas. Mun.*, ii, 5, 22–3, t. 1, c. 1.
9. See Chapter 4.
10. In Scotland this term appears at St Andrews only, where its meaning is uncertain.
11. *Glas. Mun.*, ii, 25–6. t. 3, c. 11, 13. At St Andrews, from 1415, Paris usage was followed, *AFA*, 3.
12. P. Boehner, *Medieval Logic* (Manchester, 1952), 22.
13. As at Cologne, cf. Bianco, 300.
14. *Glas. Mun.*, ii, 27–8, t. 4, c. 7, 11. Sixteen for bachelors at St Andrews, *Statutes*, 87.
15. *AFA*, cxxiii. Duncan Bunch arrived at Cologne in September 1443 and determined in May 1445, Keussen, i, 467 (218, 59).
16. E.g. two at Bordeaux (1482), Fournier, iii, 351.
17. The St Andrews programme of 1439 excludes Peter of Spain, Gilbert de la Porrée, the treatise on distribution of terms, *perspectiva*, *algorismus*, principles of Geometry, but it only lists ordinary books: *Statutes*, 94.
18. J. A. Weisheipl, 'Curriculum of the Faculty of Arts at Oxford in the early Fourteenth Century', *Mediaeval Studies*, xxvi (1964), 154–5.
19. *Glas. Mun.*, ii, 25, t. 3, c. 8.
20. 'Statuts primitifs de la Faculté des Arts de Louvain', ed. E. H. J. Reusens, *Compte Rendu des Séances de la Commission Royale d'Histoire*, ser. 3, ix (Brussels, 1867), 171.
21. The argument of Weisheipl that these 'sophisms' must have included 'questions', because bachelors argued in them also, is not therefore conclusive, *Mediaeval Studies*, xxvi, 180.
22. *Glas. Mun.*, ii, 36, t. 7, c. 7; *Statutes*, 103.
23. *Asloan Manuscript*, ii, 133, l. 185.
24. Rolland, *The Seuin Seages*, ed. G. F. Black (STS, 3rd series, 3), 16.
25. *Glas. Mun.*, ii, 36, t. 7, c. 5.
26. At terce (nine o'clock) at Cambridge.
27. M. B. Hackett, *The Original Statutes of Cambridge University* (London, 1970), 140.
28. The later 'prima quaestio' and 'quid dictum' at St Andrews seems to reflect such an important responsion and opposition: W. C. Dickinson, *Two Students at St Andrews* (London, 1952), 60, 91, 94, but on these occasions the expenses of respondents inviting masters are also involved.
29. *Glas. Mun.*, ii, 404–5.
30. J. Gagne, 'Du *Quadrivium* aux *Scientiae Mediae*', in *Actes du Quatrième Congrès Internationale de Philosophie Médiévale* (Montreal/Paris, 1969), 975–86.

ARTS: FACULTY STRUCTURE 105

31. *Glas. Mun*, ii, 26, t. 3, c. 12. St Andrews only lists ordinary books, *Statutes*, 94; but we know from James Melville that a wider course was covered.
32. J. R. Naiden, *The Sphera of George Buchanan* (n.p., 1952).
33. *Glas. Mun.*, iii, 406. The students of the *Sphere* had to make a small payment: *ibid.*, ii, 26, t. 3, c. 13.
34. *AFA*, 40.
35. L. Moonan, 'Lawrence of Lindores on Life', *Classica et Mediaevalia*, xxvii (1966), 368.
36. *Ibid.*, 359.
37. *Glas. Mun.*, iii, 405–6.
38. These were so called because, like the *Parva logicalia* and unlike the main texts, they were contained in small books.
39. *Aristote, L'Ethique à Nicomaque*, ed. R. A. Gauthier and J. Y. Jolif (Louvain/Paris, 1970), i (1), 114–16, 123, 145–52, 164–5, 179. Some seventeenth-century Scots teachers such as William Macdowell at Groningen, were to return to an enthusiasm for the *Ethics*.
40. *AFA*, 419 refers to '*themes* from the "ars disserendi" and *questions* from moral philosophy' (in 1561–2) at St Andrews. Already in the previous century it was customary to debate a moral question, Fournier, iii, 75 (Nantes), 165 (Caen), 432 (Bourges); *CUP*, iv, 730 (Paris in the time of Cardinal d'Estouteville).
41. *Auct.*, ii, 936.
42. *Glas. Mun*, ii, 27, t. 4, c. 7; *Statutes*, 88.
43. *CUP*, iv, 728.
44. *Glas. Mun.*, ii, 26, t. 4, c. 1. At St Andrews, the phrase is 'presenting themselves', *Statutes*, 88.
45. *Glas. Mun.*, ii, 285, though in this instance the record is brief and it is not certain that all formalities were completed.
46. *Ibid.*, ii, 232, 238, 263.
47. *Ibid.*, ii, 183, 266.
48. Liber Decani, 27, 'qui reperti fuerunt habere requisita ad scienciam et hoc per scedulas magistrorum regentium et iuramenta eorundem, pro sciencia autem examinanda', omitted in *Glas. Mun.*, ii, 201, line 2.
49. *Glas. Mun.*, ii, 29, t. 4, c. 16; 27, t. 4, c. 7.
50. Hannay omits the *Sophistici Elenchi* from his list of ordinary books studied at Glasgow, *Statutes*, 12.
51. *Glas. Mun.*, ii, 25, t. 4, c. 1; 183.
52. *Ibid.*, ii, 263, 269; there were five examiners at Cologne, Bianco, *Anlagen*, 64.
53. *Auctarium*, ii, 938; Reusens, 'Statuts', 156, 162.
54. *Glas. Mun.*, ii, 34, t. 6, c. 9; Hannay, *Statutes*, 100.
55. *Glas. Mun.*, ii, 26, t. 1, c. 2. The same phrase was used at Cologne (Bianco, *Anlagen*, 64), but the St Andrews procedure was different.
56. Fournier, iii, 76, 'in communibus et levibus' (principal definitions, etc.).
57. *Ibid.*, iii, 76–7.
58. Bianco, 304.
59. *Glas. Mun.*, ii, 26, t. 1, c. 3.
60. Hannay, *Statutes*, pp. 88–9.
61. This sometimes happened before the test; of one student so inscribed it is noted, that 'being examined, he did not proceed', *Glas. Mun.*, ii, 284.
62. *Glas. Mun.*, ii, c. 5, t. 1. Cf. *Statutes*, 89, 94. Also a fee to the dean and the examiners was paid, *Glas. Mun.*, ii, 27, t. 4, c. 6. Cf. also *ibid.*, 40.
63. *Glas. Mun.*, ii, 33, t. 6, c. 7.

64. E.g. 'The same year they proceeded to the degree of bachelor, preceded by the test and other requisites', *Glas. Mun.*, ii, 227.
65. *Glas. Mun.*, ii, 222, 'determinaverunt infrascripti baculariandi pro baculariatu', *Liber Decani*, f. 50.
66. *Dictionnaire de Droit Canonique*, ed. R. Naz (Paris, 1937), ii, col. 1.
67. Vives as cited in *Tudor School Boy Life*, ed. Foster Watson (London, 1908), 102–3.
68. *Glas. Mun.*, ii, 25, t. 3, c. 5; *Statutes*, 87.
69. *Glas. Mun.*, ii, t. 3, c. 9.
70. *Ibid.*, ii, 12.
71. *Ibid.*, ii, 24, t. 2, c. 2.
72. *Ibid.*, ii, 15. Cf. ii, 25, t. 3, c. 7. This circuit was cancelled for licentiands soon after the date of the 1452 statutes, *ibid.*, ii, 37.
73. *Ibid.*, ii, 18, 35, 12.
74. There is an excellent beadle's eye view of the proceedings at Cambridge, with ceremonial considerations very much to the forefront, where nevertheless it is clear that the questions were only raised on Ash Wednesday and not determined fully till later in Lent. G. Peacock, *Observations on the Statutes of the University of Cambridge* (Cambridge, 1841) appendix A, especially vi ff. Cf. Rashdall, i, 450–6. For Oxford see J. M. Fletcher, 'The Teaching of Arts at Oxford, 1400–1520', *Paedagogica Historica*, vii (Ghent, 1967), 417–454.
75. Reusens, 'Statuts', 184; *Glas. Mun.*, ii, 36, 'attendat cathedram' reads 'ascendat' in MS.
76. *Glas. Mun.*, ii, 35–6, t. 7, c. 3. Cf. ii, 38.
77. *Monumenta Historica Universitatis Carolo—Ferdinandeae Pragensis:* (*Liber Decanorum Facultatis Philosophicae*), ed. Dittrich and Spirk (1830), i, 52.
78. 'Secundum morem Studii Coloniensis', *Glas. Mun.*, ii, 36.
79. *CUP*, ii, 673.
80. *Glas. Mun.*, ii, 35, t. 7, c. 2. Ten are listed in 1462, but there were two public acts, *ibid.*, ii, 97.
81. *Ibid.*, ii, 36, t. 7, c. 9.
82. *Ibid.*, ii, 26, t. 4, c. 2.
83. Cf. Peacock, *Observations*, App. vi.
84. *Glas. Mun.*, ii, 26–7, t. 4, c. 2.
85. *Fasti Aberdonenses*, 269–70.
86. Dr Dunlop misunderstands these, *AFA*, xciii. The students she cites had determined the previous year and were responding for their licence. Cf. *AFA*, 111, 112, 191.
87. *Glas. Mun.*, ii, 27, 'sub pena iuramenti'. Cf. the later Oxford term 'juraments' for certain sophisters, disputations; Buxton and Gibson, *Oxford University Ceremonies* (Oxford, 1935), 5.
88. Fournier, i, 429; iii, 77.
89. Bianco, *Anlagen*, 65. They were short. There was a morning and afternoon session.
90. 'Unde possit habilitari', *Glas. Mun.*, ii, 25, t. 3, c. 10.
91. *AFA*, 430; *Fasti Aberdonenses*, 270.
92. *Glas. Mun.*, ii, 27, t. 4, c. 8, 9; *ibid.*, ii, 25, t. 3, c. 9.
93. *Ibid.*, ii, 25, t. 3, c. 5.
94. *Ibid.*, ii, 182–3.
95. *AFA*, 430.
96. *Glas. Mun.*, ii, 182. Apparently mainly in the bachelor's 'first responson', Fournier, iii, 57,

97. *Fasti Aberdonenses*, 270.
98. *Glas. Mun.*, ii, 27, t. 4, c. 10. The word 'crastino' after 'Julii' is faint and has been ignored by the editor. Some phrases from this statute are included in *Statutes*, 93. That 2 July was the original date is suggested by *Glas. Mun.*, ii, 184, 189.
99. *Ibid.*, ii, 16. Beside it is a marginal note (possibly in an eighteenth-century hand), 'Heer the extracte fundatioun in the paper scrool breakes off'.
100. *Glas. Mun.*, ii, 279, till 1502 at least. On one occasion, in 1478, the bishop got it postponed for a few days, *ibid.*, ii, 227.
101. *Ibid.*, ii, 224 after 'magisterii', delete 'et' and insert the above as in Liber Decani, 52-3.
102. *Ibid.*, ii, 221-2 after 'fiende' add 'antequam ingredietur temptamen prius dimedia marca super huiusmodi admodum graciose', Liber Decani, 49.
103. *Glas. Mun.*, ii, 28, t. 4, c. 13.
104. *Ibid.*, ii, 30, t. 4, c. 19. There is a reference to exercises in the regents' 'houses'; *ibid.*, ii, 29, t. 4, c. 15.
105. *Ibid.*, ii, 28, t. 4, c. 11; *Statutes*, 88, shortens this to three.
106. *Glas. Mun.*, ii, 29, t. 4, c. 18, 'unless the faculty found that (the supplicant for a grace) had done exercises elsewhere because of which he would not lack knowledge (required for the degree)'.
107. *Ibid.*, ii, 29-30, t. 4, c. 17, 18, 20.
108. *Ibid.*, ii, 28-9, t. 4, c. 15; 27-8, t. 4, c. 10.
109. *Ibid.*, ii, 27-8, t. 4, c. 10, 13. Bianco, *Anlagen*, 67-8, is not helpful.
110. *Glas. Mun.*, ii, 234-5, a postponement till Martinmas.
111. *Ibid.*, ii, 29, t. 4, c. 15.
112. Fournier, i, 430; iii, 278. Cf. St Andrews, *AFA*, cxi, cxiii, 278, 398.
113. *Glas. Mun.*, ii, 200, 203, 212, and (in statutes), 30, t. 5, c. 3, 4, if this reference can be accepted. However, the phrase 'ante introitum temptaminis' used of bachelors who had not heard the *Metaphysics* and the *Sphere* is found, *ibid.*, ii, 227.
114. Fournier, iii, 77.
115. *Ibid.*, i, 430, 'in the same room' (Angers).
116. *Glas. Mun.*, ii, 28, t. 4, c. 13. Cf. *AFA*, cix.
117. Fournier, iii, 166, 432.
118. *CUP*, 111, 414.
119. *Glas. Mun.*, iii, 518, refers to the principal's 'inner' or 'benner chalmer'.
120. D. Murray, *Memories of the Old College of Glasgow* (Glasgow, 1927), 83.
121. I owe this reference to Mr William Kelly of the National Library of Scotland who found it in the papers of Lord George Douglas.
122. *AFA*, cviii. Dr Dunlop considered the first test the decisive one.
123. *Glas. Mun.*, ii, 27-8, t. 4, c. 10. Cf. Hannay, *Statutes*, 102 (somewhat different).
124. *Glas. Mun.*, ii, 30, t. 4, c. 23, where 'oppositum' should be read for the editor's reading, 'opportunum'. Cf. *Statutes*, 94.
125. *Glas. Mun.*, ii, 194, 195, 231, 262, etc. The period is so short that the two tests may have eventually merged.
126. *Ibid.*, ii, 36, t. 7, c. 7. *Statutes*, 103.
127. *Glas. Mun.*, ii, 27, t. 4, c. 10; *ibid.*, ii, 37.
128. GUA 26620 (Clerk's Press 8), 106. But this was after the disputation, *Glas. Mun.*, ii, 52.
129. *AFA*, cxvii, Dr Dunlop speaks of the chancellor or his deputy making 'a formal disputation', which misunderstands his role at this period.
130. *Glas. Mun.*, ii, 31, t. 6, c. 2.

131. Hannay, *Statutes*, 102.
132. *Ibid.*, for corrections in brackets; *Glas. Mun.*, ii, 28, t. 4, c. 10.
133. *Glas. Mun.*, ii, 12.
134. *Ibid.*, ii, 222.
135. *AFA*, cxvi, 108.
136. Rashdall, *Universities*, i, 486.
137. *Glas. Mun.*, ii, 10 (it occurs here four times), 184 (dated 1454), etc.
138. Rashdall, *Universities*, i, 427 note, says *Principium* was occasionally preferred by universities following the model of Bologna.
139. *Glas. Mun.*, ii, 10; G. W. S. Barrow, *Robert Bruce* (London, 1965), 203. For the circuit, *Glas. Mun.*, ii, 25, t. 3, c. 7.
140. *Ibid.*, ii, 36, t. 7, c. 6.
141. Hannay, *Statutes*, 104. The wording at St Andrews suggests an inceptor-respondent rather than an opponent, but 'respondeat' here appears to be used in the general sense of replying to the debate.
142. *Glas. Mun.*, ii, 31, t. 6, c. 3, 4.
143. *AFA*, 320 and note.
144. Fournier, iii, 278. Originally four inceptors (as at Glasgow) and four responding masters and a four-cornered disputation.
145. *Fasti Aberdonenses*, 269. For numbers invited, *Glas. Mun.*, ii, 35, t. 7, c. 1.
146. *Glas. Mun.*, ii, 35, t. 7, c. 3.
147. *Ibid.*, ii, 184, 186, 194 (two groups of three), 199, 202, 285.
148. *Ibid.*, ii, 31, t. 5, c. 3.
149. *Ibid.*, ii, 25, t. 3, c. 5.
150. *Ibid.*, ii, 31, t. 6, c. 4.

6. Theology

'Let, therefore, our reason be more clearly enlightened so that it may apprehend that Wisdom to know which is Truth, to love which Virtue, to embrace which the highest Good. . . .'
Proemium to University Statutes

To WALTER KENNEDY, poet and graduate of Glasgow, it seemed that:

The schip of faythe is stormyt with wynd and rayne
Off heresye dryvand in the sey hir blaws[1]

and European internecine wars, recurrent plague, the war of words at the Councils of Constance and Basle, the Turks menacing from the East, all created a climate of mental exhaustion and physical insecurity and called for an immense effort of re-consolidation and spiritual reassurance. The need was clamant but the peril inherent was that the response might prove to be merely a temporary tiding over. By Blackadder's time the university has become something of a status symbol for his metropolitan see. Yet, on the face of it, university and college founders like Kennedy, Turnbull and Elphinstone were indeed concerned with intellectual values, though the phenomenon of Albertism itself suggests that they saw it too much as a work of restoration and not of a more searching and uncomfortable process, the 'reform in head and members' that the Councils had proposed. One way of institutionalising this process might have been to establish lively schools of theology, but poverty of resources and personnel in a small country, as well as the moral and structural inadequacies of the Church of the time, inhibited any advance towards a genuine reawakening.

When the university opened, some of its original members were men who had been at Basle: John Arrous, David Cadzow, Robert de Essy, William Lennox.[2] Of these only Essy was a theologian. But the university of Cologne had been profoundly influenced by Basle and from it came besides Essy himself, the two other theologians, Alexander Geddes, monk of Melrose, another licentiate,[3] and David Hardgate, monk of Newbattle, a bachelor.[4] If there was a Dean of the faculty, he is likely to have been Essy for this office was generally given to the senior man.[5] A 'Dean of faculty' is mentioned as being present with the Rector and others at a theological academic act in 1522,[6] but he could just have been a temporary officer or, alternatively, merely the Dean of the arts faculty. In some Italian universities there was a very meagre staff in theology, sometimes only a single lecturer.[7] Theology was one of the four faculties specifically allowed for in the Glasgow Bull of foundation and it is given a passing mention in the arts statutes, as the faculty among the four with which new masters must principally be at peace.[8]

The presence of Cistercians is noteworthy. Quite a few are found among the Scots at Cologne in the first half of this century, and the fall in numbers thereafter may be due to the subsequent creation of a separate Cistercian house of studies there.[9] The growth of Cistercian higher studies in Scotland at this time may, as in earlier ages elsewhere, have arisen under the stimulus of external heresy which left the monasteries in a dangerous state of intellectual isolation.[10] The Cistercians had produced two men of distinction, John Fogo and Thomas Livingstone, both of whom were at Basle where the latter was especially prominent.[11] Turnbull as a young man would know Melrose, which conveniently had property in Glasgow, and, for this reason, the bishop may initially have envisaged a more permanent arrangement with it. The presence of a cathedral chapter and a house of Blackfriars in the tiny city may also have encouraged hopes, though no Dominicans were in fact incorporated at this point. The Observant Greyfriars had not as yet arrived. No students from nearby Paisley abbey, a Cluniac house, are on record and this perhaps reflects a neighbourly coldness to the Glasgow bishop's schemes. Irvine, a seaport town with which Glasgow would later collaborate, was closely attached to the Benedictine house of Kilwinning, to which its parish kirk was annexed.[12] It is not too surprising then that among the very first incorporands in the university, after the university beadle, should be William Boyd, abbot, and two monks from Kilwinning, as well as the prior of the house of Augustinian canons at Blantyre, a cell of Jedburgh.[13] Members of religious orders did not at first pay university dues, a device of the founder's perhaps to attract them to Glasgow; but, with the revised statutes, if not before, these halcyon times passed away.[14]

Apart from Black and Grey friars, and—from the monastic orders—the Augustinian and Premonstratensian canons, there is no great evidence in Scotland of attachment to higher studies, though the religious may not have altogether neglected canon law, which, after all, had its practical uses.

No recorded proceedings of a faculty of theology or notes of gift of theological books—there must have been some—have come down to us. We are left to fall back on sparse indications in the Rector's book: it would be rash on the adducible evidence to postulate more

than the existence of a very small faculty, or even to be quite certain
that, even in an attenuated and undistinguished form, it had an unbroken history. A reasonable conjecture is that any statutes that
existed (and at least once their existence is implied) owed more to
Cologne and St Andrews than to anywhere else. A Cologne parentage
again is highly probable for the St Andrews theological statutes as they
were in 1439 and in which Essy and Athilmer both had a hand,[15]
though, in view of the strong Parisian affiliations of Cologne at the
time, and of subsequent constitutional development of Paris inspiration,
the significance of this can be easily overstressed.[16]

Among secular clerics in the faculty in 1453 was Adam Cockburn,
a graduate of St Andrews, who after six years of theology at Paris,
where in 1452 he was a bachelor *cursor* (taking his first course of lectures
on the Bible), was continuing his studies at Glasgow.[17] Other masters
were incorporated in this period who were obviously students in the
'higher' faculties, but only external evidence could confirm in which.
Moreover there were non-regent masters some of whom were post-
graduate students but are not identifiable as such. Duncan Bunch
himself, the first recorded principal, studied in theology, as he was
only a raw arts student of three or four years' standing when he came
to Glasgow from Cologne by way of St Andrews. He could combine
this with regency in arts, as we shall see. He is first styled bachelor
in theology in a papal supplication of May 1471, but we are not told
what grade of bachelor he held.[18] It is likely that before acting as
Quodlibetarius in 1463 he was already a 'cursor', if not earlier.[19] In
1460 and 1467 two more monks of Kilwinning entered the university,[20]
and, also in the latter year, Alexander Wemyss, described merely as
master of arts, but already a Quodlibetarius in St Andrews. He too
some years later was styled bachelor in theology.[21] Other evidences of
continuity in theological teaching, if we can judge from the presence
of religious, are the incorporation of another prior of Blantyre in 1457
along with the three first Dominican friars from the neighbouring
Glasgow house.[22] There are others in 1469 and 1470: a prior and
canon of the independent Augustinian house of Inchmahome; the prior
of the Benedictine cell of Lesmahagow.[23] John Muir, recently prior
of Glasgow but here styled vicar general of the Scots Dominicans, who
had as yet no separate Scots province, also entered the university in
1470: four years later he was bachelor in theology.[24]

Who was the doctor or licentiate lecturing in theology at this period
does not emerge from the evidence. Essy was dead by late 1466.[25]
One of the original Cistercian members may still have been there. An
important acquisition was the secular theologian, James Ogilvie,
bachelor in theology, incorporated likewise in 1470. He had been the

appointee of the Council of Basle to St Andrews in 1441 and survived long enough to become one of the first theologians at King's College, Aberdeen.[26] His letter to the university of St Andrews in 1441 or thereabouts tells us something of his attitude. It is very critical of Pope Eugenius IV for transferring the Council from Basle to Italy and shows Ogilvie as a thoroughgoing conciliarist in theology: cupidity, avarice and simony were, he said, what stood in the way of a more courageous stand on the part of Scots clerics in face of the pope's action. The doctors in St Andrews should be mountains towards which the simple could run for refuge as the storms overtook heretics, they should provide a wall of defence, be fighters for faith. In spite of these strong views and his original opposition to Bishop Kennedy, he was able to work with Athilmer at St Andrews and later succeed him as provost of St Salvator's.[27] A temporary disharmony between the two may have caused his brief residence in Glasgow.

In 1474, William Elphinstone, later bishop of Aberdeen, was Rector, and as such may have given a fresh spurt to theological studies. There seem, in any event, to be a few Cistercians about. The principal who succeeded Duncan Bunch was Walter Bunch, himself a 'formed bachelor' in theology.[28] He was, it would seem, a close relative of Duncan, who also acted on behalf of another, William Bunch, in 1474 the new abbot of Kilwinning.[29] Walter Bunch was a Cistercian monk of Balmerino, who claimed the abbacy there in succession to Richard Coventry, it would seem unsuccessfully. He studied theology at Cologne.[30] On incorporation at Glasgow he is described as prior of Gadvan (Dunbog), a cell of Balmerino, but he can hardly be distinct from a monk of Coupar Angus of the same name, described as a sexagenarian in 1486, but still alive in 1500.[31] The other Cistercians were John Crichton, the new abbot of Newbattle, and Peter Sluthman, monk also of Newbattle, and a theological student at Cologne from 1466.[32]

With the foundation of a house of Observant Franciscans in Glasgow by Bishop Laing, one might have expected some impact on the Glasgow faculty. Moreover, at Paris an important Scots theologian, John Ireland, had shared in the general swing towards a revived 'modern way'.[33] His commentary on Books Three and Four on the Sentences has not been edited, but obviously many fourteenth-century issues were still as alive as ever: predestination as viewed in the severe framework of Thomas Bradwardine; the theory of 'special help' derived partly from him and Gregory of Rimini, which convulsed theological circles again in the seventeenth century; the continual emphasis on the infinity and absolute power of God to which a devotional Marian theology, approved by the Council of Basle, may have been a counterweight; a more optimistic theory about unbaptised infants than that of another Oxford theologian cited, Richard Fitzralph; and a new attention to problems of images and iconoclasm and to some Greek authors like John Damascene and Chrysostom. These questions were in the air, especially as Ireland made a point of cultivating not only Louis XI of France, initially inclined to repress the nominalist revival, but also James III, yet the strong Ockhamist partisanship, without, however, a single reference to Lindores, does not seem appropriate as yet to the Glasgow scene. There is no trace of the 'modern devotion' either; Pierre d'Ailly and Jean Gerson seem to be the only contemporaries cited.[34] In spite of continual polemic, there is at least some mutual awareness of each other's views, even among followers of Thomas Aquinas like the Dominicans, Joannes Capreolus and later, Silvestro Mazzolini di Prierio, whose works, if not eclectic, are more syntheses of theology than analyses of new problems.

In 1474 the Dominican general chapter assigned to their Paris house as students of theology Friar David of Scotland and a French friar in the desire that 'students of honour, internal (i.e. French) and external might keep their places according to the custom kept at Paris of old'.[35] This Friar David was David Craig, professor of theology, incorporated at Glasgow along with a 'confirmed' bachelor in theology, Friar Denis (surname not found) in 1487, although they may both have attended disputations before then, as Craig was prior in the Blackfriars in 1483.[36] The year 1474 was that of the royal ban on nominalism at Paris and Ireland did not graduate in theology till two years later, but, although there had been problems between the Paris friars and the university over external students, this had ceased to be a burning issue and Craig and Ireland would meet.[37] Craig was prior of the St Andrews Blackfriars before coming to Glasgow, succeeding there a Friar John Smyth who had preceded him to Glasgow in 1478.[38] The new prior would have had a hand in the donation of a building to the Dominicans in return for the university Rector's right to appoint one of their number as chaplain. The plan presumably was that such a chaplain, being a religious[39] qualified in theology, should take over the main burden of lecturing in the faculty. Thus the early bond with the neighbouring Blackfriars, which Duncan Bunch's ties of kinship with one of them would serve to confirm, seem to be stronger than ever.[40] The Cistercians appear no more on the Glasgow theological scene, but two Premonstratensian canons regular of Dryburgh were incorporated, John Crawford in 1476, and in 1485 Robert Kennedy, vicar of Penpont.[41]

Secular masters by comparison neglected theology, but William Young, bachelor 'admitted' to the reading of the Sentences, was incorporated in 1484. He came from St Andrews, where he was licensed in arts in 1475, was probably already a bachelor *cursor* when he acted as Quodlibetarius in 1481 and had been a regent also in St Salvator's. He did not return there.[42]

Archbishop Blackadder had ideas about university expansion and attracting learned Scotsmen from elsewhere, if only to bolster up his new archiepiscopal status. Patrick Coventry arrived in the Friar Craig period and had at least completed the initial four or five years as a theological student (with a brief absence in St Andrews in 1488) for in 1491 he had already entered on his first course as he is 'bachelor of sacred theology'.[43] But his pre-occupations as a working principal in the faculty of arts must have impeded his studies and neglect in record maintenance afflicts the arts records between 1503 and 1506, while the university's own acts are blank from 1505 to 1509 with the exception of a single item concerning Coventry's theological studies.[44]

This item, dated 7 December 1507, reads: 'On this day Master Patrick Coventry, henceforward bachelor in the Bible (*biblicus*), having previously finished the requisite lectures and disputations according to the use and custom of our university, under the presidency of the distinguished man, Mr William Cadzow, professor of sacred theology, was, in the presence of several prelates, lords and masters, in our greater schools, lawfully pronounced bachelor of sacred theology by the said Mr William and acquired justly and lawfully confirmation of the said degree of bachelor as aforesaid.'[45] Cadzow is otherwise unknown in the university, but is likely to have been involved in the requisite lectures and disputations mentioned in the extract. We gather that he was something of a Court favourite, the 'Doctor Cadiou' to whom royal bounties were paid by James IV between 1504 and 1508.[46] In Edinburgh in 1505 he was in the company of the king's English chaplain when he constituted procurators to accept benefices.[47] His theological doctorate was acquired at Bologna on 5 February 1500, when, as son of John Cadzow of Aberdeen, he was licensed by Augustinus de Bononia, Franciscan, and the well-known Dominican, Silvestro di Prierio. Among the friends present was Hugh Dacre, theological scholar of Paris, later archdeacon of Carlisle.[48]

The next decade yields precious little information about any faculty till the arrival of John Mair in 1518. The new university of Aberdeen had the advantage of an abbreviated course and attracted the efforts of the Scottish Dominicans some of whom began to take the Observant Franciscan reform seriously as it had creamed off the best young men. Some were graduates of the Greyfriars' own conventual branch and others secular graduates who felt that prayerful, charismatic and penitential renewal—though renewal still within the received tradition—was more important than the intellectual: the Greyfriars even for a time refused to parade their degrees.[49] The conflict between the Blackfriars revivalists and their confrères after the death of the old provincial, John Mure, reached physical proportions in the Blackfriars kirk at Aberdeen, when the energetic, reforming prior there, John Adamson, displaced Mure's successor as provincial; it led to the arrival from abroad of a Dominican commission, members of the reformed Congregation of Holland who were supporting Adamson, to episcopal intervention and royal letters of complaint, James IV's worries being mainly about Scots Blackfriars defecting to the English province.[50] One of the new wave of Dominican strict Observants was Friar Robert Lyle who took his bachelorship in theology at King's College.[51] As such, he was incorporated at Glasgow in 1519 when he was prior.[52] As a friar he was entitled to choose a friar master as his president in academic acts and in March 1522, being already a 'formed' bachelor, he had his formal *inceptio libri* or inaugural lecture on Book Four of the Sentences in the Blackfriars monastery 'in the presence of the Rector, the Dean of faculty and other masters, under the venerable father and religious man, Friar John Adamson, professor of sacred theology, provincial of the aforesaid order in the whole realm of Scotland and thereby president'. Later he took his licence.[53] About the same time, individual religious from Kilwinning, Crossraguel and Blantyre are on record.[54]

It is less easy to identify secular masters who might have studied theology, but at least two had got beyond the stage of bachelor *biblicus* when Mair arrived, John Spreull and William Gibson, as we learn from a letter of Mair's prefaced to his short commentary on the Metaphysics.[55] There he writes, 'You both once professed arts with renown in the university (*museum*) of Glasgow, at that time enthusiastically explaining the Daedalian twists of dialectic; now, however, that you are older, you despise these tricks and wiles, following St Paul's teaching that it becomes those of riper years to put aside the things of a child. Poring anxiously over the Word of God, you did not scorn to hear me, cold lecturer though I was, analysing the Books of the Sentences. At your behest, moreover, we expounded the Books of the Ethics from beginning to end with our commentary.' Spreull and Gibson had perhaps begun their earlier studies under Cadzow or Coventry.[56]

There must have been, as we have seen, some statutes or outline of statutes, reflecting Cologne and St Andrews originals, on which Glasgow theological procedure was based.[57] We do not have the St Andrews originals, but only a copy of 1570 in a defective text, with obvious later alterations in graduation procedure in accordance with later Paris custom, as well as post-Reformation redrafting ('copied verbally from the old manuscript and separated from, and purged of,

E

superstitions and vanities')[58]; but as has already been suggested, perhaps they were more like the Cologne statutes of c. 1400.[59] The statutes were probably updated by Mair in 1518, if not before his arrival. The factors that made for the obvious resemblances between the Glasgow arts statutes of 1452 and the St Andrews arts statutes of 1439 can reasonably be conjectured to apply equally in theology.[60] The main new post-Reformation elements are in the section in religious duties and in the abolition of the Sentences of Peter Lombard and therefore the redefining of the 'formed' bachelor, but the medieval shape is still discernible, 'in part changed and reformed according to the norm of the word of God'.[61]

The course at Paris was very long. In the fifteenth century it lasted fourteen years, six till the first bachelorship course and eight more till the doctorate.[62] At St Andrews, at least in the sixteenth century, it was shorter. In January 1540 John Mair and William Manderston made a foundation for a chaplain bursar, with the requirement that on every lecturing day he should be continuously present at the acts, disputations and questions for twelve years after beginning the study of theology and should rise to the degree of 'formed' bachelor within seven years 'according to the statutes and rule of the aforesaid university'.[63] The original course at Cologne was thirteen years, but shortened often to twelve or less, except that, after the 'formed' bachelor stage, dispensation was unlikely.[64] At Paris itself dispensation for one year was given for those taking a regency in arts concurrently, but no more, 'not for all the courses of Jean Buridan'.[65] Aberdeen drastically shortened its course at first to seven, then to six, years all told, and, although it was lengthened again by papal indult, this extension was perhaps inoperative.[66] Hugh Spens in 1534 for a similar St Andrews theological bursar required attendance at lectures three times weekly, along with continuous study and disputation.[67]

The basis of the course was lectures on the Bible and the Sentences, disputations and, for practical theology, sermons. The St Andrews statutes required a studentship of four years under a regent master of the student's choice, under whom, as president, he would begin all his public acts.[68] These compulsory lectures were not only those by the masters, but of all bachelors, whether 'formed' or not.[69] The idea was that the student would gather in the wide margins of his Bible or his Books of the Sentences useful glosses as well as other notes which would help him to form his own mind and provide fuel for disputation. The Bible books as listed in the St Andrews statutes were grouped into the legal, historical, sapiential and prophetical books of the Old Testament and the New Testament. The Books of the Sentences were removed at the Reformation, 'papistry being buried and the manner of belief changed and reformed about 1560'.[70] These undergraduate studies in the Bible and the Sentences were taken concurrently. In theory, at least, the student was very busy attending all lectures from prime (seven a.m.) till later in the morning when the bachelor *biblicus* —at the end of the lecturing queue—lectured; in addition discussions and exercises, faculty and university acts, inaugural sessions of bachelors and masters, ordinary and extraordinary disputations, religious exercises, sermons required his attention. At this stage too at Paris he was required to have given two 'collations' (evening conferences) or one morning sermon and one collation.

On completing his fourth year, the theological undergraduate, now aged twenty-five, had to present himself to the Dean—if such existed at Glasgow—and faculty for admission to the next stage. The mendicant friars, such as Dominicans and Franciscans, and Cistercians at Paris at this point gave an ordinary course every day after noon. The seculars and other religious were obliged to read two lesson-series or extraordinary courses[71] on books of their choice, first in the Old, next year in the New, Testament, hence called 'cursores',[72] but often also bachelors 'of the Bible' (*biblici*). These were opened with a *principium*, a term to be explained later. The 'cursor' was expected to give a straightforward, literal exposition at this stage, one chapter at a time only, based on received glosses and concentrating on clear presentation. The post-Reformation St Andrews rules require one *principium* in the historical books involving some argument (cf. the pre-Reformation *quaestio collativa*), moving a question on the text, arguing difficulties for and against and adding certain propositions to bring out the truth of the matter clearly.[73] There is also mention of a speech of thanksgiving to all present, another pre-Reformation survival. This is the stage that Patrick Coventry reached in his theological studies under Cadzow.[74]

The next stage was Bachelor in the Sentences (*Sententiarius*); at St Andrews it opened the seventh year of study. This stage was excluded from the post-Reformation statutes. Having specialised in two books of the Bible, the bachelor could now attempt a conspectus of the whole field of theology. He had to make a *principium* on the four separate books and, after his principium on Book Three, he was a 'formed' bachelor though he had not really completed the course till the end of Book Four. Friar Robert Lyle was, therefore, already a 'formed' bachelor when he took up Book Four in March 1522—Book Four was usually reserved till after Easter.[75] Lombard's Sentences, according to an anonymous sixteenth-century St Andrews bachelor, examine in the First Book the trinity of Persons and the oneness of the divine essence; in the Second Book the order of divine wisdom (the production of creatures, God's external operations, angelic nature, man and his

Fall, sin original and actual and how God's ineffable wisdom is seen in his creation); in the Third Book, the conjunction of God and his creatures (the Incarnation); and in the Fourth Book, the divine mercy (sacraments etc.).[76] Not all of Lombard's points need be taken up by the bachelor; new issues raised since his time could be touched on. This was a more personal and demanding type of lecture than that of the *cursor*, and therefore the Bachelor of the Sentences was relieved of many other faculty chores. The shortest time taken to reach this point at St Andrews was achieved by John Lock, described as *Sententiarius* in 1455, eight years after his licence in arts; he is recorded as licentiate three years later and master in 1459, which gives us almost twelve years study in total.[77] A five-year period was required for the doctorate at Paris and Cologne, though at Cologne there were certainly dispensations given.[78] The year in which the licence was given, an even year, was called the jubilee: its original intention was to make the theological licence a specially privileged occasion. Hannay suggests that the new religious regime abolished the jubilee at St Andrews.[79] In the post-Reformation course the candidate became a confirmed bachelor after lecturing for a year on the New Testament, but the student is still said to be over thirty, indeed to have completed his thirtieth year, before licence.[80] The four years after bachelorship were, however, originally five.[81]

Disputations formed the core of the medieval study programme. Those mentioned specifically at St Andrews were the public and weekly disputations of masters, not only in *vesperiae* and *aulae*, the two solemn disputations at the end of the course. In pre-Reformation times this would include the Advent quodlibet disputations, where the *quodlibetarius* was often at least a bachelor in theology.[82] Disputants were urged, especially in the vacation disputations, to dispute modestly, 'not fighting like dogs biting each other, but like men instructing each other'.[83] The St Andrews statutes do not clarify that students began as opponents and only later were admitted as respondents, but it is evident that the bachelor *cursor* acted as respondent in vespers to the preliminary or expectatory question, while senior or 'formed' bachelors acted as opponents, though the next day in hall the respondent was a 'formed' bachelor.[84]

Disputations peculiar to theologians were the 'Sorbonic' in the long vacation. They began on 1 July in post-Reformation St Andrews (that is, after the feast of Sts Peter and Paul, in accordance with the medieval rule),[85] lasting till the beginning of October. In Paris they were held in the Sorbonne and presided over by its prior. Hence the name 'prior of vacance'.[86] He was elected on the last day of the Ordinary.[87] The disputations are said to take place for a few hours on Saturdays, but originally they would be on Fridays and last much longer.[88] John Mair, comparing lawyers with theologians, pointed out that at Paris 'nobody becomes a doctor before fourteen complete years in study in that faculty after arts; and unless he has responded without his president in public in the Sorbonne for thirteen hours without providing an opening to any opponent, not counting other public disputations under presidents for the space of four years, examining all admitted bachelors in all acts publicly and usually regenting a course or two in arts for a cycle of four or five years . . .'.[89] The 'prior' seems to have been the 'principal opponent' entitled to priority and to more arguments than anybody else.[90] A master presided, the other masters and licentiates sitting.[91] It seems to have been an arduous test.

All presented bachelors, formed and non-formed, were called upon to preach. The medieval academic sermon was a special genre, constructed to a prefixed pattern, often a scriptural, patristic or scholastic patchwork rather than a personal creation, using moral tales and allegories in profusion. Such exercises took place on Sundays and other special days, the latter listed at Aberdeen,[92] and probably at Glasgow on the days on which the Rector was expected to appear in his Rector's gown. The *sermo ad clerum* in Latin survives in the St Andrews statutes as well as the vernacular sermon.[93] A good example of such a 'vernacular sermon', heavily larded with Latin citations, can be found in a work addressed to James IV. As John Ireland, its author, admits, it is full of rhetorical rather than proof arguments borrowed from Duns Scotus and from the masters of rhetoric among whom he counts Aristotle, Cicero and Quintilian.[94] Sermons outside the university were also laid down at Aberdeen.[95]

In the original medieval regulations a distinction would be drawn between sermons and collations[96] (evening sermons, in this instance, usually by bachelors, often continuing the theme of the morning sermon of the master). 'University sermons' are merely mentioned in passing at Glasgow as being public acts at which the beadle was present.[97]

Principia were solemn acts, called *inceptiones librorum* at Glasgow, that is, solemn inaugural lectures.[98] Each bachelor 'of the Bible' had to give a preliminary conference (*collatio*) in recommendation of scripture and the bachelor of the Sentences likewise before going on to his questions.[99] These were really sermons or conferences on some broad theological theme[100] suggested by a text which was used in all his *principia*. At his final inception the young theologian returned to this text. The sixteenth-century inceptor at St Andrews (*c.* 1546), for instance, says, 'we take up that text that formerly we were in the habit of using in our *principia* to sacred letters: Concupiscite sermones meos et lumen sapientie, omnes qui preestis populis'.[101] The beadle with his mace was present at all *principia* and received fees; at St Andrews John Lock was denied the arts mace for his inaugural on the Second Book of the Sentences.[102]

In post-Reformation, as in pre-Reformation days, publication was prohibited without previous faculty censorship.[103] We do not know if the sort of propositions evidenced in the Glasgow Lollard accusations of 1494 were ever heard in the faculty; perhaps they were typical popular theology, though popular theology often affected the schools; the popular theology of one generation being often unpopular in another. On the whole the accusations seem genuine enough; and this is so even if not all the 'Lollards of Kyle' can be shown to have persisted in unorthodoxy, and at least one of the citations quoted by Knox seems to be taken from a formulary.[104] One of the accused certainly went on pilgrimage to the shrines at Canterbury and Amiens, but that might be a mere device for putting heresy hunters off the scent.

In all *principia* of bachelors, in public acts and also in the new master's *aula*, there were to be praiseworthy protestations of orthodoxy as in pre-Reformation times,[105] to the effect that the candidate did not intend 'to say, assert or affirm—expressions in ascending order of certainty—anything contrary to the orthodox faith'. Bachelors still were to lecture faithfully, according to the Catholic faith (*catholice*).[106] This statute looks like an earlier one, inherited by the 1439 statute compilers from Haldenstone, an early Dean.[107]

The medieval statutes would require some minimum requirements regarding the reception of clerical orders, though students and bachelors frequently preached without any orders at all, above the initial tonsure, which did not mean much. At Cologne before bachelorship they were required to be in the minor order of acolyte and before licence at least be subdeacon.[108] At Aberdeen there was a late attempt, not it would seem at first successful, to insist on the priesthood for theologians.[109] Besides the usual typical oaths exacted of them, bachelors were given 'exhortations' and could be denied promotion if contumacious.[110]

Before licence the 'formed' bachelor at St Andrews was required to act as responsal to one theological question in a disputation where he was opposed by everybody, by the other masters and 'formed' bachelors. Then he approached the faculty for its good will, which the faculty granted on fulfilment of the antecedent conditions. After this he was conducted by his master to the chancellor with testimonies as to his life, ability in letters, eloquence and hope of future proficiency.[111] The chancellor's duty was to send the signet, that is a notification under his seal, of the hour and place of the licence ceremony. As at Cologne the beadle carried this, not the *paranymphus* (discussed below).[112] At the licence ceremony there was the usual gathering. The president opened the proceedings with his 'collation' or conference. The chancellor or vice-chancellor then called the licentiands in their order of merit, though the St Andrews statutes only legislate for one. The oaths followed, including the promise not to spend more on the associated celebrations than three thousand *gros tournois*, as laid down in the Clementines.[113] The usual chancellor's blessing followed.

A due interval of term elapsed between licence and doctorate.[114] The usual preliminary notification took place before vespers. Those invited were given the titles of four questions,[115] two to be discussed in vespers and two in hall. Then the vesperiand sought out one of the senior masters.[116] We gather from the Cologne statutes that this master was paid as much for his 'pourboire' as the master who merely argued. The newer practice was to have two young 'paranymphs' or bridegrooms, symbolising the marriage of the new master to his science, dressed like angels and changed in appearance, wearing bright clothes and colours, and these propounded questions on the vesperiand's behalf. The Chancellor, Rector, doctors and others were brought processionally to the schools by the beadle carrying the maces (evidently two), and silver wands, and a very elaborate procedure was followed with an 'expectatory' question by a bachelor *cursor*, a bachelor of the Sentences at Paris. A general disputation followed. The second question was taken up when the masters had gathered. The vesperiand was in charge then and some senior masters took a prominent part, and it closed with the president's jocular commendation.

The *aula* or master's act, held in the morning, was even more spectacular than the vespers. Reference has already been made to his opening conference in recommendation of sacred letters. We have one of these: it is partly a speech of thanks, an oration in praise of divine wisdom, a gathering from memory (hence *collatio*) of many related passages of scripture, a commendation of Peter Lombard and a homily to the assembly. On finishing, the prospective master said, 'Let him rise who is to propound the question', the gifts of bonnets meantime having been distributed by the beadle. In the newer procedure, the greater paranymph rose to address the vesperiand's third question to a 'formed' bachelor in words similar to these, 'Most reverend *magistri nostri*,[117] I, lately capped, propound to the student of sacred religion, Master John Douglas (blank left for any degrees) and also formed bachelor in the theological faculty, this question to be determined by him as briefly as possible, etc. The third question was then debated and later there followed for the fourth question an even more ceremonial debate, 'the question of the masters', involving four seniors in a complicated intellectual tournament. After all this feast of reason, there was no further argument, but all went to the new master's more material feast.

Then followed the *resumpta*, the new master's act of determination. It was so called because he 'resumed' or took up the theme unfinished in the *aula*. It took place next day as at Cologne (not the third as at Bologna and Paris) and he took up his second question again, dealing with hanging threads of argument. Again, as at Cologne he made a short speech thanking God and also all present and absent to whom he had particular cause for gratitude. The Cologne version thanked 'the whole heavenly court and all benefactors living and dead', a phrase omitted in this post-Reformation redaction.[118]

One must ask how a course like this, tailor-made for Paris and the more thickly populated universities in Central and Southern Europe (some of which had few theological students and even fewer lecturers), could have suited the small, remote Scottish institutions. The very length and expense of the course must have frightened off students and, while no one can doubt that theology was considered so serious a subject that twelve years of study of it were all too few, one can sympathise with attempts to curtail the time-span. It is at least possible that some students, though perhaps few of them secular clerics, sampled it but did not consider later proceeding to a formal degree qualification. Yet many more must have been too disheartened at the long prospect, and remained content as ministers of religion with the more general formation given in the arts faculty.[119] The fault was perhaps too much, rather than too little, ambition.

NOTES

1. *Maitland Folio Manuscript*, ed. W. A. Craigie (STS, ser. 2, no. 7, Edinburgh, 1919), i, 235.
2. Burns, *Scottish Churchmen*, 20, 35, 41, 54.
3. Keussen, i, 314. 'Fr. Allex. de Mylros, O. Cist., de Scotia' was one of a group of three Scottish Cistercians at Cologne studying theology in 1429.
4. *Ibid.*, i, 445. 'D. David Herdghet, O. Cist., de Scotia', began theology on 1441; presumably therefore he was a bachelor of the Sentences (*sententiarius*).
5. *Ibid.*, i, 312, where he is said to be studying arts in which he had already graduated in St Andrews. Cf. Burns, *Scottish Churchmen*, 154.
6. *Glas. Mun.*, ii, 140.
7. E.g. at Pavia in 1440, a single Dominican friar, Vaccari, *Storia della Università di Pavia* (Pavia, 1948), 63. There is no record of a Dean in theology at Aberdeen.
8. *Glas. Mun.*, i, 4; ii, 31, t. 6, c. 3, 'inter quatuor facultates et maxime cum facultate theologie'; *ibid*, ii, 13, 'the faculties of arts and canon law or any other faculty'.
9. The Cologne Cistercians were either to live in a common study house in 1457 or return home; J. M. Canivez, *Statuta Capitulorum Generalium Ordinis Cisterciensis* (Louvain, 1937), v, 9.

10. D. Baker, 'Heresy and Learning in early Cistercianism', *Schism, Heresy and Religious Protest: Studies in Church History*, ix, ed. D. Baker (Cambridge, 1972), 93–107.
11. Burns, *Scottish Churchmen*, 12–13, 17–18, 60–64.
12. Cowan, *Parishes*, 91.
13. *Glas. Mun.*, ii, 55.
14. *Ibid.*, ii, 13. A monk called Reginald, of uncertain origin, was a matriculand in 1451, *ibid.*, ii, 58.
15. Hannay, *Statutes*, 112–35.
16. J. Durkan, 'St Andrews University Medieval Theological Statutes: Revised Dating Suggested', *IR*, xiii, 104–8. So far no evidence has emerged to throw light on when such subsequent development may have taken place.
17. *CUP*, iv, 737 ('Coliburn' in a list of 'cursores'); *AFA*, 61, 67, 69; *Glas. Mun.*, ii, 61, 182.
18. Reg. Supp., 705, f. 230v.
19. *Glas. Mun.*, ii, 198. Possibly before becoming principal of the Hamilton college.
20. *Ibid.*, ii, 68, 73.
21. *Ibid.*, ii, 73; *AFA*, 160; *CPL*, xiii, 613.
22. *Glas. Mun.*, ii, 65–6.
23. *Ibid.*, ii, 76, 78.
24. *Ibid.*, ii, 78; *RMS*, ii, 1164; *Liber Collegii Nostre Domine*, 180–3.
25. Burns, *Scottish Churchmen*, 54.
26. *Ibid.*, 73–5; *AFA*, li, note.
27. *Copiale*, 204–9; *AFA*, xxxii.
28. *Glas. Mun.*, ii, 83. If a 'formed' bachelor of Cologne (see below), he had studied theology for nine years.
29. *ACSB*, 247, Cardinal d'Estouteville was cardinal *ponens*; *ibid.*, 69.
30. *CPL*, xii, 192. He is probably the regular cleric, 'd. Wolt. de Scotia', student in theology in 1453, Keussen, i, 563.
31. *Charters of the Abbey of Coupar Angus*, ed. D. E. Easson, SHS, ser. iii (Edinburgh, 1947), ii, 70–3, 89, 92; *Registrum Episcopatus Brechinensis*, i, 218–20. He took his licence in theology before 1482, *CPL*, xiii, 135–6.
32. *Glas. Mun.*, ii, 82; Keussen, i, 740.
33. The best biography is in J. H. Burns, 'John Ireland and *The Meroure of Wyssdome*', *IR*, vi (1955), 77–98. On his theology Brother Bonaventure, 'The Popular Theology of John Ireland', *ibid.*, xiii, 130–46; 'John Ireland and the Immaculate Conception', *ibid.*, xvii, 24–39.
34. Aberdeen University Library, MS 264, authorities summarised.
35. A. d'Amato, 'Gli atti dei capitoli generali del 1474 e del 1486', *Archivum Fratrum Praedicatorum* (Rome, 1947), xvii, 229.
36. *Glas. Mun.*, ii, 100; *Liber Collegii Nostre Domine*, 194, 200.
37. *CUP*, iv, 626–31.
38. Craig is on record at St Andrews in 1479, SRO, General Register House Calendar of Charters, 488A; but Smyth was at Glasgow in 1478, *Liber Collegii Nostre Domine*, 190; and is active in St Andrews in 1471 and 1476, SRO, Calendar of St Andrews Chrs., 55, 65.
39. *Glas. Mun.*, i, 33.
40. Gilbert Bunch was prior of the Cupar (Fife) Blackfriars in 1460: SRO, Calendar of St Andrews Chrs., p. 468.
41. *Glas. Mun.*, ii, 86, 100; for the latter's religious status, *Prot. Bk. Simon*, 30.
42. *Glas. Mun.*, ii, 99; *AFA*, 194, 203, 212–13.
43. *Glas. Mun.*, ii, 100, 108, 112; Anderson, *Early Records*, 186.

44. *Glas. Mun.*, ii, 281; 120 (p. 85 of Liber Rectoris, 86–7 being left blank), 121 (the Coventry entry is in a different hand from the rest of the entries on p. 88).
45. *Ibid.*, ii, 120–1.
46. *ALHT*, ii, 414, 422, 425; iii, 128, 386, 399; iv, 94, 102, 105.
47. *Protocol Book of James Young*, ed. G. Donaldson (Edinburgh, 1949), pt. 6, 1542. He did in fact get presentation to the chancellorship of Brechin, *RSS*, i, 1221, but survived only till 1509 or thereabouts.
48. C. Piana, *Ricerche su le Università di Bologna e di Parma nel secolo XV* (Quaracchi/ Florence, 1963; Spicilegium Bonaventurianum 1), 220 (no. 123). Coventry later became a licentiate in theology, *Glas. Prots.*, iv, 1221.
49. John Moorman, *A History of the Franciscan Order* (Oxford, 1968), 506–7.
50. *The Letters of James IV 1505-1513*, calendared by R. K. Hannay (SHS, ser. iii, Edinburgh, 1953), nos. 30, 114, 119, 229, 348.
51. *Hectoris Boetii Murthlacensium et Aberdonensium Episcoporum Vitae* (New Spalding Club, 1894), 92; *Registrum Episcopatus Aberdonensis*, ii, 312.
52. *Glas. Mun.*, ii, 136.
53. *Ibid.*, ii, 140; described as licentiate in National Library of Scotland, Advocates MS, Hutton (Shires), ix, 13 (in 1540, when again he was Glasgow prior).
54. *Glas. Mun.*, ii, 136, 139, 146.
55. *Octo Libri Physicorum* (Paris, 1526), sig. f. iiC, to which this commentary is added.
56. Spreull graduated in arts in 1496; Gibson in 1507: *Glas. Mun.*, ii, 270, 285. Gibson alone is on record as a theologian, *Charters of the Hospital of Soltre*, 1; *St Andrews Formulare 1514-46*, ed. G. Donaldson and C. Macrae (Stair Society, Edinburgh, 1942–4), ii, 164.
57. Mention has already been made of David Hardgate in this connection. He was also at St Andrews. Hardgate, with Bunch, is mentioned as a cautioner for a student debtor in 1452, after both had gone to Glasgow, *AFA*, 94, 106.
58. Hannay, *Statutes*, 86. Hannay did not use the earliest text in NLS, Adv. MS. 29.2.7.
59. F. Gescher, 'Die Statuten der theologischen Fakultät an der alten Universität Köln', *Festschrift zur Erinnerung an die Gründung der alten Universität Köln im Jahre 1388* (Cologne, 1938), 43–108.
60. Durkan, 'St Andrews University Medieval Theological Statutes', *IR*, xiii, 104–8.
61. Hannay, *Statutes*, 112. However, cf. 'ex Cristo (sic) fundamento' (Hannay, *Statutes*, 113) and 'Cum, ubi Christus non est fundamentum' (*Festschrift Köln*, 69).
62. A Clerval, *Registre des Procès Verbaux de la Faculté de Théologie de Paris*, Archives de l'Histoire religieuse de la France (Paris, 1917), i, xxii ff. Clerval's book shows several changes from earlier medieval practice.
63. St Andrews University Archives, 'Registrum evidentiarum et privilegiorum universitatis Sanctiandree', 92v–96v.
64. *Festschrift Köln*, 74, 92 (student); 80, 82-3. One, or at most two, years at Cologne were dispensable. 'Statuts primitifs de la Faculté de Théologie de l'ancienne Université de Louvain', ed. E. H. Reusens, *Annuaire de l'Univ. de Louvain* (1882), xlvi, 391.
65. John Mair, *In Quartum Sententiarum* (Paris, 1519), f. lxii A.
66. Eeles, *King's College Chapel*, 163, 201; *Fasti Aberdonenses*, 109, 265.
67. St Andrews Univ. Archives, St Salvator's Book 'B', 98r.
68. Hannay, *Statutes*, 118, Adv. MS. 29.2.7, 2v has 'quatuor' altered to 'tres'.
69. The general background of medieval theological studies on the Parisian model is given in P. Glorieux, 'L'Enseignement au Moyen Age', *Archives d'Histoire*

THEOLOGY 125

doctrinale et littéraire du Moyen Age (1968), 65–186, but the late medieval development is not covered in Glorieux.
70. Hannay, *Statutes*, 117–18.
71. Later made 'ordinary'. Hannay, *Statutes*, 119, where legere ordinariam' should read 'legere ordinarie'. But perhaps originally 'ordinate'.
72. *Ibid.* The text is corrupt and should read 'currens bacchalaureus seu cursorius'.
73. *Ibid.*, 120. The punctuation should read 'moveat questionem, ad utramque questionis partem roborandam argumentetur, ad questionis veritatem soluendam subjungat . . .' concerning the single chapter, *ibid.*, 122.
74. *Glas. Mun.*, ii, 120. At Paris the bachelor had to give the faculty lists of his hearers. Cf. Hannay, *Statutes*, 120 concerning reading *in audientia*.
75. *Glas. Mun.*, ii, 140.
76. MS inserted in Glasgow University Library copy of the printed book, Manderston, *Bipartitum* (Paris, 1518), pressmarked BE6.b11 (f. 16r and v).
77. Anderson, *Early Records*, 26; *AFA*, 109, 127, 129.
78. *CUP*, ii, 700; *Festschrift Köln*, 82–3.
79. Hannay, *Statutes*, 126, note 4.
80. *Ibid.*, 81, 128.
81. *Ibid.*, 122. The 'quinque' has been altered to 'quatuor' in Adv. MS. 29.2.7, 3v.
82. Hannay, *Statutes*, 121; *Festschrift Köln*, 80.
83. Hannay, *Statutes*, 122. In 1512 in the Dominican church at Paris, the paranymphus or public orator describes David Cranston in the ceremony of calling the order of licentiands as usually mild and affable, but in disputation his Scots tongue would force its way past all vocal impediments and produce sounds like thunder: Paris, Bibliothèque Nationale Ms Lat 7812, f. 27.
84. Hannay, *Statutes*, 121–2 (reading 'et' between 'vacantiis' and 'bis'), 132–3. *CUP*, iii, 144, one responsion during 'cursor' stage.
85. Cf. F. Ehrle, *Statuta facultatis theologiae Bononiensis* (Bologna, 1932), 24; *Festschrift Köln*, 71.
86. *Evidence*, iii, 188.
87. Hannay, *Statutes*, 114.
88. *Ibid.*, 116.
89. *In Quartum Sententiarum* (Paris, 1521), f. clxvC.
90. Glorieux, 'L'Enseignement', 136. Hannay, *Statutes*, 114.
91. *Ibid.*, 116.
92. *Fasti Aberdonenses*, 268.
93. Hannay, *Statutes*, 114–15. Even students had to preach, *ibid.*, 121–2.
94. *The Meroure of Wyssdome*, ed. Quinn, ii, 108.
95. *Fasti Aberdonenses*, 268.
96. *Festschrift Köln*, 81.
97. *Glas. Mun.*, ii, 12, 25.
98. *Ibid.*
99. *Festschrift Köln*, 78, 82.
100. Cf. Hannay, *Statutes*, 119, 'sumpto themate ex aliquo sacre scripture loco'.
101. GUL, MS cited, note 76 above, f. 10v.
102. Hannay, *Statutes*, 123; *AFA*, 120. Dr. Dunlop discusses the faculty of theology briefly, *ibid.*, cxxxix ff.
103. Hannay, *Statutes*, 122; *Festschrift Köln*, 86.
104. D. E. Easson, 'The Lollards of Kyle', *Juridical Review*, xlviii (1936), 123–8. Knox did not agree with all their propositions.
105. Hannay, *Statutes*, 126; *Festschrift Köln*, 94.
106. Hannay, *Statutes*, 117, 126; *Festschrift Köln*, 73.

107. *Copiale*, 72.
108. *Festschrift Köln*, 74. Similarly at Paris.
109. *Fasti Aberdonenses*, 268–9.
110. Hannay, *Statutes*, 126–7. Cf. *Festschrift Köln*, 92.
111. Hannay, *Statutes*, 129–30. *Festschrift Köln*, 100, is almost identical.
112. *Festschrift Köln*, 96; Hannay, *Statutes*, 127.
113. This figure only given in the National Library manuscript.
114. Hannay, *Statutes*, 129; *St Andrews Formulare*, ii, 104–5; *Festschrift Köln*, 99ff.
115. *Ibid.*
116. *Ibid.*, 'unum de senioribus magistris', not 'eum', as in Hannay, *Statutes*, 131.
117. Hannay, *Statutes*, 134 reads 'nostro', which disagrees with the manuscripts. 'Magistri nostri' is the technical term for doctors of theology.
118. Hannay, *Statutes*, 135. *Festschrift Köln*, 104.
119. Cf. J. A. Weisheipl, 'The Structure of the Arts Faculty in the Medieval Universities', *British Journal of Educational Studies*, xix (1971), 263–271.

7. Law

'Of sewall mony volum thay rewoll,
The codyss and degestis new and ald;
Prowe and contra, strait argument thay resoll,
Sum a doctryne, and sum a nother hald.'

Henryson, *The Sheep and the Dog*

'We see it produce men . . . by whom . . . the Christian people committed
to our care may be chastised with the rod of equity and justice, faith
solidly defended, quarrelsome complaints settled and each receive
his due.'

Letter of Protection of James II

AT ST ANDREWS there is evidence of teaching in canon law from the
foundation, and, from 1432, of an attempt, not altogether successful,
to introduce civil law as well. Perhaps only in the mid-sixteenth century
was this possible.[1] At Glasgow, as we have seen, the attempt to introduce both laws was made at its foundation, and schools for the purpose
existed. Some 'ancient statutes' concerning the faculty of canon law
were in existence in 1490.[2] A chaplainry in connection with the readership was founded in 1463, and not transferred absolutely to the support
of a regent in arts till 1522.[3] On the other hand, as with theology, no
faculty act book survives, and this necessarily makes our information
somewhat fragmented.

Teaching began in July 1451, when David Cadzow, chanter of
Glasgow, licentiate in canon law, and William Lennox, graduate in
both laws, took up their lectures on canon and civil law in the chapter-
house of the Blackfriars, so chosen because it was a formal series of
inaugural lectures.[4] It has been suggested that there was in that year
another William Lennox, 'bachelor', probably William Lennox of
Cally, the second son of his mother's second marriage, which took
place about 1430. He graduated master of arts—though this degree is
not recorded either at Glasgow or St Andrews where the name also
occurs—and died in 1516. Duncan Bunch and William Arthurlie are
among witnesses to documents concerning his elder brother and he
himself had a grant of lands in 1459.[5] If he studied law for a time,
we have no record of it, and he is clearly not to be confused with the
civil law lecturer.

Of the first matriculated students in the university two are later
found as bachelors in canon law: Martin Wan, who first studied in

127

arts, and John Reston.[6] Many in this initial period are not recorded
in the arts faculty. There are possible teachers in what one presumes
was the united faculty of law in addition to Cadzow and Lennox. In
the initial incorporation a group, apparently of theologians, is followed
by what may be a group of lawyers and students of law. They include
Patrick Leitch, the chancellor of the diocese, graduate in arts of St
Andrews and a bachelor in decreets of Rome[7]; William Govan, an
aged canon who had studied at Avignon[8]; David Nairn, student of
arts and canon law at Paris[9]; William Elphinstone, senior, from St
Andrews and Louvain, had studied both laws, canon and civil[10]; Simon
Dalgleish was a bachelor in decreets in 1447 and later, by 1459, a
licentiate[11]; Stephen Ker, was master of arts and bachelor of decreets[12];
William Blair is recorded in 1468 as a bachelor of decreets[13]; Gilbert
Park was already a bachelor in decreets[14]; and so was John de Hawick.[15]
Even if some of these incorporations were purely nominal, there must
be some residue of bachelor lecturers among them.

Among those active on the original university statutes committee of
1451, besides some named above, there were John Arrous, doctor of
decreets (incorporated merely as archdeacon and unnamed),[16] and
John Dundoff, probably the same as a certain 'Dundas', bachelor of
decreets, supplicating for Maybole in 1444.[17] The name of Robert
Penven, incorporated officially in 1452, is found in a legal manuscript
(collections of William Elphinstone, senior, with a legal lexicon) and
there are other names with Glasgow associations in a manuscript copy
of the lectures of a former Bologna doctor, Petrus de Ancharano.[18]
Quintin Weir, a student of 1452, was a bachelor of canon law in 1455[19];
John Young, vicar of Stobo, a student in 1451 and later, was a bachelor
in the laws who in 1454 wished to read the laws publicly for seven
years and receive the higher degrees of licentiate and doctor[20]; John
Yrnhoss, incorporated 1453, is likewise recorded as a bachelor of
decreets in 1464[21]; Alexander Vaus, of Galloway diocese, also incorporated in 1453, can surely be identified with the priest of that diocese,
canon of Aberdeen, scholar of canon law in 1459[22]; and Gilbert
Rerik, a former student of canon law in Rome university, was presumably the man whom we find a year later, continuing his legal studies
at Glasgow.[23] It reads like a barren roll-call, but it is necessary to list
such names as long as no register of medieval graduates exists for
Scotland. It suggests that from the start canon law was on a reasonably
sound footing, whereas civil was lagging behind.

On 2 March 1463 there was a notable step forward when David
Cadzow, a few years before his death, describing himself no longer as
chanter of Glasgow but as canon and university Rector, gave the
chaplainry of the Virgin Mary in the lower church of the cathedral

to 'a distinguished, worthy and fit clerk' lecturing in the faculty of canon law in 'the public schools'. To this chaplainry was attached originally a salary of twelve merks Scots and admission was to be by the bishop on the recommendation of the Rector and his deputies. The lectures were to be the morning lectures and to be delivered 'as in other universities'. Solemn morning lectures on the Decretals were given by doctors and this may have been Cadzow's intention.[24] The first record of William Arthurlie as a doctor of decreets is in 1465, most of his career since graduating in St Andrews having been spent as a regent in arts at Glasgow.[25] The 'public schools' mentioned are the schools of canon law. Other faculties must have envied this salaried official, though later a theological chaplainry was founded for a Glasgow Dominican and some others existed to which the arts faculty also had a title.

It may be that around 1468 there was a break in the teaching of canon law, or at least a falling off in its quality so that some students went elsewhere. For some years Cadzow had been a sick man, a circumstance which, as we have seen, caused him to resign his office of chanter of Glasgow. Thomas and Vedast Muirhead went to the canon law faculty of Louvain, returning to Glasgow shortly afterwards.[26] Thomas is recorded as a licentiate in decreets.[27] Other students in canon law were Robert Houston and James Knox, who later held the readership, master of works for the school of canon law.[28] The future principal, John Goldsmith, was a bachelor of decreets by 1479.[29] The return of the wandering students to Glasgow would be helped by the arrival of the doctor of decreets, Thomas Lutherdale (or Lauderdale) in 1468.[30]

Among men of distinction in the law faculty during these decades was Robert Henryson, the poet, in 1462 a licentiate in arts and bachelor in decreets, who would probably have been recorded in the St Andrews arts faculty if he had been a graduate of that university.[31] Another was William Elphinstone, junior, about whose early career Hector Boece's biography is in some respects misleading, making his period abroad at Paris and Orleans unduly protracted. The younger Elphinstone principiated in arts at Glasgow in 1462 and, Boece informs us, continued his law studies there. He was a member of the arts faculty thereafter, had some arts determinants in his charge in 1463 and acted as regent and examiner in arts till 1465.[32] The nature of the training of a canon lawyer at Glasgow can be gathered from what Boece says about Elphinstone, who, he says, studied under approved teachers there, but also did practical work in the courts and became advocate for the poor. He is said, however, to have withdrawn himself from legal business for four years to live in his country parish, which is impossible to fit into the chronology, as are his nine years in France. Elphinstone returned home still, it would seem, a bachelor in canon law: in 1474 he was licensed with honour (*honorifice*) and only then described himself as licentiate. The 'public oration' he is said to have made which so impressed the bishop and clergy was probably an academic 'harangue'.[33] He had inherited some useful notes from his father, William Elphinstone, senior, some on civil law from Johannes Grosbeck, Richard de Tournai and Henricus Retheri, others in canon law. He had a favourite author among the canonists, Nicholas de Tudeschis, the famous Sicilian called 'Panormitanus', a guiding spirit at the Council of Basle and a notable conciliarist.[34] Conciliarism continued to be a live academic issue, and not only among lawyers.[35]

The ecclesiastical councils, however, did not have the same importance as creators of the canon law as did the papacy in its Decretals.[36] The main early collection of these Decretals or authoritative decisions was made by Gratian at Bologna about 1140. But an abundance of papal legislation followed, one set outside (*Extravagantes*) this collection in five books, to which a sixth (*Liber Sextus*) was added by Boniface VIII. The seventh book issued by Clement V (*Clementines*) completed the body of canon law (*Corpus Juris Canonici*). These were the main texts of the canon lawyer.[37] In addition, however, there was legal practice, where students were able to observe the application of these texts by their masters. John Reston, canonist, for instance acted as court scribe to Elphinstone, junior, when he was official of Glasgow and John Goldsmith and William Arthurlie were chapter scribes, that is scribes to the court of the dean of the chapter.[38] Another member of the university, John Doby, rector of Ancrum, when appointed, 'official and dean in the parts of Teviotdale' about 1523, had a long list of duties, with powers including the creation of notaries and scribes; trying cases civil, profane and mixed; promulgating sentences interlocutory and definitive and fulminating censures; holding customary chapters within his jurisdiction; receiving procurations and synodal dues; and confirming the testaments of testates and intestates. Causes regarding matrimony, benefices and crime were reserved to the central diocesan court.[39]

The Roman law or civil law was a quite separate branch of legal study, owing much to the emperors and to its transmission, after the fall of Rome, by the papacy. It had been codified by the Emperor Justinian. The first part, the *Digest*—or *Pandects*, because it dealt with all law—concerned the principles of jurisprudence; the second part, the *Code*, divided into books and titles, consisted mostly of imperial laws. New laws, *Novellae*, added by Justinian himself, were intended to provide for new contingencies. The *Institutes*, four books only, was a brief compendium of legislative principles. In addition, various commentaries and legal compendia ('summae') were used, including the 'ordinary gloss' of Accursius.[40]

At Glasgow a succession of possible teachers of civil law can be established only as far as 1472. After Lennox, or alongside him, Simon Dodds appeared in 1465.[41] Thomas Lutherdale, mentioned already, was a licentiate in laws as well as doctor in decreets.[42] Richard Cady, bachelor in both laws, is found in 1472.[43] As far as the evidence goes, however, the teaching in civil law languished utterly after the death of Bishop Andrew de Durisdeer. A probable Glasgow civil law student is Mark Muirhead, who in 1455–6 was giving the extraordinary lecture at Bologna on the *New Digest* or the *Infortiatum*, and in 1457–8 was ultramontane Rector lecturing on the *Decretum* on feastdays.[44]

In canon law there were some signs of vigour. Towards 1483 the school of canon law was being, as we saw, refurbished and the fact that some ancient statutes of the faculty were incorporated in the university statutes in 1490 might mean that new statutes had been approved. Among important students who later have a canon law qualification was Gavin Dunbar, 'well learned in canon law'.[45] Richard Robertson, canon of Aberdeen, incorporated in 1473, had a bachelorship in decreets four years later.[46] William Arthurlie, doctor in decreets, was presented in 1474 by the Rector, Elphinstone, to the readership in canon law[47]; but he is not heard of after 1478. The relevant writs for the readership were not raised in authentic form and the law schools were said to be 'ruinous'.[48] Patrick Elphinstone, who studied law at Cologne, was one of those involved in giving advice on these matters.[49] Problems of maintenance afflicted students in law, as they did David Hutcheson who hoped for a papal gift of incompatible benefices to overcome them.[50] Personal details are often wanting, but we learn from the chronicler of the bishops of Dunkeld that John Young, vicar of Dron, and later canon of Dunkeld, was a licentiate in canon law who was 'exceedingly learned and an excellent textualist, a man of great courtesy, universally beloved'.[51]

John Goldsmith, Rector in 1490, himself a bachelor in the faculty, was responsible for entering the university statutes and the early matriculations in the present parchment record (Liber Rectoris).[52] He advocated that the chaplain be compelled to read according to the tenor of the David Cadzow foundation.[53] Patrick Coventry, another principal, was also a bachelor in decreets,[54] as was James Knox, chaplain reader in 1498.[55] The school itself acquired a new gable window in 1502.[56] William Gibson, incorporated the following year, studied canon law here and there may be others of whom we have no record.[57] The exact date of Knox's demission or death is not known, though he was alive in 1512.[58]

But in 1513 the readership foundered. On 4 August in that year, the periodical inquest was made into the revenue from the chaplainries. Among these, the chaplainry of the Virgin Mary required a suitable candidate but there was no such person in the university.[59] Its funds were too low to attract men from what was otherwise a lucrative profession. It was therefore considered best to appoint an interim chaplain, to perform the suffrages for the founder and collect the rents assigned to the foundation. The onus of finding a fit person was left with the Rector and archbishop according to the tenor of the original arrangement.[60] Under these conditions a contract was arranged with a certain Andrew Smyth. He was to receive five merks for himself as chaplain and pay the rest to the university purse. In the meantime, he fell foul of Patrick Graham, the Rector. Sometime in the summer of 1514, a certain Ellen Hannay alleged that Smyth had plundered a brass cauldron from her lodging. The Rector, sitting in judgment in the aisle of St Michael in the cathedral, ordered him to restore it. The complainant was, it seems, Smyth's mother and with him co-executor of his father's will. In January 1514, however, she revoked whatever contract existed between them and this in the Drygate lodging of the Dean of arts, James Neilson. Smyth appealed to the Rector and offered, giving judicial notice, to defend the appeal in a specified time. His procurator appeared in the St Michael aisle on 1 August asserting that 31 July was assigned as the day of the diet but that the Rector had not been present on that day. Whether true or not, the suggestion was not accepted, and letters of appeal were refused.[61]

In June 1517, Graham, as Rector, and the new principal, both called for an account from Smyth, he not having rendered one for the past three years. He owed nearly two pounds from his receipts, and over two pounds more that he had not managed to collect. It was plain that the readership in canon law could not be maintained on the income available, and the previous arrangement with Smyth was renewed, except that he now had to pay five merks to 'the university and faculty of Glasgow'.[62] The way was being prepared for the complete abandonment of canon law.

John Mair, as principal, supported the liquidation of law and a more economic use of funds, for in June 1522 he was present when auditors were appointed to investigate the readership's revenues. Finally, in July, James Lindsay—by a majority decision only—was accorded them, not to teach law, but to teach arts daily in the pedagogy.[63] Even in 1530, when Mair's views on jurists had mellowed, he remarked that the magnanimous man would rather study mathematics than law: law brings in more money, but mathematics has an inner excellence.[64] Earlier he was even more specific. The ordaining bishop did not ask the ordinand if he knew both laws but if he knew both testaments, and it was in homage to these that he took off his mitre. The Church flourished more when theologians governed it; now it had come into the hands of the canonists, how it is governed, everybody knows.[65] A canonist might have retorted that in view of the lack of success of Silvestro de Prierio and Mair's friends of the theological faculty at Paris in dealing with Luther and the Reformers, the canonists might, with their lawyerly approach, have been more flexible and so risked fewer failures. Contemporary canonists were not, however, the original legal minds of earlier days.

The university statutes of 1490 are not informative about law. There were, they tell us, bachelors and students in that faculty already promoted or awaiting promotion who had abandoned their studies: these were to be pursued for their statutory debts by the university promoter; the student's dress was likewise regulated.[66] Nevertheless, with the help of further meagre fragments from the other two Scots universities of the time, especially of St Andrews, some picture of the probable pattern of study emerges.

As to the length of the course for bachelors in canon and civil law we have no precise information. At St Andrews a student who was licensed in arts in 1500 is cited as a bachelor in canon law four years later, but it is not clear when he began his law studies and his brother is not entitled bachelor till six years from his arts licence.[67] On the other hand, an Act of Parliament of 1496 required the barons' sons to study 'at the sculis of art and jure' for three years only.[68] From an incidental reference we gather that the bachelor in civil law took six years to reach that state at St Andrews, or rather that he followed six courses of forty or so months spread over six years.[69] For the bachelor in canon law no time-span is given, but we learn that he had heard ordinary lectures ('solemnly studied') and attended disputations as in the St Andrews faculty ordinances.[70] Principal John Brown at Glasgow was licensed in arts in 1473, after an unusually long period of study in the arts faculty. Five years later, in the same month, he claimed at the Roman court to be, first a bachelor and then a licentiate, in decreets: certainly he must have been at least a bachelor.[71]

The St Andrews bachelor in civil law first presented depositions regarding his praiseworthy life, that is, his studies and conduct, and his personal good name to the chancellor. Then in the presence of the audience 'decorating this act' he petitioned formally the presiding doctor in laws who received him and gave him licence to ascend the chair and publicly carry out the bachelor's act. The formulary for the act of the bachelor in decreets is very similar except that it mentions the previous oath taken in the chancellor's hands and the power given to the bachelor to perform public and private acts suited to the bachelor stage.

Of the next stage, the *propositum*, publicly determining a decretal and disengaging the general principles (*notabilia*) underlying it,[72] we hear nothing at St Andrews, but there is one reference to the 'harangue' of Robert Gardiner.[73] This was preceded by the examination regarding a certain decretal and was usually followed by a disputation against two bachelor opponents, implied perhaps at St Andrews by the use of the word 'exercised'.[74] The course for bachelorship in canon law at Caen was five volumes of the *Decretales*, the *Sext* and *Clementines*. At Aberdeen the implication is that students both in canon and civil law attend lectures in both laws and that they read in bachelor fashion on the *Institutes*. The doctor in canon law was to lecture in his faculty each lecturing day according to the form of the first regent at Paris, while the civilist doctor was to follow Orleans practice in reading from the *Institutes*.[75]

The St Andrews licentiand in civil law petitioned the chancellor to be examined, being presented to him or his deputy by two doctors of both laws. Then followed the 'rigorous and private examination' by all doctors present in the faculty, after which he was declared fit to ascend the doctoral chair.[76] In the case of the canonist we are told that the vice-chancellor, David N. (full name not given), canon of Glasgow, examined the licentiand with four or five doctors of decreets, that the candidate combined brilliance with accuracy and elegance, *puncta* or points of law having been assigned beforehand by the examiners.[77] These are defined at Caen as two chapters in canon law.[78] This was done in the morning and the student went off to study them. In one instance, Cardinal Beaton himself gave the candidate on both laws two 'points', opening the *Decretals* and chancing on a title in canon and the *Codes* for another in civil law.[79] The candidate read the text, explained it, and clarified its meaning. The doctors intervened with subtle arguments to which he had to reply.

The procedure with the candidate in both laws is more informative.[80] The candidate began with a rhetorical piece, a *collatio*, commented on the rubrics as well as the letter of the text, isolating important elements, reading, teaching, examining different conclusions to be inferred from them both, advancing additional reasons in defence of his view and finally maintaining a definite line of approach, like a judge giving his sentence. He was to allege in favour any sayings of doctors and 'summists' (famous commentators), to deal with incidental and unexpected questions and to be subtle and elegant in his replies. The candidate then went out of the place of examination and, after discussion, the doctors agreed to his licence.

The doctorate in both laws followed after an unspecified interval and could be an expensive occasion. There followed a short *collatio* in the course of which he petitioned for the insignia. The vice-chancellor then gave him all the insignia 'to the glory of God and his mother': at Caen the collation was in praise of some saint, emphasising the religious overtones of all medieval law.[81] At St Andrews there is some ceremony with the insignia in these faculties. First of all the vice-chancellor gave the candidate 'the book of sacred canons first closed, then open', or, when the degree was in both laws both the canon law and civilist books. Then he gave the 'master's crown' (*dyademque magistrale*), the coloured bonnet. Then he adorned him with the gold ring and gave the kiss of peace, after which the new master proceeded to the master's chair and so ascended to the apex of the doctorate.[82]

When studying the theoretical side of law in this period it is easy to forget the criminal cases, the marriage tribunals, the justice ayres, the settlement of wills, the cases involving property and heresy, and the whole apparatus of law, with all the notaries, commissaries, officials, sheriffs and justices. The law student, as Elphinstone's notes prove, had very practical motives for mastering his books.[83] Law was also a kind of codified theology in a society at least 'sociologically Christian'; the danger was that it might supplant theology or prevent it from evolving. Glasgow's most brilliant law student, William Elphinstone, junior, was described by the chronicler as 'like another Cusa',[84] that is like Nicholas of Cusa, whose ideas were still embedded in a medieval cosmology, but who emphasised notions of consent and representation in government and, with whatever personal drawbacks, religious regeneration within an all-embracing cosmic framework. As a reader of Valla, Elphinstone would have some consciousness too of the impact philology could make on the study of legal sources, but, by the time this impact began to be felt, the salaried reader in Glasgow had been abolished.

NOTES

1. *AFA*, cxlix–clvii. For an introduction, cf. P. Stein, 'Roman Law in Scotland', *Ius Romanum Medii Aevi*, part 5, 13b (Milan, 1968).
2. The phrase 'common law' is mistakenly used by the editor, *Glas. Mun.*, ii, page v, 19.
3. Mackie, *University*, 27.
4. *Glas. Mun.*, ii, 67.
5. *Ibid.*, ii, 55; SRO, Broughton and Cally Writs, nos 14 (witnessed by Arthurlie) 17, 19 (witnessed by Bunch); and for his death, *RSS*, i, 2815. A William Lennox determined at St Andrews in 1463–4, *AFA*, 152. Cf. Burns, *Scottish Churchmen*, 41n.

6. For Wan, *CPL*, xiii, 280; *Glas. Mun.*, ii, 56; for Reston, *ibid.*, i, 28.
7. *AFA*, 12; *CSSR*, iii, 236.
8. *CPL, Petitions*, i, 579, 595.
9. *Auctarium*, ii, 116; *CPL*, viii, 437; *CSSR*, iii, 236.
10. Durkan, *Turnbull*, 11; Reg. Supp. 473, f. 22.
11. *ACSB*, 38; SRO Broughton and Cally writs, no. 16, by which date he was both chanter and official of the diocese.
12. *AFA*, 5; *CPL*, viii, 575.
13. GUL, MS199, f. 657.
14. *RMS*, ii, 87, 183.
15. *Glasgow Registrum*, ii, 405.
16. *CPL*, x, 203.
17. Reg. Supp., 398, f. 258.
18. J. Durkan and A. Ross, *Early Scottish Libraries* (Glasgow, 1961), 33, nos. 13, 14.
19. *Glas. Mun.*, ii, 60; *CPL*, xi, 301.
20. *Glas. Mun.*, ii, 57, 180; Reg. Supp., 471, f. 122.
21. *Glas. Mun.*, ii, 60.
22. *Ibid.*, ii, 62; Reg. Supp., 521, f. 5v.
23. *CPL*, xi, 211; *Glas. Mun.*, ii, 64.
24. *Ibid.*, i, 17–18; *CUP*, iii, 643. Bachelors also read 'de mane' but not solemnly.
25. He was licensed in arts in 1448 and was at Glasgow from 1451; *AFA*, 73; *Glas. Mun.*, ii, 57.
26. Wils, *Matricule*, ii, 158, 187; *Glas. Mun.*, ii, 76. The earlier incorporations of both at Glasgow are omitted but Vedast was there in 1461, *CPL*, xii, 119.
27. *Glas. Mun.*, ii, 115.
28. *Ibid.*, ii, 95.
29. *CPL*, xiii, 627.
30. *Glas. Mun.*, ii, 73. Other bachelors in decreets are Thomas Pile (Reg. Supp. 631, f. 29v; *Glas. Mun.*, ii, 192); Thomas Forsyth (Reg. Supp. 629, f. 68; *Glas. Mun.*, ii, 71); Andrew Young (Reg. Supp. 779, f. 275; *Glas. Mun.*, ii, 66); William Foular (Reg. Supp. 742, 261v; *Glas. Mun.*, ii, 67); Thomas McKilhauch (Reg. Supp. 425, f. 89v; *Glas. Mun.*, ii, 66); John Aitkenhead (Reg. Supp. 705, f. 203v; *Glas. Mun.*, ii, 68).
31. *Glas. Mun.*, ii, 69.
32. *Ibid.*, ii, 65, 213. Boece, *Vitae*, 61. Quintin Weir was his rival for the possession of the rectory of Kirkmichael, which Adam Weir held also, Reg. Supp. 505, f. 169v; *Glas. Mun.*, ii, 203.
33. Boece, *Vitae*, 61–5; *Glas. Mun.*, ii, 83; Sir William Fraser, *The Douglas Book* (Edinburgh, 1805), iii, 22. *Historical Manuscripts Commission, Report 15, App. IX, Hope Johnstone*, xlvi, 11, shows that Elphinstone was still a bachelor in decreets *after* leaving Paris, which modifies in one respect the excellent account by Leslie J. Macfarlane, 'William Elphinstone, founder of the university of Aberdeen', *Aberdeen University Review*, xxxix (1961–2), 1–18.
34. Durkan and Ross, *Libraries*, 31ff.
35. It was also a continuing theme among theologians, John Ireland, for example, at Paris, while at Cologne in 1478 a Scots secular master, the Albertist John Hoy, held that 'the council was above the pope'. Hoy later became a Dominican. G. M. Löhr, *Die theologischen Disputationen und Promotionen an der Universität Köln in ausgehenden 15 Jahrhundert*, Quellen und Forschungen zur Geschichte des Dominikanerordens in Deutschland (Leipzig, 1926), xxi, 28, 53–4; Keussen, i, 611.

36. W. Ullmann, *Law and Politics in the Middle Ages*, The Sources of History: Studies in the Uses of Historical Evidence, ed. G. R. Elton (1975), 151.
37. *Ibid.*, 117ff.
38. Sir William Fraser, *The Lennox* (Edinburgh, 1874), ii, 22; *Glas. Mun.*, ii, 226.
39. Edinburgh Univ. Library, Laing MS III, 322, f. 179 (formulary book).
40. Ullmann, *Law and Politics*, 51ff. On the use of Accursius in the Elphinstone notes, cf. Feenstra, *Fata Iuris Romani* (Leiden, 1974), 57.
41. *Glas. Mun.*, ii, 71, 72.
42. *Ibid.*, ii, 73; in 1460, licentiate in laws, Reg. Supp. 529, f. 25.
43. *Glas. Mun.*, ii, 79, where Eady is a misreading.
44. *Ibid.*, ii, 59; Umberto Dallari, *I Rotuli dei Lettori Legisti e Artisti dello Studio Bolognese dal 1384 al 1799*, i (Bologna, 1888), 42, 47.
45. *Glas. Mun.*, ii, 77. Name mistranscribed as 'Edwinus' for 'Gavinus' in Liber Rectoris, 22. Cf. Boece, *Vitae*, 115, where Moir has mistranslated.
46. *Glas. Mun.*, ii, 81; Reg. Supp. 756, f. 285v.
47. *Glas. Mun.*, ii, 83.
48. *Ibid.*, ii, 93–5; 107.
49. *Ibid.*, ii, 94; Keussen, i, 864.
50. *Glas. Mun.*, ii, 69; Reg. Supp. 831, f. 114v.
51. *Rentale Dunkeldense* (SHS, ser. ii, 10, Edinburgh, 1915), 325; *Glas. Mun.*, ii, 83.
52. First flyleaf, 'Jhesus, Maria. Liber iste in hanc formam redactus erat et renouatus ex veteri libro papiro scripto satis corrupte tempore venerabilis viri magistri johannis Goldsmyth artium magistri in decretis bachalarii ecclesiarum de Estwode et Cathcart vicarii pro tunc Rectoris alme uniuersitatis glasguensis etc Anno domini millesimo quadringentesimo nonagesimo.'
53. *Glas. Mun.*, ii, 106.
54. *Charters of the Hospital of Soltre*, 1.
55. *Glas. Mun.*, ii, 114.
56. *Ibid.*, ii, 116.
57. *Soltre*, p. 1; *St Andrews Formulare*, ii, 164; *Glas. Mun.*, ii, 118.
58. Fraser, *The Douglas Book*, iii, 207.
59. *Glas. Mun.*, ii, 126.
60. *Ibid.*, ii, 126–7.
61. *Protocol Book of Gavin Ros* (SRS, Edinburgh, 1908), 80, 81, 117; *Prot. Bk, Simon*, 450, 503.
62. *Glas. Mun.*, ii, 130–1.
63. *Ibid.*, ii, 143–6.
64. *Ethica Aristotelis* (1530), f. lxiii verso. These lectures had been given at Glasgow.
65. *In Quartum Sententiarum* (1521), f. clxviC.
66. *Glas. Mun.*, ii, 10, 19–20.
67. *AFA*, clii; 269, 283 and note. One of them had also done some theology. 'Reading' in the phrase Dr Dunlop cites refers to the bachelor stage.
68. *Acts of the Parliaments of Scotland* (Edinburgh, 1814–75), ii, 238.
69. *St Andrews Formulare*, ii, 308–9; forty-eight months at Paris and Bologna, Rashdall, *Universities*, ii, 438.
70. *St Andrews Formulare*, ii, 309–10.
71. Reg. Supp. 773, ff. 77v, 244.
72. Fournier, iii, 169 (Caen).
73. *AFA*, 39–41.
74. Fournier, iii, 274–5; 169. At Caen the bachelorship in decreets took three years

(or less for a licentiate in another faculty), the licentiate another three. *Ibid.* iii, 247.

75. Eeles, *King's College Chapel*, 168, 213. At St Salvator's college in 1500 the bachelor chaplain was to lecture in canon law at least three times weekly, St Andrews Univ. Archives, St Salvator's Book 'B', f. 79v.
76. *St Andrews Formulare*, ii, 310–11.
77. *Ibid.*, ii, 311–13.
78. Fournier, iii, 275.
79. *St Andrews Formulare*, ii, 314.
80. *Ibid.*, ii, 313–15.
81. Fournier, iii, 275. At Aix, a harangue invoking the divine name, *ibid.*, iii, 20.
82. *St Andrews Formulare*, ii, 312–15.
83. Leslie J. Macfarlane, 'William Elphinstone's Library', *Aberdeen University Review*, xxxvii (1957–8), 253–71.
84. 'Velut alter Cusa habebatur', John Law's chronicle, Edinburgh Univ. Library MS Dc.7.63, f. 138.

8. Principals before John Mair

'These are those who bring light to the hall where the Lord's flock is gathered, who set on the right path the runners in the race, who lure some towards virtue by the fruits of their good works and attract others by their example to the desire for divine things.'
Letter of Protection of James II
Repeated in Lord Hamilton's foundation

THE EARLY years of the university and the faculty of arts are, as we have seen obscure. Obscurities also envelope the early history of the principalship. Though Turnbull's ideal was a single pedagogy, two pedagogy sites are named. It is possible that these were in the charge of different regents before the drop in numbers that followed the catastrophes that one by one struck the young university. In 1451, Alexander Geddes, theologian, monk of Melrose, is listed first among the three earliest regents in arts.[1] He is, however, never styled principal. Duncan Bunch is first mentioned as principal regent 'in the faculty of arts' in 1460 and not as principal of either pedagogy or of both, that is at the time of the Hamilton foundation,[2] and he too was on the way to being qualified in theology.

A potential rival, at least initially, to Bunch must surely have been William Arthurlie, another of the 'first regents' of 1451 and his chief colleague, and faculty members may have been tempted to take advantage of such rivalry. Yet the only recorded incident, admittedly late, shows harmony rather than tension. Bunch was Dean in 1467 when a non-regent master refused to return books belonging to Arthurlie, insulted the latter and appealed from Bunch's decision against him. The faculty took the line that the appeal was out of order, since the Dean as head of the faculty spoke in its name. The beadle was instructed to warn the appellant to return the books, or appear the following Saturday to show his reason for retaining them. This controversy was amicably settled, however, for the accused is found acting as non-regent examiner later.[3]

Bunch's role in a matter of more general university interest was the provision of a suitable mace for the university beadle. Two arts regents were appointed to collect funds for it, and immediately on the announcement of Cadzow's re-election in 1460 as Rector he gave twenty nobles to the mace fund. All faculties were further taxed for this purpose in

1465, two collectors being appointed.[4] This fine mace still exists, unhappily somewhat altered in subsequent centuries. It is of silver, the crown partly gilt and ornamented with blue enamel. The crown is composed of a polygon-shaped Gothic tower of three storeys, one storey being buttressed and with windows. On each wall surface of the lowest storey there is the half figure in relief of an angel, holding a coat of arms: the figures of saints with which it was ornamented originally were removed about 1590. It is one of the best examples of a late Gothic mace. We do not know where it was made, but Paatz points to its likeness to the Erfurt mace.[5]

After David Cadzow's death in 1466 he was succeeded as Rector by Patrick Leitch, junior,[6] Rector of the university of Paris in the previous year. At Paris he had supported John Ireland in a disputed grant towards the costs of his bachelorship in theology and for a time he was clerk of the rolls and register to James III, 'a venerable man', we are told, 'powerful in word and deed'.[7] He was aware of the rising nominalism at Paris, but had no perceptible influence in the Glasgow arts faculty.

Duncan Bunch did much for the early university. The surviving arts statutes are in his hand. He was first principal of the college, as it was styled, of arts. He had weathered the civil dissension, plague and famine of the first years and had begun the principal's house in the High Street. He was attracted, however, towards the end by prospects of royal and papal favour: rich rewards were not to be found in the university and he left Glasgow in 1473–4. On his departure, he perhaps did not neglect the claims of kin, for his Cistercian relative, Walter Bunch, prior of Gadvan, was appointed as *locum tenens*. Walter's incorporation is not recorded till 1475 when he is described as formed bachelor in theology,[8] carrying on the tradition of principal-theologians (a tradition Elphinstone, junior, was to continue at Aberdeen in the foundation of King's College).

He is never recorded as taking part in the work of the arts faculty, and it can be assumed that he devoted his time to studying for his licence in theology. All the work in the arts faculty was done by John Brown, regent, and the licence to lecture in arts formerly given to another Cistercian, Geddes, was not renewed for Walter Bunch. It was to the Dean and not to the principal that in 1475 all persons owning faculty lands in Dovehill were to show their right and title. As for the Arthurlie lands, they were now either in the faculty's possession or about to be so, for the notarial documents were ordered to be entered among the muniments.[9] Brown and not Bunch accompanied the party that rode to Ayr in 1477 to defend the university's rights in the dispute regarding the St Thomas Martyr chaplainry.[10] Bunch's status in the post was obviously precarious and Brown may have gone to Ayr as acting principal. Uncertainty may have caused some students to withdraw to St Andrews but they soon returned.[11]

There were some anomalies in the arts faculty which may have arisen partly from Brown being occupied in studying canon law as well as regenting and acting as bursar, and the faculty was anxious 'lest from this softness and leniency and lack of fulness of study, the faculty be made ridiculous and suffer shipwreck in the future'.[12] An important decision was therefore made to have a durable parchment record of all faculty acts: this was carried out in 1477, after which all acts can be taken as more or less contemporary: but how far earlier entries have been edited is a matter for speculation.[13] In all faculty activity Walter Bunch had no part. He was finally banished from the principalship when the matter came up for consideration on 25 June 1478, and expelled as being unfit to govern the college of arts and no longer acceptable as a regent. Some years later he had left the university itself, for we find him applying for the abbacy of Balmerino.[14]

John Brown who succeeded as principal on 7 October 1480 was a graduate of five years' standing who, as we have seen, had been active as a teacher and defender of the university's rights. He was born in Irvine and was the first west of Scotland principal. Among his substantial gift of books, already discussed, was a 'scriptum Johannis Burlaw', the work of an English Carmelite friar, John Burley, and this particular item reflects his origins, as Irvine, where Brown came from, was the only west of Scotland town with a Carmelite house.[15] At this time Brown was a bachelor in decreets and had obtained the prebend of Kirkbean in the collegiate kirk of Lincluden.[16] His appointment was made over the heads of his seniors, Gray and Goldsmith, the latter of whom in conjunction with John Doby had shared a joint caretakership of the college at the faculty's request after Walter Bunch's deposition, and perhaps a disputed succession lies behind it.[17] He was admitted and received '. . . according to the tenor of letters granted thereupon by the lord bishop chancellor of the university, and by the dean and faculty, and sealed with their seals'.[18] Although the interim situation had been unusual, it is hardly accurate merely to say that 'for seven years . . . they tried to do without a principal', since the caretakers were acting as joint-principals.[19] Significantly, on appointment in 1480 Brown was given the hint that he was not to be an honorary principal of the Walter Bunch type and also authorised to appoint his own regents.[20]

There were many evidences of weak finance, and strenuous remedial efforts were made in 1480. There was the running sore of the unpaid annual from the St Thomas chaplainry; the recovery of old debts, including money owed by relatives of the founder; the renewal of the wardrobe; and, most important of all, the accounts rendered for monies for the 'reform' of the college. The nature of these structural alterations we are left to guess, but a complete overhaul of the original buildings was intended, perhaps because lord Hamilton, who had died the previous year, had left something for the purpose. In 1481 the Dean drew attention to the religious services for which the faculty was obliged to his late lordship, which Brown, for himself and the students, promised to fulfil. Similarly he promised to pay a chaplain to pray for the donor of the Regent's House (Arthurlie).[21]

Before Brown's appointment the faculty depended greatly on transient junior men as examiners. David Cunningham graduated in 1478 and was examining within a few months; Laurence Purdy graduated at Paris in 1478 and next year was examining at Glasgow; John Glen presided over a determination when his master's honours were fresh upon him; while Walter Leslie graduated in Paris in the summer and was examining in Glasgow in November.[22]

Brown's election as Rector in 1482 appears to be a compromise, for we are told the electors 'condescended' to elect him.[23] He died shortly after 3 July 1483 when he left his arts books (not his law books) to the pedagogy.[24] The main faculty business, however, was the concern of the Deans, whose watchfulness over standards is more in evidence at this period; some bachelors were refused admission to the licence till they had made up their reading.[25]

The general impression is, nevertheless, one of decline. Whatever the virtues of Bishop John Laing, he does not appear to have been able to hold his university at the level his predecessor had left it and in the quarter of a century (1483–1508) during which his successor, Bishop Blackadder, held office there were five principals, which contrasts, for instance, with King's College, Aberdeen, where there were four in half a century.[26] Even when they were all men of some distinction, as they were, there could not be the same continuity of policy as in places more permanently endowed.

Brown was succeeded by a young man, Walter Leslie, son of Sir William Leslie of Balquhain. After his student days in Glasgow, he went to Paris where he was a fellow-student of James Liddell, the nominalist, an Aberdeen man, author of the first printed texts by a Scotsman.[27] He was received to the faculty at Glasgow in 1482 and is mentioned as principal in the year of Brown's death.[28]

There are problems regarding the building operations of the time which are not easy of solution. Meetings were held to examine the previous principal's account and Leslie asked the faculty to accept a certain sum received for the restoration of the stonework (*super reparacione lapicidii*) which he had received from John Smyth,[29] presumably the representative of the vicars choral or of the archdeacon (who is also later mentioned in this connection). The students may have had to take temporary occupation elsewhere while the stonework was being renewed.

The burden of the principalship, Leslie complained, was too much for him but he promised to carry on till Whitsunday meantime,[30] and in the summer of 1485, John Goldsmith took over on a temporary basis.[31] A man of mature years and high qualifications could find elsewhere less arduous employment. He was frustrated in 1485 in obtaining a canonry of Glasgow, but next year was vicar of Perth.[32] His academic career was not quite over, and it was probably to study law that he went in 1494 to St Andrews. His gifts lay in advocacy: Myln celebrates his 'wisdom and eloquence'.[33] He did not forget his Glasgow ties, founding a chaplainry of Sts Mungo and Thenew at St Nicholas kirk, Aberdeen.[34] He died at Dunkeld in 1522.[35]

Leslie's successor was, formally, George Crichton who first appears as an ordinary regent in the Rectorial period beginning in October 1484.[36] He had come from St Andrews where he had quarrelled with the provost of St Salvator's college, a quarrel settled in his favour.[37] He was the son of David Crichton, of the Crichtons of Cranston Riddell, who became bishop of Dunkeld,[38] and was at St Andrews with the poet William Dunbar.

Goldsmith acted temporarily as principal, but by the certificates of appointment by Blackadder to which the faculty added its own sealed confirmation, Crichton was appointed principal on 19 October 1485. The departing principal and bursar, Leslie, could not meet his debts to the faculty and left some books of logic with the new bursar in part payment: the faculty would give an estimate of their cost and allow for subsequent redemption. Many such temporary compositions must have been made: books not redeemed[39] would either be resold or make their way into the regents' library. The 'houses of the pedagogy', probably Arthurlie and Bunch houses, needed overhaul and the principal (Leslie) made an outlay on the 'riggin stainis'.[40]

Numbers had taken an upward climb and the arts faculty at least seemed in good fettle. Dispensations from *lectura*, the compulsory two years' reading (lecturing) after graduation, had become a matter of course[41]: the availability of printed texts made it impossible to enforce and, even before their availability, d'Estouteville had dispensed with it at Paris. Other anomalies such as early admissions to examinations may reflect rebuilding operations or civil troubles.

Crichton was soon in trouble at Glasgow too. Possibly he had spoken rashly in public disputation in this year of James III's downfall, (May–June 1488). At an arts congregation in July a letter from Black-adder, the chancellor, was read notifying the faculty that he had removed Crichton from the rule and exercise of the principalship, ordering the faculty to elect in his place a suitably learned man. Crichton continued, however, for a short time as regent.[42] The deposed principal went on to live to a good old age. He is said to have averred gruffly in an early Reformation trial that he was happy to say that he knew neither the Old Testament nor the New, but only his 'porteous' (portable breviary) and pontifical. He was an octogenarian at least when he died in 1543.[43]

John Goldsmith once again took over. An oldish man, he was elected when Dean and was the faculty's choice and not the bishop's.[44] He acquired the vicarages of Eastwood and Cathcart.[45]

Walter Leslie returned briefly to the scene to face a congregation regarding his debt (perhaps he was in a 'higher' faculty), taking his great oath to the effect that it was part of a sum loaned him by John Smyth for the repair of the stonework. The faculty thought Smyth and the archdeacon might be willing to let the money be used for the pedagogy. The matter was again referred to David Gray, chaplain of the chaplainry founded by the archdeacon for the vicars choral.[46]

Goldsmith retired with few qualms from the principalship. As Rector in 1490, he had the Liber Rectoris drawn up in its present form. He made his will on 3 April 1507,[47] his heir being Alexander Menteith, prior of Restennet, a former member of the university.[48] Goldsmith's will has few items of university interest except a gown of russet and a small one of black.

John Doby, apparently the Cologne graduate of that name, succeeded. If the identification is correct, for a short time he had charge of the grammar school at Peebles,[49] whose church was a prebend of the cathedral. At the outset of his principalship it was decided to elect a notary, David Gray, to copy legibly every conclusion, constitution, dispensation and other pertinent document. This cannot refer to the statutes book which is not in Gray's hand; nor to the Liber Decani, begun many years earlier, in 1477. Gray did, in fact, enter some deeds and dispensations in the existing Dean's book, for which as notary he had an annual fee.

An expert and hard working person was elected to act as faculty promotor in all lawsuits, for which he was to be paid a salary. Absentees from a previous congregation cited by the beadle were to have their offence remitted. The promotor was to receive all faculty goods and debts, inclusive of books and robes. But certain masters had their debts for absence from post-graduate lectures dispensed. Obviously this had become such a formality that dispensation fees caused resentment.

The laird of Hawkhead, Sir John Ross, was still being pursued for rents from faculty lands; if he did not pay up, he was to be prosecuted, especially as the faculty proposed to spend money on repairs for the St Thomas Martyr chapel. The faculty owed money to Patrick Coventry for the inner buildings of Arthurlie House, of which Coventry, as junior regent, would be in charge. Coventry promised to spend as much on roof and other repairs as he could afford.[50]

By this time Michaelmas was being preferred to St Luke for the statutory opening of session and so it was transferred to 1 October, the feast of St Remy (two days after Michaelmas). From 1490 ordinary lectures were to open then and last till the feast of St Giles (1 September).[51] On the first day of term 1497, when the choice of books was made it was decided to add the Book of Suppositions (of Peter of Spain) to the list of ordinary books. Previously all of Peter of Spain had been read by bachelors to the students: obviously more stress was now being laid on the purely logical side of teaching, as the nominalists continually advocated against the followers of the 'ancient way' of Albert and the thirteenth-century masters. It was also decided that the customary cessation from studies on the day following St Remy should only extend to formal and ordinary lectures and on such holidays students would still have extraordinary ones.[52]

The Dean of 1497–8, Thomas Forsyth, astringently observed that it was ridiculous to draw up statutes and not keep them; there ought to be a statute for keeping statutes. He urged a new policy of severity towards those who failed to continue lectures after licence. Work on the repair of the New Hall was held up for lack of money; it was no use beginning what was not to be finished. As a result of the importunity of suppliants, dispensations and infractions were the rule of the day: those failing to obey the Dean's monitions should be dealt with at once. The first point referred to a contract with Michael Waghorn, who, having begun work for the faculty, had left it. Waghorn was a skilled carpenter who had been commissioned to do elaborate work on the cathedral stalls.[53] The promotor could not be expected to fight the faculty's battles at his own expense.

In 1495 we hear of a former Dean deserving well of the faculty as regards the building of the college of arts. He had spent money on the kitchen, which had been left unfinished by the stonemason, Alexander Fleming. In connection with details for the contractors for the building, a new book of accounts is referred to (a special building account?).[54]

Space forbids citation of further incidents from this lively period. Undoubtedly the bracing effect of the new foundation at Aberdeen was being felt and the 1496 act of parliament calling for the education of noblemen's sons raised hopes. Doby was an active principal during his period of office. It cannot, however, be said that much new blood was infused into the faculty; only Walter Stewart, a former student, returned from Paris and Patrick Elphinstone, Dean in 1491, had come from Cologne.[55] Doby probably died before November 1498, when David Dun was regent. He left ten merks in his will to the faculty.[56]

Patrick Coventry, who succeeded, was an experienced regent by the time of his appointment as principal. He was a graduate on arrival, from some foreign university so far unidentified.[57] Since he belonged to the Albany nation, he must have come from north of the Forth. At the time of his appointment he was vicar of Glencairn.[58]

A problem of these years (as also at St Andrews) are the blanks in the record. There was plague in 1501, and, when the faculty met at the opening of the academic year, it was dispersed and lectures abandoned for most of that year.[59] In 1504 and 1505 there is no record even of a Dean.

There was also negligent book-keeping. Indicative are the mentions of Andrew Erskine, first in 1502 as bachelor, then (after entries about others) in 1506 as having completed the two-year post-principiation period. Neither licence nor inception is recorded for him or his fellows, for he had been dispensed as having been present at common table with the masters for over two years.[60]

William Stewart, former Dean, left money in his will, to which Coventry contributed an additional merk, to buy for the faculty a silver cup weighing seven ounces.[61] Although the faculty repaid Coventry, its funds were tight, and the Rector was present at two audits calling for help from the university purse, perhaps because of the lean years. The faculty promotor was told to collect debts come what might, *quovismodo*.[62] Other additions to the kitchen service came in 1506 from Archibald Calderwood, who, for the great labours and services done by him to the college of arts, arranged for certain masses by the regents and in return granted, besides an annual rent, four silver spoons and a mazer.[63]

Coventry was a talented administrator. Too much of the burden of teaching seems to have rested on his shoulders, though John Spreull was 'secondary regent' in July 1499.[64] Were perhaps the incomes from various rents already assigned in definite proportions to the principal and his main helper, as seems to be the case in immediate post-Reformation times? As we saw earlier, Coventry acquired useful qualifications in law and theology during his Glasgow stay and, shortly after the arrival of Archbishop Beaton I in 1509, he appeared for the last time in the university.[65] He died before 12 April 1526, when his successor as dean of the collegiate church of Restalrig is mentioned.[66]

A student of note in this period was William Manderston, who was licensed in arts.[67] He went on to Paris where he issued over a period of years little scholastic compendia in logic and morals. He cites the authors of the 'ancient way' with respect, but makes free use of those of the 'modern way' too. The former characteristic may be the Glasgow imprint upon him.[68]

When Bishop Blackadder had been appointed to the see in 1483, the choice of the chapter had been an adherent of the duke of Albany, George Carmichael, whose appointment was rejected for political reasons.[69] The university may have received Blackadder with a bad grace: they certainly proceeded to elect as Rector his rival's relative, William Carmichael, vicar of Symington, 'a noble man of great discretion'. Two Elphinstones, relatives of Blackadder's successor at Aberdeen, were appointed Rectorial deputies. Furthermore, Carmichael had some extraordinary expenses in university business, to the payment of which fines of absentees from congregation were to contribute.[70] It would even seem that the university was prepared to re-elect him as Rector in 1484, had he not 'supplicated and eloquently persuaded' against re-election. As it was, the University took the practical step of electing Nicholas Ross, who, a few months later, used his good offices with Sir John Ross, laird of Hawkhead, to recover the rent owed from Arthurlie.[71] A new gable window was inserted in the schools of canon law and a mason incorporated about this time.[72] If the example of Aberdeen inspired new zeal,[73] the thoroughgoing efforts there to provide instruction in all the higher faculties and at the same time provide facilities for grammar and music make Glasgow's own efforts seem half-hearted. From 1497, the university records vaunt the city's new metropolitan dignity and there is even a reference to the 'metropolitan university'.[74]

The attraction of the rising Parisian school of Scottish nominalists drew a few students from the Glasgow area. In 1506 one of them addressed Blackadder (in answer to a letter from the archbishop), dedicating his questions on the Posterior Analytics to him in language of some elegance.[75] 'We are accustomed to see', writes David Cranston, 'many whom idleness and negligence overcame as soon as fortune favoured them with more welcoming arms, at the peak of worldly dignity and with the arrival of affluence. We are all fired by some spark of genius within us to learn what there is to know. It is far more incumbent on those who are taken for demigods and models held up for our approval on earth, to have engaged in this struggle for knowledge.' Blackadder evidently saw the need to respond to this call but was frustrated in his efforts to annex benefices, although he left money to build a university chapel dedicated to Jesus and Mary. He used his wealth for other purposes, notably the screen and Blackadder aisle in his cathedral.

A new sense of its importance may have persuaded the university,

F

under Rector John Goldsmith, in 1490, to decree that the surviving parchment Rector's book be compiled and charters as well as university acts entered in it. Some were entered, but irregularly, and, as in the St Andrews book of 'Evidents', some important acts were probably omitted. The points made have a familiar ring: legal advice was needed regarding the Rector's jurisdiction; the rural deans (especially of Rutherglen) should have no power to summon the members; the common seal was no longer to be with the Rector but kept in the university chest; the lapsed custom of the beadle preceding the Rector to church with a sizeable retinue was to be revived and the statute concerning it integrated into the university statutes; alterations to copes, hoods and the silver mace were to be made at the general expense; Sir John Ross's and other chaplainry foundations were to be kept; bursars' accounts, after five years of neglect, were to be audited. But the Rector who ordained all this was to be dispensed personally from the new laws.[76]

In 1506, the year after Elphinstone made his endowment of King's College, Aberdeen, Glasgow too seemed about to enter on a new season of prosperity with the proposed annexation of certain vicarages. The object was to encourage the 'superior' faculties, enlarge the subjects taught and recruit some learned men. None of the benefices was in fact received, not even the nearby Cadder. The vicar of the latter was friendly, but his benefice did not come the way of the university. The new archbishop-chancellor had no intention of carrying out Black-adder's wishes and the more likely students left for elsewhere: Alexander Livingstone to St Andrews, where he was an examiner, and William Manderston, as we saw, to Paris.[77]

Archbishop Beaton I was, perhaps, a worldly man, but over his whole career he was an able administrator.[78] At the beginning of his rule, Glasgow University suffered badly, and, in the event, irremediably, from his neglect. Although a St Andrews student himself, he induced his famous nephew, David, later cardinal, to study at Glasgow, as did another close relative, Andrew Durie, later bishop of Galloway.[79] The arts faculty, however, had five successive principals in fourteen years; the faculty of canon law was abandoned; and it was only towards the end of his tenure of the chancellorship that the faculty of theology took on a new lease of life. War with England and plague added to the harm done.

There is a familiar sound about the Rector's proposals of 1509, on which deputies from all nations took decisions.[80] The first concerned the disuse of the Rector's jurisdiction; the earlier decision to make a university seal for his Court (*ad causas*) was reaffirmed (the first small seal was perhaps lost because of disuse). The rural dean was still a thorn in the flesh, contravening privileges granted by Bishop Turnbull.

This rural dean was undoubtedly Archibald Laing, dean of Rutherglen, who had influence in high places,[81] but who, as a graduate, could be summoned before the Rector. The chaplaincy of St Michael founded by Reston, of which the Rector and his council were patrons, had for long been vacant and their right of presentation was endangered by procrastination. The deputies went more warily when the Rector proposed that he ought to have precedence over the vicars general during archbishop Beaton's absence in all public acts and processions. They decided to consult Beaton before committing themselves to anything drastic.

Incorporations had begun to fall in Blackadder's time and were not improved by the aftermath of the battle of Flodden. From November 1509 we have no faculty of arts records for a quarter of a century. It is certain that the present book was either full or was mislaid for a time; the Dean of the time was Robert Hamilton and it was only under another Dean named Hamilton that it came into use again.[82] The last 1509 entries are written on a page, which was obviously in contact with a binding, if the book was bound, or at least soiled by handling, if unbound. The book at any rate was not available in 1518 to record the election of the new Dean which was entered instead in the university book.[83] Other details about the arts faculty can be gleaned from the university book, but all graduation records are lost.[84] They may have been recorded in a separate book which does not survive.

The loss was not greatly significant, as, for the present, the university was no more than a faculty of arts. In 1512, Matthew Stewart, vicar of Maybole, unable to prosecute further studies, was cited by the regent, John Spreull, commissary of the chancellor, for non-residence either at his vicarage or at the university as a student.[85] Spreull himself was in trouble in 1509 for not presenting to the chapter his dispensation to study under the archiepiscopal seal.[86] It is in this period too that the strange phrase 'Dean of the faculty of the said university' comes into use, pointing to the effective identity of university and faculty.[87]

Beaton was prepared to infuse new blood into the university, but the university was not his first priority. On 7 October 1510, Thomas Coutts, newly instituted as principal, joined the university.[88] At the time of his appointment he would be in his forties; he was born in the neighbourhood of Aberdeen and had studied at Louvain and Paris, where he was a fellow-student of Hector Boece.[89] He may have done a period of regency at King's College before coming to Glasgow. Unfortunately we have no information for this principalship. The faculty record is blank from 1510 till 1534. We have the initials of two unidentified regents[90] and the names of none. In 1512 Coutts was procurator, deputy and intrant, apparently as sole representative of the Albany nation. By

October 1514 he was no longer principal, although he acted as intrant two years later.[91] The explanation undoubtedly was that he was too useful otherwise to the archbishop and the civil power.[92]

In the Rectorial period beginning in October 1513, David Melville was incorporated as regent.[93] He was probably a Fife man, a student of St Andrews.[94] He too had come from Paris, when the Scottish nominalist school was at the height of its reputation under its leader, John Mair.[95] In October 1514 Melville is recorded as principal. Although there is no further mention of him he seems to have stayed on during the plague period, till 1517. In that year he went to become principal of the Pedagogy at St Andrews.[96] His books show his scholastic interests: John Peckham's *Perspective*, Thomas Bradwardine's *Speculative Geometry*, Pierre d'Ailly's *Commentary on the Sphere*, Jerome de Hangest's *Book of Proportions* and Jacques Lefèvre's edition of the *Sphere* and *Euclid*.[97]

The new principal, David Abercromby, like Melville, had studied at St Salvator's College, and his career as examiner, steward for the feast of St John, Quodlibetarius, and teacher of the *Summulae* of Peter of Spain can be traced in that college up to 1516.[98] He came to Glasgow in June of the following year as principal and took part as deputy and intrant in the election of Rector. In October 1518 he was styled merely 'regent of the pedagogy', it is likely that he was principal no longer. Other mentions of him include the description 'regent of the college' in 1520.[99] A copy of Sallust owned by him is still in the university library.[100]

It is improbable that the faculty could have flourished under such a bewildering succession of principals. The principal was originally meant to rule only the arts students and even in that faculty he was subject to the Dean. His power as the actual man on the spot, however, teaching and governing university property, tended to make him a key figure, liable to be elected as Dean or even Rector. He had under him usually two other regents, but in this latter period sometimes only one—though there were graduates due for a lecturing stint in the faculty to help the regents and, as examiners, non-regent students in other faculties. Even so, the whole burden of ordinary lectures rested on the regents as such, and dispensations from post-principiation lecturing became more frequent after the advent of print. It is true that in addition to the small sums raised from students, a brief stay in the faculty generally earned a benefice of some sort. But at Glasgow as this benefice was not attached to the post, and could be a distracting duty at least from time to time, not to speak of other more pastoral objections to the system, the arrangement was not ideal. The principal usually had a superior qualification: some of those named were theologians, some canon lawyers; this too in a small university involved extra obligations.

NOTES

1. *Glas. Mun.*, ii, 57, 179.
2. Watt, *Fasti*, 378.
3. *Glas. Mun.*, ii, 205–7.
4. *Ibid.*, ii, 68, 71.
5. Walter Paatz, *Sceptrum Universitatis. Die europäischen Universitätsszepter.* Heidelberger Kunstgeschichtliche Abhandlungen. Neue Folge (Heidelberg, 1953), 48, 101; plate 10. Cf. A. J. S. Brook, 'An Account of the Maces of the Universities of St Andrews, Glasgow, Aberdeen and Edinburgh', *PSAS* (1891–2), xxvi, 440ff.
6. He required some persuasion, *Glas. Mun.*, ii, 74.
7. He is not to be confused with Patrick Leitch, senior, diocesan chancellor, died before 18 February 1464: Watt, *Fasti*, 162. At Paris he was licensed in arts with Ireland, returned briefly to Glasgow (*Glas. Mun.*, ii, 196–7), was procurator of the German nation at Paris, etc., *Auctarium*, ii, 931, 956, 960, 966; iii, 17–39, 237. For his royal clerkship, *RMS*, ii, 1517, etc.
8. *Glas. Mun.*, ii, 83. Licentiate in theology later, *CPL*, xiii, 135.
9. *Glas. Mun.*, ii, 220.
10. *Ibid.*, ii, 223.
11. Michael Fleming and David Logan, the former supplicating humbly to be received, *ibid.*, ii, 214, 221. *AFA*, 191; Anderson, *Early Records*, 55, 181.
12. *Glas. Mun.*, ii, 222–4, and Liber Decani, 54–5, for omissions.
13. *Glas. Mun.*, ii, 220. Brown spent a small sum on the college of arts, *ibid.*, ii, 225. There were blank leaves left in the Liber Decani (part of pp. 55 and 56, 57, 58, all filled up much later), presumably to engross documentary material of the period as was done on pp. 46–7 (lists of gifts to the library).
14. *ACSB*, 81.
15. *Glas. Mun.*, iii, 406; Ian B. Cowan and D. E. Easson, *Medieval Religious Houses: Scotland*, second edition (London, 1976), 136.
16. *CPL*, xiii, 71. He was frustrated in his attempt to obtain the archdeaconry of Teviotdale as rival to Elphinstone and possibly also of the archdeaconry of Argyll, Watt, *Fasti*, 35, 177.
17. Goldsmith and Doby were still in charge in 1480, *Glas. Mun.*, i, 27; ii, 226.
18. *Glas. Mun.*, ii, 73, 213, 217–18, 232.
19. James Cooper, 'The Principals of the University of Glasgow before the Reformation', *SHR*, xi, 235.
20. *Glas. Mun.*, ii, 235. In this year, 'as having charge of the college of arts, he accepts the burden of lecturing for the coming year in person, and in the person of those appointed by him in the faculty of arts in the usual form', Liber Decani, 68.
21. *Glas. Mun.*, ii, 235.
22. *Ibid.*, ii, 228–30, 238; *Auctarium*, iii, 348, 387–8, 500.
23. *Glas. Mun.*, ii, 91.
24. *Ibid.*, iii, 405–6. His death is mentioned before November, probably July, *ibid.*, ii, 239.
25. *Ibid.*, ii, 235–6; after 'Hamiltone' on p. 236 the editor omits a reference to their being refused ('prius refutatos') in June, 'proxima die legibili post festum sancti

Johannis baptiste propter non complementum lecture librorum ordinariorum', Liber Decani, 69.

26. Watt, *Fasti*, 375.

27. *Glas. Mun.*, ii, 89, 230, 238; *Auctarium*, iii, 432–3, 466, 500.

28. *Glas. Mun.*, ii, 238–9. The name 'Ricardus Twedy' should read 'Ricardus Gibson tanquam pauper', followed by 'Andreas Twedy in alio actu solus', *ibid.*, ii, 240, Liber Decani, 74. This Richard Gibson (or Gilbert) entered as notary the Cadzow foundation instruments on pages 75–77 of the Dean's book.

29. Pedagogy in Rottenrow, both attached to the new St Michael chaplainry. On 30 May 1475, Leslie was to consult with the dean of faculty regarding this debt to Smyth and follow his orders: *Glas. Mun.*, ii, 242 (omissions after 'facultatis', Liber Decani, 80).

30. Before 'promisit' read instead 'libenter' as in MS.

31. *Glas. Mun.*, ii, 243.

32. *Protocol Bk. of James Young*, i, 13. Glasgow, Mitchell Library Ms 'Cartularium Glasguense', ii, 166.

33. Anderson, *Early Records*, 192; *Acts of the Lords of the Council in Public Affairs*, (Edinburgh, 1932), ad indices; *Rentale Dunkeldense*, SHS (1915), 326.

34. *Cartularium Ecclesiae Sancti Nicholai Aberdonensis* (New Spalding Club, 1888–92), ii, 341.

35. *The Black Book of Taymouth* (Bannatyne Club, 1885), 117.

36. *Glas. Mun.*, ii, 99.

37. *AFA*, xxxvi note.

38. J. Dowden, *The Bishops of Scotland* (Glasgow, 1912), 87. Cf. *SHR*, xi, 256.

39. *Glas. Mun.*, ii, 244.

40. *Ibid.*, ii, 244, 246.

41. Many dispensations are entered in the manuscript Dean's book by the bursar.

42. *Glas. Mun.*, ii, 250–1. Blackadder also spoke to them personally, 'ac vive vocis oraculum', Liber Decani, 92.

43. Cooper, 'Principals', *SHR*, xi, 258; Dowden, *Bishops*, 87–9. In 1500 he was abbot of Holyrood; from 1515 to 1528, keeper of the privy seal; in 1526, bishop of Dunkeld.

44. *Glas. Mun.*, ii, 250. He took over reluctantly, 'contradicere nolens deliberationibus et votis dictorum magistrorum', Liber Decani, 92.

45. *CPL*, xiii, 627; *Glas. Mun.*, ii, 87.

46. *Glas. Mun.*, ii, 251; Liber Decani, 93, 'Qui magister Walterus cum magno iuramento interueniens asseruit illam summam debere de pecunia sibi deliberata per dominum smyth ut cauetur in congregacione tenta Anno domini etc. lxxxvto Quam summam exigisse voluit dictus dominus Johannes smyth ab eodem magistro Waltero'; and after 'pedagogii' read 'cum consilio dicti Archidiaconi super cuius summe exposicione'.

47. *Prot. Bk. Simon*, 173–4.

48. *Glas. Mun.*, ii, 97, 246–51. Goldsmith failed in an attempt to become chanter of Glasgow, Watt, *Fasti*, 159.

49. *Glas. Mun.*, ii, 253. Keussen, *Matrikel*, i, 637 (student under Severinus de Moneta and Cornelius de Breda). A John Doby was at Paris somewhat later, *Auctarium*, iii, 196, 237. In 1482 he was rector of Kirkpatrick Fleming: Glasgow, Mitchell Library, MS. 'Cartularium Glasguense', ii, 110; *Charters and Documents relating to the Burgh of Peebles*, SBRS (Edinburgh, 1872), 155.

50. Liber Decani, 97, supplementing *Glas. Mun.*, ii, 253–5 where details of repairs on the pedagogy are also given.

51. Liber Decani, 100 (omitted in printed edition).

52. *Glas. Mun.*, ii, 27, has a number of omissions from Liber Decani, 121–2.
53. *Glas. Mun.*, ii, 271–2; *Prot. Bk. Simon*, 152–3.
54. *Glas. Mun.*, ii, 269; Liber Decani, 120. The change of policy adopted at this meeting is reflected in Gray's notes on payments for post-graduate dispensations.
55. *Glas. Mun.*, ii, 253, 271. Stewart was licensed at Paris in 1494, Paris, Archives Nationales, H2588(3), ff. 136, 142.
56. *Glas. Mun.*, ii, 272–3.
57. *Ibid.*, ii, 100.
58. *Ibid.*, ii, 109, 110.
59. *Ibid.*, ii, 278. Cf. *AFA*, 276, note 1.
60. *Glas. Mun.*, ii, 280. Liber Decani, 135 records his dispensation.
61. *Glas. Mun.*, ii, 276. After 'propria', read, 'Ego patricius cowynthre fateor me recepisse unam tasseam septem unciarum ad usum, utilitatem et commodum facultatis arcium studii glaschwensis teste manu propria', Liber Decani, 131.
62. *Glas. Mun.*, ii, 280–1.
63. *Ibid.*, i, 43–4.
64. *Ibid.*, ii, 274.
65. *Ibid.*, i, 46.
66. Watt, *Fasti*, 370. Some other details are found elsewhere in the public records.
67. His bachelorship is recorded, *Glas. Mun.*, ii, 282. His fee for licence (eleven shillings) is omitted by the editor, but see Liber Decani, 137.
68. J. Durkan, 'John Major after 500 Years', *IR*, i, 152–4 (bibliography).
69. W. M. Campbell, 'The First Archbishop of Glasgow', *Records of the Scottish Church History Society*, viii, 55–74; 135–50.
70. *Glas. Mun.*, ii, 96–7.
71. *Ibid.*, ii, 98.
72. *Ibid.*, ii, 115–16, 110.
73. Some Aberdonians were incorporated, one in 1498, two in 1501: *ibid.*, ii, 114, 117.
74. The phrase 'in capitulo ecclesie metropolitane Glasguensis' begins to be used, *ibid.*, ii, 112. 'Apud Universitatem metropolitanam Glasguensem', *RMS*, ii, 3029.
75. David Cranston, *Questiones in Posteriorum Lectura* (Paris, 1506).
76. *Glas. Mun.*, ii, 106ff.
77. Livingstone and Roger Menzies went to St Salvator's; Thomas McLellan to the Pedagogy; *Glas. Mun.*, ii, 118, 119; *AFA*, 280, 287.
78. J. Herkless and R. K. Hannay, *Archbishop of St Andrews* (Edinburgh, 1910) iii, 11. The whole of that volume is dedicated to him.
79. *Glas. Mun.*, ii, 125, 128.
80. *Ibid.*, ii, 121–3.
81. He was dispensed from his post-graduate obligation out of respect for the King, *Glas. Mun.*, ii, 284; Watt, *Fasti*, 180. The solution of the problem may have been hastened by the fact that the Arts Dean in 1514 was himself rural dean of Kyle, *ibid.*, ii, 183 (James Neilson).
82. *Glas. Mun.*, ii, 284–6. The later Dean was William Hamilton.
83. *Ibid.*, ii, 133.
84. Liber Decani, 151 records in a later italic hand, 'Anno domini 1518 creati sunt magistri Robertus Maxwell, Patricius Melvin'. This Patrick Melville (or Melvin) is not otherwise recorded.
85. *Prot. Bk. Simon*, 452. Stewart was one of the deputies consulted in 1509 and held university offices from 1519, *Glas. Mun.*, ii, 122, 136. He owned a copy of Thucydides, Durkan and Ross, *Libraries*, 150.
86. *Prot. Bk. Simon*, 314.

87. *Glas. Mun.*, ii, 134.
88. *Ibid.*, ii, 124.
89. 'Diocese of Aberdeen' at Paris, 1492–3 (B.A.), 1493 (Lic.), *Auctarium*, vi. 717, 737. 'Diocese of St Andrews' at Louvain, A. Schillings, *Matricule de l'Université de Louvain* (Brussels, 1958), iii, 240.
90. The initials are N. S. and C. A. in a formulary for licence, see Appendix.
91. *Glas. Mun.*, ii, 125–6, 128–9.
92. For some of his subsequent posts, Watt, *Fasti.* 189, 191, 326. He died about 1530.
93. *Glas. Mun.*, ii, 128.
94. Anderson, *Early Records*, 95, 190, where he was a member of the Albany nation.
95. Paris, Sorbonne, Archives de l'Université, Reg. 15, f. 116, 127, bachelor 1510–11, licentiate in 1512.
96. Watt, *Fasti*, 379, 381.
97. Durkan and Ross, *Libraries*, 129–30.
98. *AFA*, 280, 287, 293, 305, 310.
99. *Glas. Mun.*, ii, 130–1, 133, 136, 138.
100. Durkan and Ross, *Libraries*, 66.

9. John Mair

'Maister Johnne Mair, whose wourd then was holden as an oracle.'
John Knox, *History*

'Has not Amerigo Vespucci in our day discovered lands unknown to Ptolemy, Pliny and other geographers up to the present? Why can this not happen in other spheres?'
In Quartum Sententiarum

THE NEXT principal, John Mair (or Major, as he is usually called) was one of the great Scotsmen of the sixteenth century. Almost the last of the old breed of scholastics, he was not always acceptable to many of the new breed. Others continued to cite him with respect, especially the Spaniards, when the whirligig of time brought scholasticism its second wind in the university curricula of the seventeenth century. His garrulousness, his 'wagon-loads of trifling', were criticised by men of the Renaissance and the Reformation, and these criticisms have been echoed in more modern times. In one respect they were fortunate for occasionally Mair goes off at a tangent to tell us something pertinent about himself or the Scotland of his day which shows a sharp eye and an alert mind. More recently he has regained respectful attention from scholars of diverse allegiances,[1] and his work is worth treating at some length as a specimen of the best teaching available to Scots students in the pre-Reformation era.

About his life, information is abundant and only salient points can be noticed here.[2]

He was born in 1467 (not, as Burns shows, 1469) at Gleghornie, near Haddington, and was destined for the priesthood, but the harsh discipline of his Haddington schoolmaster, George Lister, almost put him off: 'he was harder than was just in beating boys'.[3] The first certain fact about his higher education is that he entered the college of Godshouse (later Christ's College) in Cambridge about 1491–2. There he seems to have remained for a year. Godshouse was a college for the training of grammar masters the head of which was a certain John Syclyng. But Mair's own master was apparently John Thorn, 'the ornament of Cambridge university'. From England he crossed over to Paris, studying first under Jean Bouillache at the college of Ste Barbe; his teacher later became regent of grammar in the college of Navarre.

He then began to study theology under Jean Standonck, the principal of the college of Montaigu of whom Mair never spoke without awe, boasting of having lived 'in the shadow of so great a man'.[4] Inspired by a school of able logicians, including Jeronimo Pardo, a Spaniard, Mair was a prominent teacher almost from the first.[5] His lectures, beginning in 1499 with the *Exponibilia*—the very title showing his nominalist affiliations—were eagerly sought after by the Paris printers. This began an incessant work of publication and editing which went on for thirty more years. At Montaigu he taught both arts and theology after taking his doctorate in 1506.[6] His commentaries on the Sentences were considered to be the liveliest, profoundest and most up-to-date. In 1518, when he received his invitation to Glasgow, he had published at Paris at least forty-six separate editions in philosophy and theology.[7] He was then a middle-aged man in his fifties, small in stature, 'major only in name', the author's joke to which George Buchanan gave an acrimonious twist. Within a month he issued his commentary on St Matthew's gospel from 'the academy of Glasgow',[8] to which he hoped to bring the ideals of the Academy of Athens. He had been a student under the restorer of Greek at Paris, the elder Girolamo Aleandro, who in 1512 entered in his diary: 'Many scholars are to be found in France who are keen students in different fields of knowledge, and several of these were among my faithful hearers, such as John Mair, doctor of theology, and David Cranston, shortly to take his doctorate, distinguished friends of mine . . .'.[9]

The dedication prefaced to Mair's edition of the gospel of Matthew is composed in the fulsome style of contemporary epistolary models and reflects his admiration of its addressee, Archbishop Beaton.[10] But the letter also preaches to him a little of his duties in intellectual matters, in the manner of David Cranston's earlier letter to Blackadder. Those who are high priests, says Mair, ought to guard the sacred books as the ancient Egyptians did theirs, all the more as they are the archetypes and models that other mortals must follow. Not for nothing did the world's Archetype lay down that the divine mysteries be handled only by those who already loved wisdom: the Jewish seers and Essenes were as devoted to it as to their priestly calling. But Beaton had already all the Pauline virtues, and if he had his responsibilities as a leader, Mair has his as a son, of the Church. 'Epaminondas seeing an army leaderless said, "I see a headless monster". Likewise this our little edition would go on to the stage lacking the dress for the part and headless, without your patronage and blessing.'[11]

It looks as though Iamblichus and Marsilio Ficino have influenced his thought and style here and we know he was amicably disposed to the elder Giovanni Pico della Mirandola.[12] It is often stated that in

1508 Mair preached at Paul's Cross in London for John Colet, an English disciple of Ficino.[13] But this was surely 'the Scottyshe doctor and ffrere of Grenewych', the Observant Franciscan, Friar Donald Gibson (Gilberti), who was guardian of the royal foundation at Greenwich,[14] the same whom Sir Thomas More heard in his youth, attacking the abuses attached to pilgrimages to Marian shrines.[15]

Mair's benign references to Pico are concerned largely with his attempts to reconcile Plato and Aristotle and to the famous letter (which Mair republished) from Pico to Ermolao Barbaro defending the 'barbaric' jargon of university philosophy against its traducers such as Lorenzo Valla, on whose attempts to marry logic and rhetoric Mair pours obsessive scorn, most notably in citing his pupil, David Cranston, in dialogue with a Scots admirer of Valla, the poet, Gavin Douglas.[16] Philosophers deliberately cultivated a pithy, non-rhetorical language.

The views of Mair in youth and in middle age on conciliar government in the Church were familiar in his day and carried on a Scottish tradition of conciliar thinking that had obvious antecedents in the period of the Councils of Constance and Basle, and subsequently in John Ireland and others. The defence of papal authority had been renewed by Thomas de Vio, a Dominican, later Cardinal Cajetan, against the French King's politically motivated summoning of the Council of Pisa. One of Mair's pupils, the Frenchman Jacques Almain, replied as did Mair himself, in more sober terms, in his commentary on St Matthew's gospel, based on earlier lectures. Using Nicholas of Lyra's text of the Bible and discussing Matthew, 16, 13–19 (the giving of the power of the keys to Peter), Mair emphasises the community aspect of the event, the desire of Jesus to win from the disciples a united confession of faith; the fact that, though Peter had a special position, he replied in the name of them all; that the rock on which the Church rested was its one foundation, Christ. The Church, for the younger Mair, was in the first instance, the 'congregation of the faithful' and elsewhere he resists humanist attempts to redefine it in pagan terms.[17] He went on to deny to the pope, as successor of Peter, the temporal power, then proceeded to emphasise his ministerial rôle and indicated, while accepting the term 'Vicar of Christ' for the pope, that this did not rule out the fact that there was an enormous distance between Christ and his vicar, as vicars did not generally have the same powers as those they represented. Though accepting the deposing power of the papacy, he turned it into a deposing power for subjects, as the pope's rôle would be purely one of persuasion. He defended the so-called Donation of Constantine to the papacy, attacked as a forgery by Lorenzo Valla and by others before him, but drew no political conclusions from it and re-emphasised the ambiguity involved in ecclesiastical wealth.[18] Likewise in his commentary on Matthew 18, 15–18, he made it the occasion for a complaint about facile excommunication procedures, explored further the relationship of the general body of Christians—especially when gathered in council—to an erring or heretical pope, conditionally accepting the proverbial phrase 'Nobody judges the pope (the first see)' only if conjoined with 'so long as he wishes to act justly' (as in the original). Mair, the proclaimed enemy of the primacy of canon law, nevertheless makes great use of canonistic authorities and his easy progress from theories of ecclesiastical to theories of secular government gives added force to the thesis of those who see in him a key influence on subsequent Scottish political theory. An unhappy illustration of his theory about the deposition of unworthy rulers was his view that Indian kings in America tolerating the cult of idols could be deposed—but by the Spanish invaders. Las Casas opposed this view on the grounds that Mair had no personal experience of Indians.[19]

Some attention has been given in recent years to Mair as an authority on international law, on which he wrote as a theologian at the peak of the first Iberian adventures in the New World. He treated questions regarding the occupation of new found lands, the property rights of the human race in land, air and water, the questions of just and unjust wars (wars of expansion, reprisals, alliances with non-Christians). He certainly influenced to a great extent future Spanish theorists on problems of international law.[20]

On ethical questions, Mair lectured in Glasgow 'from beginning to end' (*ab ouo ad malum*): these lectures must have laid the groundwork of the sole printed edition.[21] Mention has already been made of the fact that some medieval teachers were unhappy about retailing pagan ethics to Christian youth: at St Leonard's College, St Andrews, there was the option of 'one of the books of Solomon' instead.[22] Mair, on the contrary, had no scruples, as he wrote in his introduction to Cardinal Thomas Wolsey: Aristotle's attitude to the contemplative and active life is, he maintained, the same as that of the Bible when it treats of Rachel and Leah and Martha and Mary.[23] Aristotle condemns suicide, affirms free will, praises the heroic virtues and magnanimity— summing up the virtues, one might add, of a gentleman—all things which made the *Ethics* a popular vademecum for the intelligent of the period. Mair hesitates to speak of ethical knowledge: ethics is practice rather than theory.[24] His work uses the new Latin translation of Johannes Argyropoulos and also refers to the alternative version of Leonardo Bruni. The Latin of Mair's commentary is more elevated than is usual with him, and when he cites Theognis and Phocylides he no doubt does so from the edition of his Paris master, Girolamo Aleandro.[25]

More specialised aspects of moral problems are those relating to marriage. In defending pleasure in the married state, Mair, while sharing traditional prejudices, shows his usual matter-of-factness and sympathy for ordinary folk. He widens the idea of the moralists, who thought of marriage as primarily a moral remedy for concupiscence, to make it a physical one. According to one commentator, his approach shows a perceptible trend away from stressing relational and personal to individual motivation, which trend he puts down to Mair's nominalist and Scotist upbringing.[26] Cajetan made some use of Mair's work here.[27]

Probably the younger Mair was most renowned, and in his latter years, most condemned, as a scholastic logician. In view of the late sixteenth-century regeneration of Spanish philosophy, it is worth pointing to Mair's place in the chain of influences that brought it about. Lately some studies have brought to light fresh aspects of that influence. Cristobal de Medina at Salamanca university referred to Mair's work in his teaching. Juan Martinez Silicea, in his *Ars Arithmetica* (Paris, 1514) praised rather another Scot, Robert Galbraith. Domingo de San Juan declared in 1522 that at Salamanca 'in this flourishing university it was solemnly decreed, and that to no little common advantage and utility of the students, that the nominalist regents in arts should be compelled in the first year of their course to lecture on the Dialectic of the revered master John Mair, a man celebrated the world over'. At Alcala, likewise, Mair was popular. Sancho Carranza de Miranda cites him. Antonio Ramirez de Villaescusa was an associate of his pupil, David Cranston. Fernando de Enzinas was of the school of Mair and his treatise on the properties of the mental proposition was edited by a Scot, Robert Wauchope. In Spain, Mair with his school, while perhaps not the 'oracle' that John Knox claimed he was in Scotland, was nevertheless often quoted from the pulpit.[28]

The most important recent study of Mair's logic and philosophy is by T. F. Torrance, a study whose content is too technical and too densely argued to be appositely summarised in a brief paragraph. The writer is critical of the medieval 'terminist' school, as it is sometimes called, with its 'arid linguistic nominalism'. He exempts Mair from his strictures, however, emphasising his combination of severe logical analysis with a close grip on everyday experience. He stresses rather Mair's debt to his fellow countrymen, Duns Scotus and Richard of St Victor, and his rôle as a bridge between medieval and modern thought, with a possible influence on his Paris student, Calvin. Through all intermediate representation, Mair's thought, Torrance maintains, reaches out to objective realities, and for him intuitive perception is important in natural and theological science—though Mair has reservations about theology precisely as scientific. He breaks away from an exclusively visual approach to learning and emphasises affective and auditory paths to knowledge, yet according to Torrance, he suffers in theology from being untouched by the works of Jacques Lefèvre and the 'modern devotion', and from using an inadequate notion of 'authentic transmission' in tradition, though he is critical of the view that authority can replace faith.[29]

Mair's mathematical interests have had less investigation. In his treatise on the infinite, the subject is envisaged largely from a logical standpoint. As has been said, it is astonishing how men carrying so little mathematical baggage managed to get as far as they did. Towards the end of his career, he found students impatient of these hypothetical discussions (hypothetical, to escape the post-1277 censures of anything disturbing the accepted theological picture of the physical world) and duly abbreviated his infinitist references. Later, on a more favourable mathematical basis, the infinitist theme would re-emerge, to dominate the horizon of the seventeenth-century inventors.[30]

Some of his objections to a thesis whether 'local motion is a successive entity distinct from anything permanent' are again theological difficulties, which he proceeds to resolve in a way that make it difficult, one commentator suggests, to identify his own position as nominalist or realist.[31] There seems rather to be a rapprochement between the schools, for he discussed the problems in kinematics which were customarily a nominalist concern, and problems in dynamics such as the importance of cause in the velocity of local motion in realist terms. He deserves a place in the line of those who applied concepts of the infinitesimal to problems of motion and passed on the discussions of impetus raised by Buridan in Paris and by the Oxford Merton school, especially Heytesbury and Swineshead, through to Domingo de Soto and Francisco Toledo whom Galileo certainly read, though whether these influences have any central importance for his founding of a new science of mechanics is controverted.[32] In any event, medieval science was no mere rehearsal of Aristotle: some of it grew up in a basic independence of him even, as a disturbing and inharmonious annexed body of knowledge. Yet the extraordinary persistence—in spite of attacks upon it—of Aristotle's physics was due to its logical consistency which it was and continued to be intellectually convenient to maintain.

Mair taught the *Physics* in Glasgow and referred to the earth tremors there and in Paisley.[33] He also read the Sentences in Glasgow and mentions how it was customary for professors of theology (*theosophiae*) also to teach the liberal arts in Scotland.[34] From his commentaries on the *Sentences*, some evidence has been elicited on his views on social and economic questions: the precarious system of land-tenure which encouraged neglect and mismanagement; the military propensities of the farming community; inadequate rural housing; the advantages of feu-farm; relative money values in Scotland and elsewhere.[35] He was also, as a pioneering article has shown, interested in the moral problem raised by the growth of the international money-market[36]: he firmly maintained the medieval prohibition on receiving profit on a money loan, while scrutinising any extrinsic factors which would compensate the lenders. Since then it has been shown that he discussed other contemporary economic problems: 'in spite of his respect for tradition, he is less bookish than might be thought and pauses sometimes to make just remarks and cite well-chosen examples to relieve his prose, elsewhere monotonous and off-putting'.[37] Not a very promising introduction, but as the writer proceeds he becomes more enthusiastic: the scholastics did not believe in anything beyond monastic communism and had not the resources for a planned economy nor any wide programme of social change. This modern economist points out that Mair defends money exchange as against barter, for even the most arid places—Iceland—contribute to international trade. The nominalists tended to wish the establishment by authority of a fixed just price: for Mair this is the legal or market price. Mair also denounces monopolies and is hostile to corporations. He defends letters of change and disagrees with merchants who devote themselves exclusively to the speculative market. He deals benignly with problems of international borrowing, accepts maritime insurance and, more surprisingly, 'opportunity cost', arising from lost opportunities on the market, as a valid title: the latter point is a real contribution to the development of economic theory. The 'triple contract', a technique for avoiding the accusation of usury, defended by Mair, was a forerunner of modern theory though it later became the subject of a papal condemnation. His economic theory had a logical coherence, and he was a link in the chain that led to Adam Smith.

He is best known as an historian.[38] He inherited from his sources many inaccuracies, but in their deployment he was neither gullible nor prejudiced. He tried to get beyond the chronicle form and set out to look for historical patterns where possible. He is an enthusiastic Scotsman, defending the country's desire for independence, yet anxious to avoid too separatist an attitude to Scotland's neighbours. He considered that nobles were Scotland's natural leaders and yet had no illusions about their faults: churchmen too were not spared his honest criticism. Unlike his immediate successors, he wanted no truck with ancient fables about Brutus and Gathelus and the origins of the nation. He uses the phrase 'Greater Britain' which has been shown to have a longer pedigree than writers have often imagined.[39] His dedication to King James V is totally free of flattery and he made plain that he had no intention of merely setting down the record like a chronicle but would proceed to make historical judgments as well; but this he did with a modest and sober attention to the factual evidence.

Specialism has grown apace and it is not possible for anybody now to cover the range of interests exhibited by Mair in the sixteenth century. In spite of his vast learning and genial approach, he was not equal to the mental convulsions that shook Europe in his later years. Many who wrote about him do not allow sufficiently for a change and hardening of attitude as he aged. We do not really have the answer to the apparent contradictions; the signs of some sympathy with the Renaissance revival of studies, and, at the same time, the rigid conservatism in his discussion of the links between logic and rhetoric. Basically he seems to have sensed that if theologians gave up philosophy to become orators they would surrender philosophy to men of a purely secular frame of mind, which Mair as a man of deep Christian faith, was not prepared to do. In his later *Gospel Commentaries* (1529), as Ganoczy has shown, he omitted and played down conciliar themes and avoided the issue of ecclesiastical structures, but was horrified by what he saw as the renewed 'Wycliffite' attack on papal authority. In these circumstances, one must ask which of these two men, the younger or the older theologian, affected more the religious and political formation of his Roman Catholic successors as well as of John Knox, Pierre Viret, George Buchanan and John Calvin.[40]

In any event, his ideas were influential. At the time, Glasgow was fortunate to get a man of international calibre to teach in its as yet humble schools of theology and arts; and later it will be possible to show from the record number of enrolments that his teaching was fully appreciated.

NOTES

1. For some of the criticism and counter-criticism, see J. Durkan, 'John Major: After 400 Years', *IR*, i, 131–57 (bibliography).
2. The sources for his life are John Major, *A History of Greater Britain*, translated by Archibald Constable, with author's life by Aeneas J. G. Mackay (SHS, Edinburgh, 1892); J. H. Burns, 'New Light on John Major', *IR*, v, 83–100, and also his note in *SHR*, xxxi, 98; note by A. L. Gabriel and G. C. Boyce, *Auctarium*, vi, 733–4; A. B. Emden, *A Biographical Register of the University of Cambridge to 1500* (Cambridge, 1963), 384–5.

3. Lister was a St Andrews graduate, *AFA*, 196.
4. Major, *History*, 430. 'Magni enim estimaui et estimo sub umbra talis et tanti viri quiescere.'
5. Hubert Elie, 'Quelques Maîtres de l'université de Paris vers l'an 1500', *Archives d'Hist. Doctrinale et Litt. du Moyen Age*, xviii (1951), 193–243, esp. 205ff.
6. Clerval, *Registre des Procès Verbaux*, i, 5, 20.
7. Durkan, *art. cit.*, *IR*, i, 140, gives the bibliography.
8. Burns, 'New Light', *IR*, v, 90, says this dedication was dated on 22 December. It was '10 Cal. Decembris', however; i.e., 22 November (Major, *History*, 436). The book was printed in Paris.
9. Augustin Renaudet, *Préréforme et Humanisme à Paris pendant les Premières Guerres d'Italie (1494-1517)*, second edition (Paris, 1953), 614. But Mair was involved in the strife of the universities with Reuchlin, the Hebrew scholar and devotee of the Cabala.
10. The Archbishop, who was presented to the temporality of Kilwinning in 1516, *RSS*, i, 2725, in turn must have arranged for Mair to be vicar of Dunlop, a kirk annexed to Kilwinning.
11. Major, *History*, 435–6, reprinted from his commentary on Matthew. His Greek studies are reflected in the use of 'prothomiste' for 'high priests' and 'acephala' for 'headless'.
12. Major, *History*, 420, and there are other references to Pico gathered throughout his works. Nicholas of Cusa likewise uses language similar to Mair's in this letter.
13. J. H. Lupton, *A Life of John Colet, D.D.* (London, 1887), 49.
14. Bishop Richard Fox also patronised this foundation, to which other Scots (as well as Flemings and Germans) were probably attached (because their Observant reform preceded the English one), A. G. Little, 'Introduction of the Observant Friars into England', *Proceedings of the British Academy*, x (1924), 455–71, and *ibid.*, xxvii (1941), 159 note. (Among other names is one later associated with the Scottish Observant province, Louis Williamson.)
15. W. E. Campbell and A. W. Reed, *More's English Works*, ii, 62, in 'A Dialogue concernynge heresyes'.
16. Major, *History*, 427–8.
17. *Ibid.*, 342–3.
18. Alexandre Ganoczy, 'Jean Major, exégète gallican', *Recherches de Science religieuse*, lvi (Paris, 1968), 457–95. Matthew Spinka, *Advocates of Reform* (1953), 175–84, reprints the text in English. J. H. Burns, 'The Conciliar Tradition in Scotland', *SHR*, xlii (1963), 89–104. Francis Oakley, 'Almain and Major: Conciliar Theory on the Eve of the Reformation', *American Historical Review*, lxx (1965), 673–90. Francis Oakley, 'From Constance to 1688: The Political Thought of John Major and George Buchanan', *Journal of British Studies*, i (1962), 12–19. For a curialist of Bishop Turnbull's time whose papalism was more moderate than Cajetan's, cf. J. A. F. Thomson, 'Papalism and Conciliarism in Antonio Roselli's "Monarchia" ', *Mediaeval Studies*, xxxvii (Toronto, 1975), 445–58.
19. *Bartolomé de las Casas in History*, ed. Juan Friede and Benjamin Keene (De Kalb, Illinois, 1971), 303.
20. V. E. Hrabar, 'Le droit politique et le droit international dans les Questions de Jean Mair sur les Sentences de Pierre Lombard', *Académie des Sciences Oukrainienne* (Kiev, 1927), 22–35, preceded by Russian text. Chapter VI, 'El Jefe de Monteagudo: Jean Mair', of Ricardo G. Villoslada, *La Universidad de Paris durante los Estudios de Francisco de Vitoria O.P. (1507-1522)*, Analecta Gregoriana XIV, Series Facultatis Historiae Ecclesiasticae Sectio B (2) (Rome,

1938), 127–64. V. D. Carro, *La Teología y los Teológos—Juristas Españoles ante la Conquista de América*, 2 vols. (Madrid, 1944), ad indices.

21. J. H. Burns, 'New Light', *IR*, v (1954), 99–100, prints the letter (omitted in the appendix to the *History*) of Mair to William Gibson and John Spreull of Glasgow which mentions this fact. The Mair *Ethica Aristotelis* appeared at Paris in 1530.

22. Herkless and Hannay, *The College of St. Leonard*, 148.

23. Major, *History*, 449.

24. R. A. Gauthier and J. Y. Jolif, *L'Ethique à Nicomaque* (Louvain/Paris, 1970), i (1), 164.

25. G. Aleandro, *Gnomologia* (Paris, 1512), includes the Greek elegies and epigrams of both.

26. This seems an oversimplification, and based mainly on the 1521 *In Quartum Sententiarum*. L. Vereecke, 'Jean Mair: Un acte permis mais scabreux', *Mariage et Sexualité au declin du Moyen Age*, Supplément de *La Vie Spirituelle* xiv (Paris, 1961). The notion of pleasure referred to is dealt with at some length in the *Ethica Aristotelis* (1530), not used by Vereecke. I have not seen S. Concha Rodriguez 'La teología del matrimonio en Joannes Maior, El propósito del acto matrimonial' *Anales de la Facultad de Teología, Santiago, Chile*, xxii (1971), 7–13.

27. Dennis Doherty, *The Sexual Doctrine of Cardinal Cajetan* (Regensburg, 1966), 32, 223, 254, 281, suggests that Mair accepted adultery as a reason for divorce and believed that procreation was not the sole aim of marriage.

28. Vicente Munoz Delgado, 'La Logica en Salamanca durante la Primera Mitad del Siglo XVI', *Salmanticensis*, xiv (1967), 171–207; *ibid.*, 'La Logica en la Universidad de Alcalá durante la primera Mitad del Siglo XVI', *Salmanticensis*, xv (1968), 161–218. Marcel Bataillon, *Erasme et l'Espagne* (Paris, 1937), 729. For a fuller discussion of the background of Spanish philosophy of the early Renaissance see the above writer's many other contributions to the subject (often incidentally mentioning Mair) in *La Ciudad de Dios* and elsewhere.

29. Thomas F. Torrance, 'La Philosophie et la Théologie de Jean Mair ou Major', *Archives de la Philosophie* (Paris, 1969–70), xxxii, 531–47; xxxiii, 261–93. Hubert Elie, *Le Complexe Significabile* (Paris, 1937) discusses Mair's logic from a more strictly historical angle.

30. Hubert Elie, *Le Traité 'De l'Infini' de Jean Mair* (Paris, 1938), new edition with apparatus and French translation, and a useful note (220–40) on the criticisms of Mair's disciple, Luis Coronel.

31. William A. Wallace, *Causality and Scientific Explanation* (Ann Arbor, Michigan, 1972), 131–2.

32. *Dictionary of Scientific Biography*, ix (New York, 1974), s.v. Maior (32–3). W. A. Wallace, ' "The Calculatores" in Early Sixteenth Century Physics', *British Journal for the History of Science*, iv (1969), 221–32. Ibid., 'The Enigma of Domingo de Soto', *Isis* (Berkeley, Calif., 1968), 384–401.

33. Burns, 'New Light', *IR*, v, 91.

34. Major, *History*, 439 (letter to Peter Chaplain).

35. As well as much folk-lore. Cf. J. H. Burns, 'The Scotland of John Major', *IR*, ii (1951), 65–76.

36. Louis Vereecke, 'La licéité du *cambium bursae* chez Jean Mair', *Revue historique de droit français et étranger*, ser. 4, xxx (1952), 124–38.

37. Raymond de Roover, 'La Pensée Economique de Jean Mair', *Journal des Savants*, cix (1970), 65–81. The earlier part is biographical and both it and the bibliography require some updating.

38. R. G. Cant, 'John Major', *Veterum Laudes*, St Andrews University Publications

xlviii (Edinburgh, 1950), 21–31, is still the best account of this facet of Mair's scholarship.

39. Denys Hay, *Europe: The Emergence of an Idea*, revised edition (Edinburgh, 1968), 128–44.

40. Lucien Joseph Richard, *The Spirituality of John Calvin* (Atlanta, Ga., 1974), discusses Mair (144–6) as one of many converging factors influencing Calvin, at the same time firmly stressing the originality of Calvin's mind. For his influence on Viret, cf. R. D. Linder, *The Political Ideas of Pierre Viret* (Travaux d'Humanisme et Renaissance, no. 64, Geneva, 1964), 20 and note.

10. The University and the Wider Scene

'Erasmus Roterodamus schawis . . . na thing in moir admiracioun
to the pepill than werkis of kingis. . . . And sen na thing is that the
pepill . . . kepis in moir recent memorie, than werkis of nobill men,
of ressoun thair besynes suld be moir respondent to vertew than of
ony uther estatis. . . .'

John Bellenden, Translator's Preface to Boece's History

'There wes Faustus, and Laurence of Vale. . . .
With mony other clerkis of gret auayle,
Thare wes Brunell, Claudyus and Bocace.
So gret a pres of pepill drew us nere,
The hunder part thare namys is not here . . .
Of this natioun I knew also anone
Gret Kennedy and Dunbar yit undede.'

Gavin Douglas, The Palice of Honour

CHURCH and state, town and gown, lords and commons all had their
rôle in the promotion of higher studies and sometimes in their retarda-
tion. The university did not exist in a vacuum and was fortunate in
that it had teachers prepared to give a tiny burgh on the edge of the
civilised world the benefit of their training and experience in a wider
cosmopolitan context. The misfortune of three separate small universities in a small and relatively backward land has to be balanced
against some good fortune in the presence of three alternative traditions
of local learning with, nevertheless, a community of educational bonds
that could act as a countrywide force for national unity.

The rôle of the bishop-chancellor in the medieval universities of
Scotland was certainly more prominent than in England, for instance,
where neither Oxford nor Cambridge were episcopal sees. But it can be
exaggerated, at least in Glasgow. There is no pre-Reformation
chancellor's oath and, as a *deus ex machina* for granting the licence for
the final degree, he generally respected the university's autonomy and
appointed from the university body a vice-chancellor. As a protector
of its privileges and as patron in a more material sense, that is, as
founder or the potential source of further endowment, or again as a
final court of appeal in a crisis, he could play a key rôle, however.
Generally his priorities were elsewhere: in his membership of the royal
bureaucracy or in his cathedral. There is no sign at Glasgow of the

existence of any episcopal commission of visitation but bishops did from time to time attend academic functions, especially principiation ceremonies, and were entitled to be presented with an expensive bonnet on such occasions.[1]

Strong episcopal backing would have been particularly important in the university's first years, and Turnbull appeared at the Rectorial election of 1452 when university 'nations' were being set up.[2] Again, when in 1453 the university took further steps towards constituting itself an autonomous corporation in proposing a common seal and signet as tokens of exemption from the bishop's delegated jurisdiction, a personal approach to Turnbull had to be made.[3] The designs on the seals both of the university and of the arts faculty reflected their common origin in the see of St Kentigern,[4] but the university was not a mere cathedral school writ large.

In July 1461, Bishop Andrew de Durisdeer confirmed the Rector's powers of separate jurisdiction and his precedence over all other prelates.[5] It was in his episcopate too that another symbol of Rectorial authority, the university mace, was acquired; and subsequent moves to regulate the Rector's retinue and Rectorial dress, in relation to the varying solemnity of the occasion, again stressed his precedence—after the presiding prelate—in all processions, sessions and councils.[6] It has already been shown how the university successfully fought the desire of the conservators of St Andrews university to poach on Glasgow's preserves and how both bishop and king joined forces to solicit papal protection. This recourse to the Curia in Rome was a last resort. There were no university rolls petitioning the pope for presentation of qualified academics to benefices as in the previous century.[7] Moreover, whether the explanation is increasing venality in the Curia or the complex situation resulting from the indult of 1487 by Innocent VIII, higher degrees ceased to gain the same automatic rewards and so the Vatican supplications are no longer the rich quarry they once were for details about academic qualifications.[8]

Of Bishop John Laing we know little, although, as we saw, he was a donor to the arts faculty library. In 1481 he acted as the university's intermediary in presenting Patrick Leitch, junior, with an expensive red hood.[9] Nominally in the appointment and deposition of principals the bishops had some say, and this of course would affect teaching trends. In the deposition of Walter Bunch and the appointment of temporary joint-principals, the bishop had no rôle: as far as we can see this was totally a faculty initiative.[10] But after Glasgow became a metropolitan see in 1492, the evidence suggests that the faculty's say in the appointments was nullified and this remained true for the rest of the period. For instance, George Crichton was both inserted in office by Bishop (later

Archbishop) Blackadder and despoiled of it within three years.[11] The faculty of arts would have preferred to see even the appointment of principals as a joint concern of themselves and the chancellor,[12] and in 1490 the university sought legal advice regarding Rectorial jurisdiction and the privileges as set out in charters and letters of erection.[13] Blackadder had some academic ability and was himself a former student both of Paris and Louvain.[14] But, in spite of good intentions on paper, his metropolitan and cardinalatial ambitions inhibited him from gaining the chapter's confidence with undesirable consequences all round.[15] It is explicitly stated again during Blackadder's regime that the licence was given 'by authority of the chancellor'[16]; on the other hand, the faculty risked rejecting a Blackadder in the examination with no adverse consequences.[17] Archbishop Beaton's advice was sought on provisionally terminating the canon law readership[18]; the date of a Rectorial election was postponed at the request of the second Archbishop Beaton—to allow the election of a relative of his[19]—but this was on the eve of the Reformation. The placing of some candidates on the roll for licence was postponed in 1462 till the chancellor's coming, William Elphinstone, junior, then leading the field.[20] Doubtless, there were other such pressures that passed unrecorded, but Andrew de Durisdeer, the same bishop, on an earlier occasion left such matters in the faculty's hands.[21] The vicar general acquired importance in the bishop's absence and in 1456 he delegated his duties as chancellor, while at a later date the University took the precaution of electing one of the vicars general as Rector.[22] That the bishop was not considered irrelevant to the future fate of the institution is suggested by the high hopes that Gavin Dunbar would assist its advancement.[23]

The members of the cathedral chapter were not, however, always in accord with their bishop, and, throughout the medieval period, it was they who controlled both university and faculty. There were thirty-two prebends at least,[24] and as many vicars choral. Yet, as Mair wryly observed, 'in Scotland canons who are graduates in theology are as common as snakes in Ireland or dormice in Glasgow'.[25] Canon lawyers were more plentiful in the Glasgow chapter, some of them trained in the university and able to practise in the diocesan official's Consistory Court or in the course of chapter business. University lawyers are found closely associated with such ecclesiastical courts as well as the court scribes proper and a little army of notaries, some of whom had university training: John Morison, Thomas Hamilton and William Reid are only three such scribes incorporated.[26]

The chapter's own independence of the new archbishops seems to have been at the university's expense. The university echoed their defiance, for when Blackadder was first appointed to the see they supported the chapter's own choice, George Carmichael, and were about to re-elect his relative William as Rector in 1484 when he eloquently dissuaded them from doing so.[27] In 1491, a document in the classical hand of the capitular president, Archibald Whitelaw recalled nostalgically how 'blessed were our predecessors who flourished in the best of republics under prelates adorned with meekness, justice, virtue and liberty so that they could pass their lives in freedom, that in business they might exist free from danger or live in leisure with dignity'. A solid phalanx of twenty-four canons signed this protest, including John Ireland; clearly they would find it hard to accept Blackadder's protestations that he 'had lever have our said bretheris hartis than thar gudis'.[28] Delaying by the chapter seems to have accounted for Blackadder's, and later Dunbar's, inability effectively to endow the university with minor benefices. Blackadder's project for a university chapel dedicated to Jesus and Mary to be funded from his personal legacies had perhaps better hopes of fulfilment.[29]

The chapter, however, put their own meeting place, the chapter-house of the cathedral, freely at the university's disposal. The earliest meeting recorded in the upper chapter-house completed by Bishop Turnbull was that of the faculty in June 1453.[30] Innumerable other meetings of faculty and university occur, mostly in the lower chapter-house, though for a time the university made greater use of the upper.[31] When mass was said in the lower chapter-house, the reference is clearly to the adjacent altar of St Nicholas sited beside the doorway. These locked places provided privacy and security for the conduct of business. On one occasion the faculty met 'at the west door', the great ceremonial door.[32] Between this door and the south porch of the nave stood the aisle of St Michael and this was the Rector's 'auditorium' where he heard the cases referred to his tribunal.[33] Adjacent to the upper chapter-house stood St Catherine's altar, where a meeting is recorded in 1480, and adjacent to St Martin's (behind the high altar) where the faculty met in 1496.[34] Altars in the lower church used once only were St Andrew's and St John Evangelist's (the latter, the parish altar).[35] When the Cadzow foundation at the St Mary altar in the lower church was transferred to the arts faculty they met there on most occasions.[36] But the St Nicholas altar was the statutory place.[37] Most university services and sermons would take place in the cathedral, though the Blackfriars and Greyfriars churches must have been used on the occasions when the preacher was a friar.

Among other ecclesiastical bodies who impinged on the university were the vicars choral who substituted daily in the cathedral for the canons of the chapter. Their highly elaborated singing and organ music would compensate in some measure for the seeming lack of training in musical theory. A master of the song school, Hugh Brown, was certainly incorporated in 1476,[38] and, like later vicars of the choir he may have prosecuted further studies.[39] The court of the barony of Glasgow was conducted in the hall of the vicars to the north of the cathedral, and some of them had certainly legal expertise.[40] One such vicar choral, William Tod, a student, was left a lute in the will of Walter Beaton, rector of Govan, and former university Rector.[41]

A minor official in whose deanery Glasgow was situated was the dean of Rutherglen who summoned university members to his deanery chapters and against whom the bishop's help had to be invoked.[42] The chapel of St Thomas Martyr and the collegiate church also made some contribution to university life, though the latter was the town's kirk in the main.

The Blackfriars kirk was, and continued after the Reformation to be closely identified with the neighbouring college. The Dominicans had occupied the site on the east side of the High Street since the mid-thirteenth century and for a short time before 1454 the Hamilton building was in their hands. The Blackfriars kirk and bell were important for the neighbouring university. Meetings are said variously to take place in the church, chapter-house, place or monastery of the Friars Preachers and the Blackfriars bell may have regulated these as well as other university activities.[43] Some time after the Reformation the university constructed a new place for the bell.[44] One result of the reform of the order to be mentioned later was a concentration of its material resources. The old 'parvis' (*paradisus*) was leased out to tenants as Paradise Yards. The upper paradise yard, for instance, leased to tenants in 1558, was described as lying with the pedagogy yard immediately to the north; before its conversion into gardens this area could well have been at the university's disposal.[45]

Since in subsequent times the university was to acquire the whole area, it is interesting to note the other boundaries of the 'parvis': the western boundary was the grass meadow yard, the eastern their 'mekill grit ʒaird', and there is mention also of their coalhouse yard and west yard that ran in line with a brewhouse and hedge, 'that gangis lyinlie with oure brewiss and ascheyn hege'.[46] But there were earlier leases and at the back of their 'auld borne' the friars sowed mustard and also grew fruit such as 'pipanis and ympis'.[47] The destruction of their bell-tower referred to earlier led to much rebuilding, which accounted in 1534 for royal gifts 'to the bigging of the kirk'.[48] The prior, Alexander Barclay, had a special gift at the king's hands in 1528.[49] He was indeed a bit of a courtier, proud of his ability to write in a court hand.[50] He can be identified with the person of that name from Moray diocese found at Paris in 1506 and subsequently at Orleans,[51] who was incorporated at Glasgow in 1530.[52]

In Scotland the Blackfriars or Dominicans had for long been an order with intellectual interests. For instance, a Friar William *Scotus*, regent and master in theology, preached two university sermons in Paris in 1281,[53] and several further examples of the kind could be cited. It is not surprising, then, that early meetings of the university often took place in their chapter-house in Glasgow, that is to the south of their church in the east cloister, to which their school was perhaps adjacent. Friar Thomas Robison, of Chester priory but a native of Glasgow, was in 1476 given permission to transfer to the Glasgow house to teach the liberal arts.[54] He was ordained priest as Friar Thomas of Scotland in December 1469 at Bologna where presumably he studied theology[55]; he was still a member of the Dominican study house there in 1471–2.[56] He was in the order's Edinburgh house in 1509.[57] His name is not, however, in the Glasgow university records, where the first friars recorded are Patrick Sharp, John Symson and Andrew Hasting in 1457, presumably as students or teachers of theology.[58] One of the disadvantages of the friars from a university viewpoint was their constant mobility from town to town and occasionally from country to country. Sharp was later prior successively at St Monance (1467) and Inverness (1501).[59] Hasting was later with Robison in Edinburgh. In 1470 the vicar general (there being as yet no separate Scottish province), John Mure, was incorporated. In 1487, Friar David Craig, professor of theology from Paris, was in the university with his bachelor, a Friar Denis.[60] The Dean's book in this year records the foundation of a Dominican student's chaplainry by William Stewart, canon of Glasgow, who also built up their west cloister; the Rector and regents shared the patronage of it along with the burgh's provost and bailies.[61]

In 1481—and this was the century of Savonarola with his prophetic sermons on the Apocalypse—the Scots Dominicans acquired the status of a province and began to feel the breath of reform. John Mair has described the riots provoked by the Paris pastry cooks and other tradesmen (who foresaw a decline in their order books) when the reform of the Congregation of Holland was adopted there.[62] A parallel struggle, involving royal and episcopal intervention, took place in Scotland.[63] The older group of friars had been inclined to accept commendatorships of Trinitarian houses like Failford and Houston: the younger group, led by an energetic and inspiring professor of theology, John Adamson, backed by Bishop Elphinstone and the Congregation of Holland, looked more to the example set in Scotland by the Observant Franciscans who were then in their first reforming fervour.[64] There were still learned Dominicans, but reactionary in their learning, like the enemy of Reuchlin, Benedict of Scotland, mentioned in the 'Epistles of Obscure Men'.[65]

The first centre of the new group appears to have been Aberdeen university. John Spens, who was in the Aberdeen house in 1507, appeared as prior of Glasgow and bachelor in theology in 1517.[66] Robert Lyle studied theology at both Aberdeen and Glasgow, in the latter under Adamson's auspices. He was subprior at Perth in 1545, and it is he who, as licentiate of theology, must have attended the Church provincial council of 1549.[67] Not all the inhabitants of the Glasgow Blackfriars would by any means be theologians, and the learning of some, acquired in the Lutheran Rhineland, also involved them in trouble with the ecclesiastical authorities. In any event, both they and the Greyfriars tended to settle their best men in St Andrews, the ecclesiastical capital, or Edinburgh, the royal capital.

The Grey Friars or Observant Franciscans were brought to Glasgow by Bishop Laing and Thomas Forsyth, parson of Glasgow, sometime between 1473 and 1479,[68] though Alexander Vaus, originally of Galloway, rector of Lochmaben and later canon of Aberdeen, became a bachelor of decreets at Glasgow before entering the order as a Conventual Franciscan at Padua in 1460.[69] Glasgow regents who joined the Observant branch of the order included John Whiteford and James Pettigrew, the latter becoming their provincial.[70] The pious chronicler of the Scots friars says that they heard student confessions; less credibly, that the Glasgow house held twenty friars, and that the first recruits were 'converts' of Friar Cornelius of Zieriksee.[71]

Two interesting observant friars turn up as witnesses in a university document of 21 February 1495.[72] The first, Friar Patrick Ranwick, is said to have advised James IV to wear his iron girdle; he became provincial and warden (guardian) of their house in Stirling.[73] The second is Friar William Touris who may have written in Glasgow his poem, 'The Contemplacioun of Synnaris', a work of some learning and great spiritual earnestness, published in London in 1499 by Wynkyn de Worde, and extant in three manuscripts. (The print was sponsored by Richard Fox, bishop of Durham from 1494 to 1501, whom we have already met as patron of the Greenwich Observant friary of which the guardian was a Scot.[74]) But few names of consequence are associated with the Glasgow Greyfriars. Friar John Paterson, warden in 1531, described also as a 'theologian', attended the provincial church council of 1549.[75] He retired in 1560 with some friars into voluntary exile in Lower Germany and died abroad.[76] Others include Friar Andrew Cairns and Friar Andrew Cottis, the latter warden of the house in St Andrews in 1549, involved there with an English Dominican in a rather trivial dispute about prayer to the saints.[77] Cairns acted as mediator between James V and the earl of Angus and, according to the Greyfriars obituary, was qualified in canon law and theology when he died in 1543 in Edinburgh.[78] A difficulty facing Black and Grey friars in the immediate pre-Reformation period was that the more defections to Protestantism there were from their ranks, the more establishment-minded the others had to show themselves as official preachers and inquisitors, with, therefore, the possibility of conniving at, instead of flaying, abuses.

By the early sixteenth century, Glasgow had three hospitals, a leper hospital of St Ninian, bishop Durisdeer's foundation of St Nicholas and Roland Blackadder's hospital. How much genuine medical knowledge was available to the hospital masters is doubtful, but at least there would be some interest in herbal gardens or in sections of kitchen gardens devoted to their cultivation. Mark Jamieson, vicar choral particularly associated with the hospital of St Nicholas and a member of the Rector's council in 1555, had two herbal books of Marco Brasavola and Leonhard Fuchs on which he has entered the herbs' names in Scots.[79]

A number of other medical men are known to have had university connections. For instance, William Baillie, who graduated in Glasgow in 1468,[80] proceeded some time later to study medicine at Bologna where the medical faculty was conjoined to the arts faculty and he appears there among the 'artists' lecturing on feast days in 1486-7 as 'D. M. Gulielmus Balce de Scotia, artistarum et medicorum dignissimus Rector'.[81] In 1490 he is described as parson of Carrington and assignee of Alexander Baillie of Carfin, presumably his father, as later the laird of Carfin was described as William's brother.[82] He had ecclesiastical pluralities showered upon him and royal gifts, for in 1508 he was described as doctor in medicine and prebendary of Provand. As rector of Restalrig he was witness to a deed concerning the will of Bishop Elphinstone, whose death-bed in Dunfermline he must have attended.[83] A matriculated student of 1469, William Wallace, was nine years later royal physician to James III.[84] About October 1469 Andrew Gorleth, master of arts and doctor of medicine, was received at St Andrews and about the same time a doctor of medicine, whom the later scribe interprets as Andrew de 'Garleis', was received at Glasgow. George Buchanan's account of him suggested that royal envoys brought him back to Scotland from the court of Charles the Bold, whose death and that of James III he predicted. Buchanan calls him Andreae, the Latinised form of the Flemish Andries, but he was, in fact, a Dane[85]; his stay in the university was of the briefest. Equally mysterious is Gerard of Brabant, physician (*medicus*), who lived in High Street in 1486.[86]

Andrew Borde, ex-Carthusian from London, in Glasgow in April 1536 to collect opinions on Henry VIII's differences with the papacy, was a medical man of some native ability and a protégé of Thomas Cromwell, to whom he wrote that he was 'now . . . in a lytle Unyuersyte or study named Glasco, wher I study and practyse Physyk'.[87] Another student in Glasgow who, after matriculating in 1505, went on to become a doctor of medicine at Paris was William Manderston, whose medical interests did not prevent him writing handbooks in logic and morals and becoming a professor in theology. He later lectured at St Andrews.[88] The young George Buchanan acted as his servant at the Ste Barbe college in Paris.[89]

The grammar school near the Greyfriars and close to the university on the other side of the High Street taught the first two liberal arts, grammar with versification and rhetoric and possibly also some logic. Soon after 1461, when, with the gift of this separate building, the grammar school became dissociated from the pedagogy, the university apparently began to be dissatisfied with the new arrangements and a conflict arose with the diocesan chancellor who resisted interference in an appointment he considered his statutory perquisite.[90] On 13 September 1494 Martin Wan, the chancellor, obtained Blackadder's support in prohibiting Master David Dunn from openly teaching grammar to boys and youths in town and university as he had been publicly contemptuous of the idea of getting the necessary permission from him.[91] This looks like an influential member of chapter forcing the archbishop's hand. Dunn, a Glaswegian and graduate of 1490, had become a university official and a non-regent and regent master, and the university must have been trying to improve the standard of university Latin.[92] Clearer evidence emerges in 1501 when Blackadder, armed with a papal indult, felt strong enough to deprive the existing St Nicholas hospital master of his chaplainry and appoint in his place Cuthbert Simson with the duty of residing daily in the pedagogy and teaching grammar there to the students every day.[93] Simson, a student at Paris with Hector Boece and other Scots, was before his arrival in Glasgow schoolmaster in Irvine and may have introduced new textbooks.[94]

Of masters of the city grammar school, John Reid was closely associated with the university in 1508.[95] Matthew Reid was bursar from 1521 to 1525;[96] Alexander Crawford from 1549 to 1555.[97] These schoolmasters could ensure a hearing for the claims of a more elegant Latin on the examining board. Robert Maxwell, previously grammar 'preceptor' in Paisley, held the Glasgow post by the Reformation when he disputed with the Reformers: and a sample of his Latin verse has been printed.[98] The new Latinity is, however, in no distinct way reflected in the entries in the extant Dean's and Rector's books. As to the proportion of scholars from local grammar schools, the few names of such scholars, garnered from Glasgow, Ayr and Dumbarton records, were not traceable in the university.

The relations between town and gown were regulated by Bishop Turnbull in line with the original grant of Rectorial jurisdiction by Bishop Wardlaw in St Andrews. Turnbull obviously had Wardlaw's charter of privileges before him as he made his own grant, later confirmed by his own seal and that of his diocesan dean and chapter. Both grants gave power to the Rector, doctors, masters and other members to buy and sell their own goods in the city, all over the regality and in the diocese's lands and ports. Goods brought for trade were excluded, but the sale and purchase of all necessities relating in particular to food and clothing were included, and that as often as and whenever they so desired, without the need to apply for a licence or pay customs duty.[99]

The largest single item of food was bread and ale. All members had to observe the burgh's laws and customary practices regarding the assise of bread and ale and the pricing of foodstuffs. Delinquents were to be punished, when their names were intimated to the provost or any bailie. Unless correction took place within eight days (Wardlaw allowed only a single day), the Rector himself could transfer the case to his tribunal. If a difference of opinion were to arise between town and gown, the case automatically became the bishop's responsibility. Wardlaw's phraseology is more severe on the provost and bailies than Turnbull's, allowing for possible neglect and even guilt in their administration of justice, and he takes account of the baronies of the prior and the archdeacon in the town. Wardlaw expressly gave the Rector's court jurisdiction in cases of injury, except severe cases, inflicted on university members by clerics or layfolk. Turnbull is less specific: he reserves the cognition of all major cases, inclusive of severe injury, to himself. Wardlaw's Rector was to have jurisdiction in all civil causes, actions and complaints raised by scholars against anyone in the city, regality or other lands of the bishopric at the scholars' will, and the Rector was to employ a summary procedure and dispose of the case according to legal process. Turnbull restricts the jurisdiction specifically to minor cases and those financial cases or contentions, disputes, fights and quarrels between university members and citizens or anybody within the episcopal jurisdiction.[100]

Summary justice was characteristic of the Rector's court. Andrew de Durisdeer in 1461 amplified Turnbull by explaining that the Rector had power to cite, admonish, suspend and excommunicate and inflict Church censures on any culprit, and in fact do all the bishop himself could do in the circumstances.[101]

Wardlaw laid down that, in contractual or civil questions members need not appear before any judge, ecclesiastical or lay, in preference to the Rector, but they might prefer to choose another Church court. More precisely, Turnbull granted the faculty in minor cases and disputes, but only to such members as were resident in Glasgow, the right to choose as judge the Rector, the bishop or his official—saving the privileges of dean and chapter: appeals to the bishop, who was mostly absent, would delay judgment and Durisdeer limited jurisdiction to Rector and official. Turnbull had added that anybody complaining of the Rector's jurisdiction could appeal to the bishop.

Wardlaw and Turnbull both allow that hostels and houses in the burgh should be rented at a rent fixed by a composite body of 'taxers' made up equally of university and civic representatives elected and sworn. One who duly paid the rent and whose conduct as tenant could not be faulted could not be evicted by his landlord 'except for other causes expressed in law'. Beneficed men in both dioceses, acting regents, students or those wishing to take up study could not, if they were able to benefit from a course of study and had the bishop's permission, be forced to reside personally in their benefices. Meantime they could enjoy the fruits of their livings, but must see that curates carried out divine service in praiseworthy fashion in their absence.

In both dioceses also esquire beadles, familiars, servants, scribes, stationers (about whom at Glasgow we know nothing) and parchment sellers, along with their wives, children and maidservants, were included in this privileged body. Sometimes we find such people incorporated; for instance, in 1534, John Spottiswoode, Rector's servant[102]; in 1451, the university beadle, John Moffat[103]; in 1514, William Baxter, elder, burgess of the university.[104]

The provost, bailies and other burgh officials on assuming office each year would take oath in the Rector's hands and at Glasgow, in the bishop's presence; or in his absence, in the presence of one or more deputies of the Rector or university. They took an oath to respect all the privileges and liberties granted up to the present or in future to the university and to see to their observance. There might be some significance in Wardlaw speaking of 'your university' and Turnbull of 'ours'.

Wardlaw added a section concerning the wills of scholars omitted by Turnbull. What happened to the books of a scholar who had failed to pay his rent was not specified. Both founders exempted their members from all burghal tolls, exactions, vexations, capitations,[105] nightwatches, guards, collections, burdens, 'angarii et perangarii' (services and additional services), imposed for any cause in future. The impression is given that, in spite of the near identity of both documents, the Rector's tribunal at Glasgow was less firmly based than that at St Andrews.

The town was never involved, except for a perhaps involuntary grant from the income from Tron customs, in the payment of salaries to the university, and, in the absence of the records of the Rectorial tribunal and the burgh court proceedings of the period, no conclusions can be drawn as to how town and gown collaborated or conflicted at this time.

The king, as we saw, had his rôle in securing the university foundation. The original aim was to stem the outflow of currency by students travelling abroad, but, since many of the high officials in the royal offices had of necessity to train abroad, the aim was modified, if not nullified, from the start. One Glasgow student of 1456 even entered the service of a papal physician; Thomas Dalgleish was scribe to the physician of Pope Paul II.[106] The Stewarts founded no royal lectureships as at King's College, Aberdeen. James II did grant the usual tax exemption and promises of protection on 20 April 1453,[107] echoing verbally James I's grant of privilege to St Andrews. He expresses the wish that the Christian people under his rule may benefit from the production of men of knowledge, good counsel and good life so that justice might be promoted and orthodoxy preserved. He therefore exempted from various national duties and services certain named officials (Rectors, Deans, Procurators of nations, regents), and masters, beadles and other minor officials and scholars, unless they were prelates and so long as their studies continued. In 1472, William Glendinning, Rector, complained that these privileges were under attack: 'certain consuls of our supreme lord, the King, have stirred his serenity' to impose taxes on beneficed students. It was decided to send to the 1472 parliament three orators with a transcript of the original exemption— Rerik, the archdeacon, William Elphinstone, junior, and Duncan Bunch. Bunch, with Athilmer from St Andrews, had also been present in parliament on 6 May 1471.[108] The end-result was that the home universities were encouraged by the renewal, under the great and secret seal,[109] in December 1472 by James III of their grant of exemption and the usual warning against the export of Scots coin was reinforced. James IV's privilege, granted on 7 June 1509 (after Blackadder's death), confirmed previous grants, but mentioned 'dayly officiaris', as the number of university officers had swollen since the date of the original grants.[110] All these grants were confirmed by the Duke of Albany on behalf of the young James V on 20 May 1522, but an attached endorsement informs us that the Rector of the time and the principal, John Mair, had to dip into their own pockets to cover the expense of this renewed exemption.[111] A similar exemption was granted by Mary of Lorraine and Governor Arran at the request of Walter Beaton, Rector, on 6 July 1547.[112]

Kings, like bishops, were also important sources of patronage for graduates, but this is a field where little work has been done for this period. Duncan Bunch's merits were recognised after his appearance in parliament by appointment to a royal embassy to Rome, and there are more personal examples of royal patronage. Mr John Blair who was incorporated at Glasgow along with Andrew Stewart, uncle of the king, was in 1467 paid for writing out for James III 'a book called Mandvile', that is, Mandeville's travels.[113] Dr William Baillie was summoned to Edinburgh to the queen and prescribed certain drugs for her, and about the same time he or Dr Robert Shaw, it is not clear which, prescribed six pounds of fine green ginger and four pounds of citron 'comfits' for the king.[114] In 1508 the treasurer's accounts mention a payment 'that nycht, to the King to play at the tables with Maister William Bailzee'.[115] At a humbler level, an incorporated student of 1474–5, John Caird (Kerd), was already chaplain of the king at the chapel of Holy Trinity of Christ's Well, also called 'the Kingis bred hous of Cristiswell' near Inverkip.[116] Indeed, the doctor or lawyer or theologian must have been a useful counsellor to any man of substance.

Another area of future enquiry is the influence of local lairds. Lord Hamilton's foundation was unique in Scotland during the medieval period. It replaced a system of unendowed hostels or pedagogies with no security of tenure beyond the term of the lease. It may have saved the future of the infant university: but it could also have helped the increasing trend to satisfaction with a simple qualification in arts, at that time a qualification in Aristotle. It may indeed be that a training in Aristotle was as good a way as any to prepare a young student from a tiny burgh or a modest farming family, who did not want him to follow an 'illiberal' craft, to hold his own at all levels of fifteenth-century society.

NOTES

1. *Glas. Mun.*, ii, 18.
2. *Ibid.*, ii, 59.
3. *Ibid.*, ii, 63. George W. Campbell, 'The Seals of the University of Glasgow', *Transactions of the Glasgow Archaeological Society*, new series, iv (1903), 65–74.
4. Sir John Horne Stevenson and Marguerite Wood, *Scottish Heraldic Seals* (Glasgow, 1940), i, 165. There is a medieval representation of the motto 'Via, veritas, vita' in the Rossdhu Book of Hours, for which, cf. George Hay and David McRoberts, 'The Rossdhu Book of Hours', *IR*, xvi, 7. However, our earliest surviving seal is post-Reformation.
5. *Glas. Mun.*, i, 16.
6. *Ibid.*, ii, 75.
7. J. A. F. Thomson, 'Innocent VIII and the Scottish Church', *IR*, xx, 23–31.

8. D. E. R. Watt, 'Scottish Masters and Students at Paris in the 14th Century', *Aberdeen University Review*, xxxvi (1955); and 'University Clerks and Rolls of Petitions for Benefices', *Speculum*, xxxiv (1959).

9. *Glas. Mun.*, ii, 90.

10. *Ibid.*, ii, 226.

11. Watt, *Fasti*, 378.

12. *Ibid.*, the case of John Brown.

13. *Glas. Mun.*, ii, 105.

14. *Auctarium*, iii, 27 (procurator of the German nation); Wils, *Matricule*, ii, 456.

15. Leslie J. Macfarlane, 'The Primacy of the Scottish Church', *IR*, xx, 111–29, puts the matter in context.

16. *Glas. Mun.*, ii, 248–9.

17. *Ibid.*, ii, 284. Cf. *ibid.*, ii, 253, where 'Blakcae' should read 'Blakcader' (Liber Decani, 97).

18. *Glas. Mun.*, ii, 127.

19. *Ibid.*, ii, 174.

20. *Ibid.*, ii, 196.

21. *Ibid.*, ii, 186.

22. *Ibid.*, ii, 190, 149.

23. *Ibid.*, ii, 145.

24. Cowan and Easson, *Medieval Religious Houses*, 208.

25. Burns, 'New Light', *IR*, ii, 74.

26. *Glas. Mun.*, ii, 126, 153–4.

27. *Ibid.*, ii, 96–7.

28. *Glasgow Reg.*, ii, 475–8, 483. Lever = rather.

29. J. Durkan, 'Archbishop Robert Blackadder's Will', *IR*, xxiii, 139.

30. *Glas. Mun.*, ii, 182.

31. Arts faculty in upper, *ibid.*, ii, 97–146 (with breaks), 231, 257.

32. *Ibid.*, ii, 221.

33. *Ibid.*, ii, 126, 129, 137.

34. *Ibid.*, ii, 232, 268.

35. *Ibid.*, ii, 238, 214.

36. *Ibid.*, ii, 287ff. In Liber Decani, f 149, an inaugural meeting was held there in October 1555.

37. *Ibid.*, ii, 23, 84 (the latter a reference to the altar 'in the chapter-house').

38. *Ibid.*, ii, 86.

39. *Ibid.*, ii, 86, 109, 126, 134, 137 etc.

40. A vicar choral was clerk of a barony court held in 'ye wiccares place of ye Qweir' on 10 December 1527, a lay court presided over by the archbishop. GUL, Murray Ms 645, 430–1.

41. He left Tod 'meum le luyt', SRO, Commissariot Record, Glasgow Testaments, i, 99. For Tod, *Glas. Mun.*, ii, 168, 172.

42. *Ibid.*, ii, 105.

43. *Ibid.*, ii, 55, 67, 140, 198, 206, 208.

44. *Ibid.*, iii, 558–9, 570. Further details about these Blackfriars buildings can be found in Appendix B.

45. GUA 16299. Within their cloister there was a 'knot' or elaborately cultivated garden, *Glas. Mun.*, i, 120.

46. A hedge of seven 'aspens and ash-trees' was near the west cloister gate, *Liber Collegii Nostre Domine*, 183.

47. GUA 11615 (December 1554); other leases are in 11616, 21017, 21487, 22003.

48. *ALHT*, vi, 200.

G

49. *ER*, xv, 425; xvi, 24. He had come from Wigtown priory, *ibid.*, xiv, 279, 425.
50. National Library of Scotland, printed book, Marko Marulič, *Evangelistarium* (Basle, 1519), has 'frater Alexander Barclay with ye curt hand'.
51. Paris University, Sorbonne, Reg. 91, f. 80. *Miscellany of the Scottish History Society*, ii (Edinburgh, 1904), John Kirkpatrick, 'The Scottish Nation at the University of Orleans', 96. This identification is supported by R. J. Lyall, who has written about the other Barclay, 'Alexander Barclay and the Edwardian Reformation 1548–52', *Review of English Studies*, New series, xx (1969), 457–61.
52. *Glas. Mun.*, ii, 156.
53. One at Christmas, Paris, Bibl. Nationale, Ms Lat. 14947, ff. 188v–189r, 197v–198r.
54. British Library, Additional Ms 32446, f. 10. A. B. Emden, *A Survey of Dominicans in England based on the Ordination and Episcopal Registers, 1268-1538* (Rome, 1967), 436, identifies him wrongly with another English friar of similar name.
55. C. Piana and C. Cenci, *Promozioni a Bologna* (Quaracchi/Florence, 1968), 162.
56. C. Piana, *Ricerche su le Università di Bologna e di Parma nel secolo XV* (Quaracchi/Florence, 1963) Spicilegium Bonaventurianum i, 113.
57. SRO, Elibank writs GD 32/21/14. Along with Friar Andrew Hasting, below.
58. *Glas. Mun.*, ii, 66.
59. *ER*, vii, 438, 513; xi, 84, 365.
60. *Glas. Mun.*, ii, 100. If Denis is his second, not his first, name, he might be Friar Robert Denis, at Stirling in 1526, SRO, Duntreath Muniments, section 1 (45).
61. Printed *ibid.*, i, 337.
62. Cited in R. A. Villoslada, *La Universidad de Paris* (Rome, 1938), 71.
63. Anthony Ross, 'Notes on the Religious Orders in Pre-Reformation Scotland', *Essays on the Scottish Reformation*, ed. McRoberts, 191.
64. The ejected, 'unreformed' Provincial held the Trinitarian house at Houston, Reg. Supp. 1442, f. 77.
65. In Ulrich von Hutten, *Operum Supplementum* (Leipzig, 1867), ii, 725, the editor, Edvardus Bocking, unaware of Scots Dominicans at Cologne, identifies him mistakenly with Thomas Lyle of Scotland, a Scotist defender of the Immaculate Conception. John Hoy, a Scots Dominican and Albertist at Cologne *c.* 1480, on the other hand, emerges as a man of some intellectual adventurousness, cf. Löhr, *Die Theologischen Disputationen*, which also quotes other Scots disputants. A Friar Andrew of Scotland was at Cologne in 1483, and a Friar John Prod of 'Ercht' convent in Scotland (Perth? Edinburgh?) at Heidelberg in 1482. B. M. Reichert, *Registrum Litterarum Salvi Cassettae et Barnabi Saxoni* (Quellen und Forschungen, etc., vii), 2, 46, 64.
66. *Liber Collegii Nostre Domine*, 213; P. J. Anderson, *Aberdeen Friars, Red, Black, White and Grey*, Aberd. Univ. Studies (1909), 66.
67. R. Milne, *Blackfriars of Perth* (Edinburgh, 1893), 169. 'Leitch' was Joseph Robertson's interpretation of the strange form given by the scribe of the Baluze manuscript, *Concilia Scotiae*, Bannatyne Club (Edinburgh, 1846), 83, 208 ('Lieu' for 'Liell'?).
68. Cowan and Easson, *Medieval Religious Houses*, 131.
69. *Glas. Mun.*, ii, 62, 184; Reg. Supp. 521, f. 5; and 523, f. 247. He was friar at Dundee, W. Moir Bryce, *The Scottish Grey Friars* (Edinburgh, 1909), ii, 129.
70. *Glas. Mun.*, ii, 221–88, 243. Bryce, *Scottish Grey Friars*, ii, 308, i, 329, 345.
71. Bryce, *Scottish Grey Friars*, ii, 187.
72. GUA, 16375; shortened version without witnesses is in *Glas. Reg.*, ii, 462.
73. Bryce, *Scottish Grey Friars*, ii, 177.

74. *Devotional Pieces in Verse and Prose*, ed. J. A. W. Bennett, STS, third series, 23 (1949), 64–169. Regarding the English edition, see the Introduction, xxv–xxxii. Friar Touris is mentioned in the customs expenses of Aberdeen in 1502, *Exch. Rolls*, xii, 87.

75. *Concilia*, 84.

76. *Essays in the Scottish Reformation*, 199–200 and note.

77. *Ibid.*, 226; *Glas. Mun.*, ii, 147.

78. *Ibid.*, ii, 104, 261; Bryce, *Scottish Grey Friars*, 76–7, 316.

79. *Glas. Mun.*, ii, 174; Durkan and Ross, *Libraries*, 119–20, nos. 4 and 6.

80. *Glas. Mun.*, ii, 208 (not dispensed from post-graduate lecturing).

81. U. Dallari, *I Rotuli dei Lettori Legisti e Artisti dello Studio Bolognese dal 1384 al 1799* (Bologna, 1888), 130.

82. *Acta Dominorum Concilii*, 151; *RSS*, i, 318, 1430.

83. *Acts of the Lords of the Council in Public Affairs*, ed. R. K. Hannay (Edinburgh, 1932), 29; *ALHT*, iv, 361, shows he held both Restalrig and Provand.

84. Fraser, *The Lennox*, ii, 117; *Glas. Mun.*, ii, 75.

85. *AFA*, 168; *Glas. Mun.*, ii, 74; and see the review notice of *AFA* by J. Durkan in *English Historical Review*, lxxxi (1966), 112.

86. *Glas. Reg.*, ii, 450.

87. Mackie, *University*, 28.

88. *Glas. Mun.*, ii, 120; *AFA*, clviii.

89. *IR*, xv, 186.

90. In October 1477, George Lorne, master of the grammar school, was incorporated as a member of the university, for what purpose is uncertain: *Glas. Mun.*, ii, 87.

91. *Ibid.*, ii, 37–9.

92. *Ibid.*, ii, 110, 251 (where 'Downye' should read 'Dwyne'), 257, etc. A few months earlier the grammar schoolmaster's living was augmented by the grant of St Ninian's hospital chaplainry: *Glas. Reg.*, ii, 488.

93. *Glas. Mun.*, i, 39–41.

94. Durkan, *Turnbull*, 57. A scholar of his at Irvine was a future graduate William Gibson, *Prot. Bk. Simon*, 6, 24.

95. See Appendix G. *Prot. Bk. Simon*, 267; chaplain of the altar of St Ninian, he had wounded two youths, one of whom had David Muirhead as his master (pedagogue?); the latter was chaplain of St Roch, *ibid.*, 465, 501.

96. *Glas. Mun.*, ii, 139, 149–50.

97. *Ibid.*, ii, 170, 297, 299 (Archibald is a scribal error).

98. *Essays on the Scottish Reformation*, 165–6.

99. *Evidence*, iii, 173–4; *Glas. Mun.*, i, 7–9.

100. It is possible that the Rector's tribunal at St Andrews no longer conformed in some respects to Wardlaw's original design.

101. *Glas. Mun.*, i, 16.

102. *Ibid.*, ii, 160.

103. *Ibid.*, ii, 55. The same probably as John de Montefixo alias Moffeth, priest of Glasgow diocese, notary in 1452, GUA, 12425. Described in 1468 as priest of Dunkeld diocese, bachelor in decreets, when acting as notary in Dumbarton, GUL, Murray Ms 643, f. 473.

104. *Glas. Mun.*, ii, 129.

105. The Glasgow text reads 'capitulationibus'.

106. *Glas. Mun.*, ii, 64, 193; *Essays on the Scottish Reformation*, 279.

107. *Glas. Mun.*, i, 6.

108. *Ibid.*, ii, 79. *APS*, ii, 98; parliament also hindered projects for endowment by

preventing the annexation of benefices, which may account for the subsequent confinement to minor chaplainry endowments.

109. *Glas. Mun.*, i, 25–7.
110. *Ibid.*, i, 47.
111. *Ibid.*, i, 47–9.
112. *Ibid.*, i, 54–6.
113. *ER*, vii, 500. He is one of two John Blairs at Glasgow, *Glas. Mun.*, ii, 64, 65, 191, 192.
114. *ALHT*, ii, 445, 477.
115. *Ibid.*, iv, 95.
116. *Glas. Mun.*, ii, 83; *RSS*, i, 400.

11. The Student

'Item . . . of the haly preching making to the peple without ony rehers
of opinable materis bot in the sculis . . .'
                    Complaint of James V to Lords of Council, 1534
                'Clerkis diuine wyth problewmys curius . . .
                To the Palice of Honour all thay go.'
                        Gavin Douglas, *The Palice of Honour*

A STUDENT'S-EYE view of the university is not what immediately
emerges from books of statutes and records of university and faculty
acts. This chapter will therefore inevitably contain a miscellany of
matters and leave many questions either unanswered or, at most,
treated superficially and fleetingly.

The young student arriving at the university had to learn to listen to
lectures in Latin and even to speak Latin in his leisure time as far as
possible. If there was no grammar taught in the university, he needed
a grammar school education, which he could acquire in the university
town, living with relatives or clerical friends, or in his home town.
The technical jargon of unfamiliar subjects could certainly leave the
young student at sea, but we have no evidence in medieval Scotland
of cruel initiation ceremonies for 'bejants' ('yellowbeaks', fledglings),
as new students were called.

He could not be a bachelor till he was fourteen, but he could, of
course, arrive earlier. In 1556 at an enquiry regarding the archbishop's
powers in relation to the provost of Glasgow, Mr John Colquhoun,
parson of Stobo, stated that he was fifty-four and had been a canon
of Glasgow for thirty years or so.[1] As it is likely that he came up to
the university in 1513 at the age of eleven,[2] the probability is that he
is the same as the vicar of Glasgow who graduated at St Andrews six
years later, aged seventeen, certainly before—by statute—he should.[3]
An even younger graduate was Robert Houston, licensed in arts for
special reasons, perhaps episcopal favour, though a mere fourteen-
year-old.[4] John Houston, his brother one presumes, licensed with
him, was just as young, about fifteen, and was afterwards to remember
how Archbishop Dunbar 'wes crabbit' when a certain Michael Lindsay
was made bailie: he later became a regent.[5] On the other hand, William
Hamilton, afterwards parson of Cambuslang, went up to university at
fifteen.[6] John Hall, Glasgow burgess, was eighteen on incorporation
in 1524[7]; he remembered Archbishop Beaton I and how he 'tuik na
tent to the chusing of the ballies'. Mr John Laing, later parson of Luss,

lived with Sir Robert Clerk, subchanter, in the time of the same archbishop: he went up to university in 1519 at the age of twenty-one.[8]
Mr David Wilson, 'citiner', claimed to be forty-three: he thus would
be nineteen on incorporation and was about twenty-three before final
graduation in 1536.[9] Some of these students were natives of Glasgow,
others stayed with other clerics, and the Houstons, it would seem,
lived in the bishop's castle.

Another source records that in 1564 various notaries appeared in
Edinburgh for confirmation by the Lords of the Council.[10] Mr James
Blair of Orchard was a married man of forty-two: he was therefore
licensed in arts in 1537 at the age of fifteen,[11] and was created a notary
two years later. George Brownside and Ninian Swan were both entering
university in 1551, the former at the age of twenty-three and the second
at nineteen.[12] Henry Gibson was created a notary in 1549 by William
Salmond, count palatine (*comes palatinus*); but he was a bachelor
two years later at the age of seventeen and over twenty when he
graduated at St Andrews.[13] Salmond was perhaps still in the university:
he was already master of arts when he was incorporated in 1546.[14]
On the whole, it appears that the statutes regarding age were kept:
but they plainly did not have the force of the laws of the Medes and the
Persians. Evidence concerning St Andrews graduates is a little more
abundant and the age range there could be quite considerable.

On coming up to university, students might already be beneficed
clerics though this in itself is no sure guide to age. Andrew Stewart,
subdean of Glasgow, entering university in 1456, was stated to be
fifteen the previous year: he was the brother, however, of James II.[15]
Some were future prelates; one, David Beaton, was a cardinal-to-be.[16]
He probably graduated in arts (the Dean's book lacks entries for these
years) before proceeding to Orleans to study law.[17] There are future
bishops like William Elphinstone, founder of Aberdeen university, who
entered the university in 1457 and did not graduate till he was twenty-
five, if Boece is to be believed: certainly Boece has the time-span
between incorporation and graduation right, for Elphinstone took five
years, unusually long unless perhaps he did some law concurrently.[18]
Robert Cockburn, later bishop of Ross, was already a master when he
entered Glasgow in 1491.[19] He became a friend of Symphorien
Champier, a French disciple of Marsilio Ficino, and was something
of a humanist himself.[20] While at university, Andrew Durie probably
stayed with the archbishop for he was a witness in the castle close in
1514.[21] His 'indolence and absorption in secular affairs' made him a
worthless abbot of Melrose, but he was something of a court poet
and not without learning when he died as bishop of Galloway.[22]

Most of the canons, parsons and vicars incorporated are from

Glasgow diocese, naturally, though there are a few from Argyll: John, rector of Kilmore in Lorne, for instance, whose surname defied the scribe's interpretative powers.[23] There were also the odd arrivals from Galloway, Sodor, Dunkeld, Dunblane, St Andrews, Brechin, Aberdeen and even Ross dioceses. Other clerics range from provosts of collegiate churches, such as Bothans, Methven and Kilmun,[24] to simple parish clerks, two from Govan, one each from Cadder and Paisley.[25]

Occasionally persons with no indication of nobility in the university records describe themselves in papal supplications as having vague baronial and even royal connections and it is hard to know how far to believe them, but there is an impression of at least some increase in the number of sons of lairds at the university after the 1496 Education Act. A few are sons or brothers of great barons: Alexander Sinclair, son of the earl of Orkney; various sons of earls of Lennox; John Campbell, son of Argyll; Patrick Graham, brother of Montrose.[26] About the time that the earl of Glencairn was secretly entertaining John Knox, his brother, John, and his son, James, were in the university.[27] There is a fair sprinkling of local lairds, and, from further afield, James Stewart, the son of the laird of Rosyth, and William Livingstone, son of the laird of Easter Wemyss.[28] An occasional burgess of Glasgow also appears on the lists, but several names are entered with no note of origin attached and the St Andrews habit of mentioning the student's nation is not followed. To get a fair picture it would be necessary to compile a biographical register with the help of printed and manuscript sources. Occasionally, however, the native place of more humble members is duly recorded: Thomas Bennett of Linlithgow, Robert Ellem of Coldingham, Robert Mure, cleric, of Stirling, Thomas Watson of Dumbarton.[29]

Christian names are mostly John, James and Robert in drab succession; Andrews, Patricks, Thomases and Williams are common. Dougal, Aeneas, Eugenius (for Ewan?), Colin and Lachlan occur each only once. Of Old Testament names Adam is most favoured, but Abraham and Eliseus occur once. There appears to be a single Vedast (Vaast, an associate in France of St Remy).[30] Some names were automatically Latinised by the scribe: Neil becomes Nigellus and Duncan, in one case, Dominicus.[31] Strangely, in medieval Glasgow, there is just a single Kentigern and he was from north of the Forth[32]; one Fergus and a few Constantines, Gavins and Ninians.[33] Saxon-sounding names like Cuthbert, Oswald, Roger, Hugh, Herbert and even Edward occur in ones and twos: but George and Henry are more frequent. Humphrey had some popularity.[34] There is a single Jasper.[35] Norman was so unusual that the scribe did not feel the need to enter the surname.[36] Maurice, Denis, Roland and Charles occur likewise in ones and twos.

There is a single Lancelot, who seems to have been popularly called Lansy for short.[37] But the most promising future philosopher should surely have been Aristotle Crawford.[38]

The students were posted on arrival to their 'nations' or provincial groupings. Unfortunately the representatives of nations are not always indicated. There were generally no problems at Rectorial election time with the first nation (Clydesdale) or the second (Teviotdale). But in the sixteenth century the third nation (Albany) was seldom able to muster a single name: not surprisingly when the chancellors Archbishop Dunbar and Cardinal Beaton were battling with croziers.[39] There was nobody from the fourth nation (Rothesay) in 1470, but thereafter it managed a representative. The nation system was perhaps a practical way of teaching geography, for, unlike Aberdeen, where 'cosmography' was part of the course,[40] geography was left at Glasgow to be picked up incidentally, possibly even at the dinner table!

Ireland had no university and as one might expect there was the occasional Irish student in the Rothesay nation, though there does not seem to be any rationale for their appearances. Patrick Odechane, probably the modern surname Deane, is found in 1511,[41] and a clutch of Irish students arrived in 1527, for reasons not immediately obvious, though Irishmen must occasionally have taken up residence in schools in Scotland. Cermacus Turnlewe is probably Cormac Turley; Cognatius Ocheyll possibly O'Kelly or O'Keily; Nicholas Ogalquhoir is O'Gallagher; Duncan Odoneyle is O'Donnell or O'Donnelly; Duncan McThenocht is McKenna.[42] In 1547 Cornelius Ardochadye is presumably O'Docherty.[43] On the whole, a poor harvest from Ireland.

We have no extensive information at Glasgow about conditions of residence. We are told in the 1452 statutes 'that no student in arts who is rich (*potens*) may bide at table except with the regents of the arts faculty by weekly payment (*bursaliter*) or by the pedagogy method as at Paris. Those who are unable (*impotentes*) to stay in this way will pay to the regents a Scots noble, but, if anybody has sworn poverty, this will be remitted.'[44] There were thus three social grades: the rich student paid the maximum burse, that is, the same as the regent, or in some cases more; those who could not afford the maximum paid one noble in lieu and did not eat with the regents but separately, making their own arrangements; the poor, being financed by their betters, may have been required to act as servants or, as at Paris, beg from neighbouring religious houses.

With the foundation of the Hamilton College, however, there was a new state of affairs.[45] The statute was then reworded to read, 'Each student in the arts faculty who is rich will bide at the same table (*commensaliter*) with the regents and will not be admitted to the study of arts otherwise, and concerning this there will be no dispensation at all. Poor students or those unable to stay in this way with the regents, will pay the price laid down in the faculty statutes, and, as many as can be suitably and honourably placed there, will sleep in the college rooms, the price of a room being first arranged with the regents.' From this it appears that the poor also made some token payment, and that all were expected to rent rooms on a sliding scale related to their individual purses. A later modification of the second part stated that 'students not rich enough to bide at the same table as the regents will have a room inside (*infra*, i.e. in college) for a price to be fixed by the regents', later again, fixed by the principal. Any infringement of these dispositions was to involve perjury on the student's part. The picture seems reasonably clear. Certain well-off students got the same food as the regents ('commons'); others got less ('short commons'); the poor served the tables of the rich and ate afterwards. There would be herrings and eggs on fish days, again measured out according to status, and wheaten bread would be confined to high table, while the rest had rough oaten bread. Exceptions to these boarding rules may, however, have been made for townsmen and burgesses.

The calendar is said to go back to the time of the first foundation.[46] The opening day of First Term was originally 19 October (the morrow of St Luke)[47] and it ended on 20 December (vigil of St Thomas, apostle). Second Term began on 8 January (two days after Epiphany) and continued till the vigil of Palm Sunday (a variable date, dependent on Easter). Third Term opened on the day after Low Sunday and went on till the vigil of Whitsunday (both variable dates). Fourth Term lasted from the Thursday before Trinity Sunday (again variable) till 13 September (the vigil of the Exaltation of the Holy Cross).

These first arrangements on the whole endured, but a second calendar altered the end of the Easter break to follow the Glasgow synod, which was held on the Tuesday of Low Week. The final holiday was at first lengthened to begin on 1 September (St Giles) and that shortened the final term, but this break was cut again at the other end by making First Term start, as at St Andrews, on 1 October (St Remy), allowing for a break at Michaelmas of 29–30 September.

If the academic year seemed a long and sombre prospect to a fledgling student, it was at least broken by Sundays and other feast days; lectures could take place even then, but not the formal 'ordinary' lectures. The most important of these were generally overtaken in the first two terms, though they could be given throughout the year. At the end of Fourth Term, though, there would be no academic activity at all ('cessations in all faculties').[48]

The custom of celebrating not only the greater feasts, but the morning after ('morrow') as well, was in the spirit of the French expression 'la tristesse des lendemains des fêtes.' The great feasts, the morrow of which was also free, were (*a*) certain feasts of our Lord: the Epiphany (6 January), the Ascension (variable), Corpus Christi (variable); (*b*) certain feasts of the Virgin Mary: Candlemas (2 February), the Annunciation (25 March), the Visitation (2 July), her Assumption (15 August), her Nativity (8 September), her Conception (8 December); (*c*) feasts of certain saints: the Nativity of St John Baptist (24 June, Midsummer); Peter and Paul (29 June); Translation of Thomas Martyr (7 July); and Andrew (30 November). The appearance of Thomas Martyr (Becket) in this list might raise an eyebrow, but in view of the close Hamilton connection with the university and of David Cadzow, its first Rector, with the saint's chapel, it is readily explicable.

St Kentigern (13 January) was eventually also allowed the privilege of a free morrow, the excuse being the feast of relics on that day; though one might ask why there had been no exposition of relics before. Single holidays were apportioned as follows:

January:	Kentigern (13), Conversion of Paul (25).
February:	Chair of Peter (22), Matthew (24).
March:	Thomas Aquinas (7), Gregory, pope (12).
April:	Ambrose (4), Mark (25).
May:	Philip and James (1), Finding of the Holy Cross (3), John before the Latin Gate (6).
June:	Barnabas (11).
July:	Mary Magdalene (22), James (25).
August:	Peter in Chains (1), Laurence (10), Bartholomew (24), Augustine (28), Beheading of John the Baptist (29).
November:	Martinmas (11), Clement (23), Catherine (25).
December:	Nicholas (6).

This may seem a long list, but compared with some foreign institutions, holidays in Glasgow were relatively restricted. Later, for more mundane reasons, the feast of St Patrick (17 March), was added, with the limp explanation that it was James IV's birthday and also the date of one of the Dumbarton fairs.

The holidays, however, were not complete holidays, as on certain days mass attendance would be obligatory and on others there might be university sermons. The beadle or his deputy had to celebrate mass on the morrow of St Luke and likewise on the day of the Rectorial election (which was also the cordiners' feastday, Sts Crispin and Crispinian). This particular decision was due to William Elphinstone, junior, Rector in 1474, and the mass was to be said at the altar in the cathedral chapter-house, that is at the altar adjacent to which was the St

Nicholas altar in the lower church. It involved a fine of two shillings for non-attendance and the obligation could not be dispensed except by common consent. The mass for the session opening was to be attended by all university members, from doctors to new students, who were to wear ankle-length gowns for the occasion, their Sunday best, so to speak, and give an offering to be put to the beadle's use: the fine for absence or leaving before the service ended was to be decided by the Rector in council. The Rector was expected to put on a special show on certain days, probably university sermon days on which the beadle had to be present. These days are listed in the manuscript, though omitted in the printed edition, in this order: the 'days of Pentecost, the Ascension of the Lord, the Trinity, Corpus Christi, the Assumption of St Mary, All Saints, St Andrew apostle, the Lord's Nativity and Epiphany, the Glasgow synod, the feast of St Kentigern, the Purification of St Mary, Palm Sunday and the Translation of St Thomas Martyr'.[49]

Lord Hamilton's college foundation of 1460 was meant to favour a more collegiate religious life. New regents in their first institution to the college by the bishop had to promise to fulfil the desires of the founder in this regard. At the end of midday and evening meals regents and students were obliged to rise from table and recite prayers for the universal Church, the King and Queen and the souls of his lordship and lady Euphemia, his wife. If the regent were a priest, he was to say mass and especially at the readings stand at the corner of the altar and ask the people for their prayers on the founders' behalf. For this he was to be shown special favour. Should an oratory or chapel be built—and this was obviously part of the original plan, though it does not seem to have matured till Blackadder's time—regents and students were to foregather there every Saturday and after vespers or evensong recite the anthem to the Virgin Mary, 'Ave Gloriosa', with collect and commemoration for the founders. In the interim they were to recite it in a low key in the Blackfriars kirk. They had also to attend his obit in the cathedral.[50]

On 2 May 1462 it was decided with the assent of all masters (not student members, as this was a faculty of arts decision) that there would henceforth be a notifiable general congregation on the feast of the Translation of St Nicholas (9 May).[51] Its purpose was to choose two discreet masters to be stewards to make necessary and useful provision for a perpetual annual faculty feast to be held in the college of arts on the nearest Sunday or feastday after 9 May. The faculty would decide on the procedure annually, dependent on the mildness or otherwise of the weather. To finance it, a compulsory charge of three shillings on all beneficed men present in congregation or in town, of eighteen pence on non-beneficed, and of like sums on under-graduates was to be exacted by these stewards. Attendance was obligatory under pain of a fine of two shillings. On the day set for the feast, all were to be present at mass at eight in the morning in the St Thomas Martyr chapel to the north of Glasgow, not the chapel of the same dedication given to the university by Thomas Arthurlie.[52]

The stewards of the feast were to bring to the chapel a supply of flowers and leafy branches bought from the special fund and there distribute them to university members after the service. There was then to follow a procession on horseback along the public highway from the 'upper part' of the city downhill to the mercat cross and back to the college of the faculty.[53] This was to be a solemn and serious affair like that at St Andrews, though it was also a 'regal procession', that is, headed by the king of the feast,[54] possibly comparable to the King of the Bean celebrations at Epiphany where there was a mock king in fancy dress.[55] Members were to arrange themselves in the correct order before setting off. At St Andrews there had been disputes about precedence.[56]

Not so at Glasgow, where peace and concord were to reign. On the return to college there would be refreshment available, a joyful occasion where, however, masters could still discuss the future of the faculty and its numerical progress. Any discordant conduct in word or deed arising from personal dislikes, litigation or past involvement in controversy was to be forgotten and forgiven in an atmosphere of mutual congratulation as they honoured the 'prince of peace and joy'.[57] After the banquet all the masters were to proceed in the company of the students to a suitable 'place of solace' where some masters and students were, on the advice of other masters, especially faculty regents, to take part in the performance of a short play (*interludium*) or something similar that people would enjoy. Performers were not to suffer academically because of the time given to rehearsing these plays, and the faculty would even give a readier ear to their just petitions. If arts students or clerics in town were willing to share in the expense of the faculty spread on this occasion, they too could attend.[58] The price must, however, have put this banquet beyond the normal student purse.

From time to time the death of some master or student[59] would provide a more sobering interruption in the life of study. On the funeral day there were to be no ordinary lectures and all masters and students, on notification by the beadle, were to attend the mass and burial service and not slip away before it finished but to stay and recite the seven penitential psalms and the litany at least, or devoutly read vespers for the dead. The penitential outlook of an earlier day is reflected

most clearly in the former student, Walter Kennedy, who certainly
had his lighter side, if William Dunbar's *Flyting* is to be trusted. The
gamesome Dunbar teased him as 'prince of Lollards', but Kennedy
could be a very serious-minded young man as his verses show.[60]
Kennedy arrived in 1476 and his studies covered the period in which
the first wave of Observant Greyfriars arrived in Glasgow.[61] It may
be that it is to their house he refers when he writes of the octogenarian
that:

> I hard in till ane place of freirris
> Off ordour gray makand grit dule.

His devotional verse meditation, 'The Passioun of Crist',[62] is not, like
that of Friar Touris, divided according to weekdays, but based rather
on the hours of the divine office (from matins to vespers and compline
of the week before Easter): but it is enlightening to think that these
two poets may have lived close by each other.

Student devotion did not rule out, however, student vice on occasion,
although our statute makers explicitly drew attention to the contradiction involved. All graduates and students were warned against wild
behaviour for which their new-found freedom gave scope. The usual
list of student offences follows: gluttonous over-eating, excesses with
loose women, frequentation of public taverns, late-night meals, dicing,
the allurements of street-walkers and all carnal pleasures. If ugly
rumours were in circulation about anybody in this respect, the person
concerned was to be directed by the university or faculty to mend his
ways. He was also to be denied privileges if a master, or promotion
if a student, until he had done so.[63] But there must have been increasing
external criticism of student behaviour and this may have been the
main factor in encouraging the production of new and more drastic
procedures.

The earliest hint of such procedures was under James Stewart,
Rector, provost of the collegiate church of Dumbarton in 1522. The
first change proposed was fairly harmless. It concerned graduates
failing to take their masters' insignia, customarily taken some time
after licence, following a period of withdrawal of as much as four
months. They ignored the Rector's letters reminding them of their
obligation taken under oath. Henceforward no bachelor was to be
admitted to licence, unless he took caution in the hands of the college
steward, if there was one, or otherwise in the hands of the Rector or
Dean or their councils, to complete the formalities within a mere
eight days.[64] An example of this new practice of the principiation
following hot on the heels of the licence was when licentiates of 1543
were licensed on 22 December and principiated on Christmas eve.[65]

With regard to the rest of the agenda put forward by Stewart as Rector, the university preferred to adhere for the present to the ancient statutes. The Rector wanted at least one regent to accompany the band of students to mass in the cathedral on Sundays and other solemn feasts as had become customary, but in addition wanted him to call out their names both on leaving and entering college and note and punish the absentees. Both Rector and Dean were united in wanting the regents when the college gates closed to carry out their inspection of the rooms, note absentees and punish likewise accordingly. Moreover, the whole policy of the university, it was suggested, would collapse in ruins if the masters, students and other members neglected to appear at congregations: therefore both Rector and Dean called for the collaboration of all if their offices were not to be made to look ridiculous. One wonders if there must not have been a deeper reason for this general apathy in the lack for some time of genuine participation of the whole body in university and faculty government. Or perhaps the collegiate peace of the period was exacting too high a price in decreasing student freedom: tighter regulations then being enforced in the Paris colleges would encourage this trend to a more iron control.

But Stewart's stringency is echoed a decade later in regulations to cope with the increased lay influx. In 1532, under Rector Adam Colquhoun and Dean James Neilson, there was a new, stricter regulation regarding student attendance at mass ('the supreme sacrifice') and vespers. The ankle-length gowns are not this time mentioned but students were to be dressed according to quality as they answered the bell calling them to congregate with their teachers (*preceptores*) in the place fixed by the regents.[66] The changed religious terminology reflects contemporary controversies over the sacrament. No student of whatever dignity, faculty or pre-eminence (the last word may refer to nobles) was to carry a weapon in the shape of a sword or dirk either in the college or out of it, except for special reasons to be approved by the regents, and, if any scholastic vandal did so, he was to lose the weapon and be expelled till he improved his manners.[67]

The nearest thing to a student spy or 'wolf' was one of the theological students at Aberdeen.[68] But the 1532 stringency at Glasgow made the regents into 'wolves', who now were to insist on attendance under pain of expulsion and had to note down the absentees from ordinary and extraordinary lectures. After the little college bell struck for silence and for the regents to begin their nightly scrutiny, no student was to leave his cubicle without leave. The birch had now been introduced and for the first offence the offender against this rule had to loosen his breeches for punishment, which grew sharper for the second offence and for the third brought permanent expulsion. Moreover, to improve the quality of spoken Latin, no student, even if only a boarder, could bring in a servant or relation unless he could speak school Latin under penalty of the expulsion of the servant concerned and of his master if he tried to oppose his removal. A curious rule with a blend of harshness and realism referred to students playing permitted games in the open. If they ran into the Rector, Dean or regents on such occasions, they were not to continue playing without their leave, but to withdraw and flee as best they could. If found wandering in the streets without their preceptors' licence they were to be whipped as before in the presence of their fellows as an example to other transgressors. If they proved incorrigible, perpetual expulsion again was the answer.[69]

Probably for good reasons there were alterations in faculty procedure and disregard of the ancient statutes to meet the requirements of a new age, but when as many as thirteen determinants of 1539 proceeded to bachelorship on one single day, the element of serious disputation must have been sadly curtailed. In the same way their masters' act in the first term of the following year was also now very formalised and shows yet another Parisian trend towards abbreviated courses.[70]

The tendency for servants to be incorporated, especially Rector's servants, may mean that they too were not only subject to college rules but found this a cheap way of paying for their studies. The whole question of university costs bristles with difficulties because of sliding scales in use for the different categories and the unfamiliar system of tipping one's betters which we shall examine. And while a poor student could expect a richer student to help him through his degree fees—*noblesse oblige*—he might need to beg as well.

In theory learning was free, so elaborate casuistic explanations existed for charging fees. The young student had two main types of charge, one on the university and the other a faculty charge. The university scribe got a small fee for writing each name at incorporation. Before determination, a fee had to be paid to the Rector.[71] For the fees in the faculty of canon law we are referred to lost statutes.[72] It is not clear if, by the time of our revised university statutes, faculty and university beadles have coalesced and there is a vagueness about the beadle's salary and domicile. We are told that henceforward student religious were not to be excused the beadle's fee, but friars seem to be exempted.[73] Licentiands also had to pay the Rector a substantial sum apart from what the faculty burse had to pay him.[74] Before determination there was a faculty fee of one Scots noble, with eighteen pence to the faculty beadle, as well as a small offering by undergraduates to him on 1 November (All Saints). From the examinee for bachelorship similarly there was a small payment to the beadle before admission. Stiffer sums were exacted from the faculty bursar before licence and in mastership. The examiners for licence also received a small fee, and on principiation the candidate's masters. There were also fees to the university bursar.[75] The Dean of faculty, by a decision of 1454, collected small fees at bachelorship and inception.[76] Dispensations, moreover, from the two-year post-graduate lectures were costly affairs.

Some students found it impossible to pay these fees and had to find some security or other. The result was that the faculty of arts especially began to amass a number of such cautions for payment which were not always honoured. Lists of these are to be found here and there in the records. In 1463 Duncan Bunch, for example, had in his faculty fund £7 Scots and three books handed in as pledges at an estimated value of twelve shillings in all.[77] They were either redeemed or sold or perhaps found their way into the library.

University members often had to stand security in other circumstances. For instance, in January 1491, the Dean obtained the consent of the rest of the masters of arts that William Ker who had been licensed two years previously should principiate by the next feast of St Peter in Chains (1 August) for which Robert Braidfoot stood caution for five merks Scots.[78] Braidfoot was a chaplain and otherwise not known to be in the university. About 1488 he and a Mr George Ker had a licence from James III and letters of protection to help them visit the apostolic see and other places in Europe for the prosecution of their affairs.[79] He was a scribe and has left a manuscript he copied in 1481 containing Eutropius's *Roman History* in a recension of Paulus Diaconus and a transcript of Raimundo Marliano's Index to the *Commentaries* of Julius Caesar. Braidfoot may have acted as scribe to Archibald Whitelaw, the royal secretary and a considerable classical scholar.[80]

Gaps in the records make any exact counting of heads in the medieval university a hazardous affair. It was approximately a quarter of the size of St Andrews,[81] with about 1113 incorporations in all recorded in the period 1451–1558.[82] The first half-century accounted for well over half of these, and the average for the whole period was a mere ten per annum. Some years had more sparkle than others: in 1451 there were over sixty matriculations (though some of these were evidently staff members)[83] and in 1518, with the arrival of John Mair, forty-three. It is doubtful if the college buildings had room for more than fifty students at one time. In the early period at least the bulk of students were in the nations of Clydesdale and Teviotdale; the western ports of Rothesay nation had to wait another century before beginning to expand. The first staff arrivals were from the east. They had, as we saw, the royal blessing in bringing the light of civilised ways to Scotland's darker corners. But any royal plans to stem the export of currency by sponsoring home institutions seem to have foundered on the king's own propensity for European-trained counsellors as well as the unbroken stream of Scots abroad to Cologne, Louvain and increasingly, Paris. Occasionally, if only on visiting the city, he must have consulted its learned men and James II even sent his brother to Glasgow university. Robert III wanted to know from the French theologians of his time if it was possible to proceed against anybody up to four 'defects' (presumably, legal defeats) in a criminal case involving no criminal intention and in that way win the case: perhaps Principal Mair, at least, was faced with similar questions.[84] Where too would the Governor Arran's consort of viols find a more appropriate setting for their 1547 Glasgow performance than in the college founded by his ancestor?[85]

It was certainly customary for important visitors to appear at great academic occasions especially when the nobility graduated. When Alexander Erskine took his bachelor's degree, the scribe got carried away and wrote that he 'celebrated a really glorious act and paid out huge sums'.[86] The expenditure would be not only in banqueting but in gifts. Knowledge was a gift of God, a pearl of great price,[87] and could not be adequately compensated. Just as fees were scaled according to the donor's wealth and nobility, so likewise were gifts. But these lost their spontaneous quality and became almost entitlements. Bishops received better bonnets and gloves than regents, though the gloves were originally meant to be mere gages of loyalty to the other members of the guild of masters and scholars: hence in arts at Glasgow all masters in the faculty were entitled to an invitation and therefore to a gift.[88] The feast in the hall after the schools ceremony was another form of gift. The possibilities for venality in all this are, however, evident.[89]

An interesting three-cornered Parisian conversazione exists between John Forman, Jean Dullaert of Ghent and John Annand, then a regent in Paris, about the Paris custom of new students in logic having to present their regent with a cope. Hardly a day passed without him reminding them of the obligation. The cope was not exigible at Louvain and Cologne, so why Paris? Annand cited Aristotle. Had he not said that nobody could properly thank the gods, his parents and his masters? At Paris the regents went through a stupendous amount of work and thus like the Roman empire enjoyed privileges. Forman still was oblivious to the justice of the demand so Annand resorted to that last refuge of the pedant, the pun: Take money from rich arts students (*Cape a potentibus artistis pecuniam*); to which Dullaert retorted: Beware of taking money for arts students (*Caueas accipere pecuniam pro artistis*). With a final pun, Dullaert replied that those arts men who were richer (in ideas) were the poorest of men (in financial terms) and that most of the rich men were poor arts students. Mair was genial enough to air the problem, a purely Parisian one, though typical of other features of current academic practice that provoked grumbles.[90]

Academic dress is controversial and difficult and a subject in itself. The most frequent epithets attached to it are not 'elegant', but 'becoming' and 'honourable', sufficiently vague to allow for the vagaries of fashion.[91] Basically it refers to dress that becomes persons enjoying clerical privilege. Thus St Leonard's students who were non-bursars had not to wear secular clothes with slashed openings or whose cut was too short but tailored of woollen and linen material such as became grave persons of the clerical sort.[92]

The cope itself had assumed many diverse shapes in the course of its history. The great cope (or 'ordinary') was a round cope of ankle-length.[93] The small cope (or 'extraordinary') was a shorter version. At least two copes were presented to the Glasgow Rector on election.[94]

At his determination, a bachelor acquired the right to wear a bachelor's cope. This cope was pleated, the wrinkles evidently being appropriate to this stage of study: each group of three was required to have one between them, but even this requirement seems to have proved beyond ordinary means.[95] The arts Dean's cope at Glasgow was to be made at the common faculty expense in 1452.[96] Whether this was made or not, the gift of a scarlet hood by Patrick Leitch, senior, a hood perhaps Italian in style, seems to have been behind the move to authorise the tailoring of a master's cope with furrings in 1464.[97] Unfortunately, the colour of that is not specified; presumably it was scarlet to match the hood. By statute Glasgow conformed to Bologna usage, as far as Scottish clerical custom allowed.[98] At Bologna, all students were required to wear 'cloth of the statute' or alternatively 'black cloth', but Rashdall found this hard to reconcile with the fact that students of the German nation wore red.

The main requirement for the Glasgow Rector's dress in 1469 was that it should be recognisably distinct from that of other university members. On double feasts he was to turn up for processions in his better academic outfit. There is a reference in 1490 to a single university cope,[99] but the Rector had at least two.

The *toga* or gown is almost as elastic in its definition as a cope. The 1483 university statutes of Glasgow modified an earlier statute whereby all students in arts and canon law had to wear their gowns loose without girdles. These gowns probably persisted in use in later times. There are many other variations of the gown, but only a close comparative study of other Scottish universities would further the discussion of them.

The hood was, as its name itself declares (*caputium*), essentially a head covering, but whether always detachable or not is another question. In the fifteenth century it is already clear that the wardrobe keeper at Glasgow was mainly a custodian of hoods, who hired them out to students. The Glasgow records are singularly uninformative about dress, but in 1464 four to six arts hoods were ordered for the faculty of arts. Five years later, new hoods with furring were ordered for the faculty.[100] By 1479 there were five furred hoods, four blue and one red.[101] The use of blue may have been an attempt to conform to Bologna usage. The shade of blue is not given and it could have verged on bluish grey.[102] That these were hoods held in common and for student use is clear from the order of 1490 for the purchase and tailoring of six blue hoods with adequate furring.[103]

At Glasgow in 1481, the bishop chancellor gave Patrick Leitch, junior, the Rector, a hood well-furred with ermine and miniver above and underneath.[104] But this was only for special occasions and may have gone with a cope to match. Adam Colquhoun, a former Glasgow Rector, had in his possession a cope 'firrit with spottit arming' (ermine).[105] According to an arrangement of 1469 he also wore a hood with furred edges that fell around the shoulders or one lined inside with taffeta.[106] University hoods being re-tailored are mentioned in 1490.[107] Obviously all orders about hoods and their shapes were at the mercy of changes in fashion. In 1452 a Glasgow arts statute stipulated that no student might wear hoods 'swelling out too much in the circle of the face, which are plain evidence of light-headedness'.[108] For such dress offences there was a penalty of loss of the time that counted towards degree requirements.

An early statute ruled that no student in arts or canon law could wear a loose gown without a girdle, but this was modified later to remove the menace of perjury.[109] They would be handy items of dress, with scrips or even swords and daggers hanging from them and might have been of a different colour again from the gown. The reason for the original insistence on its use at Glasgow may have been that the loosening of the girdle was one of the master's insignia, a sign of his new freedom. The bonnet is another ever-changing item of academic wear. The bonnet presented at academic functions to the bishop had to be twice the cost of that offered to the Rector and other officers. The 'cornett cap' was denounced as a badge of idolatry after the Reformation. At first, however, bonnets were cylindrical, then became squarish in shape.

Glasgow required all arts students and graduates to wear ankle-length clothes at public acts, general congregations, church services, university and faculty sermons and similar rules existed for Rectorial elections. The faculty also forbade open stomachers of any colour, shawls (*humeralia*), beaked or laced shoes and over-ample hoods.[110] As to colours, it is clear that black was interpreted fairly broadly, Brereton[111] mentions in 1636 that grey and red gowns predominated during his Glasgow visit, but while the grey gowns could have been the serviceable equivalent of the modern denims they may have been a bluish grey relic of earlier times and the red gown a late importation from St Andrews. It may indeed be that, headgear and copes apart, the vestiarian controversy affected university wear less than did student fashions.

A 1533 statute at St Andrews shows that the university considered games and honest recreation necessary for the young as a rest for the spirit, a reward for work done and a preparation for future study.[112] Certain games were regarded as 'illiberal', unfit for freemen and as such entirely forbidden, such as dicing and especially, because of accompanying dangers, football.

These strictures against the medieval passion for gambling are found in the Glasgow arts statutes, and repeated in the university statutes, which echo almost word for word an earlier St Andrews statute.[113] Medieval football was so unregulated as to be positively perilous and the clerical status of the average student made it imperative that he suffered no bodily harm that might act as an impediment to orders. Nevertheless, ball games were extremely popular, though opposed by parliament as distracting the youth from archery.[114] The Glasgow students presumably used the Muir Butts in the college lands beyond the Molendinar.[115] Shrove Tuesday was an exception at St Andrews and no doubt everywhere. There, in 1535, sixpence was expended on a football by the arts bursar, but in 1537 a great 'schism' broke out on the links because the beadle removed the football. The town's provost (the game was probably with the town) seems to have confused the new ball with one of the old, with riotous consequences.[116]

If regents were nervous about the consequences of ball-game incidents, that is not too surprising. Robert Ross, a student who determined in 1471,[117] did not proceed to his licence. The reason is that while playing in the grounds of Hamilton's college of arts another student accidentally hit him on the left eye with a cabbage stalk, perhaps from a cabbage used, in default of something better, as a football. A film formed over the pupil and blinded the eye, but left it otherwise undamaged.[118] The immediate result of this was grave parental displeasure and Sir John Ross of Hawkhead began his efforts, related earlier, to wrest the St Thomas chaplainry of the Arthurlie foundation from the university. Eventually the quarrel was patched up. The offended student returned to the university and was continuously associated with it from 1490 to 1505 when he was archpriest of Dunbar.[119]

John Mair,[120] with reference to Sunday teaching, pointed out that, as feast days were free from lectures, youths would lie about in their rooms and other places hatching schemes and forming useless gangs. In the afternoon, he suggested, they could play at jumping or archery, but not engage in dancing. After expatiating on the need for games, Mair condemns some, such as dicing, as disreputable. Some are honourable: keeping a parrot or cage-birds or a monkey, making music on the monochord, all leisure pursuits which were to prelates and students as hunting and poaching to layfolk. (He did not mention cock-fighting, on record at St Andrews, which appealed to the student's aggressive instincts.[121]) The older folk, priests and lay, were free to play for a pint or a quart at board games in which they used checkers as well as men (chessmen!). Card games like trumps were allowable ('Eodem modo de chartis pro triumpho, cleka, beldosa et ceteris id genus').[122]

The earliest reference to billiards is post-Reformation. But 'cache', a kind of hand tennis, was played. Skittles ('kylis'), bowls, possibly alley-bowls, were common: and some early form of golf. In 1557, Thomas Forret of Glasgow sold a place of amusement (*lusorium*) called 'ly caichepule' near Ashkirk manse in the city. There was also a playfield near the Green mentioned in 1559.[123]

The game called *pugna numerorum*, the battle of numbers, is mentioned by Robert Gardiner in his St Andrews harangue of 1435.[124] This was a scholastic game—the ancient equivalent of Fun with Arithmetic—with two players who drew up their counters facing each other, odds versus evens, as in other board games. The counters were of different geometrical shapes (square, circular, triangular), of different colours and each numbered on its face. The leading numbers in each group were called either earls or dukes and the groups were arranged according to numerical types, a system that goes back at least as far as Jordanus Nemorarius. The counters could be built in pyramids to teach, it would seem, the theory of progressions. 'The Buke of the Howlat' with its mention of 'bernes batalland on burde' seemingly refers to this game.[125]

At Glasgow from 1462 the celebration of the Maytime feast of St Nicholas looks like a typical 'inbringing of summer' festival. The branches with bunches of flowers and leaves are reminiscent of maypoles. The 'locus solatii' ('solace place') could also have been an open-air playfield rather than an interior setting.[126] But the northern chapel of St Thomas Martyr that had been mentioned in connection with this festival probably disappeared a few decades after its union with the collegiate church of Hamilton.

Beyond all this study and play, however, the student had still to look to his career prospects at the end of the academic day. It would have been helpful to draw up an exact and neatly categorised statistical survey covering these, but this would involve the compilation of a biographical register of all Scots students such as we do not yet have. In the circumstances perhaps a few impressionistic observations may be excused. There does appear to be some increase in the number of lay students towards the end of the medieval period and these may have been the men who clamoured for a participation in the affairs of Church and State hitherto denied them. A preponderance of these and even of the clerk-students (apart from the mass of clerical non-students content with their abysmal ignorance) were by this century graduates in arts alone with little law and less theology, but, so it seems, with spiritual energies which the lack-lustre leadership of the period appeared prepared rather to stifle than to release.

Even before final graduation, students had their eye on their future. For example, Michael Fleming, while still a bachelor of arts at Glasgow in 1472 and only eighteen, was already making approaches to the Roman curia.[127] A sample of the effects of the sort of patronage a country youth might obtain from the presence of the great at university functions is William Lawtie, future minister at Banff and Inverboyndie, who, as a youth, must have caught the eye of the archdeacon of Glasgow. He graduated master in Glasgow in July 1543, aged about seventeen,[128] and is later found with the archdeacon in Peebles, the archdeacon's prebendal kirk. From there he went to Cullen, where the collegiate church was of the archdeacon's foundation, becoming chaplain of St Anne and song schoolmaster.[129] It is only because he was registered as a notary in February 1564 that we learn that before moving to Cullen he was a clerk of Glasgow diocese and born, in fact, near Glasgow at Lochwinnoch.[130] Future readers in the kirk who were in the university about this time were Patrick Wodrow and Ninian Swan.[131] Glasgow as well as the east coast ports may have been invaded by 'the disputaris of the bukis and opinionis' of Luther.

Some schoolmasters were university-trained. A Dumbarton schoolmaster c. 1512 to c. 1540 was Matthew Forsyth, a Glasgow graduate of 1500.[132] There are few Ayr men in the university records. One of these was a schoolmaster, Gavin Ross, whose graduation is, however, not recorded. Great precision in these matters is not possible with such defective records.[133]

Even so, some picture of the medieval university and the medieval student emerges. He was not cut off from society nor from the questions raised in it by enquiring minds, however second-rate some masters may have been or however shop-soiled the philosophy had sometimes become that they handed down. Opinions would often be aired in the schools before they got a general airing. The major defect was the small size of the institution, but its survival probably meant that as many as a thousand more Scots got higher education than otherwise would have happened and, of course, the university's presence was a fortunate chance for the development of industrial Glasgow in centuries to come. The best of our vernacular writers (and Henryson and Bellenden were at Glasgow) were university men. John Mair was prepared in his Paris days to give a certificate of approbation even to such an untoward personality as Ramon Lull, but he was ageing when his geniality was tried by the 'Wycliffite' excesses, as he saw them, of Luther as well as of the 'Radical Reformers'.[134] There must have been some opening-up and relaxation of tensions in the final decade before 1560 with the rhetorical logic of Rudolph Agricola[135] infiltrating into St Andrews and the philosophical gadfly Peter Ramus, long enjoying the clear patronage of a relative of the Queen Dowager, the Cardinal of Lorraine; yet there is no hard evidence (rather the contrary) that in Scotland he had as yet penetrated any college portals. Indeed, one has the impression that some layfolk and schoolmasters outside the universities were, in this respect at least, more intellectually venturesome. Nevertheless, the university's double didactic and moral function was not fated to cease, while the student himself was not so cocooned that he would not survive immersion in a world where both abstraction and rhetoric could soon be purged of their unreality.

NOTES

1. Various papers regarding Glasgow, SRO, RH.11.32/1.
2. *Glas. Mun.*, ii, 128.
3. *AFA*, 329.
4. *Glas. Mun.*, ii, 286.
5. *Ibid.*, ii, 287; RH.11.32/1. Information regarding age is taken from this document, unless otherwise stated.
6. *Glas. Mun.*, ii, 136.
7. *Ibid.*, ii, 149.
8. *Ibid.*, ii, 137. Clerk was subchanter 1510–39, Watt, *Fasti*, 169.
9. *Ibid.*, ii, 158, 287.
10. J. Spencer Muirhead, *The Old Minute Book of the Faculty of Procurators 1668–1758* (Glasgow, 1948), 18–19.
11. *Glas. Mun.*, ii, 287, 289.
12. *Ibid.*, ii, 171.
13. *Ibid.*, ii, 298; *AFA*, 403. A 'count palatine' had the faculty of creating notaries and could delegate it to a 'viscount palatine'. SRO, NP2/1, f. 91
14. *Glas. Mun.*, ii, 168.
15. *Ibid.*, ii, 64; *CPL*, xi, 1–2.
16. *Glas. Mun.*, ii, 125.

17. *Miscellany of the Scottish History Society*, ii, 98.
18. *Glas. Mun.*, ii, 65, 196; Boece, *Vitae*, 60.
19. *Glas. Mun.*, ii, 108.
20. 'Robert Cockburn, Bishop of Ross, and French Humanism', *IR*, iv, 121–2. He became almoner to Louis XII in 1517: Paris, Bibl. Nat. MS fr. 22861, no. 28.
21. *Glas. Mun.*, ii, 128; *Protocol Bk. of Gavin Ros*, 96.
22. A. Ross, 'Notes on the Religious Orders', *Essays on the Scottish Reformation*, 217. He was a student at Montpellier in 1515, *ibid.*, 310 note. John Rolland mentions his poetic gifts.
23. *Glas. Mun.*, ii, 75.
24. *Ibid.*, ii, 214, 82, 84.
25. *Ibid.*, ii, 81, 146, 170, 277.
26. *Ibid.*, ii, 195, 80, 102, 160.
27. *Ibid.*, ii, 173, 176.
28. *Ibid.*, ii, 205, 286.
29. *Ibid.*, ii, 69, 109, 111, 187.
30. The Vedast Anderson and Vedast Muirhead are probably identical: *ibid.*, ii, 77, 197.
31. *Ibid.*, ii, 61, 147–8, 154, 156.
32. *Ibid.*, ii, 97, 102. There are, however, four Quintins.
33. *Ibid.*, ii, 93, 117, for the two Constantines.
34. *Ibid.*, ii, 76, 117, 128, 137, 292.
35. *Ibid.*, ii, 68.
36. *Ibid.*, ii, 64. It was Scott, GUA, 14235 (witness in 1455).
37. *Ibid.*, ii, 86, 225.
38. *Ibid.*, ii, 140.
39. *Ibid.*, ii, 147–63. St Andrews was much nearer and better equipped. Some former Galloway students such as Michael Agnew, Wigtown sheriff and notary, will be found in *Wigtownshire Charters*, ed. R. C. Reid (SHS, ser. 3, Edinburgh, 1960).
40. *Fasti Aberdonenses*, 265.
41. Edward MacLysaght, *More Irish Families* (Galway, Dublin, 1960), 82.
42. *Glas. Mun.*, ii, 153.
43. *Ibid.*, ii, 176. E. McLysaght, *Irish Families: Their Names, Arms and Origins* (Dublin, 1972), 106, 117, 120–1, 153, 195, 197.
44. *Glas. Mun.*, ii, 30. The 'burse' was reckoned on a weekly basis, but paid by the term. The Glasgow muniments only occasionally record a student as 'pauper'.
45. *Ibid.*, ii, 17–18.
46. *Ibid.*, ii, 16–17.
47. *Ibid.*, ii, 22–3 (where the original dates have been erased from the manuscript).
48. *Ibid.*, ii, 16–17.
49. *Ibid.*, ii, 5, 22–3, 84; Liber Decani, 100; Liber Rectoris, 151.
50. *Glas. Mun.*, i, 11. For his cathedral obit, *Glas. Reg.*, ii, 616.
51. This was in imitation of St Andrews, which celebrated the May feast of St John before the Latin Gate, until the sixteenth century, *AFA*, lviii, note. Some of these congregations were recorded at St Andrews in the faculty record, but not so at Glasgow.
52. See above, p. 26.
53. *Ibid.*, ii, 39.
54. *AFA*, 322.
55. *Ibid.*, 38.
56. *Ibid.*, cxxxiii, note.

57. There is an echo of a phrase from the Hamilton foundation, 'ad locum unde exierunt flumina', Ecclesiasticus 1, 7. Cf. *Glas. Mun.*, i, 11.

58. *Ibid.*, ii, 40. For 'communio' read 'conuiuio', GUA 26615.

59. *Ibid.*, ii, 23, t. 1, c. 3, should probably read 'magistri seu incorporati'. The 'students' may have been missing from the original version.

60. Cf. *Maitland Folio Manuscript*, i, 255, 342, 364.

61. *Glas. Mun.*, ii, 86.

62. *Devotional Pieces in Verse and Prose*, ed. J. A. W. Bennett, 7–63.

63. *Glas. Mun.*, ii, 19; 23–4, t. 2, c. 1. Hannay, *Statutes*, 86.

64. *Glas. Mun.*, ii, 142–3.

65. *Ibid.*, ii, 295. The older term for inception, principiation, had now, however, fallen into disuse.

66. *Ibid.*, ii, 40ff.

67. Such expulsions are not recorded and may have been temporary, but other regulations explicitly lay down the penalty of expulsion for good and exclude any possibility of further promotion to degrees.

68. *Fasti Aberdonenses*, 264.

69. *Glas. Mun.*, ii, 41.

70. *Ibid.*, ii, 290–1.

71. *Ibid.*, ii, 13, 20, 30, 40.

72. *Ibid.*, ii, 20.

73. *Ibid.*, ii, 13. The last beadle recorded, David Kirkland, was chaplain of St Mungo in the lower church, and as such occupied the building immediately to the south of the principal's house.

74. *Ibid.*, ii, 20, 40 (there are variations in the sums named).

75. *Ibid.*, ii, 19–20, 30.

76. *Ibid.*, ii, 38.

77. *Ibid.*, ii, 198. These were often expensive law codices as the Bursar's Book at St Andrews shows.

78. Omitted in printed edition. Liber Decani, 102.

79. Edinburgh Univ. Library, Laing MS iii, 322, f. 1. Though a graduate, George Ker's graduation is not recorded but he was listed among absentees from congregation in 1482, *Glas. Mun.*, ii, 237. He was presumably in a 'higher' faculty. Cf. *ibid.*, ii, 90.

80. National Library of Scotland, Adv. Ms. 18.3.10. Braidfoot witnessed Whitelaw's charter of gift to Currie Kirk in 1493, *RMS*, ii, 2154.

81. *The Scottish Tradition: Essays in honour of Ronald Gordon Cant*, ed. G. W. S. Barrow (Edinburgh, 1974), 'The Provinces of the Scottish Universities', 92, by R. N. Smart.

82. Some names are absent from the index of *Glas. Mun.* and some are recorded in faculty but not in university acts.

83. The incorporations in *Glas. Mun.* ii, 67, Patrick Houston to William Haliburton, belong to 1451.

84. *Questiones Johannis Galli*, ed. Marguerite Boulet, Bibliothèque des Ecoles françaises d'Athènes et de Rome, 156 (Paris, 1944), 384. Lord Hamilton's foundation laid down that the regents were to give counsel to his family, *Glas. Mun.*, i, 11.

85. *ALHT*, ix, 127; their conductor seems to have been John Fethy, the well-known musician. Cf. *ibid.*, viii, 54.

86. *Glas. Mun.*, ii, 266.

87. The *scienciae margarita*. Cf. Bulls of Nicholas V (*Glas. Mun.*, i, 3); of Alexander VI (Eeles, *King's College Chapel*, 136); of Pius II (Cant, *St Salvator*, 66).

88. *Glas. Mun.*, ii, 18.
89. Gaines Post, and others, 'The Medieval Heritage of a Humanistic Ideal: "Scientia Donum Dei est, Unde vendi non potest" ', *Traditio* (New York, 1955) xi, 195ff.
90. *Acutissimi artium interpretis magistri Johannis maioris in Petri Hyspani summulas commentaria* (Lyons, 1505), unnumbered leaves at beginning, 'Trilogus inter duos logicos et magistrum'. The pun is, of course, on *cappa* (cope).
91. W. N. Hargreaves-Mawdsley, *A History of Academic Dress in Europe* (Oxford, 1963), esp. 139–42. One of the earliest uses of the word 'elegant' is in 1505 to describe Alan Stewart of Cardonald, *Registrum de Passelet* (1877), 433.
92. Herkless and Hannay, *St Leonard*, 153.
93. Ordinary lectures in schools by masters were to be given in 'ordinary' dress, *Glas. Mun.*, ii, 24.
94. *Ibid.*, ii, 90.
95. *Ibid.*, ii, 182–3. But the term is the vaguer 'habit'.
96. *Ibid.*, ii, 180.
97. *Ibid.*, ii, 199–201. He had studied laws at Rome, *CSSR*, ii, 73.
98. Rashdall, ii, 94–5, note. Malagola, *Statuti*, 132–3.
99. *Glas. Mun.*, ii, 75, 106.
100. *Ibid.*, ii, 201, 210.
101. Liber Decani, 62, 'quinque capucia foderata, quatuor videlicet blodei coloris et unum rubei coloris et cum hiis habet cappam foderatam'. The present writer pointed out the mistranslation of 'blodeus' by previous writers on the subject, in J. Durkan, *The Scottish Universities in the Middle Ages* (unpublished Edinburgh Ph.D. thesis, 1959), 438. The red hood was given by Patrick Leitch, senior, for the Dean.
102. A genuinely blue hat (*ceruleus*) was forbidden at Aberdeen in 1641 and may have been a relic of an earlier blue hood; *Fasti Aberdonenses*, 226.
103. *Glas. Mun.*, ii, 256.
104. *Ibid.*, ii, 91.
105. Warrack, *Domestic Life in Scotland* (London, 1920), 47.
106. *Glas. Mun.*, ii, 75.
107. *Ibid.*, ii, 106.
108. *Ibid.*, ii, 24.
109. *Ibid.*, ii, 19.
110. *Ibid.*, ii, 5, 24. The 'caligae', 'breeches' or 'hose', loosened for birching purposes in Glasgow, could have been worn with doublets.
111. Brown, *Early Travellers*, 152–3.
112. St Andrews University Archives, Univ. Statutes, Title 5.
113. *Glas. Mun.*, ii, 13, 23. Hannay, *Statutes*, 86, 108.
114. *APS* ii, 5, 48, 226. Francis P. Magoun, 'Football in Medieval England', *American Historical Review*, xxxv, 33–45.
115. *Glas. Mun.*, i, 67.
116. *AFA*, cxxxii, 381.
117. *Glas. Mun.*, ii, 78, 214.
118. *CPL*, xiii, 237.
119. *Glas. Mun.*, ii, 96ff and 119.
120. *In Quartum Sententiarum* (Paris, 1521), f. lxxx, C and D.
121. *AFA*, cxxxii, 4.
122. Cf. Dunbar, 'ane cleik of kirkis with ane fals cairt into his sleif'. 'Tabillis' was also a card game, cf. *Scottish National Dictionary*, s.v.
123. *Glasgow Protocols*, ii, 354, 469. A scholar of Glasgow diocese, aged twelve, had a

lunchtime swim with his fellows and was drowned *c.* 1478; Reg Supp. 763, f. 121.

124. *AFA*, 40. Cf. the *Rithmimachia* (Paris, 1514) of Lefèvre.

125. In *Scottish Alliterative Poems*, ed. F. J. Amours (STS, ser. i, 27, 38, Edinburgh, 1892–7), 73, line 775.

126. *Glas. Mun.*, ii, 39, and see above.

127. Reg. Supp. 683, ff. 158v–159. *Glas. Mun.*, ii, 76. His bachelor's degree is not on record, but he went on to St Andrews: Anderson, *Early Records*, 181.

128. Not in *Glas. Mun.*, indices, and not incorporated, but cf. *ibid.*, ii, 294–5.

129. *RMS*, iv, 254, 1626. W. Cramond, *The Church and Churchyard of Cullen* (Cullen, 1883), 37, 66, 68. For more details of him, SRO, Cullen Writs GD248/ 548.

130. SRO, Register of Admission of Notaries (NP2/1), i, f. 71.

131. *Glas. Mun.*, ii, 165, 171. Charles H. Haws, *Scottish Parish Clergy at the Reformation 1540-1574* (SRS, new series, 3, Edinburgh, 1972), 315, 322.

132. *Glas. Mun.*, ii, 114, 272–3, 276–7. Fergus Roberts, *The Grammar School of Dumbarton* (Dumbarton, 1948), 3, 15.

133. *Glas. Mun.*, ii, 123. *Essays on the Scottish Reformation*, 167.

134. *Florilegium Historiale: Essays presented to Wallace K. Ferguson*, J. G. Rowe, etc., editors (Toronto, 1971); Eugene F. Rice, 'Jacques Lefèvre d'Etaples and the medieval Christian mystics', 93.

135. *Essays on the Scottish Reformation*, 283 note.

12. The Shadow of Religious Change

'That in every cathedral church there be a theologian and a professor
of canon law . . . both of whom . . . shall commence to lecture and teach
about the feast of St Michael. . . . This holy synod enacts that lecturers
in the several colleges shall seek to expound the scriptures as accurately
as possible according to the sense of the Catholic Church; while others
shall, at different hours, on different days of every week, apply themselves to lecturing in theology . . .' (1549).

Statutes of the Scottish Church

JOHN MAIR'S reputation attracted new students, forty-three of them
in 1518, the largest annual inflow since the university's foundation, and
understandably, there was enticement from St Andrews.[1] Some notable
future regents were also among the matriculands of this remarkable
year, among them John Douglas, later bachelor of medicine at Paris,
member of the commission for the first Book of Discipline and post-
Reformation archbishop of St Andrews.[2] Fewer new students in 1519
perhaps resulted from pressure on space, but in 1521 thirty-four were
admitted.[3] These were high numbers relative to the average of the time.
There may too have been a limit to the numbers of what were mainly
poor students who could be absorbed and some migrated to St Leonard's
college. If George Buchanan was one of the migrant students of this
period, and his later devotion to the university might imply that he was,
his name is curiously absent from the printed record. Mair as principal
must meantime have been extraordinarily busy, yet he managed to
write his history of Scotland then: at this period he appears as a man of
immense energy.

A point worth noting, in view of the place occupied by grammar
instruction in Mair's own upbringing at Cambridge, and conceivably
also under Bouillache at Paris—for whom he retained considerable
respect as two of the dedications bear witness—is that we first find the
master of the grammar school active in the university councils during
Mair's principalship, for in 1521 the schoolmaster was bursar.[4]

Finance was a source of anxiety during these developments. In 1522
the university was still ingathering the fruits of the canon-law readership. All university and faculty bursars were to render accounts.
Arthurlie House needed reconstruction beyond the resources of the
common purse. The Rector proposed that it should be let to a rich man
who would pay a rent and repair it, but this device was for a time

shelved. Archbishop Andrew Forman of St Andrews had died: James Beaton I was to succeed him; and the university hoped for much from Beaton's successor in Glasgow.[5] The brief absence of Mair in Paris in 1521 would draw away some numbers, as would the earthquake which set the Blackfriars spire on fire, leaving not a single place unaffected. It is likely to have been this act of God rather than accumulated neglect that caused Arthurlie House to be in so parlous a state,[6] and it would also account for the absence of students from the east of Scotland.[7] The principal was back in Glasgow in October and seems to be there throughout 1522, but in early 1523 he was in Paris once more.[8] He soon left Glasgow for St Andrews, where the rest of his career may be followed.

In spite of the spurt of renewed action on Mair's arrival, the impression is that the university, at least as a home for several faculties, has somehow contracted. To have imitated Aberdeen, which Mair calls a 'noble college', would have necessitated fat endowments, which he hints that Glasgow could well afford.[9] He had taught logic, physics, ethics and theology during his brief occupancy of the principalship; the class which he took for physics he had taken at an earlier stage for logic, so that the system of 'regenting' was in force.[10] It may even be that new arts statutes, which have not survived, were drawn up at this time, though it could have been at any time in the period from 1510 to 1535 for which the arts records are missing for, when they are resumed, statutory dates for degree congregations had already been abandoned.

Archbishop Beaton I had brought principals of quality to the university, but they had been rapidly spirited away. He had repaired the Clyde bridge, added to his castle, augmented cathedral altarages and carried out extensive repairs in the choir, where his arms are visible in the north choir aisle. Perhaps it was too soon after Flodden to attempt much more.[11]

John Mair did not wait for Archbishop Gavin Dunbar, who succeeded Beaton in 1524. He was a lawyer and Mair had spoken unsympathetically of lawyers, so that the newcomer might not be friendly to his schemes. Some years later, however, Mair dedicated to him his commentary on St Luke.[12] The advent of Lutheranism had softened his opposition to canonists and Dunbar had perhaps surprised him. Mair could now say of him what Aristotle said of Pittacos of Mitylene, that his conduct in office had revealed his true nature.[13] Dunbar and Mair had both studied in the same 'Parisian academy' and while there both had held posts of authority, Dunbar had corrected and prepared editions of Mair's works before leaving Paris to become a doctor in both laws at the 'gymnasium of Angers', to the admiring applause of all in that 'museum of learning'. Mair agreed that some careerists took up law to serve their own ends, 'greeting it from the threshold merely', like an Egyptian dog drinking a few hurried drops out of the Nile for fear of crocodiles. Not so Dunbar; he rather, like Bitias in Virgil, drank up the nectar of pontifical and Caesarean law, not like Dido with the tip of her lips, but out of the fulness of an appreciative heart.[14]

This dedicatory letter was worth paraphrasing at length; firstly because it supplies biographical facts about Dunbar which have been overlooked.[15] It also shows that, by 1529 at least, Mair had a high opinion of his learning, an opinion shared elsewhere, as by Alexander Kinghorn, professor of medicine at Copenhagen.[16] The university, therefore, had some reason to be hopeful about its new chancellor.

There is already something ominous about the articles put forward by the Rector in the university congregation of December 1522.[17] Congregations had come to be purely formal affairs where Rectorial decisions were rubber-stamped. Not surprisingly they were ceasing to muster members who were contemptuous of the threat of fines. As the fourth article of James Stewart, the Rector, complained, it seemed as if the Rector and Dean of arts were elected to be ridiculed rather than obeyed. The first article concerned insignia and licentiates who ignored the Rector's monitorial letters. They were henceforward to be obliged to become masters within a mere eight days after licence and give security to the steward (or otherwise to the Rector, Dean or deputies) that they would do so before they could be licensed.

The regents were evidently restive under government that had lost some of its old authority. At least one regent must lead a sufficient number of students to church for Sunday mass; a roll-call was necessary both on leaving and returning to college. The students had little of the early medieval freedom. The Rector was legislating for a college, not a university. To encourage study and virtue, the customary scrutiny was to be carried out by regents once the college gates shut, the names of absentees being noted and the 'usual animadversion' employed.

For a few years the university carried on with the impetus it had recently gained. But again a congregation of the arts faculty was called in June 1532, curiously not by the Dean's sole authority, but also by the wish of the Rector, Adam Colquhoun. Many appeared at this congregation, which was obviously a continuation of the meeting at which the Dominican prior and others were incorporated.[18] An army camp regime was imposed by a Rector whose personal morals were not above cavil. His own ordinary dress was a doublet of velvet lined with scarlet, his sports were hunting and archery and he kept expensive pets like a parrot, a hind and a crane. In fact, one could almost fit him into a Flemish Renaissance painting.[19] His library, besides two courses of the law with commentaries, theology and other sciences, consisted of two shelves of 'librell bukis'.

There is every indication that the annual Rectorial election had become a formality. Colquhoun was Rector from 1529–1532, James Houston from 1533 until 1541 and John Bellenden from 1542 until 1545. The dignity of elections vanished when two intrants alone could take part as in 1529, or when a bachelor of arts was both intrant and deputy in 1537; and when the habit of electing as intrant for a nation someone not of that particular nation began to be regularised.[20] It is also significant that the name of the nation which intrants and deputies represented began to be omitted.

Rectorial record-keeping was also negligent. In some years a lack of new students is comprehensible; in 1523, the vacancy of the see may have had some effect; in 1528 there were no matriculations at St Andrews either, the three names entered being repeated the following year; in 1545 even the election was cancelled because of plague; in 1547 there were none in St Andrews either.[21] Yet in 1540, where the Rector records no matriculands, there must have been at least the eight who were bachelors in 1542, and similarly in 1541 at least the seven bachelors of 1543. Editorial negligence has compounded the difficulties as the records of book selection at the opening of the new ordinary in arts are occasionally omitted; for instance in 1540, 1543, 1551, 1554, and on 3 October 1555.[22] There is still the odd hiatus between 1542 and 1544 in both Rector's and Dean's records, the explanation of which, it is suggested, is that Dunbar had started a scheme of reconstruction of the buildings which went on fitfully for years; this would account for the unfinished appearance of the site two decades later.

In 1537 on Assumption day (15 August), Dunbar at last contemplated the setting up of a college as rival to the projected Beaton foundation in honour of St Mary of the Assumption in St Andrews. The moving spirit may have been the dean of the chapter, George Lockhart, formerly of the Sorbonne, professor of theology, disciple of Mair at Paris.[23] As far as one can understand, it was a scheme for a university college for all faculties: 'collegium universitatis magistrorum et scholarium'. It was to be endowed in the way that Blackadder had earlier planned, with the vicarages of Erskine, Cadder and Monkland, Colmonell, to all of which the dean and chapter had collation. Burses, somewhat tenuous in value, would be supported out of this new foundation (*alimonia* and *sustentatio*). The Cadzow and other chaplainries were re-annexed to this foundation, whose existence did not meet the same stone-walling approach of earlier days; but one capitular member, the prebendary of Ayr, at once recorded his dissent as regards the chaplainry of St Michael which he then held. On this 'new foundation', the Rector—not the Dean or principal—took instruments.[24] If, as we may reasonably believe, Dunbar intended to bring this plan to fruition, some otherwise inexplicable hiatuses in the record can be explained.

Precious little is known of James Lindsay, principal from 1523 to 1527. He is first heard of as a 'professor of arts' in October 1519, which suggests that there was also a grammar teacher in the College. His previous history is unknown, but he may have belonged to the family of the Lindsays of Dunrod; he certainly was a member of the Clydesdale nation. In May 1522 he is mentioned as 'secondary regent' and chaplain of the Cadzow chaplainry.[25] The first overt reference to him as principal is on 25 October 1526, when he was intrant in the Rector's election. During this rectorship he received payment from the university purse, but the next payment went to his successor.[26] Apart from the passing mention of him in the letter of Mair prefixed to the metaphysics section of the *Octo Libri Physicorum*, he is not otherwise found in the university. His presence in Glasgow in 1536 is attested; he had a royal presentation to the vicarage of Dunlop in 1548, as had also a subsequent principal. He became vicar of Cambuslang and is mentioned as curator of John Lindsay of Greenlees.[27]

There is no definite indication that his successor, Alexander Logan, was more than a senior regent. The office of principal may even have lapsed in the period 1527–1538; but as faculty records are available only for the last three years of Logan's term of office, it would be rash to be too positive. The phrase 'dean of the university', already noted, is paralleled by another, 'regent of the university'.[28] The payments mentioned above may mean not university subvention, but university absorption, of the college of arts.

Logan is to be distinguished from his namesake, the rector of Restalrig, also associated with the university.[29] He was a student under Mair, being incorporated in 1518; in 1525 he was regent in the pedagogy, holding other offices as well as being deputy of the Dean in 1537.[30] His seniority to his fellow-regent, Alexander Hamilton, is indicated by the fact that his name precedes his in signatures to the accounts.[31] The system of 'regenting' (that is, one regent taking a class through the whole arts course) had been abandoned again, as most of the bachelors presented for licence by him in 1537 were at an earlier stage, under Hamilton.[32] He was still in the university in 1538.[33]

Alexander Hamilton likewise is never recorded as principal, and since his term of office as senior regent extended till 1547 it looks as though the president of Dunbar's university college was not expected to be an arts principal. This Alexander Hamilton is the suppliant who on 27 March 1526 asked to be received at Paris as a licentiate and graduate

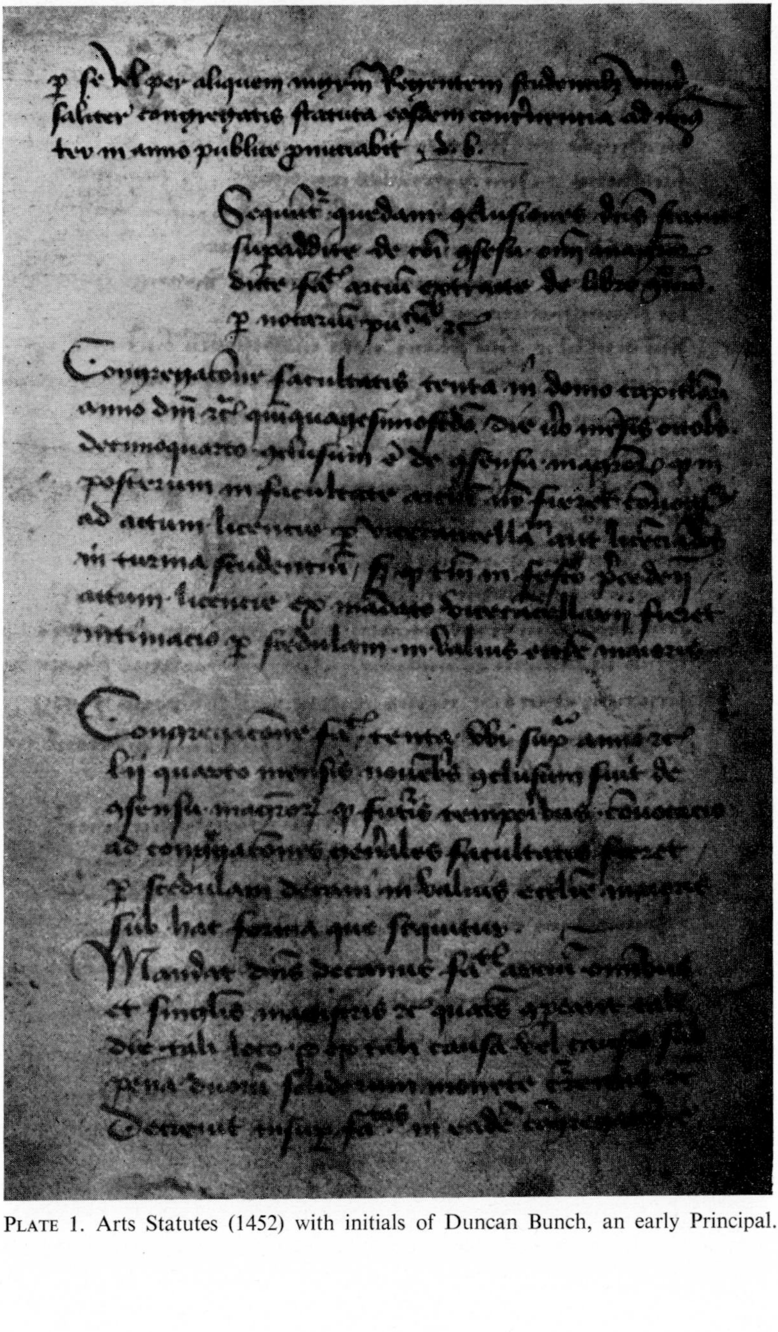

PLATE 1. Arts Statutes (1452) with initials of Duncan Bunch, an early Principal.

Acutissimi artium interpretis magistri
Johannis maioris in Petri hyspani summulas Comentaria.

PLATE 2. John Mair lecturing at Paris (*c.* 1505). From *In Petri Hyspani Summulas Commentarii.*

The COLLEDGE of GLASGOW

PLATE 3. The University and Blackfriars in the seventeenth century. From *Captain Slezer's Theatrum Scotiae, 1693.*

of Glasgow: 'in solempni studio universitatis Glasguensis in Scotia': he returned at once to Glasgow, where he had been incorporated in 1518.[34] He may have succeeded to the Cadzow chaplainry on Logan's death for in February 1539–40, a new regent, John Houston, began to preside at graduations.[35]

The habit of holding faculty congregations at the Lady altar in the lower kirk of the cathedral, an altar with strong Hamilton associations, had now developed. The chaplainry founded at this altar was attached to the arts faculty now, and at his death, Alexander Hamilton left money received from the altar offerings to buy a chasuble for it. To John Hamilton, who followed him as regent, he left his second best gown as well as his books, of which there is one—Appianus's *Historia Romana* (Venice, 1477)—in Aberdeen university library, one of two brought north (with another of John Hamilton's books) by Peter Blackburn.[36]

Under the terms of Alexander Hamilton's will, Mr Robert Laing, evidently the steward of the pedagogy, and his wife, were to have his house for three years. To the pedagogy he left £8 due to it from William Hamilton, former dean of faculty. Two other debts received by him had been spent on the repair of the pedagogy, which shows that it was being reconstructed rather than replaced. The will adds: 'Moreover, if it should happen that I die before the return of my bulls from Rome, my executors will exact from Mr John Thornton 252 crowns of the sun, of which sum 100 crowns are to be spent in the construction of the place of the pedagogy of Glasgow. The rest is to be divided among my brothers and the sons of William, my brother,' etc. He also left money to a hitherto unknown chapel in Hamilton, that of St Arungill (a Breton saint like St Malo, patron of Lesmahagow) which stood at a place shown on later maps as Armeidahill. From this testament it can be seen that he died in 1547.[37]

In 1530, Friar John MacDowell,[38] subprior of the Blackfriars, was incorporated, along with his prior, Alexander Barclay; MacDowell, it seems, was a bachelor in theology in Cologne of about 1525.[39] Cologne was the Dominican study house most involved in the campaign against the Hebraist, Johann Reuchlin, the Franciscans being his defenders and defenders also of the Cabala, a system of Biblical interpretation involving a sacred numerology: the letters of the Hebrew alphabet also represented numbers, so that certain words could, if made up of the same letters, add up to the same meaning.[40] MacDowell, by then prior of Wigtown, fled to England in the summer of 1534. At first he was accused by his enemies of condemning all singing and reading and organ playing, and his own letters show him as a diehard opponent of the new learning and a proponent of necromancy. He won the patronage

H

of Thomas Cromwell, however, preached to the recalcitrant London Carthusians—and this may be the background of the ex-Carthusian Borde's Glasgow visit—and with his fellow Dominican, John MacAlpine, former prior of Perth, became attracted to the Reformed bishop of Salisbury, Shaxton. When Knox wrote his history he was a burgermeister in a city of Germany or Friesland.

In February 1539, there was another heresy case in Glasgow. The accused was a Premonstratensian canon of Holywood, Donald Makcarny, who, after a series of accusations of heretical views as set out on a certain paper bill the contents of which, unfortunately, were not recorded, abjured them and was absolved outright. It is likely that with him were associated two others, a Conventual Franciscan of Dumfries, Jerome Russell, and a young man of some poetical promise called Kennedy. Russell refused to abjure and, Knox informs us, prophesied the eventual triumph of the opinions for which he died.[41] On the whole, however, heresy seems to have been ignored by Dunbar, but 1539 seems to have been a busy year for heresy trials in Scotland.

A better-known convert to Protestantism is John Spottiswoode, later a member of the commission to draw up the first Book of Discipline. He was licensed as a student of Alexander Logan in 1536, and was a Rector's deputy in 1543.[42] He might be the 'John Spottyswood, Skotishman', who on 4 May 1557 was granted leave to trade in England.[43] He certainly can be identified with the John Spottiswoode who, with Robert Colville of Cleish, signed a contract on 14 May 1558 with the Parisian master printer, Jean Cavalier.[44] They were perhaps in France with other Scots gentry for Queen Mary's marriage to the Dauphin. The printer promised, conditionally on the approval of the Paris faculty of theology, to deliver them two hundred copies of Patrick Cockburn's *De vulgari Sacrae Scripturae phrasi* (first edition, 1552) for two 'deniers tournois' a page, the delivery to be made within a month of the next Whitsunday. An advance payment was made and the rest, it was arranged, would follow on delivery; but the print, it was also agreed, need not be confined to the number of copies commissioned. Cockburn was at the time lecturing in St Andrews,[45] but it is interesting to see that vernacular Bible translation, to which Dunbar had been opposed, was an issue on which these two future Reformers were prepared to invest heavily on the eve of the religious change.

It is not recorded that the Dominican prior of Glasgow in 1545, Friar Andrew Abercromby, taught in the university, though he appears on record as a professor of theology.[46] Friar George Crichton, incorporated as prior in 1532, left within two years to replace the runaway Friar MacAlpine at Perth while Friar Abercromby replaced Friar MacDowell at Wigtown.[47] Circumstances increased the native mobility of these friar theologians. Crichton too was perhaps trained abroad with the Congregation of Holland.[48]

In 1546 the university elected Walter Beaton as Rector, doubtless mainly as a gesture of sympathy for the Cardinal murdered by the supporters of the martyred George Wishart, though the new Rector had studied law at Orleans.[49]

Archbishop Dunbar himself did not long survive, dying in April 1547. Buchanan has a flattering epigram recalling the table talk of Dunbar, when, in the presence of a small company of learned men, the archbishop discoursed eloquently on the majesty of God and the frailty of men[50]; themes that recall Jacques Lefèvre of Etaples. His library, of which little remains, did include Josse Clichtove, Lefèvre's disciple, but it contained also the Paris theological faculty's condemnation of Erasmus and the work of the anti-Lutheran Johannes Cochlaeus (or Dobneck) against the Scots Protestant refugee, Alexander Alane.[51] It is not surprising then that John Knox thought Dunbar a glorious fool.

Reading over John Mair's dedicatory letter of 1529 in the light of later events, one senses a prophetic irony. The careerists, he said, were like pirates, 'greedy for the strange goods of merchants borne in frail craft, not for the treasures of the mind against which neither fortune nor the lust for booty can prevail. Cicero praised Bias, one of the seven sages of Greece, who said, "All my goods I carry with me".'[52] Dunbar's whole career was politically oriented and the damage done to the Church's image by the Dunbar–Beaton feud was incalculable. It looks as though he did at least begin work on the university's reconstruction; but otherwise, as far as attracting the best men to teach there, and as far as his personal interest may be gauged from the records (there is no mention of it in his will), one must confess to disappointment that such a learned head had done so little for learning.

From 1544 to 1550, the only entries in the arts record are the elections of a Dean.[53] In 1551 two regents, John Hamilton and John Houston, selected books for the new session[54]; the former was perhaps senior regent, even as early as 1547 when John Houston, vicar of Rutherglen, was described as 'one of the regents'.[55] John Hamilton was a student of 1532, graduate of 1536 and thereafter non-regent master.[56] The number of Houstons and Hamiltons in the University give it the appearance of an inbred community. John Hamilton had royal presentation to the cathedral subchantership in July 1551 and presumably gave up his regency shortly thereafter, though he continued to attend congregations.[57] The incorporations for these years tell a sorry tale, and if the sorry appearance may be partly due to defective record-keeping, as in 1551, none the less two of the students who took their bachelor degree in December 1551 were forced to go to St Andrews to finish their course.[58]

Apart from religious divisions, Scotland had also suffered from acute civil divisions. After the disaster of Solway Moss in 1542, the death of James V and the rise to power of the Governor, James Hamilton, earl of Arran, Scotland was a profoundly disturbed land. In the west, moreover, the earls of Lennox and Glencairn had allied themselves with England against the Governor, as did many local lairds such as Houston and Buchanan. In March 1544 the archiepiscopal castle in Glasgow was besieged; about the same time Lennox held Dumbarton Castle and it was not till May that year that Arran defeated Glencairn in the battle of the Gallowmuir near Glasgow. According to Leslie the 'hoill citie was spulyeit' and only the pleading of lord Boyd saved it from being burnt down entirely. Whether the university suffered or not, one regent, a Hamilton, gained the Stablegreen from Lennox's escheat.[59] In this turmoil, the college could do little more than survive.

The evil situation of the college was not mitigated by the long vacancy of the see following the death of Dunbar, with a flock of contending claimants: James Hamilton, Donald Campbell, Alexander Gordon and finally James Beaton II. In the end, after five years of an ecclesiastical power struggle, Rome consecrated Beaton in August 1552; but he may not have been in his see till that winter.

He was the cardinal's relative who had gone with the cardinal's sons and nephews to study at Paris, where he still was at the time of his postulation to Glasgow. His teacher there was Giovanni Ferrerio,[60] the Italian who had been employed from 1531 as tutor to the Cistercian monks at Kinloss and who, while in the north, had gained the friendship of Hector Boece, the historian, and of other teachers at King's College, Aberdeen. He had reprinted Giovanni Pico della Mirandola's defence of the immortality of the soul and was associated with an edition of Marsilio Ficino. In addition to acting later as editor of Boece's history, modelled on Livy but fabulous in content, he collaborated in editing the chronicle of Johannes Carion whose view of world chronology was more biblically based, but bore special reference to the four monarchies in the visions of the Book of Daniel. In Europe Carion's view of history was propagated most assiduously by Melanchthon.[61] In Scotland, the most notable propagator of Livy was John Bellenden, Rector of the university from 1542 to 1544: and of Carion, Sir David Lindsay in his 'Monarche', though John Knox and other Reformers were also influenced by him. Ferrerio was also associated with Guillaume Postel, the eccentric French Hebraist and specialist in the Jewish cabala, whom he knew personally. The library of James

Beaton II, part of which may have been given to the university, bears the impress of Ferrerio, whose distinctive monogram has been placed on some of the books.[62] This 'coincidence of opposites' in Ferrerio—the attempt to marry Livy and Carion, Plato and Aristotle—is characteristic of his politic spirit of religious orthodoxy and intellectual moderation.[63] Beaton therefore, we may surmise, was a person totally out of sympathy with the Protestant Reformation; but in many respects he was also a man of contemporary intellectual outlook.

The arrival of James Beaton II in 1552 had tonic consequences. Yet apart from the unstable state of the country, there may have been little accommodation to spare in a college under partial reconstruction. From 1546 the Rector had been Walter Beaton, who in November 1551 had deputed his vice-Rector in legal form, giving him power to hear, cognosce and terminate all cases and pleas of members with the necessary clauses as set out more fully in the formula of Speculator.[64]

The provisions of the will of Alexander Hamilton for the reconstruction of the pedagogy point to a large scheme of at least partial rebuilding. If the money came to hand, it was supplemented by a gift of Mr Gilbert Kennedy who in July 1552, on the strength of his claim to have spent large sums on the same object, was given a tack of the vicarage of Colmonell, annexed under the Dunbar foundation.[65] This arrangement was terminated in January 1558, when the vicarage was demitted to the principal for the common use of masters and regents.[66] For university officials there is quite a crop of exemptions from taxation beginning in 1547 and ending ten years later.[67]

There was some break in the monotony of Rectorial appointments. John Steinston, senator of the College of Justice, succeeded John Bellenden as chanter of Glasgow and likewise as Rector. His reading matter included Melanchthon's *Rhetoric* as well as Livy with the addition of the lost books recently discovered at Lorsch.[68] John Colquhoun succeeded him, but then there followed, by the archbishop's evident persuasion, his relative, the chanter of Aberdeen, Archibald Beaton. Notable members of the university council at this period were Archibald Crawford, a Greek and Hebrew scholar; and William Baillie, another learned man.[69]

John Houston, regent, may have been principal during part of this period, but there is only a single reference to his status as such and that in an endorsement to a letter asking for tax remission, obtained by himself and other university officers, so that he may have continued merely as senior regent.[70] He was vicar of Rutherglen in 1546 and of Dunlop, in succession to Principal Lindsay; canon of the vicarage of Glasgow in 1547, in succession to John Spreull.[71] He was still regent in

1555 when, as was customary, he selected the books to be lectured on.[72] As vicar of Glasgow he should have been responsible for preaching under the terms of the Scots provincial council's mandate of 1549.[73] The statutes of the various provincial councils achieved little, however, in the way of immediate results; the enjoined flow of monastic students to the universities did not take place and, as late as April 1559, Beaton was summoning them from Melrose and Jedburgh for four years' study of theology[74]; a shorter course than would have earlier been regarded as normal. In a document of the immediate post-Reformation period, the Dominican prior and subprior are designated as being 'otherwise of Glasgow university'.[75] Of these, Andrew Leitch and John Law, the second later received a pension from the university which, however, does not appear to have been related to university duties proper. Andrew Leitch, whom Beaton took with him to the siege of Leith,[76] would defend a traditional approach armed with his copy of Jan van den Bundere, a friar of the Congregation of Holland whose theological compendium he owned.[77] John Hunter, prior from c. 1553 to 1558, appears in a few university deeds in the archives concerning Blackfriars property, and when he went into religious exile he was, in 1574, confirmed by the Dominican order as a master in theology.[78] On the other hand, some Dominican friars in the west of Scotland were active Protestant Reformers.

John Davidson was principal from 1556 till 1574. He was born about 1520 at Meikle Folla or Folla Rule, near Fyvie, in Aberdeenshire, the eldest son of William Davidson and Elizabeth Galloway, his wife. Since he was already master of arts in May 1543, he must have begun his studies at Aberdeen before 1540 and is described as a student there in 1542.[79] After graduating at King's College, he became a regent in arts and student in theology. As such he was presented to the vicarage of Alness in Ross.[80] He left Aberdeen for France in September 1549.[81] His object was to continue his theological studies and in his treatise in reply to Quintin Kennedy's defence of Church authority, he refers to his long-standing friendship with this Roman Catholic apologist. There can be little doubt that he knew Giovanni Ferrerio, who may have recommended him to Beaton. He held a benefice in the Glasgow diocese for a time, but had to yield it in 1552.[82] His first arrival in Glasgow was in October 1556, no doubt already invited to be principal. Davidson was a man of the new times and had learnt oriental tongues at Aberdeen and Paris as well as Greek, which he quotes in his treatise of 1563. His appointment was thus an act of deliberate policy on the part of the chancellor and university.

The last pre-Reformation act to be entered in the faculty book (Liber Decani) mentions the presentation of bachelors by Robert

Cunningham, regent, in 1555, probably November. John Laing was Dean, as he had been for the previous three years.[83] His successor was Houston, whom Davidson had replaced as principal.[84] It is likely that there was some delay at least by Laing in handing over the Dean's book or, as it was almost full, the time might have seemed ripe for a new book. Laing did deliver the arts statutes to Davidson.[85] A few deeds concerning the university's patrimony were entered subsequently in both books by Davidson, from originals now lost.

All the world of ideas characteristic of Ferrerio would be shared by Davidson. If any history was taught or implied in the teaching of other subjects, it would be the mixture of Carion and Livy. The influence of Erasmus and Ficino was powerful at Aberdeen.[86] Davidson inherited his copy of Aristotle's *Politics*—in Leonardo Bruni's translation—from Bishop Stewart at Aberdeen and brought it to Glasgow with him.[87] From the fact that he presented Archbishop Beaton with a copy of Quintin Kennedy's treatise in favour of orthodoxy, because of the 'aulde Parisiane kyndness' between himself and Kennedy, it has been assumed that his conversion to the Reformation party was slow. Not so, for he joined it almost at once in 1559. We learn from a letter of Ferrerio to Beaton, dated in September from Paris, deploring Davidson's 'foolish choice', that Ferrerio could hardly credit the report of Davidson's action, because 'if he had been so far confirmed in one ancient faith as at first he wished to appear, he would not have left the Catholic Church with so few qualms and turned to the Congregation'.[88] The same letter refers to a good friend of his (Postel) who might be able to help in obtaining a trilingual Bible for the dean of the chapter, Henry Sinclair, a 'cunning letterit' man of 'singular eruditioun', to whom Ferrerio had earlier presented his copy of Pico and to whom Sinclair had donated Bellenden's translation of Boece.[89] Davidson's brother, William, stayed on in Paris and was an associate of Ferrerio.

From all of this it cannot be concluded that Davidson actually taught the 'tongues' at Glasgow in spite of his Hebrew *Biblia Bombergiana* and Chaldee dictionary[90]: but that he applied philological tools to his Bible studies can scarcely be doubted. He possibly influenced the arts course of the period, for the physics compendium was a book by the Louvain Franciscan, Frans Titelmans, which tried to avoid contentious and subtle matters and concentrate on what might advance piety more than on strictly scientific enquiry. The first six books of the Physics are hastily treated but the last—on the universe and the soul—are expatiated on at some length with pious home-made psalms sandwiched between. The aim was to promote a sense of religious awe and wonder rather than to grapple with abstruse difficulties. But

Aristotle remained the basis. Two Glasgow students of this period owned Titelmans' compendium.[91]

The role of the Hamilton family (Davidson became their minister in the kirk of Hamilton) in the fate of the Hamilton college might have been a signal one. In France the earl of Arran was the recipient in 1555 of a dedication by the French translator of Aristotle's ethics. He was also commended to Barthélemy Aneau at Lyons by Florence Wilson, as Aneau pointed out in his French edition of the *Emblemata* (1549) of Andrea Alciati.[92] To him also was dedicated the fine French translation by Gaspard d'Auvergne of Macchiavelli's *Prince* (1553), where the earl was commended for his conduct in bringing up his children in literary studies in France. Arran at first was neutral about the Congregation and in 1558 promised to help Beaton 'in this perillous and dangerous tyme quhen detestable heresies ryses and increases in the diocy'.[93]

Under Beaton, the university was beginning to recover some of its lost dignity. The presence of lawyers and theologians shows that he hoped to carry out the prescriptions of the Church councils, which everywhere were so tardy of fulfilment. Anxious for its material prosperity, he had the Dovehill lands measured and, finding that the tenants had been encroaching on lands given by the first Lord Hamilton for the common table, referred the question to the burgh.[94] But until his advent, and for a time after it, as a result of apathetic management, there had arisen a growing crisis of rising religious expectations and diminishing returns, which exploded into a civil revolution from which Archbishop Beaton II retreated to France. The Rector, James Balfour, then diocesan treasurer, following the chancellor to Paris, went so far as to remove the mace, which was later restored.[95] He also removed the Rector's book, which was at length restored to the university by his descendant, James Balfour of Tarrie, in 1625.[96] Beaton's valuable books were removed too and stored, it would seem, in the castle from which they re-emerged in a donation by the Post-Reformation chancellor, James Boyd.[97]

In the university, the pace of such renewal as there was had lagged too far behind the dramatically quickened pace of events in the world beyond its walls. The national Church councils had not called for the teaching of the 'tongues' as such, yet the new principal had some familiarity with them and this would account in part for his appointment. But they had called for renewed attention to canon law, and of that there was at Glasgow as yet no sign. Moreover, although—apart from the key figure of the principal, Davidson—there appeared to be among them no public enthusiasm for the Reformers, no members of the university staff are on record as defenders of traditional beliefs. The duty of accepting the burden of open disputation with a seasoned campaigner like John Willock, the new superintendent of the west, former friar of Ayr, friend of Heinrich Bullinger and Marian exile in Emden, fell on the shoulders of the 'preceptor of the grammar school', Robert Maxwell.[98] The clear impression is given that the 'provisioune for the pouir bursaris and maisteris to teche ceissit' because in 1559 the university authorities could still scarcely credit that collapse was at hand and that it was indeed their eleventh hour.

NOTES

1. *Glas. Mun.*, ii, 134–6. John Lion, probably from St Andrews; Anderson, *Early Records*, 211; Thomas Brady, licensed St Leonard's 1517, *ibid.*, 107. The following later left for St Andrews: David Coventry, pauper, St Leonard's, 1523; John Still, St Leonard's 1519; William Hepburn, St Leonard's, 1520; Henry Forrus, St Leonard's, 1526; *ibid.*, 113, 118, 215, 216.
2. *AFA, ad indices*, but Dr Dunlop confused him with a later Douglas, rector of Newlands. Robert Fergushill became regent at St Andrews, *AFA*, 352; Alexander Logan a regent at Glasgow.
3. *Glas. Mun.*, ii, 136–40. Of these William Henderson may have been at St Leonard's in 1520 and William Barclay in the Pedagogy in 1526; *Early Records*, 110, 118.
4. Burns, 'New Light', *IR*, v, 98; Major, *History*, xci, 430; *Glas. Mun.*, ii, 139.
5. *Glas. Mun.*, ii, 145.
6. Burns, 'New Light', *IR*, v, 91.
7. *Glas. Mun.*, ii, 147–8. In 1522 there was no intrant for the Albany nation. John Heriot and James Mosman appear as poor students at St Andrews pedagogy in 1525, while Adam Kinghorn went to St Leonard's, Anderson, *Early Records*, 221–2.
8. *Glas. Mun.*, ii, 139, 146–7. Paris, University Archives, Reg. 91, f. 217.
9. Major, *History*, 28–9.
10. *Octo Libri Physicorum* (Paris, 1526), sigs. ciiA, fiiC. That these physical questions were also read at Glasgow is clear from the reference to 'templum sancti Kentigerni' (sig. giiA).
11. Herkless and Hannay, *Archbishops of St Andrews*, iii, 30.
12. Reprinted in Major, *History*, 444–5.
13. The reference should be to Bias, not Pittacos.
14. Mair is the first in Scotland to use the Greek terms for a university (academy, gymnasium, museum). The reference to the dog drinking out of the Nile recurs curiously in a letter of Johann Eck to Joachim von Watt (Vadianus), Rector at Vienna, just prior to a reference by Eck to Mair's discussing at Paris (*c.* 1517) questions that the lawyers thought were their own province, P. Goldast, *Epistolicae Quaestiones et Responsiones Variae* (Frankfurt, 1614), 144–5.
15. 'He does not appear to have gone abroad', D. E. Easson, *Gavin Dunbar*, 3.
16. *Letters of James V*, ed. Hannay and Hay, 151.
17. *Glas. Mun.*, ii, 141–3.
18. *Ibid.*, ii, 40, 157.
19. D. McRoberts, 'The Manse of Stobo in 1542, Part 2', *IR*, xxii, 101–9; John Warrack, *Domestic Life in Scotland, 1488–1688* (1920), 37ff.
20. *Glas. Mun.*, ii, 155 (where these are said to be three intrants, though none are

named from Clydesdale and Albany), 163. Two students were incorporated from St Leonard's in 1537 (Archibald Douglas and Patrick Ballantyne; Anderson, *Early Records*, 239).

21. *Glas. Mun.*, ii, 149, 154, 168–9; *Early Records*, 225, 252.
22. *Glas. Mun.*, ii, 292–3; Liber Decani, 143, 145, 147, 148, 149.
23. J. Durkan, 'George Lockhart', *IR*, xv, 191–2.
24. *Glas. Mun.*, i, 493–5. Mr T. Graham informs me that Reg. Supp. 2415, f. 116 shows the St Michael chaplain in Rome in 1541 securing the chaplainry to his own person.
25. *Liber Collegii Nostre Domine*, 72; *Glas. Mun.*, ii, 146, 151.
26. *Glas. Mun.*, ii, 155; this payment was for the chaplainry of St Mary, part of the income from which had to go to the university bursar (*ibid.*, ii, 146).
27. Renwick, *Glasgow Protocols*, iv, 1235; i, 196. *RSS*, iii, 2585; *ibid.*, iv, 584.
28. *Glas. Mun.*, ii, 155–6, 158; but cf. *ibid.*, ii, 40.
29. *Ibid.*, ii, 150, 154, 157.
30. *Ibid.*, ii, 150, 154, 157.
31. Liber Decani, 106, 108.
32. *Glas. Mun.*, ii, 287–9.
33. *Ibid.*, ii, 290.
34. Paris, Univ. Archives, Reg. 15, f. 99v; Reg. 91, f. 235. *Glas. Mun.*, ii, 135.
35. *Glas. Mun.*, ii, 291. The 'xxxiv' should read 'xxxix'.
36. His signature, on a torn initial leaf, is not recorded in Durkan and Ross, *Scottish Libraries*, 159 (under Archibald Whitelaw). The other John Hamilton book, Quintilian's *Institutiones* (Venice, 1494), edited by Lorenzo Valla and others, is recorded, *ibid.*, 111.
37. Appendix D.
38. *Glas. Mun.*, ii, 156.
39. J. Durkan, 'Some Local Heretics', *Transactions of the Dumfriesshire and Galloway Natural History and Antiquarian Society*, xxxvi, 67–71.
40. An example of this alphabet used in a book owned by John Greenlaw of Haddington (*Glas. Mun.*, ii, 120) is illustrated in the plate in Durkan and Ross, *Libraries*, facing p. 117.
41. Durkan, 'Some Local Heretics', 71–2.
42. *Glas. Mun.*, ii, 286, 167.
43. *Calendar of Patent Rolls, Philip and Mary*, iii, 295.
44. Annie Parent, *Les Métiers du Livre à Paris au XVIe siècle (1535–1560)* (Paris 1974), 101, 295.
45. St Andrews University Archives, Acta Rectorum, ii, 54, shows him as lecturer in sacred letters in St Leonard's college in 1556.
46. National Library of Scotland, Advocates MS. 34.7.2, f. 61. He got a canonry of Dunkeld after the Reformation, Charles H. Haws, *Scottish Parish Clergy at the Reformation 1540-1574*, SRS (Edinburgh, 1972), 187. For his degree, *Protocol Book of Gilbert Grote*, 276.
47. *Glas. Mun.*, ii, 157; *ER*, xvi, 378, 384.
48. Friar George of Scotland, hardly likely to be Crichton, was transferred in 1536 from the Lille to the Antwerp Dominican house, *Acta Capitulorum Provinciae Germaniae Inferioris 1515-1569*, ed. S. P. Wolfs (The Hague, 1964), 144.
49. *Glas. Mun.*, ii, 168; *Miscellany of the Scottish History Society*, ii, 84.
50. Cited in D. E. Easson, *Gavin Dunbar*, 100.
51. Durkan and Ross, *Libraries*, 30–31.
52. Major, *History*, 444–5, the citation is from Cicero, *Paradoxa*.

53. *Glas. Mun.*, ii, 295–7.
54. Liber Decani, 147; omitted in printed edition.
55. *Glas. Mun.*, ii, 169, 296, though Houston was probably regent since 1540, *ibid.*, ii, 291.
56. *Ibid.*, ii, 159, 286–8.
57. Watt, *Fasti*, 170.
58. Robert Cunningham, son of the laird of Craigends, and Henry Gibson brought certificates from the university authority and 'from him who taught them' at Glasgow. The former was a regent, the latter an examiner at Glasgow in 1555: *Glas. Mun.*, ii, 170, 299; Anderson, *Early Records*, 150–1.
59. Renwick and Lindsay, *History of Glasgow*, i, 369; *RSS*, iii, 1758, 1401.
60. A brief chronology of Ferrerio's career, on which the present writer is still working, is given in Appendix F.
61. Melanchthon's grammar and rhetoric, Rudoph Agricola's logic, etc., were part of Ferrerio's educational programme at Kinloss, John Stuart, *Records of the Monastery of Kinloss*, Society of Antiquaries of Scotland (Edinburgh, 1872), 54. On Ferrerio and Ficino, cf. P. O. Kristeller, 'L'Etat présent des études sur Marsile Ficin,' *Platon et Aristote à la Renaissance. XVIᵉ Colloque international de Tours* (Paris, 1976), 71.
62. Durkan and Ross, *Libraries*, 24–27, 169. No. 23, has a note of donation to the college. Nos. 37, 38, 40, 41 and a copy of Lucian (not listed) have the Ferrerio mark. I have to thank the staff of Glasgow University Library for noting three of these.
63. On the neglect of Livy by the German Reformers, cf. *Livy*, ed. T. A. Dorey (London, Toronto, 1971), 108.
64. *Glas. Mun.*, ii, 172; the formula cited is omitted after 'deputavit' (Liber Rectoris, 121). Speculator was Durandus, author of the *Speculum Judiciale*.
65. *Glas. Mun.*, i, 56; Mackie, *University*, 47, is sceptical about Kennedy's donations. David Gibson was presented to the vicarage in 1552, *RSS*, iii, 1640, and was closely connected with the university till 1558, *Glas. Mun.*, ii, 177.
66. *Glas. Mun.*, i, 62; scholars are not mentioned in this subsidy.
67. *Ibid.*, i, 54–61.
68. Durkan and Ross, *Libraries*, 145–6.
69. *Glas. Mun.*, ii, 173–4. For Crawford's and Baillie's books, see Durkan and Ross, *Libraries*, 73, 84–5. The Colquhouns and the city were at odds in 1553, *Liber Collegii Nostre Domine*, lxiii.
70. *Glas. Mun.*, i, 59.
71. *Ibid.*, ii, 179; *RSS*, iii, 2767; Fraser, *Memorials of the Montgomeries, Earls of Eglinton* (Edinburgh, 1859), ii, 162. Cooper exaggerates in making him a confirmed pluralist, and confuses him with the older James Houston, founder of the collegiate church, *SHR*, xi, 262.
72. Liber Decani, 149 (omitted in print). His reading tastes seem relatively conservative, Petrus Comestor and Virgil; Durkan and Ross, *Library*, 116. 118,
73. *Statutes of the Scottish Church, 1225-1559*, ed. David Patrick (SHS, ser. 1, 49, Edinburgh, 1907), 121.
74. *Ibid.*, 107; *Melrose Regality Records*, ed. C. S. Romanes (SHS ser. 2, 13, Edinburgh, 1917), iii, 167, 173.
75. *RMS*, iv, 1970.
76. *Liber Collegii Nostre Domine*, lxiv note.
77. Durkan and Ross, *Libraries*, 180.
78. *Acta Capitulorum Generalium Ordinis Praedicatorum*, v (Rome/Stuttgart, 1901), 181 (under the date, 1574): 'In desolata provincia Scotiae magisterium fr.

Ioannis Unter (sic) pro fide et religione exulis et multae eruditionis viri'. Cf. McRoberts, *Essays on the Scottish Reformation*, 199 (the French house referred to was Bordeaux). Hunter had studied at Cologne: David Camerarius, *De Scotorum Fortitudine* (Paris, 1631), 180.

79. *Protocol Book of Sir John Cristisone*, 326, 344, 360.

80. *RSS*, iii, 402.

81. *Fasti Aberdonenses*, 264.

82. *RSS*, iv, 1850. As vicar of Nigg, he witnesses a deed of the bishop of Aberdeen, William Gordon, in Paris: Wodrow Society, *Miscellany*, i, 177. He was also receiving a pension from the parsonage of Kinkell, *Glas. Mun.*, i, 63.

83. *Glas. Mun.*, ii, 229, 298–9.

84. *Ibid.*, i, 61.

85. Liber Decani, f. 170, 'Johannes houstoun scripsit'. Arts statutes, f. 21, 'Johannes houstoune vicarius de Dunlop'.

86. Cf. for Ficino owned by Boece, Durkan and Ross, *Libraries*, 78.

87. *Ibid.*, 89, cf. also 64.

88. McRoberts, *Essays on the Scottish Reformation*, 330. Davidson's wife seems to have had a foreign origin. Her name was Barbara Deirik, SRO, Nasmith Writs, no. 66.

89. *A Diurnal of Occurrents* (Bannatyne Club, Edinburgh, 1883), 98. Durkan and Ross, *Libraries*, 54, 57.

90. *Ibid.*, 89.

91. Alexander Douglas (*Glas. Mun.*, ii, 175) and Donald MacLachlan (*ibid.*).

92. J. Durkan, 'The Beginnings of Humanism in Scotland', *IR*, iv, 12.

93. *Glasgow Reg.*, ii, 582–4.

94. *Glas. Mun.*, i, 67.

95. *Ibid.*, iii, 517, 523.

96. Liber Rectoris, last leaf, 'This buik is delyuerit be me Ja. balfour of tarrie in anno 1625'.

97. *Glas. Mun.*, iii, 408–9.

98. J. Leslie, *The Historie of Scotland*, trans. J. Dalrymple, ed. E. G. Cody and W. Murison (STS, Edinburgh, 1895–1898) ii, 464–5. *Glasgow Protocols*, v, 1413, 1480. The latter shows that Maxwell had ceased to be schoolmaster by November 1563.

II

THE NEW FOUNDATION

13. Prelude to Reform

'For as the youth must succeed to us so we ought to bee carefull that
they have knowledge and erudition to profit and comfort that which
ought to be most deare to us, to wit, the kirk and spouse of our Lord
Jesus.'

The First Book of Discipline, 1560

THAT Scotland, a country so frequently described as backward and
impoverished, should possess at the close of the fifteenth century no
less than three separate universities is without doubt a creditable
achievement not only of the late medieval church which helped to
sustain them, and of its bishops who were their founders, but of the
society which created them, which valued their existence and which
responded to the opportunities that they offered. This accomplishment
is all the more remarkable when contrasted with the picture earlier in
the Middle Ages. Before 1410, or thereabouts, Scotland had no *studium
generale* of its own,[1] and Scots seeking a higher education had to
pursue their studies abroad. Yet, by the end of the century, the country
could provide not only a native university education for its scholars but
even a choice of universities where they could study; and the creation
of a university at Glasgow, as the papal bull indicated,[2] remedied a
deficiency in the west of Scotland. By 1600, the number of centres of
learning, where a university education might be sought, had risen from
three to five, and attempts were also made, with limited success, for the
founding of a sixth at Fraserburgh.[3]

The proliferation of universities in the fifteenth century is, of course,
a well attested European phenomenon,[4] and in this rapid expansion of
higher education Scotland seemed poised to participate to the full. Yet
how far these developments marked a sustained advance in university
education is not easy to assess. The increase in the quantity of available
education need not have been matched by an increase—or even by a
decrease—in quality. There are indications, however, that by paying
scant regard to the limited material resources at their disposal, the
Scots in their endeavours were liable to overreach themselves. The very
fact that the accelerating pace in the growth of universities should take
place in a country whose population may be reckoned at little more
than half a million may suggest that the founders were inclined sometimes to be rather too ambitious. Certainly the difficulties which beset
Glasgow university in those years were substantially 'hose which

confronted St Andrews and Aberdeen as well. Their development was subject to frequent setbacks and, on more than one occasion, their continued existence seemed to hang in the balance.

The two related problems of inadequate endowment and a shortage of distinguished teachers merely helped to prolong the decidedly precarious existence of universities which, at best, remained but pale reflections of Bologna or Paris[5] and which, at worst, came close to extinction. A scholar like George Buchanan, at any rate, spent more of his life teaching abroad than at home; and the poverty of the universities, to which Mair drew attention, offered little financial incentive for teachers to remain.[6]

Universities everywhere, it is true, originally had few funds on which they could draw. They were essentially guilds or associations of teachers and students. They need own no buildings; it often sufficed to rent accommodation for board and teaching and to utilise perhaps a neighbouring church for assemblies and meetings. The lack of any financial provision in the foundation charter of Glasgow university in 1451, far from being unorthodox, is comparable with the initial situation at the universities of both Paris and Oxford, neither of which possessed any significant endowment.[7] But, whereas the collegiate movement abroad had provided many universities, including Paris and Oxford, with numerous constituent colleges, often richly endowed,[8] in Scotland a different pattern prevailed where, with the exception of St Andrews which came to possess three colleges by 1538,[9] no multi-collegiate structure emerged. As a result, teaching remained highly centralised. What endowment the Scottish universities and colleges did receive was met, all too often, at the expense of the parishes through the familiar device of appropriating a portion of the parish revenues for their upkeep. Thus, at St Andrews, St Salvator's college, founded in 1450, was endowed with revenues from the parish churches of Cults, Kemback, Dunino and Kilmany; St Leonard's in 1512 was granted the revenues of the church and hospital of St Leonard; and St Mary's, erected in 1538, eventually came to be financed from the teinds of Tyninghame, Tannadice, Conveth, Inchbrayock and Tarvit.[10] Similarly, at Aberdeen, a royal grant in 1497, made fully effective in 1505, conferred on the university the revenues of the churches of Aberluthnet, Glenmuick and Abergerny, to which were added Slains by 1498, St Mary ad Nives in 1499, and Auchindoir in 1514.[11] It was not, however, until 1506 that the poverty-stricken college of Glasgow was promised the vicarages of Cadder, Stobo, Linton and Kilbirnie, and the parsonage of Garvald, none of which it acquired, and it was only in 1558 that it effectively received the grant of the vicarage of Colmonell, initially annexed without apparent success in 1537.[12]

All this, however, was a practice neither satisfactory to the parish which saw its finances rapidly diminish nor to the university which was likely to incur the responsibility of providing for the cure of souls in the parish whose revenues it had in part appropriated. Imperceptibly, Glasgow university, like St Andrews and Aberdeen, became integrated into the complex, sometimes chaotic, system of ecclesiastical finance. Nor were the university's links with the church in any sense purely tenuous. If, in the later Middle Ages, it came to be 'generally recognised that the academic guild was a legally constituted autonomous entity standing outside the ecclesiastical structure',[13] it would still seem to be true that Glasgow and her sister universities remained subject to strong ecclesiastical influences and pressures. There may have been no outright attempt by the ecclesiastical authorities at Glasgow, or elsewhere, to impose any rigid control over the universities, but there may also have been no sound reason why they should. The close relationship of the university to the church was sufficiently well understood to render this unnecessary. It was, after all, founded by an ecclesiastic and confirmed by papal bull; it was presided over by a chancellor who was also a bishop; it was staffed by teachers who were clerics in the main, and who were sometimes established in benefices as well; it was sustained by ecclesiastical endowments and it was also subject to episcopal supervision.[14]

This being so, any wholesale assault upon the church could not but affect the university as well. It formed part of the ecclesiastical system; it possessed a theological faculty; it was therefore a preserve of the clergy and a nursery of the priesthood; and, with the growth of heresy, it was expected to use its resources in the defence of orthodox Catholic teaching.[15] But, just as protestantism succeeded even in penetrating the religious houses,[16] whose heads were instructed in 1549 to 'ransack the cells of their monks' in the search to uncover heretical literature,[17] so too did each of the universities succumb, in varying degrees, to those same influences at work. Whereas St Andrews appears to have been the most receptive, and Aberdeen the least receptive,[18] to reforming tendencies, all that can be said with confidence about Glasgow, owing to a scarcity of information, is that on the eve of the Reformation its principal had renounced Catholicism and had become a protestant.[19] It was within this context, therefore, that Glasgow university had to brave the Reformation crisis. Nor was it particularly well-equipped to do so. By conforming, however, John Davidson, the principal, kept the university in being, saving it from possible extinction, and his decision to side with the reformers was a serious blow to Archbishop Beaton, the chancellor, and to those conservatives who may have wished to frustrate any bid to take over the university by the protestants.

Any attempt to reconstruct the pattern of events at Glasgow during the Reformation is hampered by a lack of evidence, but some instructive comparisons may be made with the situation at St Andrews in 1560. Some disruption and dislocation was, of course, inevitable. Yet it is also easy to exaggerate this. That the formalities of examination and graduation at St Andrews should be suspended in 1560 'because of the universal upheaval in the state and reformation in religion'[20] ought not to obscure the fact that the university continued to function without any irrevocable damage or serious interruption. In many ways, the changes which had taken place by 1560 were a good deal less drastic than might be supposed. Two of the three colleges conformed, and only at St Salvator's was some token resistance offered.[21] In St Andrews, the reformers were able to look for encouragement to lord James Stewart, a leading member of the Congregation and commendator of the priory there, who had also been a student at the university and who used the full weight of his influence on the side of the reformers.[22] As early as 1559, the town, which in a formal sense at least was still the archbishop's seat, possessed an established ministry, supported by the magistrates, with an active kirk session where members of the university from 1561 sat regularly as elders of the church.[23] In St Andrews, then, the general picture is one of conformity with the Reformation in both university and town; and in Glasgow, where no university records—other than the odd charter—exist for the 1560s, and where no ecclesiastical or burgh court records survive for those years, a not wholly dissimilar situation may have prevailed.

In so far as the fate of the church and the future of the universities were inextricably interwoven, the Glasgow college could not expect to remain aloof for long from the activities of the reformers in the town. For a spell, however, the burgh witnessed something like a coexistence of the old faith with the new. All in all, it was a rather odd situation while it lasted. By the summer of 1559, the principal of the college was a protestant—fortified, no doubt, by the periodic visits of the lords of the Congregation—but there must have been those on his staff who were not. As late as November 1560, two friars who were already graduates could describe themselves as being 'otherwise of the university'.[24] In the town, the chaplains in 1559 were not yet compelled to recant; indeed, in February 1559 the cordiners of Glasgow had petitioned *inter alia* for 'augmentatioune of devine service at the alter of Sanct niniane situat in the metropolitane kirk of Glasgw';[25] the friary adjacent to the pedagogy was not dissolved, and as a property-owning corporation, at least, it continued to function; the archbishop still retained his ecclesiastical jurisdiction, if he chose to exercise it, and he continued to receive revenues from his see. Similarly, priests who possessed a legal title to benefices continued to enjoy the fruits. Nor does it seem that Glasgow possessed a regular minister in 1559.

During those critical months, the state of the university can only be surmised. If teaching at the college was not suspended, some of its activities were soon to be terminated. No longer could the principal, as a protestant, be expected to justify the repetition of multiple masses for the souls of the founder and subsequent benefactors.[26] Other religious practices in the college were bound to come under scrutiny. The observance prescribed in 1460 that the regents and students should assemble in chapel every Saturday after vespers to sing on bended knees the anthem of the Blessed Virgin with a collect and remembrance for the founders' souls must also have disappeared at the Reformation, if indeed it had endured so long.[27] Similarly, the calendar of festivals and holy days observed by the university, to which the reformers took exception, could not for long survive persistent criticism.[28] Members of the college could no longer remain untouched by the changing religious climate around them. Nor can the reformers be said to have been exactly idle in the town.

The fate of the friary beside the college merely served to underline what the reformers meant by reformation. It was the regents of the college, no less, who claimed in 1578 that in August 1559:[29]

'be the space of twa monethis immediatlie preciding or thairby the haill places of Freiris within this realme wes demolischit and cassin downe and the conventis quhilkis maid residence within the samen wer dispersit sua that efter that tyme thair wes na convent bot the places and monastereis than and continewallie sensyne dissolvit in sic sort that for that tyme the haill landis and rentis pertening to the saidis Freiris returnit to oure Soverane Lordis derrest motheris and his Grace dispositioun to sic usis as mycht best aggrie with the word of God and sinceir religioun'.

It would be unsound, however, to accept this statement, without qualification, as evidence of what befell the friars preachers in Glasgow at the Reformation. The college, after all, had a vested interest in asserting what it did, for it was engaged in a successful action of reduction before the lords of Council against an individual who had acquired property from the friars in 1560, and it was therefore argued that the friars were in no position to dispone property at that date.[30] There is, however, no evidence of any violent destruction of the friary or, for that matter, of any damage done to the adjoining college buildings by the reformers in 1559. Indeed, all the evidence points in the opposite direction. Far from having suffered destruction by the reformers, or by anyone else, the buildings of the friaries in Glasgow survived the Reformation, and in February 1562 the privy council exhorted the city magistrates to maintain for the benefit of the burgh 'the places of freris as yit standand undemolissit'. Indeed, the manse and 'kirkroom' of the friars preachers seem to have been still intact in 1563 when they were conveyed by a royal grant to the college.[31] The friars minor in Glasgow, who received a royal gift of herring at least as late as November 1559, look almost as if they were still in business, and it was not until June 1560 that we hear of a friar minor in Glasgow 'now ejected' (*nunc explosus*) from his convent, which thereafter is described as 'the place sometime of the Friars Minor'.[32] The 'dissolution' of the friaries in Glasgow evidently took a rather different form from that suggested by the college regents in 1578, and even if individual instances of hardship occurred with the dispersal of their community, the friars were of course still entitled to receive their 'friars' wages' after the Reformation.[33] This, however, was but one aspect of the comparative moderation which accompanied the religious change. It was a moderation which manifested itself in many ways, not least in the coexistence of the structure of the old church with that of the new. There was ingenuity as well as irony in the attitude adopted by Henry Sinclair, first parson, then dean, of Glasgow and later bishop of Ross, described by Knox in 1563, as 'ane perfyct hypocrite and ane conjured ennemye to Christ Jesus'.[34] He was no convert to the reformed faith but he was content 'to furneis breid and wyne to the halie communion continewalie sen the Reformatioun of religioun within this realme, and nevir maid obstakill nor refusall thairin'.[35] It was, he seems to have thought, a small price to pay for his continued possession of the fruits of the parsonage of Glasgow.[36]

It was with apprehension, nonetheless, that conservatives like Archbishop Beaton, the university chancellor, viewed the future. By 1558, he was only too painfully aware of 'this perillous and dangerous tyme quhair detestabil heresies ryses and increasis in the diocy of Glasgow', and he therefore concluded a bond of maintenance with the indecisive Chatelherault[37] who later joined the Congregation. In declaring its support for the reformers, Glasgow was decidedly more cautious than some prominent burghs, and it is rather significant that Knox does not include Glasgow among the eight burghs which possessed an established ministry in September 1559.[38]

The support of the nobility was, without doubt, a key factor in determining the success of protestantism in that network of local societies which comprised the nation. In the west country, the movement had its aristocratic and baronial supporters in Argyll, Glencairn, Ochiltree and Boyd,[39] but a city and episcopal burgh, like Glasgow, still dominated by Beaton and his associates, could claim no lord

James Stewart as St Andrews undoubtedly did. Not only did Beaton continue to assert his right to nominate the provost and to select the bailies from leets submitted to him,[40] but Chatelherault, already bailie-principal of the regality of Glasgow[41] and later to aspire to becoming the 'second person in the realm', was not finally won over to the protestant cause until the summer of 1559.[42]

The privy council's proclamation in February 1559 inhibiting the inhabitants of Glasgow (as well as those of Irvine, Ayr and Linlithgow) from menacing priests and disturbing the services used in churches—coming as it did within a month of the Beggars' Summons—suggests that the reformers in the city had already resorted to overt action.[43] Even so, it was really only with Chatelherault's switch in allegiance that Glencairn and the gentlemen of the west, in the summer of 1559, 'purged the churches in Glasgow of idolatrie',[44] but their mission, if correctly reported, was evidently not wholly successful, for in January 1560, Chatelherault, Argyll and Arran arrived in Glasgow 'and caused take done the images and altaris and intromitted with the bischoppis castell and rents and pat in certane gentill men to keip the samyn'.[45] Nor were matters likely to improve in March 1560 when Beaton and the French on marching to Glasgow 'recovered the castell againe and tareit ane nycht in the cittie' before retiring to Edinburgh.[46]

Despite the marching and countermarching which took place, the reformers still succeeded in retaining possession of the bishop's palace as well as the steeple, the two local strongholds, and they were sufficiently in command by October 1560 to order those priests who declined to recant to be banished from the town.[47] The assumption is, therefore, that the town had a protestant preacher by that date. It is known that John Willock had been assigned to preach in Glasgow by August 1560,[48] though in what capacity is less than clear. Knox assigns Willock's initial nomination as superintendent of the west to July 1560, and in August the chamberlain to the Catholic archbishop of Glasgow described how Willock had been 'maid Bischop of Glasquo now in your Lordschippis absens, and placit in your place of Glasquo'. As he succeeded in obtaining a stipend from the revenues of the archbishopric and ultimately took up residence in the dean's house, it may not be entirely surprising that his office might be mistaken for that of bishop.[49]

But whatever the tentative plans—if plans there were—to nominate superintendents in 1560, the prevailing political situation was such as to render their appointment inoperative until 1561.[50] The likelihood is, therefore, that Willock undertook the work of the parish ministry at Glasgow in 1560. The first mention of a regular minister comes only with David Wemyss's appointment which cannot have been much before 1562, since Wemyss himself claimed in January 1572 that 'he hes servit in the office of ministerie at the said citie be the space of ten yeris bipast in sum troubill and without certantie of his stipend'.[51] Yet it would be rash to conclude that before his appointment Glasgow lacked the regular services of the reformed church. It is scarcely conceivable that John Willock, as superintendent in 1561, should ignore the needs of the inhabitants of the principal town of his province; and if Glasgow did not initially possess a regular minister which it could call its own, it could at least claim the services of a reader in James Hamilton, a graduate, possibly of the pedagogy,[52] and prebendary of the New College in the town,[53] who conformed at the Reformation and who is on record as reader in the kirk of Glasgow in 1561.[54] Neither university nor town was to be deprived of reformed teaching.

What interest Willock may have taken in the university is unknown, but he could scarcely ignore it. One of his duties as superintendent was to consider 'how the youth be instructed', and it was envisaged that he should exercise a certain supervision over the university in matters of finance and in the appointment of a rector.[55] He would also be able to count on the support of John Davidson who, of course, remained a key figure in determining the fortunes of the college in those years, and it is all the more remarkable, given the burgh's initially qualified reception to the Reformation, that the university principal should conform so early. In part, he may have taken his cue from Chatelherault, the dominant magnate in the area, but there is no reason to doubt the sincerity of his religious conversion. There was, at any rate, little financial incentive to conform, so unequivocally, when he did. The outcome of the Reformation could not be foreseen in the summer of 1559 and by becoming a reformer Davidson stood to lose as much as he might conceivably gain: he might be threatened with the loss of his benefices, his salary, his office and even a roof over his head. After all, until July 1560, Archbishop Beaton, the man who had initially appointed him, was still active in Scotland,[56] if less noticeably in his diocese, but although Davidson risked the prospect of prosecution by the ecclesiastical authorities, no attempt was made to remove him from office; or at least if there was, it was not successful.

Davidson himself was a relative newcomer to the university. He had studied first at Aberdeen and then at Paris,[57] where his relation, William Davidson, who remained a Catholic, was to become regent.[58] By 1556, he had arrived in Glasgow,[59] and two years later he was still manifestly a Catholic. In 1558, his fellow student at Paris, Quintin Kennedy, the abbot of Crossraguel, published his *Compendius Tractive* on the 'matters that are in debate concerning faith and religion', and before publication he had sent Davidson a summary of the book to be presented to the archbishop. At that stage, the work was 'approvit

baith to be gude and godly' by Davidson as well as Beaton, but afterwards Davidson was not entirely happy with what he had read.[60]
Within a short space, a marked transformation took place in Davidson's
religious outlook, and in a letter to Archbishop Beaton from Paris in
September 1559, the humanist Giovanni Ferrerio expressed surprise
that their friend, John Davidson, should have joined the reformers.[61]
Thereafter, Davidson took up the challenge presented by Kennedy's
tract and in 1563 published a reply which he dedicated to the earl of
Glencairn,[62] whose son, James, had been incorporated as a student in
the college in 1557.[63] By publishing his tract, Davidson had publicly
demonstrated his protestant convictions. Though an avowed protestant
with an aversion to 'papistry', the principal was no extremist. His tract
altogether lacks the bitter invective of polemicists like John Knox or
Ninian Winzet. In theology, he and Quintin Kennedy were poles apart.
The whole purpose of his book was to undermine Kennedy's arguments,
yet he still found space to recall that 'aulde Parisiane kyndnes that was
betuix us', and though estranged from Archbishop Beaton, he still saw
reason to regard him as one 'quha was my gude maister and liberall
freind'.[64]

Amidst these religious changes, the college itself must have remained
in a somewhat confused and unsettled state. Not only did a survey of
the college lands conducted 'be the baronie men at the bischops
command' in 1557 reveal an encroachment 'fra the nychtbouris nixt
adjacent', but by Whitsun 1559 no remedy had yet been found 'bereasone
the bischop passit to France to the quenis mariag and the controversie
rays betuix the protestants and the papists for the religione'.[65] Then,
in 1560, came the expulsion from the town of the university chancellor
along with the French. Bereft of its chancellor, the college was confronted with the advent of the Reformation which directly affected
established patterns of teaching, particularly in the higher faculties. The
teaching of theology, for one thing, could not remain the same, but
since this was the duty of the principal, himself a reformer, the change-
over in 1560 may have been less radical in practice than might be
imagined. Certainly, the teaching of canon law would be harder to
justify after 1560, though a knowledge of it would not be completely
irrelevant, since the work of the commissary courts after 1560 was
based on earlier ecclesiastical law. But none of this, in any event, was
likely to cause much of an upheaval in a college like Glasgow which had
already ceased to teach canon law well before the Reformation. In the
only faculty which could be said ever to have flourished, the faculty of
Arts, there was a less pressing need, in religious terms, for any immediate
or drastic overhaul of the curriculum. Nor did the university witness
any wholesale purge of devotional literature at the Reformation.

Catholic works, no doubt, were quickly superseded by others more carefully attuned to the new ecclesiastical environment, but as late as November 1580 the college could claim to possess 'xvj buikis or thareby of musik of sangis and messis'.[66] Books for which there was no longer any obvious purpose evidently still possessed an intrinsic value and were not subjected to wanton destruction in 1560.

It may therefore have been not so much in teaching practice but in personnel that problems were likely to occur. Once again, however, the picture is obscured by an absence of adequate information, and it is within the wider framework of the Reformation settlement that an appreciation can best be gained of how the university reacted to the changes of 1560. It was certainly indicative of the 'alteration of religion within the realm' that the rector of the university in 1560 should take the prudent precaution of placing the custody of the mace, the symbol of authority, with the Catholic archbishop, and university chancellor, who promptly 'cariit the same with all the silver warke and hail juels of the Hie kirk to Paris with him'.[67] Yet the archbishop's over-hasty action, in deserting his flock if not his faith, served little purpose, and it must have dismayed those clerics and teachers who looked for a lead but who saw no sound reason to imitate his example. Since the Reformation, in certain of its aspects, was accomplished with comparatively little dislocation, it is not at all surprising that many who held office in the old church should fail to perceive a need for precipitate action on their part in 1560. There was often a significant continuity in personnel: men who hitherto held office in the old church often opted to serve in the new. This may have been less true of Glasgow than it was for certain other areas of Scotland.

Even so, a number of chaplains in the city conformed in 1560 and continued to serve as ministers, exhorters and readers in the post-Reformation church. Not only did Mr James Hamilton, a prebendary of the New College of Glasgow, accept office as reader in the city after 1560,[68] but Thomas Knox, chaplain of St Stephen and St Laurence in the cathedral, became reader or exhorter at Eastwood after the Reformation.[69] It seems conceivable that Mr Archibald Crawford who appears on record as cathedral chaplain of St John the Baptist in 1547, 1558 and 1575, was the same Mr Archibald Crawford who became minister of Kilmacolm.[70] Mr Robert Houstoun, who held the chaplainry of the Holy Rood in the cathedral, may be identified with the person of that name who became exhorter at Kilpatrick.[71] Other chaplains in the area also conformed. James Laing, a clerk in the diocese of Glasgow and later chaplain, was in all probability the same individual who served as reader at Luss, itself a prebend of Glasgow cathedral.[72] Nor is it hard to identify Adam Landels, a notary and chaplain, with the individual of that name who became reader at Ochiltree.[73] William Jackson, another chaplain, accepted office as reader in the reformed church at Inchinnan,[74] and Ninian Swan, who was also chaplain, undertook to serve as reader at Carmichael after 1560.[75] John Miller is a common enough name, but it is conceivable that the John Miller who served as chaplain before 1560 is the same John Miller who became exhorter at Symington[76] whilst John McGhie who served as chaplain in 1555 may be identified with the person of that name who became minister at Kirkcowan.[77] Moreover, a few of the friars preachers in Glasgow, whose convent lay beside the university, conformed after 1560. Of the sixteen friars whose names appear as witnesses in three charters between 1554 and 1558,[78] at least three are known to have accepted office in the reformed church: Helecius McCulloch became reader at Balmaclellan, James Fotheringham became minister at Walston and James Carruthers, reader at Eastwood.[79]

There were also teachers and graduates of the university who joined the protestant cause. One of the earliest was John Macdowell, the Dominican prior of Wigtown, who as subprior of the friars preachers in Glasgow was incorporated in the university in 1529. By the mid-1530s, however, he had become involved in the movement for reform and had fled for safety to England before eventually leaving for the continent.[80] Outstanding among the graduates who not only accepted the Reformation but also undertook to work in the reformed church was John Spottiswoode who entered the university in 1534. Disillusioned with the policy of persecution at home, he chose, on graduating, to study divinity in England where he met Cranmer, and after a spell in France 'he made no great stay in any one place till the work of Reformation began'.[81] Thereafter he undertook to serve concurrently as minister at Mid-Calder and as superintendent of Lothian. Others, too, found a place within the ranks of the reformed ministry. Rather less distinguished was the career of Mr David Hamilton, parson of Cambuslang, who matriculated in 1531 and who may be identified with the post-Reformation exhorter at Monkland who was sentenced by the general assembly in 1569 to be deposed and excommunicated for alleged 'double fornication'.[82] Identification is at best tentative in the absence of corroborative evidence, but it seems likely that John McCorquodale and Adam Colquhoun, both of whom matriculated in 1539, subsequently served after 1560 at Killin and Linton respectively.[83] Of the students who entered the university in 1549, it is safe to conclude that Thomas Knox became reader at Eastwood, that James Hill, parish clerk of Govan, later acted as exhorter at Cathcart,[84] and that Andrew Hay, a former canon of the cathedral, became minister at

Renfrew, an appropriate enough appointment since he was also parson of Renfrew, and he went on to serve as university rector.[85] Ninian Swan and John Miller, the two conforming Glasgow clerics, were also students at the university in 1551 and 1557 respectively.[86] All in all, a continuity of a sort is demonstrable in the personnel of the old church who chose to conform and serve in the new.

There are, of course, certain qualifications to be made, for there were also those who declined to conform. While it is true that the 'reformation parliament', whose very composition and legality were called in question, did legislate against papal authority and the celebration of mass, as well as adopt a reformed Confession of Faith,[87] it is equally true that there was still no statutory compulsion for the adherents of the old order to conform to the new. The permanence of the Reformation in 1560 was not assured. Neither protestant nor Catholic regarded the revolution of 1560 as irreversible, and it was hardly a sign of undue pessimism on their part that the prior and subprior of the friars preachers in Glasgow, who vaguely styled themselves 'otherwise of the university', should make provision in a feu charter of November 1560 for the eventuality that the friars would be restored along with their order.[88]

Not only so, but benefice holders, irrespective of their religious convictions, continued to enjoy legal title to their livings, and this held good for school and university teachers alike, for it was only after 1567, with Mary's deposition and the accession of her infant son which provided the reformed church with formal establishment, that parliament finally decreed that schools, universities and colleges should be reformed and that henceforth no teacher be appointed unless approved by a superintendent or visitor of the kirk.[89] The general assembly, it is true, might well urge, as it did in 1563, that only teachers who professed the reformed faith should receive appointments and that nonconformists should be deposed,[90] but it is plain that only something akin to a parliamentary statute could have the force of making the assembly's requirements legally binding. Parliament's action in 1567 plainly set the pattern for future appointments, but it was still no easy matter, as the assembly found, to eject existing incumbents of suspect religion, and, in the case of benefice holders, it was only in the aftermath of the 'civil war' and with the undisputed dominance of the king's party that a religious test was applied to existing benefice holders: in 1573 parliament presented them with the choice of accepting the reformed faith or of suffering deprivation as a consequence of refusing.[91]

This, then, was the context within which Glasgow and the other universities had to operate after 1560. What it all meant was that, despite the religious change, there need be no immediate break with the past. In 1560 there was plainly no recognised mechanism for the wholesale deposition of teachers—or of anyone else—on religious grounds alone; and the likelihood was that teachers would continue in office after 1560 and that many would conform to the new regime. This is what happened at St Andrews where the decision of influentia. members of the academic community to support the new order stimulated others into doing likewise. If William Cranston, the principal of St Salvator's, and 'a great favorer of papystes', decided to leave for France in 1561 only to be threatened with excommunication if he returned,[92] others like John Duncanson, principal of St Leonard's till his death in 1566,[93] continued to serve. Duncanson's colleague, John Douglas, principal of St Mary's since 1547 and rector of the university, also conformed, and even after his elevation to the archbishopric of St Andrews he succeeded in retaining his university commitments, though not without criticism, till his death in 1574.[94] Whilst there is little indication of any concerted attempt at St Andrews to adhere to the old faith, the situation at Aberdeen demonstrates clearly enough the difficulties which the reformers experienced in attempting to eject those teachers whose religious convictions did not coincide with their own. Although Alexander Anderson, the acting principal of King's college, declined to conform or recant, he nevertheless retained his appointment till 1569 when he and several other teachers at Aberdeen were deposed by the privy council for their refusal to accept the reformed Confession of Faith.[95]

Sufficient evidence has been adduced to illustrate how substantially the same people remained on the staff at both St Andrews and Aberdeen after 1560, but when attempts are made to trace a parallel development at Glasgow, where the position is much more uncertain, it is doubtful whether this pattern was repeated. No accurate assessment can be made since the records of the faculty of Arts abruptly end in 1555 and those of the university cease in 1558.[96] With the conspicuous exception of the principal, however, it seems to be true that none of the officers of the university in the 1550s reappears on record in that same capacity after the Reformation. The trouble is that there are no university records for some fifteen years after the Reformation. Without question, Beaton's intransigence deprived the university of a chancellor who would not have complied with the Reformation, and his departure no doubt facilitated the way for further change. Yet, not all the members of the university were quite so uncompromising as Beaton. James Balfour, the university rector and treasurer of Glasgow, who placed the mace and other valuables in Beaton's custody, may have been no supporter of the Reformation, but the very fact that he managed to retain his benefice as late as the 1580s—long after the application of a religious test in 1573—suggests that he finally made peace with the new regime.[97]

238   THE NEW FOUNDATION

Even so he did not serve in the reformed church and, after his partisan action in 1560, it is highly improbable that he took any further part in university affairs in Glasgow at least, though he reappeared as deputy rector of St Andrews university in 1580.[98]

On the other hand, it is certainly indicative of the continued co-existence of the structure of the old church with that of the new that the bailies and magistrates of Glasgow in 1566 should present John Law, the former subprior of the friars preachers to the chaplainry of St Machan in the cathedral, and it is an interesting commentary on the times that collation should be granted not by a superintendent or commissioner of the reformed church but by James Balfour, then dean and vicar-general, who instructed any chaplain or notary public in Glasgow to go to the altar of St Machan in the metropolitan church and there give Law institution to the chaplainry.[99] It is equally illuminating that Thomas Knox, a notary and public clerk of the city, should witness the document as 'notary by apostolic authority';[100] and as late as 1569 James Balfour was still described as 'vicar-general of James, archbishop of Glasgow, then in foreign parts'.[101]

It is all too apparent that much of the organisation of the old church in Glasgow, as elsewhere, remained intact after 1560, and while it would be misleading to read too much into the archaic and stylistic forms employed by notaries public in charters of this kind, it is nonetheless remarkable, in a burgh which had accepted the Reformation, to find the same John Law receiving the chaplainry of St Nicholas in the cathedral in July 1564 'by the real and actual handing over and delivery into his hands of the chalice and priestly ornaments in the best method, way, form, right and cause . . . nobody at the time opposing or contra-dicting'.[102] In view of the continuing duality of the two structures, it is scarcely surprising that neither John Colquhoun, a canon of the cathedral, who was university rector in 1556, 1559 and still in office in June 1560, nor John Laing, another canon of the cathedral, who was dean of faculty in 1556 and again in 1560, saw any need to serve in the reformed church.[103] At the same time, unlike Balfour who did his best to prevent the rector's book falling into the hands of the reformers,[104] John Laing who had possession of the arts faculty records in 1560 did nothing to prevent Robert Hamilton, the regent in the 1560s, from acquiring them;[105] and the dean's book which bears the signature of John Houstoun (but which was presumably in Laing's keeping in 1560) also passed into the possession of the reformers and was later signed by Peter Blackburn and Andrew Melville.[106] John Houstoun himself, who occurs as principal regent in 1556 and dean of faculty in 1557, declined to conform in 1560, and by 1567 his benefice was declared to be vacant through death.[107] It may be conjectured that his demission as principal regent, if such he was, in favour of Davidson in 1556 was the result of incapacity or old age, but, in any event, he could not be accommodated within the ministry of the reformed church. Not only did he give canonical institution on Beaton's behalf to a clerk in December 1560 but he was also accused shortly afterwards, it seems, of baptising according to Catholic rites, though by 1562 he had apparently settled down to a career as a commissary.[108] A somewhat similar attitude was adopted by Archibald Beaton, chantor of Aberdeen and university rector in 1556 and again in 1557, who was less uncompromising than his kinsman, the archbishop, and willing to accept an appointment in the secularised commissary court of Glasgow. He had, after all, already occupied the post of official general.[109]

While we cannot be certain that none of these men continued to hold office in the university for a spell after 1560, the distinct impression is that they had deserted what was already an ailing institution. And what seems true of the university officers is also true of the college regents. Thus Robert Cunningham who was regent in 1555[110] does not reappear after 1560; and whatever the status of John Law and Andrew Leech, the two friars who were 'otherwise of the university', neither seems to have had any function in the college after the Reformation. In fact, it sounds rather as if Law was content to receive his 'freiris wageis' of £16 Scots a year and to enjoy the fruits of at least three chaplainries in the city free of commitment.[111]

Despite what looks like the disappearance of most of the staff in 1560, teaching, it seems, did not quite come to a halt. Davidson's continued presence there ensured that at least a skeleton teaching staff—albeit of one—survived, and he was able to count on the assistance of Robert Hamilton who is on record as regent in the college from 1562 till 1565.[112]

The university had been saved from extinction. It had survived the shock of the Reformation. There can be no denying, however, its unhealthy state or its exceedingly uncertain future. Glasgow's plight was much more extreme, its condition far more critical than, say, that of St Andrews or even Aberdeen. The university was smaller, far from flourishing and ill-prepared to weather the religious upheaval. Whilst it might therefore be tempting to ascribe the deterioration purely to the Reformation, reflection would suggest that such an emphasis is rather misplaced, for it is evident that the sorry state of the university can be traced back beyond 1560 to pre-Reformation times.

In the early sixteenth century, John Mair was scarcely flattering when he described the university as 'poorly endowed and not rich in scholars'. Yet if he was critical of Glasgow, Mair had few compliments to pay to her sister institutions and his censorious verdict on them all was: 'I look with no favour on this multitude of universities'. His idea of a flourishing academic community was one in which 'a large number of students together will sharpen one another's wits', and Scotland's universities plainly did not measure up to his exacting standards. A university, like Glasgow, 'poorly endowed', associated with a church which 'possesses prebends many and fat' whose 'revenues are enjoyed *in absentia*', typified a practice which Mair held 'to be destitute at once of justice and of common sense'.[113] This is, of course, an indictment which can fairly be levelled against the late medieval church, but it was a situation, no less, which the crown and nobility had a vested financial interest in perpetuating.

If Glasgow university languished in those years, explanations are not hard to find. The years immediately preceding 1560 seem to disclose a record not merely of unfulfilled ideals and lost opportunities but of inadequate resources and endowment—in short a record of neglect and dilapidation. The envisaged reconstruction of the college buildings[114] had never fully materialised, and in 1563 the university's ruinous state was firmly placed on record: the schools and chambers stood half-built and the endowments for its teachers, together with provision for poor scholars, were said to have ceased.[115] With a keen eye for profitable business transactions, pope and prelate alike had neither incentive nor inclination to initiate any drastic reform in church or university. What is more, the increasing burden of clerical taxation imposed in the 1530s,[116] which often led clerics to dilapidate their benefices, meant that ecclesiastical funds needed for the university's support were less likely than ever to be sufficiently forthcoming; and the unsettling effect which this may have had was matched only by the rapid succession of principals which the college witnessed in the earlier years of the century. Indeed from 1547 to 1550, the university altogether lacked a chancellor at its head.[117] It is also indicative of the college's critical condition in the decade or so before the Reformation that the university found itself unable to attract students in sufficient numbers on a regular basis. By the 1550s matriculation numbers were lower than they had ever been. Only twice do the figures exceed a dozen. Four members of the university are recorded as incorporated in 1550 and again in 1551, one in 1552, nine in 1553, one in 1554, thirteen in 1555, three in 1556, seventeen in 1557 and none in 1558.[118] Gone were the days when the university could boast of a thriving student community, and it is a sobering thought that within a century of its creation the university had almost ceased to function.

The matriculation figures, if fairly accurate, may not be wholly discreditable, but they would seem to compare unfavourably with those of St Andrews,[119] the only other Scottish university with surviving statistics for the period. It may, of course, be possible in part to attribute the apparent decline in student numbers at Glasgow to defective book-keeping and even to periodic outbreaks of plague like that of 1545,[120] which caused some dislocation; but, whatever the position, neither factor was likely to enhance the college's reputation. The overall trend for half a century, in any event, had been a depressing one, and there is no reason to doubt an English visitor's impression in 1536 that Glasgow was 'a lytle unyversyte or study'.[121] It may also be something of a left-handed compliment to Glasgow that in the 1550s, two of its students on gaining their B.A.—students which it could ill afford to lose—should choose to continue their studies at St Andrews.[122]

Though the Glasgow college before the Reformation was in worse shape than other universities, there is little reason to believe that either Aberdeen or St Andrews fared particularly well. By the early sixteenth century, a detectable decline had set in which may be linked with the poor performance of the late medieval church. That an archbishop and chancellor should remark in 1512 that his university was almost extinct and in ruins because of the failure of the foundation and a lack of men of letters does little credit to the situation which existed at St Andrews; and if his action in annexing to the pedagogy the parish church of St Michael was designed to remedy matters, it was less than successful.[123] By the 1540s, at any rate, the university rector voiced the complaint that St Andrews had become 'sa desolate and destitute bayth of rederris, techarris, and auditours yat it is neir perist and meretis nocht to be callit ane universitie'.[124] The matriculation records for those years would seem to confirm that impression.[125] Nor was Aberdeen in much better form where the college had departed somewhat from its founder's intentions. The visitation of 1549 suggests that there was something amiss. It commented on the lack of discipline and the disrepair of the buildings, it criticised the staff for negligence and urged them 'to commence' their duties, it chided the students and some of the teachers for non-residence, it exhorted the principal to provide privies as soon as possible and in all it contributed over fifty recommendations on how the university should be run.[126] If anything was subsequently done, it was soon to be undone, for by 1562 the English agent in Scotland, accompanying the queen to Aberdeen, described the university as 'one college with 15 or 16 scholars'.[127]

The immediate impact of the Reformation may have had a less than beneficial effect on the universities. Yet it is still a little difficult to escape the conclusion that the Scottish universities as a whole—and not just Glasgow—were in a bad way well before the Reformation. To attribute the decay of the Glasgow college solely to the Reformation, therefore, is to overlook a none too edifying record in the years preceding the crisis of 1560, and it might be more realistic to remark that pope, plague and protestantism had each played a part in the college's fall from grace. In any case, it was not the reformers' intention to weaken the fabric of university education in Scotland but rather to augment it. They had ambitious plans for strengthening the whole university system. The Book of Discipline in 1560 recognised the universities as the training ground of the ministry as well as of the commonwealth, and as much, if not more, attention is devoted in that document to the future welfare of the universities than to any other single topic included for discussion.[128] Glasgow, it proposed, should consist not of one college but two—one for arts, the other for philosophy, civil law, Hebrew and divinity. Provision was to be made for forty-eight bursars; and the principal was to be assigned a stipend of £200. Nor were the reformers so naïve as to assume that their programme would not cost money. They had done their sums. Their estimates were that the yearly expenses at Glasgow would amount to a precise £2,922, and that the total annual expenditure of all three universities would reach £9,640. At the same time, their proposal to finance all this from the temporality of the bishoprics and collegiate kirks was less than realistic,[129] and it was likely to be frustrated so long as the worldlings 'greedily gripped to the possessions of the Kirk'.[130]

Nowhere is any hint given of the actual situation which the reformers found at Glasgow university, but John Willock, who helped draw up the first Book of Discipline, was well placed to provide the reformers with a first-hand account. There was plainly a limit, however, to what could be expected from the two existing teachers who were apparently working on what amounted to a part-time basis, for there can be no doubt that John Davidson, the principal, concurrently served as minister of Hamilton. That this identification is correct is confirmed by Davidson's renunciation in 1575, when he was minister of Hamilton, of the tenement called Arthurlie's place in favour of the university; and not only is this property known to have been in the possession of John Davidson, the principal, who was still in office in 1571, but it is also on record that Davidson, the minister, served at Hamilton at least as early as 1563.[131] In later life, Davidson himself remarked in April 1592 that he had acted as minister for thirty-three years, which rather suggests that he had become minister as early as 1559.[132] It seems very likely that Robert Hamilton, the regent on record from 1562 to 1565, was the same man as the Robert Hamilton who appears as minister of Hamilton in 1562,[133] the year before John Davidson is recorded as minister there.

The situation was not entirely hopeless. At Hamilton, Davidson had the assistance of John Rayse, 'exhorter and teychar of the youth' who,

PLATE 4. Andrew Melville. From an engraving in St Andrews University Archives, apparently based on an original at Sedan.

PLATE 5. University Seal of 1588 (80 mm × 64 mm).

PLATE 6. Opening lines of the *Nova Erectio* charter (GUA 21134). Signs of nineteenth-century damage are visible.

in Davidson's absence, would be able to perform any of the duties of the parish ministry except the administration of the sacraments.[134] This would certainly enable Davidson, if he chose, to devote more of his time to college affairs, but it was scarcely a satisfactory arrangement either for the parishioners of Hamilton or for the students of the college. Although the university after 1560 was an exceedingly modest establishment by any standards, it would be wrong to assume that it had been noticeably larger in the years immediately preceding 1560; and if the university could claim only two teachers in the 1560s, there is no reason to believe that the size of the teaching staff was particularly impressive in the 1550s. Indeed, by 1555, there is only mention of two regents—John Houstoun and Robert Cunningham,[135] one of two students who had found it expedient to complete their studies at St Andrews. This was the situation which the reformers inherited and there can be no denying that the university which survived the Reformation was in a sorry state.

An official description of the college in the queen's name in July 1563 records that:[136]

'within the citie of Glasgow ane College and Universitie wes devisit to be hade quhairin the youth mycht be brocht up in lettiris and knawlege, the commoune welth servit and vertew incressit, of the quhilk college ane parte of the sculis and chalmeris being biggit, the rest thairof alswele dwellingis as provisioun for the pouir bursouris and maisteris to teche ceissit, swa that the samin apperit rather to be the decay of ane universitie nor ony wyis to be reknit ane establissit fundatioun'.

These remarks are singularly revealing. They help to explain a good deal about what was happening at the college. They have even been used as evidence by those who have casually assumed that the university was already defunct, but such a verdict is ill-considered and unwarranted. Nowhere does the document claim that the university had ceased to function. What it does explain is why Davidson and Hamilton had ministerial charges: there was simply insufficient money forthcoming from college funds to pay their stipends. Provision for the teachers, it was said, had ceased, but teaching itself was not said to have stopped. Adequate financial support for the regents had somehow to be secured, and one temporary solution was that the regents should combine their teaching duties in the college with a ministerial charge which could be expected to provide a reasonable stipend. Nor was it purely accidental that first Robert Hamilton and then John Davidson, in 1563, should become parish ministers at Hamilton where Chatelherault resided. As minister, however, Davidson could be assigned

I

neither benefice of Hamilton. The parsonage constituted the prebend of the dean of Glasgow cathedral, and at the Reformation the benefice was occupied, first, by Henry Sinclair and, then, by James Balfour who succeeded to the deanery in 1561.[137] The vicarage of Hamilton, on the other hand, was annexed to Hamilton collegiate kirk, of which Chatelherault was patron, but it was already occupied by the provost and was unavailable for Davidson, whose stipend was assigned instead from the thirds of benefices under the scheme devised in 1562.[138] Chatelherault, however, may well have asserted a right to present to the parish church, as distinct from the benefice, and, in any event, his views could not be disregarded. Andrew Hay, minister of Renfrew and later university rector, was also commissary of Hamilton,[139] and it seems likely that his support for Davidson would also be influential. For Chatelherault, however, whose ancestor James, lord Hamilton had been the original founder of the college of Glasgow in 1460, the device adopted may have had the twin attractions of acquiring a well-educated minister for the parish as well as keeping the college afloat.

The first surviving college rental dates only from 1575, but it reveals that the finances of the 'auld fundatioun' amounted to less than £100 in all, and in a subsequent account drawn up at some point between 1578 and 1605, the income from the old foundation stood at no more than £115.[140] Both rentals included the revenues of the vicarage of Colmonell which added up to little more than £40. On the basis of the income derived from the old foundation in the second of these rentals, the first master would receive a stipend of only £66,[141] a figure considerably less than the generous £200 suggested for the principal by the Book of Discipline in 1560 and even less than the more modest £100 recommended for the principal of a college in Buchanan's scheme for St Andrews in 1563.[142] The second master's burse was valued a little more than £10.[143] With an income insufficient to sustain the two existing regents, there could be little hope of attracting any additional help. As regards the financial position of the two regents, that of Robert Hamilton was the more precarious. From the university, he could expect little reward for his labours, but by becoming minister first at Hamilton and then apparently at Bothwell[144] he could claim a stipend which bore some relation to the cost of living. Davidson, however, was in the more fortunate position of being able to supplement his stipend as minister with income derived from other sources. By 1556—the date at which he took up his appointment at Glasgow—he was already vicar of Alness; he also held the vicarage of Nigg in the diocese of St Andrews and in 1559 he was chaplain of St Michael's altar in Glasgow cathedral.[145] As principal, he held the vicarage of Colmonell and even although it yielded a rather modest return, he may have been no more successful in obtaining the fruits than the canons of Glasgow who held the parsonage and who ruefully remarked in 1564 that they had not received payment for the last four years.[146] Even his right to the title of the vicarage was disputed in 1568 when he successfully defended an action against James Greig who, as minister of Colmonell, claimed both parsonage and vicarage.[147] Davidson was also in receipt of a pension of £40 from the parsonage of Kinkell, the third of which was remitted in accordance with 'the ordour tane be hir majestie with the remanent collegeis'.[148] The thirds of the vicarages of Alness and Colmonell were likewise remitted during his tenure as principal of the pedagogy.[149] And this was not all; he was also in receipt of a pension of 100 merks from the parsonage of Glasgow; he was due a pension from the chaplainry of Muirhall in the barony of Carnwath,[150] and as late as 1578 he claimed from the university a small pension of £5 for the Whitsun term.[151] Moreover, as minister of Hamilton, Davidson was entitled to a stipend of £120.[152] Although he had the churches of Dalserf, Cambuslang and Blantyre committed to his charge, there were of course readers in attendance at these churches who could undertake much of the parish work.[153] Even so, it is not really surprising that by 1572, or thereabouts, Davidson should finally decide to set aside his university duties and concentrate instead on his ministry at Hamilton.

The dilapidated state of the college, on which the queen had reason to comment in 1563, poses the problem of what had happened to its revenues at the Reformation. It must have been little consolation to a college already on the verge of bankruptcy that Mary, like her predecessors, should grant it immunity from clerical taxation—an immunity, indeed, which was to extend in perpetuity.[154] Yet, a flourishing scholastic community remained difficult to attain. The finances of the college had never been in a particularly healthy state, and even before 1560 the greater portion of a teacher's income was likely to be derived from the ecclesiastical benefices which he held independently of his university office. The only benefice which the college could claim after 1560 was the vicarage of Colmonell, recently annexed in 1558 'pro augmentatione annualis redditus'.[155] Any benefices previously sought had evidently not been acquired. The record, in short, had been one of unsuccessful appropriations. Nor was the college's dwindling income likely to be much improved by the fees paid by the few students which it managed to attract. Impoverished through lack of funds, the college's main source of income consisted of the revenues and rents obtained from what property the college possessed, that is, from the lands, tenements and yards which it leased and from those of the chaplainries which it had acquired.[156] But it was not always an easy matter to collect the rents as subsequent litigation was to show.

The coming of the Reformation perhaps gave added incentive, as happened at St Andrews,[157] for adherents of the old order to dissipate college revenues, possibly to avoid their falling into the hands of the reformers, but more probably to secure some financial return for themselves and their kinsmen in the years ahead, though to what extent this happened is now difficult to discover. The mere fact that Davidson became a protestant was no guarantee that it would not happen. Nor would this in itself prove any great impediment to those intent on diverting property, for certain property including chaplainries in university patronage could be disponed simply with the consent of the rector or also with the consent of the dean of faculty, without recourse to the principal.[158] And it is true that the university rector and dean of faculty in 1560 were not committed to protestantism in the way in which the principal was.

But if there were losses there were also gains. After the Reformation, college revenues were gradually augmented with the acquisition of property previously owned by the friars preachers and vicars choral, as well as by the gaining of a number of chaplainries in the city.[159] This process of secularisation was facilitated by an edict of the privy council in 1562 which not only permitted the town council to convert the friaries into suitable accommodation for schools and colleges, but which also conceded the reallocation of 'all annuellis, males and dewiteis within fre burrowis or utheris townis of this realme, alsweill pertenying to chapellanreis, prebendariis as to freris, togidder with the rentis of the freris landis quhairevir thai be' for such godly uses as the support of schools and hospitals.[160] It was not, however, until March 1567 that the queen formally granted to the town council and burgh the lands and rents of the churches, chapels, prebends, altarages and chaplainries in the city together with the places, lands and revenues of the friars preachers and friars minor in Glasgow.[161] Since the existing chaplains, prebendaries and friars were permitted to enjoy the emoluments of their possessions for the duration of their lives, the envisaged returns assigned to the town were slow to materialise. The town council, however, by the terms of the grant, was required to support the ministry of the burgh, and when the magistrates showed reluctance to pay their minister £80 from the rents disponed by the queen for that purpose, the privy council intervened to ensure that payment was made, by sanctioning the imposition of a general tax on the inhabitants of the burgh.[162] This merely demonstrated the inadequacy of the grant of 1567, and, as a remedy, in 1568 the thirds of the revenues derived from all chaplainries, altarages, prebends, kirks and colleges within the town were assigned to the town council, lest any 'impediment succeid throw non payment of the stipend appertening to the ministeris thairof'.[163] In all these proceedings, the claims of the university were disregarded, but in 1573 its pressing needs were recognised when the town council formally conveyed to the college the revenues of the various ecclesiastical properties which the burgh had acquired.[164]

Attempts to alleviate the plight of the university had already been made in a bequest by the queen in 1563 in favour of five poor bursars to be financed from the rents and lands, extending to thirteen acres, of the friars preachers beside the university.[165] Although it has sometimes been assumed that the college did not acquire this property until at least 1573, the fact that the college received the rent in 1563 for the lease of these thirteen acres, as a result of action taken by the town council, sufficiently indicates that effective superiority of these lands already lay with the university.[166]

The rather optimistic expectation in 1563 was that the queen's foundation would provide the college with 'sic ressonabile leving that tharin the liberale sciences may be planlie techit siclike as the samyn ar in utheris collegis of this realme'.[167] In practice, this did not prove to be the case. Even so, bursars could be admitted to the university once more to take their place along with fee-paying students in the pedagogy. Some, indeed, were fortunate enough to obtain the gift of a benefice. On the other hand, since 'the poverte of mony is in sic sort that thay may not hauld thair children at letteris', parliament in 1567 encouraged patrons of provostries, prebends, altarages and chaplainries to present bursars to these livings when they became vacant to enable students 'to studie vertew and letteris within ane college of ony of the universiteis of this realme'.[168] With this boost in morale, the prospect was that the college would receive a new lease of life. As a result of this enactment, in November 1569, David Gibson received a gift of a prebend in the collegiate kirk of Lincluden 'for his sustenatioun at the scolis within the universitie of Glasgw quhair he presentlie studiis for the space of sevin yeris nixtocum, providing that in the menetyme he continew his study in the said universitie . . . quhilk tyme being expyrit or the said David desisting of his study in the menetyme the said prebendarie to be gevin to ony uther student that the supreme power findis maist indigent'.[169] Archibald Herbertson, another student at the college, was likewise provided to the vicarage of Maybole in December 1569,[170] and the chaplainry of St Michael in the cathedral was made available in January 1570 for the support of bursars in the university.[171] In October 1570, Archibald Gibson also obtained a gift of a prebend in the collegiate kirk of Lincluden to support him in his studies at the college, and provision was made in September 1571 for the annexation to the college of the vicarage pensionary of Glasgow, which Wemyss as minister demitted, 'for sustening of ane student or studentis thairin'.[172]

The university, it is plain, continued to provide instruction and students continued to attend. As a teacher, Davidson may have shown no exceptional gifts, but there is no reason to doubt his competence. By replying to Quintin Kennedy, he at least provided posterity with an insight into his theological outlook which might be described as mildly Calvinist. The tract itself is pedestrian rather than inspired, though it does reveal a knowledge of the primitive and apostolic church.[173] As a theologian, Davidson had evidently a certain interest in biblical languages. He is known to have owned some books in Hebrew as well as Sebastian Munster's dictionary of Chaldaic.[174] It is therefore reasonable to suppose that he possessed a knowledge of both these languages, though he need not have taught them to his students. Quite what he did teach them is not known, but, at most, all that he could hope to offer them was a training in Arts with possibly some instruction in theology.

Despite the intervention of church and state with schemes for reforming St Andrews and Aberdeen, little thought was given either by general assembly, parliament or privy council to remedying the situation at Glasgow. The university, it almost seemed, could be conveniently forgotten. Apart from confirming a grant in 1573,[175] it was only in 1574 that parliament turned its attention to Glasgow—and then only fleetingly—when it decreed that any university students not licensed to ask for alms should be treated as vagabonds, a measure to be applied in all three universities.[176]

Whether the university possessed a revised constitution after 1560, or indeed any formal constitution at all, is hard to determine. It presumably no longer had a chancellor at its head. After the Reformation, it could no longer recognise its former chancellor, the papalist archbishop, who still remained 'in foreign parts' and by 1572 was described as 'sumtyme archebischop'; and it was not until November 1573 that the first protestant archbishop of Glasgow was effectively elected and consecrated.[177] The situation was not unlike that which later occurred at St Andrews when during a visitation in 1576 the criticism was voiced:[178]

'as to the office of chancellarie that the visitouris that ar to be appointit be the kirk and regentis grace supplie the office until ane chancellar be appointit'.

The Book of Discipline, it is true, had nothing to say of the office of chancellor, but the town's foundation in January 1573 certainly regarded the office as an integral part of the university's constitution.[179] By that date, however, with the conclusion of the Leith agreement in 1572, there was once more the prospect that Glasgow would receive its first protestant archbishop.[180] It was, however, no foregone conclusion that the next archbishop would automatically be the next *cancellarius superintendens universitatis*. On the other hand, since Willock retired to England in 1568,[181] Glasgow no longer possessed a rival in the superintendent, and the 'vice-superintendent' (in effect the commissioner) to which the document referred was none other than Andrew Hay, the minister of Renfrew, who first appears on record as university rector in 1569.[182] The town's charter also recognised the office of dean of faculty, and from an incidental reference it is known that David Cunningham, minister of Cadder and subdean of Glasgow, was dean of faculty in 1573.[183]

The foundation of 1573 was the first significant step in restoring the university's fortunes, but it was a gloomy picture which the charter painted of the college's rundown state. Through a lack of funds to spend upon it, the pedagogy was said almost to have gone to ruin, so that 'through excessive poverty the pursuit of learning has become utterly extinct'.[184] The town council had therefore taken upon itself the task of restoring the college and endowing it anew in order that 'the study of the liberal arts should revive'. The temporality and spirituality of those ecclesiastical properties which the town had received from the queen were transferred to the college for its upkeep. But the intervention of the town council did not end there. Not only did the magistrates regard it as 'a duty entrusted to us' to restore the ailing state of 'our pedagogy of Glasgow', they also proceeded to rewrite much of its constitution and to prescribe the curriculum and subjects for study as well as to impose a strict code of discipline. The conditions of service for the teaching staff were also drawn up by the town council, and of the twelve bursaries which it proposed endowing the stipulation was that preference should be given to the sons of Glasgow burgesses and that the right of presentation should be vested in the town council. In addition to all this, the bailies were also to be included amongst the visitors of the university, with power to audit the college accounts and to deprive teachers of their office.[185]

After a hundred and twenty years of existence, it looked almost as if the college was destined to become a 'tounis college'. For some there is something shameful or unworthy in this, but this was not the attitude of ecclesiastical and educational reformers in the sixteenth century who saw no sound reason to venerate papal bulls. For them, there could be few finer examples than the city colleges of Strasbourg, Lausanne, Geneva, and the numerous newly-established French protestant academies, modelled on those of Nîmes and Bordeaux, where native Scots sometimes chose to study in preference to their own universities.[186] And in Edinburgh, where the 'tounis college' owed its origins to the sponsorship of the burgh ministers and magistrates, a university came into being, dependent on no papal bull, its status confirmed solely by royal charter in 1582, which empowered it to establish higher faculties as well as studies in the liberal arts.[187] If, in the end, as has been confidently asserted, 'Glasgow never became the "tounis college"',[188] it was less because a benevolent town council chose not to interfere, than that the town's foundation of 1573 was superseded four years later by a royal foundation which averted any threatened domination by the town council.[189]

It is questionable whether studies were 'utterly extinct' at the university by January 1573. If, by that date, Davidson had already left, as may have been the case, then it is of course a reasonable inference that instruction had come to an end, as the charter asserted. On the other hand, as late as July 1573, Blaise Lawrie appears on record as 'student in the university of Glasgow',[190] which suggests that the college was still functioning. Not only so, in 1578 to support him in his studies of philosophy in the university, Duncan Nairn received a gift of the vicarage of Maybole, vacant on the expiry of the gift of the benefice granted for seven years to Mr Archibald Herbertson in 1569.[191] Now it is evident that Herbertson had already taken his master's degree, and as he is known to have been a student at Glasgow university,[192] the deduction might be that he was also a Glasgow graduate, but Archibald Herbertson, the Glasgow student of 1569, may well be the student of that name who matriculated in 1571 at St Salvator's college, St Andrews, where he eventually graduated in 1575.[193] Another Glasgow student, Archibald Gibson, who in 1577 resigned to his brother, John, the benefice he had obtained in 1570,[194] does not seem to have gained his master's degree, possibly because the college had been disbanded or equally possibly because he failed to last the pace, whatever the pace may have been. Even so, there are distinct signs that all was not well at the pedagogy. It says little for the university's wellbeing that Blaise Lawrie, the Glasgow student of July 1573, should proceed to St Andrews where he matriculated at St Mary's college in 1573 and graduated in 1577[195] before returning to Glasgow as a college regent. Certainly the university was in dire straits by the summer of 1573.

That the town's charter should solely acknowledge 'the constant and oft-repeated exhortation, persuasion, advice and help' of Andrew Hay,[196] the university rector, without mention of any assistance from Davidson, strongly suggests that the principal wished to take no further part in college affairs and that he had probably returned to Hamilton, though it was only after the arrival of Andrew Melville, as principal, that Davidson finally renounced in favour of the college in January 1575 all rights to the vicarage of Colmonell.[197] Nor is it really surprising that he should retire to Hamilton. There were practical enough reasons why the new constitution was not likely to appeal to him. For one thing, there was no hope of obtaining a higher salary. The proposed stipend for the principal was not to be increased: he was assigned the revenues and teinds of the vicarage of Colmonell, plus twenty merks from the college rents,[198] which, if anything, on paper at least, was rather less than what he might expect. No longer would the principal be able to receive recompense from other sources, for he was prohibited from undertaking outside work or holding other offices. He was also forbidden from residing 'elsewhere than within the walls of the college'. There were other aspects, too, of the new constitution which had a medieval air about them. Earlier traditions, or rather ideals, of celibacy and the communal life were not easily effaced, even under a protestant regime. The foundation of 1573 grudgingly recognised, as a concession to the times, that teachers might marry: 'if they be not able to bear the life of chastity and cannot contain themselves, let them marry wives in the Lord'.[199] But they were plainly not encouraged to rush into matrimony; it might not be too much to say that obstacles were placed in the way. There is surely a strange ambivalence in a provision which required teachers to live in college but which excluded their wives—and indeed all women—from the college precincts. None of these arrangements was likely to prove satisfactory either to Davidson or his wife. That he was married is indicated by his acting as administrator for his daughter, Margaret, in the transfer of college property to which she had rights in 1575.[200]

The new constitution contained little that was novel, except perhaps the rigour with which it was to be upheld. It provided for a professor of theology, 'gravely and earnestly travailling in that faculty' who would also serve as principal of the college. This was simply a reaffirmation of earlier practice, though the term 'professor' may have had an innovating ring about it. The principal was to be elected *ad vitam aut culpam*, and the power of election was to lie with the chancellor, rector, dean of faculty and with the 'dean parson' (*decanum rectorem*) of the church of Hamilton and the parson of the church of Glasgow, if the latter two were ministers. The principal was expected to read and to expound the scriptures daily in the college pulpit. This was similar to the practice observed at St Andrews where in 1576 James Wilkie, as principal of St Leonard's college, 'techis in Latin ilk Fryday the epistill to the Hebrues, and on Settirday and Sonday reidis the prayeris and techis the prophet Ezechiel in Inglische'.[201] There were also to be two regents, elected by the rector, principal and dean of faculty, who would teach philosophy: the principles of dialectics, logic, physics, moral philosophy and metaphysics. For their labours, they were assigned a stipend of £20 each, a figure which ill compares with St Mary's college, St Andrews, where the recommended salary scale in 1576 commenced at £40 increasing to £100 for the first master. It is only fair to add, however, that St Andrews had its own financial problems: St Mary's college was said to be in debt in 1576 and one of the regents there had not been paid for two and a half years.[202] At Glasgow, the two regents were subject to possible removal from office every sixth year after they had conducted two classes through the whole curriculum. They were also required to read the prayers in the Blackfriars church beside the college, at the discretion of the elders on the kirk session, and in church the students and people were expected to assemble to hear the prayers. In addition to fee-paying students, who were evidently permitted 'to live there for the sake of study', there were to be twelve foundationers who were to reside in college and who had to complete their master's degree within three and a half years, no extensions being granted. All matriculands were obliged to subscribe to the reformed Confession of Faith.[203] Students of unsound religious convictions were to be excluded from a university education.

The envisaged size of the college with a principal, two regents and twelve foundationers was modest enough. Yet it was not absurdly small, if compared with the St Andrews colleges: St Leonard's had a principal, four regents and six bursars in May 1576, and St Salvator's had apparently a principal and three regents.[204] With so small a staff, there were limitations in what could be taught, and the Glasgow college, it seems, was designed to operate exclusively as a college of philosophy and theology. No provision was made for the appointment of a grammarian. Students were evidently expected to be already proficient in grammar before arriving at the college. It was required of bursars that they be already 'so well grounded in the knowledge of grammar as to be fit auditors for philosophy and that they have skill in speaking and writing correctly'.[205] This attitude, however optimistic, was in accord with the ideas of the first Book of Discipline, with its elaborate schemes for the erection of grammar schools, and arts colleges 'in every notable town' where 'at least logick and rhetorick, together with the tongues, be read by sufficient masters, for whom honest stipends must be appointed'.[206] Reality, however, dictated that both St Andrews and Aberdeen universities should have their own grammarians.[207]

With its concentration on philosophy and theology, the proposed curriculum could scarcely be said to contain the full spectrum of the medieval Arts course which, in theory at least, was based on a study of the seven liberal arts: the *trivium* consisting of grammar, logic and rhetoric, and the more advanced *quadrivium* subjects of arithmetic, geometry, astronomy and music. Nor was attention paid to what the first Book of Discipline had to say about the teaching of mathematics and economics as well as civil and Roman law at Glasgow.[208] Equally, any similarity between the curriculum outlined in 1573 and George Buchanan's 'Opinion', some ten years earlier, for a philosophy college at St Andrews would seem to be at best coincidental, for unlike St Andrews there was no suggestion that Glasgow's philosophy course should incorporate 'the medicinis lesson' or the 'principis of mathematick'.[209] That George Buchanan, nonetheless, had an interest in educational developments at Glasgow is indicated by the college's recognition in February 1579 of the 'singular favour that ane honorable man Maister George Buchannan, teachar of our soverain lord in gude lettres, hes borne and shawen at all tymes to our college'.[210] There is, however, no evidence of his involvement in the scheme of 1573; and, as a friend of Andrew Melville,[211] his more immediate interest may have lain in the proposals associated with the new erection of 1577. Shortly afterwards, at any rate, he donated a number of books to the college library.[212]

Responsibility for composing the foundation charter in 1573 lay firmly with the town council and Andrew Hay, the university rector. In the aftermath of the 'civil war' between the king's men and the queen's men, the dust of which settled only in 1572, the town council judged it appropriate that a fresh start should be made. Sir John Stewart of Minto, the provost, had evidently commended himself to the king's cause; not only had he been made keeper of the castle in Glasgow by the Regent Moray, but he had also been appointed by the Regent Lennox bailie of the lordship and regality of Glasgow.[213] His views on teaching methods in the college were likely to be less informed, and to that extent less influential, than those of Adam Wallace, a bailie on the council, who became the town's procurator, and who was also a graduate of the university;[214] but it would seem that the dominant figure behind the town's charter was Andrew Hay, himself a Glasgow graduate, who could claim unrivalled experience and knowledge as rector, minister, commissary, commissioner of the churches in the west and, ultimately, moderator of the general assembly.

Whatever the merits of the new foundation, the test would only come in its application, and the first priority was to find a new recruit to act as regent. The choice fell on Peter Blackburn. The son of a Glasgow burgess, Blackburn had been educated at St Mary's college, St Andrews, matriculating in 1568 and graduating master of arts in 1572.[215] At some point, he seems to have visited France: it was presumably there that he purchased a copy of *Commentaires de Jules Cesar, de la guerre de la Gaule*, published at Lyons in 1555, which bears an inscription in

French of his ownership.[216] Described as 'new come from St Androis', where he had been appointed a university procurator as late as 1573, Blackburn arrived in Glasgow to accept office as regent in the college.[217] The precise date of his appointment is unknown, but he was already teaching by April 1574 when David Wemyss, the city minister, handed over certain property to the 'principal and masters and regents' of the college, sasine being given to Blackburn as 'regent or one of the masters of the said pedagogy in name of the university and pedagogy of Glasgow and of the principal and regents and masters thereof'.[218] It is doubtful whether the stylised form of the document recording the transaction can be taken as sound evidence that Blackburn had colleagues at the college. Certainly, when Andrew Melville, as principal master, arrived in November 1574 to 'sie the beginning of a collage ther', he found neither an out-going principal nor masters, but merely the solitary figure of Peter Blackburn, who taught 'conform to the ordour of the course of St Androis'.[219]

Despite the measures taken for the financial resuscitation of the college, first by the queen in 1563 and then by the town council in 1573, it looked rather as if the demise of the university which had been long predicted could scarcely be further postponed. Its life expectancy had nearly run out. That it should recover at all was no mean feat, and it is to Andrew Melville that credit must go for giving university education at Glasgow, and elsewhere in Scotland, a new lease of life. Only then was the university's reputation placed beyond cavil. Indeed, not the least of his achievements as principal was the *nova erectio* or new foundation of the college in 1577 which bears the imprint of his thinking and which had important consequences for the university's development in the next three centuries.

NOTES

1. Teaching at St Andrews began in 1410; Bishop Wardlaw granted a charter of incorporation in 1412 which was confirmed by papal bull in 1413. See Cant, *University of St Andrews*, 1.
2. *Glas. Mun.*, i, 4.
3. See Cant, *University of St Andrews*; Mackie, *University*; R. S. Rait, *The Universities of Aberdeen* (Aberdeen, 1895); D. B. Horn, *A Short History of the University of Edinburgh* (Edinburgh, 1967); Fraserburgh, *RMS*, v, no. 2117; vi, no. 1167; *APS*, iv, 147–8.
4. Rashdall, *Universities*, i, p. xxiv, ii, *passim*.
5. In the papal bull of 1451, Glasgow was granted the privileges and immunities enjoyed by Bologna (*Glas. Mun.*, i, 4–5; ii, 4), and both the papal bull of 1495 and the royal charter to Aberdeen in 1497 were granted 'cum omnibus privilegiis Universitatibus Parisiensi et Bononiensi . . .' (*Evidence*, iv, 131; *Fasti Aberdonenses*, 4, 11).

6. P. H. Brown, *George Buchanan* (Edinburgh, 1890), 47–177; Major, *History*, 28–9.

7. Rashdall, *Universities*, i, 406.

8. *Ibid.*, i, 497–539; ii, *passim*; iii, 169–235, 293–324; Cobban, *Medieval Universities*, 122–59.

9. Cant, *University of St Andrews*, 22–40; also Cant, *College of St Salvator*, Herkless and Hannay, *College of St Leonard, passim*.

10. St Salvator's: the parsonage of Cults and the parsonages and vicarages of Kemback and Dunino were erected into specific prebends within the college for the maintenance of the provost, licentiate and bachelor of theology respectively, whilst the parsonage revenues of Kilmany were assigned in common to members of the college. See Cant, *College of St Salvator*, 55–7, 63, 67, 71; *Evidence*, iii, 269–73; Cowan, *Parishes*, 41, 52–3, 93, 104.

   St Leonard's: *Evidence*, iii, 356–7; Herkless and Hannay, *College of St Leonard*, 128–9, 137–8.

   St Mary's: *Evidence*, iii, 357–67; Cant, *University of St Andrews*, 36; Cowan, *Parishes*, 35, 85, 194–6, 203.

11. *Evidence*, iv, 131, cf. 135, 139; Cowan, *Parishes*, 3, 76, 183–4 (Slains), 2 (St Mary), 9 (Auchindoir); Rait, *Aberdeen*, 44–5 (St Mary).

12. *Glas. Mun.*, i, 42; cf. 42–3. For Colmonell, *ibid.*, i, 56–7, 62–4; Cowan, *Parishes*, 34. Dunbar's foundation of 1537, to be endowed with the vicarages of Erskine, Cadder, Monkland and Colmonell does not seem to have taken full effect, *Glas. Mun.*, i, 49, 493–5; Cowan, *Parishes*, 24, 62, 150.

13. A. B. Cobban, 'Episcopal Control in the Medieval Universities of Northern Europe', *Studies in Church History*, v (1966), 1–22 at 2.

14. *Glas. Mun.*, ii, 243–4, 250.

15. Cf. *Statutes of the Scottish Church*, ed. D. Patrick (SHS, Edinburgh, 1907), 106–7, 125, 176; *Melrose Regality Records*, iii, 167–75.

16. Knox, *Works*, i, 36, cf. 55, 192; *History*, i, 15, cf. 23, 86.

17. *Statutes of the Scottish Church*, 123.

18. J. Durkan, 'The Scottish Universities in the Middle Ages' (unpublished Edinburgh Ph.D. thesis, 1959), 367–8; G. Donaldson, 'Aberdeen University and the Reformation', *Northern Scotland*, i, 129–42.

19. *Essays on the Scottish Reformation*, 330–1.

20. *AFA*, i, p. lxvii; ii, 415; *Early Records of the University of St Andrews*, 157, 266–7.

21. Durkan, 'Scottish Universities in the Middle Ages,' 367–8.

22. *Early Records of the University of St Andrews*, 252; Knox, *Works*, i, 346–50; *History*, i, 180–3; *CSP Scot.*, i, no. 469; *Narratives of Scottish Catholics under Mary Stuart and James VI*, ed. W. Forbes Leith (London, 1889), 80; M. Lee, *James Stewart, Earl of Moray* (New York, 1953), *passim*.

23. *St Andrews Kirk Session Records* (SHS, Edinburgh, 1889, 1890), i, 2–5.

24. *RMS*, iv, no. 1790.

25. W. Campbell, *History of the Incorporation of Cordiners of Glasgow* (Glasgow, 1883), 248; *Glasgow City Charters*, i, pt. i, 18.

26. *Glas. Mun.*, i, 9–12, 17–18, 20.

27. *Ibid.*, i, 9–12.

28. *Ibid.*, ii, 16–17; *The First Book of Discipline*, ed. J. K. Cameron (Edinburgh, 1972), 88.

29. *Glas. Mun.*, i, 118.

30. *Ibid.*, i, 116–19.

31. *RPC*, i, 202; *Glas. Mun.*, i, 68.

32. *ER*, xix, 142; *Glasgow Protocols*, v, nos. 1370, 1374.
33. *Accounts of the Collectors of Thirds of Benefices, 1561–1572*, ed. G. Donaldson (SHS, Edinburgh, 1949), 98, 256.
34. C. Haws, *Scottish Parish Clergy at the Reformation 1540–74* (SRS, Edinburgh, 1972), 97; Watt, *Fasti*, 156; Knox, *Works*, ii, 398; *History*, ii, 90.
35. *RPC*, i, 492.
36. Technically, Sinclair was by then liferenter or *usufructuarius* of the parsonage (Edinburgh University Library, MS Dc.4.36. Rental of Assumptions, f. 17v) since he had resigned the title, though not the fruits, on appointment to the deanery in 1550.
37. *Registrum Episcopatus Glasguensis*, ed. C. Innes (Bannatyne and Maitland Clubs, Edinburgh, 1843), ii, no. 526; *Glasgow City Charters*, i, pt. ii, 125–6.
38. Knox, *Works*, vi, 78.
39. *Ibid.*, i, 340, 345, 367, 382, 414, 434; *History*, i, 175, 179, 195–7, 207, 230; *CSP Scot.*, i, no. 1023.
40. SRO, RH11/32/1. Archbishopric of Glasgow: Charters, depositions of witnesses and productions relative to the claim of the archbishops to appoint the provost and bailies of the city of Glasgow, 1543–1557; SRO, Register of Acts and Decreets, xv, ff. 6r–10r; *Registrum Episcopatus Glasguensis*, ii, no. 523; *Glasgow City Charters*, i, pt. ii, 119–21.
41. *HMC 11th Report*, App. vi, 221; *Glasgow City Charters*, i, pt. i, 16; pt. ii, 125. In 1564, Chatelherault was ordered to renounce his lease of the bailiary and justiciary of Glasgow. *RPC*, i, 290–1.
42. *CSP Scot.*, i, nos. 480, 525, 530, 551, 665.
43. *ALHT*, x, 416. For the Beggars' Summons, Knox, *Works*, i, 320–1; *History*, ii, 255–6.
44. *Wodrow Society Miscellany* (Edinburgh, 1844), i, 62.
45. J. Leslie, *The Historie of Scotland* (STS, 1895, and Bannatyne Club, 1830), 281.
    The phrase 'caused tak done' may well be appropriate. Bishop Leslie, writing as a Catholic commentator, does not hint at violent destruction. Argyll, Ruthven and Stewart, it is true, gave the following instructions to the city magistrates in 1560:

    'pray you fail not to pass incontinent to your kirks in Glasgow and tak down the hail images thereof and bring forth to the kirk zyard and burn thaym openly. And sicklyk, cast down the altaris and pure the kirk of all kynd of monuments of idolatrye. And this ze fail not to do as well as ye will do us singular emplesure, and so committis you to the protection of God; bot ze tak guid heyd that neither the dasks, windocks, nor durris be ony ways hurt or broken, either glassin wark or iron wark'.

    Whatever the effect of these directions, archbishop Beaton in July 1560 was able to carry off 'all the Silver Warke and hail Juels of the Hie Kirk to Paris with him' (*Glas. Mun.*, iii, 523). He apparently took not only records of the see but 'all the vestments, and image of our Saviour in beaten gold, the twelve Apostles in silver, gold and silver crucifixes, chalices, platters, candlesticks, maces etc.' (cf. J. Cleland, *Statistical Tables relative to the City of Glasgow*, Glasgow, 1823, 166-7). That the cathedral should be denuded of its ornaments was as much the result of action by Catholics as it was by protestants.
46. Leslie, *Historie*, 281.
47. *CSP Scot.*, i, no. 694; R. Keith, *History of the Affairs of Church and State in Scotland* (Spottiswoode Society, Edinburgh, 1844–50), iii, 7 n. 2.
48. *CSP Scot.*, i, no. 891.

49. Knox, *Works*, ii, 87; *History*, i, 334; Keith, *History*, iii, 10, 7 n. 2.
50. *CSP Scot.*, i, nos. 967, 1023; Keith, *History*, ii, 87.
51. *RPC*, ii, 114.
52. *Glas. Mun.*, ii, 288, 289, 293.
53. I.e. the college of St Mary and St Anne. Edinburgh University Library, MS Dc.4.32. Rental of Assumptions, f. 20v.
54. *Thirds of Benefices*, 92, 150, 261, 265; *RPC*, i, 499.
55. *First Book of Discipline*, 123, 145, 148, 152.
56. *CSP Scot.*, i, nos. 566, 876.
57. *Fasti Aberdonenses*, 264; *Officers and Graduates of the University and King's College, Aberdeen*, ed. P. J. Anderson (New Spalding Club, Aberdeen, 1893), 51 n. 1; *Wodrow Society Miscellany*, i, 257.
58. SRO, CC10/1/1. Act Book of Hamilton and Campsie Commissary Court, i, (15 April 1564–7 May 1566), f. 40r; W. A. McNeill, 'Scottish Entries in the *Acta Rectoria Universitatis Parisiensis*, 1519 to *c.* 1633', *SHR*, xliii, (1964), 66–87, at 73.
59. *Glas. Mun.*, ii, 175.
60. *Wodrow Society Miscellany*, i, 175–94, 187, 256.
61. *Essays on the Scottish Reformation*, 330–1.
62. *Wodrow Society Miscellany*, i, 181–258.
63. *Glas. Mun.*, ii, 176.
64. *Wodrow Society Miscellany*, i, 257, 187, cf. 256.
65. *Glas. Mun.*, i, 67.
66. *Ibid.*, iii, 518.
67. *Ibid.*, iii, 517, 523.
68. *Thirds of Benefices*, 92, 150, 261, 265.
69. J. Durkan, 'Notes on Glasgow Cathedral', *IR*, xxi (1970), 54; *Thirds of Benefices*, 164, 264.
70. *IR*, xxi, 65; *Glasgow Protocols*, ii, no. 454; *Thirds of Benefices*, 262.
71. *IR*, xxi, 69; *RSS*, iv, no. 727; *Thirds of Benefices*, 264.
72. Haws, *Parish Clergy*, 173; *Thirds of Benefices*, 265; Cowan, *Parishes*, 141.
73. Haws, *Parish Clergy*, 287; *Thirds of Benefices*, 264.
74. *Glasgow Protocols*, i, no. 222; v, no. 1394; Haws, *Parish Clergy*, 283; *Thirds of Benefices*, 265.
75. *Glasgow Protocols*, i, no. 142; ii, no. 510; v, nos. 1324, 1340, 1345, 1403; Haws, *Parish Clergy*, 315; *Thirds of Benefices*, 264, 266.
76. *Glasgow Protcols*, ii, nos. 285, 286, 598; Haws, *Parish Clergy*, 231, 295.
77. *Glasgow Protocols*, i, no. 78; v, no. 1416; Haws, *Parish Clergy*, 146, 292.
78. GUA. MSS 11615, 11616, 16299. (20 Dec. 1554: John Hunter, prior, Robert Lyle, subprior, David Dawson, Robert Aken, John Johnstoun, George Denewoll, Andrew Hunter, John Law. 6 November 1557: John Hunter, prior, Robert Aitken, 'baggit' Dawson, Mark Hamilton, George Denewoll, John Law, James Carudderis, James Fodringham, John McKursche. 6 December 1558: Andrew Leche, prior, John Law sub-prior, David Dawson, Mark Hamilton, Symon Cornwall, John Forton, John Meyk, James Carudderis, James Fodringham, Helecius MacCullocht.).
79. *Thirds of Benefices*, 293 (McCulloch), 187, 193 (Fotheringham), 265, 291 (Carruthers).
80. *Glas. Mun.*, ii, 156; J. Durkan, 'Some Local Heretics', *Trans. Dumfries and Galloway Nat. Hist. and Antiqu. Socy.*, 3rd ser. xxxvi (1957–58), 67–77, at 67–71.
81. *Glas. Mun.*, ii, 160; Spottiswoode, *History*, iii, 336.
82. *Glas. Mun.*, ii, 157; *Thirds of Benefices*, 263; *The Booke of the Universall Kirk*

of Scotland: Acts and Proceedings of the General Assemblies of the Kirk of Scotland (Maitland Club, Edinburgh, 1839–45), i, 158–9 (hereafter *BUK*). He was still 'reader' at Monkland in 1574. *Wodrow Society Miscellany*, i, 380.

83. *Glas. Mun.*, ii, 165; Haws, *Parish Clergy*, 126, 163.

84. *Glas. Mun.*, ii, 170; *Thirds of Benefices*, 264 (Knox and Hill).

85. Vatican Archives, Reg. Supp. 2855, ff. 140–1; 2876, f. 25; 2963, f. 291r; *Thirds of Benefices*, 67, 92–3, 137, 150, 261–2; *Glas. Mun.*, i, 76–7.

86. *Ibid.*, ii, 171, 176.

87. *APS*, ii, 526, 535.

88. *RMS*, iv, no. 1790.

89. *APS*, iii, 38 c. 16.

90. *BUK*, i, 33, 60, 108; Calderwood, *History*, ii, 226, 288, 380.

91. *APS*, iii, 72; *BUK*, i, 212; Calderwood, *History*, iii, 175–6.

92. Knox, *Works*, vi, 144; *CSP Scot.*, i, no. 1139, (where he is reported to have died by 1562); *CSP Scot.*, i, no. 1031; *St Andrews Kirk Session Records*, i, 169–70.

93. *AFA*, ii, 427n.

94. *Ibid.*, lxii n. 6, lxv, lxvii, lxix; *BUK*, i, 241–2; Calderwood, *History*, iii, 210–11.

95. *RPC*, i, 675; *BUK*, i, 141–4; Calderwood, *History*, ii, 491–2; cf. *RPC*, ii, 238.

96. *Glas. Mun.*, ii, 177, 299.

97. *Ibid.*, iii, 517, 523; Haws, *Parish Clergy*, 104.

98. St Andrews University Archives, MS Acta Rectorum, ii, 99. In 1580, Balfour was also appointed to a commission to visit the universities, *Evidence*, iii, 192.

99. GUA, MS 16472.

100. *Ibid.*

101. *Glasgow Protocols*, vi, no. 1616.

102. GUA, MS 16471.

103. *Glas. Mun.*, i, 59, 60, 65; *Glasgow Protocols*, v, nos. 1368, 1369.

104. In 1560 Balfour removed the rector's book which came into the possession of Balfour of Tarrie and it was not restored to the university until 1625. The last folio of the rector's book bears the comment that 'this buik is delyverit be me James Balfour of Tarrie in anno 1625'. GUA, MS 26613. 'Annales Universitatis Glasguensis, 1451–1558'.

105. GUA, MS 26615. 'Liber Statutorum Facultatis Artium Studii Glasguensis'. The title page contains the signature of Mr John Laing as well as that of Mr Archibald Crawford, styled dean of the faculty of arts. The final fly leaf bears the name of Robert Hamilton. The signature of John Houstoun, vicar of Dunlop, appears on f. 21r. Elsewhere the signatures of Andrew Melville and his colleagues are entered which demonstrates that they had at their disposal the earlier faculty records.

106. GUA, MS 26614. 'Annales Collegii Facultatis Artium in Universitate Glasguensi, 1451–1555'.

107. *Glas. Mun.*, i, 59, 61; Watt, *Fasti*, 379; *RSS*, v, no. 3242.

108. *Glasgow Protocols*, v, no. 1399; Durkan and Ross, *Libraries*, 118; *Crosraguel Charters*, i, 130-1; *Edinburgh Burgh Charters, 1557-71*, 152-3.

109. *Glas. Mun.*, i, 60; ii, 177; *Glasgow Protocols*, vi, no. 1787; Watt, *Fasti*, 191–2; J. S. Muirhead, *The Old Minute Book of the Faculty of Procurators in Glasgow, 1668–1758* (Glasgow, 1948), 16, 229.

110. *Glas. Mun.*, ii, 299.

111. *Thirds of Benefices*, 98, 256; *Glas. Mun.*, i, 97, 170.

112. *Glasgow Protocols*, iii, no. 683; v, no. 1515.

113. Major, *History*, 28–9.

114. *Glas. Mun.*, i, 49, 493–5.

115. *RSS*, v, no. 1423; *Glas. Mun.*, i, 67–9.
116. *APS*, ii, 335–6, 371; R. K. Hannay, *The College of Justice* (Edinburgh, 1933), 1–78.
117. A vacancy in the see ensued on Dunbar's death when successive candidates nominated by the crown failed to obtain papal confirmation. Watt, *Fasti*, 149–50.
118. *Glas. Mun.*, ii, 171–7.
119. *Early Records of St Andrews University*, 254–67.
120. *Glas. Mun.*, ii, 168.
121. *Letters and Papers, Foreign and Domestic of the Reign of Henry VIII*, ed. J. Gairdner (London, 1887), x, no. 605.
122. *Glas. Mun.*, ii, 170, 299; *Early Records of St Andrews University*, 150–1.
123. *Evidence*, iii, 356–7.
124. Cant, *University of St Andrews*, 35.
125. *Early Records of St Andrews University*, 250–3.
126. *Fasti Aberdonenses*, 259–72.
127. *CSP Scot.*, i, no. 1136.
128. *First Book of Discipline*, 137–55.
129. *Ibid.*, 143, 149, 150, 151.
130. Knox, *Works*, ii, 128; *History*, i, 344.
131. *Glasgow Protocols*, vii, no. 2113; v, no. 1500; cf. iii, no. 683; vi, no. 1794; *Thirds of Benefices*, 261–2. See also GUA, Drawer F5. Discharge by John Davidson to Peter Blackburn, 16 March 1576.
132. Porteous MS. 4 April 1592.
133. *BUK*, i, 16. In June 1562 the assembly remitted the trial of Robert Hamilton, minister of Hamilton, to the superintendent of Glasgow who was 'to remove him out of the ministry if he thought expedient'.
134. *Thirds of Benefices*, 264. Raes, who was aged 52 in February 1564, was born in Hamilton and created notary public in 1540. SRO, NP2/1. Register of Admissions of Notaries, i, f. 153r–v.
135. *Glas. Mun.*, ii, 299.
136. *RSS*, v, no. 1423; *Glas. Mun.*, i, 67–9.
137. Cowan, *Parishes*, 80; Watt, *Fasti*, 156; Edinburgh University Library, MS Dc.4.32. Rental of Assumptions, f. 17v.
138. Cowan, *Parishes*, 80; Watt, *Fasti*, 361; *Thirds of Benefices*, 262.
139. SRO, CC10/1/1. Act Book of Hamilton and Campsie Commissary Court, i, f. 41r.
140. *Glas. Mun.*, i, 91–3, 157–85.
141. *Ibid.*, i, 91, 157.
142. *First Book of Discipline*, 150; *Vernacular Writings of George Buchanan*, ed. P. H. Brown (STS, Edinburgh, 1892), 7.
143. *Glas. Mun.*, i, 157–8.
144. *BUK*, i, 16; *Fasti*, iii, 258; Edinburgh University Library, MS Dc.4.32. Rental of Assumptions, f. 19v; *Fasti*, iii, 230.
145. *Glas. Mun.*, ii, 175 (Alness); Vatican Archives, Reg. Supp. 2855, ff. 90v–91; 2905, f. 104 (Nigg); *Glas. Mun.*, i, 65 (St Michael's).
146. Edinburgh University Library, MS Dc.4.32. Rental of Assumptions, f. 56r; SRO, CS7/17. Register of Acts and Decreets, xvii, ff. 228v–229r, 7, 56.
147. SRO, Register of Acts and Decreets, xlii, ff. 405r–407r. By 1569 Davidson had resumed his right to dispone lands of the vicarage. SRO, GD27/20, Dalquharran Writs.
148. *Thirds of Benefices*, 89, 221.

149. *Thirds of Benefices*, 91, 147, 148, 261.
150. Edinburgh University Library, MS Dc.4.32. f. 17v. 'Item, Mr Johne Davidsoun hes i° merk pensioun of the said personage for the quhilk is contentit and satisfiet yeirlie thir xviij yeiris bygaine or thairby one siklyke man be yeirlie dureing his fyftyme'. See also SRO, Register of Acts and Decreets, xlviii, f. 195r–v. For Muirhall, see Edinburgh University Library, MS Dc. 4.32. f. 22v.
151. GUA, Drawer F5. John Davidson to Thomas Jack, 12 September 1578.
152. *Thirds of Benefices*, 262. Cf. SRO, E47/1. Register of Assignations and Modifications of Ministers' Stipends, f. 50v, where by 1576 Davidson's stipend was reckoned at £133 6s 8d.
153. *Register of Ministers, Exhorters and Readers*, 32.
154. *Glas. Mun.*, i, 59–62.
155. *Ibid.*, i, 62.
156. *Ibid.*, i, 91, 157, 159, 183.
157. Durkan, 'The Scottish Universities in the Middle Ages', 367.
158. *Glas. Mun.*, i, 58.
159. *Glas. Mun.*, i, 157–85; *Glasgow Protocols*, vii, no. 2044.
160. *RPC*, i, 202.
161. *Glasgow City Charters*, i, pt. ii, 131–7.
162. *RPC*, i, 508–9.
163. *RSS*, vi, no. 295.
164. *Glas. Mun.*, i, 82–90; *Glasgow City Charters*, i, pt. ii, 140–62.
165. *Glas. Mun.*, i, 67–9.
166. *Ibid.*, i, 69–70.
167. *Ibid.*, i, 68–9.
168. *APS*, iii, 25, c. 13.
169. SRO, CH4/1/1. Register of Presentations to Benefices, i, f. 31r–v; *RSS*, vi, no. 787.
170. SRO, CH4/1/1. Register of Presentations to Benefices, i, f. 31v; *RSS*, vi, no. 805.
171. *Glas. Mun.*, i, 76–7.
172. SRO, CH4/1/1. Register of Presentations to Benefices, i, f. 46v; *RSS*, vi, no 980 (Lincluden); SRO, CH4/1/1. Register of Presentations to Benefices, i, f. 57r; *RSS*, vi, no. 1261 (Glasgow vicarage).
173. *Wodrow Society Miscellany*, i, 181–258.
174. Durkan and Ross, *Libraries*, 89.
175. *CSP Scot.*, iv, no. 514.
176. *APS*, iii, 87.
177. SRO, Register of Acts and Decreets, xlvii, f. 171r. cf. f. 200r; Watt, *Fasti*, 150.
178. SRO, PA10/1 (the bundle is unfoliated). Papers relating to the visitation of St Andrews University, 1574–76.
179. *First Book of Discipline*, 137–55; *Glas. Mun.*, i, 85, 87; *Glasgow City Charters*, i, pt. ii, 153, 156–7.
180. *BUK*, i, 207–32; Calderwood, *History*, iii, 169–96.
181. *CSP Scot.*, ii, no. 728.
182. *Glas. Mun.*, i, 76.
183. GUA, MS 26615. 'Liber Statutorum Facultatis Artium Studii', f. 20v.
184. *Glas. Mun.*, i, 83–4; *Glasgow City Charters*, i, pt. ii, 149–50.
185. *Glas. Mun.*, 82–90; *Glasgow City Charters*, i, pt. ii, 140–62.
186. C. Schmidt, 'Mémoire de Jean Sturm sur le projet d'organisation du gymnase de Strasbourg (Fév. 1538)', *Bulletin Historique et Littéraire, Société de l'Histoire du Protestantisme Français*, xxv (Paris, 1876), 499–505; L. Junod and H. Meylan, *L'Académie de Lausanne au XVIᵉ siècle* (Lausanne, 1947);

C. Borgeaud, *L'Académie de Calvin 1559–1798* (Geneva, 1900); P. D. Bourchenin, *Etude sur les Académies Protestantes en France au XVIᵉ siècle* (Paris, 1882).

187. *Charters, Statutes and Acts of the Town Council and the Senatus, 1583–1858*, ed. A. Morgan (Edinburgh, 1937), 12–16.
188. Mackie, *University*, 63.
189. *Glas. Mun.*, i, 103–13; *RMS*, iv, no. 2693.
190. *Glasgow Protocols*, vii, no. 1974.
191. SRO, CH4/1/1. Register of Presentations to Benefices, i, f. 31v; *RSS*, vii, no. 117.
192. *RSS*, vi, no. 805.
193. *Early Records of St Andrews University*, 171, 173, 280.
194. SRO, CH4/1/1. Register of Presentations to Benefices, i, ff. 46v., 144r; *RSS*, vii, no. 1117. See also *RSS*, vi, no. 980.
195. *Early Records of St Andrews University*, 174, 178, 283.
196. *Glas. Mun.*, i, 84; *Glasgow City Charters*, i, pt. ii, 150.
197. *Glasgow Protocols*, vii, no. 2112.
198. *Glas. Mun.*, i, 86; *Glasgow City Charters*, i, pt. ii, 154.
199. *Glas. Mun.*, i, 88; *Glasgow City Charters*, i, pt. ii, 157.
200. *Glasgow Protocols*, vii, no. 2074, 2113.
201. SRO, PA10/1.
202. *Glas. Mun.*, i, 86; *Glasgow City Charters*, i, pt. ii, 154; SRO, PA10/1.
203. *Glas. Mun.*, i, 89; *Glasgow City Charters*, i, pt. ii, 160.
204. SRO, PA10/1.
205. *Glas. Mun.*, i, 88; *Glasgow City Charters*, i, pt. ii, 157.
206. *First Book of Discipline*, 131.
207. *Officers and Graduates of the University and King's College, Aberdeen*, 45; SRO, PA10/1.
208. *First Book of Discipline*, 143.
209. *Vernacular Writings of George Buchanan*, 11–14.
210. *Glas. Mun.*, i, 123.
211. Melville, *Diary*, 48, 120–1, 313.
212. *Glas. Mun.*, iii, 407.
213. *RPC*, ii, 302; 697–8.
214. *Glas. Mun.*, i, 83; *Glasgow Burgh Records*, i, 54; *Glas. Mun.*, ii, 163, 165, 175, 290, 291.
215. *Glasgow Protocols*, vii, no. 2045; *Early Records of the University of St Andrews*, 166, 167, 276.
216. Aberdeen University Library, Press Mark π, 87812G.
217. Melville, Diary, 48; St Andrews University Archives, MS Acta Rectorum, ii, 80.
218. *Glasgow Protocols*, vii, no. 2044.
219. Melville, *Diary*, 48–9.

14. Andrew Melville and the *Nova Erectio*

> 'And it is not our will that these three regents change every year into new courses, as is the custom in the other colleges of our kingdom, whereby it comes to pass that while they profess many branches of learning they are found skilled in few; but they shall exercise themselves in the same course that young men who ascend step by step may find their preceptor worthy of their studies and gifts.'
>
> James VI's charter of New Erection, 13 July, 1577

IN SCOTLAND, religious discontent, social unrest and recognition of the need for educational reform had all been manifest in varying degrees during the crisis of 1560. Each was reflected in the first Book of Discipline, with its desire for a purified faith, its detestation of the 'tyrannie of the lord and laird', its solicitude for the 'poor labourers and manurers of the ground', its provisions for the needy and its ambitious programme for educational reform.[1] Yet despite urgent advocacy, the Book of Discipline's paper schemes for a drastic reorganisation of university teaching and its proposal to establish two colleges at Glasgow had come to nothing. Moreover, it is not to John Knox with all his evident distrust of the universities—a distrust not altogether ill-conceived in view of their tardy reformation—but rather to Andrew Melville that recognition should be given for remoulding, at least in part, the structure and content of university teaching in Scotland: Glasgow, St Andrews and even Aberdeen were each affected by the impact of his reforms.[2] But whereas the John Knox of history is a well-known figure both within Scotland and beyond, Andrew Melville, his successor, has fared less well. When he is remembered at all, it is usually for his services to Scottish presbyterianism. His purpose on returning from Geneva, however, albeit reluctantly, in 1574 was not to revise the constitution of the church but rather to revive and reorganise university education in post-Reformation Scotland. The recovery of Glasgow university in these years is directly attributable to Melville's work as principal; and it is really only in terms of his earlier career that his reforms and their precedents become readily explicable. He is also the first principal for whose career we have something like an adequate account.

His family background was that of the lesser gentry or lairds: the Melvilles of Baldovy in Angus. Born in 1545, the youngest of nine sons

262

whose father died at Pinkie in 1547, Melville was afforded a somewhat remarkable education, particularly for one orphaned at the age of twelve. The picture which emerges of the young Melville is of 'a seiklie tender boy' who 'tuk pleasur in na thing sa mikle as his buik'.[3] Such was his devotion to his studies that on completing his formal schooling at Montrose under Thomas Anderson, he remained for a further 'year or twa', at his own expense, to be taught 'the Greek grammar and something of that language' by the Frenchman Petrus de Marsiliers, whom Erskine of Dun had welcomed to Montrose. This was indeed an uncommon opportunity, denied to most Scots: 'a rare thing in the countrey nocht hard of befor'.[4] It is not wholly surprising, therefore, that after matriculating at St Mary's college, St Andrews, in 1560 he should startle his teachers by studying Aristotle's logic from the Greek text 'quhilk his maisters understud nocht' and that he should complete his course at St Andrews 'with the commendation of the best philosopher, poet and Grecian of anie young maister in the land'.[5] The claim, of course, is not that all knowledge of Greek had hitherto eluded the Scots—they could always learn it abroad; it is that the teaching of Greek, other than a rudimentary training in the alphabet, was something of a novelty in Scotland. But even here, it seems, James Melville was inclined to exaggerate the dearth of Greek in Scotland for something of that language was certainly taught at Aberdeen.[6]

There was possibly little incentive for Andrew Melville to embark on an intensive study of theology in a university like St Andrews, caught up in the midst of the religious upheaval, whose revised theology statutes were still substantially the same medieval enactments.[7] Even more than a decade later, his nephew's lasting impression was of the 'ignorance and negligence of tham that sould haiff teatched theologie', so that 'regents and schollars carit na thing for divinitie'.[8] Nor is Melville's interest in protestant theology immediately apparent in his choice of Paris as the university where he could best further his studies.

There can be little doubt, however, that Melville inherited something of his family's reforming tendencies. Not only were several of his brothers to become ministers in the reformed church, as did Thomas Anderson, his former schoolteacher, but his eldest brother, Richard, it seems, had studied at the Lutheran university of Greifswald, where he matriculated in 1546, and he also accompanied James Erskine, the laird of Dun's son, as his pedagogue to Wittenberg.[9] There they are said to have studied for two years under Melanchthon, before proceeding to Denmark to meet John Macalpine or Machabaeus who by 1542 was teaching theology in the university of Copenhagen.[10] Associations such as these are but one aspect in the steady infiltration of Lutheran thought into Scotland by North sea routes, before it was finally overtaken by the more austere protestantism associated with the Swiss reformers, and with the mission in 1544 of George Wishart, who visited Montrose and met Erskine of Dun.[11]

If these, then, were influences which were likely to affect his outlook, Melville's own religious instincts were probably still at a formative stage as he embarked on his university studies at St Andrews. It may be indicative of his inclinations, or his family's, that he should study at St Andrews where 'heretical' views had found sympathy in certain of the colleges well before 1560, rather than at Aberdeen which was still inclined towards 'papistry' well after 1560.[12] Yet he enrolled not at St Leonard's, the most protestant of the colleges, but at St Mary's where John Douglas, the provost, who conformed at the Reformation and contributed to the Book of Discipline, befriended him.[13] Although it is less than clear which regent conducted him through his course of studies, Melville may have been attracted to St Mary's by William Ramsay, who had not only studied at Wittenberg and taught at the college of Guyenne in Bordeaux, but also had an interest in Greek, as his books reveal.[14]

It might even emerge that the Alexander Ramsay whom Thomas Dempster describes as Melville's teacher[15] is in reality none other than a mistaken identity for William Ramsay himself. Later, in some verses written in praise of George Buchanan, Melville spoke of this celebrated humanist as his *praeceptor* or teacher; and although it has been suggested that the description should not be taken literally, there is good reason to believe that Melville did receive instruction from Buchanan.[16] Although he is named as 'lector public' in a document which is to be related to the intended reformation of St Andrews in 1563, it is improbable that Buchanan did much, or indeed anything, in the way of teaching at St Andrews until his appointment as principal of St Leonard's college in 1566.[17] In a letter which Melville wrote to Peter Young in 1572, however, there is evidence that Melville and Buchanan met during the latter's brief visit to France in the winter of 1565; Melville not only praised Buchanan's erudite conversation but recalled how on being admitted to Buchanan's company he had the more difficult parts of the psalms and epigrams explained and how he went on to interpret the works of Buchanan both privately and in the public schools.[18]

In any event, as a student interested in classical languages, Melville could hardly fail to be aware through contact with John Douglas, and others, of the educational reforms of the Book of Discipline with its concern for 'the tongues', and of Buchanan's 'Opinion', which favoured providing St Andrews *inter alia* with a college of humanity.[19] And parliament's unprecedented intervention in 1563 added a further dimension to the efforts at securing a measure of educational reform at

St Andrews.[20] It was within the context of reform, amidst changing attitudes and a radical reappraisal of existing structures both ecclesiastical and educational, that Melville received his university education. Yet far-reaching reforms at St Andrews were not immediately effected. There was probably no sudden break with the past in a university, the majority of whose teachers conformed, leaving few posts to be filled by new men; and it is doubtful if the Arts curriculum of the 1560s was much altered from that of the 1550s.[21]

Among his fellow students at St Mary's in the class of 1559–60[22] were James Lawson, later to become regent first at St Andrews and then at King's College, Aberdeen before aspiring to the presbyterian leadership as minister at Edinburgh; and Thomas Maitland, the younger brother of William Maitland of Lethington, the queen's secretary.[23] Although the graduation rolls for the eleven students of this class have not survived, Melville is known to have 'past his cuirse' and graduated M.A. before embarking for France.[24] The accepted date of his graduation and departure is 1564[25] but this is apparently based on no more than mere guesswork. If, as seems to be the case, he entered St Mary's in the autumn or winter of 1559, then 1563 is a much more probable date for his graduation. Thomas Maitland, who presumably graduated along with Melville, is known to have left for France in October 1563;[26] and Melville's own departure was not likely to be much delayed. He is said to have left St Andrews and made preparation for France 'with all possible diligence', sailing first to England and then to Bordeaux and Dieppe before finally reaching Paris 'whar he remeanit in the Universitie twa yeiris at his awin studies'.[27]

In pursuing his studies overseas, Melville was simply following in the path of earlier generations of Scots who can be found in the universities of most countries in Europe. An impression of the incessant wanderings of Scots from one centre of learning to another is conveyed not only in official university records but also in the few personal *alba amicorum* which have survived.[28] Nor did the Reformation necessarily interrupt this trend. Far from discouraging scholars from studying abroad, the general assembly, as late as 1575, lamented the lack of financial assistance available for promising students 'to visite other countreyes and Universities for thair furtherance in learning'.[29] Indeed, not until 1579 did the assembly complain of how 'many young scholars are sent out of this realme to Paris and other Universities professing papistrie wherethrough the youth of this realme is corrupted by pestilent poprie in place of godly virtue'.[30] Even so, there were still Scots like Robert Bruce at Louvain[31] who experienced no difficulty in studying at Roman Catholic centres abroad and in preserving their 'godly virtue' intact. The pattern of university-going might change, but the pursuit of learning abroad continued much as before. Alexander Cockburn, the reforming laird of Ormiston, might choose to study at Basle in 1555, Peter Young, who later tutored James VI, might go to Geneva in 1559, Gilbert Walker to Rostock in 1562 and Alexander Arbuthnot, the future principal of King's College, Aberdeen, might select Bourges, but Andrew Melville had understandably set his sights on Paris.[32] Despite the outbreak of the wars of religion, Paris was still an important international centre of education with a long tradition of receiving numerous Scottish scholars, and some of the teachers at St Andrews, including Douglas and Rutherford, had earlier studied at Paris, as George Buchanan himself had done.[33] It is not surprising, therefore, that Melville should be attracted there.

When he arrived, there was already a sizeable Scottish, though largely Catholic, community. The exiles after 1560 included the archbishop of Glasgow and John Hunter, the Dominican from Glasgow who had arrived shortly after the Reformation,[34] as well as three regents from St Salvator's college, St Andrews: Edmund Hay, who joined the Jesuits, Thomas Smeaton, the future principal of Glasgow university, who became a Jesuit before ending up a Calvinist, and William Cranston who remained a Catholic.[35] Scots like John Dempster, William Davidson and Henry Blackwood were regents in the university.[36] Scottish protestants, however, as well as Catholics, were also to be found in Paris. Patrick Adamson, adjudged fit to minister by the general assembly in 1560 and later to become Melville's adversary as archbishop of St Andrews, not only published a book in Paris in 1566 but was briefly imprisoned there, before proceeding to Bourges and ultimately to Geneva where he met Theodore Beza.[37] Melville's friend from St Mary's, James Lawson, whose later career was that of a staunch presbyterian, also turned up in Paris in 1568 as tutor to John Lindsay of Menmuir;[38] and it was presumably before he left Paris, and not on his return in 1574, that Melville himself met up with Thomas Maitland, his old classmate from St Andrews, who was evidently a convinced protestant: 'a young gentilman of guid literature and knawlage in the treuthe of religion'. Whilst there, he also became acquainted with Gilbert Moncrieff, who went on to study at Geneva,[39] which for so many protestants had become the 'oracle of the Christian world';[40] and there, too, he had also discussions with Thomas Smeaton, who though still a Catholic was deeply troubled with doubts about the very nature of salvation.[41] These, then, were the circles in which Melville might be expected to move during his student days at Paris.

It seems clear from the names of his teachers that Melville attended the public lectures given in the Collège de France, the Royal Trilingual College, founded by Francis I in 1530, primarily for the study of Latin,

Greek and Hebrew.[42] He need not therefore be an incorporated or matriculated member of the university: the lectures were open to the public; and this may also explain his nephew's remark that Melville remained 'at his awin studies' whilst in Paris. On the other hand, the comment that 'he declamit and teatchit lessones', while it is not necessarily proof of incorporation, does suggest that he played an active part in the formal academic exercises at Paris.[43] An awakened interest in biblical philology demanded a specialised knowledge of the oriental tongues, and this, it seems, led Melville to the Royal Trilingual College. To obtain a first-hand understanding of these languages, some Scots, indeed, were prepared to go to almost any length: George Strachan, for example, arrived in Paris in 1592 and, after studying at a variety of French protestant and Catholic universities as well as at Rome, he made his way eastward to Persia where he was last to be heard in pursuit of the tongues.[44] Melville, more modestly, contented himself with the instruction available in Paris; and in two years he seems to have heard a remarkable number of lecturers.

He attended the Hebrew lectures given by Jean Mercier and Jean de Cinquarbres; he heard Greek and Latin philosophy taught by Peter Ramus who, though a convert to protestantism in 1561, was also principal of the Collège des Prèsles, but he also listened to Ramus' great opponent, Adrien Turnèbe, lecture on the same subject; in mathematics, he was taught by Pierre Forcadel, Jacques Charpentier, another critic of Ramus, and apparently by Pascal Duhamel; and he is said to have attended the medical lectures of Louis Duret, who does not seem to have received an appointment in the college till 1567, after Melville's departure. Added to all this, he also heard Scaliger on Hebrew and François Baudouin on law, once again, teachers who had no official status in the Collège de France.[45] But it was on studying Hebrew, above all else, that Melville was 'speciallie set', and in Greek he became so expert, it was said, that 'he declamit and teatchit lessones, uttering never a word bot Greek with sic readines and plentie as was mervelus to the heirars'.[46] All this conveys something of the intellectual flavour of his university days at Paris: the whole emphasis of his studies was on the humanities with some instruction in medicine and law; he received no theological training while in Paris.

Despite a gap in the records of the 'Acta rectoria' between 1554 and 1567, more than a dozen Scottish students are known to have studied in Paris during Melville's stay, though Melville's own name has not been found in any of the surviving documents. Present with him in the Collège de France (or Collège Royal), already suspect for the protestant tendencies of some of its teachers, were two other St Andrews graduates: George Bellenden and David Cunningham.[47] The latter, who was to become dean of faculty at Glasgow university, went on to study civil law, with Patrick Adamson, at Bourges;[48] and by 1566 Melville had also decided to further his legal studies, not indeed at Bourges but at Poitiers.[49]

The progression from Paris to Poitiers was one which a good many Scots had made in the past. Its law school had attracted Scottish teachers as well as students. Robert Ireland, whose remarkable career in France spanned six decades, taught law at Poitiers till his death in 1561; Henry Blackwood, from St Andrews diocese, had taught philosophy at Poitiers in 1551, before proceeding to Paris where he was elected rector by 1568 and styled 'baccalaureus medicus humaniorum disciplinarum et philosophus professor annos tredecim';[50] Duncan McGruder, a student of St Andrews and Paris, was a regent in law at Poitiers in 1562;[51] Richard Lawson appears to have studied law there in the 1560s;[52] and Thomas Bicarton, Adam Blackwood, William Hegait and Thomas Barclay were four other Scots who were later to teach there.[53]

At Poitiers, the Guise family evidently had an interest in the university and, indeed, Charles of Lorraine, the future cardinal, was conservator of ecclesiastical privileges at the university from 1548 to 1552.[54] Nor was Archbishop Beaton, the exiled chancellor of Glasgow university who had served Mary of Guise in Scotland, exactly devoid of influence in that quarter. As well as acting as an administrator, on the death of Francis II in 1560, of Mary's dowry which included lands in Poitou as well as Champagne and Picardy, he also had claims to certain benefices in the area including the priory of Absie-en-Gatine.[55] What Beaton seems to have been doing, in the absence of a viable Scots college in Paris, was to provide Scottish students there, and possibly at Poitiers, with bursaries, and his prestige in Poitiers was greatly enhanced with his election as chancellor of the university from 1573 till 1582.[56] Having lost Glasgow university, he could now claim Poitiers instead. It is not improbable therefore that Beaton in the 1560s was directing Scots from Paris to Poitiers. Whether Melville was in receipt of a bursary from Beaton and whether the latter was in any way influential in securing his appointment at Poitiers is, in the absence of evidence, merely speculative. Certainly some Scots, like David Graham of Fintry, who arrived to study in Paris in 1571, were fortunate enough to have their expenses met by the archbishop, possibly from the bishop of Moray's Grisy foundation.[57] If, however, Melville was in any sense indebted to Beaton, then there were perhaps added grounds for the archbishop's indignation and irritation when, at lord Ogilvie's invitation, Melville arrived in 1574 at the Jesuits' college in Paris where, fresh from Geneva, he disputed with Tyrie for several days until Beaton's 'minassing speitches' put an abrupt end to the proceedings.[58]

There also exists a possible Ramist connection which might help explain Melville's arrival in Poitiers. That Melville was deeply interested in the anti-Aristotelian philosophy of Ramus, under whom he had studied in Paris, is a recurring theme throughout his career; and Duncan McGruder at Poitiers, who evinced a marked interest in Ramist method, had already edited a work of Talon, Ramus' disciple, entitled *Tabulae in Rhetoricam*, published in Paris in 1559.[59] It is conceivable, too, that George Buchanan, who knew Ramus, may also have influenced Melville, on meeting him in Paris, in the direction of Poitiers. In 1554, Buchanan's brother, Patrick, as pedagogue in Paris to Hamilton, abbot of Arbroath, had connections with Chatelherault near Poitiers.[60] Once there, Melville appears to have taught as regent in the university for three years, presumably in the Collège Royal de Sainte-Marthe, and not in the non-existent college of St Marcean to which his nephew assigns him. 'Ther', it was said, 'he haid the best lawers, and studeit sa mikle thairof as might serve for his purpose, quhilk was theologie wherto he was dedicat from his mother's wombe'.[61] Although Poitiers had taken on something of the complexion of a Catholic city besieged by Huguenot forces, this ought not to obscure the reality that some teachers in the faculty of law had strong Calvinist tendencies. Indeed, Poitiers had sent representatives to the first national synod of the French protestant churches in Paris in 1559, and the second synod had met in Poitiers itself in 1560.[62] If the faculty of theology in the university remained orthodox in its traditional allegiance, a number of lawyers in the law faculty had defected to Calvinism. The lawyer, Charles le Sage, had been the friend of Calvin, while Albert Babimot and Vernou, who also taught law there, were both convinced Calvinists.[63] In the legal faculty, therefore, where he would be anxious to further his studies in the law, Melville was likely to find allies in these co-religionists, and it was presumably this circle which provided him with introductory letters when he chose to leave for Geneva in 1569.

With the disruption of classes because of the siege, Melville acted as tutor to the son of 'an honourable councellar', to whom he taught Greek; but when his pupil was killed by a stray bullet, Melville had to seek employment elsewhere. He was already suspected of being a Huguenot, and therefore deemed it expedient to leave for Geneva where his classical learning secured him an appointment to teach humanity in the Genevan college. If he had shown any interest in theology at Poitiers, it must have been apparent that Poitiers, a city besieged by the protestant Coligny and defended by the Catholic duke of Guise, was no fit place to pursue an interest in divinity, and it was only in Geneva where he attended Beza's 'daylie lessons and preatchings' that Melville finally made divinity 'his cheiff studie'.[64] Yet, what is known of his earlier career hardly supports the view that he possessed any great desire from the outset to visit Calvin's city or to study the Genevan system at first hand. His earlier work, after all, had been carried out in France rather than in Switzerland and his immediate preoccupation seems to have lain in the field of the humanities. Moreover, it was really only because of the resumption of the religious wars in France that Melville was prompted to seek refuge in Geneva. All in all, had different political conditions prevailed, it is hard to see why Melville should not have remained in Poitiers, or at least in France, without ever having visited Geneva. However, it was not to La Rochelle, nor even to England, which could also have afforded him shelter, but to far-distant Geneva that Melville journeyed determinedly through France on foot in 1569. And it was to Geneva and to Beza that Melville owed much of his theological training.

As the inheritor of Calvin's system of church government, Beza had assumed the leadership of the Calvinist cause in Europe, and in Geneva he was strategically placed to become the principal international protagonist of presbyterian theory and discipline. Wherever the influence of Geneva reached far and deep, Beza's views won wide acceptance. Within its confines, therefore, Geneva attracted an international group of scholars whose representatives in the early 1570s included two Englishmen and a Scot, Thomas Cartwright, Walter Travers and Andrew Melville, who were to assume the leadership of the presbyterian movements in their own countries. Dismissed from the Lady Margaret chair of divinity at Cambridge, Cartwright in the invigorating atmosphere of Geneva had gained admittance, with the Flemish van Til, to the Genevan consistory to observe 'l'ordre qu'on y tient et y profiter et s'en servir non seulement aux gouvernements de leurs Eglises, mais aussi pour respondre a ceux qui parlent de nostre Consistoire autrement qu'il ne fault'.[65] As a fellow resident, Travers produced for the puritan world his *Ecclesiasticae disciplinae . . . explicatio* during his Genevan stay,[66] but Andrew Melville, the third member of this academic coterie, wrote nothing of substance. Instead, he employed his talents by teaching humanity, not indeed in the academy or university (*schola publica*) but in the college (or *schola privata*) where Beza secured his appointment in November 1569 as regent of the second class.[67] Yet, Melville's interest in Travers's treatise was evidently substantial, for after his return to Scotland he presented a copy of the work to Alexander Arbuthnot, principal of King's College, Aberdeen, presumably with a commendation of its presbyterian principles.[68]

In Geneva, Melville's relentless pursuit of learning was sustained not only by studying theology with Beza but also by acquiring a knowledge of the Chaldaic and Syriac tongues from Bertram, the professor of

Hebrew. At one point, he even had the audacity, to question the pronunciation of Portus, the professor of Greek, and himself of Greek extraction, which drew from the exasperated teacher the natural enough retort: 'vos Scoti, vos barbari, docebitis nos Graecos pronunciationem linguae nostrae, scilicet'.[69] What Melville was probably doing here was adopting the new pronunciation of Greek which Ramus 'appears to have been the first to introduce' at Paris.[70] With the influx of more Huguenot exiles after the massacre of St Bartholomew in 1572, Melville had the opportunity to hear François Hotman, the French lawyer and political theorist, whose *Franco-Gallia*, published in Geneva in 1573, reasserted the ultimate sovereignty of the people over their king.[71] He also knew Joseph Scaliger, who taught philosophy in Geneva, as a French exile, with whom he maintained a lasting friendship.[72] As was to be expected, he was also 'weill acquented' with Henry Scrimgeour, the uncle of James Melville the diarist, and professor of law at Geneva.[73] Earlier in 1570, he was able to hear Ramus, his former teacher at Paris, lecture in Geneva on Cicero according to his 'method', and although the French philosopher incurred the opposition of Beza who remained a convinced Aristotelian, he evidently won the admiration of Melville who, together with Gilbert Moncrieff, followed Ramus to Lausanne where they attended his lectures in July 1570, before Ramus returned to Paris.[74]

If Melville's arrival in Geneva owed more to accident than design, his subsequent departure for Scotland was scarcely less fortuitous. During an absence of more than a decade, he seems to have corresponded exceedingly little with friends at home; and during his five years at Geneva, relations, on hearing no news of him, feared he had become a victim of the religious strife in France.[75] When, at last, word came that Melville was living at Geneva, his countrymen, having failed to secure for Scotland the services of the aged Henry Scrimgeour, finally prevailed on Melville to return.[76] Yet it was not without considerable persuasion that he left, which may suggest the absence rather than the presence of any missionary zeal. There is certainly no reason to suppose that he left for home with a view to establishing 'presbyterianism', and indeed his object on returning was to revitalise teaching in the universities, particularly so at Glasgow.

Having bidden farewell to Beza, and to Geneva, in April 1574, Melville travelled home in the company of Alexander Campbell, who had been provided to the bishopric of Brechin in 1566, and Andrew Polwarth, later minister at Paisley and dean of faculty at Glasgow university. He returned in July, 'a lytle befor Lammbes', with testimonials from Beza, as moderator of the Venerable Company, and from Jean Pinaud, rector of the college, in which they warmly praised his abilities and commended him to the Scottish church.[77] For Beza and the Genevan pastors, so James Melville remarked, 'the graittest taken of affection the Kirk of Genev could schaw to Scotland' was to allow Melville to return home so that, through their own loss, the Scottish church might benefit from the services of an outstanding scholar. News of Melville's erudition and fame, which preceded his return, resulted in competition to obtain his services. Since he 'lyked nocht to be in Court bot rather to be in sum Universitie', he declined the offer to become the Regent Morton's domestic chaplain. He may, however, have viewed with more favour the proposal which the commissioners from Fife placed before the general assembly in August 1574 that he be made provost of St Mary's college, St Andrews, in succession to John Douglas, the archbishop, who had died in July.[78] Already, in April 1574, because of 'sum abuse and negligence', the Regent Morton had initiated a visitation from the further 'reformation'[79] of a university which would seem to offer Melville ample scope for his reforming activities.

Yet, in the end, he chose with the assembly's blessing to go not to St Andrews, despite a pressing invitation, but rather to Glasgow, as a result of the 'earnest dealing' of James Boyd, the protestant archbishop of Glasgow, and Andrew Hay, commissioner of churches in the west.[80] It is certainly one of the ironies of the period that a man who is best remembered for his opposition to bishops should himself owe his appointment to an archbishop and university chancellor, whose episcopal office he was intent on abolishing. Even so, Melville's criticisms of diocesan episcopacy—unscriptural 'pseudo-episcopacy'[81] as he called it—need not preclude friendship with the men, or at least some of them, who held the office. In later life, though exiled to Sedan in France for his opposition to King James's bishops, he was still able to write amicably to Andrew Knox, a Glasgow graduate, who had become bishop of the Isles in 1608.[82] In the case of the Glasgow archbishop, Melville apparently had already met Boyd, who had studied civil law under Cujas at Bourges, during their peregrinations on the continent in the 1560s,[83] and it was probably this contact which helped to secure his appointment as principal master of the college of Glasgow. It was not for nothing that Melville's presbyterian nephew should characterise the archbishop as 'a guid man and lover of lerning and of lernd men'.[84]

Since a college of sorts already existed, what Melville presumably found when he arrived to 'sie the beginning of a collage ther and heir what conditions sould be offered to him'[85] was the college as it stood after its re-foundation by the town in January 1573. It is doubtful if the college buildings were in any better state than they had been in 1563 when they were said only to be partially built. Indeed, the charter of

1573 had spoken of how the pedagogy had 'almost gone to ruin' through lack of funds to spend upon it. Even so, the buildings, or some of them, continued to be used by Melville, as principal, and the nature of their ruinous state in 1574 may simply have been that the roofing for lack of repair was no longer watertight and therefore in need of thatch and slate. This picture would seem to be confirmed by the action taken, just before Melville's arrival, to make good the necessary renovations. In July 1574, the university authorities had proposed demolishing the manses of the vicars choral, which the university owned, and utilising the 'rediast sclaittis thairof' for the 'reparatioun' first of the pedagogy and, then, the cathedral.[86] At any rate, within two years of Melville's principalship, the college became so renowned, it is said, that with the influx of so many students 'the roumes war nocht able to receave tham'.[87] This encomium scarcely suggests that total dereliction confronted Melville when he took over what looked like a moribund institution in November 1574.

The prospect for recovery already seemed brighter with the appointment of James Boyd of Trochrague as archbishop of Glasgow in 1573. For one thing, it meant that the university could once more have a chancellor at its head, something that it had, in effect, been denied since 1560. For another, there was now a recognised agency for securing the resignation of the last principal and for arranging the appointment of the next. Although by 1573 Davidson had evidently retired from teaching—nothing more, indeed, is to be heard of his university activities—he was apparently reluctant formally to resign his office as principal, and with it the revenues of the vicarage of Colmonell. When Peter Blackburn was recruited from St Andrews to take over teaching in the college, there was no suggestion that he should occupy Davidson's place as principal. Any lingering doubt, however, was terminated with Melville's appointment which took effect in November 1574.[88] Yet Davidson still retained a modest pension from the university[89] possibly in recognition of his demission in Melville's favour. Moreover, in a receipt dated 16 March 1576 Davidson also acknowledged payment from Peter Blackburn of twenty merks 'consignit for the thryds of the vicarage of Colmonel apertening to me for that tyme as maister of the pedagog and tharfor gif the said soume of xx merkis be requirit of the said Maister Peter for the thryds of Comonel, I the said Maister Jhone oblesis me to refound the said soume of xx merkis againe to the Maister Peter be this writt subscrivit with my hand'.[90] Davidson may have quit, but arrears of stipend had still to be met.

If Boyd's election to the see, at the instance of his kinsman lord Boyd, seemed to be a dynastic appointment of the unreformed variety, and if he incurred criticism for accepting the bishopric without first having served as preacher, there could be no doubting his abilities as a university chancellor. Before his death in June 1581, he had not only presided over the university in one of its most formative periods but had approved a new constitution for the university, had installed two new principals, had helped augment college revenues by mortifying to the college all the tron customs in his episcopal burgh of Glasgow, and he contributed by way of a bequest what was then the largest single donation of over forty volumes—most of which had belonged to Beaton—to the college library.[91]

Before taking up his appointment, the new principal first 'conferrit at lynthe' with George Buchanan, the king's preceptor, at Stirling;[92] and there need be little doubt that the college of Glasgow figured prominently in their discussions. As one interested in educational reform, Buchanan had a wealth of knowledge and experience to impart, first as regent at Paris and then at the college of Guyenne at Bordeaux.[93] At home, he had been appointed by parliament in 1563 as one of the commissioners to visit St Andrews university, and he produced schemes of his own for the projected reformation of St Andrews.[94] Before becoming tutor to the king, he had served from 1566 until 1570 as principal of St Leonard's college; but he is also known to have taken an interest in the Glasgow college. Principal Robert Baillie, an admittedly late authority, writing in 1660, spoke of Buchanan as 'much conversing in our college, the chief instrument to purchase our rents from Queen Mary and King James; he left our library a parcell of good Greek books, noted with his hand'.[95] Buchanan, it is suggested, paid periodic visits to the college, and he may also have visited Glasgow, if not the university, in 1563 when he resigned certain lands which he held in the west.[96] Indeed, he may not have ruled out the possibility, were Davidson to be displaced, of obtaining the principalship at Glasgow for himself, for his brother, Patrick, was already tutor in the service of Chatel-herault,[97] the descendant of the college's original founder. Whatever the case, there can be no doubt that the college found it useful to have a friend at court in the person of Buchanan, and his good offices help explain the college's rather cryptic comment in February 1579, following the *nova erectio* of 1577, when he was praised for the 'singular favour' which he had 'borne and schawen at all times to our College'.[98] He may even have been instrumental in securing the queen's charter of 1563 in favour of five poor bursars at the college, but to attribute the town's foundation of 1573 to Buchanan merely on the strength of a classical allusion in the charter to the Trojan horse[99] is to go further than the evidence would seem to warrant. After all, Archibald Hay, who may have been related to Glasgow's Andrew Hay, also thought fit to introduce an allusion to the Trojan horse in his *Panegyricus* on the planned reconstruction of St Mary's college in St Andrews in the 1540s.[100]

At court, Melville also had conversations with the nephews of Henry Scrimgeour, Peter Young, tutor to the king, and his brother Alexander, who had conveyed Melville's correspondence from Geneva. Also present were Melville's friend from Geneva, Gilbert Moncrieff, now royal physician, and Thomas Buchanan, George's nephew and schoolmaster at Stirling, who 'of his kindnes' accompanied Melville and his nephew to Glasgow.[101]

Once installed at Glasgow, Melville taught, it was said, 'things nocht hard in this countrey of befor';[102] but, already, James Melville, who joined the staff in 1575, had experienced a foretaste of what was to come, during the summer he spent with his uncle at Baldovy in 1574. Although James had newly graduated from St Andrews in 1574, Melville was less than satisfied with the training he had received: 'he fand me bauche in the Latin toung, a pratler upon precepts in Logik without anie profit for the right use, and haiffing sum termes of Art in Philosophie without light of solid knawlage'.[103] Perceiving him 'yit of ingyne and capacitie guid aneuche', Melville embarked on what amounted to a crash course to make good the deficiencies he found in his nephew's education at St Andrews. Beginning with Buchanan's Latin psalms,[104] Melville proceeded to instil in his nephew a better appreciation of the works of Virgil, Horace, Terence, Caesar, Sallust and Cicero's Catiline Orations; then, as something of a novelty, he embarked on the study of history according to the 'method' of Bodin, the French political thinker; and on to Greek grammar, the New Testament and finally an intro-duction to Hebrew grammar from the works of Martini and Reuchlin. If all this amounted to 'bot pleying and craking', then there was good reason for James Melville to remark that he learned more from his uncle 'in daylie conversation' than 'ever I lernit of anie buik'.[105]

The new principal, who read Virgil as his 'chieff refreschment efter his grave studies', was evidently a man of unusual talent and of un-accustomed learning in Scotland. Initially, he assumed most of the teaching duties in the college and personally conducted students through a bewildering galaxy of courses which included classics, logic, rhetoric, mathematics, geography, moral philosophy, physics and history as well as theology, which he taught 'verie exactlie and accuratlie', but the brightest star in his firmament was Hebrew and such unfamiliar languages as the Chaldaic and Syriac dialects. If all this is true, then it is easy to understand how his 'lerning and peanfulnes was mikle admired'. Instead of students from Glasgow being attracted to St Andrews, as once they were, Melville succeeded in turning the tables: 'sic as haid passed ther course in St Androis came in nomber ther and

K

entered schollars again' at Glasgow so that the college could no longer accommodate them all.[106] His outstanding reputation as an academic was clearly not ill-deserved. It was his ability as a teacher to attract students, much as Mair had done between 1518 and 1522, which infused the college with new life. Glasgow's revival, in a very real sense, was Melville's personal achievement. Within a few years of his arrival, the reputation of the college soared, and teaching at Glasgow could again be compared with other universities in Europe.

Although every inch a scholar's scholar, Melville did not quite conform to the accepted mould. Rebellious and innovating, contemptuous of traditional structures and curricula, he typified an attitude of mind not unknown among radical protestants. Principal at twenty-nine, audaciously go-ahead and wholly convinced of the rightness of his cause, he attempted to effect something akin to a major educational revolution at Glasgow. Like many a young radical, he readily succumbed to new fashions in educational thought. He had already absorbed, first at Paris and then at Lausanne, the Ramist critique of the traditional scholastic logic and Ciceronian rhetoric which had dominated university teaching for so long. As a pioneer of new academic trends in Scotland, Melville had his own contribution to make to the educational revolt, associated with Ramus, which so upset the pedagogic world by its call for far-reaching reforms of the curriculum and teaching methods in the universities. Ramus' new approach to logic, to 'the art of discoursing well', based on a simplified, more easily communicated, 'method' of dichotomised classifications, was designed to help teachers and learners alike; for one thing, it provided a new way of memorising subjects, but it also discredited the Aristotelian logic of the schoolmen who, Ramus felt, had misrepresented the real Aristotle.[107] By applying the rules of logic to each subject, Ramist principles were soon extended to cover the whole Arts course, including the *quadrivium* as well as the *trivium*; and by 1562 Ramus had produced his own programme for academic reform at Paris in his *Advertissements sur la réformation de l'université de Paris au roy*, which included the proposal that the king should appoint a number of public professors, paid by the state, to teach in the various faculties.[108] Nor was this lesson entirely lost on Melville who expressed the wish, on returning home in 1574, 'to be in sum Universitie and profess thair as the King's Lectors in Parise'.[109] His recollections of the Collège Royal, and of the teaching of Ramus, had evidently not dimmed in the ten years which had passed.

As an admirer, therefore, of the anti-scholastic philosophy of Peter Ramus, Melville assumed responsibility for introducing reforms at Glasgow along Ramist lines. No longer was the teaching of Aristotle accorded the unquestioning veneration of times past, and the challenging and even disturbing works of Ramus and his staunch supporter Omer Talon, were given their due place in the revised curriculum. He began in 1574 by introducing Ramist logic, based on Ramus' own *Dialecticae*, before proceeding to teach the *Rhetorica* of Talon, who worked out the principles of Ramus in this field. In mathematics, a subject rooted in logic which Ramus was keen to develop, Melville employed the *Geometriae* of Ramus; and when it came to history, on which he also lectured, he is known to have owned a copy of the *Methodus ad Facilem Historiarum Cognitionem* (1566) by Bodin who had strong Ramist connections.[110] Although ownership of the works of Ramus and Talon cannot now be traced to Melville or, for that matter, to the college at this date, Ramus' signature is to be found on two mathematical books, by other authors, which found their way at some date into the college library where they still remain.[111] Even after his departure in 1580, the Ramist tradition which Melville established continued to be upheld. Under Smeaton's principalship, the works of Ramus and Talon were still prescribed texts in the newly drafted constitution and an obligatory part of the curriculum; and on the testimony of a Glasgow student, Ramus continued to be taught in the 1590s.[112] If, by the early seventeenth century, scholastic philosophy gained ascendancy once more and Glasgow students like John Livingston were once again taught 'logick and metaphysick and the subtilties of the schoolmen' by Robert Blair as regent,[113] the Ramist inheritance did not altogether disappear. Mathematical works by Ramus were acquired by the college library as late as 1652, and it also obtained the works of Alsted who owed something to the influence of Ramus.[114] Ramist teaching, it seems, had not entirely evaporated.

Melville, of course, was neither the first nor the last Scot to become attracted to Ramist philosophy. George Buchanan, for one, was on friendly terms with Ramus, who in 1567, exhorted him to make better provision for teaching mathematics at St Andrews,[115] but no evidence has been found that Ramist principles at that stage were being taught by Buchanan, or anyone else, in that university. However, the logic of Ramus does seem to have won the approval of Buchanan and Peter Young, as tutors to the king, for four of his works, including the *Dialectica*, figure among the books acquired for the king's library in the decade between 1573 and 1583,[116] a date well after Buchanan's teaching connection with St Andrews had ended. Other Scots, too, were interested in Ramus' novel teaching methods. Two illegitimate sons of James V are said to have been the guests of Ramus in Paris.[117] One may have been lord James Stewart, subsequently earl of Moray, who was taught first at St Andrews and then at the Collège des Prèsles under Ramus, and the other the John Stewart who wrote a commentary at Paris on one of Ramus' works.[118] When the bishop of Galloway's son, John Gordon, a graduate of St Andrews, whose pretensions in scholarship ran to numerous languages which he did not always comprehend, returned to England from France in July 1568, he brought with him a letter for Cecil from Ramus, and in the same month he was in touch with the earl of Moray with a story that 'Ramus hes obtinit licence to pas out of France and hes promisit me to visit Scotland befoir his returnyng; and that cheifly to visit your graice, to quhom abuive al uthers he beris singuler luif and affection, quhois godlines, luif to justice and happines in wear, he extollis aboive ony uther'.[119] Another St Andrews graduate, Roland McIlmain, has the distinction of being the first to produce an edition in English of Ramus' *Dialectica*, published in London by Vautrollier in 1574, the year of Melville's return from Geneva.[120] Yet McIlmain's interest in Ramism, like Melville's, seems to have been the product of his university studies at Paris, where he had matriculated by 1571,[121] and not the direct result of teaching at St Andrews, where he had studied between 1566 and 1570. It was, no doubt, as a result of influences of this sort that Ramist literature began to circulate in Scotland, and it is not surprising to find the 'cataloge of Adame Bischope of Orknayis buiks, 1594', listing a remarkable collection including the Koran, two works of Peter Ramus: his *Dialectica* and his *Commentaria de religione*.[122]

That many of the men who became attracted to Ramism should happen to be St Andrews graduates is not in itself proof of Ramist teaching at St Andrews, but a measure of the less flourishing state of Scotland's other two universities. When James Melville attended St Leonard's college as a student in the early 1570s, before becoming regent at Glasgow, he was taught the logic of Aristotle by his regent William Collace, who produced his own compendium of philosophy and 'haid the estimation of the maist solide and lernit in Aristotle's Philosophie'.[123] Even a decade later, when Andrew Melville arrived with his Ramist notions at St Andrews as principal of St Mary's theological college, a heated debate soon ensued between Melville and the philosophy regents of St Leonard's college who insisted on defending the traditional teaching of Aristotle, presumably from the Latin texts of the schoolmen.[124] All this would suggest that Aristotelian teaching was still well established and that Ramism in that college, at least, had made little headway in the intervening years. Some evidence, however, of dislocation, and even altercation, is indicated during a visitation of that university in 1576 when, without further explanation, it was:

thocht expedient that ther be chosin be the maisteris and regentis [ane] certane compendium contening the summe of dialectik quhilk salbe observit in all the collegis and nane othir techit; gif thai can not agree that the morne be avys of the principall maisteris there be ane compendium appointit to thame to be techit, beysidis the quhilk compendium thai sall also teche the logickis of Aristotell and als the Offices of Cicero for practising and exercising the youtheid in the precepts and that alsua thai teiche the preceptis of Rhetorik, and to knaw the practise therof sa mony or few of the Orisonis [recte, Orationes] of Cicero as the principallis sall think expedient; thairefter in everie colleg thai begyn at the morall philosophie and teche the Ethickis, Economikis and Politikis'.125

What this advice amounted to in practice it might be hard to say, but it does not suggest the sustained assault of Ramism on teaching methods at St Andrews.

Melville, it would seem, as principal of Glasgow university, is to be credited with introducing in university circles, on an official basis, the teaching of Ramist principles in Scotland. The appearance of Ramism at Glasgow in 1574 is directly paralleled with its introduction at Cambridge where, to the horror of traditional Aristotelians, Ramism won support from, amongst others, George Downham (later Melville's opponent on episcopacy) who as fellow of Christ's college and a university reader in logic popularised Ramist logic; and at Oxford, too, though not without fierce criticism, Ramism found both teachers and adherents.126 Even at Glasgow, where he had more or less a free hand, Melville encountered opposition from Peter Blackburn who, significantly enough, as a St Andrews graduate was 'a bitter propugnar of Aristotle' until won over by Melville. The new principal, by contrast, was determined 'to schaw that Aristotle could err, and haid erred, contrar to S. Androis axiom *Absurdum est dicere errasse Aristotelem*', and so 'being sure of a truethe in reasoning, he wald be extream hat and suffer na man to bear away the contrar'.127 Such was the forceful personality which Andrew Melville displayed at Glasgow.

Melville, however, was no slavish imitator of Ramus in every field. In moral philosophy, if not in logic, Andrew Melville still taught certain of Aristotle's works at Glasgow; and if James Melville provided instruction in the dialectic of Ramus and the rhetoric of Talon in his first year as regent at Glasgow in 1575, he proceeded the following year to teach Aristotle's logic and ethics, the logic from the Greek text and not from the Latin of the schoolmen—'the first regent', so James Melville claims, 'that ever did that in Scotland'.128 It was presumably as a result of Andrew Melville's campaign that the general assembly in October 1583 condemned those aspects in philosophy 'directlie impugning the grounds of religioun, and speciallie in the philosophie of

Aristotle' which caused students to drink 'erronious and damnable opiniouns'.[129] Such a pronouncement, however, was simply in accord with the critical spirit of biblical humanism which, not surprisingly, had found much that was pagan in Aristotle's writings. Aristotle, though deposed, was reassessed, not ousted.

Nor was Melville prepared to go all the way with Ramus in matters of church government where he seems to have sided with Beza instead. In opposition to Beza, Ramus had criticised both the deacon's exclusion from church government and the oligarchic tendencies in the Calvinist polity of the French church. Beza, in turn, had accused 'that pseudo-dialectician' of stirring up 'a very serious discussion concerning the whole government of the church' by declaring that it 'ought to be more democratic, not aristocratic, leaving to the council of elders only the proposal of legislation; wherefore, the synod at Nîmes, in which I participated, upon my advice condemned that view, which is most absurd and pernicious'.[130] On this subject, something of Melville's thinking is to be found in the second Book of Discipline in 1578 which was antipathetic to Ramus' ideas on polity, for not only did it propose excluding the deacon from a share in the church's government, through its courts, but it had also recommended that voting membership in the general assembly should consist purely of 'ecclesiasticall personis'.[131] On this issue, Melville chose to ally with Beza, not Ramus.

With these qualifications, it is nonetheless significant that the new intellectual ideas associated with Ramist humanism should find a firm footing and outlet in Scotland at so relatively early a date. At Glasgow, both the form and content of university education was studiously reassessed, and before his six years' stay was over, Melville had succeeded in introducing the concept of specialist teaching in place of the outmoded practice of regenting, the system of conducting students through the whole course of study by men who 'profess many subjects but are found expert in few'.[132] As a result, Blaise Lawrie, a new recruit, undertook to teach Latin and Greek; James Melville concentrated on logic, moral philosophy and mathematics; Peter Blackburn specialised in physics and astronomy; and Andrew Melville devoted his energies to the teaching of theology and biblical languages.[133] This far-sighted experiment in teaching methods, which Melville pioneered in Scotland, did not endure, for under the covenanting regime of the 1640s the old system of regenting was restored, and it is a little odd that Melville's presbyterian successors should bear the responsibility for undoing this aspect of his work. Not until the reforms of the early eighteenth century when regenting was finally abandoned in favour of fixed professorships were Melville's methods vindicated.[134]

Melville's reforming programme at Glasgow was not effected overnight. It took time and it cost money. For a start, since he initially had only one other member of staff, Peter Blackburn, whom he had appointed *œconomus* or steward, Melville had little choice but to assume the role of the polymath and undertake most of the teaching himself. He began his work, therefore, 'with a few number of capable heirars, sic as might be instructars of uthers thairefter'.[135] What this meant, in financial terms, was that until the number of students rose, as it subsequently did, little income could be expected in the way of fees. Consequently, any prospect of increasing the teaching staff did not look bright. On the other hand, Melville and Blackburn were, at least, working on a full-time basis and whilst they might therefore be entitled to expect full-time salaries, the situation looked more promising than it had been in the 1560s under Davidson and Hamilton. One source of income was the vicarage of Colmonell, but by leasing it for nineteen years to Gilbert Kennedy in 1570 for an annual return of little more than £40, of which £16 had to be 'paid to the vicar pensionary until his demission in 1580, Davidson had effectively committed his successors in the university to an arrangement which was unlikely to be altered until the expiry of the lease in 1589.[136] Besides the vicarage of Colmonell, the college could also claim the revenues derived from the annual rents of properties in the town which it leased.[137]

Even so, 'the Collage leiving', as James Melville knew from experience, remained 'but verie small, consisting in litle annualles then',[138] and although the revenues of the chaplainries, prebendaries and altarages in the burgh had been formally assigned to the university in 1573 to help augment its finances, Melville and Blackburn had still to resort to litigation before the lords of Council to secure payment. In June 1575, the lords of Council ordered the 'fewaris, anuelleris, tennentis and occupyaris' of the various ecclesiastical properties disponed to the university to make due payment of their rents to the college on pain of imprisonment in Dumbarton castle. Melville then followed this up, in December 1575, by obtaining from the lords of Council an inhibition against those who had legal title to the numerous chaplainries, over which the university had acquired the superiority, from dilapidating their benefices by granting tacks, liferents or wadsets to the defraud of the university.[139]

As a result of these activities, university finances looked in rather better shape than they had been for quite some time. A third member of the academic staff could therefore be recruited. The nature of Scottish society being what it was, with its affection for ties of kinship, no one was likely to raise an eyebrow of protest, or even surprise, when the principal's nephew was appointed regent 'about Michaelmas' 1575. In his first year, he taught Greek grammar, rhetoric and dialectic. This constituted, in effect, the course for first-year students in Arts, a course which his uncle had conducted the preceding year.[140] In structure, though not in content, it bore some resemblance to the first-year course at St Andrews where, in true medieval fashion, rhetoric and dialectic provided the staple fare, but the introduction of Greek at Glasgow for first-year students was startlingly novel, and although it went well beyond the recommendations of the first Book of Discipline, which in somewhat traditional form prescribed dialectic, it was in accord with the aims of educational reformers on the continent.[141] In his second year, James Melville went on to teach mathematics, logic and moral philosophy.[142] This presumably comprised the course for second-year students. Although as a student at St Andrews James Melville had studied mathematics in his second year, it was not until his third year that he was taught moral philosophy, which in the traditional medieval curriculum was taken towards the end of the M.A. course.[143] At Glasgow, natural philosophy or physics came to be taught by Peter Blackburn to students in their third year,[144] which conformed to accepted practice. Whether Andrew Melville, as principal, provided instruction in theology and biblical languages for the remainder of the Arts course, a course which would normally be of three and a half years' duration,[145] or whether this was reserved for more advanced, post-graduate study after licence had been granted is less than clear.[146] Such, at any rate, was the Arts course which Melville formulated at Glasgow.

As was to be expected, there were traditional elements in the course; certain of the works studied can be traced back to Glasgow in the fifteenth century and to Oxford and Paris in the thirteenth century. Aspects of the *trivium* and *quadrivium*, which by the later Middle Ages had begun to disintegrate, still survived, along with the three philosophies, but although a continuity of a sort remained in the subjects recognised for instruction, meaningful changes had been introduced in both the content and structure of the curriculum. Alterations in teaching methods are also apparent in James Melville's remark that by 1577 'that profession of the Mathematiks, Logic and Morall Philosophie, I keipit (as everie ane of the regents keipit their awin, the schollars ay ascending and passing throw) sa lang as I regented ther'.[147] If initially under Melville regenting of a kind existed, which was understandable enough in a situation where there were so few teachers, it did not survive for long, and, as James Melville's comment bears witness, Melville soon succeeded in introducing the principle of specialist teaching, in an elementary form at least, to replace the old regenting system which continued to dominate current teaching practice in Scotland's two other universities.

Reforms at Glasgow were carried one stage further with the charter of new foundation—the *nova erectio*—in July 1577 which not only made formal provision for abolishing regenting but also established an adequately endowed collegiate organisation within the university.[148] By way of benefaction, the king bestowed on the college the whole benefice of Govan, both parsonage and vicarage, and engrossed in the charter were details of the revised constitution and curriculum. After reciting something of the earlier distress which had befallen the college, the charter pointed the way forward. Since college revenues were 'so small that they are not sufficient' to sustain the staff, assistance was necessary 'for making and erecting therin some appearance of a college', a remark rather reminiscent of the wording in Queen Mary's benefaction of 1563. The king's intervention, therefore, was designed to 'gather together the remains of our university of Glasgow which we found to be pining in poverty and now well nigh ruined' and so 'to provide against that calamity and to obviate the sting of poverty which is wont to be most adverse to persons studious of the liberal arts', a statement which calls to mind the description of the college in the town's charter of 1573.[149]

The picture painted is not a flattering one, but there are indications that it may be somewhat overdrawn. The college was certainly short of funds and its fabric stood in need of further, indeed constant, repair. Yet, despite all, its teaching continued and, what is more, its quality improved. In James Melville's estimation, the college's reputation once more began to rise.[150] Since it had been low indeed, this may not have been difficult to achieve. Even so, it is evident from the graduation records which begin in 1578 that there were at least ten students ready to enroll when Melville took over in 1574.[151] Sustenance was the remedy; and a measure of financial stability seemed to be guaranteed in the annexation to the college of the benefice of Govan, vacant by the death of Stephen Beaton, the last possessor. The college was now to receive the annual rental from Govan of twenty-four chalders of victual which, being computed in kind with its in-built safeguards against inflation, might be reckoned at something like £480.[152] Most of this income, in almost monastic fashion, was to sustain twelve foundationers in food and drink 'without extravagance and waste that by means of frugal fare they may be incited to more earnest application to their studies'. The college, therefore, was to comprise a principal, three regents, an *œconomus*, and four poor students, together with a servant for the principal, a cook and a porter.

The new foundation prescribed a constitution for the college, not the university. The principal was endowed with 'ordinary jurisdiction over every one of the persons of our college', but he was required to reside in college, a not unreasonable demand, particularly in the aftermath of

Davidson's apparent lack of residence. Nor was he to undertake 'any considerable journey' without first notifying the rector, dean of faculty and teaching staff. Absence of more than three days without leave would result in dismissal. The appointment of a new principal resembled the procedure in episcopal appointments. Presentation was to lie with the crown; examination and election were vested in the archbishop of Glasgow, 'who is the chancellor of the university', the rector, dean of faculty and ministers of the churches of Glasgow, Hamilton, Cadder, Monkland and Renfrew (all prebends of Glasgow cathedral); and, in the event of the crown's failure to exercise its powers within thirty days, the right of presentation was to devolve on the examiners and electors, who were also empowered to depose as well as to appoint. At the same time, during a vacancy, regents from St Andrews and Aberdeen, as well as Glasgow, were to be invited to apply, so that the final choice could be made 'without favour nor influence of party but for worth and superiority in learning', a stipulation which might be held to infringe rights of presentation. The appointment and dismissal of the three regents, however, were to lie with the rector, dean of faculty and principal. As for the four poor students, presentation to the bursaries was vested in the Regent Morton and his heirs male, whilst the power of admission lay with the principal, who was charged 'to take heed that rich men are not admitted instead of poor'.[153]

As well as establishing a collegiate constitution, the royal charter also prescribed the curriculum which embodied Melville's attitudes in education. For a start, it was enacted that 'it is not our will that these three regents change every year into new courses, as is the custom in the other colleges of our kingdom, whereby it comes to pass that while they profess many branches of learning they are found skilled in few; but they shall exercise themselves in the same course that young men who ascend step by step may find their preceptor worthy of their studies and gifts'. This, in effect, gave formal recognition to the reforms which Melville had already begun to introduce. Accordingly, the first regent was to provide instruction in rhetoric and Greek so that students may become 'more fit to receive the principles of philosophy'. The second regent was, therefore, assigned the teaching of dialectic and logic, and moral philosophy from Cicero, Plato, Aristotle and similar 'best authors'. He was also required to teach arithmetic and geometry 'which are of no small importance for the acquisition of learning and sharpening the intellect'. Natural philosophy was to be taught by the third regent who was also 'to profess geography and astronomy and likewise general chronology, or history, 'and computation of time from the creation of the world'.

All this comprised the Arts or 'philosophic course', but the principal was to provide the theological content. As one well versed in scripture, it was his task 'to open up the mysteries of the faith' and so to 'unfold the hidden treasures of the word of God'. These were, of course, the duties of the office of doctor, a recognised ecclesiastical function to which Melville gave added emphasis; and it was by virtue of this office that he claimed a seat in the courts of the church. Indeed, at one point, the wording of the *nova erectio* is echoed in the second Book of Discipline in 1578 when it explained how it was for the doctor 'to oppin up, be simple teacheing, the mysteris of the fayth'.[154] Combining the office of principal with that of the theology professor was by no means new. John Davidson had already served in both capacities, as well as in some others, before and after the Reformation; and the town's charter of 1573 had explicitly reserved to the principal the office of professor of theology (*professor . . . theologiae*). But the *nova erectio* went further; it also charged the principal to be skilled in biblical languages, particularly in Hebrew and Syriac; in this, few Scots were as suitable as Melville. From Monday to Friday, he was to lecture daily for at least an hour on theology and, on alternate days, on the sacred languages.

In certain aspects, the foundation of 1577 resembled its predecessor of 1573.[155] The college's constitution was evidently modelled on the earlier scheme, though with provision for rather fewer foundationers. But there were clearly differences, not least in the subjects to be taught. In the curriculum of 1573, emphasis had been firmly placed on the philosophies to the exclusion of arithmetic, geometry and astronomy, geography and history, and Greek and Hebrew. The *nova erectio* redressed this imbalance. Similarly, the supposition in 1573, that regenting would continue, stood in sharp contrast to what the *nova erectio* had to say about specialist teaching. Yet if this innovation was at variance with established patterns of teaching in the Scottish universities, it was at least in accord with educational developments on the continent where in the course of the sixteenth century there had developed fixed professorships in distinct subjects.[156] Although collegiate instruction in some universities had displaced public university lectures, Ramus, for one, had greatly favoured the establishment of public chairs;[157] and in the newly created academies, modelled on the reforms of Baduel and Sturm, specialist teaching had evolved. At Nîmes, founded in 1539, there were, in addition to regents in grammar and rhetoric, three specialist, public lecturers in philosophy, mathematics and Greek;[158] and this pattern was repeated in the numerous protestant academies established in France and also in Switzerland where by 1547 Lausanne was equipped with public lectors or professors in Greek, Hebrew, philosophy, and theology, and Geneva, founded in 1559, had public chairs in these same subjects as well as in law and medicine.[159] If, in the Scottish universities, notably at St Andrews, attempts at establishing public lectors sometimes met with success,[160] regenting still remained the recognised method of teaching in the constituent colleges. The Glasgow charter of new erection, by contrast, stands out as a pioneering effort. Not only did it give a lead to St Andrews and Aberdeen, it also showed a sensitive awareness of European trends. That Melville himself kept in touch with changing continental patterns of education is also suggested in the copy which he owned, admittedly in later life, of Sturm's *Institutionis literatae tomus primus*, published in 1586.[161]

With all its advantages, the *nova erectio* contained some defects. If the principal's stipend of two hundred merks was assigned from the existing college rents which on paper were said to amount annually to £300, the remaining salaries of fifty merks apiece for the first and second regents and £50 for the third and senior regent had evidently to be found from the additional revenues assigned in 1577. These new revenues, however, were forthcoming only by resorting to the well-tried expedient of appropriating benefices, in this case Govan, a method of financing universities and other higher institutions which had caused difficulties in the past. Although the second Book of Discipline in 1578 called for the separation and division of churches annexed to prelacies, it tacitly ignored the university colleges whose revenues were largely drawn from the parishes. Far from reforming the practice, the *nova erectio* merely confirmed this trend, which was carried one step further in 1617 when the benefices of Kilbride and Renfrew were annexed to the college.[162] Temporal lands, from one source or another, were evidently too precious to be used for the endowment of the universities whose links with the church in any event were sufficiently close to serve as a pretext for continuing to finance them from the patrimony of the church. This was something to which the first Book of Discipline had been by no means averse, although it had admittedly envisaged subverting the old benefice structure instead of incorporating it intact into the structure of the reformed church.[163]

Though designed to relieve the college's financial distress, the annexation of Govan also meant that the college would have to undertake the cure of souls at Govan. There was already a reader to give assistance,[164] for Stephen Beaton, the former parson, played no part in the ministry of the reformed church; but under the *nova erectio* the principal had now to undertake preaching in the parish. Just as Davidson had voluntarily undertaken to serve as minister of Hamilton as well as principal, so too was Melville now required to preach the sermon on the Sabbath to the parishioners of Govan, since it was only right that 'they who furnish the temporal things should receive of the spiritual and not be defrauded of the bread of life, which is the word of God'. Not only was this likely to prove a distraction from college duties, hence the requirement that the principal should reside in college, but it also infringed the second Book of Discipline's insistence that 'nane be intrused upoun ony congregatioun'.[165] Patronage remained the order of the day, confirmed by statute law; and for the parishioners the right to choose their own minister was not conceded. Despite the fact that Melville's immediate successors continued to perform their duties as principal and preacher, it did not always prove easy to reconcile what were in effect two separate occupations. Only in 1621 was this unsatisfactory arrangement terminated when Robert Boyd of Trochrague, as principal, was freed from his obligations at Govan. Though retaining its patronage of the benefice, the college undertook to provide a full-time minister to serve the cure of souls in the parish of Govan.[166]

Defects in practice as well as in principle are also apparent, not least in the difficulties experienced in acquiring the full revenues to which the college was entitled from the benefice it acquired in 1577. Although the patronage of Govan had lain with the archbishop in pre-Reformation times, the crown on assuming this right after 1560 had presented Stephen Beaton, a kinsman both of the exiled archbishop and of the previous parson of Govan, to the benefice in October 1561, and he, in turn, in February 1575 had leased the teinds of Govan for nineteen years to his brother, Archibald Beaton, the university rector in 1556 who became the 'read-faced' commissary of Glasgow, for an annual rent of three hundred merks.[167] When the college failed to obtain payment of the teinds, it resorted to litigation, but the judgment of the lords of Council in November 1577 upheld the terms of the existing lease 'during the yeris to ryn'. By October 1578, however, agreement was reached between the college and Beaton who renounced his lease at the king's request so that the college 'may instantlie cum in possessioune of the said personage and vicerage'. In return, the college granted Beaton a new lease of fifteen years on the same terms, and Beaton not only agreed to pay two years' arrears of rent and to free the college of all sums payable from the teinds for these years and for the remainder of his lease, including a £10 pension to the vicar pensionary, £16 for the reader's stipend and £7 for the almshouse of Glasgow, but he also undertook to uphold the fabric of the parson's part of the church and to provide the communion elements at Govan for the duration of his lease.[168] Not until 1593 would the college be likely to obtain full access to the teinds on their reversion to the college and the expiry of the lease.

The *nova erectio* was a landmark in Scottish university organisation, and it was recognised as such by the other universities which sought to imitate features of the scheme. Melville had rescued Glasgow university and had raised its stature immeasurably. The new foundation, with some subsequent modification, remained the basis of the college's constitution for three centuries. Even in the nineteenth century legal decisions still rested on interpretations of the charter of new erection.[169] That the university should obtain such a grant in 1577 was in itself no mean achievement, for the ecclesiastical views of its principal ran counter to those of the crown. The Regent Morton, in attempting an erastian settlement for the church along the lines of a 'conformity with England', had accused Melville and his presbyterian associates of disturbing the peace of the church 'be thair conceats and oversie dreames, imitation of Genev discipline and lawes'.[170] Much of the initiative in guiding the general assembly away from the settlement of Leith in 1572, professedly based on Anglican procedure,[171] towards a more presbyterian constitution for the church was undoubtedly taken by Melville in those years as principal of Glasgow university. There may therefore be some substance in the remark that Morton offered Melville the benefice of Govan 'provyding he wald be the Regent's man and leave aff the persut of the bischopes' and that, on Melville's refusal, Morton deliberately postponed any settlement for the college by leaving the benefice of Govan vacant for two years and so blaming Melville for denying the 'collage and him selff bathe of sic a benefit because of his new opiniones and oversie dreames anent the kirk discipline and polecie'. This caused Peter Blackburn and others to complain that Melville was 'a grait hinder of a guid wark'; and only on the advice of Patrick Adamson, the minister of Paisley and then a 'grait frind and companion' of Melville, was Morton persuaded to make 'a new erection and reformation of the Collage of Glasgw . . . quhilk was the best turn that ever I knew ather the Regent or Mr Patrik to do'.[172]

Melville, of course, remained the dominant figure in Scottish theological education, and there is good reason to believe that some of his educational theories penetrated and influenced current thinking at St Andrews and Aberdeen. It was not fortuitous that Glasgow's foundation of 1577 should be followed by a new foundation of the St Andrews colleges in 1579, an intended new foundation for King's College, Aberdeen in 1583, and the creation and foundation in 1593 of Marischal College, Aberdeen, all of which owed something to Melville's innovations.[173] It was with Arbuthnot, the principal of King's, that Melville had first 'communicat anent the haill ordour of his Collage in doctrine and discipline'.[174] Nor was Arbuthnot likely to need much persuading, for he, too, was aware of continental patterns of education during his sojourn at Bourges in the 1560s.[175] As early as 1575, they had agreed on a common line of action and initiated a programme of reform in both universities. Melville was again in touch with Arbuthnot in 1579, and his nephew, as an informed observer, attributed Aberdeen's projected foundation of 1583 to the joint activities of Melville and Arbuthnot.[176] The Aberdeen foundation certainly conformed to the Glasgow model. The earlier offices of canonist, civilist and mediciner were to be abolished, and the reconstituted college was to become a college of arts whose principal would teach theology as well as preach in St Machar's church. The foundation also provided for four regents, twelve bursars, a grammarian, *œconomus*, cook and two servants. The regenting system was to be replaced by specialist teaching, and the subjects studied were closely related to those of Glasgow.[177] If all this fitted the Glasgow pattern, there was noticeably no mention of Ramus in the curriculum. Not till 1641, it would seem, did the works of Ramus and Talon become prescribed texts at King's.[178] It may, however, be more than just coincidence that both John Johnston and Robert Howie, on graduating from King's in 1584, should decide to pursue studies abroad which finally imprinted upon them a definite Ramist outlook.[179] Johnston subsequently became Melville's friend and colleague at St Andrews in the 1590s and a committed opponent of episcopacy whilst Howie, who also condemned the 'pseudo-episcopacy' of the English church in 1592, entered the ministry in Aberdeen before becoming the first principal of Marischal College in 1593 and his appointment by the king in 1607 as Melville's successor in St Mary's college, St Andrews, in recognition no doubt of his conversion to the episcopal cause.[180] It was not, however, until 1597 that the new foundation of King's began to take effect and those who have found the initial failure of the 1583 foundation inexplicable would do worse than to attribute it to the repercussions following the deaths in 1583 of Arbuthnot in Aberdeen and Smeaton in Glasgow.[181] Nor did the prospect for change look bright with the 'Black Acts' of the conservative Arran regime in 1584 and with the flight of the presbyterian leaders to England.[182] It was even rumoured in 1584 that Archbishop Adamson of St Andrews wanted to abolish theological teaching at St Mary's and to replace it with a school of philosophy.[183] It was, by contrast, in the more favourable presbyterian climate following the 'Golden Act' of 1592 that the earl Marischal founded his own college at Aberdeen in 1593, employing phraseology in his charter borrowed from the Glasgow one of 1577.[184] Nor is this altogether surprising. His father, to whose earldom he succeeded in 1581, had witnessed the Glasgow charter of new erection in 1577, and he himself on returning home in 1580 after visiting Paris and Geneva, as well as Germany and Italy, became identified with 'the maist wacryff [wakeful] and cearfull of the breithren' who met under Melville's leadership in 1589 to consider 'the dangers threatned to the professors of the true Religion within the Realme'.[185]

Like the Glasgow college, Marischal was designed as a college of Arts, 'where young men might receive a godly and liberal education in letters and in arts', to be staffed with a principal, three regents, six bursars, a steward and a cook. The principal 'must be well versed in the Scriptures, able to unfold the mysteries of faith and the hidden treasures of the Word of God' and he 'must also be skilled and learned in languages, and especially in Hebrew and in Syriac'. Not only so, specialist professorships were introduced on the Glasgow model, 'so that the youths who ascend step by step may have a teacher worthy of their studies and talents'.[186] All this recalls the language of the Glasgow charter of new foundation which plainly had repercussions for the universities as a whole.

The humanist and Ramist values associated with Melville's teaching were also introduced at St Andrews where they made some headway. In 1580 Melville himself left Glasgow 'sear against his will' to become principal of St Mary's college,[187] following the reorganisation of that university in 1579 and the reconstruction of St Mary's as a college of divinity to be staffed with five theology 'professouris' or 'lectors'.[188] George Buchanan, whose name was attached to the Glasgow project of 1577, was also associated with the report of the visitation which produced the schemes for reform at St Andrews in 1579;[189] and although accorded no official status, Melville was undoubtedly influential in the ideas behind the remodelling of St Mary's. While at Glasgow, he and Smeaton, it was said, 'war the first motioners of an anti-seminarie to be erected in St Androis to the Jesuist seminaries for the course of theologie'.[190] Thereafter St Mary's functioned as 'ane seminarie for planting of the haill kirkis within the realme,' and Melville established himself as 'chief doctor and master of the education of the youth in knowledge of the tongues and theology'.[191] Nor was it long before he confronted his more conservative colleagues, particularly the philosophy lecturers of St Leonard's with the full force of his radical, anti-scholastic, Ramist philosophy. Within a year of his appointment turmoil had broken out in St Andrews university as his opponents attempted to fight a rearguard action. If Ramus were right and Aristotle wrong, the implications were clear: 'thair breadwinner, thair honour, thair estimation, all was gean, giff Aristotle sould be sa owir-harled in the heiring of thair schollars; and sa dressit publict orationes against Mr Androe's doctrine'. The same domineering attitude which Melville displayed at Glasgow was also brought to bear at St Andrews where 'Mr Andro insisted mightelie' against the exponents of the old scholastic philosophy 'in his

ordinar lessones' until they finally 'acknawlagit a wounderfull trans-
portation out of darknes unto light'.[192] Over the years, despite 'mikle
feghting and fascherie', Melville's will eventually prevailed in certain
quarters.

To attain 'that perfectioun of teaching which this learnit aige craves',
the reorganisation of 1579 had provided for the introduction in the
colleges of specialist teaching on the Glasgow pattern. In St Salvator's
and St Leonard's, the second regent was to teach 'the precepts of
inventioun, dispositioun and elocutioun the second yeir, schortest,
easiest and maist accurate with practice thairof in the best authors of
bayth the toungis' and the third regent was required to teach only the
'maist proffitable and needful pairtis of the logiks of Aristotle'. All this
may be indicative of Ramist tendencies, or at least of a new approach;
and although a visitation of these colleges in 1588 disclosed that neither
kept 'the reformatioun in changing of thair discipulis fra maister to
maister', it also revealed that in St Salvator's the mathematician, Homer
Blair, was teaching the arithmetic of Ramus and that Robert Wemyss
was instructing his class in Talon.[193] Plainly, what the curriculum
prescribed and what the masters chose to teach need not always have
agreed. As was to be expected, Ramist teaching in the universities
inevitably spilled over into the wider church: in 1596 John Rutherford,
the minister of Kilconquhar, submitted to St Andrews presbytery as 'the
penner of that infamous and godles lybell intitulat the head of blackeare
doctrein resolvit in a Ramist method';[194] and Rutherford was the son
of the former provost of St Salvator's whose Aristotelian taste in logic
does not seem to have advanced beyond Rudolph Agricola.

Similar tendencies were at work in Edinburgh too. James Lawson,
who had been sub-principal of King's College before becoming minister
in Edinburgh, was instrumental in the successful institution of this new
university; and through its first principal, Robert Rollock from
St Andrews, where he had studied Hebrew under James Melville,
Edinburgh also became affected by Ramist teaching. Rollock's own
attitude is clearly revealed in one of his sermons where, attacking
Aristotelian scholasticism, he accused its followers of turning 'the gospel
of Jesus to Aristotle, all thair writings are bot spreitles. Thair is not sa
mekle as ane smel of the spreit of Jesus in them all'.[195] Much of this is
reminiscent of Luther's earlier criticisms of the German universities
'where only the blind heathen teacher Aristotle rules far more than
Christ'. Luther had indeed proposed banishing many of Aristotle's
works, though he had conceded that Aristotle's *Logic* could 'be read as
it is without all these commentaries', for 'the whole thing has become
nothing but a matter for disputation and a weariness to the flesh'.[196] In
Edinburgh, however, Rollock's students were subjected to the novel

works of Ramus and Talon, as prescribed texts in the curriculum,[197] and one graduate, Charles Ferme, the presbyterian minister at Fraserburgh, who also became principal of the ill-fated college there, applied Ramist logic to theology in his *Logical Analysis of the Epistle of Paul to the Romans*.[198] The logical analysis of scripture had also been undertaken by Rollock in his study of The Epistle to the Hebrews.[199]

Here, then, was something of the ethos which characterised university education in Scotland from the 1570s onwards, and it was against this background, amidst these new academic influences, that many of Melville's younger disciples spent their formative years. In the late sixteenth century, at least, a close affinity existed between presbyterianism, radicalism and Ramism and between episcopacy, aristocracy and scholasticism.[200] 'Most of the great English Puritans', it has been observed, 'were followers of Ramus',[201] and in Scotland, using Glasgow as his base, Melville advanced these new academic values which spread from Glasgow to St Andrews, Edinburgh and in some sense perhaps to Aberdeen. At Glasgow, he established something of a Melvillian dynasty by appointing James and then Patrick Melville as members of the academic staff,[202] and when he left for St Andrews it was Thomas Smeaton, his presbyterian associate, who became his successor, so that with Arbuthnot at Aberdeen and later with Rollock at Edinburgh, Scottish theological training was for a time supervised by men sympathetic to the Melvillian cause. The victory, however, was far from complete. The most that may be said is that some headway had been made. In the end, the reforms proved to be short-lived. Whereas in the late sixteenth century, scholasticism had looked like yielding place to humanism and even to Ramism, the early seventeenth century witnessed the revival of scholasticism in the universities and of episcopacy in the church. Consequently, Melville's reforms in the universities, as in the church, were soon eclipsed, and he himself was removed from the scene, first as a prisoner in the Tower of London and then as an exile in France.

The history of the universities of Poitiers and Geneva can readily be written without the name of Andrew Melville. Abroad, his contribution was unexceptional rather than notable and at most his name deserves only the briefest mention. Yet for Glasgow, and indeed for Scotland as a whole, Melville's name assumes a greater significance. As an educational reformer, he sought to bring Glasgow and the other universities into closer contact with the latest continental trends, and his abilities lay basically in the vigour with which he applied to the Scottish situation the new techniques in education which he had learned in France and Switzerland.

NOTES

1. *First Book of Discipline*, 85-209.
2. Knox, *Works*, vi, 619, 630; Melville, *Diary*, 26.
3. Melville, *Diary*, 38-9.
4. *Ibid.*, 39.
5. *Early Records of St Andrews University*, 267; Melville, *Diary*, 39.
6. *Essays on the Scottish Reformation*, 152-3.
7. Melville, *Diary*, 40; *The Statutes of the Faculty of Arts and the Faculty of Theology at the period of the Reformation*, ed. R. K. Hannay (St Andrews University Publications, no. 7, St Andrews, 1910), 67-85, 112-35.
8. Melville, *Diary*, 124; *ibid.*, 14-15, 39; T. McCrie, *Life of Andrew Melville* (Edinburgh, 1899), 1-2; *Fasti*, v, 191, 405, 423.
9. Th. Fischer, *The Scots in Germany*, 314. For Anderson, see Melville, *Diary*, 22, 38; *Fasti*, v, 409.
10. Melville, *Diary*, 14.
11. Knox, *Works*, i, 125, 132; *History*, i, 60, 64.
12. Knox, *Works*, i, 36; *History*, i, 15; Donaldson, 'Aberdeen University and the Reformation', *Northern Scotland*, i, 129-42, at 136ff.
13. *Early Records of St Andrews University*, 267; Melville, *Diary*, 39.
14. Durkan and Ross, *Libraries*, 137.
15. T. Dempster, *Historia Ecclesiastica* (Bannatyne Club, Edinburgh 1829), ii, 561.
16. Buchanan, *Opera Omnia*, i, 20; cf. Dempster, *Historia Ecclesiastica*, ii, 497: 'Andreas Melvinus discipulus Georgii Buchanani'; McCrie, *Melville*, 7.
17. SRO, PA10/1. St Andrews University Archives, MS 'Liber Comptorum Divi Leonardi', 1549-91, p. 200: £5 to Mr George Buchanan for the Pentecost term, 1567. Even after he became principal, there was criticism of his evident lack of industry in college.
18. Bodleian, Smith MS, 77, f. 27r.
19. *First Book of Discipline*, 138, 141; *Vernacular Writings of George Buchanan*, 6-11.
20. *APS*, ii, 544, c. 26.
21. Cf. *The Statutes of the Faculty of Arts and the Faculty of Theology in the period of the Reformation*, 1-66, 86-111.
22. *Early Records of St Andrews University*, 267.
23. *RSS*, vi, nos. 518, 663; *Fasti*, i, 51-2; cf. *CSP Scot.*, ii, no. 33.
24. Melville, *Diary*, 39.
25. McCrie, *Melville*, 8.
26. *CSP Scot.*, ii, no. 33 (and PRO, SP52/8, f. 3r). Though not there described as 'Mr', he is so styled in Melville, *Diary*, 73.
27. Melville, *Diary*, 39-40.
28. Cf. *The Alba Amicorum of George Strachan, George Craig, Thomas Cumming*, ed. J. F. K. Johnstone (Aberdeen, 1924).
29. *BUK*, i, 339.
30. *Ibid.*, ii, 437.
31. *Sermons and Life of Mr. Robert Bruce*, ed. W. Cunningham (Wodrow Society, Edinburgh, 1843), 5.
32. *Die Matrikel der Universität Basel*, ed. H. G. Wackernagel (Basle, 1956), ii, 181; *Le Livre du Recteur de l'Académie de Genève*, ed. S. Stelling-Michaud (Geneva, 1959) i, 81; *Die Matrikel der Universität Rostock*, ed. A. Hofmeister (Rostock, 1889), ii, 148; Francisque-Michel, *Les Écossais en France, les Français en Écosse*, i, 119 and n. 6.

33. W. A. McNeill, 'Scottish Entries in the *Acta Rectoria Universitatis Parisiensis*, 1519 to *c*. 1633', *SHR*, xliii, 66–86, at 73, 79, 86; P. H. Brown, *George Buchanan*, 15.

34. *CSP Scot.*, i, no. 876; Durkan and Ross, *Libraries*, 118.

35. Melville, *Diary*, 72–4; *CSP Scot.*, i, nos. 1031, 1139.

36. McNeill, *SHR*, xliii, 66–83, at 73 (Dempster); for Davidson see above, 232; Dempster, *Historia Ecclesiastica*, i, 116 (Blackwood).

37. *BUK*, i, 4 (i.e. Patrick Constane); Francisque-Michel, *Les Écossais en France*, ii, 52 n. 2; J. Durkan, 'George Buchanan: Some French Connections', *The Bibliotheck*, iv, 66–72, at 71 where the text is given of Adamson's letter from Bourges, citing Berne Burgerbibliothek, MS 141, f. 213r; *DNB*, i, 112.

38. Lord Lindsay, *Lives of the Lindsays* (London, 1849), i, 331–3.

39. Melville, *Diary*, 73. *Le Livre du Recteur de l'Académie de Genève*, i, 96.

40. Cf. P. Collinson, *The Elizabethan Puritan Movement* (London, 1967), 110.

41. Melville, *Diary*, 73.

42. A. Lefranc, *Histoire du Collège de France* (Paris, 1893; Geneva, 1970), 101ff.

43. Melville, *Diary*, 39–40.

44. *The Alba Amicorum of George Strachan, George Craig, Thomas Cumming*, 1–17.

45. Melville, *Diary*, 39–40; Lefranc, *Histoire du Collège de France*, 381–2; A. Lefranc *et al.*, *Le Collège de France, 1530–1930* (Paris, 1932), 15–16, 18–22.

46. Melville, *Diary*, 40.

47. W. A. McNeill, *SHR*, xliii, 85.

48. *The Bibliotheck*, iv, 71–2.

49. Melville, *Diary*, 40.

50. P. Boissonnade, *Histoire de l'Université de Poitiers passé et présent (1432–1932)* (Poitiers, 1932), 167–8; Francisque-Michel, *Les Écossais en France*, ii, 211; W. A. McNeill, *SHR*, xliii, 71.

51. *Early Records of St Andrews University*, 251; W. A. McNeill, *SHR*, xliii, 78; Boissonnade, *Poitiers*, 171 (Elias Donat MacRodor).

52. St Andrews University Archives, SS110 AP2. Testament of William Skeyne. I owe this reference to Dr J. Durkan.

53. Boissonnade, *Poitiers*, 173–4, 254; Francisque-Michel, *Les Écossais en France*, ii, 205–21.

54. Boissonnade, *Poitiers*, 46.

55. SRO, GD30/897. Shairp of Houstoun Muniments; Boissonnade, *Poitiers*, 45.

56. Francisque-Michel, *Les Écossais en France*, ii, 139; Boissonnade, *Poitiers*, 45.

57. SRO, GD151/13/13. Graham of Fintry Muniments, Letter book of Sir David Graham of Fintry; cf. Francisque-Michel, *Les Écossais en France*, ii, 139; *Warrender Papers*, i, 275–6.

58. Melville, *Diary*, 44.

59. E. D. English, *Rare Books in the McKissick Library* (New York, 1952), 11 (no. 70). I owe this reference to Dr J. Durkan. McGruder's edition is not listed in W. J. Ong, *Ramus and Talon Inventory* (Cambridge, Mass., 1958).

60. Edinburgh University Library, MS La.III.321, ff. 43r-v, 105r, 106r, 107r, 123v, 146v, 187v. Instruments and letters relating chiefly to the see of Glasgow.

61. Melville, *Diary*, 40.

62. Quick, *Synodicon in Gallia Reformata* (London, 1692), i, 2–20.

63. Boissonnade, *Poitiers*, 111.

64. Melville, *Diary*, 40–42.

65. *Registres de la Compagnie des Pasteurs de Genève*, edd. O. Fatio and O. Labarthe (Geneva, 1969), iii, 49.

66. S. J. Knox, *Walter Travers* (London, 1962), 28–9.

67. C. Borgeaud, 'Cartwright and Melville at the University of Geneva, 1569–74', *American Historical Review*, v, 284–90, at 287.
68. A. F. S. Pearson, *Thomas Cartwright and Elizabethan Puritanism 1535–1603* (Cambridge, 1925), 142.
69. Melville, *Diary*, 42.
70. J. B. Mullinger, *The University of Cambridge* (Cambridge, 1884), ii, 63 n. 1.
71. Melville, *Diary*, 42; J. W. Allen, *A History of Political Thought in the Sixteenth Century* (London, 1961), 308ff.
72. McCrie, *Melville*, 20.
73. Melville, *Diary*, 42; C. Borgeaud, *Histoire de l'Université de Genève: l'Académie de Calvin, 1559–1798* (Geneva, 1900), 73ff.
74. C. Borgeaud, *AHR*, v, 288; F. P. Graves, *Peter Ramus and the Educational Reformation of the Sixteenth Century* (New York, 1912), 99.
75. Melville, *Diary*, 30.
76. Buchanan, *Opera Omnia*, ii, *Epistolae*, no. viii; GUL, Wodrow's MS. Biographies, iii, Life of Henry Scrimgeour, ff. 5–9; Melville, *Diary*, 30, 42.
77. C. Borgeaud, *AHR*, v, 288–9; P. Mellon, *L'Académie de Sedan* (Paris, 1913), 258–9.
78. Melville, *Diary*, 42–3, 45, 47.
79. SRO, PA10/1; *Evidence*, iii, 187–9.
80. Melville, *Diary*, 47; Calderwood, *History*, iii, 329–30.
81. NLS, Wodrow MSS, folio vol. xlii, f. 11r.
82. SRO, GD1/371/1, Warrender Papers, f. 12.
83. Wodrow, *Biographical Collections* (Maitland Club, 1834–35), i, 206, 208, 210.
84. Melville, *Diary*, 47.
85. *Ibid.*
86. GUA, Drawer F5, 23 July 1574.
87. Melville, *Diary*, 50.
88. *Ibid.*, 48.
89. GUA, Drawer F5. Discharge by John Davidson, minister of Hamilton, to Peter Blackburn, 3 October 1575.
90. *Ibid.*, 16 March 1576. Davidson had resigned in favour of the college all rights to the vicarage of Colmonell in January 1575. *Glasgow Protocols*, vii, no. 2112.
91. *Glas. Mun.*, i, 132–4; iii, 408–9.
92. Melville, *Diary*, 48.
93. Brown, *Buchanan*, 50ff, 105ff, 126ff.
94. *APS*, ii, 544, c. 26; *Vernacular Writings of George Buchanan*, 6–17.
95. *Letters and Journals of Robert Baillie*, ed. D. Laing (Bannatyne Club, Edinburgh, 1841–2), iii, 402.
96. *Glasgow Protocols*, iii, no. 756; cf. iit, no. 761; v, no. 1420.
97. Edinburgh University Library, MS La.III.321, ff. 43r-v, 106r, 107r, 123v, 146v, 187v.
98. *Glas. Mun.*, i, 123.
99. Brown, *Buchanan*, 243.
100. A. Hay, *Ad Reverendissimum in Christo patrem D. Jacobum Betoun . . . pro Collegii Erectione Archibaldi Hayi Oratio* (Paris, 1538), 9v.
101. Melville, *Diary*, 48.
102. *Ibid.*, 49.
103. *Ibid.*, 46.
104. Cf. I. D. McFarlane, 'Notes on the Composition and Reception of George Buchanan's Psalm Paraphrases', in *Forum for Modern Language Studies: Renaissance Studies*, vii, no. 4 (1971), 319–60.

105. Melville, *Diary*, 46–7.
106. *Ibid.*, 49–50.
107. F. A. Yates, *The Art of Memory* (London, 1966), 231–42; W. J. Ong, *Ramus Method and the Decay of Dialogue* (Cambridge, Mass., 1958); W. S. Howell, *Logic and Rhetoric in England, 1500–1700* (Princeton, 1956); Graves, *Ramus and the Educational Reformation;* cf. P. Miller, *The New England Mind* (New York, 1939) and L. Jardine, *Francis Bacon: Discovery and the Art of Discourse* (Cambridge, 1974), 41–7.
108. Graves, *Ramus and the Educational Reformation*, 78ff. See also P. Sharratt, 'Peter Ramus and the Reform of the University: the Divorce of Philosophy and Eloquence?' *French Renaissance Studies, 1540–70*, ed. P. Sharratt (Edinburgh, 1976), 4–20.
109. Melville, *Diary*, 45.
110. N. Nancelius, *Petri Rami Vita*, ed. P. Sharratt, *Humanistica Lovaniensia*, xxiv (1975), 161–277 at 201–3; P. Sharratt, 'The Present State of Studies on Ramus', *Studi Francesi*, 46–8 (1972), 201–13 at 204–7; Melville, *Diary*, 46, 49; K. D. McRae, 'Ramist Tendencies in the Thought of Jean Bodin', *Journal of the History of Ideas*, xvi (1955), 306–23; K. D. McRae, 'A Postscript on Bodin's Connections with Ramism', *ibid.*, xxiv (1963), 569–71.
111. GUL, Archimedes, *De Insidentibus aquae* (Venice, 1565); Nicomachus Gerasinus, *Arithmeticae, libri duo* (Paris, 1538).
112. *Glas. Mun.*, ii, 45–6; see below, 371.
113. *Select Biographies*, ed. W. K. Tweedie (Wodrow Society, Edinburgh, 1845, 1847), i, 132.
114. GUA, MS 26624. Library Accounts, 1630–1745, p. 29 (pagination at front of volume); ff. 9r, 10v (foliation at end of volume).
115. I. D. McFarlane, 'George Buchanan and French Humanism', in *Humanism in France*, ed. A. H. T. Levi (Manchester, 1970), 295–319 at 298.
116. 'The Library of James VI', *SHS Miscellany*, i, xlii, xlviii, lxvii.
117. Ong, *Ramus Method*, 372 n. 14.
118. *Early Records of St Andrews University*, 252; *HMC Sixth Report*, pt. i, 647; *Humanism in France*, 314 n. 20; J. Durkan, 'Alexander Dickson and S.T.C. 6823', *The Bibliotheck*, iii, 183–90 at 184.
119. D. M. Quynn, 'The Early Career of John Gordon, Dean of Salisbury', *Bibliothèque d'Humanisme et Renaissance: Travaux et Documents*, vii (Paris, 1945), 118–38. But see also *RMS*, iv, no. 1804, where Gordon is said to be expert in Hebrew, Chaldaic, Syriac, Greek and Latin; *The Sutherland Book*, ed. W. Fraser (Edinburgh, 1892), ii, 111; *CSP Scot.*, ii, no. 729.
120. *Early Records of St Andrews University*, 164, 165, 273; Ong, *Ramus Method*, 301.
121. W. A. McNeill, *SHR*, xliii, 78.
122. *The Warrender Papers*, ii, 404.
123. Melville, *Diary*, 24–5.
124. *Ibid.*, 123–4.
125. SRO, PA10/1.
126. Edinburgh University Library, MS Dc.6.45. Melville, Short Confutation of Dr. Downames Apologetic Sermon; Calderwood, *History*, vi, 741–6; J. B. Mullinger, *The University of Cambridge* (Cambridge, 1884), ii, 404–13; M. H. Curtis, *Oxford and Cambridge in Transition, 1558–1642* (Oxford, 1959), 119, 253.
127. Melville, *Diary*, 67.
128. *Ibid.*, 49, 54.
129. *BUK*, ii, 640–1.

130. Graves, *Ramus and Educational Reformation*, 200–1.
131. *BUK*, ii, 500–1.
132. *Glas. Mun.*, i, 109.
133. Melville, *Diary*, 54; *Glas. Mun.*, iv, p. xciii.
134. *Ibid.*, ii, 467; *Evidence*, ii, 260; Mackie, *University*, 161, 181.
135. Melville, *Diary*, 49, 63.
136. *Glas. Mun.*, i, 81–2, 132. But see also *ibid.*, i, 125.
137. *Ibid.*, i, 91–3, 157ff.
138. Melville, *Diary*, 49.
139. *Glas. Mun.*, i, 94–8.
140. Melville, *Diary*, 49, 53.
141. *The Statutes of the Faculty of Arts and the Faculty of Theology at the period of the Reformation*, 61; Melville, *Diary*, 24–5; *First Book of Discipline*, 143; cf. Jules le Coultre, *Maturin Cordier et les Origines de la pédagogie dans les pays de langue française* (Neuchâtel, 1926), and M-J. Gaufrès, *Claude Baduel et la Réforme des études au XVIe siècle* (Geneva 1969).
142. Melville, *Diary*, 54.
143. *Ibid.*, 27–8; *AFA*, i, p. lxxxiv.
144. *Glas. Mun.*, iv, p. xciii.
145. *Ibid.*, i, 86; Rashdall, *Universities*, i, 464.
146. See below, 318-19, 333.
147. Melville, *Diary*, 54.
148. *RMS*, iv, no. 2693; *Glas. Mun.*, i, 103–12. For the text of the charter of *nova erectio* see Appendix K.
149. *Glas. Mun.*, i, 67, 83, 103, 105.
150. Melville, *Diary*, 49–50.
151. *Glas. Mun.*, iii, 3.
152. *Ibid.*, i, 106. On any reckoning, much depends not only on the proportion of 'beir' and 'meill' which went to make up the 24 chalders, but also the current regional prices of 'beir' and 'meill'. The rental of Govan was very largely derived from 'meill' with an insignificant proportion of 'beir', (*Glas. Mun.*, i, 184–5); and the average price of 'meill' in 1578 was about 25/- per boll, (SRO, E45/12. Accounts of the Collector-General of Thirds of Benefices, 1578, f. 78v.). The thirds of the parsonage and vicarage of Govan were estimated at £66 13. 4d. in 1578, (*ibid.*, f. 33v). The benefice was already set in tack, and under the terms of a new lease drawn up in 1578 the rent was fixed at 300 merks a year for 15 years, (*Glas. Mun.*, i, 124–6).
153. *Ibid.*, i, 106–8, 110. See Appendix K.
154. Knox, *Works*, vi, 293–4; *BUK*, i, 305; ii, 495; *Glas. Mun.*, i, 106.
155. See Appendix K.
156. Rashdall, *Universities*, ii, 284–5.
157. *Ibid.*, i, 518ff, 527ff; Graves, *Ramus and Educational Reformation*, 83.
158. P-D. Bourchenin, *Etude sur les Académies Protestantes en France au XVIe et au XVIIe siècle* (Paris, 1882), 100, 157, 232, 241; Gaufrès, *Claude Baduel et la Réforme des études au XVIe siècle*, 13–14.
159. Bourchenin, *Académies Protestantes en France*, 107–52; 'Leges Scholae Lausannensis, 1547', in L. Junod and H. Meylan, *L'Académie de Lausanne au XVIe siècle*, (*Etudes et Documents*), 11–34; Borgeaud, *l'Université de Genève: l'Académie de Calvin*, 52ff, 87ff.
160. *Evidence*, iii, 188.
161. Edinburgh University Library, T.19.45. J. Sturm, *Institutionis literatae tomus primus* (Torunii Borussorum, 1586). See also Appendix I.

162. *BUK*, ii, 504; *Glas. Mun.*, i, 200–2.
163. *First Book of Discipline*, 150.
164. *Wodrow Society Miscellany*, 382.
165. *BUK*, ii, 509.
166. *Glas. Mun.*, i, 215–17.
167. Cowan, *Parishes*, 77–8; *RSS*, v, no. 856; Edinburgh University Library, MS Dc.4.32. Rental of Assumptions, f. 31v; *Glas. Mun.*, i, 115; Melville, *Diary*, 64.
168. *Glas. Mun.*, i, 114–16, 124–6.
169. *Information: College of Glasgow v. Lockhart* (1808).
170. Melville, *Diary*, 68.
171. *BUK*, i, 203–6; *CSP Scot.*, iv, no. 149.
172. Melville, *Diary*, 53–4.
173. *APS*, iii, 178–82; *Evidence*, iii, 183–6 (St Andrews); *APS*, iii, 214; *BUK*, ii, 594, 614 (King's); *APS*, iv, 35; *Fasti Academiae Mariscallanae Aberdonensis*, i, 39–77 (Marischal).
174. Melville, *Diary*, 53.
175. Spottiswoode, *History*, ii, 319.
176. NLS, Wodrow MSS, folio vol., xlii, f. 11r; Melville, *Diary*, 53.
177. *Officers and Graduates of the University and King's College, Aberdeen*, 335ff.
178. *Fasti Academiae Mariscallanae Aberdonensis*, i, 231.
179. *Letters of John Johnston and Robert Howie*, ed. J. K. Cameron (Edinburgh, 1963), xvi, xxv, xxix.
180. *Ibid.*, xlviii, lviii, lxiv, lxvi, 134, 139, 303, 310, 316–17.
181. Spottiswoode, *History*, ii, 319.
182. Calderwood, *History*, iv, 12, 34, 63–4.
183. *CSP Scot.*, vii, no. 146.
184. *Fasti Academiae Mariscallanae Aberdonensis*, i, 39–77.
185. *Glas. Mun.*, i, 112; *Scots Peerage*, ed. J. B. Paul (Edinburgh, 1914), vi, 51; *BUK*, ii, 740–1.
186. *Fasti Academiae Mariscallanae Aberdonensis*, i, 39–77.
187. Melville, *Diary*, 83; *Evidence*, iii, 191–2.
188. *APS*, iii, 179; *Evidence*, iii, 183–4.
189. *Glas. Mun.*, i, 112; *APS*, iii, 182.
190. Melville, *Diary*, 76.
191. MS. St Andrews Presbytery Records, 5 November 1590; Calderwood, *History*, iv, 422.
192. Melville, *Diary*, 123–4.
193. *APS*, iii, 180; *Evidence*, iii, 184, 194–5.
194. MS. St Andrews Presbytery Records, 3 June 1596.
195. A. Grant, *The Story of the University of Edinburgh* (London, 1884), i, 105–7; *Extracts from the Records of the Burgh of Edinburgh, 1573–1589*, ed. J. D. Marwick (Edinburgh, 1882), iv, 103, 105; *Maitland Club Miscellany* (Edinburgh, 1833–40), i (pt. ii), 287–91 (Lawson); Melville, *Diary*, 86; R. Rollock, *Select Works*, ed. William M. Gunn (Wodrow Society, Edinburgh, 1844, 1849) i, 388.
196. *Luther's Works*, ed. H. Lehmann (Philadelphia, 1966), vol. 44, 200–2.
197. *Charters, Statutes and Acts of the Town Council and the Senatus*, ed. A. Morgan, 60–1, 63.
198. C. Ferme, *A Logical Analysis of the Epistle of Paul to the Romans . . . and a Commentary on the same Epistle by Andrew Melville*, ed. W. L. Alexander (Wodrow Society, Edinburgh, 1850).

199. Rollock, *Analysis dialectica in Pauli apostoli Epistolam ad Romanos* (one edition, Edinburgh, 1594).
200. H. Kearney, *Scholars and Gentlemen: Universities and Society in pre-Industrial Britain, 1500–1700* (London, 1970), 46–70.
201. C. Hill, *Intellectual Origins of the English Revolution* (Oxford, 1965), 292.
202. Melville, *Diary*, 53, 84.

15. The New Constitution

'Finalie, I dar say ther was no place in Europe comparable to Glasgw
for guid letters during these yeirs for a plentifull and guid chepe mercat
of all kynd of langages, artes and sciences.'

James Melville's *Diary*, 1574

IN SO SMALL a community where a pedagogy of somewhat indeterminate status assumed the focal point in academic life, the distinction
between the university and the college was sometimes apt to become
blurred. John Davidson, in 1557, could well be described as 'principall
regent of the said universite and pedagoge', and even in 1574 the
regents might be termed 'the maisteris of the universitie of Glasgw'.[1]
The creation of a firm collegiate structure in 1577, however, not only
lessened this tendency but it may also have prompted a revision of the
statutes governing the university's constitution. The charter of new
erection, in prescribing a constitution for the college, had nothing to
say about the government of the university. The need for university
statutes therefore became all the more necessary, and the first significant
step towards drafting a new constitution for the university was taken
during Melville's principalship in 1578. Up to this point, reliance was
presumably placed on earlier, pre-Reformation enactments with such
adaptation as the new situation would require. Certainly, Melville and
his colleagues would not be completely unaware of the pre-Reformation
procedures regulating the appointment and duties of the university
officers. Admittedly, they would have no knowledge of the contents of
the rector's book removed by James Balfour in 1560 and recovered only
in 1625, but they did have access to the dean of faculty's book, and the
town's charter of 1573 had spoken of the 'statutes of that faculty'.[2] Yet
it was only after Melville's arrival that the initiative was taken to
formulate a revised university constitution.

How much of this revision was undertaken by Melville himself and
how much was additional material incorporated by his immediate
successors is a question which cannot readily be resolved. The printed
text certainly conveys nothing of the complexities in composition and
dating. The trouble is the original drafting of the new constitution, as
such, does not survive, and the final text,[3] which provides the regulations for the university officers, the academic course and the graduation
ceremony, is merely a rather late copy which cannot be dated much

before 1606. This full version, possibly written in the hand of Patrick Sharp, principal from 1586 till 1614, contains an intrusive entry in another hand under the heading '4 *Kalends Januarii* 1606' (29 December 1605), inserted after the section on the promotion of candidates to the master's degree. The scribe, however, on realising his error has abruptly cancelled the entry only to repeat it on a subsequent folio where the entry in full is interposed between the chancellor's benediction at graduation ceremonies and the form of the university's testimonial for its graduates.[4] This interpolation, in which the examiners complained how students had sometimes evaded payment of their regents' honoraria, is not to be found in variant versions of the statutes; and it has been omitted, without comment, from the printed text. Possibly it was only the testimonial which was copied out at a later date, that is, at a point after December 1605. Nonetheless, this scribal error, if error it be, provides some evidence for approximately dating this copy of the statutes; that it is no more than a copy is suggested by the testimonial which, though in the same hand as the rest of the document, bears the much earlier date of 1583,[5] so placing its composition in the period of Thomas Smeaton's principalship. Beyond that, the copy sheds no further light on the earlier drafts of the new constitution.

The reason why a copy of the statutes should be made at all around 1606 is not hard to find. It must surely be related to the appointment after 1603 of John Spottiswoode as the new archbishop of Glasgow and university chancellor, who effectively began his duties in 1605.[6] Before this, in the years of the presbyterian ascendency, Glasgow lacked an archbishop recognised by the church, and the university was without a chancellor, or, at least, it was without a chancellor who was also an archbishop. Robert Montgomery, the last active protestant archbishop, found himself excommunicated by the church and was deprived of his see in 1585.[7] His successor, William Erskine, whilst exercising no ecclesiastical or academic function, merely enjoyed the temporality of the archbishopric.[8] Nor were matters helped when James Beaton, the exiled Catholic archbishop, was restored to his see in 1598, but with Beaton's death in France in 1603 and with the reappearance of episcopacy in the church the way was again open for the more respectable appointment of John Spottiswoode, a graduate of the university, as archbishop and chancellor.[9] There would consequently be a more pressing need to clarify those university procedures relating to the office of chancellor which had partly fallen into abeyance. Hence the copy which was made shortly before 1606.

Earlier efforts, composed in various hands, at drafting new post-Reformation statutes for the university are to be traced in what was the pre-Reformation dean of faculty's book. Inserted where space permitted among earlier enactments is a *testimonium academiae* bearing the date the Ides of January 1581 (13 January 1581).[10] This, like the testimonial of 1583, falls within the principalship of Melville's presbyterian associate, Thomas Smeaton, but Melville himself had clearly a hand in drawing up some of the new regulations. A surviving fragment of the chancellor's benediction at graduations, jotted down in the pre-Reformation dean of faculty's book, is dated 9 Kalends September 1578 (24 August 1578) and can be therefore assigned positively to Melville's principalship. A second copy of this benediction, in a different hand, is also inserted in the dean's book together with other, undated, statutes on examination and graduation whose text is incorporated in the extended version made around 1606.[11] Now it is plain that the chancellor's benediction at graduation ceremonies was not formulated in complete isolation in 1578. It must have belonged to a larger corpus of enactments, and it is fair to assume that Melville with his colleagues was responsible for composing the related entries on the curriculum and graduation and on the election of the chancellor, rector and dean of faculty, which appear in final form in the 'copy of 1606'. Other considerations likewise suggest that these entries were composed at a relatively early date, most probably under Melville. For one thing, the statutes begin with the chancellor's oath, and since it had not yet occurred to anyone that the chancellor could be someone other than the archbishop, the regulations must have been designed to meet the needs of the university at a time when Glasgow possessed an active archbishop. Equally, at this point the only archbishop of Glasgow acceptable to the general assembly, dominated as it was by the presbyterians, was James Boyd who died in 1581. It is certainly hard to see how the section on the chancellor could have been written after 1581, for Boyd's successor, Robert Montgomery, was strenuously opposed both by the general assembly and by Thomas Smeaton as principal, whilst the college students took to demonstrating at his election to the see.[12]

All in all, it seems likely that Melville had a hand in composing much more than the chancellor's blessing at graduation ceremonies. Even the text of the testimonial of 1581 need not have been composed then, any more than the testimonial of 1583 was composed in that year for the texts of both documents are virtually identical[13] and were probably based on whatever form of testimonial was used during Melville's principalship. On the other hand, a separate page of statutes in the dean's book on student discipline was without doubt compiled in the period when Smeaton was principal.[14] They are written in a distinctive hand which was probably Smeaton's own and were subsequently incorporated with some alteration in the 'version of 1606',[15] but the original entry in the dean's book also contains the signatures, omitted in the later version, of James Boyd, archbishop and chancellor, Andrew Hay, university rector and minister at Renfrew, David Wemyss, dean of faculty and minister at Glasgow, Thomas Smeaton, principal, Peter Blackburn, professor of physics, Patrick Sharp, who was presumably still master of the grammar school and possibly university examiner, Blaise Lawrie, professor of Greek, Patrick Melville, the nephew of Andrew Melville who had newly joined the teaching staff of the college, and the names of what appear to be four graduates of the university who may have been engaged in post-graduate studies.[16] Since Smeaton became principal in November 1580 and Archbishop Boyd died in June 1581,[17] this series of statutes may be readily dated without difficulty.

In addition to all this, a further fragment of the statutes, badly stained, bearing a close resemblance to the 'version of 1606' though in more truncated form, has come to light on an inserted leaf which has been used apparently as a paste-down in the binding of the volume subsequently entitled 'Jura Leges Instituta'. It evidently comprises an earlier drafting of the statutes relating to the chancellor, rector, dean of faculty and quaestor, for the text, where legible, is less complete than the later version and, on the top left hand corner, it bears the inscription 'decanus Mr John Blak[burn]' which may not necessarily be strictly contemporaneous with the document itself. John Blackburn, the younger brother of Peter Blackburn, graduated from the university with Patrick Melville in 1578 before succeeding Patrick Sharp as master of the grammar school in November 1582, and he is unlikely to have been elected dean of faculty before that point.[18] Although he appears on record as dean in 1592,[19] little is known of the men, other than Andrew Polwarth, who held the office in the 1580s.

A final copy of the university statutes is to be found not indeed in Glasgow but in Trinity College, Dublin, where there exists not only an annotated copy of the second Book of Discipline of 1578 but also certain writings by Andrew Melville on the book of Daniel.[20] Melville himself in 1580, while still principal at Glasgow, had invited his English presbyterian counterparts, Walter Travers and Thomas Cartwright, to become theology professors at St Mary's college, St Andrews.[21] In the event, however, both declined though in 1594 Travers did accept an appointment as second provost of Trinity College, Dublin.[22] The links with Scotland were evidently close and this may help to explain not only the interest in Scottish presbyterianism but also why the early library of Trinity should contain numerous works in Scottish theology by such authors as John Knox, Robert Rollock, Robert Bruce, Alexander Hume and, significantly enough, Thomas Smeaton and Patrick Sharp, the two Glasgow principals, together with other items relating to Scotland.[23] As in Glasgow, Ramist literature was much in evidence where it was bound to be fostered by Trinity's fourth provost, William Temple, who had earlier pioneered Ramist teaching at Cambridge.[24]

Since the original college statutes have not survived, the purpose in acquiring a copy of the Glasgow statutes remains conjectural, and it is impossible to trace any direct Glasgow influence on the statutes of Trinity College, Dublin. The earliest extant collection of statutes, other than a fragment composed during the provostries of Temple (1609-27) and Bedell (1627–29) are the Caroline statutes drawn up by Laud,[25] but it is not unreasonable to suppose that with the founding of Trinity in 1592[26] an interest would be taken in the Glasgow statutes, especially when it emerges that two Scots, James Fullerton and James Hamilton, not only helped establish Trinity College but were afterwards elected fellows in recognition of their services. Furthermore, although two Scots with those names matriculated along with Andrew Melville at St Mary's college in 1559,[27] the Trinity men are not to be identified with these St Andrews students but with two graduates of Glasgow university. James Fullerton, the son of the laird of Dreghorn, who graduated from Glasgow in 1581, and who was presumably related to 'Mr Fullerton, the Scottish agent' in Ireland in 1579, was appointed schoolmaster in Dublin by 1587, and he had as his assistant James Hamilton, son of the minister of Dunlop, who had recently graduated from Glasgow university in 1586.[28] Not only had Fullerton studied much of his course under Melville's principalship, but he remained one of Melville's 'special friends' with whom he corresponded in later life. As the nephew of lady Trochrague, the widow of Archbishop Boyd, Fullerton may have owed something for his appointment as schoolteacher in Dublin to lord Boyd, a key figure in Glasgow, who had visited Ireland in 1586.[29] As fellows of Trinity, both Fullerton and Hamilton assisted Travers, as provost, in augmenting the finances of a college which was said to be 'in danger of dissolution' for want of means.[30] All this conveys something of the connections between Glasgow and Ireland, and it helps to provide an explanation for the existence of a copy of the Glasgow statutes at Trinity College, Dublin. The copyist was possibly a Glasgow student with a neat enough hand and a less than perfect knowledge of Latin, but, in all essentials, the text corresponds to the 'version of 1606' with two noticeable exceptions. The university's testimonial, with the date 1583, is missing from the Dublin copy, though the latter, by way of an addition, does incorporate the text of the relevant section of the *nova erectio* on the principal's office[31] which is merely alluded to in the 'version of 1606'. All in all, it seems very likely that the Glasgow material was sent to Dublin soon after Trinity's foundation in 1592.

The Glasgow university statutes, written in Renaissance Latin, begin with the officers (*moderatores*) of the university, and first with the chancellor, who presided at the examination of candidates presented for the master's degree. The oath which the chancellor had to swear is new and is not found among the pre-Reformation statutes: he had to promise to promote the welfare and dignity of the university and to defend the religion of Jesus Christ, as set down in the written word of God; he was not to tolerate any malicious disputation or thesis; he was faithfully to examine the students to be awarded the master's degree; he was not to intercede 'with any extraordinary grace', nor to permit others to intercede, on their behalf; he was to bestow the title of master only on those who had meritoriously completed the ordinary curriculum; he was to reject from the degree those whose impious and wicked lives would disgrace the master's dignity; nor was he to attempt to conduct any university business except with the assent of the officers and masters.[32]

The chancellor, then, as head of the university was the person who was to award the degrees. Nothing, however, was said of his election. Nor was this necessary, for the assumption was that the chancellor would continue to be the archbishop, as had been customary in the past. During Melville's principalship, there was certainly no attempt to alter this arrangement. Melville, and others, might wish to abolish the episcopal office, but Archbishop Boyd proved accommodating to the wishes of the general assembly that bishops should exercise a parish ministry, by at least agreeing in 1576 'to haunt to ane particular kirk and to teach therat quhen he dwells in the sheriffdome of Air . . . and quhen he is in Glasgow to exerceise lykwayes at some part'.[33] But after 1581, with Boyd's death, the university had no acceptable archbishop as chancellor and, for a spell after 1585, there was simply no consecrated archbishop at all.

A similar difficulty had already occurred at St Andrews during the vacancy in the see between Douglas's death in July 1574 and Adamson's election by 1576 when it was resolved regarding 'the office of chancellarie that the visitouris that ar to be appointit be the kirk and regentis grace supplie the office untill ane chancellar be appointit'.[34] Then, with Adamson's death in 1592, and the eclipse of episcopacy in the church, rather more drastic action had to be taken when, in the absence of an archbishop, Lindsay of Menmuir, lord Balcarres, was appointed lay chancellor of that university.[35] Not until 1604, with Gladstone's election to the see, did St Andrews receive a new archbishop. During these years, Glasgow's experience was not dissimilar, but no evidence has come to light to show that Glasgow adopted the St Andrews expedient of a lay chancellor. Nor is there any evidence, for that matter, of the appointment of a vice-chancellor to preside at graduations in the chancellor's absence. Only in 1642, with the election of James, marquis of Hamilton, did Glasgow receive its first-known lay chancellor.[36] For much of the later sixteenth century, the office of chancellor seems simply to have fallen into disuse, only to be revived with Archbishop Spottiswoode's appointment to the see.

On the office of rector, the statutes are rather more revealing. The rector had to be a grave person of virtue, prudence and authority, elected annually on 1st March, or on the following day if the first were a Sunday. This marked a break with the pre-Reformation statutes which had originally prescribed 25 October, the feast of St Crispin and St Crispinian. The decision to adopt a different date was designed perhaps to ensure a measure of continuity from one academic year to the next. On the day preceding the election, the retiring rector had to affix a notice on the doors both of the college and the adjacent Blackfriars church or 'temple', but if he failed to do so the masters, after fixing the notice themselves, were to proceed to the election. The outgoing rector had first to lay down his office in congregation and his performance over the preceding year was subject to scrutiny by all who were present. In a rectorial election, everyone enrolled as members of the university had the right to vote, and voting was to take place within the respective 'nations'. In the event of a tie, the issue was to be settled by the casting vote of the retiring rector. The rather complicated procedure seems to have been that the procurators of the four nations would collect the votes and opinions both on the performance of the retiring rector and on the choice of his successor. Thereafter, four elected 'intrants' would meet together in conclave to consider the voting pattern and after deliberation would announce the new rector. The verdict would then be reported to congregation for promulgation.[37] How the intrants were elected is not indicated but in the pre-Reformation statutes it was the procurators who elected the intrants and they, in turn, appointed the rector. In much of the rectorial procedure, including the adoption of a different date for the rector's election, the imprint of St Andrews practice is detectable; and it is of course true that Melville and his colleagues were mostly St Andrews men.

Once elected, the rector had to carry out his duties with the assistance of several assessors, and he had also to appoint a public apparitor to act as bedellus. Official record of rectorial elections begins only in March 1594 when 'comitiis academiae, omnium nationum suffragiis designatus est rector universitatis in annum sequentem David Wemyss evangelii minister'. After election, Wemyss proceeded to nominate as assessors the principal and three regents of the college, and in accordance with the statutes John Alan was chosen as apparitor. In the following year, the rector, John Hay, nominated as his assessors the dean of faculty, principal and masters, and this was the form observed in subsequent elections.[38] In no case was an outsider unconnected with the university appointed to serve as assessor. At the same time, no teacher in the college was actually created rector. This differed from the pattern at St Andrews where Andrew Melville,[39] amongst other members of the teaching staff, held the rector's office but in both Glasgow and St Andrews the office was still confined to ecclesiastics, to ministers and doctors or teachers.

Like the chancellor, the rector designate had to swear an oath for the welfare of the university: he was to promise to maintain the university's freedom and dignity; he was to defend the pure religion of Jesus Christ, founded on sacred scripture, against the malice of the enemies of the truth; he was to expel from the whole university all rebels and any who refused to obey the instructions of the university officers; he was to defend discipline strenuously and to deal with scandals and wickedness with vigilant coercion; he was to attend with the civil magistrates to matters regarding food, drink and candles and other items of that nature accorded to him by first obtaining the judgment of his assessors; and, finally, he was to promise to fulfil the duties of his office as he would render account before God and his blessed angels.[40]

The rector's book might have disappeared in 1560 but the format of rectorial elections did not deviate substantially from pre-Reformation arrangements. The division of the members of the university into four nations also conformed to traditional practice but the names of the nations were altered. The Albany nation of the pre-Reformation statutes emerged as *Transforthiana* in the new statutes and was defined as the region north of the Forth with the district round Stirling, but this, it seems, was only after it had passed through the intermediate stage of being called *Angusiana* which appears, though only partially legible, in a variant text in an almost obliterated fragment of the statutes discovered as forming part of the binding of another volume.[41] The other three nations comprised Clydesdale or *Glottiana*, Teviotdale renamed *Laudoniana* or Lothian, and Rothesay now called *Siluriana*.[42] The adoption of *Angusiana* and *Laudoniana* is indicative of a St Andrews influence where the terms had long been employed to describe two of the nations in that university. At Glasgow, the terminology might change but with some minor alterations, the geographical areas represented by the nations remained basically unaltered from the definition made in 1482. The first nation of Clydesdale was then defined as the area extending from Errickstane, the meeting-point of the shires of Dumfries, Peebles and Lanark, to Dumbarton, including the barony of Renfrew; the nation of Teviotdale was described as Lothian, Stirling and all to

L

the east of the Urr water in Dumfries; Albany consisted of the lands
north of the Forth; and the nation of Rothesay was made up of the
sheriffdom of Ayr, Galloway beyond the Urr water, the Isles, Lennox
and Ireland.[43] No one then, it seems, regarded it as artificial to talk
about the 'nations' of what was, in effect, one country. In this, as in
other matters, regional diversity helped to determine many of the
characteristics of Scottish society.

In essence, the rector was the civil magistrate of the university, and
when Andrew Melville was dismissed from his rectorship of St Andrews
in 1597 he gladly demitted office on the grounds that 'it importeth a
mixture of the civill magistracie with the ministerie ecclesiastic'.[44] All
offences affecting university personnel were referred to the rector for
judgment, and his seal had the same kind of authority as if the seal of
the whole university had been appended. In the medieval university, so
long as it remained a corporation with a genuine diversity of faculties,
where students were not concentrated in one building, the rector was
the effective ruler, but where the university became less important as a
corporation and more important as a place, the principal of the college
assumed a greater say than had hitherto been so. This was evident at
Glasgow. When faced with the rebellious conduct of Mark Alexander
Boyd, Melville, as principal, took immediate action and 'commandit all
the schollars to thair bedds, perceaving them to be incensit', before
convening the rector and city magistrates next day to investigate the
incident in which Boyd, who was the kinsman of lord Boyd, had
threatened his regent with a 'baton' whilst his associate, Alexander
Cunningham, held him at swordpoint with 'monie bludie words'.
Rumour had it that the Boyds and Cunninghams 'wald slay the maisters
and burn the collage' and so the college took the prudent precaution of
having their judgment ratified by act of privy council, charging the
offender to submit or enter ward. Foreseeing trouble ahead, the rector
advised that the college should 'quyt that decreit and forgiff it seing ther
was na evill done', but he was overruled by Melville who refused to be
intimidated by a show of armed force lest it be thought 'we dar nocht
correct our schollars for fear of bangstars and clanned gentlemen'.
When the earl of Glencairn and lord Boyd rode into town with their
followers, Melville remained steadfast and by declining all compromise
secured a submission and confession.[45] From this incident, as recorded,
it is plain that it was the principal, rather than the rector, who took the
initiative in deciding the action to be pursued. The inference might even
be that only the faculty statutes were then available for guidance.

Outstanding in his length of service to the university as rector was
Andrew Hay, minister of Renfrew. His brother, George, was minister
of Rathven in the diocese of Aberdeen, and both had pursued ecclesias-

tical careers before and after the Reformation.[46]According to Edmund Hay, George and his brother had studied Greek at Paris before the Reformation. Thereafter, as 'a man of grait moyen in the countrey', Andrew Hay held the rector's office for much of the period from at least 1569 to 1586.[47] In view of his numerous other commitments, it is not wholly surprising later to find him censured by the presbytery in April 1592 for neither executing discipline at Renfrew nor possessing a reader, for failing to preach on Sunday afternoons and for administering the sacrament on Palm Sunday contrary to the acts of assembly.[48] By then, however, old age had taken its toll and he died in the following year. His successors as rector included Archibald Crawford, parson of Eaglesham, David Wemyss, minister of Glasgow, and his son John Hay, minister of Renfrew.

The next university officer defined in the statutes, the dean of faculty, was to be elected annually on 26th June (6 Kalends of July). He was to be a person of rare probity and learning able to judge and examine all subjects on which lectures were given in the university. Notification of the dean's election was to be made according to the form observed in the rector's case, and the retiring dean was to demit office in congregation. The new dean, however, was to be chosen not, like the rector, by all members but only the officers and masters. The students, in other words, were to be excluded from any say in his election. Once appointed, the dean was to swear an oath to perform his duties to the best of his abilities not only in appointing and supervising the masters and examiners but also in examining the students in the liberal arts without favour or hatred, without listening to entreaties or being influenced by bribes. He was to conduct himself according to the commands of the divine will and the laws of the university, so that he could render account before men and before God, the witness and judge of all.[49]

Since no more than a college of arts existed in the university, only one faculty was necessary and so the dean could simply be styled 'dean of facultie of the said universitie'.[50] His main duties lay in supervising, teaching and in examining students for their degrees. The dean's office, unlike the rector's, was held by a greater variety of men, but the same ecclesiastical emphasis was all too apparent. David Cunningham, for example, dean of faculty in 1573 and 1576, was minister of Cadder, before becoming bishop of Aberdeen. Patrick Sharp, dean in 1577, later became principal of the college. As master of the grammar school, he attended Melville's lectures and probably acted as a university examiner.[51] As a teacher, he was recognised as occupying the doctor's office within the church. Such an office, the second Book of Discipline maintained, comprehended 'the ordour of the scoles' and comprised one of the 'foure ordinarie functionis or offices in the kirk of God'.[52]

Sharp therefore was eligible to sit on the courts of the church. Another dean, in 1580, was David Wemyss, minister of Glasgow, who later served as university rector. Andrew Polwarth, Melville's 'friend and companion' in Geneva[53] became dean in 1582, was minister first at Paisley and then, from 1578, at Cadder. John Blackburn, dean for much of the 1590s and 1600s, was reader at Cathcart in 1578, then master of the grammar school and from 1615 minister of the Barony church in Glasgow. The links between university and church were seemingly indissoluble.

The fourth officer mentioned was the quaestor or bursar, a man of proven truth, fidelity and constancy. Only a regent, however, was eligible for the post. The date of his election, 26th June, was to be intimated by the bedellus; his electors were the dean of faculty and masters of the university; and on demitting office he was to render an account of his activities. The quaestor's duties consisted in keeping charge of the treasury, out of which he could make no payment except at the command of the masters, and also of the library where he had to take care that no books were lent without the consent of the masters. For each book lent he was to obtain a receipt with the signature of the borrower. As with other officers, the quaestor was to take an oath for the honest administration of his office.[54] Since the only mention of the quaestor in the library catalogue occurs in 1577, it seems very probable that this particular statute originally took shape during Melville's principalship.[55]

The library itself, though modest enough, was largely augmented by gifts from a number of donors such as Andrew Hay, George Buchanan, Archbishop Boyd, Thomas Jack, the university quaestor and minister of Eastwood, Peter Blackburn, Archibald Crawford, parson of Eaglesham, and Mark Jamieson.[56] It also became customary for students on graduating to donate books to the library.[57] It was not, however, until 1641 that a keeper or librarian was appointed, as a result of Hutcheson's mortification 'for ordoring, preserving and enlargeing of the Common Bibliothec'.[58] Apart from the books in the library, there were also the private collections of individual masters, including Melville's own, 'ritche and rare, of the best authors, in all languages, artes and sciences', which was carefully transported home; and James Melville is on record, borrowing some books from the university rector, Andrew Hay.[59]

The method for the election of the principal and four regent masters was the prescription in the *nova erectio*. No more was said. Only the Dublin copy, for obvious reasons, had the appropriate section of the *nova erectio* inserted in the statutes. Before the students were admitted to lectures, the rector was to impose an oath on all members enrolled in the university in which they promised to embrace the true religion of Jesus Christ founded in the written word of God and not elsewhere, and comprehended in the Confession of Faith and catechism of the reformed church. They were therefore to eschew all ways of worship and superstitions devised by the Roman pontiff and his followers, or indeed by anyone else, without foundation in the word of God. This conformed with what the *nova erectio* had to say about the imposition of a religious test.[60] The students had also to swear to abide by the rules and laws of the university and to ensure that they were kept by others; they had to obey the rector, the masters and professors; they were expected to be present not only at all meetings for study but were obliged to attend councils in each 'estate' or faculty of the university (though in practice only one faculty could be said to exist); they were forbidden to disclose any university secrets; and in later life they were to the best of their power to enhance the university's standing and prestige.[61]

Whereas the statutes spoke of a principal and four masters,[62] the *nova erectio* had only specified a principal and three masters, and during Melville's own principalship no more than three masters are known to have taught. This entry in the statutes must therefore have been written, or at least modified, at a date after Melville's translation to St Andrews in 1580. Although Patrick Sharp's name occurs amongst those of the college masters who signed the statutes on student discipline drawn up between November 1580 and June 1581,[63] it is plain that he must have subscribed in his capacity as master of the grammar school or university examiner and not as a fourth regent. But with Archbishop Boyd's grant to the college of the tron customs in May 1581, funds were available to support a fourth master and by 1582 John Bell had joined the staff as an additional teacher.[64] At this point, with Smeaton as principal, the teaching staff consisted of Peter Blackburn, 'physicae professor', Blaise Lawrie, who continued to teach Greek, Patrick Melville, who after graduating in 1578 from the university succeeded to James Melville's 'roume'[65] and would therefore teach logic, mathematics and moral philosophy, and finally John Bell, who graduated from the university in 1581[66] and who, as a new recruit, probably taught rhetoric to first-year students.

In the event, however, this stability did not endure. Blackburn resigned his office later in 1582 to become minister at Aberdeen; Smeaton died in December 1583; and Patrick Melville later switched to teach Hebrew at St Andrews university. With insufficient information from the college records, it is now impossible to reconstruct the sequence of masters elected to fill these vacancies. There can be little doubt, however, that the situation deteriorated rather than improved, and the fortunes of the college were further disrupted by the 'Black Acts' of

1584 and by other measures taken by the 'anti-presbyterian dictatorship' which characterised the conservatism of the Arran regime whilst it remained in power. But even with the appointment of a fourth master by 1582, the pattern of studies prescribed in the new statutes closely followed the curriculum of Melville and the *nova erectio*. What redrafting took place was probably not an effort at a major revision or reconstruction of the course but simply an attempt at accommodating an additional teacher within the existing framework with the minimum of dislocation.

The first master, according to the statutes, was to read from 1st October, the start of the academic session, till 1st March the precepts or rules of Greek grammar. This he was to do very briefly and readily without going into the subject too intensively. The aim clearly was to provide a survey course designed to introduce students to the principles of Greek grammar without undue specialisation. The teacher was then to demonstrate the practical use of these linguistic techniques from the writings of Isocrates and Lysias, the Greek orators, and from the Epistle of Libanius, the Greek sophist. After this, from March until 1st September (the feast of St Giles in the pre-Reformation calendar) the first master was to explain the principles of eloquence from Talon, who applied the teaching of Ramus in rhetoric, and their practical use in the shorter orations of Cicero and Demosthenes, and in the works of Homer and Aristophanes, as well as in the Greek epigrams.[67]

All this comprised the first-year course in Arts. Emphasis was firmly placed on the Greek authors, and the assumption was, of course, that students entering the college would be already proficient in Latin. This, after all, was the task of the grammar school and in Glasgow school and university were aware of the necessary entrance requirements. Patrick Sharp, as schoolmaster, was himself the friend of Melville and so became his 'ordinar heirar' in college, whilst Melville, in turn, instructed him 'in the maist commodius bringing upe of the youthe in grammer and guid authors'.[68] This made for close liaison between school and university. Nor can there be any doubt that the course for first-year students was demanding both in content and in duration. Latin, of course, was the medium of instruction, and with subjects like philosophy, complex to master in English or Scots let alone in Renaissance Latin, it was a natural enough reaction for James Melville, as a fourteen-year-old student entering St Andrews university, to dissolve into tears:[69]

'at the beginning, nather being weill groundet in grammer, nor com to the yeirs of naturall judgment and understanding, I was cast in sic a greiff and dispear, becaus I understood nocht the regent's langage in teatching that I did nathing bot bursted and grat at his lessones, and was of mynd to haiff gone ham agean, war nocht the luiffing cear of that man comforted me, and tuik me in his awin chalmer, causit me ly with him selff and everie night teatched me in privat, till I was acquented with the mater'.

But for students such as James Melville who still 'lyked the schollar's lyff best', more was in store.

At Glasgow, the second master began by propounding in detail the universal art of speaking from such sources as Aristotle's *Rhetoric* dedicated to Theodectes, and from Cicero's *De Oratore*. The master was then to show how the rules of rhetoric were applied in Demosthenes, the *Orationes* of Cicero, Sophocles and Pindar. In the second half of the year, from March till September, he was to explain as briefly and as accurately as he could the principles of invention and disposition or arrangement from Peter Ramus and to illustrate this from Plato, Plutarch, Cicero's *De Finibus* and from his *Tusculan Questions*. All this constituted the art of dialectic on which Ramus had written at length. To scholars trained to write and speak in ornate Renaissance Latin, part of the appeal of Ramism was precisely its claim to simplify and systematise the intricacies of logical method and to stimulate the art of memory.[70] But if logic had occupied a disproportionately large space in the medieval curriculum, it was now assigned to be taught only for half a year in the post-Reformation statutes. This was in contrast to rhetoric which was studied for a whole year over two academic sessions.

It is not really surprising that this detailed description of the curriculum for first and second-year students in Arts does not wholly conform with James Melville's account for the 1570s. For one thing, James Melville's description was written in later life and to that extent may therefore be less than accurate; for another, it is not improbable that a number of changes in the prescribed texts would be made from time to time after Andrew Melville's departure in 1580. If, however, what James Melville says is to be accepted then it seems that rather different classical authors were studied in the 1570s than subsequently. There is, for example, no mention in the statutes of Horace and Virgil or of Hesiod, Phocylides, Pythagoras, Theognis and Theocritus which James Melville claims his uncle taught from 1574,[71] together with Homer, Isocrates and Pindar which are included in the statutes. On the other hand, James Melville has nothing to say in that part of the course of Cicero or Aristophanes, Demosthenes, Libanius, Lysias, Plato, Plutarch, Sophocles or the Greek epigrams which are prescribed in the statutes. Even so, it is more than just coincidence that whilst in Geneva,

Melville had been afforded an opportunity to become acquainted with some of the works in manuscript of the Greek authors assiduously collected by his kinsman Henry Scrimgeour for the Fugger library. With the exception of Isocrates and Phocylides which are stated to have been taught at Glasgow, all the Greek works listed by James Melville and also those prescribed in the statutes had already been acquired by Henry Scrimgeour.[72] Not even the library of the Genevan academy in 1572 possessed copies of the works of Lysias, Libanius, Phocylides, Theognis or Pythagoras.[73] The notes and copies which Scrimgeour had taken from some of the works collected for the Fugger library were intended for publication, and they could not but make a deep impression on Melville as a classical scholar. This influence may therefore be detectable in the Greek texts prescribed for study at Glasgow. At any rate, there can be no doubt that the groundwork was firmly laid during these years of Melville's principalship.

At the same time, it is also possible that some of the works listed in the curriculum were additions by Patrick Sharp, while John Blackburn, who succeeded Sharp as grammar schoolteacher, may have been influential in securing the inclusion of Aristophanes, a copy of whose works he is known to have owned. But it is noticeable that there is no mention of Ovid or Catullus, and Melville himself seems to have studied the more philosophical writers in preference to these Latin authors. An examination of the library lists for Greek and Latin works, other than those whose themes were purely theological, shows little sign of any interest in the Italian or French Renaissance in their strictly humanistic aspects. There is, for example, no mention of Montaigne, Lipsius, Boccaccio or Ronsard. The course so conceived was markedly linguistic in content, though it appears to have lacked linguistic authors like Johannes Tzetzes, whom Buchanan had taught, and it remained basically Aristotelian with little indication of any excessive Platonism. Not only so, the emphasis tended to be on oratory with rather less time devoted to mathematics and physics, subjects in which Glasgow lagged behind many continental universities.

The third-year course remained much as it was in Melville's day. The statutes laid down that the third master should start by teaching mathematics, arithmetic and geometry before proceeding to the *Logic*, *Ethics* and *Politics* of Aristotle, the *De Officiis* of Cicero and selected *Dialogues*, chosen with discretion from Plato.[74] When teaching mathematics, Andrew Melville from 1574 had lectured on the *Elements* of Euclid, the *Arithmetic* and *Geometry* of Ramus and the *Tables* of Honterus. This was the course to which James Melville succeeded in 1576, but 'for schortness' he chose to teach the elements of arithmetic and geometry from Michael Psellus, not Ramus.[75] This was evidently the volume entitled *Sapientissimi Pselli opus . . . in quattuor mathematicas disciplinas arithmeticam, musicam, geometriam et astronomiam*, of which editions had been published at Venice in 1532 and Paris in 1545,[76] and this seems to have been the work which James Melville had studied as a student at St Andrews when he learned 'the four speaces of the Arithmetik'.[77] In the statutes, however, no prescribed texts are cited for mathematics, unlike philosophy where the works of Aristotle, Cicero and Plato are recommended. In the philosophical part of the third-year course, Andrew Melville had taught the *Ethics* of Aristotle, the *De Officiis* of Cicero, Aristotle's *De Virtutibus*, Cicero's *Paradoxes* and *Tusculan questions*, Aristotle's *Politics* and certain of Plato's *Dialogues*,[78] but he seems to have omitted Aristotle's *Logic*, the collection of logical treatises known as the *Organon*, and it was only in 1576 that James Melville, on taking over this class, included Aristotle's *Logic*, from the Greek text, as well as his *Ethics*, the *De Officiis* of Cicero, Plato's *Phaedo*,[79] and the *Axiochus*, attributed to Plato. Since the *nova erectio* had itself recommended 'the best authors such as Cicero, Plato and Aristotle on life, morals, policy and government',[80] there could scarcely be said to be anything innovating in the statutes when they prescribed the *Logic*, *Ethics* and *Politics* of Aristotle as well as Cicero's *De Officiis* and Plato's *Dialogues*. In essential aspects, the statutes continued to reflect the patterns of teaching established by the Melvilles.

The fourth master, in accordance with the statutes, was to lecture on the *Physics* of Aristotle, which came in eight books, the book called the *Sphere* and also on cosmography, the science of the geographical world. He was then to pass on to an easy method and introduction of world history but he was also assigned to teach the principles of Hebrew with some practice in the language.[81] This formed the final-year course in Arts, and once again it more or less conformed to what Melville had done after 1574. In natural philosophy, he had taught the *Physics* of Aristotle, the *De Ortu*[82] and *De Caelo* as well as Plato and Fernel, and had then lectured on history from Sleidan and Melanchthon, whilst in geography he had employed Dionysius and the *Tables* of Honterus, and in 'astrologie' he used Aratus.[83] An edition of Dionysius Periegetes' *De situ orbis* containing Aratus's *Astronomicon* in the same volume had been published at Basle *circa* 1523,[84] and this may have been Melville's text. The *Tables* of the Hungarian reformer, Honterus, who edited Dionysius Periegetes, consisted of the *Rudimentorum Cosmographicorum, libri III cum tabellis geographicis*, an edition of which had been published at Zurich in 1548.[85]

The science of the universe which Melville taught at Glasgow and which then consisted of a mixture of astronomy and astrology was silently dropped from the curriculum depicted in the statutes. Although

Copernicus had died in 1543 there was as yet no hint of any particular interest in Copernican theories at Glasgow. At the same time, Melville's friend, Peter Young, from at least 1586, and later James VI himself, was in regular correspondence with the famous Danish astronomer Tycho Brahe[86] who of course did possess Copernican treatises. In cosmography, the works of Ptolemy were still available, but amongst newer works to appear was the *Cosmographia* of Sebastian Munster, already well-known for his Hebrew lexicon and grammar, and these texts with others had begun to find their way into Scottish libraries in the course of the sixteenth century.[87] At Glasgow, Peter Blackburn, who apparently succeeded Melville in teaching the subject, possessed 'Ane New General Cart stentit upon buirdes sett out be Gerardus Jode' (Antwerp 1575), and subsequent students on graduation presented copies of several works on cosmography to the college library.[88] As the titles of some works on the subject suggest, the study of cosmography had important practical implications for navigation.

The prominence accorded to history in the Glasgow curriculum mirrors the renewed humanist interest in history as a subject worthy of serious study. There had of course been histories or chronicles of Scotland by Hector Boece and John Mair; and despite his poem in honour of Gathelus which might indicate that Melville followed the Hector Boece tradition, what seems to have been envisaged here was not the study of Scotland's history, mythical or otherwise, nor even that of classical antiquity; nor was it just to be the history of the Christian church, but history viewed from the perspective of the four monarchies which, in turn, was capable of a chiliastic interpretation. The pattern of the four monarchies might be held to herald the imminent arrival of the fifth monarchy, the reign of Christ and his saints on earth. As an historical event, the Reformation enabled protestants to examine the history of the church from a new perspective, and in the Apocalypse, as a guide to history, many found a pattern and an explanation for past events as well as a prophecy of things to come. To the reformers, Antichrist came to be identified with the person of the pope, the 'man of sin', and with the papacy as an institution, the second beast of Revelation. On the basis of the beast's number 666, predictions could be made on how much longer the beast would remain before the beginning of the end. Melanchthon, who prophesied the fall of Antichrist for 1588,[89] had not only produced his *Chronicorum ab orbe condito pars secunda, historiam continens a Christi natali Augustique imperio* (Basle edition, 1560) but he had also edited Carion's *Chronicon absolutissimum* with its treatment of the four monarchies.[90] Sleidan, another German historian, wrote his history of the Reformation entitled *De Statu Religionis et Reipublicae Carolo quinto Caesare*

Commentarii (1555), of which the Glasgow college had certainly a copy in its library in the 1580s,[91] but Sleidan also wrote *De quatuor summis imperiis* (Genevan edition, 1559). The Genevan academy had copies of both works in 1572;[92] Sleidan was also being read in Trinity College, Dublin;[93] and at Glasgow, Sleidan's *Four Monarchies* was probably taught by Melville and by 1648 was prescribed reading[94] at a time when apocalyptic ideas were to the forefront.[95]

Apart from recommending Sleidan to his Glasgow students,[96] Melville had also copies of Heliodorus's 'Ethiopic Historie' and Bodin's *Methodus*.[97] Bodin, however, as a vigorous opponent of the apocalyptic theory of history, had devoted a chapter of his *Methodus* as a 'refutation of those who postulate four monarchies and the golden age'.[98] Even so, Melville's interest in the four monarchies, by inference, was probably substantial. He is known to have been attached to the study of salvation history, sacred rhetoric as well as sacred numerology, and Jewish economics. In the Book of Daniel, with its vision of the fall of four empires and the coming of 'one like the Son of man' to whom is given everlasting dominion over all nations, the apocalyptic element is all too apparent, and Melville himself had written on Daniel chapter ix;[99] he had also preached on Daniel iv, with the result that he had been summoned before the privy council in 1584 for describing the king as Nebuchadnezzar.[100] In Daniel, Melville found a guide to universal history and in his versified account of chapter ix, he sought to estimate the different ages of the Old Testament and even introduced episodes from Greek history such as the battle of Marathon and the crossing of the Hellespont. Robert Rollock at Edinburgh published a commentary on the prophet Daniel,[101] and Calvin himself, though declining to write a commentary on Revelation through fear of apocalyptism, had nevertheless shown considerable interest in Daniel's dream of the four monarchies and in the intricacies of computation posed by Daniel who understood 'in books the number of the years for filling up the desolation of Jerusalem'.[102]

Although the existence of chiliastic ideas has not been recognised in late sixteenth-century Scotland, it is nonetheless significant that Christopher Goodman should preach on the Apocalypse in St Andrews; that John Knox, in his first public sermon at St Andrews in 1547, should preach on the four monarchies from Daniel, chapter vii, and that he should return to the 'prophecie of Daniel' in his sermon at St Andrews in 1571; that James Melville should own a copy of Bullinger's *In Apocalypsim*; that Spottiswoode, the superintendent of Lothian, should donate a copy of Bullinger's sermons on the Apocalypse to James VI; and that the visitors of St Andrews university in the year of the Armada should speak of 'this confused tyme quhen all folkis ar loukand to the weltering of the warld'.[103] Judgment day, it almost seemed, was close at hand. Nor is this all. Knox in his *History of the Reformation* had borrowed from Foxe's *Acts and Monuments*[104] where the Apocalypse is treated as a key to history. James VI may have had little in common with John Knox but he certainly saw himself as a theologian, and on discovering that 'the Booke of the Revelation is most meete for this our last age, as a prophesie of the latter times', he devoted his attention to writing two works on the Apocalypse.[105] John Napier of Merchiston also produced *A plaine discovery of the Revelation of Saint John*, an edition of which was published in Edinburgh in 1593. In the complex calculations for discovering the day of judgment, there was ample scope for Napier's mathematical talents, and another Scot, George Thomson, translated Napier's work into French where it was published at La Rochelle under the title *Ouverture des secrets de l'Apocalypse . . . de S. Jean*.[106] Patrick Forbes, who had studied under Melville at Glasgow and St Andrews, was yet another Scot who wrote a treatise on Revelation in which he identified Rome with the 'mystical Babylon of the Apocalypse'.[107]

By itself, none of this necessarily amounted to millenarian extremism about which orthodox Calvinists remained highly suspicious; but if this interest in prophecy and the fulfilment of prophecy foreshadowed the emergence of millenarianism in the seventeenth century then explanations should not ignore the kind of history students read any more than the theology which they absorbed.

In the fourth-year course, minor changes were no doubt introduced when Peter Blackburn assumed responsibility for teaching that class, but even after both Melville and Blackburn had left, their successors evidently adhered to the same essential framework. The prescription in the statutes that the fourth master should also teach Hebrew is, however, rather odd. For one thing, the *nova erectio* had assigned to the principal the teaching of theology and the sacred tongues. It is hardly likely that the statutes were intended to include the principal as one of the four masters, but were this so it would perhaps provide grounds for dating that section of the statutes before 1582, when a fourth teacher was appointed. On the other hand, the inclusion of Hebrew among the duties of the fourth master may be indicative of a certain confusion in redrafting the statutes to accommodate the fourth master. It may even be that when the statutes were revised the current principal had insufficient knowledge of Hebrew and therefore assigned the teaching of the subject to another. All this, however, would contravene the *nova erectio* which stipulated that the principal had to be skilled 'particularly in Hebrew and Syriac'. Whatever the explanation, it is less than clear that Hebrew was regarded as forming an integral part of the Arts curriculum and that all students before graduating would be drilled in Hebrew. It may have been expected that only students proceeding to theology would undertake the study of Hebrew. On the other hand in 1620, as a fourth-year student, John Livingston, with the rest of his class, was expected to have studied Hebrew, even though his intention then was to pursue a career in medicine rather than the ministry.[108]

A hint of flexibility in the curriculum is at least suggested by the rubric that each master must consult the dean of faculty and principal on 1 October, and again on 1 March, for approval of the prescribed works and of the passages from each author to be read aloud or dictated to the students.[109] It was the dean's responsibility to announce not only the texts but also the times of classes.

The timetable itself was stringent. Everyone in the college had to rise at 5 a.m. and an hour later the teachers were to enter their schools or lecture rooms where they were to instruct their students and also question them on the previous day's lectures until 8 a.m. After an interval for prayers, which was not to exceed half an hour, the students were to resume their studies, and to revise and repeat the morning's lectures until 9 a.m. when they breakfasted for three-quarters of an hour. By 10 a.m. they were to return to their studies or rooms, but senior students in the two upper classes at 10 a.m. were to attend the public lecture in theology. At 11 a.m. the masters, on returning to their classes, were to supervise their students as they contined to revise the morning lectures. At 11.15 a.m. the cook was to be notified so that final preparations could be made in the kitchen for the midday meal. On the resumption of classes at 1 p.m., except on days when games were played, the masters were to hear disputations in which each student took it in turn to defend a thesis on a subject announced by noon on the preceding day, and his fellow students were to produce arguments opposing what he said. From 1 April until 1 August, however, and also on games days, disputations were to be held after supper. On Mondays, Wednesdays and Fridays, when no games were held, students at 2 p.m. were to proceed to their studies, and from 3 p.m. till 4 p.m. they were to revise their public lectures. The masters were then to undertake further teaching and questioning of their students from 4 p.m. till 5 p.m. when all classes were to meet for disputations in the public schools, as distinct from the masters' own classes. Prior notice before noon on the preceding day was to be given of the argument for daily exercise in Greek and Latin alternately.[110]

It is rather improbable that the discussion itself would be conducted mainly in Greek; Latin would be the normal medium for communication; and the assumption is that only the text to be debated might be composed in Greek. The new erection at St Andrews in 1579, it is true, recommended that second-year students should 'begyne to declame anys in the moneth in Greik and Latyne alternatim',[111] but these exercises were not disputations but declamations, set speeches read aloud to show the students' proficiency in rhetorical oratory. It was one thing to compose a set speech in Greek but quite another matter for students to display their verbal agility in Greek during debates or disputations. Some printed theses at St Andrews, however, were written in Greek. Students certainly received ample practice in disputing; and on Saturdays from 10 a.m. till noon, the three upper classes in the Glasgow college were to take part in public disputations in which the two upper classes were first to dispute a thesis with each other and then with the lower class, while the masters who were present noted the names of absentees and latecomers.

The persistence of the essentially medieval teaching methods of lectures, disputations, declamations and other academic exercises such as repetitions is well illustrated in these post-Reformation statutes. Lectures might either take the form of public university lectures, such as those in theology which senior Arts students attended, or else lectures delivered by the regent masters to their own classes in the college. At St Andrews, the visitation of 1575 had recommended an elaborate scheme of public lectures. The intention was that every week the principals of the three colleges should each 'reid a publict Latin lessoun of Theologie' to which 'salbe ordinar auditours all the publict lectouris in the Universitie, the Regentis in Philosophie, Maisteris of Grammer-sculis, Studentis and Bursaris in Theologie, all minsteris and reidaris resident within the citie and utheris studentis that salbe desirous to proceid in the Facultie of Theologie'. In addition, four public lectures of an hour's duration were to be given each week on a number of other subjects: on Hebrew by the second master of St Mary's to the same audience; on Greek by his counterpart in St Salvator's; on mathematics by the third master in St Mary's; on rhetoric by his opposite number in St Salvator's whose audience was to be 'the haill Studentis of Philosophie and utheris within the Universitie that sall pleis frequent the same'; and on law by the lawyer of St Mary's whose audience was to consist of 'all the advocattis and scribis in the consistorie and sic utheris as ar desirous to proceid in the Faculty of the law'. All these public lectures, it was envisaged, were to be 'teichit frelie to the auditouris without ony dewitie to be pait to them yairfore'.[112]

A somewhat similar scheme, if less developed, may have operated in Glasgow, but the distinction between public university lectures and college lectures, which was more marked at St Andrews with its three constituent colleges, was probably less apparent at Glasgow with its single college or pedagogy as the sole teaching unit. In lectures, the prescribed texts were read and discussed and problems resolved in orderly fashion. The notebooks of Glasgow students have not survived for this period, but with the increasing availability of printed books dictation may have been no longer the necessity which it once was. Students, however, still favoured copious note-taking, and it was not until 1648 that the commissioners for visiting the universities urged that 'the unprofitable and noxious paines in writeing be shunned . . . and that the Regents spend not too much time in dyteing of thair notes'.[113] After lectures, students had to memorise what they had learned. Hence the need for daily repetitions and revision exercises. More arduous were the frequent disputations in which the disputants acquired a practical training in dialectics by resolving questions or theses put forward for debate. These academic exercises might take place, first of all, privately in the masters' own classes where students received an introduction to the art, but for more advanced students, who had acquired an understanding of the techniques, there were the public disputations held on a formal basis in the schools where students' ability to dispute was rigorously tested. Under a presiding master who, as moderator or *praeses*, began proceedings with an introductory address, students, in their turns participated both as opponents of the theses or questions formulated and as respondents or defendants of their own theses. Where a respondent faltered in debate, his regent as 'father', who may already have delivered a preliminary speech in his support, would be likely to come to his assistance. Finally, the debate would be ended by the moderator who summed up the findings and pointed out any errors in reasoning which may have occurred.

The theses which the candidates disputed in open debate could consist of any topics studied in the course—on, perhaps, philosophy, or mathematics, or theology. The graduation theses in philosophy at St Andrews included such themes as *De disciplinarum natura in genere, De Universalibus, singularibus et secundis notionibus* and *De natura logicae*.[114] Disputations, however, could be more than mere academic exercises. They could tread dangerous political ground as well, and could be regarded as controversial and even subversive. Melville, for one, was accused at St Andrews of causing 'the questione of the lawfulnes of deprivatione of kings and princes be ther subjectis to be publictlie disputit' in which it was affirmed that 'a successioun of kingis was lawfull but that all suld be electit'.[115] Such themes, it was felt, were not 'questionis disputable in this cuntrey befoir the youth quha certanlie lernis nathing soever in that uneversetie nor to tak ane evill opinione of his majestie, his hienes counsell and all ther proceidingis quhilk may sumtym produce evill effectis'.[116] The Melville of Glasgow is unlikely to have differed much from the Melville of St Andrews. And if the universities looked like becoming hotbeds of radical presbyterianism, there was good reason for royal intervention. By gradually re-imposing episcopacy in the church, removing the presbyterian leadership and prescribing the catechism *God and the King* to be read in the universities and schools,[117] James may have felt satisfied by the end of his reign that he had succeeded in overcoming the worst excesses of Melvillianism in church and university.

As well as disputations, which on occasion could prove troublesome, declamations, in private and in public, also formed an integral part of university studies. There the emphasis was placed on a stylised speech, composed in advance, in which students displayed their erudition in classics by incorporating apposite quotations, which they had collected in their commonplace books, from the works of classical antiquity. In St Andrews, there were to be monthly declamations for students in Arts and Divinity.[118] The bachelor's degree at St Andrews was conducted, as James Melville recalls, 'according to the solemnities then used of declamations, banqueting and playes', and at Glasgow declamations were certainly held at graduations for the master's degree.[119]

In charge of all these scholastic activities were the regent masters to whom the statutes assigned a number of additional duties. Each of the masters was to take it in turn to waken the students living in college every morning at 5 a.m., and at night he was to note the names of students missing from their rooms. On sports' days, he had to escort the students to the fields for games which were to be held after the midday meal until 4 p.m. on Tuesdays, Thursdays and Saturdays. In ecclesiastical affairs, the teacher on duty was to take up the prayers in church, and in times of sermon all masters and students were of course to be present without exception. There were also administrative duties to be fulfilled. Academic meetings held in the mornings, be they for discussing studies, the appointment of university officers or the promotion of students, were to be attended by all officers, masters and even graduates, if so required.[120]

In the series of miscellaneous statutes on student discipline, composed between November 1580 and July 1581, which were to be publicly announced each year by the dean of faculty or by the principal, it was decreed that no one enrolled in the university should keep the company of scandalous or lost citizens, presumably persons excommunicated, or those who lead wicked, profane or shameful lives. Graduates were not to be permitted to remain in college without embarking on further studies, and those who did remain after receiving the master's degree, and the licence to teach, were to give proof of progress in their studies and in attending lectures, whilst the principal, for his part, was to assess them at least once a month by questioning them in writing or by asking them to interpret a classical author. Nothing was said on whether those recent graduates pursuing further studies were expected to contribute as non-regent masters to teaching in the college by giving 'extraordinary' or 'cursory' lectures to supplement the 'ordinary' or prescribed lectures conducted by the regents. This customary obligation had fallen into disuse long before the Reformation, though efforts were made to revive the practice after the Reformation. At St Andrews, it was decided in 1574 that no one should be given the seal of the university unless, after receiving licence, he had taught publicly and had accepted the master's cap according to the statutes of the faculty and the customs of the students and masters of St Salvator's and St Mary's.[121] What the Glasgow statutes did require, however, was that all post-graduates should attend the public lectures in theology. They had, of course, to converse in Latin, and those who wished to pursue theology were to defend or oppose theses in public every fortnight in the presence of the principal and regent masters.[122]

Any student who attacked the name of another with a notorious libel was to be ignominiously expelled. Those who obtained the master's degree were not to mix with undergraduates, and no student was to dare to keep their company. Unless express permission were granted, scholars were not permitted to leave the college, and to enter the kitchen was deemed unworthy of scholarly honour, an expression designed perhaps to prevent student raids on the pantry. Similarly, nobody was allowed to enter an inn or tavern; nor were they to play hand tennis or to frequent tennis courts. Games could only be played at the stated hours and no one was to remain in the fields beyond 4 p.m. but must return to college with the rest of the students. After meals, the boarders were to rise and await grace and the singing of a psalm. At the times appointed for grace, psalm-singing and sacred reading, the masters, graduates and students were all to be present with their books, presumably the Book of Common Order with the Psalm book appended. They were also to attend church for prayers and sermons held both in the lower church (or Blackfriars) and in the upper church (the High kirk or cathedral). On the day preceding the celebration of the Lord's Supper, the masters were to prepare their students for the communion service by reading the appropriate lesson and on the appointed day the teachers, graduates and students were all to communicate at the last table.

Nor was this all; in the aftermath of earlier disturbances, the prudent precaution was taken of forbidding everyone to carry swords, daggers and other weapons or arms. These were all to be deposited with the principal. If anyone secretly retained a weapon he was to be punished and the weapon confiscated. Anyone who wounded another by shedding blood was to be ignominiously punished and expelled from the university. If a graduate was the culprit he was to be deprived of his degree. The exchange of books, or anything else, amongst the students or graduates was also forbidden. Boarders who spent the night in the town and any members of the university who passed the night in nocturnal games and wanderings were to be severely punished. Anyone who broke into other people's gardens was to repair the damage and undergo similar punishment. Because of the 'sad and mournful example in those who swim in the waters', the university also decided to place a prohibition on swimming—presumably because of a drowning accident —and were any to contravene this enactment, they were to be chastised with 'many whips'. Finally, private tutors and pedagogues were forbidden to teach or exercise discipline. Matters of this nature were reserved for the principal and professors. Offenders in breach of the regulations were first to be privately admonished by the principal and masters but if the culprits persisted without making amends they were to be sharply rebuked and publicly punished by the officers of the university and, on remaining contumacious, were to be expelled.[123] All this, of course, had a parallel in the disciplinary proceedings exercised in the ecclesiastical courts.

The standards of behaviour imposed by these 'laws concerning conduct and piety' issued in 1581 certainly convey an impression of the rigorous and exacting nature of college life. It was a regulated regime designed to restrain the exuberance of youth. The disciplines imposed on personal conduct were the necessary counterpart of those disciplines involved in training young minds through study. In prescribing 'a sound education and right training of youth in learning' the *nova erectio* had emphasised how 'the exercise of good discipline and order' should accompany 'instruction in letters and languages',[124] and the statutes, in turn, gave more tangible expression of what form this might comprise. For a start, it was considered unbecoming in 'this seminary of piety' that anyone should live in a disorderly manner.[125] The model of an ordered, disciplined community was undisguisedly monastic, and even though the monastic ideal in post-Reformation Scotland had lost its earlier relevance and purpose, its spirit persisted in the university colleges and was perpetuated in statutes such as these. It is also appropriate that these enactments should have been sanctioned and promulgated in 1581 by none other than an ex-Jesuit, Thomas Smeaton, the principal, a man 'verie wacryff [wakeful] and peanfull' who, abstaining from 'lang denners and suppers at Generall Assemblies', was 'verie frugall in fude and reyment and walked maist on fut'.[126] The life of austerity and self-denial, dedicated to preaching and teaching, had an appeal for Jesuits and stricter Calvinists alike. If Erasmus had found, as was said, that the rules of the English universities 'far exceeded all the monastic institutions that were ever devised',[127] then there is reason to suppose that in the discipline of the Scottish universities he would not have been disappointed. Boyd of Trochrague, as a later principal, also appreciated this aspect of the monastic ideal. Not only had he a melancholy disposition, seeking to retreat from the world to pursue his studies, but under his principalship the students were termed 'novices'. In all this was reflected the conservatism of the new scholasticism.

A prominent feature of university ordinances is the examinations programme, and in appointing a 'rule for examination and promotion'[128] the statutes gave some impression (though less specific than might be wished) of the standards students were expected to have attained before they proceeded to graduation. There were, of course, no written examinations, but at each significant stage in the four years of a student's career in Arts, searching oral examinations, in the form of disputations, were held to test a candidate's fitness for promotion from one year's class to the next until he finally attained the coveted master's insignia. The examination of senior students for the master's degree took place in the last week of August, but for the rest of the students, as well as for those entering the university, examinations were held on 7 October at the beginning of the new academic session. The examiners comprised the dean of faculty, the principal, the regent masters and the master of the grammar school. Graduates who were non-regents were also permitted to question and test students, but the promotion of students to 'higher degrees' was to be only at the discretion of the appointed and recognised examiners who were obliged to take an oath before examining. By 'higher degrees' (*superiores gradus*) may be meant promotion to the senior classes, but it more probably signifies the master's degree and whatever degree was awarded in theology, and the inference might then be that the bachelor's degree, though nowhere mentioned in the statutes, was nonetheless still recognised. Candidates were eligible to present themselves for examination only on the production of a signed testimony from their regent of their good conduct, diligence, and their gratitude and liberality to their regent together with details of the subjects they had studied that year. The honorarium payable by a student to his regent before the examination was on a fixed scale according to a student's rank. Students of the first order who were the sons of earls, lords and barons were required to pay their regent at least £3 each year by way of an honorarium; students of the second order whose parents were below the rank of baron but endowed with sufficient funds were to pay 40/- regardless of whether they lived in the country or in the towns; and those of the third order, with fewer resources, were to pay 20/-. The poor were exempt from all payment.

Before undergoing examination students were obliged to make payments also to the lord rector, bursar and bedellus. The rector was to receive 12d from each student entering university and the bedellus was to be given 2/- from students in each year of their course. Students of the first order before examination, were each to pay the quaestor 20/- in their second year, 30/- in their third year and 45/- in their fourth year; students of the second order paid 13/4d in their second year, 20/- in their third year and 30/- in their fourth year; whilst students of the third order paid 6/8d in the second year, 10/- in the third year and 15/- in their final year.[129] This scale was in keeping with the division of students according to their social background into 'primars' ,'secondars' and 'ternars'.[130] Social niceties were preserved and students were expected to pay each according to his means. To ensure that payments were duly made, only students who could produce a receipt from the bursar were admitted to examination; and it was the evasion of payment on the part of some students promoted to the master's degree which prompted the insertion in one manuscript version of the statutes the entry of 4 Kalends January 1606 condemning this abuse.[131]

Students presented for the M.A. degree were first required to give an exact account of the subjects which they had studied, both in the humanities and in philosophy, during the four years of their course to the chancellor, dean and examiners. They had also to take an oath as students to be examined for the master's degree promising to render account of all their studies, to submit to the examiners' decision and to the place assigned them in the promotion and finally to set a good example to posterity by their lives and conduct, unlike some recent graduates who by their bad behaviour had brought the university's honour into disrepute through nocturnal wanderings, games and insolence. The second part of the oath was to be exacted again at the graduation ceremony between the chancellor's prayer and the benediction.[132]

The examiners, for their part, had their own oath to take before each examination and particularly before the magisterial act. The chancellor, it is to be observed, was now included with the dean of faculty and other examiners who in the name of God and his blessed angels promised faithfully and honestly to examine and place candidates for promotion in order of merit, and they were to punish the ignorance and idleness of the others.[133] Individually, the examiners' opinions of candidates were to remain secret and not for disclosure. At the examiners' meeting, the dean and other examiners were to draw up lists of the students to be promoted in order of merit on a 'schedule' or roll subscribed by the examiners and sealed with the dean's ring. This was the form to be observed in all promotions, and on the day assigned for promotions to the master's degree, after the public debates and disputations of theses had been performed, the dean was to render the schedule to the chancellor and rector. The bedellus was then publicly to announce the names of those students who had qualified for the degree and those who had failed. The magistrands in order of merit were to take up their place and after falling on their knees, the chancellor was first of all to offer prayers and finally to bestow the benediction. The rubric enjoining kneeling was itself an insertion in the draft of 1578 (though written in the same hand) but none of this was likely to be objectionable to presbyterians who were averse not to kneeling at prayer but, as the Five Articles later showed, to kneeling at communion, especially if enforced by royal decree, lest their action be misconstrued as idolatry.[134]

All who were to receive the master's degree were to kneel and so be incepted masters, but first the chancellor was to give thanks in Latin to 'the eternal God and most clement father' for renewing his image, present in man at the creation but since obliterated by sin only to be restored once more by Christ. Prayer was also offered to God for having 'led us not only from a wild and rustic life to this human and civilised culture but also from the deep abyss of superstition and from the dense darkness of ignorance in which we lay drowned with our ancestors under the water' until called into 'this sublime light both of heavenly wisdom and evangelical truth and into this admirable splendour by your incredible power and outstanding goodness', thereby imparting 'knowledge of these arts and letters by which our minds may be informed by more liberal teaching towards all virtue and honesty and our spirits nourished by a holier discipline towards the hope of a blessed immortality and everlasting happiness'. The hope was expressed that these 'incomparable treasures of all understanding and knowledge' would be transmitted to posterity and that the sparks of divine light in the students would be rekindled for the rest of time with heavenly fire of God's spirit, so that from these beginnings they might aspire to that goal of perfection in which learning and a godly life would be joined together to the honour of God and his church, and the university. With the words 'to thee Father, Son and Holy Ghost be praise, honour and glory', the chancellor and masters of the university were to rise and there followed the chancellor's address to the graduands who remained on bended knees. By the authority of God and by command of the university, the chancellor granted the magistrands the honourable title of master and with it 'the power of interpreting and teaching humane letters and explaining universal philosophy in Greek and Latin'. Then 'with the greatest simplicity and scarcity of ceremonies with the favouring prayer of the gathering', the new masters were to arise from their knees, after being adorned with the master's insignia, and were to be greeted by the chancellor, rector, dean and regent masters with the right hand of fellowship. After the benediction, they were to cover their heads and sit down, whilst those who were appointed to give the declamations and lectures customary at that time would carry them out. All that remained was the formula for the university's testimonial which ran in the name of the rector and university and, signed by the rector, dean, principal and four regent masters, testified that the student, born of an honourable place and family, had studied for a full four years in the university and had gained the title of master to which was added the university's commendation of its alumnus.[135]

Only the broadest outline of academic procedures is presented in the statutes. This is perhaps to be expected. For one thing, there was much which was common knowledge, requiring no elaboration. Accepted practices and routine duties were assumed rather than defined. The examination system of which the statutes tell so little was too well known in academic circles to warrant extended comment. Of the baccalaureate, however, nothing whatsoever is said. The process by which a 'determinant' reached the bachelor's standard usually in his third year after a series of responsions and disputations was certainly a well-known feature both of the pre-Reformation university and of James Melville's student days at St Andrews in the early 1570s,[136] but in the post-Reformation Glasgow statutes no trace is to be found of the bachelor act. The omission may well be significant and probably betrays Melville's own disregard for the bachelor's degree. Such an impression is strengthened by the pattern of events at St Andrews where, in the years of Melville's ascendency, the B.A. also underwent a decline in status.[137] The hand of Melville may also be detected in the tendency at Glasgow, as at St Andrews,[138] to assimilate 'licence' (conferring the right to teach) with 'inception' (admission to the fellowship of masters and to the formality of teaching) in one graduation ceremony for the master's degree.

After graduation divinity students, as the statutes testify, had the opportunity of pursuing their studies in theology, but with this exception, emphasis of necessity was on teaching Arts students in a university which consisted of one faculty and one college. The Convention of Leith in 1572 could readily approve plans to provide bursaries to help students 'study thair art, theologie, the lawes or medicine within the pedagogy of Glasgow',[139] and the university statutes could vaguely speak of the 'higher degrees', but much of this was pious talk which bore little relation to reality. In both medicine and law, the university could offer no formal instruction. The presence of an English physician in the college for a brief spell in 1536 where he studied and practised his art 'for the sustentacyon off my lyvyng'[140] does nothing to alter the impression that from the university's inception the teaching of medicine never became established, and there was consequently no medical tradition for the post-Reformation university to inherit. The college might possess a herb garden[141] but this was perhaps for culinary rather than for medical purposes. On the other hand, the gift to the university of some herbal books by Mark Jamieson might modify such an impression, and Peter Blackburn's donation of the *Anatomy* of Vesalius is also indicative of an interest in medicine in certain circles. If, however, the university lacked a medical faculty, Glasgow, as a town, was not to be denied its Faculty of Physicians and Surgeons, founded in November 1599. Among the numerous medical practitioners in the burgh was one surgeon of distinction who won the confidence and support of the town council.

This was Peter Lowe, a native of Errol, who returned to settle in Glasgow after service for more than twenty years in France, Spain and Flanders. He described himself as a 'doctor in the facultie of chirurgy in Paris and chirurgian ordinary to Henry the fourth', and he was plainly a theorist as well as a practitioner of his art as his *Spanish Sicknes* (1596) and his *Chirurgerie* (1597) amply demonstrate.[142] It was probably at his behest that the town council decided in April 1599 to exercise a measure of control over medical practitioners by appointing examiners to improve standards. Nor did the university stand entirely on the sidelines, for the town enlisted the services of the principal, Patrick Sharp, and a regent, Blaise Lawrie, the Greek professor, in examining the 'mediciners and chyrurgianes quha dayele resortis and remanis within this towne and ar not able to discharge thair dewtey thairintill inrespect thai have not cunyng nor skill to do the same'.[143] By intervening, the university may have hoped to resist the establishment of a rival faculty in its midst, and there is certainly evidence of later friction, but if this were the purpose then it was not successful. Reforms were carried one step further in November 1599 with the king's grant to Peter Lowe and Robert Hamilton, a 'professoure of medecine' in the town, and their successors of the right to supervise the practice of medicine and surgery in the west of Scotland.[144] This established the Faculty of Physicians and Surgeons which helped make good the lack of medical training in the university until the appointment in 1637 of a university professor in medicine.[145]

When it came to teaching medicine, St Andrews also experienced difficulties. According to the *nova erectio* of 1579, the principal of St Salvator's was to become professor of medicine,[146] but a visitation of 1588 disclosed that although the principal 'affirmis he teichis tuyis ilk oulk the Aphorismes Hippocrates quhill October last, sensyne he hes teichit na thing', and the masters 'sayis he nevir teichis skantlie anis in the moneth'.[147] In 1599 he was found to have 'teichit medicine', but by 1616 the plea was advanced 'that ther be wirthie men socht and gotting for the professione of medicen and lawis without quhom our universitie quhilk suld be ane moder of all knawlege is ane universitie only in name'.[148] Aberdeen, on the other hand, seems to have maintained an interest in the study of medicine.[149]

Even although he had attended medical lectures at Paris and was the friend of Gilbert Moncrieff, who became the king's mediciner, and although he had studied law at Poitiers and had maintained an interest in that subject at Geneva, Melville did nothing to encourage the pursuit of either of these studies at Glasgow. Nor, for that matter, did any of his immediate successors who continued to ignore the claims of both law and medicine. As was the case with medicine, there had been no strong tradition of legal teaching at Glasgow, and as early as the 1520s the outlook for canon law was decidedly bleak, for teaching seems to have come to a halt and its fate was irrevocably sealed with the Reformation. For the reformers after 1560 there was plainly nothing to be gained in teaching the canon law of a discredited church whose jurisdiction had been abrogated by acts of parliament. On the other hand, the forensic services of men already skilled in canon law continued to be sought in the secularised commissary courts, and Andrew Hay, the university rector, acted as commissary of Hamilton.[150] Even in this field of law, the Edinburgh commissary court retained a general competence for the country as a whole, and although the reformers envisaged the teaching of civil law at Glasgow,[151] it is evident that the tendency to centralise the practice of law, at higher levels, in Edinburgh did nothing to advance the cause of legal studies in the west. Yet when the king threatened to remove the law courts from the capital after the Edinburgh riot of December 1596, Glasgow town council on 24 December 1596, in reply to a letter from the lord treasurer, was not slow in pressing its own claims by discussing 'quhat offer and conditiounes the towne will mak to his Majestie incace he culd be movit to plant the Sessioune and College of Justice in this towne'.[152]

The demise of canon law by 1560 was no argument for ignoring other branches of the law, but if Glasgow lacked a legal faculty, so too did St Andrews where the solitary lawyer, William Skeyne, the commissary of St Andrews, gave public university lectures.[153] As a student, James Melville had heard him 'teatche Cicero de Legibus and divers partes of the Institutiones of Justinian' and he had also visited the commissary court where 'the comissar wald tak pleasour to schaw us the practise in judgment of that quhilk he teatched in the scholles'.[154] But when

Skeyne's successor, William Welwood, the friend of Melville, was deprived in 1597, the post was promptly abolished, 'it being fund that the professioun of the lawes is na wayes necessar at this tyme in this universitie'.155

Unless remedied, the decline in legal studies was bound to lead to a shortage of trained men. It was presumably for this reason that Robert Pont, himself a minister, had been appointed a senator of the College of Justice in 1572, 'provydeing alwayes that he leave not the office of the ministrie' and that such a step be not interpreted as a 'preparative to other ministers to procure sick promotioun'.156 It was indeed as much on these grounds—a scarcity of qualified candidates—as in an attempt to embarrass an assembly intent on maintaining a separate ecclesiastical jurisdiction that the Regent Morton in 1573 had sought to recruit further ministers as senators, only to be met with the assembly's discouraging reply that 'nane was able or apt to beare the saids twa charges, and therefore inhibits that any Minister occupying the voca- tioun of the Ministrie take upon him to be a Senatour, Mr Robert Pont only excepted'.157 What Morton may have been seeking was the restoration of the ecclesiastical membership of the College of Justice. All in all, for Scots who wished to obtain a sound legal training, the best advice might be to study at Bourges or Poitiers or some such centre overseas. It was, for example, at Bourges that Edward Henryson,158 Alexander Arbuthnot, Patrick Adamson and David Cunningham159 had all studied, and whilst three of them later pursued ecclesiastical rather than legal careers it was nevertheless to Bourges that David MacGill, the kinsman of the lord clerk register, was sent where he duly received his degree certificate as a licentiate in civil law on 21 July 1579.160 At Glasgow, however, it was not until the beginning of the seventeenth century that the claims of law received attention when the proposal to appoint a 'professour off the lawes' was justified on the grounds that there were established within the city 'divers judicatoreis, viz., synodall assemblie, presbitrie, sessioune, haldin be ministeris; consistorie be commissaris; burghe and baroune courtis be bailzeis; quhais proceidingis aught all to be terminit be the boundis off lawe, the ignorance quhairoff breidis and fosteris mony confusiones'. The expectation was that the lawyer's stipend would be financed from revenues at the disposal of the archbishop and canons. The scheme, however, went no further and it was only after the Restoration that the creation of a chair in civil and canon law was seriously canvassed in 1664 by the commissioners for visitation.161

If judged by the St Andrews yardstick of 1616, Glasgow might be considered 'ane universitie only in name' in so far as it lacked teaching in the higher faculties of law and medicine. Andrew Melville may have brought to Glasgow a 'plentifull and inexhaust theassour of all guid letters and lerning, bathe of humen and devyne things',[162] but both he and his successors purposely concentrated on Arts and theology where they could claim some competence. Staffed as they were by ecclesiastics, the universities were still the nurseries of the church, 'the fountaine fra the quhilk ministers must flow'.[163] Provision had therefore to be made for theological instruction. After a visitation of St Andrews university in 1574 it was decided that entrance to the ministry from 1577 should be restricted to those who had studied philosophy 'in ane of the universities of this realme' and had reached at least the bachelor's standard in theology, and it was recommended that bishops should possess a doctorate.[164] The general assembly, however, in 1575 was perhaps more realistic when it imposed the more modest requirement that candidates for the ministry should possess a knowledge of Latin.[165] Nevertheless, the universities exercised an important rôle in teaching divinity and in ensuring that the ministry in Scotland was, on the whole, a well-educated ministry. In the invitation to Cartwright and Travers in 1580, it was even said that none should be admitted to the ministry without first completing the theology course in the tongues, the Old and New Testaments and the commonplaces of religion.[166]

Not all aspiring ministers, however, were graduates in theology. Candidates for the ministry, irrespective of their earlier education, had to undergo a series of trials by preaching on the exercise, a meeting set aside for interpreting scripture and biblical study, and which from 1581 formed an integral part of presbytery meetings. Designed to maintain, and even improve, the educational standards of graduate and non-graduate ministers alike, the exercise took one of two forms: the discussions could take place in public before the congregation and kirk session of the principal town where the presbytery met, or they could be held behind closed doors where divinity students and inexperienced or ignorant candidates could be heard by the presbytery in private. Every entrant to the ministry was therefore placed on the exercise. In Glasgow, the presbytery instructed the principal of the college to ask the new graduates if they were willing to enter the privy exercise,[167] and all candidates who were admitted to the privy exercise, which was sometimes held in the college,[168] were expected to have attended the principal's lectures on theology in the college.[169] While still at university, divinity students as a matter of course regularly attended the exercise.

According to the statutes, post-graduate students of theology were to take part in disputations once a fortnight. These were likely to be on such themes as original sin, grace, predestination, justification, the church or the sacraments. All that is on record, however, is that the principal in 1586 lectured on Calvin's commonplaces and that the students undertook their disputations.[170] A clearer picture emerges from the printed theology theses which have survived at St Andrews where Melville acted as moderator or *praeses* during disputations on *De praedestinatione sive de causis salutis et damnationis aeternae disputatio, De libero arbitrio theses theologicae, Scholastica diatriba de rebus divinis, De Justificatione hominis coram deo, Theses theologicae de peccato, Utrum Episcopus Romanus sit Antichristus necne?, De Sacramentis et missa Idololatrica,* and so forth.[171] As at Glasgow, theology students attended the exercise, which was often held in St Mary's,[172] and there can be little doubt that St Mary's college under Melville was considered to offer the most comprehensive teaching in theology. That Glasgow presbytery in 1599 should ask Patrick Sharp, the college principal, to deliver a letter from the presbytery to Melville at St Andrews requesting him to send a qualified student to enter the ministry in Glasgow presbytery[173] says much for Melville's reputation at St Andrews and perhaps rather less for Patrick Sharp's work as principal at Glasgow.

Yet Melville's first allegiance as college principal had been to Glasgow, not St Andrews, and although the content of the theology course at Glasgow is shrouded in some mystery, it is apparent that from 1574 Melville gave instruction in Hebrew, Chaldaic and Syriac grammar with practice of these languages in the psalms, the works of Solomon, David, Ezra and the Epistle to the Galatians. Thereafter, he proceeded to teach the Old and New Testaments as well as the commonplaces of theology. He is also known to have lectured on Calvin's *Institutes.*[174] His matured ideas, however, were worked out, while still principal at Glasgow, in the new foundation of 1579 for St Mary's college as a school of divinity at St Andrews. The plan was for a four-year course in theology to be taught by five lectors. The format, though more ambitious, conformed to the Glasgow model. The course began with instruction in the precepts of Hebrew grammar with practice in David, Solomon and Job, followed by the precepts of Chaldaic and Syriac with their application in Daniel, Ezra, the paraphrases and the Syriac New Testament; the second master was to 'interpreit out of the ebrew and sensiblie oppin up the law of Moses and the historie of the auld Testament, conferring with the paraphrasis, septuaginits and uther learnit versions quhair neid beis'; then came instruction in the prophets from the third teacher; while the fourth lector was to teach the Greek New Testament and make comparisons with the Syriac version; and the fifth lector was assigned the teaching of the commonplaces of theology. By daily repetitions, weekly disputations, monthly declamations and three examinations, the intention was to produce 'perfit theologians'.[175]

It was, however, recognised that there was a 'grait raritie at this present of men learnit in the knawledge of the toungis' and this was one consideration which led the assembly to endorse the king's proposal to translate Melville from Glasgow to the principalship of St Mary's in 1580.[176]

The assembly's decision, taken only after 'farder disputation' was opposed by Andrew Hay, the university rector who in the name of the university made a formal protestation 'disassenting from the removeall of Mr Andro in any wayes'.[177] Melville, himself, who regarded Glasgow as his 'eldest bern' left for St Andrews 'sear against his will'[178] and it may therefore have been in a bid to retain his services at Glasgow that Archbishop Boyd, as chancellor, Andrew Hay, as rector, Thomas Smeaton, as dean, together with Melville and David Wemyss, the city minister, wrote to Cartwright and Travers inviting them to accept appointment as theology professors at St Andrews.[179] Neither accepted and Melville took up his post in St Andrews in November 1580. In his own words he was transported 'by the advice and authoritie both of generall assembly and three estats, at his majesties command, from Glasco (where six yeers the Lord had blessed my labours in letters and relligion to the comfort of the church and honour of the countrie) unto St Androis for reforming of the universitie and erecting a colledge of divinitie for the profession of learned tongues and theologie against the seminaries of Rems and Rome, wherein I was placed by commissionars both of church and counsell, authorized with his majesties commission in most solemn manner'.[180] Accompanying him was his nephew James who was 'glad to be frie from the daylie labor of regenting in philosophie' and who had intended to leave for France but was persuaded by his uncle 'to ascend to the profession and daylie travell in theologie'. With their departure, the Glasgow college was faced with the loss of what amounted to half of its teaching staff, but this was soon made good with the appointment of Patrick Melville to succeed James Melville and with the presentation under the privy seal of Thomas Smeaton to the principalship in January 1581.[181]

A native of Gask in Perthshire and once clerk in the diocese of Dunblane,[182] Smeaton had come as a late convert to Calvinism. His adherence to the old faith had led to his removal from St Salvator's college at the Reformation and with his departure for France he had entered the Jesuits college at Paris, the Collège de Clermont, 'understanding that the ordour of the Jesuits was the maist lerned, halie and exquisit in the papistrie'. Yet even this did not resolve his doubts about 'the trew way of salvation'. Nor did his journey from Paris to Rome *via* Geneva, where he met Melville, do anything to lessen his uncertainties. By 1572, however, he had finally decided to quit the Society of Jesus, and with the onset of the massacre of St Bartholemew he had sought refuge in the home of Francis Walsingham, the English ambassador in Paris, with whom he returned to England where he taught for five years as schoolmaster at Colchester before returning to Scotland.[183] Once home, he was 'gladlie content' to be in Melville's company and 'sa aggreit to be minister at Pasley',[184] a difficult charge even for a former Jesuit in view of the recusancy prevalent in the parish. Andrew Polwarth, his predecessor, had left Paisley with the assembly's blessing 'because of the contempt of the discipline, thair manifest vyces, minacing and boasting of him in doing his duetie'; and Melville himself had been a member of the assembly committee which had recommended the move.[185] As a prominent presbyterian and former moderator of the general assembly, Smeaton was well suited to inherit Melville's post at Glasgow. Nor were his more precisely academic credentials likely to be ignored. He was already dean of faculty and, as such, had supervised examinations in the university. At Melville's instance in 1579, he had published a reply to Archibald Hamilton's attack on Scottish Calvinism, and was regarded as 'a man learned in the languages' and well versed in the patristic writings, who taught 'with great profit' during his three years as principal of the college.[186]

The issues in the church, however, could not but affect the university as well, particularly with the crown's nomination in 1581 of Robert Montgomery, minister of Stirling, as Boyd's successor to the vacant archbishopric of Glasgow and so to the chancellorship of the university. Montgomery's bargain with the duke of Lennox allowing the duke access to the temporality of the see[187] did nothing to commend him to the general assembly which had already condemned the episcopal office. The thirty or so ministers who composed the chapter consequently declined to elect the king's nominee. Not only so, university personnel were directly involved in the issue. As parson of Govan, Thomas Smeaton was himself a member of the chapter and so too, under the Leith arrangements of 1572, were Andrew Hay, the rector, and Andrew Polwarth, the dean of faculty, as well as John Davidson, the former principal. Faced with the chapter's refusal to elect, the privy council declared in April 1582 that the right to dispone the bishopric had devolved on the king, and Smeaton with his colleagues were summoned before the council where Andrew Hay protested on behalf of the church.[188]

The church replied first by suspending and then excommunicating Montgomery but the privy council countered this by declaring the excommunication to be null and void.[189] When Montgomery attempted to preach in Glasgow, students from the college succeeded in excluding him from the church and reserved the pulpit instead for their principal who, taking as his text 'He that enters not by the door but by the window is a thief and a robber', proceeded to criticise Montgomery for 'his simoniacal entry and the levity he had showed in all his proceedings'. Some forty people, it was claimed, including a number of students, 'all bodin in feir of weir with jakkis, steilbonettis, hagbuttis, pistolettis' had 'enterit be leddirs in the revestrie of the Hie Kirk of Glasgow and detenit the same be force of armes the space of sex houres or thairby of mynd to have attemptit sum uther heich interpryse'. All this was said to have taken place at the instigation of the college and presbytery, and so Thomas Smeaton and the ringleaders were called before the council to answer for the 'riot'.

The general assembly, however, saw matters in a rather different light. It was particularly concerned at the treatment meted out to John Howieson, minister of Cambuslang and moderator of Glasgow presbytery, who was 'rugged out of the judgement seat' during a discussion of the Montgomery case and 'lyke a theife' was thrown into prison by the provost and bailies. David Wemyss, the city minister, also found himself being pulled out of the pulpit by the king's guard on the 'day of the communion in presence of the haill congregatioun' to make way for Montgomery. In its list of grievances to be presented to the king, the assembly also complained of how the 'ministers, masters of colledgis, and scholers of Glasgow in tyme of publick fast were be letters of horning compellit to leave thair flockes and schooles destitute' and how 'the scholers of Glasgow were invaidit and thair blood cruellie shed be the bailzies and commountie gatherit be sound of the commoun bell and straik of drum and be certaine seditious men inflamit to have slaine them all and to have brunt the colledge'.[190]

With the *coup d'état* known as the Ruthven raid and the collapse of the Lennox regime in August 1582, a declaration was issued to justify the palace revolution in which were recounted the misdemeanours of the previous administration. Wemyss's ejection from his church was condemned; so too were the summoning of 'the maisters of the universitie and regents' to compear before the privy council, and the troubling of the scholars, 'all being the sonnes of noblemen, barons and others of good qualitie', who were 'furiouslie invaded and their blood drawin'. It was also said that 'papists and men weill knowne infamous' were deliberately appointed 'as magistrats in that citie and universitie to trouble the kirk and studies of the schollers'.[191] This looks like an allusion to the Hegaits, a prominent Glasgow family; and the next assembly in October 1582, taking advantage of the well-disposed government of the Ruthven lords, reiterated its complaints asking that the Hegaits and others 'be punischit according to justice for the seditioun and uproare made be them, being magistrates and counsellours, against the students of Glasgow and shedding thair blood'. The laird of Minto, as provost of the city, promptly submitted to the assembly and was referred for censure to Glasgow presbytery but some of his associates were ordered to be excommunicated 'for haunting companie of Mr Robert Montgomerie being excommunicat' and for 'other enormities committed by them'.[192]

So long as the Ruthven raiders remained in power Montgomery could look for little support from the new administration which was sympathetic to the presbyterians. The new government, however, chose to remind the assembly in April 1583, 'seing his Majestie is patron and erector of the college of Glasgow', that it should 'meddle not with the removing of any of the members thereof and especially of the principall',[193] which rather suggests that the assembly had been contemplating some such change. A new appointment had presumably been made with Patrick Sharp's resignation from his post as master of the grammar school in November 1582[194] to become regent in the university, but when change did come, it was only with the sudden death of the forty-seven-year-old principal in December 1583.

By that date the political complexion of the government had undergone a further change with the fall from power of the Ruthven raiders in July 1583 and the onset of the Arran regime which was decidedly hostile in its attitude towards the presbyterians. Since the crown chose to make no immediate appointment of a successor to Smeaton, the principalship remained vacant. The ecclesiastical policies of the Arran administration were also made explicit in the 'Black acts' of May 1584 which asserted royal supremacy over the church, reaffirmed episcopacy and proscribed presbyteries.[195] The prospects looked bright for Montgomery now 'reponit to his former estait'[196] as archbishop; and for refusing to hear Montgomery preach, the regents of the college were summoned before the privy council in July. They rested their case on the church's excommunication of Montgomery and they denied that the government had any power to absolve him from that sentence. The council therefore ordered 'the whole foure regents' to be imprisoned, two in the castle of Glasgow and two in the castle at St Andrews. The college itself was closed and the students charged by proclamation to return home until new masters were appointed.[197] Nor were the university rector and dean of faculty immune from prosecution. Andrew Hay and Andrew Polwarth had both been denounced as rebels in May for failing to appear before the privy council on an undisclosed charge.[198] Hay was warded north of the Tay but Polwarth withdrew 'for fear of apprehension' and joined the presbyterian leaders who had sought refuge in England,[199] where Melville and his associates, using London as their base, wrote to Geneva and Zürich with their version of events to counteract Archbishop Adamson's propaganda to the reformed churches abroad.[200]

The fate of the college at that point lay largely at the mercy of the government which deferred appointing a new principal. How long the college remained closed and the masters imprisoned is unknown, but the damage inflicted was not irreparable. At least fifteen students are known to have graduated in 1584 and the graduation lists for 1588 suggest that the college received an intake of a dozen students presumably at the start of the new academic session in October 1584.[201] Patrick Sharp, one of the imprisoned regents, is said to have acted as minister at Paisley in 1584, but David Cunningham, subsequently bishop of Aberdeen, to whom the Arran government granted 'the haill dewtie appertening to the office of the principall of the college' in 1584, may well have undertaken some duties in the college.[202] Arran's rule, however, was open to challenge. The return of the exiled lords and ministers in November 1585 marked the downfall of Arran's government and the formation of a coalition ministry which without delay deprived Montgomery of his archbishopric in December 1585, and appointed Patrick Sharp in January 1586 as Smeaton's successor in the university.[203] On returning from England, Melville himself spent the winter of 1586 at Glasgow 'being ernestlie intreated to visit that collage', before proceeding to St Andrews.[204]

By pursuing a conciliatory policy, Sharp, who was apparently related to the Sharps or Shairps of Houstoun, did at least keep the college free from serious political trouble for more than twenty-seven years. During Sharp's principalship, however, a dispute between the college and town council over college revenues derived from the town's foundation of 1573 and the king's foundation of 1577 led to the privy council's intervention in June 1602 and to the appointment of commissioners who were empowered 'to visite the said college, sicht and considder the fundationis thairof, call for a perfyte rentall of the revenewis mortefeit thairto, urge the saidis maisteris with the last yeiris compt of thair haill rentis, informe thame treuly of thair sufficiencie for thair saidis functionis als weill in lyfe as letteris, and of the haill estait of the said college in every point and thairof and of the haill doubtis and difficulteis quhilk thay find in the saidis fundationis'. The visitors were instructed to report their findings to the king 'at his repairing to the said citie that be thair guid avyse his hienes may put ordour to thair present difference, and settle thame in a steadfast unioun and concord, to the weill and quyetnes of the said citie and furtherance of vertew in that college in all tyme comeing'. The visitors' recommendations for the future management of college revenues and their proposed regulations for the masters' and bursars' rations were subsequently approved by the privy council in August 1602.[205] Although the details of the dispute remain partially obscured, the town's objective may have been to assert a measure of control over college finance in an effort to acquire a greater say in college affairs. The control which Edinburgh town council exercised over the recently-founded college in the capital clearly formed a precedent for Glasgow which the university was anxious to resist.

It was probably these developments which led to the composition of an undated document, newly discovered, entitled 'controverseis betuix the fundationes of Glasgow college', which depicts the discrepancies between the two foundations and proceeds to recommend that the town should resign to the king its foundation of 1573 and that the crown should approve a new foundation of nineteen persons to replace the fifteen foundationers of 1573 and the twelve foundationers of the *nova erectio*. New regulations were presented for the principal, regents, bursars, provisor and cook. The document was evidently composed in the interests of the college rather than the town, and two outstanding novelties are the suggestions, first, that the principal should no longer act as minister of Govan, a proposal which did not take effect until 1621, and, secondly, that a professor of law should be appointed and financed from revenues at the disposal of the archbishop and canons, but no such appointment materialised. The contents of the document, it would seem, are exhortatory rather than mandatory, and whatever the significance of the document as a whole, it is plain that its recommendations were at most only partially fulfilled.[206]

During all these discussions, first with the town council in 1601, and doubtless with the privy council and its commissioners in 1602, Sharp as principal played a central role, and seems to have successfully resisted any pressure exerted by the town council. In more strictly scholastic matters, Sharp, while principal, produced his *Brief Explication of Christian Doctrine*, printed in 1599, which he dedicated to the king,[207] and he later gained the reputation, amongst his opponents at least, of being something of a courtier. Certainly, at Hampton Court in 1606 he argued against the Melvilles that the Aberdeen assembly which the king had prohibited was indeed an unlawful assembly.[208] He also accepted appointment as constant moderator of Glasgow presbytery by 1607 and was equally prepared to serve as a member of the High Commission in 1610. His compliance in these matters, however, did not win him the full confidence of the king who, in December 1613, ordered a visitation of the university because of certain 'enormiteis'. Attention was drawn to the 'old age of the principall and utheris many defectis', and the visitors were to investigate whether 'brybrie' had influenced the appointment of either regents or bursars. Seeing his 'utter disgrace' in

M

sight Sharp chose to demit office rather than be deposed, and Robert Boyd, son of the former archbishop, who had pursued a distingushed career in France after graduating from Edinburgh, was admitted principal in 1615.[209] By 1621, however, he too resigned office after refusing to kneel at communion, as enjoined by the Five Articles approved by the Perth assembly of 1618.[210]

Each of the principals from Melville to Boyd had thus incurred the displeasure of the crown for one reason or another, but during those years there was progress as well as setback. College finances were augmented particularly with the annexation in 1617 of the benefices of Renfrew and Kilbride, to which Torrance was united in 1618.[211] Student numbers also showed signs of increase with over forty new students matriculating in 1621,[212] and a new building programme was undertaken in the 1630s. This steady expansion set the pattern for much of the seventeenth century. Melville's 'bairn' had finally come of age.

NOTES

1. *Glas. Mun.*, i, 61; GUA, Drawer F5. Unfoliated bundle, 23 July 1574.
2. *Glasgow City Charters*, i, (pt. ii), 153.
3. *Glas. Mun.*, ii, 42–54.
4. GUA, MS 26619, 'Jura Leges Instituta' (Clerk's Press no. 7), f. 7v, 8v.
5. *Ibid.*, 8v; *Glas. Mun.*, ii, 54.
6. Watt, *Fasti*, 151; GCA, MS Glasgow Presbytery Records, 2 January 1605; Porteous MS, 87. But see also SRO, CH4/1/4, f. 20v, Register of Presentations to Benefices, where Spottiswoode received a grant of the archbishopric as late as 24 May 1608.
7. Watt, *Fasti*, 151; see 335–8.
8. Watt, *Fasti*, 151; *BUK*, ii, 693.
9. Watt, *Fasti*, 151; *APS*, iv, 169–70; Porteous MS, 10, 4 April 1587, where the synod of Glasgow complained at Beaton's restitution (though not effective till 1598); *Glas. Mun.*, iii, 4.
10. GUA, MS 26614, 'Annales Collegii Facultatis Artium in Universitate Glasguensi, 1451–1555' (Clerk's Press no. 2), 149.
11. *Ibid.*, 150, 160–2; GUA, MS 26619, 'Jura Leges Instituta', ff. 7r–8r; *Glas. Mun.*, ii, 52–4.
12. See 335–8.
13. GUA, MS 26619, 'Jura Leges Instituta', f. 8v (*Glas. Mun.*, ii, 54); MS 26614, 'Annales Collegii Facultatis Artium', 149.
14. GUA, MS 26614, 'Annales Collegii Facultatis Artium', 158.
15. GUA, MS 26619, 'Jura Leges Instituta', f. 6r-v; *Glas. Mun.*, ii, 48–9.
16. GUA, MS 26614, 'Annales Collegii Facultatis Artium', 158; Wodrow, *Biographical Collections*, i, 530–2.
17. Watt, *Fasti*, 150, 380.
18. *Glasgow Burgh Records*, i, 4, 99; *Glas. Mun.*, iii, 3.
19. *Glas. Mun.*, iii, 348.
20. Trinity College, Dublin, MS 510, 'Jura Leges Instituta Academiae Glasguensis',

ff. 83–9; TCD, MS 533 (Book of Discipline); TCD, MS 416, 'Andreas Melvini, Scoti. Dan. 9', ff. 2r–4v.

21. T. Fuller, *Church History of Britain* (London, 1845), v., 180–2.

22. *CSP Ireland, 1592–1596*, 262.

23. TCD, Library Muniments, MS Catalogues, nos. 1 and 2.

24. *Ibid.*; Mullinger, *Cambridge*, ii, 356, 404–5, 409.

25. TCD, MUN/P/1/201. Early University Statutes, caps. v–xvii, with signature of Temple and fellows and a note at the end by Bedell; for the Laudian statutes, see J. W. Stubbs, *The History of the University of Dublin* (Dublin, 1889), 69, 76.

26. *CSP Ireland, 1588–1592*, 437, 438, 455, 461.

27. *Early Records of the University of St Andrews*, 267.

28. *Glas. Mun.*, iii, 4; *CSP Scot.*, xi, no. 578; *CSP Ireland, 1574–1585*, 163; W. Urwick, *The Early History of Trinity College, Dublin, 1591–1660* (London, 1892), 9; *The Montgomery Manuscripts*, ed. G. Hill (Belfast, 1869), 30n; *The Hamilton Manuscripts*, ed. T. K. Lowry (Belfast, 1867), 4; *Glas. Mun.*, iii, 5.

29. Andrew Melville to Sir James Semple of Beltrees, 1 December 1610, in T. McCrie, *Melville*, 486–7; *CSP Scot*, xi, no. 531; *CSP Ireland, 1586–1588*, 6, 35.

30. TCD, MUN/P/32. Papers relating to college estates, nos. 6–10, 13, 15–24; MUN/P/1. Papers, General and Miscellaneous, nos. 19, 33, 41; *HMC, Salisbury MSS.*, vii, 151–2.

31. TCD, MS 410, ff. 84–5.

32. *Glas. Mun.*, ii, 42.

33. *BUK*, i, 379.

34. SRO, PA10/1.

35. *The Calendar of the University of St Andrews, 1976–77* (p. 78), lists the following chancellors: 1572–74, John Douglas, archbishop of St Andrews; 1576–92, Patrick Adamson, archbishop of St Andrews; 1592–95, John Maitland of Thirlestane; 1597–98, John Lindsay of Balcarres; 1599–1604, John Graham, earl of Montrose; 1604–15, George Gladstanes, archbishop of St Andrews. But according to SRO, CH4/1/3, Register of Presentations to Benefices, vol. iii, f. 16r, George Gladstanes was appointed chancellor on 29 September 1598 on the decease of John Lindsay: 'Ure soverane lord being informed that the office of chancelarie of the universitie of Sanctandros being now vaicand in his majesteis handis and at his gift and dispositioun be the deceis of umquhile Mr Jhonne Lindsay of Balcarras, last chancelair thairof and possessor of the said office, and understanding of the qualificatioun and litterature of Mr Georg Glaidstains, minister of Chrystis Evangell, being meit and able to use and exerce the said office, thairfore ordanis etc., gevand, grantand and disponand to the said Mr George during all the dayis of his lifetyme the foirsaid office of chancelarie of the said universitie with all and sindrie priviledges, casualties and pertinentis quhatsumevir appertening or that hes bene accustumat or knawin to appertene thairto according to the laws and constitutiouns of the said universitie, statutis and actis of this realme with command to the lordis of counsall to grant and direct lettres. *Subscribitur*, at Dalkeith the penult day of September, 1598'.

   In July 1599, however, Gladstanes is styled 'vice-chancellor of the university', and the earl of Montrose, lord chancellor of the realm, was 'created likeways chancellour of the university'. *Evidence*, iii, 198.

36. *Glas. Mun.*, iii, 307.

37. *Ibid.*, ii, 42–3; for the pre-Reformation date, *ibid.*, ii, 6.

38. *Ibid.*, iii, 313ff.

39. *Evidence*, iii, 196–7.

40. *Glas. Mun.*, ii, 43.

342   THE NEW FOUNDATION

- 41. GUA, MS 26619, 'Jura Leges Instituta'.
- 42. *Glas. Mun.*, ii, 43.
- 43. *Ibid.*, ii, 6.
- 44. Melville, *Diary*, 418.
- 45. *Ibid.*, 69–72.
- 46. *RMS*, v, no. 728; cf. *RMS*, iv, no. 1615; Vatican Archives, Reg. Supp. 2855, ff. 140–1; 2875, ff. 186–7; 2876, f. 25; 2963, f. 291r; Resignationes, series A, 171, f. 7v; 208, f. 29v.
- 47. H. Chadwick, 'A Memoir of Fr. Edmund Hay, S.I.', *Archivum Historicum Societatis Jesu*, viii (1939), 66–85, at 84–5; Melville, *Diary*, 71; for a list of rectors, see Appendix G.
- 48. Porteous MS, 45, 4 April 1592.
- 49. *Glas. Mun.*, ii, 44.
- 50. *Ibid.*, i, 119.
- 51. Melville, *Diary*, 50; *Glas. Mun.*, ii, 50.
- 52. *BUK*, ii, 491, 495.
- 53. Bodleian, MS Smith 77, f. 29r.
- 54. *Glas. Mun.*, ii, 44.
- 55. *Ibid.*, iii, 409.
- 56. *Ibid.*, iii, 407ff. In his *Onomasticon Poeticum* (GUL copy Bi7–h22), Thomas Jack, the university quaestor, mentions in a prefatory letter addressed to James Hamilton, son of Claud, lord Paisley, that he came to Glasgow to teach eighteen years ago and that he gave up teaching on 5 Kalends September 1574. He also refers to Andrew Melville's arrival in Glasgow in November 1574; he indicates that he had met George Buchanan while the latter was writing his history at Stirling; and he recalls that no students were more deferential to their regents than were James Hamilton and John Graham, younger, when they were Arts students at Glasgow university (*gymnasium*). In his letter, which was written at Eastwood on 7 Kalends August 1592, Jack took the opportunity of recommending his nephew, Gabriel Maxwell, who was later regent in the university. Jack's work contains a prose composition by Hadrian Damman and poems by Damman, Robert and Hercules Rollock, Patrick Sharp, Andrew Melville and Thomas Craig.
- 57. *Glas. Mun.*, iii, 411ff.
- 58. *Ibid.*, iii, 424–6.
- 59. Melville, *Diary*, 45, 50–1.
- 60. For the text of the *nova erectio*, see Appendix K.
- 61. *Glas. Mun.*, ii, 45.
- 62. *Ibid.*
- 63. GUA, MS 26614, 'Annales Collegii Facultatis Artium', 158; Wodrow, *Biographical Collections*, i, 531.
- 64. *Glas. Mun.*, i, 132–4, 141.
- 65. *Ibid.*, iii, 3; Melville, *Diary*, 84.
- 66. *Glas. Mun.*, iii, 4.
- 67. *Ibid.*, ii, 45–6.
- 68. Melville, *Diary*, 50.
- 69. *Ibid.*, 25.
- 70. See above, 276.
- 71. Melville, *Diary*, 49.
- 72. *Eine Geschichte der alten Fuggerbibliotheken*, ed. P. Lehmann (Tubingen, 1956 and 1960), ii, *passim*; cf. Bodleian, MS Cherry 5, ff. 188r–89v.
- 73. A. Ganoczy, *La Bibliothèque de l'Académie de Calvin* (Geneva, 1969).

74. *Glas. Mun.*, ii, 46.
75. Melville, *Diary*, 49, 54.
76. *BM, Catalogue.*
77. Melville, *Diary*, 27.
78. *Ibid.*, 49.
79. *Ibid.*, 54.
80. *Glas. Mun.*, i, 108–9.
81. *Ibid.*, ii, 46.
82. I.e. *De Generatione et Corruptione.*
83. Melville, *Diary*, 49.
84. *BM, Catalogue.*
85. *Ibid.*
86. Bodleian, MS Smith, 77, ff. 67r–83v.
87. Durkan and Ross, *Libraries*, 57, 77, 104, 113, 149.
88. *Glas. Mun.*, iii, 409, 411–12.
89. C. Hill, *Antichrist in Seventeenth-Century England* (Oxford, 1971), 161.
90. BM, *Catalogue.*
91. *Glas. Mun.*, iii, 410.
92. Ganoczy, *La Bibliothèque de l'Académie de Calvin*, 117, 194, 259.
93. TCD, Library Muniments, MS Catalogue no. 2.
94. *Glas. Mun.*, ii, 316. Andrew Melville is accredited by his nephew (Melville, *Diary*, 49) with teaching at Glasgow 'Sleidan, Menarthes and Melanchthon', but since no such author as Menarthes can be traced, it seems very likely that this is an error for 'Sleidan *Monarchies* and Melanchthon', which does make sense.
95. S. A. Burrell, 'The Apocalyptic Vision of the Early Covenanters', *SHR*, xliii (1964), 1–24.
96. Melville, *Diary*, 49.
97. *Ibid.*, 46, 84.
98. E. L. Tuveson, *Millennium and Utopia: A Study in the Background of the Idea of Progress* (Gloucester, Mass., 1972), 56ff.
99. TCD, MS 416, ff. 2r–4v; Bodleian, Cherry MS 37, f. 37r.
100. Calderwood, *History*, iv, 3–10.
101. Rollock, *In Librum Danielis Prophetae . . . Commentarius* (Edinburgh, 1591). Copy in GUL.
102. H. Quistorp, *Calvin's Doctrine of the Last Things* (London, 1955), 109, 113ff. Calvin, *Commentaries on the Book of the Prophet Daniel* (Edinburgh, 1852, 1853), i, 250; ii, 141, 197ff.
103. *DNB*, xiv, 60; M. Napier, *Memoirs of John Napier of Merchiston* (Edinburgh, 1834), 86–7; Knox, *Works*, i, 189–92; *History*, i, 84–6. (In his sermon at St Andrews in 1547, Knox 'maid a schorte discourse of the foure Impyres, the Babyloniane, the Persiane, that of the Greakis, and the fourte of the Romanes; in the destruction whairof, rase up that last Beast, which he affirmed to be the Romane Church'. *Ibid.*); Melville, *Diary*, 26; GUL, Bn8 c3. Henry Bullinger, *In Apocalypsim*, (Basle, 1570). (In 1619, the college obtained Winkelmann's *In Apocalypsim* as part of a bequest by John Howieson, the minister of Cambuslang, *Glas. Mun.*, iii, 415); *SHS Miscellany*, i, p. lxvi, cf. xli; *Evidence*, iii, 193.
104. Knox, *Works*, i, 14; *History*, i, 11.
105. Tuveson, *Millennium and Utopia*, 52–4.
106. Copies of both works in GUL. Napier was nonetheless critical of what he called 'the great error of Cerinthus and his sect of Chiliasts or Millenaries who

thought our reign with Christ to be on earth, and temporal for a thousand years, and we then again to die and ly dead another thousand years'. Napier, *Memoirs of John Napier of Merchiston*, 208.

107. W. G. S. Snow, *The Times, Life and Thought of Patrick Forbes, Bishop of Aberdeen, 1618–1635* (London, 1952), 142ff.
108. *Select Biographies*, i, 132.
109. *Glas. Mun.*, ii, 46.
110. *Ibid.*, ii, 47.
111. *Evidence*, iii, 185.
112. *Ibid.*, iii, 188.
113. *Fasti Aberdonenses*, liii.
114. R. G. Cant, 'The St Andrews University Theses, 1579–1747', *Edinburgh Bibliographical Society Transactions*, ii, 106–50, at 121.
115. Bodleian, MS Fairfax, 30, f. 62r.
116. NLS, Adv. MSS 29.2.8 (Balcarres Papers), f. 116r.
117. *RPC*, x, 530–1; cf. *BUK*, iii, 1123.
118. *Evidence*, iii, 182.
119. Melville, *Diary*, 28; *Glas. Mun.*, ii, 54.
120. *Ibid.*, ii, 47.
121. St Andrews University Archives, MS Acta Rectorum, 87.
122. *Glas. Mun.*, ii, 48.
123. *Ibid.*, ii, 48–50.
124. *Ibid.*, i, 105.
125. *Ibid.*, ii, 50.
126. Melville, *Diary*, 75.
127. D. Cressy, *Education in Tudor and Stuart England* (London, 1975), 116.
128. *Glas. Mun.*, ii, 50.
129. *Ibid.*, ii, 51.
130. *Ibid.*, ii, 324; cf. *Evidence*, iii, 37.
131. See above, 301.
132. *Glas. Mun.*, ii, 52.
133. *Ibid.*, ii, 51.
134. GUA, MS 26614, 'Annales Collegii Facultatis Artium', 150; W. McMillan, *The Worship of the Scottish Reformed Church, 1550–1638* (London, 1931), 151ff; I. B. Cowan, 'The Five Articles of Perth', *Reformation and Revolution*, ed. D. Shaw (Edinburgh, 1967), 160–77.
135. *Glas. Mun.*, ii, 52–4.
136. Melville, *Diary*, 28.
137. Cant, *The University of St Andrews*, 57.
138. *Ibid.*
139. *BUK*, i, 215.
140. *Letters and Papers . . . of Henry VIII*, x, no. 605.
141. *Glas. Mun.*, iii, 521.
142. J. Finlayson, *Account of the Life and Works of Maister Peter Lowe* (Glasgow, 1889), 3ff.
143. *Glasgow Burgh Records*, i, 193.
144. Finlayson, *Maister Peter Lowe*, 20.
145. *Glas. Mun.*, iii, 379–80.
146. *Evidence*, iii, 184.
147. *Ibid.*, iii, 194.
148. *Ibid.*, iii, 198, 201.
149. *ER*, xix, 12, 45, 86, 116, 177, 202, 226, 301, 329, 373.

150. See above, 244.
151. *First Book of Discipline*, 143.
152. *Glasgow Burgh Records*, i, 183.
153. *Evidence*, iii, 184, 190.
154. Melville, *Diary*, 28–9.
155. *Evidence*, iii, 198.
156. *BUK*, i, 206.
157. *Ibid.*, i, 264.
158. *Essays on the Scottish Reformation*, 292.
159. See above, 266, 268.
160. SRO GD135/Box 121. Stair Muniments.
161. See Appendix J; *Glas. Mun.*, ii, 480.
162. Melville, *Diary*, 44.
163. *BUK*, i, 339.
164. *Ibid.*, i, 322.
165. *Evidence*, iii, 188.
166. Fuller, *Church History of Britain*, v, 182. See also *APS*, iii, 180.
167. Porteous MS, 73, 25 December 1599.
168. *Ibid.*, 4 November 1586.
169. GCA, MS Glasgow Presbytery Records, [28] May 1594; cf. Porteous MS, 38, 6 October 1590.
170. Porteous MS, 8, 11 October 1586.
171. Cant, 'The St Andrews University Theses, 1579–1747', ii, 143–7.
172. MS St Andrews Presbytery Records, e.g. 30 April, 7 May, 14 May, 28 May, 22 October 1590; 17 August, 8 September 1597; 26 May 1603.
173. GCA, MS Glasgow Presbytery Records, 19 June 1599.
174. Melville, *Diary*, 49, 55.
175. *Evidence*, iii, 183–4. Neither Cartwright nor Travers accepted the St Andrews invitation, and a visitation of 1588 disclosed that 'anent the teiching of the fyve maisteris, thair enterit nevir bot thrie; the uther twa sould have bene strangearis quha refusit to cum, and als na leiving was appointit to thame as was promissit; thrie quhilk enterit war thir, Mr Andro Melville, Mr Johnne Robertsoun, and Mr James Melvill.' *Ibid.*, 193.
176. *Ibid.*, 184; *BUK*, ii, 466.
177. *Ibid.*, ii, 466, 471.
178. Melville, *Diary*, 83, 244.
179. Fuller, *Church History of Britain*, v, 180–2.
180. Melville, *Diary*, 83; McCrie, *Melville*, 487.
181. Melville, *Diary*, 83–4; Watt, *Fasti*, 380.
182. Vatican Archives, Reg. Supp. 2930, ff. 9v–10r.
183. Melville *Diary*, 73–5; Spottiswoode, *History*, ii, 319–20.
184. Melville, *Diary*, 75.
185. *BUK*, i, 396.
186. Melville, *Diary*, 75; Spottiswoode, *History* ii, 320.
187. *Ibid.*, ii, 282.
188. *RPC*, iii, 474–6.
189. *BUK*, ii, 557–8, 560, 562, 565, 573–5; Porteous MS, 2, 25 June 1582; *RPC*, iii, 476–7.
190. Spottiswoode, *History*, ii, 287; *RPC*, iii, 490; *BUK*, ii, 579, 583–4; Spottiswoode, *History*, ii, 288.
191. Calderwood, *History*, iii, 655–6.
192. *BUK*, ii, 598–9, 604.

193. *BUK*, ii, 620.
194. *Glasgow Burgh Records*, i, 99.
195. *APS*, iii, 292–4, 303–4.
196. *Glasgow Burgh Records*, i, 108.
197. Calderwood, *History*, viii, 271–2.
198. *RPC*, iii, 662, 663.
199. Calderwood, *History*, iv, 71; *CSP Scot.*, vii, no. 119; G. Donaldson, 'Scottish Presbyterian Exiles in England, 1584–1588', *RSCHS*, xiv, 67–80, at 69.
200. Bibliothèque Publique et Universitaire Genève, MS Fr. 410, f. 26r–v; Staatsarchiv des Kantons Zurich, MS E. II. 382, ff. 1057r–1059v. One version is given in Calderwood, *History*, iv, 158–67.
201. *Glas. Mun.*, iii, 4–5.
202. SRO, E4/1, f. 3r. Exchequer Act Book, 22 July 1584, where Sharp is said to have been minister of the kirks of Paisley, Neilston and Kilbarchan since 1583. It is not clear whether he undertook teaching in the college concurrently with his ministry at Paisley. For Cunningham, GUA, Drawer F5 (unfoliated bundle). David, bishop of Aberdeen, to the principal and regents, 26 November 1586, endorsed 'the discharg of the bischoip of Abirdein'.
203. Watt, *Fasti*, 380.
204. Melville, *Diary*, 244.
205. *Glasgow Burgh Records*, i, 217–9; *RPC*, vi, 408–9, 452–4; see also Appendix J.
206. See Appendix J.
207. *Doctrinae Christianae brevis explicatio* (Edinburgh, 1599).
208. Calderwood, *History*, vi, 573.
209. GCA, MS Glasgow Presbytery Records, 25 March 1607; *RPC*, viii, 418, 775; x, 195–7; Wodrow, *Biographical Collections*, ii (pt. i), 116–17.
210. *Ibid.*, ii (pt. i), 156–62.
211. *Glas. Mun.*, i, 200–2, 206–11.
212. *Ibid.*, iii, 75.

16. The College Community

> 'And finally we commend over and over again to thee these adolescents
> in whose mind as a result of our labours and their industry thou hast
> deigned to arouse and enkindle with thy fan the tiny sparks of that
> divine light and ask you to favour them for the rest of time with the
> heavenly fire of thy spirit.'
>
> The Chancellor's blessing at graduation

IN ITSELF, the Reformation did nothing to impair the medieval purpose
of a university. The university remained as before an association of
scholars bound together in the pursuit and diffusion of learning. Within
this academic community, there were almost by definition two clearly
defined groups: first and foremost the teaching guild of masters, the
principal and four regents endowed with considerable authority in
college affairs; and secondly the general fraternity of students, who for
the most part lived and worked together in college for four years until
they, too, after graduation, were admitted to the incorporation of
masters but not necessarily to a share in the government of the faculty.
The separation of these two groups was a marked feature of the post-
Reformation statutes which not only decreed that students should be
obedient to their teachers but also prohibited them from keeping
familiar company with the masters. Magisterial authority was firmly
asserted and faithfully enforced. There was no tendency other than
mere participation in rectorial elections for power to rest with the
student community, as had once been the case at Bologna.

As a corporate association of students and masters pursuing common
interests, the university formed a distinctive, elitist and competitive
society with its own special privileges and immunities, its own members
and officers sworn to secrecy, its own magistrates, its rules and regulations, its own government and its distinctive academic dress and ceremonial. It had all the attributes of the medieval guild and more. It
constituted an academic republic, a *literaria civitas* separated from the
rest of society. It was physically enclosed from the outside world by the
college gate and walls, its two quadrangles, the inner and outer court-
yards, from whose precincts no student could leave without special
permission. Nor was this all. The gulf between the world of learning and
the outside world was deepened by a linguistic barrier. Latin alone could
be spoken in college.[1] The Reformation might be regarded as the series
of events which broke the largely illusory unity of Christendom but

Latin remained, and continued to be recognised, as the language of the educated world. The majority of works in theology and philosophy, in the sciences as well as the humanities, and in medicine as in law continued to be written in Latin, or at least in a language other than Scots or English. Proficiency in Latin, then, was an essential passport for the scholar at home or abroad. Preaching alone was undertaken in the vernacular, and when the Melvilles took to preaching in English before a wider audience the king tried to render any subversive utterances innocuous to the ordinary people by insisting that they preach only in Latin.[2]

The independent legal status which the university enjoyed also contributed to a sense of separate identity, but here qualifications must be made. The university, for one thing, was still financed in part from ecclesiastical resources granted to it by the crown, and it remained subject to external control from both church and crown. The general assembly exercised a vigilant supervision of both schools and colleges. From the 1560s, it asserted a right to restrict appointments in universities and schools to candidates found 'sound and abill in doctrine' by superintendents or visitors of the kirk.[3] It authorised visitations of the university colleges by appointing commissioners, sometimes on its own initiative, sometimes jointly with commissioners chosen by parliament or privy council.[4] It saw fit to voice its opinion on whether the king could translate Melville from Glasgow to St Andrews, and it had no hesitation in proposing to translate Arbuthnot from the principalship of King's College, Aberdeen to the ministry of St Andrews, which drew from the king the retort that the matter was not 'so proper to the Kirk or so improper to the civill estate' that his own views could be lightly disregarded.[5] Yet it was only if 'he be commandit be the Generall Assemblie', that Charles Ferme agreed to accept the principalship of the proposed college of Fraserburgh.[6] On more detailed issues, the assembly intervened in 1582 to complain of the treatment of the Glasgow masters and students in the Montgomery affair; it issued directions for teaching Aristotle in the universities; and by 1593 it had decided that no disposition of college rents could be made 'without the advyse and consent of the Assemblie Generall under the pane of depositioun'.[7] There could be no doubting the assembly's attitude to the universities. It regarded them as extensions of the church, and it looked rather as if it intended to integrate them more fully into the ecclesiastical structure.

Such solicitude, however, did not preclude royal intervention. Nor could the crown afford to abrogate its responsibilities. The government enquired into the state of the universities, ordered visitations, settled disputes, had sometimes a say in appointing personnel and where necessary granted additional endowment.[8] Even so, none of this really compensated for what amounted to ecclesiastical control of the univer-sities. Nowhere is this more clearly illustrated than in the choice of university personnel. The chancellor, the dean of faculty and the rector were all ecclesiastics whose prime allegiance lay with the church.[9] The principal was not only the theology professor but also minister of Govan. It is often said that Melville never served as minister, but two of his successors, Patrick Sharp and Robert Boyd, are explicitly styled as ministers of Govan,[10] and it is more than a guess that Melville also served in that capacity. Even the college regents were regarded as occupying the teaching office of doctor within the church[11] and so were eligible to sit on ecclesiastical courts. Whether Melville served as elder on the kirk session, as he later did at St Andrews,[12] cannot now be established, but there can be no dubiety about his successor, Thomas Smeaton, who was currently elder in 1583 when the surviving records start, as were the regents in the college, Blaise Lawrie, Patrick Melville and Patrick Sharp.[13] Despite frequent changes in the teaching staff, Sharp and Lawrie continued to be re-elected elders of the session.[14] They also sat on the presbytery at least until the king's general prohibi-tion of non-ministerial members in 1597.[15] Patrick Sharp, who was himself a minister, was sometimes chosen as commissioner to the general assembly.[16] All this served to increase rather than lessen what looked like the church's monopoly of the universities.

Normally, the regents were recent graduates whose ultimate intention was to pursue a career in the ministry. Of the Glasgow regents, Blaise Lawrie alone stayed on as regent in Glasgow to make university teaching his career. The remainder all but invariably proceeded to the parish ministry. After more than eight years as regent, Peter Blackburn chose to enter the ministry at Aberdeen in 1582 and James Melville later became minister of Anstruther Wester in 1586.[17] But whereas the earlier regents under Andrew Melville had all been St Andrews men, increasingly reliance was placed on Glasgow's own more promising graduates. John Bell who was promoted to the third place in the graduation lists of 1581 stayed on as regent; there was even talk in 1591 that he should become a minister in Glasgow but he proceeded instead to the ministry of Kilbarchan.[18] The same sort of picture was true of John Millar, first among the graduates of 1586 who, after a spell of college teaching, was appointed minister of Logie Wallach near Stirling in 1592.[19]

On the other hand, John Forbes who acted as regent after coming third in the graduation of 1587[20] does not appear to have followed an ecclesiastical career, at least in Scotland. Normal practice was resumed with John Gibson who won first place in 1589, was then regent and subsequently minister at Eastwood in 1599.[21] Similarly, after graduating first in 1590, Archibald Glen was appointed regent of the first class in 1592 before being presented by the commendator of Paisley to Rutherglen parish church in 1596.[22] It is harder, however, to identify the later career of William Dunlop who served as regent on graduating first place in 1593.[23] The principal's son, David Sharp, won second place in 1596 and so taught as regent before his election as minister of Bothwell in 1606.[24] John Cameron, however, who was first in 1599 taught for only a year, and his appointment as principal of the college in 1622, after a remarkable ecclesiastical career in France, was of equally short duration.[25] His successor as regent in 1600 was Archibald Hamilton who gained fifth place in 1599 and later became minister of Paisley in 1610.[26] This same pattern continued to be observed in subsequent appointments. Nor was there difficulty in obtaining suitable recruits.

Open competition and selection by disputation seems to have been a recognised principle if not always a recognised practice. By an act of privy council in 1602, a teaching post in the college was to be filled, after fifteen days' notice, by 'the competitour that previs worthiest be tryall to be preferrit to the vacand place'.[27] Yet when John Livingston sought appointment to a vacancy in the college, after coming first in the graduation lists in 1621, he 'studied hard and prepared to disput for the regent's place but when the time came, I heard that one without any dispute was placed', and so he proceeded to the ministry instead.[28] The new foundation in 1577 had placed the election of regents with the rector, dean of faculty and principal who were charged to 'provide for the college the best and most learned preceptors they can find'.[29] This, however, did not prevent the king from exercising a right to nominate a regent to the college in at least one instance in 1586 when the presentation was directed to the rector, dean of faculty, principal and 'utheris haifand voit in the election of ane regent in the samin'.[30] Explicit mention of the archbishop as chancellor was tacitly omitted. By 1602, however, the electorate was widened to include the chancellor of Scotland, the archbishop of Glasgow, the rector, dean of faculty, the principal and regents, and the ministers of Glasgow, Cadder, Hamilton, Monkland and Renfrew, or any eleven of them convened in chapter.[31] In practice, the views of the principal and regents counted for much. They were certainly decisive in the appointment in 1615 of Robert Blair who got the job despite 'opposition from Archbishop Law who had promised the place to another', but in this instance the principal and regents 'would not give way to his motion'.[32]

The nature of the regent's employment was vocational rather than remunerative. His stipend, if viable, was still considerably lower than that which a beneficed parish minister with manse and glebe, might hope to earn. Benefices, of course, varied enormously in value from one district to another. Nor were all ministers financed from such a source. Although on entering the ministry many of the regents acquired a slender stipend well below the average, they were as a rule still marginally, sometimes substantially, better-off than they had been as regents. The *nova erectio* had assigned £50 to the senior regent and 50 merks (£33 6s 8d) apiece to the remaining regents,[33] and while some subsequent augmentation of stipends did take place,[34] salaries still remained low. After leaving the college, John Bell, as minister of the Tron church in 1595, could claim £200 in stipend paid by the town. John Millar's stipend in the rural parish of Logie near Stirling in 1595 was £138 13s 4d plus 5⅓ bolls of wheat, though John Gibson was earning a meagre £80 in 1599 as minister at Eastwood. This stood in sharp contrast to the wealthy neighbouring benefices of Renfrew with a stipend of 1,090 merks and Paisley with 800 merks.[35] Within the college, it was not until 1602 that a review of regents' salaries fixed the first or senior regent's fee at £80 and that of the other three at 100 merks (£66 13s 4d) each with a supplement of four merks for 'every toun bairne and aucht merkis of utheris duelland to landwart'.[36]

By annexing to the college the benefice of Govan, however, the *nova erectio* did at least guarantee the regents a stipend assigned from an independent source, so reducing their financial dependence on income derived from student fees. At the same time, while promoting a greater measure of stability than had hitherto been the case, endowment of this sort did little to foster the idea of university teaching as a permanent career. Prevailing attitudes still tended to regard tenure of the regent's office as temporary, usually as a stepping-stone to the ministry. This was particularly so in the case of men who were too young to become ministers. A bright young graduate of eighteen or nineteen destined for the ministry might well find it attractive to teach in college for six or seven years until he reached the age at which he was eligible to enter the ministry. Unless they were exceptionally gifted, candidates were not normally accepted for the ministry until they were twenty-five.[37] This, at any rate was the theory; and congregations, ever ready to indulge in fraternal correction, were liable to find fault with the excessive youth of prospective ministers.[38] For the university, however, recruitment of its own best graduates meant that the regents were often young, possibly energetic and enthusiastic, but also inexperienced and unskilled in the art of teaching.

Other considerations, not least the prospect of marriage, might induce a young regent to settle down in alternative employment. At a visitation of St Andrews in 1574 it was decided that 'the wyffis, bairnis and servandis of the principallis and utheris maisteris in the universitie be put apart in the cietie out of the collegis sua that wemen, to a slanderus and evill exempill, haif not residence amangis the young men studentis'.[39] But 'quhat ordour salbe tane with maisteris of colleges quha heirefter sall marie ane wyf' was a related question on which there was continuing discussion, and one entry, before deletion, even asked whether a married regent 'salbe removit fra his office furth of the college'.[40] Not until the conservative Arran administration was the issue determined, though not necessarily observed, with the privy council's ruling in 1584 that no married regents should remain in college.[41]

In Glasgow, earlier university statutes had reluctantly permitted regents to marry insisting that they live in college whilst barring their wives from the college precincts. Andrew Melville never married and strongly discouraged his nephew from re-marrying, but Melville's successor, Thomas Smeaton, as a Jesuit in Paris, had taken the advice of his superior to return home and find a wife. Patrick Sharp also married.[42] This presented little difficulty for the principal who had a house of his own attached to the college, but the problem of accommodating the wives and families of young married regents on lower stipends could be acute. Blaise Lawrie did, however, brave the obstacles. He had his wife, Isobell Ross, installed in the bellhouse of the adjacent Blackfriars church, whilst retaining his own rooms in college, rooms recently modernised, apparently at his own expense, for which the university at his death had still to reimburse him, and consisting of a chamber and study where he kept his 'haill librarie and buikis' valued at £150.[43]

Although Lawrie was entitled to the same increase in stipend which 'wes allowit to Mr James Melvill at his departure out of the said college', it was not long before he found a supplementary source of income. The Lawries apparently rented spare rooms in their bellhouse to students anxious to find accommodation in an overcrowded college. This would seem to be the inference from the entries in Lawrie's testament where amongst the debts owing him were £50 'be the lady Glengarnik for Thomas Cunynghame hir sonnes buirde', £90 'be the laird of Innerweik for the buird and scole wage of his sone Claud Hammiltoun' and £29 'be my lord Glencairne for his sonnes buirding'. Only the sons of nobles or lairds seem to have been accommodated in the Lawrie household. There is no evidence, however, that the principal took in boarders. At his death on 19 August 1599 Lawrie left an estate of over £2,000 whereas Patrick Sharp, as principal, who died somewhat later in May 1615 left net assets of only £1,362.[44]

Another factor contributing to the mobility of university teachers may well have been the repetitious and wearisome nature of the job. The regents were in more or less constant supervision of their students each day from 5 a.m. until after supper.[45] There was seemingly little respite or relaxation. But none of this prevented James Melville from accompanying Thomas Smeaton when he went off to Edinburgh to 'fetche ham his wyff'. His students, however, were not entirely left to their own devices: 'befor my going I tuk exact ordour with my schollars, injoyning large task to tham and apointing of censurers and deleattors of all ther behaviour'.[46] College life no doubt suited the dedicated like Andrew Melville who after teaching each day and twice on the Sabbath had still energy to hold 'an ordinar conference with sic as war present efter denner and supper';[47] but for others the regime could be monotonous if not oppressive. Five years of teaching philosophy were enough for James Melville who was 'glad to be frie from the daylie labor of regenting in philosophie', and after teaching for a year John Cameron, by 1600, 'resolved to travell that he might the more perfect himself in litterature'.[48] Somewhat later, Robert Blair, though a regent in Arts, found theology more absorbing:[49]

> Being entered to this charge, my elder colleagues, perceiving that I had some considerable insight in Humanity, urged me to peruse all classical authors; and I, hearkening to the motion, began to peruse the most ancient fragments, and read over all Plautus. But the Lord being displeased with this design, diverted me thus: Having the charge of the library, I fell upon the ancients who are called fathers, especially Augustine, who had another relish with me, and who, in his Confessions, inveighs sharply against the education of the youth in heathen writings. I therefore betook me to the reading of the Holy Scriptures and the ancient fathers, who breathed out much piety; yet even then I perceived our reformed divines much purer according to the Scriptures; yet I resolved to peruse these ancient monuments, beginning at the eldest, wherein I made considerable progress in the hours I could spare from my charge.

After eight years so employed 'being now wearied of teaching philosophy and considering in how dangerous company I was', the presbyterian Robert Blair 'demitted my place in the college to the great grief of my fellow-regents, the students and good people of Glasgow' and left for Ireland to become minister at Bangor at the invitation of James Hamilton, the Glasgow graduate and fellow of Trinity College, who as lord Clandeboye had become an Ulster planter, and patron of the church at Bangor.[50] Blair's predecessor as minister at Bangor was another Scot, John Gibson, who had been appointed dean of Down and Connor in 1609,[51] and it may emerge that this is the same John Gibson as the Glasgow regent who disappears from record as minister of Eastwood by 1606.

Although the social background of a number of the regents cannot

readily be identified, the underlying pattern is clear; they were of intermediate status. As in the ministry, recruits were sometimes the younger
sons of lairds or lesser gentry. This was so in the case of the Melvilles
and possibly of William Glen who is said to have belonged to the Glens
of Bar, and of Patrick Sharp who was associated with the Sharps of
Houstoun.[52] Thomas Smeaton seems to have come from a tenant
farming background in Gask, whereas Peter Blackburn came of solid
burgess stock.[53] Robert Blair's family, on the other hand, had ties both
with the land and with commerce; he is described by his son-in-law as
having been born in Irvine in 1593, the sixth son of John Blair 'a
gentleman living in the town of Irvine, son to Alexander Blair, the
good-man of Windyedge who was brother-german to the Laird of Blair'.
His mother, 'Bessie Muir, out of the ancient and honourable family of
Rowallan', was widowed when he was six, but Blair nonetheless
profited from his 'bairnly studies' and so was 'fitted to go to the college
of Glasgow where I appeared to be inferior to none of my fellow-
students', gaining first place in the graduation lists of 1614.[54] Two of his
elder brothers became provosts of Irvine and a third was regent in the
college and minister of Dumbarton.[55] Another regent, David Sharp was,
of course, the principal's son, but John Cameron's origins may have
been humbler than some. He was born in Glasgow about 1580 and
according to his French classmate Guillaume Rivet, he obtained a
bursary of '25 mercarum annua pensione pauperum aliquot civium
filiis destinata', though a later tradition suggests that he was the son of
the minister of Dunoon.[56]

By far the more populous element in the academic community was,
of course, the student body about which little evidence has survived
other than the list of unidentified names in the matriculation and graduation rolls beginning in 1591 and 1578 respectively.[57] Much has been said
of the democratic tradition in Scottish education. Both before and after
the Reformation, the sixteenth-century experience in grammar school
education in the burghs was not an unworthy one. The universities were
plainly dependent on the supply of Latin scholars from the grammar
schools, and in the early seventeenth century the grammar school in
Glasgow was accredited with having 'above three hundred children'.[58]
But the universities, like the schools, were fee-paying institutions.
Whilst recognising that 'the children of the poore must be supported
and sustained of the charge of the kirk', the protestant reformers in 1560
had insisted that the sons of the 'rich and potent' should be educated at
'their own expenses because they are able'.[59] Not only so, they included
among the university entrance qualifications an attestation of the
parents' ability to sustain their sons at university 'and not to burden the
commonwealth with them'.[60]

Education was an expensive business even for the better-off. One Scottish student pursuing his studies abroad wrote home from Montpellier in 1620 complaining of the 'hudge expences' of living in France, which was making him short of money, and asking for more funds since 'in this countrie the nam of a stranger is able to mak him pay ten schillingis quhair a Frenchman wald have payed bot one'.[61] Although his father later commanded him to return home, he succeeded in gaining permission to remain for a further spell to complete his studies.[62] When David Graham left to study in Paris in 1571 he kept a careful account of the expenditure incurred in travelling, his board on ship, the hiring of a horse, the cost of clothes, meals, wine and candles, 'thre buikkis in french and llatin', 'ane belt to my rapper', 'ane buik namit de corrupti sermonis emendatione in frenche and llatin', and a host of other necessary expenses.[63]

For those who remained at home, university education could still be costly. From matriculation to graduation the student was confronted by a series of expenses: the cost of board either in college or in alternative lodgings in the burgh; lecture fees to the regents, perhaps tuition fees for private exercises and honoraria payable to the regents before examinations; the cost of academic dress, the purchase of text-books and note-books, and finally graduation expenses including the banqueting and feasting traditionally associated with graduation ceremonies. All this could prove prohibitive for the less well-off, but the universities were conscious of their social obligations. Charges were levied according to a student's social standing and, for those who could plead real poverty, the payment of fees was waived altogether.[64]

To be exempt from fees was certainly an incentive, but the poor scholar had still to find the wherewithal to live for four academic years if he wished to complete the course and take his M.A. Some poor students managed to find a place as servants in the college and so combined their studies with menial work of that nature. Andrew Melville deliberately 'schosed for his servantes onlie schollars, and giff they haid done anie guid at thair book, he cared nocht what they did to him'.[65] The practice of students acting as servants to the regents was also customary at St Andrews where William Collace 'haid a lytle boy that servit him in his chamber called David Elistone wha amangs threttie-and-sax schollars in number (sa manie war we in the class) was the best'.[66] Poverty was not always a barrier to ability, but it was no great advantage either. That some students had a lean time of it and were sometimes reduced to begging is attested in the act of parliament in 1574, repeated in 1579, which called for the punishment of 'all vagaboundis scollaris of the universiteis of Sanctandrois, Glasgow and Abirdene not licencit be the rector and dene of facultie of the universitie to ask almous'.[67] This suggests that the university authorities were empowered to licence genuinely poor students to earn a living by begging.

For the more fortunate, financial hardship could be mitigated by the acquisition of a bursary. This could be done in a number of ways. Some bursaries were founded by the crown, others through the generosity of individual benefactors. These might be foundation bursaries or simply bequests or mortifications. Alternatively, a patron might present a student to a provostry, prebend, chaplainry or altarage to sustain him at the schools.

Since 'provisoune for the pouir bursouris' was said to have ceased, Queen Mary in her grant of 1563 had endowed places for 'five pouir childrene bursouris' within the college and a decade later the town council's charter had made allowance for twelve poor scholars. Yet when effective endowment came with the *nova erectio* of 1577 only four poor students were allocated places as foundationers.[68] Machinery for the disposition of provostries, prebends, chaplainries and altarages to students came with an act of parliament in 1567 which recognised that 'the poverte of mony is in sic sort that thay may not hauld thair children at letteris'. Patrons were therefore required to present 'ane bursar quhome thay pleis to name to studie vertew and letteris within ane college of ony of the universiteis of this realme thair to remaine for sic space as the patroun foirsaid plesis to hauld him at vertew and leirning'.[69] Clearly, the enactment was intended to be compulsory rather than permissive. The Convention of Leith, however, in 1572 endorsed this method of financing students.[70] Much of course depended on the attitude of the patron. There was sometimes a tendency to keep benefices within the family and to utilise them in the interests of educating kinsmen.[71] The better-off, or less poverty-stricken, looked like profiting at the expense of poorer students.

Of the students who were elected to foundation bursaries within the college, little evidence has survived. But one instance occurred in April 1593. Since the 'presentatioun of the ane half of the bursaris places within the university or college of Glasgew pertenis to his majestie', John Lindsay, son of the minister at Lanark, was presented to a bursar's place for four years on the next vacancy either 'be deceis, removing or finisching of the cours of ony of the said present bursairis'. Lindsay was accredited with having 'alredy leirnit his grammar and is hable and meit to enter to the said college for attening to further knawlege and lettres that thairby threw the providence of God he may be sum instrument proffitable in the kirk or commonwealth'. The principal and regents were therefore charged to examine his qualifications and on finding him fit 'to authorize him with thair testimoniall of admissioun'.[72]

The town council also exercised a right to present bursars. In 1613, it nominated two students, one of whom was the son of the minister at Greenock. Some subsequent council presentations are on record in 1623, 1625 and 1626.[73] Nor was it always the burgess élite who succeeded in having their sons promoted to bursaries. In one case, the son of a webster or weaver won a bursar's place vacant 'be maister William Spang, laitlie laureat thairin, to indure for the space of thrie yeiris, in respect he has bein ane yeir alreddie trainet up thairintill'.[74] Both father and son evidently prized the opportunities afforded by a university education. It offered a ready means of social mobility enabling men to rise in the world, and although in this case no bursary was available in his first year, the family were still prepared to send their son to college without the initial benefit of financial support from this source.

To support a bursar in philosophy presented by the grantor and his heirs, Thomas Crawford of Jordanhill in 1576 granted sixteen bolls of oatmeal from the mill of Partick.[75] Rather later in 1613, John Howieson, the minister of Cambuslang, bequeathed 1,000 merks 'for the help and supplie of the intertenyment of ane bursor' presented by the deacons and visitors of the Glasgow crafts. Significantly enough, tenure was to be restricted to the sons of Glasgow craftsmen.[76] A similar grant to the Edinburgh college, though on a smaller scale, was made in 1611 by the widow of an Edinburgh merchant burgess who provided the annual rent of two hundred merks for two bursars to be presented by the deacon and quartermasters of the Edinburgh tailor craft.[77] These bequests not only display a certain burghal pride in the colleges, they also hint at the increasing prominence and assertiveness of the crafts-men in burgh politics after the conflicts of the sixteenth century between the merchants and craftsmen. What is more, the bequests underline the genuine aspirations of a number of craftsmen's sons to pursue their studies beyond the grammar school. By fostering their colleges, burgesses were looking for tangible benefits. The colleges were as much for themselves as for outsiders. Outsiders, however, could still feel gratitude. Michael Wilson of Eastbourne in Sussex, a graduate of 1585 who for his support had obtained a chaplainry from the town in 1582, donated £500 sterling to the university in 1617 'to be imployed con-tinuallie from tyme to tyme to the redifying of the decaied parts and places of the sayd universitie and to the educatione in meat drink apparell and guid letters of all such of my kinred as shall stand in neid of such educatione and in default . . . all such burgesses sonnes of the sayd citie whose parentis ar not able' to support them.[78] In the earlier seventeenth century, further bursaries, specifically for divinity students, were instituted first by William Struthers, minister at Edinburgh, and a Glasgow graduate of 1599, who in 1633 mortified to the colleges of Glasgow and Edinburgh an equal share of 6,000 merks, a portion of which was assigned for the maintenance of two divinity students in each of the two colleges for four years; and secondly by Zachary Boyd, who had studied at Glasgow, St Andrews and Saumur before becoming minister of the Barony church in Glasgow and dean of faculty and rector of the university, and who endowed the college with three bursaries for theology students.[79] The gradual accumulation of these bursaries did much to obviate the stigma of poverty for some.

The utilisation of smaller benefices without the cure of souls in the interests of students had also a contribution to make. In accordance with the act of 1567, the crown and other patrons made presentations in favour of grammar school scholars and university students. The university's own chaplainry of St Michael was made available for the support of bursars in October 1569 when Andrew Hay as rector granted the chaplainry to John Davidson, the principal, 'in name and behalf of the universite and college . . . for the sustentatioune of bursaris', the patronage lying with the rector.[80] Further provision was made in 1571 for annexing to the college the vicarage pensionary of Glasgow 'for sustening of ane student or studentis thairin according to the ordour to be tane thairanent be the rectour and maisteris of the said college'.[81]

The criteria for the distribution of these benefices and the terms of the grants varied considerably. On the death of Mr David Gibson, the pre-Reformation parson of Ayr, who also possessed a prebend in the collegiate kirk of Lincluden, the crown immediately chose to keep the grant within the family by disponing the prebend in November 1569 to David Gibson, brother of Mr Henry Gibson in Glasgow 'for his sustentatioun at the scholis within the universitie of Glasgw quhair he presentlie studiis for the space of sevin yeris nixtocum, providing that in the menetyme he continew his study in the said universitie . . . quhilk tyme being expyrit or the said David desisting of his study in the menetyme the said prebendarie to be gevin to ony uther student that the supreme power findis maist indigent'.[82] Nor was this all. Lincluden continued to finance the education of Gibsons in Glasgow. Archibald Gibson obtained a prebend of Lincluden in 1570 and demitted it in favour of his brother David in 1577.[83] Not only so, by 1584 Hugh Gibson, son of Mr Henry Gibson, the commissary clerk of Glasgow, received a gift of a prebend of Lincluden for his support for seven years 'at the sculis within the citie of Glasgow quhair he presentlie studeis' by demission and resignation of his brother David.[84] This must have been for his support at the grammar school because in 1591 David Gibson, son of the commissary clerk, as a student once more received the gift of a prebend of Lincluden.[85] David is known to have matriculated in the university in 1593, graduating in 1596, whilst Hugh's matriculation is recorded in 1591 and his graduation in 1594.[86] All in all, the commissary clerk's family benefited substantially from the prebends of Lincluden and they established a record which it would be hard to rival.

A benefice was frequently granted for seven years, rather than for the minimum four years of study in Arts, perhaps to allow the bursar to undertake some post-graduate theological training. Archibald Herbertson, a student at the university, thus received the vicarage of Maybole, a prebend of the New College, in December 1569 for seven years.[87] On expiry, the vicarage in 1578 was then bestowed for a further seven years on Duncan Nairn, son of Duncan Nairn in Bannockburn, who was 'of convenient aigis to entir in the studie of philosophie and apt and disposeit thairfoir sa alsua hes promist to be subject to discipline and continue thairin'. The principal and regents were charged to receive the presentee 'and at the end thairof incaice of his not continuance in his studie to report the same to his hienes that ane uther may be of new nominat to the said prebendarie'.[88] The injunction in this case proved not to be necessary, for Duncan Nairn graduated first place in 1580 to become regent under Robert Rollock in the recently founded Edinburgh college.[89] With his premature death, the vicarage in March 1586 passed to Robert Herbertson, 'student in the scholis of Glesgow', possibly the graduate of 1596, who obtained the benefice for life 'for his better intertenyng at the scuilis and doing of utheris his effairis', and the whole 'prebendarie of the halie trinitie foundit off auld within the new kirk of Glesgow', which Nairn had also held, was bestowed in April 1586 upon Andrew Ross, 'student in the universall schoile of Glesgow', and son of Thomas Ross, a Glasgow burgess, who had also received a presentation to the vicarage of Maybole in February 1586.[90] The vicarage of Strathaven was yet another benefice which was allocated to a bursar with its disposition in 1571 to John Hay 'for his sustentation at the scoles within the universitie of Glasgow quhair he presentlie studies for the space of sevin yeris nixtocum'.[91]

It was by no means uncommon for a student to receive a benefice for life rather than for a term. In 1581, Dougal Campbell, the son of Donald Campbell of Auchmuling, obtained from the king the gift of the chaplainry of Christ's Well in the diocese of Glasgow for his support 'at the sculis during his life', and David Sharp, the principal's son, who graduated in 1596, acquired a gift for life of the vicarage of Maybole in 1591 'ffor his intertenement at the scules and doing of utheris his effairis'.[92] Support could also be forthcoming from sources other than benefices. In 1587, the king granted to Patrick Anderson, son of John Anderson, a Glasgow burgess, the common lands of Dunkeld for his support for seven years at the schools, and the recipient is presumably to be identified with the student of that name who matriculated in the university in 1593.[93] The Exchequer records from 1588 also disclose payments made to students and bursars in the college from the burgh fermes of Rutherglen, and in Glasgow the town council made available to students prebends in its patronage.[94]

To be distinguished from such students, sometimes loosely termed bursars, were the college bursars who, so far as is known, were likely to be recruited from the sons of burgesses and ministers in the Glasgow area. One instance of a highland student being presented to a college bursary in October 1591 was possibly exceptional. On being 'informit of the qualificatioun, literature and habilitie of Donald McOlvorie and of his eirnest affectioun to be ane proffitabill member in the kirk of God for instructioun of utheris in the pairtis of the Ilis and hielandis', the king presented him to a bursar's place in the college 'with all aliment, leveray and intertenement dew thairto during the ordinare tymes thairof'. MacGilvray, who had already matriculated in the university in January 1591, was described as 'the first and maist leirnit student of the said college abill now for the said roume and place'. This was indeed a warm encomium for a student coming from an area less equipped with educational resources than most parts of the lowlands. He had even sustained himself at university for at least a year, possibly two years, before receiving the bursary. His schooling, however, was likely to have taken place not in the highlands but rather in Glasgow grammar school which probably accepted Gaelic-speaking highlanders in the same way as it received a number of 'Irishmen scholars', causing the university in 1595, on the presbytery's directions, to examine their beliefs in the 'heads of religion'.[95] Coming from an area where John Carswell, as superintendent of Argyll and bishop of the Isles, had pioneered his *Foirm na n-Urrnuidheadh* as a Gaelic adaptation of the Book of Common Order,[96] MacGilvray would be literate in Gaelic, Scots and Latin, and for his future career he chose to enter the ministry, seeking licence from the presbytery of Glasgow to be admitted not indeed to a highland parish but initially to the Barony church of Glasgow in 1594. Almost immediately, however, he left for Rothesay and then Glenaray.[97]

One of the most persistent criticisms of bursaries was that they were often assigned to the wrong people and that the really deserving were sometimes deprived of a place. In St Andrews university, it was resolved in 1576 that 'the principallis of ilk college sall sweir and gif thair bodelie aithe that thai sall ressave nay bursaris bot sik as thai ondirstand and knaw to be pure and to be worthie of the benefite belangand to the pure and that thai sall do diligence to knaw the samyn befoir thai ressave only sik within thair collegis'.[98] Even so, it was nonetheless claimed in 1578 and again in 1579 that university foundations 'alsweill in rentis as provisionis of maisteris and burserris' were sometimes 'misusit be particular personis to thair awin advantage'.[99] Not only so, the act establishing the new foundation of the St Andrews colleges in 1579 proceeded to speak bluntly of how 'thair hes been and is greit corruptioun and abuse in ressaving of the bursaris in everie facultie rather upon favor and sollisitatioun than for vertew or in support of povirtie'.[100] A visitation in 1588 showed that St Salvator's college had failed to examine the qualifications of its bursars at their admission, as required by act of parliament.[101] In the case of Glasgow university, the visitors appointed in 1613 were ominously charged 'to try gif the poore be receaved burseris and not sick by brybrie placed as have meanes of thair awne'.[102] Without vigilant supervision the system was no doubt open to abuse. James Melville, whose family was hardly poverty-stricken, was certainly promised 'the benefeit of a bursare's place' at St Andrews, but since he lived in lodgings in the town and not in college, his expectation of a bursary may well have been disappointed.[103] If so, this may be a vindication rather than a criticism of the system.

A further source of finance sometimes allocated by the crown to bursars and students 'to help and hald thame at the scuillis' were the revenues from the thirds of benefices which had been utilised since 1562 in the interests of the crown and reformed ministry.[104] As well as a number of grammar-school scholars who were sustained by grants from the thirds, the recipients were frequently St Andrews students. Some were even post-graduate students in theology and law.[105] But several Glasgow students can also be detected. It might not be readily apparent that Thomas Nicholson, son of James Nicholson, writer and clerk of the collectory, who received 'the third of the Trinitie freris of Abirdene togidder with the few maillis of the landis of Drumgranis' was a student in the Glasgow college were it not for the scribe's gratuitous entry in 1583, in one solitary instance among many, where he is styled 'student in the universitie of Glasgw'.[106] In the other entries of what was a lengthy tenure of the thirds which stretched back at least to 1573 and which continued until as late as 1595 (when the records end),[107] Nicholson's status or activities, other than that he was a 'student' are not revealed. But he is undoubtedly the Glasgow graduate of 1585.[108] His brother, John, who studied law after graduating from St Andrews, was also in receipt of a grant from the thirds.[109] James Duncanson, a son of the manse, who graduated with Thomas Nicholson in 1585 was financed from the revenues of a prebend of the chapel royal and continued so to be in 1586 even after his graduation;[110] and although he is described as 'master' in the accounts of thirds for 1581, it looks rather as if the John Hay, who, as a student in Glasgow, received the prebend of Lammelethame, was the graduate recorded in the rolls of 1582.[111]

The thirds from eight prebends and chaplainries in the city were also assigned to the university for the support of students.[112] All this went some way towards offsetting the considerable expenses incurred by students in the course of receiving a university education.

The living conditions of bursars and other boarders in college are harder to assess. In an inventory of 1582, the number of 'studentis studeis' was placed at 'xxv or thairby'. As well as these, there were rooms or chambers assigned to individual students. Accommodation, however, was at a premium. 'In the haill college', there was said to be 'xxvj timmer bedis by the portaris in his ludgin'.[113] There was even talk in 1582 of moving the college from its location in the High street beside the Black-friars church to the site once occupied by the vicars choral near the cathedral.[114]

The foundation bursars ate with the other boarders and masters, though not necessarily at the common table, in the college hall which also contained a pulpit[115] from which grace may have been said at meals and a chapter of the Bible read. This seems to have been custo-mary in St Mary's college, St Andrews, where the 'burdouris exponis the cheptour and giffis notes at denner and supper ilk day, thair day about'.[116] The fare, if wholesome, was somewhat monotonous. For breakfast, the principal and masters, by an act of 1602, were entitled to receive wheaten bread in soup 'with the remanis of a peice [of] beif or muttoun resting of the former day' and a pint of ale. At the midday meal and again at supper, they were to be served 'ordinarlie quhyt breid aneuch, with fyve choppins of sufficient guid and better nor the commoun sell aill in the toun, with ane dische of bruise and ane uther of skink or kaill, a peice of sodden muttoun, another of beif, salt or fresche, according to the seasoun, ane roist of veill or muttoun with a foull or cunyng or a pair of dowis or chikkins or uther siclyke secund rost, as the seasoun gevis'.

After the Reformation the observance of fasts, rather than feasts, was a religious tradition for which there were strong economic arguments, particularly so during Lent when the eating of flesh was normally forbidden. This regulated eating habits; and in college on fish days breakfast was to consist of eggs with bread and drink. On offer for the midday meal and supper were kail, eggs and fish. The bursars who also ate in college enjoyed a less nutritious diet. On so-called flesh days, they were to receive an oaten loaf in soup for breakfast and at other meals, oat bread, kail or brose, 'ane peice of beif' and some ale, but on fish days breakfast was reduced to bread and drink supplemented at other meal times with kail, eggs and fish.[117] The menu for fee-paying boarders was not prescribed.

By 1608, however, the college had resorted to hiring an outside contractor to provide the catering 'in all things requisite for honest buirdouris'. He was to provide a 'skillit cuik' and attend to the fire in the hall at midday and evening. The fare remained much as before. On flesh days, from Sunday to Thursday, the masters and 'utheris that payis as they pay' were to be served at breakfast, held at 9 a.m., with 'ane soupe of fyne quheit breid or ane portioun of cauld meit as best may be had with sum dry breid and drink'. At twelve o'clock after the table had been covered and set, the meal took the form of 'broois skink sodden beif and muttoun the best in the mercat, roistit muttoun or veill as the commoditie of the sessoun of the yeir sall serve, with ane foull or the equivalent thairof, with gud quheit breid the best in the mercat without scairstie, and gud staill aill aucht or ten dayis auld'. The same could again be expected at supper. For the bursars, the contractor was to provide 'ane soup of ait breid and ane drink' at breakfast, followed by 'broois with ane tailye of fresch beif with suffi-cient breid and aill to drink' at midday and supper. On 'fish' days, some meat was evidently permissible. Masters and fee-paying students were to receive 'everie ane in the morning ane callour fresch eg with sum cauld meit or milk and breid and sum dry breid and drink'. This was followed at noon and at supper by 'kaill and eggis, herring and thrie course of fische give thai may be had or the equivalent thairof in breid and milk fryouris with dry breid as of befoir'. On fish days, the bursars had to content themselves with bread and drink, an egg at breakfast, eggs, herring 'and ane uthir course' at noon and supper.[118]

If judged by the yardstick of the college accounts, a more varied fare is discernible in the college catering by the 1620s. In addition to wheaten and oat bread, kail and eggs, there was also to be found honey, cheese, sour milk and curdled cream, and salt and fresh butter; there was salt, pepper, ginger, vinegar and saffron for seasoning, flavouring and colouring; there were 'ploumdames' or damsons, and raisins by the pound, and even onions made a brief appearance. For drink, there was milk and wine by the pint as well as the ubiquitous ale. Malt, meal, barley and flour were ordered in quantity. For fish, there was herring by the barrel; there were 'codlings' or 'killing', occasionally haddock and 'troutis', some salmon (sometimes a whole salmon, sometimes a half, sometimes a quarter) and 'sevin dosen and ane halfe of hard fische'. Despite some seasonal adjustment, there was also more variety in the meats consumed. As well as salt and fresh beef and mutton, there was bacon, pork, lamb and tongue; 'young beif' and veal made their appearance in January, supplemented by 'twa hochis', 'a haire', 'ane pair of midretis' (perhaps heart or kidneys) and 'ane neat feit'. Amongst the fowl, there were 'snype and wodcoks', 'horskokis' and 'blakcock', 'wyll foulis', partridges, 'a duik', a goose, 'a cok', 'a hen', 'vij and a half chickens', 'a capoune', two 'foullis for broth', and 'laverokis' or larks were ordered by the dozen. There were even 'som cakes at xvjd.'[119]

The sons of the nobility appear to have been accorded the privilege of sitting at high table with the masters.[120] This was certainly so at St Andrews where it was explicitly stated in the 1570s that 'nane be admittit to sitt at the first mes of the first tabill with the principall maisteris except thai be lordis eldest sonis and lordis of parliament'.[121] Social distinctions were preserved rather than ignored.

The dining hall like the other chambers and schools was likely to be cold and draughty, particularly in winter. Hence the need to ensure a well-stocked fire during the midday and evening meals, but nothing was said of heating the building for breakfast. Students suffering from cold and damp conditions were no more immune than the rest of the population from illness and disease. The hours of study were long; the discipline was strict; and sickness took its toll. 'To the great detriment of my studies', the conscientious Robert Blair succumbed for four months to a 'tertian fever', and in order to gain more time for study he 'chose every other day to forbear one meal of meat'. In his final year at college in Glasgow, John Livingston suffered from a 'fistula in my left leg' and so was 'long detained in Edinburgh under doctors and chirurgions'. As a result, he missed his regent's lessons in Hebrew, but by private study in his father's manse, he managed to acquire 'some knowledge' of that language.[122]

The cost of board involved considerable expenditure. In 1603, the boarding of eight foundation bursars, four of whom were presented by the king and four by the town, amounted to more than £444 a year. By 1608, board for a master worked out at £30 quarterly compared with £16 13s 4d for a bursar.[123] Not every burse, however, was paid in cash. An additional bursar was supported from endowment in kind. A chalder of meal was the burse which John Couper, a minister's son, received in 1602. As a token payment, it became customary for bursars to present a spoon in lieu of boarding fees.[124]

The age at which students entered the university might vary, but it was usual for students to matriculate straight from grammar school about the age of fifteen or sixteen. Robert Blair, born in 1593, matriculated at the beginning of the rectorial year on 1 March 1611, having presumably entered university in the preceding October at the age of seventeen, graduating in 1614.[125] John Livingston, however, was rather younger. He had been taught at Stirling grammar school where he was frequently thrashed by the schoolmaster, William Wallace, a Glasgow graduate, and a 'learned humanist'. After one incident in which he was beaten 'with a stick in the cheek so as my face swelled', his father reprimanded the teacher who promised 'to forbear beating of me and after that I profited an great deall more in my learning'.[126] He even stayed on at school for an extra year because of his youth and delayed entering university till 1617 at the tender age of fourteen, matriculating in March 1618 and graduating in 1621.[127] Some students, however, must have been considerably older. Even allowing that some on graduating in Arts might pursue post-graduate studies in theology, the first Book of Discipline nevertheless envisaged the possibility of students studying until the more advanced age of twenty-four, when 'the learner must be removed to serve the church or commonwealth'.[128]

The 'bejan',[129] or first-year student, on arrival at university entered an academic community with a population, on the evidence of the graduation lists, of perhaps little more than thirty students in 1578. By 1610, however, there are on record 106 matriculated students for the four classes, and the figure by 1620 had risen to 139, with an annual intake, on average, of thirty-five students.[130] It was a small, self-contained society. Its population amounted to less than half the number of students said to have attended the city grammar school.

Although the academic session began in October and ended in July, the newcomer would be obliged to matriculate during the rectorial year of his entry to the university. He had to swear obedience to the university statutes and by way of a religious test to acknowledge the Confession of Faith and teaching of the reformed church. If he was a bursar or benefice holder, he was required under the terms of the Convention of Leith in 1572 to recognise the 'kingis authoritie' as the 'only lauchfull supreme governour of this realme als weill in thingis temporall as in conservatioun and purgatioun of the religioun, and that na foreyne prince, prelat, state or potentate hes or aucht to have ony jurisdictioun, power, superioritie, preheminance, or authoritie ecclesiasticall and spirituall within this realme'.[131] This was a carefully-worded statement devised in part from the phraseology of the Elizabethan oath of supremacy and in part from the Scots Confession of 1560, and it not only abrogated papal or foreign jurisdiction but it also avoided offending the scruples of those within the reformed church who were reluctant to concede an outright supremacy of the crown in matters ecclesiastical.[132]

After finding accommodation in the college or in a hostel or digs in town, the 'bejan' settled down to academic life. He rose early, attended lectures and classes, copied down the regent's notes and learned the intricate art of declamation and disputation on which so much hinged. Parental pressure, keen competition, strict discipline and the vigilant eye of the regent were all conducive to hard work. It meant that a student was anxious to do well irrespective of whether he was a bursar or fee-paying student. To have gained a place at university and to earn the coveted title of master, prefixed to his name as the mark of the educated man, was a genuine aspiration as well as a sign of social status, an indication of his standing in the wider community. The student, then, was expected to work for his promotion each year from one class to the next and was censured if he failed.

In the absence of any contemporary account, student life in the university is difficult to assess. After entering the college, Robert Blair could 'remember no remarkable thing till the fourth year' other than solid study and some sport. That he was unable to recall anything memorable about his college days was more the fault of Blair than of the university. He suffered from the same problem after becoming a school-teacher in Glasgow 'where I remember no remarkable thing' save the wearisome nature of the job. Yet it is to Blair that we owe our know-ledge of the college ghost. To find a peaceful spot for studying Blair was accustomed to resort to 'a chamber wherein none was permitted to lie by reason of apparitions in the night season'. There he 'resolved to spend my waking nights, and did so the whole summer, and was never troubled nor terrified a whit', even after seeing 'a spirit in likeness of one of my condisciples whom I, having a lighted candle in my hand and supposing verily it had been that boy, chased to a corner of the chamber where he seemed to hide himself but when I offered to pull him out I could find nothing'.[133]

The abolition of saints' days and holy days as religious festivals after the Reformation meant a substantial reduction in the number of holidays. Certainly, under the presbyterians, students could look for no special holidays at Christmas or Easter. The academic session from October until the end of July was a lengthy stint. The post-Reformation statutes which fixed the start of the academic year on 1 October had prescribed the last week in August for the final examination before laureation,[134] but in practice graduation ceremonies came to be held in July,[135] and in 1604 mention was made of 'two monethis of vacans'[136] which presumably took place in August and September before the start of the next academic session in October. August and September, then, remained fallow months, free from academic labour, but even this break did not go uncontested. At St Andrews in the 1570s it was pro-posed 'that the vacance be alluterlie tane away'.[137] In practice, however, the long vacation remained. Moreover, in 1598 parliament appointed Monday as a weekly holiday throughout the land, and students were to be given a rest from their studies on Monday afternoons.[138]

According to the university statutes, games were only to be held as organised college activities at stated hours. Catchpole or hand tennis and swimming were altogether prohibited.[139] Yet Robert Blair, as a student, had indulged in 'the exercise of my body by archery and the catchpole'. After completing his course, in which he had his elder brother William as regent, Robert spent a few days 'hawking and hunting' with friends in the country before entering 'a very laborious task' as schoolteacher in Glasgow.[140] At school, James Melville had been taught archery, golf, fencing, running, jumping, swimming and wrestling; and at university he had taken up archery and golf. His father had given him a 'bow, arrose, glub and bals, but nocht a purs for catchpull and tavern; sic was his fatherlie wisdom for my weill'. This, however, did not prevent him from playing some tennis: 'now and then I lernit and usit sa mikle bathe of the hand and racket catche as might serve for moderat and halsome exerceise of the body'. Whilst at college, he also 'lerned my music' from the principal's servant who had been trained by the monks of the priory. He received instruction, as a result, in 'the gam, plean-song and monie of the treables of the psalmes wherof sum I could weill sing in the kirk'. He was also keen to learn some musical instruments. A number of the students were able to play the virginals, the lute and guitar, and Melville practised on the spinet which his regent had in his chamber. But divine wisdom intervened and prevented further progress, 'for giff I haid atteined to anie reasonable missure thairin I haid never don guid utherwayes in respect of my amorus disposition wherby Sathan sought even then to deboiche me, bot my God gaiff me a piece of his fear and grait naturall shamfastness, quhilk by his grace war my preservatives'.[141]

Although music no longer formed an integral part of the Arts curriculum as once it had done as part of the *quadrivium*, students were still encouraged to take an interest in the subject. In the Glasgow college, John Livingston found that the principal, Robert Boyd, a 'man of an soure like disposition and carriage', would 'call me and some other three or four and lay down books before us and have us sing setts of musick wherein he took great delight'. An inventory of 1582 also reveals that the college possessed some books of 'musik of sangis'.[142]

The wearing of academic dress was not simply a practice reimposed as an extension of the ecclesiastical and liturgical innovations begun by James VI and pursued by Charles I. Even under Andrew Melville, in the years of the presbyterian ascendancy, gowns were worn in college on certain occasions by both teachers and students.[143] Yet no mention of prescribed forms in academic dress are to be found in the post-Reformation university statutes. The matter may have been regarded as too trivial for formal legislation. All that the general assembly had decreed for ministers was that they 'apparell themselves in a comely and decent cloathing as becometh the gravity of their vocation' and that none wear plaids in times of divine service.[144] It might be expected that the regents in the college would wear the black teaching gown, sometimes known as the Genevan gown, but there is no firm evidence that students were obliged to wear a uniform type of gown. Bursars were, however, expected to wear distinctive dress.[145] James's Act of Apparel in 1609, which simply prescribed 'black, grave and comelie apparrell' for ministers, did not extend to undergraduates at university, but in setting up a commission to visit Glasgow university in 1613 the king took the opportunity of instructing the members 'to appoint deceint and comelie habites and formes of vesture for the studentis, licentiatis, regentis, doctoris and governoris' of the college.[146] Whether the practice had lapsed, was not enforced or needed alteration is less than clear, but Charles I had the same complaint in 1634 when he wrote to the archbishop of Glasgow, requiring the students and teachers in the college to attend divine service in the cathedral 'in decent maner with their gownes according to their severall degrees in schooles respectively and that they do use the said habite of gownes according to their degrees in the schooles, universitie and streets'.[147] This was an attitude which was upheld even during the presbyterian revolution of the 1640s.[148]

Graduation, of course, was a highlight in any student's career. It was the goal for which he had been aiming all along. Few students could afford the luxury of pursuing a totally dispassionate, altruistic interest in study for study's sake, as an end in itself without tangible return. University education was costly, it involved sacrifices for many and there were very practical reasons why students should embark on such a course of study. Nor were the subjects which were taught necessarily divorced from the needs of contemporary society. The universities were seen to be fulfilling a useful social function as agencies for 'the spread and growth of learning, and the instruction of youth to the end that useful members may be reared, instructed and educated for serving the church of God and the commonwealth within this our kingdom'.[149] This was the language of the *nova erectio* of 1577. Bursaries were therefore founded to encourage 'the erudition of the yuithe at the scholis for lerning off vertew, lettres and guid maneris to the effect that thay may be proffitabill instrumentis of the kirk of God and commoune weill'.[150] And the universities themselves aimed at providing 'that perfectioun of teacheing which this learnit aige cravis'.[151]

The sons of some nobles and increasingly the sons of the gentry found a university education profitable; for aspiring ministers it was all but essential; and for those intent on a professional career it was becoming more and more desirable. Some on graduating even pursued a career in commerce or trade. The aspirations which brought students to college are to be explained partly in the relevance of a university training to the needs of society, partly in the status it conferred and the prospect of further advancement. A knowledge of logic and rhetoric and an ability to dispute and declaim were useful attributes in many aspects of professional life. The increasing interest in the sciences, in mathematics, arithmetic, physics and cosmography had a relevance and application in commerce, in 'industrial' enterprises and in navigation. Napier of Merchiston, the inventor of logarithms, was educated at St Andrews,[152] despite his uncle's advice in 1560 that he should be educated abroad[153] but he chose to send one of his sons to Glasgow university,[154] while Melville's friend at St Andrews, William Welwood, who had taught mathematics and law, not only produced what is claimed to be the first treatise of maritime law in Britain but also patented an invention in 1577 for 'the elevatioun of watteris out of coill pottis, sinkis and utheris law places'.[155]

Above all, however, the appearance of Ramism on the academic scene, with its new approach to education, caught the imagination of contemporaries in a way which it is now hard to fathom. In his English translation of Ramus' *Logic*, the Scot Roland MacIlmaine set out to show the reader 'howe easye it is above all others to be apprehended, howe thou shalt applye it to all artes and sciences and shortlie that no arte or science maye eyther be taught or learned perfectlie without the knowledge of the same'. Ramism was recommended to the preacher, in his logical analysis of scripture, and to the lawyer, physician and mathematician. In short, the Ramist 'perfecte methode maye be accommodate to all artes and sciences'.[156] It all served a very practical purpose. Far from purveying an arid scholasticism, the universities were attempting to measure up to the educational needs of society.

Graduation, then, came as the climax to an academic career which augured well for the future. According to the post-Reformation statutes, graduation was to take place with simplicity and the minimum of ceremony.[157] This was consistent with the Reformation ethos in Scotland, with its distaste for elaborate ritual and ceremonial. Graduation ceremonies took place in the Blackfriars church[158] beside the college where the chancellor conferred on the graduands the master's insignia and the 'power of interpreting and teaching humane letters and explaining universal philosophy in Greek and Latin'.[159] Under Smeaton's principalship, with all his distaste for festivities and dinner parties, the traditional banqueting at graduation may have been somewhat curtailed or, at least, not encouraged. The expenses at graduation were considerable. There were degree fees, payments to be made to the regents; there was the cost of academic dress and expenses in banqueting. This hit the poor scholar hardest, and after the Reformation the traditional practice probably continued whereby a poor student graduated along with a richer colleague who bore the burden of expenses. In one known instance, the town council in Glasgow even granted a bursar in the university twenty merks 'to help to by him cloithis at his laureatioun'.[160] Because of the costs involved, one university even sought to abolish completely the expensive custom of banqueting. At a visitation of King's College, Aberdeen, in 1628, it was resolved that 'sic banquettis ar altogether improfitable and onnecessar', being merely 'ane occasioun to the saidis studentis parentis to exclame and cry out against the said colledge memberis for the coist charges and expensis of the said banquettis, nor anie weill or credit to the said colledge'.[161]

With graduation a student's career was at an end except for those who opted to pursue post-graduate studies in theology under the principal's personal supervision. The outlines of the theology curriculum have already been discussed and there can be little doubt that Melville's presbyterianism left its mark on a number of his students. In church government, as in doctrine, he seems to have accepted the substance of the teaching of Beza under whom he had studied divinity. While at Glasgow, he commended Beza's Confession of Faith to his nephew and he is known to have lectured on Calvin.[162] There can be little doubting his devotion to Calvinism, as a system of theology, or to presbyterianism, as a system of church government. His left-wing brand of protestantism was curiously reflected in the letters of commendation which he granted to the Brownists on their arrival in St Andrews from England in 1584, though any friendship quickly vanished when Edinburgh presbytery ordered their imprisonment for criticising the discipline of the Scottish church.[163] In later life, he seems to have desisted from condemning, and indeed lent tacit approval to, the somewhat novel theological views, at any rate among Calvinists, of Piscator, a prominent Ramist and theologian at Herborn, whose teaching on the doctrine of justification caused considerable controversy in both France and Switzerland, and led in 1603 to his condemnation by the Synod of Gap, which wrote to the Scottish and other universities in an effort to gain overseas approval of their action,[164] though no reply from Glasgow university has come to light. Melville, however, even as an exile in Sedan, remained sympathetic towards Piscator. In 1611, it was rumoured that he was 'of the opinion of Piscator', but he remained resolute in his defence of the absolute decree of reprobation (*de decreto absoluto reprobatione*) and was vigorous in his opposition to 'all that verge towards Arminianisme'.[165]

Whatever his theological abilities, Smeaton as his successor in Glasgow, defended the Calvinist position when it came under attack,[166] and Patrick Sharp, if less involved in theological controversy, may also have stimulated an interest in divinity among his students. Within the fast-flowing waters of Calvinism, the changing emphases are not always easy to detect. Melville, like several of his successors, committed little to print. Yet, if his attitudes, on the whole, lay within the main stream of Calvinist thinking as it developed, the views of John Cameron were seen in the eyes of many Calvinists to be decidedly unorthodox. Cameron had been taught under Patrick Sharp before becoming regent in 1599 and ultimately principal for a brief spell in 1621 after a distinguished career on the continent where he had served as professor of classics at Bergerac and of philosophy at Sedan, as pastor at Bordeaux, as tutor, then as scholar at Geneva and Heidelberg and particularly as theology professor at the French protestant academy of Saumur, founded by the Calvinist du Plessis-Mornay.[167] As an Arts student in Glasgow in 1595, Cameron is known, on the testimony of a fellow student, to have been 'addicted to the philosophy of Ramus and defended it with zeal';[168] he would also have attended Sharp's public lectures in theology, but it was only after further study on the continent that Cameron expounded his theological views on the three covenants which seemed at odds with Calvinist teaching on the two covenants.[169] His views had more immediate repercussions on the continent than they did in Scotland, and it was to Cameron in particular that Amyraut, who claimed that Calvinism had deviated from Calvin, acknowledged his indebtedness.[170]

Cameron's distinctive contribution to the development of French Calvinism serves as a reminder of the close connections which had existed from at least the 1550s between the Scottish and French protestant movements.[171] This became apparent at Glasgow where numerous French students arrived in the 1580s and 1590s. Their numbers included 'Isaacus Mazerius, Gallus', who graduated in 1585; 'Jeremias Barbaeus, Celta', a graduate of 1589; and 'Jacobus Choquetus' in 1596, but there were others who studied at the university without necessarily graduating. Three French students matriculated in 1591 and three more in 1593, two in 1594, six in 1595 including Guillaume Rivet, the brother of André Rivet, the Leyden theologian, and two in 1598.[172] Their appearance may have been brief yet their presence was not inconsiderable and they gave something of a cosmopolitan colour to a university whose student body was very largely composed of Scots from the homeland and from Ulster.

The interest which some French protestants displayed in Scottish reformed theology and in the education offered by the Scottish universities was matched by the increasing prominence of Scottish teaching personnel in the French protestant academies. By the early seventeenth century, Scottish teachers were to be found at such centres as Bordeaux, La Rochelle, La Rochefoucauld, Sedan, Saumur, Montauban and Puylaurens, Orthez, Die, Nîmes and Montpellier.[173] For Scots, French protestantism still held out great promise despite the reversals in its fortunes. At Glasgow, James Melville, after learning the language, longed

N

to visit France. So too did John Livingston who was 'very earnest to go to France'.[174] Neither succeeded, but others did. James Sharp, the eldest son of John Sharp of Houstoun, advocate and procurator for the university, was a Glasgow graduate of 1582, who continued further studies in Paris where he kept in touch through correspondence with the Glasgow college.[175] He seems to have developed an interest in the writings of the Jesuit Toledo whose 'haill wourkis of Toletus in thrie volumes' he sent to his brother Patrick. Calvinists and Jesuits showed considerable interest in each other's philosophical treatises, but to avert parental criticism James Sharp thought it wise to explain that 'I menit not in my lettres send to my father quhairin I wrett of the Jesuites diligence of ony disputes of theologie as it apperes ye understand, bot only of disputes in philosophie'.[176] In the library of the protestant academy of Saumur, Robert Boyd included the works of Toledo with those of other Spanish and Italian scholastics[177] for enlightenment as well as criticism. Even earlier, the college library in Glasgow possessed in the 1580s a copy of Toledo on Aristotle and it acquired various philosophical works by the Italian Zabarella and the Spanish Jesuit, Antonio Rubio.[178] Later, Heidelberg and, increasingly, Dutch influences are detectable. Abraham Schultz of Heidelberg, who had Ramist leanings, was read at Glasgow, though it is not always easy in this earlier period to trace the presence of Glasgow students at Heidelberg or Leyden, or even, for that matter, in France.

Several Glasgow graduates were drawn to England for a period of further study rather than to France. Thomas Smeaton in 1583 enlisted the support of Walsingham, whom he had known in Paris, to help gain a place at Cambridge or Oxford for William Lynne, who 'having ended his course is determined to follow forth the study of divinity'. In his letter to Walsingham, Smeaton remarked that 'in our colleges here there is no small number of youth well trained up in Latin, Greek and Hebrew, and all parts of philosophy', but he thought fit to explain that 'being once pastmasters in art, there is no means to entertain those who have dedicated themselves to serve God in His Church, such is our misery and confusion, whereby the greatest part, by extreme necessity, are driven to France, and there "mak shipp wraik of conscience and religion"'. In much of this there may have been special pleading, and Smeaton also took the opportunity to request 'some piece of favour' for another graduate, Hugh Fullerton, 'a godly and well learned gentleman' who had 'com to England for sum condition', before entering the ministry at Dumfries by 1586'.[179] Nor was it regarded as unorthodox that a Scottish presbyterian principal should seek the support of a puritan patron to secure the entry of a divinity student to one of the English universities. The Scottish presbyterians maintained close links with their English counterparts, and certain colleges in both Oxford and Cambridge retained a strong puritan tradition. Melville himself made a point of visiting the English universities in 1584 where he 'conferrit with the most godlie and lernit there'.[180] He was also to recommend several students for admission to Oxford.[181]

As a Glasgow graduate in 1583,[182] James Hegait, son of the town clerk in Glasgow, undertook a period of further study at Cambridge where he obtained his M.A. in 1598 and served as chaplain to Ludovic, duke of Lennox.[183] Somewhat later, in 1610, David Foules, as a Glasgow graduate seeking admission to Magdalen Hall, Oxford, obtained letters of testimonial from his university which ran in name of John Hay, the rector, John Blackburn, dean of faculty, Patrick Sharp, as principal, Archibald Hamilton, professor of physics, Michael Wallace, professor of logic, Gabriel Maxwell, professor of eloquence, and William Blair, professor of Greek.[184] In 1613, three other Glasgow graduates, Robert Spottiswoode, the archbishop's son, Gavin Stewart and Gavin Hamilton, were engaged on further work at Oxford where they were permitted access to the Bodleian library.[185] If, on the whole, Scottish scholars still developed closer associations with continental centres of learning, they did not altogether ignore the educational opportunities afforded by the English universities. Nor was the traffic entirely one way. Some English students came north to the Scottish universities, and the Edinburgh college, in particular, had more than a tendency to produce graduates who, on returning south, caused trouble as puritan preachers in England.[186]

That a proportion of the university's graduates undertook post-graduate work at home or abroad need not be doubted. How many remained at Glasgow for further theological training cannot readily be assessed for no university records relating to the study of divinity in this period remain. Added to this was the apparent disregard by presbyterians for the bachelor of divinity degree and their scarcely concealed distaste for the higher degree of doctor of divinity,[187] which seemed to conflict with their conception of the doctor's office, which included schoolteachers, within the church.

Earlier discussions on 'degrees to be usit be ministers' had been remitted to the general assembly in 1569 for consideration.[188] It was parliament, however, in approving the new foundation of the St Andrews colleges, which enacted in 1579 that entry to the ministry should be restricted to those who had 'compleitit thair cours in theologie or be rigorous examinatioun be the facultie sal be found worthie and qualifeit to ressave all thair degreis in the said facultie'[189] A degree in theology was clearly envisaged, but Glasgow could not compete with the specialised theology course of four years' duration offered in St Mary's college,

St Andrews. Students might therefore proceed to 'the cours of theologie' and be examined in their work without necessarily obtaining any degree qualifications at the end.

That students in increasing numbers should embark on a university career and succeed in obtaining an Arts degree depended on an assortment of factors. It has to be related to changing patterns in demographic growth, to the multiplication of schools, the supply of grammar school students, the competition for available places, the availability of financial aid for the less prosperous in the form of bursaries, benefices and other aspects of patronage. Added to this were the prospects of social advancement, of the employment opportunities offered through the acquisition of a university degree, particularly in the reformed church or in schoolteaching which usually required a degree, and the social status which such degrees conferred. Again, much depended on social conventions and aspirations, on the Reformation ideal of an educated society and the enthusiasm for education which this engendered among some. Parental influences and motivation were also crucial. The humbler a student's background the stronger was the temptation to find immediate employment to earn a living as early as possible; but often sacrifices were made to ensure that a bright student could make full use of the country's educational resources. The reputation of the college and of its teachers, as well as the relevance to society of the education which was offered were also key issues. Even communications had a part to play. Geographical remoteness from a university centre was no great asset, but, on the whole, the country was well-served by the regional distribution of its five institutions of higher learning. The universities were accessible both geographically and socially to a fairly wide section of Scottish society.

Yet a reliable statistical examination of the social and geographical origins of the student population cannot proceed on the scanty nature of the material available. The list of unidentified names in the matriculation and graduation rolls generally gives no indication of the social background or geographical location of the students who were recruited. The rolls convey nothing of the status of a student's parents, his place of birth or earlier schooling or even his age at matriculation. The distinctive appellations of *dives*, *potens* and *pauper*, characteristic of St Andrews and sometimes used at Glasgow, are no longer recorded at Glasgow after the Reformation. In short, the social categories of university entrants are not delineated. No clues other than the stark list of names remain.

A tentative exploration, in the absence of firm data, may nonetheless be attempted. A starting-point can be made with students who proceeded to a career in the ministry. Although they did not necessarily comprise a majority of students, they did form the largest single group in the student community and are the most readily identifiable. It is certainly easier to trace the subsequent careers of graduates who entered the ministry than it is for those who followed other professions. One of the main functions of the university, after all, was to produce a supply of ministers for the church. Indeed, one of the criticisms levelled against parish clergy in the pre-Reformation church, and recognised to be so by the provincial councils of that church, was their 'crass ignorance of literature and of all the liberal arts'.[190] The Reformation emphasis which elevated preaching of the Word to a position of co-centrality with the administration of the sacraments made the education of ministers a top priority. The number of clergy might be drastically reduced after the Reformation, but the need for training ministers after 1560, far from diminishing, actually increased. It is important to appreciate the novelty of the idea that parish ministers should be university-trained. No longer was it to be confined to a ruling élite of bishops, canons and dignitaries, as had been largely the case before.

Of the ten students who graduated under Melville's principalship, when the records begin in 1578, at least five are known to have entered the ministry: John Blackburn, son of a Glasgow burgess, was reader at Cathcart in 1578, later minister at Cardross, dean of faculty and grammar schoolmaster; Hugh Fullerton, whom Smeaton had recommended to Walsingham, became minister at Dumfries by 1586; Ninian Young was appointed reader at Ayr in 1580; and John Ross, a burgess's son, entered the ministry at Dumbarton in 1580; while a sixth, Patrick Melville, the son of a Dundee merchant, seems to have pursued further studies at college before becoming regent in 1580.[191] At least four, and perhaps five, of the six graduates in 1579, also became ministers: Andrew Knox, younger son of the laird of Ranfurly, who after continuing his studies in the college[192] became minister at Lochwinnoch in 1581, then at Paisley and in 1605 was appointed bishop of the Isles; Robert Darroch, apparently the son of a Glasgow burgess, was minister at Kilmarnock in 1580; Patrick Walkinshaw, son of the laird of Walkinshaw, was minister at Stevenston in 1581; Dougal Campbell, younger son of the laird of Ardkinglass and younger brother of the bishop of Brechin who had known Melville on the continent, became minister at Farnell and dean of Brechin in 1581; while James Cunningham, a fifth graduate in 1579, seems to be the same man as the reader at Dumbarton who became minister at Bonhill in 1588.[193] In the lists for Melville's final year at Glasgow in 1580, in which only five students are entered as graduates, two out of the three students identified became ministers: William Douglas, younger son of the laird of Whittinghame, and Richard Ogill, younger son of the laird of Hartwood, both of whom continued post-graduate studies,[194] before becoming ministers at Drainie and Innerwick respectively, and the third, Duncan Nairn, son of Duncan Nairn in Bannockburn, became regent in the Edinburgh college.[195]

It is noticeable, however, with Melville's departure for St Andrews in 1580 that fewer Glasgow graduates in 1581 entered the ministry. In the midst of his studies, Patrick Forbes, the eldest son of the laird of Corse, chose to leave Glasgow and follow Melville, his kinsman, to St Andrews.[196] There can be little doubt that the reconstitution of St Mary's as a specialist college of theology under Melville's principalship had attracted many prospective divines to St Andrews. Of the eight Glasgow graduates in 1581, only one proceeded straight to the ministry, John Spottiswoode, son of the superintendent of Lothian and future archbishop, who was appointed assistant and successor to his father's parish of Mid-Calder in 1583.[197] John Bell, who graduated with Spottiswoode in 1581, became minister at Kilbarchan in 1591, while David Blyth, who may be the Glasgow graduate of 1581, taught as schoolteacher at Kirkcudbright before becoming minister there by 1589.[198] Nor did recruitment to the ministry improve in 1582 when only one graduate out of the ten, John Hay, the eldest son of Andrew Hay, became minister at Mearns in 1588, though two others later succeeded to ecclesiastical office in England and Ireland.[199] Thereafter, at least three out of 18 graduates in 1583 subsequently entered the ministry and at least four out of 15 in 1584 and probably five out of 15 in 1585 followed a career in the church, and this sort of pattern was maintained at a similar level for the rest of the century.[200]

Competition was also forthcoming from the newly-founded college of Edinburgh which from 1587 was producing its own supply of graduates for the ministry. At least fifteen of the forty-seven graduates in 1587 became ministers, twelve of the thirty graduates in 1588, seven of the thirteen graduates in 1590, six of the fourteen graduates in 1591 and twelve out of twenty-eight graduates in 1592.[201] Indeed, the threat from Edinburgh was such that it was even suggested in 1616, albeit by St Andrews, that Edinburgh's 'power be restranit to the bernis of ther awine citie'.[202]

Socially, these graduate recruits to the ministry came from the ranks of the lairds, usually younger sons, or from burgess stock. By the end of the century, the acquisition of a good benefice or burgh charge made the parish ministry attractive to the sons of the lesser gentry as, perhaps, never before. Thus Walter Stewart, son of the laird of Barscube, entered the ministry of Kilpatrick in 1587 after graduating from the university in 1584. Thomas Muirhead, son of Muirhead of Lauchope and a Glasgow graduate of 1591, became minister at Shotts in that year.

Andrew Law, the son of the laird of Spittal and brother of the future archbishop, was a graduate of 1591 and subsequently minister at Stonehouse. On leaving the university in 1596, George Lindsay, son of the laird of Blackhom, served as minister at Bonhill in 1599. Similarly, after obtaining his M.A. in 1597, William Wallace, son of Wallace of Johnstone, chose to become minister at Eastwood in 1606. More varied was the career of Archibald Hamilton, son of Hamilton of Barnes, who on graduating in 1599 became regent in the college, then served as minister at Paisley and later in Ireland as bishop of Killala and as archbishop of Cashel and Emly, before ultimately leaving for Sweden.

Others who were the eldest sons of local lairds also found the ministry an attractive enough career after a university education. John Cunningham, a Glasgow graduate of 1595, is identified as the eldest son of Cunningham of Baidland and was minister at Houston in 1599; and it seems to be accepted that Claud Hamilton who obtained his M.A. from the university in 1596 and became minister at Monkton and Prestwick in 1599 was the eldest son of John Hamilton of Newton. A number of burgess's sons also aspired to the ranks of the ministry. Alexander Rowat, who graduated from the university in 1587 and became minister at Cambusnethan in 1588, was the son of a prominent Glasgow burgess who served as bailie on the town council. Similarly, David Cunningham who received his M.A. in 1600 and served as minister at Dunscore in 1609 was the son of a Glasgow burgess. This was also true of George Clydesdale, the eldest son of a Glasgow baxter burgess and another graduate of 1600, who entered the ministry at Glasford in 1607. Others yet again were the sons of ministers. William Livingston, a graduate of 1595 who became minister at Lanark in 1613, was himself the son of the minister at Kilsyth, while David Sharp, who was admitted to the parish of Bothwell in 1606, was the son of the principal of the university and minister at Govan.[203]

Most of these graduates were drawn from the west of Scotland, particularly from the Glasgow area and they tended to remain as ministers of parishes in the west of the country. Indeed, the university had a particular responsibility for supplying graduate ministers to serve the west-coast parishes. Some, however, were attracted to Glasgow for reasons other than geographical proximity. It is hard to resist the conclusion that Dougal Campbell, the younger brother of the bishop of Brechin, was attracted to Glasgow in preference to St Andrews or Aberdeen by the reputation of Melville who had travelled home from Geneva with Brechin and his pedagogue, Andrew Polwarth, who became minister at Paisley and dean of faculty, and whom Melville once described as his 'friend and companion' in Geneva.[204] It may also be significant that John Spottiswoode, superintendent of Lothian and minister at Mid-Calder, should send his two sons to his own university of Glasgow and not to St Andrews which was scarcely more distant. John, the elder, a graduate of 1581, became minister at Mid-Calder before his promotion as archbishop, first of Glasgow and then of St. Andrews; and James, the younger son, entered the university at the unusually early age of twelve, after being tutored at home by William Strang, the father of the later university principal, and schooled in Edinburgh and Linlithgow. A graduate of 1583, he later became bishop of Clogher in Ireland.[205]

It was probably family connections with Glasgow which determined that William Douglas, the son of Douglas of Whittinghame in East Lothian, should study at Glasgow university, graduating in 1580.[206] His father, a prominent reformer suspected of complicity in Rizzio's murder, and a member of several general assemblies, was later as a lord of Council involved in the lawsuits associated with the reorganisation of the university under Melville, and his uncle, Archibald Douglas, was archdeacon of Glasgow.[207] That Richard Ogill, the son of another East Lothian laird, should also choose Glasgow—he also graduated in 1580—is probably attributable to the ultra-protestant traditions of his family which, like that of Douglas, became manifest in their support for the Ruthven raiders in 1582.[208] Nor is it without relevance that John Duncanson, minister of the king's household and once closely associated with the presbyterian campaign, should send his son, James, to Glasgow, under Smeaton's principalship, where he graduated in 1585.[209]

On entering the ministry, some of these graduates became prominent presbyterians. William Douglas, for example, who was educated under Melville later signed the protest of 1617 in favour of the liberties of the church.[210] It may also have been his sympathy for presbyterianism which led Richard Ogill, as minister at Innerwick, to answer before the privy council in 1600 'for sum impertinent applicatiounes maid in his sermones'.[211] John Livingston, the graduate of 1621, was the presbyterian son of a presbyterian father, the graduate of 1595, who had been 'all his dayes straight and zealous in the work of reformation against episcopacy and ceremonies'.[212] Another committed presbyterian was Robert Blair. Yet Blair discloses that it was not as a student but only after graduating that he 'laid to heart the controversy about church government', resolving that 'prelacy itself was the worst of all corrupt ceremonies'.[213]

Other graduates showed sympathy to episcopacy as a system of church government. Spottiswoode, who became archbishop, seems to have received no specialised theology training from Melville who in a later letter to his nephew described Spottiswoode as 'your schollar'.[214] Another product of the presbyterian regime who ended up a bishop was

Andrew Knox, bishop of the Isles, who succeeded in maintaining friendly relations with Melville in later life.[215] Most of the Glasgow graduates who entered the ministry left no testimony of their views on ecclesiastical polity or of their adherence to one party or the other. They seem to have been prepared to acquiesce in the prevailing system depending on whichever party was in power. But a few students like Hugh Semple and Thomas Maxwell opted out of the fellowship of the reformed church altogether and turned Catholics, some seeking refuge on the continent in France or Spain.[216]

So far attention has been largely focussed on graduates who became ministers but even the most cursory examination discloses that only a certain proportion entered the church and that a majority of students came to university with the intention of pursuing a secular career outside the ministry. As contemporaries never ceased to remark, the university was certainly the nursery of the ministry, but it was the training ground for careers in the commonwealth as well. Much depended on the supply of jobs in professions other than the church. Some graduates chose college lecturing or schoolteaching: James Fullerton and James Hamilton in Dublin, Duncan Nairn in Edinburgh and William Wallace in Stirling and Glasgow.[217] Alternatively, there was the prospect of becoming a tutor or pedagogue to a nobleman's son. After graduating in 1612, William Forret, a younger son of a Glasgow merchant and bailie, served for a spell as pedagogue to the eldest son of the earl of Montrose.[218]

A more promising avenue for advancement was the law. Some Arts graduates after acquiring a knowledge of law perhaps by studying overseas or even by private study went on to undertake work of a legal nature. James Sharp, the son of Sharp of Houstoun, graduated from Glasgow in 1582, went on to study in France and then took up a career in law as an advocate until incapacitated by 'infirmitie of bodie and mynd'.[219] Another graduate of 1582 with an interest in law was Alexander Sym who may be identified as the son of the commissary of Edinburgh and who succeeded his father as advocate and commissary.[220] Yet a third graduate of 1582 who became an advocate was Adam Newton, the son of an Edinburgh baker, who contributed a small pension for the support of James Melville, his former teacher, when the latter was exiled in England.[221] Newton was recommended in 1594 as a teacher in the laws or humanity in the Edinburgh college, though his appointment was disputed by the town council which claimed the right to elect, and he subsequently became tutor to prince Henry.[222] This marked his entry to a career in royal service which led to his appointment as dean of Durham in 1606.[223] After graduating from the university in 1583, George Erskine who may be related to the

Erskines of Gogar sought a career in law, became procurator and adviser to the earl of Argyll and was later promoted as lord Innertiel to a lord of session in 1617.[224] Not all aspired to high office. Commissary court work sufficed for some. David Hay, a graduate of 1594 and a younger son of Andrew Hay, minister at Renfrew and sometime commissary at Hamilton, succeeded his brother-in-law Archibald Gibson as commissary clerk of Glasgow in 1609.[225]

Nor was a career as an officer in the army to be despised. Until the wars of the covenants, there may have been little opportunity to serve at home in a Scottish army, but a career as a professional soldier in a foreign army had attractions for some. Although his name does not appear in the surviving university records, Hugh Montgomery, the eldest son of Adam Montgomery of Braidstane in Ayrshire, is known to have attended the university, probably in the 1570s. After leaving college, he travelled in France, visited the French court and finally settled in Holland where he became captain in a Scottish regiment under the Prince of Orange. It was only with news of his parents' death and the debts to be settled on the estate to which he had fallen heir that he returned home, was received at court and subsequently pursued a career as an Ulster planter for which he was created viscount Montgomery of the Great Ards.[226]

Though openings were limited, a career in royal service offered opportunities for certain graduates as professional administrators, officials, bureaucrats and even courtiers. There was certainly nothing novel in employing educated men of lesser standing in such a capacity, but after the Reformation, with the elimination of clerical administrators, there was perhaps added scope for laymen in royal service as never before. Although his career was largely ecclesiastical, George Montgomery won the king's favour, spent considerable time at court and served as privy councillor in Ireland. A graduate of 1582, Montgomery was the second son of the laird of Braidstane, the younger brother of Hugh, who had attended the college, and the elder brother of John who 'graduated doctor in physick in some French university or college'. After leaving Glasgow, Montgomery sought preferment in England, and was recommended by Bowes, the English agent in Scotland to Cecil in 1594. When James asked Elizabeth to accord Montgomery letters of denization in 1596, he was said to have 'spent ten or twelve years in your realm', but he also applied for a passport to visit France for his 'edification'.[227] Through correspondence with his brother, Hugh, he supplied James with information on English attitudes to the succession and was later rewarded with the deanery of Norwich, was appointed a royal chaplain and was subsequently elevated to the episcopate in Ireland, though his latter years were spent at court in London.[228]

Two others who aspired to favour at court were Fullerton and Hamilton, the Dublin schoolteachers and fellows of Trinity College. Hamilton became a prominent Ulster planter as viscount Clandeboye and worked in association with Hugh Montgomery, a fellow Glasgow graduate, while Fullerton, who also received grants of land including forfeited estates of Irish rebels, showed a preference, instead of becoming an Irish magnate like Clandeboye, for 'ready money and to live in court more than in waste wildernesses in Ulster' and so was retained in royal service by Charles I.[229]

Connections with the court were greatly to be prized. James Spottiswoode, after graduating in 1583, entered the king's service, accompanied James as a gentleman usher to Denmark in 1590, and remained at court as a secretary, accompanying an embassy to Germany in 1598. On James's accession to the English throne, he became almoner to the queen, a post which he relinquished in favour of a clerical career and so was provided to the benefice of Wells juxta Mare in Norfolk and finally to the Irish bishopric of Clogher in 1621.[230]

Influence and patronage counted for much in obtaining office at court or elsewhere. Andrew Knox, bishop of the Isles, who sent his son Thomas to his own university of Glasgow had the problem of finding suitable employment for his son on his graduation in 1608. He therefore sent him to London, presumably for preferment, 'to receive the court's direction and that in God where he may upon reasonable conditions without offence in religion serve God with the talent which God has bestowed upon him', but Knox also took the precaution of writing in 1608 to Boyd of Trochrague for advice about Thomas's future 'in furnishing him for France and to sic end as ye would prescribe and advise me'.[231] In the end, he assisted his father in administering a turbulent diocese, was taken hostage when the MacDonalds of Islay seized Dunivaig castle in 1614 but was rewarded by the crown with lands in Ulster and eventually succeeded to his father's bishopric in 1619, after being admitted minister at Eaglesham in 1616.[232]

One Glasgow graduate who rose to particular eminence in royal service was Sir Gideon Murray, a younger son of the laird of Black-barony in Peeblesshire, who came first in the M.A. lists of 1581. A kinsman of Beaton, he succeeded as chantor of Aberdeen, an office previously held by Archibald Beaton, the commissary of Glasgow; and although he entered the ministry at Auchterless, he soon abandoned it on being put to the horn for murder, for which he was imprisoned in Edinburgh castle in 1585-86. On entering the service of Scott of Buccleuch as chamberlain, he came to the notice of the king who appointed him to a commission of justiciary for the Borders in 1603; he was knighted in 1605, and appointed to the privy council. He became one of the 'Octavians' or treasury officials in 1611, and lord high treasurer in 1613, an office he combined with a host of others.[233]

While a university education might be regarded as a useful acquisition for access to a particular career in the professions, there was still a fair number of students for whom a university training had no particular utility whatsoever. In terms of a subsequent career, there was no practical reason why the eldest sons of lairds who would inherit their fathers' estates should embark on a university education. The training which they received was of no immediate advantage to the running of their estates. Yet there they were entering university: William Edmonston of Duntreath matriculating in January 1591, together with James Sandelands of Calder, who had his own pedagogue Mr John Brown;[234] and William Livingston, the son of lord Livingston.[235] Four heirs of lairds, so styled, came up to university in 1601, five in 1609, two in 1611 and six in 1612.[236] Their appearance has therefore to be explained on social rather than on strictly economic grounds. It was a reflection of the lairds' social aspirations. To be trained up in letters and respected as an educated man was a definite sign of social status. It enhanced the lairds' prestige and social standing in the localities and served as the educational complement to their ecclesiastical involvement as elders in kirk sessions, presbyteries and general assemblies.

On leaving university, John Shaw of Greenock returned to his estates and secured a charter for erecting Greenock into a burgh of barony. He acquired the patronage of the parish church at Greenock, supported the covenants, sat as a ruling elder on the presbytery of Paisley, attended the general assembly and was elected to parliament for Renfrewshire.[237] A similar pattern is discernible in the career of John Brisbane of Bishopton, who matriculated in 1612 and subsequently settled down to follow the normal life of a country gentleman. He managed his property; like Shaw, he served as ruling elder in the presbytery of Paisley, attended the assembly and represented Renfrewshire with Shaw in parliament.[238]

If some lairds were rising, others were depressed, threatened with insolvency and mounting debt. Their lands might already be placed in wadset or mortgaged. While a university education did not help offset their financial or social insecurity, it could at least serve as insurance if alternative employment had to be sought. Loss of land meant a sharp decline in social standing. A hard-up gentleman, without a university degree, might have to earn his living as a burgess. Roger Melville, as a younger son of the Melvilles of Baldovy, became a merchant in Dundee; 'a man of singular giftes of nature and God's grace, bot was nocht traned upe in lettres'. If he, by all accounts, had fallen in the world, he did at least ensure that his son, Patrick, received a university training at Glasgow.[239]

For some, however, Ireland seemed the answer to their problems. The land-hungry or landless who still considered themselves to be gentlemen, set off to seek their fortune in Ireland. Others seem to have incurred debts as a consequence of doing so. William Edmonston of Duntreath, who apparently left university without graduating in the 1590s, negotiated along with his father and brothers grants of land in Ulster from Montgomery of Braidstane, but the enterprise cost money and this was perhaps one reason that the family fell into debt, pledging their lands at Duntreath to Livingston of Kilsyth for fifteen years.[240]

It was not just the planters and their tenants who found their way to Ireland. An assortment of Glasgow's graduates had a habit of re-appearing in Ireland: Fullerton and Hamilton initially in Dublin, George Montgomery and James Spottiswoode as bishops of Irish dioceses, James Hegait as archdeacon of Clogher and bishop of Kilfenoragh, John Gibson as dean of Down, and John Blackburn as archdeacon of Down.[241] Another category of ecclesiastics were those who, far from seeking promotion in the church of Ireland, had been forced to leave Scotland as presbyterian nonconformists rather than submit to episcopacy at home—ministers like Robert Blair and John Livingston who arrived in Ulster with their brand of presbyterianism.[242] Nor was the traffic one-way. A number of Irish students and clerics came to Glasgow for their education. Some were said to speak 'Irish and Latin'; others were versed in 'Irish, Latin and Scots'.[243]

If the local gentry, burgess élite and merchant community were intent on exploiting the available educational resources to the full, elements of the nobility also took an interest in what the university could provide. Unlike the sons of burgesses and lairds who normally attended grammar school together and then, if fortunate, went on to university, the nobility had their own tutors and pedagogues. Frequently, they chose to visit a continental centre of learning. That some decided to attend university at home was purely a matter of social convention. Their attendance served no utilitarian purpose. In pursuing their studies, however, they might wish to acquire a further knowledge of the classics and perhaps a smattering of Hebrew and theology. One of Glencairn's sons attended Glasgow university on the eve of the Reformation; another went to St Andrews in the 1570s.[244] The presbyterians might complain that 'the nobilitie and gentlemen ar unlerned them selffs and takes na delyt to haiff thair childring and frinds brought upe in lettres to the grait reprotche and schame of the countery and thair awin grait hurt and dishonour'.[245] But this remark has to be placed in its proper context: it was made by embittered exiles in 1584. Nor is its accuracy necessarily trustworthy. Their chief opponent, the earl of Arran, had a knowledge of the classics; the earl Marischal established a university college; and the young earl of Gowrie was a scholar of considerable promise. Indeed, by the early seventeenth century the claim was actually advanced that the Scottish nobles were 'learned scholars, read in best histories, delicately linguished the most part of them'.[246]

Certainly by the 1620s, the sons of several nobles took up residence in the college at Glasgow in considerable style. The earl of Eglinton's three sons arrived with their pedagogue in 1628 and received 'ane pynt of beir everie nicht'. Then came the earl of Linlithgow's son with his pedagogue and servant, followed by the earl of Wigtown's son 'with ane servant' in 1629.[247]

Not all students, of course, lasted the pace. There was, for example, less pressure on sons of the nobility to proceed to graduation. Others dropped out through lack of finance, sickness or incapacity. Most, however, endured the course and received their due reward. On the surface, at least, there was little evidence of alienated intellectuals. Students seemed more intent on securing a niche within the existing social order rather than challenging the basic assumptions underlying post-Reformation Scottish society. The ethos may have been that of an educated and sanctified society obedient to the will of God in which none, be he great or small, was exempt from ecclesiastical censure. Yet the renewed protestant emphasis on vocation, on following a calling rather than passively accepting the station in life into which an individual had been born, did not mean an end to the hierarchical structure of society in which godly kings and magistrates were the Lord's appointed lieutenants. The exercise of ecclesiastical discipline might involve an element of social insubordination: it might result in a questioning and censuring of one's social betters. Presbyterianism might stand for a plurality of votes. The rejection of a hierarchy in the church might even be at odds with the hierarchical nature of society. Yet the axiom that the abolition of the one was but the prelude to the end of the other had still to be put to the test. It was also a proposition from which most Scots would have recoiled in horror.

As it was, apart from the Melvillian interlude, episcopacy remained the established order in the church and it was not until the presbyterian revolution of the 1640s that the tables were once more turned. Even then, the underlying belief in one national church and in the university's rôle as a fountain for the ministry still went unchallenged and seemed as strong as ever. If, in the wider perspective, it was Melville's contribution to presbyterianism which ultimately proved enduring, the fresh life and renewed purpose which he brought to the university of Glasgow were of inestimable value.

Ecclesiastical and educational revolutions which set aside much of the teaching of the Roman church and of the Aristotle of the schoolmen have come and gone, but something of the medieval purpose of a university survived the Reformation crisis. And the essence of that medieval ideal was preserved and passed on to succeeding generations. Melville may have stood if not for a completely new educational system then at least for a drastic overhaul. Yet amidst the changing structures and ideas, an essential continuity remained; and in the transmission of this academic heritage Andrew Melville had manifestly his contribution to make.

NOTES

1. *Glas. Mun.*, ii, 45, 48.
2. Calderwood, *History*, iv, 607.
3. *BUK*, i, 33, 60, 108; *APS*, iii, 24, 38; *RPC*, i, 535.
4. *BUK*, i, 360; iii, 811; jointly: *ibid.*, ii, 593–4, 624–5; *RPC*, iii, 199.
5. *BUK*, ii, 466, 471, 644, cf. 634.
6. *Ibid.*, iii, 958.
7. *Ibid.*, ii, 583, 640–1, iii, 811.
8. *RPC*, ii, 561–3; iii, 57–8, 199, 243, 274–5, 713; iv, 74–5, 266–7; v, 58–9, 129.
9. See above, 305–10.
10. GCA, Glasgow Presbytery Records, 24 October 1592: 'The names of the brethrene on the exercise within the presbitrie of Glasgw and of thair kirkis and offices'; *Glas. Mun.*, i, 215–7.
11. See above, 285, 309–10.
12. *St Andrews Kirk Session Records*, ii, 694, 751, 760, 788, 802.
13. SRO, CH2/550/1. MS Glasgow Kirk Session Records, f. 2r [7] November 1583.
14. *Ibid.*, ff. 20v, 52r, 80r, 100r, 119r, 137v, 158v, 181r. 25 April 1585, 13 October 1586, 20 October 1587, 10 October 1588, 9 October 1589, 15 October 1590, 21 October 1591, 19 October 1592.
15. GCA, MS Glasgow Presbytery Records, ff. 47v, 51v, 57r. 8 April, 15 July, 18 August 1595. SRO, CH2/121/2. MS Edinburgh Presbytery Records, 8 February 1596/7; MS St Andrews Presbytery Records, 15 July 1597; *Evidence*, iii, 197.
16. GCA, MS Glasgow Presbytery Records, ff. 45r, 65r, 148v. 5 March 1594/5, 17 February 1595/6, 11 March 1600.
17. *Fasti*, vi, 36; v, 182.
18. *Glas. Mun.*, iii, 4; *ibid.*, i, 139–41; SRO, CH2/550/1. MS Glasgow Kirk Session Records, f. 164; *Fasti*, iii, 149.
19. *Glas. Mun.*, iii, 5; SRO, CH4/1/2. Register of Presentations to Benefices, ii, f. 157r. 23 September 1586 (cf. *Glas. Mun.*, i, 149); *Fasti*, iv, 354.
20. *Glas. Mun.*, i, 149; iii, 5.
21. *Ibid.*, iii, 5, 373; *Fasti*, iii, 133.
22. *Glas. Mun.*, iii, 6, 373; *Fasti*, iii, 486; GCA, MS Glasgow Presbytery Records, f. 66r-v. [21] March—13 April 1596.
23. *Glas. Mun.*, iii, 6, 374.
24. *Ibid.*, iii, 7, 374; *Fasti*, iii, 230.
25. *Glas. Mun.*, iii, 8, 374; Wodrow, *Biographical Collections*, ii (pt. ii), 81–223.
26. *Glas. Mun.*, iii, 8, 374; *Fasti*, iii, 162.
27. *RPC*, vi, 453.
28. *Glas. Mun.*, iii, 14; *Select Biographies*, i, 132.

29. *Glas. Mun.*, i, 109.
30. SRO, CH4/1/2.
31. *RPC*, vi, 453.
32. Blair, *Life*, 11.
33. *Glas. Mun.*, i, 109.
34. SRO, CC8/8/34. Register of Testaments, Blaise Lawrie, 4 June 1600.
35. SRO, E47/6. Register of Assignations of Ministers' Stipends, f. 45r (Bell); f. 30r (Millar); *ibid.*, E47/8, f. 43r (Gibson); cf. W. R. Foster, 'A Constant Platt Achieved: Provision for the Ministry, 1600–38', *Reformation and Revolution*, 124–40 at 126.
36. *RPC*, vi, 453.
37. SRO, CH2/252/1. MS Synod of Lothian and Tweeddale Records, f. 9v. 2 April 1589; cf. f. 24r. 7 October 1590.
38. SRO, CH2/121/1. MS Edinburgh Presbytery Records, 5 September 1592.
39. *Evidence*, iii, 189. See also *APS*, iii, 181.
40. SRO, PA 10/1.
41. *RPC*, iii, 713.
42. *Glas. Mun.*, i, 88; McCrie, *Melville*, 295–9; Melville, *Diary*, 75; SRO, CC9/7/11. Register of Testaments, ff. 113r–114v.
43. *Ibid.*, CC8/8/34, 4 June 1600 (unfoliated).
44. *Ibid.*; CC9/7/11, ff. 113r–114v.
45. *Glas. Mun.*, ii, 46–7.
46. Melville, *Diary*, 69.
47. *Ibid.*, 49.
48. *Ibid.*, 83; Wodrow, *Biographical Collections*, ii (pt. ii), 82.
49. Blair, *Life*, 11.
50. *Ibid.*, 45–6, 55, 58.
51. *Ibid.*, 58; J. M. Barkley, 'Some Scottish Bishops and Ministers in the Irish Church, 1605–35', *Reformation and Revolution*, 141–59, at 145; M. Perceval-Maxwell, *The Scottish Migration to Ulster in the Reign of James I* (London, 1973), 268.
52. Melville, *Diary*, 14, 38; *Fasti*, iii, 378; for Sharp see SRO, GD30/1632, Shairp of Houstoun Muniments.
53. Spottiswoode, *History*, ii, 320; *RMS*, iv, no. 1536 (Smeaton); *Glasgow Burgh Records*, i, 4 (Blackburn).
54. Blair, *Life*, 3, 7, 112; *Glas. Mun.*, iii, 12.
55. Blair, *Life*, 9, 112; *Fasti*, iii, 341; *Glas. Mun.*, iii, 376.
56. Wodrow, *Biographical Collections*, ii (pt. ii), 84; *Memoirs of Sir Ewen Cameron of Locheill*, 63; Fasti, iv, 22.
57. *Glas. Mun.*, iii, 3, 60.
58. *Essays on the Scottish Reformation*, 145–68; Blair, *Life*, 9.
59. *First Book of Discipline*, 132.
60. *Ibid.*, 150.
61. SRO GD30/1696.
62. *Ibid.*, GD30/1697.
63. SRO, GD151/13/13. Letter Book of Sir David Graham of Fintry.
64. *Glas. Mun.*, ii, 51.
65. Melville, *Diary*, 46.
66. *Ibid.*, 25.
67. *APS*, iii, 87, 140.
68. *Glas. Mun.*, i, 67–8, 85, 88, 110.
69. *APS*, iii, 25, c. 13.
70. *BUK*, i, 214–15.

71. *RPC*, ii, 565–6.
72. SRO, PS1/65. Register of the Privy Seal, f. 52r-v. For an earlier example in 1591 see 360.
73. *Glasgow Burgh Records*, i, 336, 340, 345, 351, 352.
74. *Ibid.*, i, 351.
75. *Glas. Mun.*, i, 100–1.
76. *Ibid.*, i, 196–7.
77. SRO, GD1/12/42. Inventory of Titles pertaining to the Edinburgh Incorporated Craft of Tailors.
78. *Glas. Mun.*, iii, 5; *Glasgow Burgh Records*, i, 96; *Glas. Mun.*, i, 200.
79. *Ibid.*, iii, 8; *Deeds instituting bursaries, scholarships and other foundations in the College and University of Glasgow*, 25–32, 33–47.
80. *RSS*, vi, no. 868; *Glas. Mun.*, i, 76–7.
81. *RSS*, vi, no. 1261.
82. *Glasgow Protocols*, v, nos. 1327–9; SRO, CH4/1/1. Register of Presentations to Benefices, i, f. 31r-v; *RSS*, vi, no. 787.
83. *RSS*, vi, no. 980; vii, no. 1117.
84. SRO, CH4/1/2. Register of Presentations to Benefices, ii, ff. 113r, 115v.
85. SRO, PS1/62. Register of the Privy Seal, f. 98v.
86. *Glas. Mun.*, iii, 7, 60–1.
87. *RSS*, vi, no. 805.
88. GUA, MSS 28800, 28801; *RSS*, vii, no. 1541.
89. *Edinburgh Burgh Records*, iv, 305; *Glas. Mun.*, iii, 3.
90. SRO, CH4/1/2. Register of Presentations to Benefices, ii, f. 143r; GUA, MSS 28802–28805; *Glas. Mun.*, iii, 7.
91. SRO, CH4/1/1. Register of Presentations to Benefices, i, f. 53r; *RSS*, vi, no. 1157.
92. SRO, CH4/1/2. Register of Presentations to Benefices, ii, f. 57r; *Glas. Mun.*, iii, 7; SRO, PS1/62. Register of the Privy Seal, f. 17r; GUA, Drawer C6b.
93. SRO, CH4/1/2. Register of Presentations to Benefices, ii, f. 162v; *Glas. Mun.*, iii, 61.
94. *ER*, xxi, 402; xii, 147, 223, 305, 394; xxiii, 52, 231, 284, 323, 352; *Glasgow Burgh Records*, i, 83, 96.
95. *Glas. Mun.*, iii, 60; SRO, PS1/62. Register of the Privy Seal, f. 193. GCA, Glasgow Presbytery Records, f. 59v, 28 October 1595.
96. See D. Meek and J. Kirk, 'John Carswell, Superintendent of Argyll: A reassessment', *RSCHS*, xix, 1–22.
97. GCA, Glasgow Presbytery Records [27 December] 1594, [4 February] 1594/5; *Fasti*, iii, 391; iv, 9, 39.
98. SRO, PA10/1.
99. *APS*, iii, 98; c. 5, 178; cf. *RPC*, iii, 199; *Evidence*, iii, 183.
100. *APS*, iii, 179; *Evidence*, iii, 184.
101. *Evidence*, iii, 196.
102. *RPC*, x, 196.
103. Melville, *Diary*, 24, 29.
104. SRO, E45/1-25. Accounts of the Collector-General of the Thirds of Benefices, 1561–97. The volume for 1597 is merely fragmentary. The accounts before 1572 are printed in *Thirds of Benefices*. Excerpts of grants allocated to students between 1573 and 1579 are printed as an appendix to the *Early Records of St Andrews University*, 297–311.
105. SRO, E45/13, ff. 99v, 100v, 102r; *Early Records of St Andrews University*, 298, 301, 305, 307, 310, 311.

106. SRO, E45/17, f. 92r.
107. *Ibid.*, E45/24, f. 105r; *Early Records of St Andrews University*, 297.
108. *Glas. Mun.*, iii, 5.
109. SRO, E45/13, f. 102r; *Early Records of St Andrews University*, 307.
110. SRO, E45/14, f. 101r; E45/15, f. 102r; E45/16, f. 99r; E45/17, f. 93r; E45/18, f. 98r; E45/19, f. 102r; E45/20, f. 103r; *Glas. Mun.*, iii, 5.
111. SRO, E45/13, f. 100v; E45/14, f. 100v; E45/15, f. 101v; *Glas. Mun.*, iii, 4.
112. SRO, E45/13, f. 101r.
113. *Glas. Mun.*, iii, 518.
114. *Ibid.*, i, 139–40.
115. *Ibid.*, iii, 518.
116. *Evidence*, iii, 194. See also Appendix J.
117. *RPC*, vi, 452.
118. *Glas. Mun.*, iii, 519–22.
119. GUA, MS 26730. Schedule of Boarders and Accounts relative to them (unfoliated).
120. *Glas. Mun.*, iii, 530.
121. SRO, PA10/1.
122. Blair, *Life*, 7–8; *Select Biographies*, i, 132.
123. *Glas. Mun.*, iii, 554 (1603), 520 (1608).
124. *Ibid.*, i, 100–1, 186–9; iii, 553, 257ff.
125. *Ibid.*, iii, 12, 69; cf., Blair, *Life*, 3, 7, 112.
126. *Select Biographies*, i, 130–1.
127. *Ibid.*, 130; *Glas. Mun.*, iii, 14, 73.
128. *First Book of Discipline*, 135.
129. *Glas. Mun.*, ii, 345.
130. *Ibid.*, iii, 3–4, 67–8, 72–4.
131. *BUK*, i, 230–1.
132. *Statutes of the Realm*, iv, pt. i, 350–5; Knox, *Works*, ii, 118; *History*, ii, 271.
133. Blair, *Life*, 7–9.
134. *Glas. Mun.*, ii, 50.
135. *Select Biographies*, i, 130.
136. *Glas. Mun.*, iii, 554.
137. SRO, PA10/1.
138. *APS*, iv, 160; *RPC*, v, 462.
139. See above, 323–4.
140. Blair, *Life*, 8–9.
141. Melville, *Diary*, 17, 29–30.
142. *Select Biographies*, i, 134; *Glas. Mun.*, iii, 518.
143. Melville, *Diary*, 72.
144. *BUK*, i, 322, 334–5; ii, 441.
145. See Appendix J.
146. *APS*, iv, 435; *RPC*, viii, 612–4; *ibid.*, x, 196.
147. *Glas. Mun.*, i, 248–9.
148. Cf. *Evidence*, iii, 206.
149. *Glas. Mun.*, i, 103.
150. SRO, CH4/1/2. Register of Presentations to Benefices, ii, f. 143r.
151. *Evidence*, iii, 183.
152. *Early Records of St Andrews University*, 271.
153. Napier, *Memoirs of John Napier of Merchiston*, 67.
154. *Glas. Mun.*, iii, 61.
155. McCrie, *Melville*, 391, 476; *RSS*, vii, no. 1264.

156. *The Logike of the Moste Excellent Philosopher P. Ramus Martyr*, translated by Roland MacIlmaine (1574), ed. C. M. Dunn (Northridge, Cal., 1969), 3, 7–8.
157. See above, 327–8.
158. Wodrow, *Biographical Collections*, ii (pt. ii), 78.
159. See above, 327.
160. *Glasgow Burgh Records*, i, 374.
161. *Fasti Aberdonenses*, 283–4.
162. See above, 333; Melville, *Diary*, 55.
163. Calderwood, *History*, iv, 1–4.
164. *Letters of John Johnston and Robert Howie*, ed. J. K. Cameron, lix–lx, 195ff, 209ff, 214f, 273ff, 339ff, 343ff; Quick, *Synodicon*, i, 227.
165. Wodrow, *Biographical Collections*, ii (pt. i), 102, 105, 106.
166. See above, 335.
167. Wodrow, *Biographical Collections*, ii, (pt. ii), 81–223.
168. B. A. Armstrong, *Calvinism and the Amyraut Heresy* (London, 1969), 46 and n. 129, citing A. Rivet, *Opera*, iii, 897, 2.
169. *Ibid.*, 47.
170. *Ibid.*, 42–3.
171. Cf. J. Kirk, 'The Influence of Calvinism on the Scottish Reformation', *Records of the Church History Society*, xviii, 157–79 at 168–71.
172. *Glas. Mun.*, iii, 5–7, 60–3. They may have come from the Poitou region. Cf. Wodrow, *Biographical Collections*, ii (pt. i), 11–12.
173. MSS Archives Municipales de Millau (for James Hart, principal regent at the protestant college of Millau, 1613, and Robert Monroe, another Scot, 1623); 'Diaire de Jacques Merlin ou Recueil des choses [les] plus mémorables qui se sont passées en ceste ville [de la Rochelle] de 1589 à 1620', ed. C. Dangibeaud; *Archives Historiques de la Saintonge et de l'Aunis*, vol. v (1878), 133–4, 368; *Inventaire Sommaire des Archives Départementales antérieures à 1790*, ed. Bligny-Bondurand; *Gard, Archives Civiles*, série E, vol. 2 (*Notaires*), (Nîmes, 1900), 182, 189, 221; Bourchenin, *Les Académies Protestantes en France*, 77–8, 87, 122, 145, 463–70; M. Nicolas, *Histoire de l'Académie protestante de Montauban (1598–1659), et de Puylaurens (1660–1685)* (Montauban, 1885), 155–68; *Alba Amicorum of George Strachan, George Craig, Thomas Cumming*; Boissonnade, *Poitiers*, 96, 171, 173–4, 232; Dempster, *Historia Ecclesiastica*, i, 238–40; ii, 393, 541, 577; Wodrow, *Biographical Collections*, ii (pt. i), 27, 34, 51, 59, 93.
174. Melville, *Diary*, 83; *Select Biographies*, i, 133.
175. *Glas. Mun.*, i, 115, 117, 127–8, 136, 143, 145; iii, 4; SRO, GD30/1632. Shairp of Houston Muniments. Mr James Sharpe to Mr John Makcalzeane, Paris, 10 June 1585.
176. SRO, GD30/1632.
177. Wodrow, *Biographical Collections*, ii (pt. i), 25.
178. *Glas. Mun.*, iii, 410.
179. *CSP Scot.*, vi, no. 671.
180. Melville, *Diary*, 219.
181. *Register of the University of Oxford*, ed. A. Clark (Oxford 1887), ii (pt. i), 372, 373.
182. *Glas. Mun.*, iii, 4.
183. *University of Cambridge: Book of Matriculations and Degrees, 1544–1659*, edd. J. Venn and J. A. Venn (Cambridge, 1913), 344; *Fasti Ecclesiae Hibernicae*, ed. H. Cotton (Dublin, 1847–50), iii, 91.
184. *Register of the University of Oxford*, ii (pt. i), 373.

185. *Register of the University of Oxford*, ii (pt. i), 275.
186. R. A. Marchant, *The Puritans and the Church Courts in the Diocese of York, 1560–1642* (London, 1960), 249, 264, 273.
187. Calderwood, *History*, vii, 222.
188. SRO, PA10/1; *BUK*, i, 140.
189. *APS*, iii, 180; *Evidence*, iii, 184.
190. *Statutes of the Scottish Church*, ed. D. Patrick (SHS, Edinburgh, 1907), 84.
191. *Glas. Mun.*, iii, 3; *Fasti*, ii, 264; iii, 55, 104, 335, 341, 381, 392; Melville, *Diary*, 84.
192. *Glas. Mun.*, iii, 518.
193. *Ibid.*, iii, 3; *Fasti*, iii, 122, 152, 162, 267, 273, 280, 331, 350; v, 392; Watt, *Fasti*, 45, 206; *Clan Campbell Papers*, ed. H. Paton (Edinburgh, 1922), vi, 46 and *passim; RPC*, vii, 604; R. Keith, *An Historical Catalogue of the Scottish Bishops*, ed. M. Russell (Edinburgh, 1824), 166.
194. Wodrow, *Biographical Collections*, i, 531.
195. *Glas. Mun.*, iii, 3; SRO, PS1/60. Register of the Privy Seal, f. 129; *Fasti*, i, 409, 426; ii, 36; vi, 382; *Edinburgh Burgh Records*, iv, 305.
196. Snow, *Patrick Forbes, Bishop of Aberdeen*, 27.
197. *Glas. Mun.*, iii, 4; *Fasti*, i, 176.
198. *Ibid.*, ii, 416; iii, 149, 335.
199. *Ibid.*, iii, 154; for George Montgomery and Adam Newton (*Glas. Mun.*, iii, 4), see 379–80.
200. *Fasti*, iii, 222, 289, 338–9 (1583); 209, 353, 381, 386 (1584); 78, 122, 327, 367; iv, 291 (1585).
201. *A Catalogue of the Graduates . . . of the University of Edinburgh* (Edinburgh, 1858), 7–11. There are no figures for 1589.
202. *Evidence*, iii, 201. See also the statistics presented by R. N. Smart, 'Some observations on the Provinces of the Scottish Universities, 1560–1850', *The Scottish Tradition: Essays in honour of Ronald Gordon Cant*, ed. G. W. S. Barrow (Edinburgh, 1974), 91–106 at 94.
203. *Glas. Mun.*, iii, 4–8 for most of the persons named; *Fasti*, iii, 353 (Stewart); 240, 276 (Muirhead); 157, 253, 280 (Law); 331, 362 (Lindsay); 133 (Wallace) 162; *Fasti Ecclesiae Hibernicae*, iv, 67 (Hamilton); *Fasti*, iii, 84, 139, 142 (Cunningham); 55 (Hamilton); 240, 248, 373, 391, 486 (Rowat); ii, 272; iii, 90 (Cunningham); 253 (Clydesdale); iii, 306–7, 478; *Select Biographies*, i, 129–30 (Livingston); *Fasti*, iii, 230, 267 (Sharp).
204. Bodleian, MS Smith 77, f. 29r.
205. *Glas. Mun.*, iii, 4; *Fasti*, i, 176 (John); *Spottiswoode Society Miscellany*, i, 97–164; *Fasti Ecclesiae Hibernicae*, iii, 78–9 (James).
206. *Glas. Mun.*, iii, 3.
207. *RPC*, i, 437, 462; *BUK*, i, 110, 113, 145, 289; *Glas. Mun.*, i, 94, 99, 114, 135, 142.
208. Calderwood, *History*, iii, 645; *Glas. Mun.*, iii, 3.
209. *Glas. Mun.*, iii, 5; *Fasti*, iv, 291; SRO, E45/15, f. 102r. Accounts of the Collector-General of Thirds of Benefices; E45/16, f. 99r; E45/17, f. 93r; E45/18, f. 98r; E45/19, f. 102r.
210. Calderwood, *History*, vii, 256.
211. Although the synod of Lothian in 1589 heard a report from the presbytery of Dunbar that 'Mr Richard Ogill being admitted be thame to the office of the ministrie hes now desisted bayth from teiching and from thair exerceis, quhairof they had divers and sindrie tymes admonischit him', Ogill continued in the ministry at Innerwick until 1608. (SRO, CH2/252/1. Synod of Lothian

and Tweeddale Records, ff. 3r, 94r; *Fasti*, i, 409.) He was presented by the crown to the vicarage of Innerwick on 11 May 1590 (SRO, PS1/60, Register of the Privy Seal, f. 129). In the Register of the Assignations and Modifications of Ministers' Stipends for the years 1590 and 1591 a blank space has been left for the name of the minister at Innerwick, but from 1593 Ogill's name is entered as minister. (SRO, E47/5, ff. 40v., 39v., 35r; E47/6, ff. 34r (1593), 34r (1594). For the quotation see *Fasti*, i, 409.

212. *Select Biographies*, i, 130; *Glas. Mun.*, iii, 7, 14.
213. Blair, *Life*, 11, 15.
214. Edinburgh University Library, MS Dc.6.45, Melvini Epistolae, 29.
215. *Glas. Mun.*, iii, 3; Watt, *Fasti*, 206; SRO, GD1/371/1, Warrender Papers, f. 12.
216. *Glas. Mun.*, iii, 67, 72; J. S. Diaz, *Impresos Del Siglo XVII* (Madrid, 1972), no. 1216; *Bibliothèque de la Compagnie de Jésus*, ed. C. Sommervogel (Paris, 1896), vii, 1117. Other Glasgow students who became Roman Catholics include John Main, Alexander Baillie, Archibald Anderson, George Hegait, William Hegait, David Landels, James Bryson and (for a spell) Patrick Crawford.
217. *Glas. Mun.*, iii, 10; *Select Biographies*, i, 130–1; *Glasgow Burgh Records*, i, 477.
218. *Glas. Mun.*, iii, 11; *Memorials of Montrose*, ed. M. Napier (Maitland Club, Edinburgh, 1848–50), i, 108, 110, 136–8.
219. *Glas. Mun.*, iii, 4, 518; SRO, GD30/111, 816, 1632.
220. *Glas. Mun.*, iii, 4; *RMS*, v, no. 1604; *RPC*, v, 665, 707–8.
221. *Ibid.*, iii, 4; *Edinburgh Burgh Records*, iv, 265, 568–9; v, 48, 58; *RPC*, v, 318, 490; Melville, *Diary*, lii.
222. *Edinburgh Burgh Records*, v, 115, 116, 131, 134, 137, 202; *Charters, Statutes and Acts of the Town Council and Senatus, 1583–1858*, 83, 99–100; W. C. Dickinson, 'The Advocates' Protest against the Institution of a Chair of Law in the University of Edinburgh', *SHR*, xxiii (1926), 205–12; *RMS*, vi, nos. 1291, 1326.
223. *HMC Salisbury MSS*, xviii, 29, 141, 279, 284. For Newton's correspondence with Peter Young see Bodleian, MS Smith 77, ff. 49r-v, 51r.
224. *Glas. Mun.*, iii, 4; *CSP Scot.*, xi, *passim*; *RPC*, v, 741; vi, 213, 229, 484, 508, 713, 715; xii, *passim*.
225. *Glas. Mun.*, iii, 7; *Glasgow Protocols*, x, nos. 3226, 3228; J. S. Muirhead, *Old Minute Book of the Faculty of Procurators of Glasgow* (Glasgow, 1948), 231.
226. *Montgomery Manuscripts*, 9–149.
227. *Ibid.*, 10; *Glas. Mun.*, iii, 4; *CSP Scot.*, xi, no. 404; xii, nos. 135, 138, 154, 159, 184.
228. *HMC Salisbury MSS*, xv, 57; *Montgomery Manuscripts*, 9, 96–8, 100; *Fasti Ecclesiae Hibernicae*, iii, 78, 117–18, 315–16, 350.
229. *Montgomery Manuscripts*, 30–2, 42, 49–50.
230. *Spottiswoode Society Miscellany*, i, 97–164; *Glas. Mun.*, iii, 4.
231. Wodrow, *Biographical Collections*, ii (pt. i), 64; *Glas. Mun.*, iii, 10.
232. *RPC*, x, 719; *Fasti*, iii, 386; Watt, *Fasti*, 206.
233. *Glas. Mun.*, iii, 4; *DNB*, xxxix, 364–5; *Fasti*, vi, 248–9; *Glasgow Protocols*, viii, no. 2433.
234. *Calendar of Writs preserved at Yester House, 1166–1625*, edd. C. C. Harvey and J. Macleod (SRS, Edinburgh, 1930), 1536–98, no. 877.
235. *Glas. Mun.*, iii, 60.
236. *Ibid.*, iii, 64, 67–9.
237. *Ibid.*, iii, 68; *APS*, v, 440; vi (i), 4, 95; vi (ii), 125, 377; SRO, CH2/294/2, Paisley Presbytery Records, 22 September 1638, 17 June 1641, 9 February 1642, 25 May 1643; G. Chalmers, *Caledonia*, iii, 846.

238. *Glas. Mun.*, iii, 69; *APS*, vi (i) , 95, 285, 430, 441; SRO, CH2/294/2. Paisley Presbytery Records, 2 January 1640, 19 March 1640, 25 August 1642.
239. Melville, *Diary*, 38; *Glas. Mun.*, iii, 3.
240. *Montgomery Manuscripts*, 56–7.
241. *Fasti Ecclesiae Hibernicae*, iii, 78, 117–18, 315–16 (Montgomery and Spottiswoode), 91 (Hegait), 224 (Gibson), 231 (Blackburn).
242. Blair, *Life*, 53ff; *Select Biographies*, i, 140ff. See also J. M. Barkley, 'Some Scottish Bishops and Ministers in the Irish Church, 1605–35', in *Reformation and Revolution*, 141–59; Perceval-Maxwell, *Scottish Migration to Ulster*, 363–5.
243. *Analecta Hibernica* (Dublin, 1943), xii, 102, 103, 104.
244. *Glas. Mun.*, ii, 176; *Early Records of St Andrews University*, 280.
245. Melville, *Diary*, 190.
246. W. Lithgow, *Totall discourse of the rare adventures* (1632), 499, cited in G. Donaldson, *Scotland: James V–James VII* (Edinburgh, 1965), 256.
247. *Glas. Mun.*, iii, 530.

Appendix A

This list of contents of the statutes of the faculty of arts has been omitted from the printed edition of the statutes in *Glas. Mun.*, ii, 20–37, and was presumably made by Duncan Bunch. It precedes the statutes in the little parchment volume in Glasgow University Archives 26615 (or Clerk's Press 3).

Incipiunt capitula statutorum secundum titulos eorundem quorum quodlibet incipit Item etc.
Capitula primi tituli qui est de hiis que pertinent ad laudem et honorem dei
  Capitulum primum De tempore et modo inchoandi nouum ordinarium omni anno
  Capitulum secundum De tempore electionis decani facultatis arcium singulis annis
  Capitulum tertium De funeracione magistrorum cum contigit
Capitula secundi tituli qui est de moribus et habitibus suppositorum
  Capitulum primum De modo corrigendi delinquentes tam magistros quam studentes in vite honestate
  Capitulum secundum et tertium De correctione studencium in diffamitate habituum et qualiter in eis se habent
Capitula tertii tituli de disposicione lectionum numero librorum ordinacione actuum et modo legendi
  Capitulum primum De modo legendi in studio glasguensi in habitu ordinario
  Capitulum secundum De tempore eleccionis quodlibetarii et de officio eius
  Capitulum tertium De electione librorum ad legendum ordinarie
  Capitulum quartum et quintum De intimacione festorum per bedellum et actum Et qui sint actus publici
  Capitulum sextum et septimum In quo loco fuerint congregaciones publice Et qualiter uocabuntur magistri ad actus
  Capitulum octauum et nonum Quo tempore incipient disputaciones in vico Et quod non legatur quando fuerit publicus actus
  Capitulum decimum Quod quilibet bachalarius in artibus potest legere tractatum petri hispani

Capitulum undecimum et duodecimum De modo docendi Item de electione receptoris burse facultatis

Capitulum decimum tertium De libris audiendis a studentibus tam ordinarie quam extraordinarie

Capitulum decimum quartum Quantum studentes soluere debent pro quo libet libro magistris regentibus

Incipit capitulum primum quarti tituli De die quo aperitur examen pro bachallauriis

Capitulum secundum et tertium De electione temptatorum pro bachallariatu Et de modo creandi bachallarios

Capitulum quartum et quintum De disputacione bachallariorum in quadragesima Et quot in una scola disputent

Capitulum sextum et septimum De etate bachallariorum et quantum debent solui decano (et) temptatoribus quando admittantur

Capitulum octauum et nonum De tempore quo fiant disputaciones in vico Et ad questiones respondebunt

Capitulum decimum De tempore aperiendi temptamen pro magisterio et modo procedendi ad licenciam et forma licenciandi

Capitulum undecimum Quot annos habebunt qui insignia magistralia recipiunt in studio uniuersali

Capitulum duodecimum De tempore inchoandi temptamen post eleccionem temptatorum

Capitulum decimum tertium De non dispensando in audicione librorum pro forma Et de dispensacione tertie responsionis

Capitulum decimum quartum De literis testimonialibus super audicione librorum presentaturis facultati per bachalaurios

Capitulum decimum quintum De modo quo decanus examinabit bachalaurios ante admissionem

Capitulum decimum sextum Quot annos integros complebit aliquis antequam admittatur

Capitulum decimum septimum De non admittendo eos qui allegant se habuisse scienciam preteritam

Capitulum decimum octauum Quod non admittantur qui non impleuerunt tempus a facultate ordinatum immediate ante eorum presentacionem ad cancellarium

Capitulum decimum nonum Quod nullus presentet se ad temptamen nisi sub aliquo magistro regente

Capitulum vicesimum Quod nullus gradum capiat de gracia cancellarii tantum

Capitulum vicesimum primum et vicesimum secundum Quod potentes stent commensaliter cum regentibus Et non potentes sic stare soluant decem solidos

Capitulum vicesimum tertium Quod nullus capiat gradum nisi prius temptatus per facultatem

Capitula quinti tituli de hiis que debent solui a promouendis

Capitulum primum Quod quilibet determinans antequam admittatur soluat facultati x s bedello xviii d rectori xv

Capitulum secundum Quod quilibet studens soluat bedello singulis annis in festo omnium sanctorum viii d

Capitulum tertium et quartum Quantum licentiandi soluent facultati et bedello et magistris regentibus ante introitum

Capitula sexti tituli qui est de Iuramentis

Capitulum primum De iuramentis bachallariandorum

Capitulum secundum De iuramentis licentiatorum

Capitulum tertium De iuramentis magistrorum de nouo incipientium

Capitulum quartum De dispensacione iuramenti cum magistris de lectura et de penis leuandis

Capitulum quintum De iuramentis receptoris

Capitulum sextum De iuramentis bedelli

Capitulum septimum De iuramentis decani

Capitulum octauum De iuramentis magistrorum superueniencium antequam recipiuntur

Capitulum nonum De iuramentis temptatorum pro bachallariandis

Capitulum decimum De iuramentis temptatorum pro licentiandis

Capitulum undecimum De iuramentis regencium antequam admittantur ad regendum in facultate

Capitula septimi tituli de modo procedendi ad magisterium

Capitulum primum Quot magistri erunt vocati de necessitate in aula magistrali et (de) ordine facultatis

Capitulum secundum et tertium Quot determinabunt uno die et quot magistros inuitabuntur Et quot magistri uno die

Capitulum quartum Quod presidens nunquam ascendat cathedram quousque (facultas) sit contenta

Capitulum quintum Quod in actibus scole conforment se magistri forme studii parisiensis et coloniensis

Capitulum sextum Quod in aula magistrali respondebit unus bachalarius ad questionem etc

Capitulum septimum Quod decisiones questionum digeste et mature fiant

Capitulum octauum Quod alia sequuntur in hoc septimo titulo ut clare patet intuentibus

Appendix B

THE BLACKFRIARS AND OTHER BUILDINGS

The buildings and yards to the south of the university site in the High Street present some problems which need elucidation. They include the Principal's House, the tenements of the chaplainry of St Mungo in the lower church of the cathedral, and the whole complex of tenements and yards surrounding the Blackfriars precinct. This may help to position the friars' chapter-house (used at times for university meetings) and other places mentioned in 1579, 'the West Freir Yaird' and the 'colhowse and Closter Knot, the Paradyce Yairds uver and neather with the remanent small yairdis' of the Blackfriars (*Glas. Mun.*, i, 119–22).

If we start from Slezer's print in the *Theatrum Scotiae* (published in 1693 but drawn many years earlier), we have a picture considerably altered from the medieval one, but one which can yield some information in conjunction with documentary evidence.

The small house on the High Street immediately adjacent to the college on the south represents the site in whole or in part of the original Principal's House as constructed by Duncan Bunch to the south of the Hamilton College of Arts with access to a room or rooms in the adjacent college. This site was developed in the early seventeenth century when the contiguous building to the south was acquired.

This second building (immediately north of the entry with steps shown by Slezer) represents the site of the house given by Robert Forstar to the St Mungo chaplainry concerning which foundation a tablet commemorating the patrons, the Blackadders of Tulliallan, still existed when the university site was moved to Gilmorehill. This gift was described in 1499 as consisting of fore and back tenements, to the north of which stood the tenement of the Pedagogy, to the south the place of the friars and to the east their graveyard (GUA, 16391). The graveyard, therefore, shown in Slezer was in part a new one, having been extended east into the site of the former Cloister.

The open entry leading into the precinct as shown in Slezer was at an earlier period (1478) overarched by yet another building of Robert Forstar's (*Liber Collegii Nostre Domine*, 190–1) with a window looking towards the friars' statue of the Virgin. By 1630, however, this had gone, and the southern boundary here is now stated to be an imaginary line drawn from the (north) gable of the Blackfriars kirk to the street (*Glas. Mun.*, i, 235). One of the houses owned by the St Kentigern chaplainry founded by Andrew Stewart on the opposite, west side of High Street faced directly the friars' entry, 'coram introitu ad ecclesiam fratrum predicatorum' (GUA, 16406). The university beadle, David Kirkland, was chaplain of the Forstar chaplainry just before the Reformation when he let this house to tenants (GUA, 16571, and for subsequent history GUA, 16574, etc.). It was later re-acquired for the university. Behind this house in 1557 stood no longer the northern section of the friars' graveyard but a little meadow, and this in turn by 1630 had become part of the Principal's Garden (*Glas. Mun.*, i, 235).

The Blackfriars kirk as shown in Slezer is not, as has been suggested, in part imaginary, but represents what Slezer saw before the old kirk had gone to ruin and had been repaired (he may, of course, have borrowed from an earlier print). At its north-west end stood the Bellhouse Yett (not in Slezer) which was a gatehouse similar, it would seem, to the present Tron Kirk tower and replacing an earlier bell-tower destroyed, as mentioned elsewhere in this volume, by lightning. It was part of the friars' property (*Glas. Mun.*, i, 181) which the university inherited at the Reformation; after 1600 it was inhabited by Isobel Ross, widow of the regent, Blaise Lawrie, whose ownership she was forced to renounce (*Glas. Mun.*, iii, 246). However, she acquired another Blackfriars property by 1631 (*ibid.*, i, 246).

The yards to the north of the kirk beyond the little meadow were the Over and Nether Paradise yards, divided probably by an alleyway leading to a conjectured North Porch, providing easy access from the college. This, it is suggested, was the 'porche Kirk dure' of 1553 in which sanctuary was sought (*Liber Collegii Nostre Domine*, lxiii). Before being turned over to garden use, this area was perhaps merely a 'paradise' or *parvis*, such as was commonly found in proximity to church porches. Already before the Reformation it was let for cultivation (GUA, 11615–6, 22003, from 1554).

Directly in front of the Blackfriars kirk in Slezer can be seen the site of the Old Mealmarket, previously the first of a succession of great tenements leading southwards to Blackfriars Wynd. Some of the ground intermediate between this and the kirk was part of the friars' graveyard and at the extreme south was their west yard (*Liber Collegii Nostre Domine*, 182). On the west end of the cloister, a high vaulted building was constructed from the kirk (on the north) to the dorter (on the south), about 1487 (*ibid*, 198–201). The interior of the cloister was the 'Closter Knot' and to the east of the cloister and south of the kirk were, apparently, the chapter-house and school. Beyond that again were outhouses including the coalhouse with its yard. An alley running north to south divided this area off from the Great Orchard which extended back east to the Molendinar burn and can be seen in the Slezer print.

The kirk suffered from a thunderclap in 1670 and was deserted though repairs are mentioned in 1688–9 (R. Renwick, *Glasgow Memorials* (Glasgow, 1908) 197–8). The site of the new Blackfriars kirk was to the north of the old, immediately facing the entry or College Open, and not south of it as was the old. In a sketch of *c.* 1764, a 'Plan of the city and the course of the Molendinar Burn' reproduced at the end of the preface to *Records and Charters of the Burgh of Glasgow* (ed. Robert Renwick, Glasgow, 1902, vii), the site of the original church can be gauged from the comparative narrowness of the tenements formerly facing it on the same side of the High Street in relation to other longer tenements west of what must have been the original cloister area.

Of the tenanted buildings south of the College Open and on the north side of Blackfriars Wynd the history can be pieced together partly from city Protocol Books, deeds in the university archives and, in the case of the Thomas Caird (Kerd) house, in the Dumbarton Town Archives. At the west end of the founded buildings but to the east of the tenements fronting the High Street was a brewhouse and a pathway, shaded by ash and aspen, leading away from the cloister (*Liber Collegii Nostre Domine*, 183–4). Cf. also GUA, 16299, dated 6 December 1558, which also shows that the 'pettecok yard' was adjacent on the north to the 'ower paradise' yard.

Appendix C

The following formulary of Archbishop Beaton I empowers both or either of the regents, whose initials alone are given, to act as vice-chancellor(s) and grant the licence in arts. It is dated at Glasgow, 31 July 1514 (Edinburgh University Library, Laing Ms Div. iii, 322).

(f. 123) Commissio ad actum licencie in artibus

Jacobus miseratione diuina glasguensis Archiepiscopus dilectis clericis nostris magistris N.S. et C.A. uniuersitatis nostre regentibus salutem cum benedictione diuina Quia ex relatione vestra concipimus nonnullos bachalarios in artibus ad gradum licencie ascendere volentibus, quemquidem gradum conferre ad nos tanquam ad cancellarium dicte uniuersitatis pertinere dinoscitur Quia nos variis et arduis prepediti negotiis predicto actui interesse non valemus vobis igitur et vestrum cuilibet coniunctim et diuisim predictum actum celebrare gradumque licencie conferre nostram per presentes concedimus potestatem, facultatem pariter et auctoritatem. Datum sub nostra subscriptione manuali Apud glasgw die ultimo julii anno domini mvc quingentesimo xiiii°.

399

Appendix D

WILL OF ALEXANDER HAMILTON, REGENT IN THE PEDAGOGY

The inventory of the belongings of Alexander Hamilton, regent in the pedagogy, was made at Glasgow on 30 August 1547, in the presence of Mr John Hamilton, Quintin and James Hamilton, and Mr David Robeson, notary, commissary of Hamilton. It is to be found in the National Library of Scotland, Advocates Ms 25.9.4 (Riddell Collection 44), ff. 15v–16.

Assets. Hamilton had £160 in ready money and various furnishings, etc., including two 'Irish' pieces of clothing, one white and one multi-coloured. Some of his belongings were in Hamilton, and some in the dean of Glasgow's lodging near the cathedral. He owned some books which along with some clothes and small items were worth £20. At the time of his death he was obviously trying to obtain the deanery of Glasgow, vacant by the death of George Lockhart (cf. Watt, *Fasti Medii Aevi*, 156).

Some outstanding debts were owed him by the parishioners of Hamilton and Dalserf for crops due since 1540, over and above what was owed to the dean of Glasgow (whose prebend Hamilton was). This was presumably for the St Mary chaplainry founded by Cadzow, the sources of whose income (distinct from the Cadzow obit) have not been traced. Hamilton had lent money to Mr Robert Lang, former student (*Glas. Mun.*, ii, 140), evidently at this point the steward of the pedagogy. Others in debt to him were Walter Spreull and Robert Bracanrig in Arthurlie (for part of the revenue of the St Thomas Martyr chaplainry). He had a pension payable from Dalry.

Debts. Hamilton owed Mr Robert Lang for the table of Quintin Hamilton (*Glas. Mun.*, ii, 162, 289–91) from 8 July to date of inventory, 50 shillings; for the table of William Wilkyne from 16 July likewise, 42 shillings; for his own and Mr John Hamilton's from 1 August, 56 shillings; and for advance payment for William Wilkyne till Martinmas following, £4 13s (Wilkyne was his servant). He owed William Fleming 13s 4d for lime, and £8 to the pedagogy for the debts of William Hamilton. All other debts to the pedagogy received by him, including part of the said £8, he had spent on its repair. (The Liber Decani, f. 143, notes that in 1542 he was exonerated for debts expended on the repair of the place.) He owed to Mark Jamieson (as procurator for the vicars choral?) for offerings received at the altar of St Mary in the lower church of the cathedral and for a covering (*casula*) to be purchased for it: and to Mr John Ray for an annual rent due to the chapel of St Arungill 13s 4d, and to the executors of the dean of Glasgow about £80.

Legacy. He wished to be buried near the tomb of his father in Hamilton, or otherwise near the altar of the Virgin Mary wherever he died. Among his bequests were sums to the grey and black friars of Glasgow and for an annual celebration on 26 August by the chaplains of Hamilton. The annual dues were to be paid to the vicars choral and Archibald Dickie (cf. *Glas. Mun.*, ii, 176), chaplain of the altar of the Virgin Mary in Glasgow. His books in Glasgow were to be distributed among his brothers, including Mr John Hamilton. Mr Robert Lang (that is, the steward) and his wife were to continue to occupy his house for four more years. His executors were Michael Hamilton, vicar of Mearns, Mr John and Quintin Hamilton, and James Nasmyth, chaplain in Hamilton.

Moreover, if it should happen that I die before the return of my bulls from Rome, my executors will exact from Mr John Thornton 252 crowns of the sun, of which sum 100 crowns are to be spent in the construction of the place of the pedagogy of Glasgow.' He left his grey gown to Michael Hamilton. His executors were to note that he had in his keeping over £600 in his iron chest in Hamilton (of which William Wilkyne had the key); that is, the sum left by Archbishop Gavin (Dunbar) with the dean of Glasgow for the purchase of gold copes and other church ornaments.

The chapel of St Arungill referred to above is not otherwise on record. A witness in Hamilton in 1584 was Armagill Carbarnis (SRO GRH charters, RH6/2754). In a corrupt form the site is found as a place-name on early maps.

Appendix E

KITCHEN FURNISHINGS

The following excerpts from the Muniments regarding kitchen furnishings have been omitted in the printed edition.

(1) Liber Decani, f. 111
   7 August 1492. After 'archangeli' (*Glas. Mun.*, ii, 260):

Item in hoc computo et eciam allocacione deliberauit idem Johannes dicto collegio unum caminum ferreum iii parapsides stanneas et vii discos eiusdem metalli ii mappas et ii manutergia Item idem Johannes deliberauit dicto collegio bona infrascripta eidem pertinencia videlicet tres pipas a hoghed ii barellis in le larder Item in coquina ii ollas i pan a caldron and a cruk Item in Brasiatorio i led and in panataria unum almariolum.

(2) *ibid.*, f. 120
   1 November 1496. After 'circa edificium nove coquine' (*Glas. Mun.*, ii, 269):

tam de bonis receptis a domino archidiacono glasguensi quam de tribus libris receptis ab archibaldo craufurd bursario moderno approbarunt et eundem Magistrum Joannem de huiusmodi summis exonerarunt in cuius testimonium dicti decanus et auditores se suis propriis manibus subscripserunt Salua tamen condicione stare cum alexandro flemyn super complemento dicte coquine quod decanus et facultas intendit prosequi coram domino officiali et domino rectore uniuersitatis
   Ego Thomas forsyth decanus facultatis huiusmodi computo interfui teste manu propria.

(3) *ibid.*, 2nd flyleaf
   17 March 1522/3

xvii martii Anno millesimo quingentesimo xxii deliuerit be wellem to master James yir gudis undirwrittin imprimis iii siluer spwnis ane brass basyn iii pottis ii ald pannis ane caldroun viii dischis Item ix plaitis of ye quhilks ii ar small i chargeour x trunschoris twa yrne chymnais ii rakis ii spetis Irn ladil a tayngis i pare of pot bowlis i mortare i pestel i gyrdyl ane half galone stop i pynt stop of chad (?) i half bare(l) iii ald chandlaris i ald dornyk brod clat ii new towelis of dornyk twa new bordclatis and ane ald of lynyn Item ii new towelles of lynyng i salt fat i rostin irne ane almory Item willelmus is oblist to deliuer a playt Item schot of pewder togidder with ye pypis barellis and hogsheids as ye bil of compt beris.

(4) *ibid.*, f. 2

Inventarium domiciliorum et utensilium pedagogii glasguensis de quibus oneratur prouisor Willelmus Layng factum coram venerabili viro Magistro Willelmo hammyltoun decano facultatis et auditoribus computi deputatis die 2° mensis Julii anno domini millesimo quin-gentesimo xxxvt^{to}

Inprimis una tassia argentea ponderis nouem unciarum aut circiter in custodia magistri alexandri logane Item in manibus dicti prouisoris quatuor candelabra ennea Item una olla duarum quartarum Item duo camini unus pro aula et alius pro coquina Item una peluis ennea Item unus cacabus Item unum circingulum ly girdil Item una olla ennea continencie quinque pinctarum Item una patella ennea vi quartarum Item duo patelle una continencie duarum quartarum altera trium Item nouem parapsides stannee cum quinque discis stanneis ly luggit et duobus discis circularibus xi scissoriis stanneis ly trunsholis Item unum mortarium enneum ly mortar cum tusorio enneo Item unum pendulum ferreum ly cruk Item unum colum ferreum ly irne ladil unam fuscinulam ly elcruk Item unum par ly pot bowlis Item duo ly spettis maius et minus Item ly rakkis Item unum ly almory Item una pipa lignea Item duo ly hogheidis Item duo coclearia argentea Item unum salsarium stanneum Item una quarta stannea Item una amphora stannea duarum quartarum Item forceps Item ly gard enneum trium s. Item in ly napry duo mappe confecte anno immediate precedente continentes unaquaque quinque ulnas de ly bertane kenwiss Item noua de ly dornik Item una mappa antiqua pro studentibus Item duo manutergia ly smal claith cum duobus ly seruiettis Et premissa acta erant coram prescripto decano regentibus loci et Magistris dauid bruyce et Nicolao Witherspone auditoribus dicti computi deputatis.

o

Appendix F

GIOVANNI FERRERIO: A BRIEF CHRONOLOGY

As no good biographical source for the life of Ferrerio exists, the following skeleton summary of his life may be of use to the reader:

1502   25 February, born at Riva di Chieri, near Turin

c. 1527   In Paris, student at the college of Lisieux

1528   In Paris, introduced to Robert Reid, abbot of the Cistercian abbey of Kinloss

            to Scotland; at the court of James V

1531   Teacher of monks at Kinloss

            Friendly with Hector Boece, the historian and principal at Aberdeen university

1536   Introductory letter to the reprint of Marsilio Ficino's translation of *Plato's Phaedo* edited by Francesco Zampini

1539–40 Issued various works in Paris including a reprint of Pico della Mirandola in defence of the soul's immortality

            Also *De vera cometae significatione*, an attack on astrology

1541   Easter, returned to Scotland

1544   Left Scotland for Paris

1547–53 At the Collège des Lombards in Paris

            Met Guillaume Postel, cabalist and Hebraist, royal lecturer there

1549   Edited a work of Alessandro Alessandri; in his dedication he mentions that Cardinal Beaton's nephews were his pupils

1551   Began to supply Scottish historical material to Paris editions of Johann Carion's chronicle

1552   Witness in house of Archbishop Beaton II in Paris

1556   Biographical introduction to Chrysostom *Opera*, ed. Ph. Montanus

            Bought books in Paris for Beaton in Glasgow

1559   Letter to Beaton *re* John Davidson, Principal

1563   Along with Davidson's brother, William, testifies to the Catholic faith of Gilbert Skene on latter's appointment to the college in the town of Rennes

1566   Edinburgh edition of John Vaus *Rudimenta* with verses by Ferrerio

1574   Ferrerio's edition of Boece's History printed at Lausanne

Refers to Scottish historical collections of the former dean of Glasgow (Henry Sinclair)

1576   Postel wrote that Ferrerio's health was failing

1577   Italian translation of anti-astrological work gives the Italian form of his name as Ferrerio

1579   His collection of proverbs added to Jean Gillot's edition of the *Adagia* of Erasmus (Gillot was in the Cistercian college in Paris)

Appendix G

Dates on the left in roman type are precise dates of appointment; in italic, they record the first known occurrence in office. Dates on the right are those of death or demission of office.

Information is taken from the printed *Munimenta* unless otherwise indicated. For bishop and archbishop chancellors, however, it is taken from D. E. R. Watt's *Fasti Medii Aevi*.

Procurators of Nations, Intrants and Members of the Rector's Council (Deputies or Assessors) have been omitted.

Chancellors

1451, 7 Jan.	William Turnbull	1454, 3 Sep.	
1455, 7 May	Andrew de Durisdeer	1473, 20 Nov.	
1474, 28 Jan.	John Laing	1483, 11 Jan.	
1483, 19 Mar.	Robert Blackadder	1508, 28 Jul.	
1508, 9 Nov.	James Beaton I	1523, 5 Jun.	
1523, 15 Aug	Gavin Dunbar	1547, 30 Apr.	
1550, 6 Jan.	James Beaton II	1560, Jul. (left for France)	
1573	James Boyd	1581	
1581	Robert Montgomery (?)	1585	
1603(?)	John Spottiswoode	1615	

Vice-Chancellors

Not strictly an office, but regular appointments were made. The vice-chancellor performed the chancellor's duty of granting the licence, a duty he seldom performed personally.

Rectors

1451	David Cadzow
1452, 16 Sep.	David Cadzow
1453, 25 Oct.	Thomas Cameron
1454	Blank
1455	Blank
1456, 25 Oct.	William Herries
1457, 25 Oct	William Herries
1458	Blank

1459, 24 Aug.	David Cadzow	
1460, 25 Oct.	David Cadzow	
1461, 25 Oct.	David Cadzow	
1463, 25 Oct.	David Cadzow	
1464, 25 Oct.	David Cadzow	
1465, 25 Oct.	David Cadzow	
1466, 25 Oct.	David Cadzow	
1467/8, 26 Jan.	Patrick Leitch	1468, 9 Jul.
1468, 25 Oct.	Duncan Bunch	
1469, 25 Oct.	William Arthurlie	
1470, 25 Oct.	Thomas de Lutherdale	
1471, 25 Oct.	William Glendinning	
1472, 25 Oct.	William Glendinning	
1473, 25 Oct.	William Semple	
1474, 25 Oct.	William Elphinstone	
1475, 25 Oct.	William Glendinning	
1476, 25 Oct.	Thomas Montgomery	
1477, 25 Oct.	Thomas Montgomery	
1478, 25 Oct.	William Carmichael	
1479	Thomas Montgomery	
1480, 25 Oct.	Thomas Forsyth	
1481, 25 Oct.	Patrick Leitch	
1482, 25 Oct.	John Brown	
1483, 25 Oct.	William Carmichael	
1484, 25 Oct.	Nicholas Ross	
1485, 25 Oct.	Patrick Elphinstone	
1486, 25 Oct.	John Stewart	
1487, 25 Oct.	John Stewart	
1488, 25 Oct.	Thomas Muirhead	
1489, 25 Oct.	David Cunningham	
1490, 25 Oct.	John Goldsmith	
1491, 25 Oct.	John Doby	
1492, 25 Oct.	Nicholas Ross	
1493, 25 Oct.	Thomas Forsyth	
1494, 25 Oct.	David Cunningham	
1495, 25 Oct.	George Montgomery	
1496	George Montgomery	
1497, 25 Oct.	John Goldsmith	
1498, 25 Oct.	Patrick Elphinstone	
1499, 25 Oct.	Thomas Muirhead	
1501, 25 Jul.	Alexander Inglis Deputed Patrick Coventry vice-Rector	
1501, 25 Oct.	Thomas Forsyth	

1502, 25 Oct.	Thomas Forsyth
1503, 25 Oct.	Thomas Forsyth
1503/4, 17 Feb.	Deputed Patrick Coventry vice-Rector
1504, 25 Oct.	Thomas Forsyth
1505, 25 Oct.	Patrick Elphinstone
1506	Blank
1509, 19 Jun.	Martin Reid
1509, 25 Oct.	George Montgomery
1511, 25 Oct.	George Montgomery
1512, 25 Oct.	James Stewart
1513, 25 Oct.	Patrick Graham
1514, 25 Oct.	Patrick Graham
1515, 25 Oct.	Plague, no election
1516, 25 Oct.	Patrick Graham
1517, 25 Oct.	Adam Colquhoun
1518, 25 Oct.	Alexander (sic) Colquhoun
25 Jun.	Deputed John Doby vice-Rector
3 Nov.	Deputed John Doby vice-Rector
1519, 25 Oct.	Robert Maxwell
23 Nov.	Deputed James Neilson vice-Rector
1520, 25 Oct.	Robert Maxwell
19 Nov.	Deputed James Neilson vice-Rector
1521, 25 Oct.	James Stewart
1522, 20 May	James Stewart
1523, 25 Oct.	James Stewart
1524, 25 Oct.	Adam Colquhoun
1525, 25 Oct.	Walter Kennedy
1526, 25 Oct.	John Reid
1527, 25 Oct.	Thomas Campbell
1528, 25 Oct.	Adam Colquhoun
1529, 25 Oct.	Adam Colquhoun
1530, 25 Oct.	Adam Colquhoun
1531, 25 Oct.	Adam Colquhoun
1532, 25 Oct.	Adam Colquhoun
1533, 25 Oct.	James Houston
6 Nov.	Deputed James Neilson vice-Rector
1534, 25 Oct.	James Houston
1535, 25 Oct.	James Houston
1536, 25 Oct.	James Houston
1537, 25 Oct.	James Houston
1538, 25 Oct.	James Houston
1539, 25 Oct.	James Houston
1540, 25 Oct.	James Houston

1541, 25 Oct.	James Houston
1542, 25 Oct.	John Bellenden
1543, 25 Oct.	John Bellenden
1544, 25 Oct.	John Bellenden
1545, 25 Oct.	Plague, no election
1546, 25 Oct.	Walter Beaton
1547, 25 Oct.	Walter Beaton
1548, 25 Oct.	Walter Beaton
1549, 25 Oct.	Walter Beaton
1550, 25 Oct.	Walter Beaton
1551, 26 Oct.	Walter Beaton
1551, 5 Nov.	Deputed John Stewart vice-Rector
1552, 26 Oct.	John Steinston
1553, 25 Oct.	John Colquhoun
1554, 25 Oct.	John Colquhoun
1555, 25 Oct.	Archibald Beaton
1556, 25 Oct.	Archibald Beaton
1557, 25 Oct.	Archibald Beaton
1558, 25 Oct.	James Balfour
1559	John Colquhoun
1569	Andrew Hay
1570	Andrew Hay
1573	Andrew Hay
1574	Andrew Hay
1577	Andrew Hay
1579	Andrew Hay
1580	Andrew Hay
1582	Andrew Hay
1586, May	Andrew Hay
1586, July	Archibald Crawfurd
1594	David Wemyss
1595	John Hay
1596	David Wemyss
1597	David Wemyss
1598	David Wemyss
1599	David Wemyss
1600	John Hay

University Bursars (or *Receivers*)

Before 1482	Unknown
1482	William Carmichael (continued)
1485	John Hutchinson
1486	William Stewart

1487	William Stewart
1489	Thomas Forsyth
1490	Thomas Forsyth
1491	John Glen
1492	Patrick Coventry
1493	Patrick Coventry
1496	Patrick Coventry
1497	Archibald Calderwood (continued)
1498	Archibald Calderwood
1499	Archibald Calderwood
1501	Archibaid Calderwood
1502	Archibald Calderwood
1503	John Spreull
1504	James Neilson
1505	James Neilson
1510	William Gibson
1512	Thomas Lees/15 Oct. James Houston
1513	James Houston
1514	James Houston
1516	James Houston
1517	James Houston
1518	James Houston
1519	James Houston
1520	James Houston
1521	Matthew Reid
1522	Matthew Reid
1524	Matthew Reid
1525	Matthew Reid
1526	David Smyth
1527	David Smyth
1528	(David Smyth) 1528/9 Feb. Alexander Hamilton
1529	Alexander Hamilton
1530	Alexander Hamilton
1531	Alexander Hamilton
1532	Alexander Hamilton
1533	Alexander Logan
1534	Alexander Logan
1535	Alexander Logan
1536	Alexander Logan
1537	Alexander Logan
1538	Alexander Logan
1539	Alexander Hamilton (continued till 1544)
1547	John Houston (continued till 1554)

1555	Archibald Crawford
1556	John Laing (continued till 1558)

University Promotors (and/or *Procurators*)

1483	John Gray
1490	Archibald Crawford 1492
1493	David Dunn
1497	John Hutchinson (Hugonis) 1499
1501	John Bigholm (continued in office)
1505	Unnamed (but continued)
1510	David Dunn
1512	Andrew Smyth
1513	Unnamed (continued)
1514	James Houston
1516	James Houston (Procurator), Andrew Smyth (Promotor)
1517	Michael Hutchinson (Hugonis)
1518	Nicholas Wotherspoon
1519	Matthew Stewart (and Procurator)
1520	Nicholas Wotherspoon (Procurator), James Lindsay (Promotor)
1521	Nicholas Wotherspoon (Procurator), Andrew Smyth (Promotor)
1522	Nicholas Wotherspoon (and Procurator)
1524	Nicholas Wotherspoon
1525	Alexander Logan
1526	David Smyth
1528	Alexander Logan
1529	David Smyth (and Procurator)
1530	David Smyth
1531	William Hamilton (and Procurator)
1532	Nicholas Wotherspoon (and Procurator)
1533	David Smyth (and Procurator)
1534	David Gibson (and Procurator)
1535	Nicholas Wotherspoon (and Procurator)
1536	Nicholas Wotherspoon
1537	Nicholas Wotherspoon
1538	David Gibson (and Procurator)
1539	William Hamilton
1540	David Gibson (and Procurator)
1541	David Gibson
1542	David Gibson (Promotor), David Robeson (Procurator)
1543	David Gibson (and Procurator)
1544	Alexander Crawford (and Procurator)

1547	David Gibson (and Procurator)
1548	David Gibson
1549	Robert Houston (or Procurator)
1550	David Gibson (and Procurator)
1551	David Gibson (or Procurator)
1552	Andrew Laing (or Procurator)
1553	Andrew Laing (and Procurator)
1554	Andrew Laing (or Procurator)
1555	Henry Gibson (or Procurator)
1556	Robert Herbertson (or Procurator)
1557	Henry Gibson (or Procurator)
1558	Henry Gibson

University Scribes or Notaries

1488	John Gray 1493
1497	John Scott
1498	Stephen Provand
1501	David Dunn (Liber Rectoris, f. 81); and 1554
1502	John Bigholm
1517	Andrew Smyth
1518	Nicholas Wotherspoon, 1522; 1547; 1552
1553	Thomas Knox

University Beadles

1451, Jun.	John Moffat
1451, Sep.	Archibald McNelsone (entry out of place)
1519	William Hutcheson
1521	Thomas Crawford
1528	James Shaw
1546	David Kirkland (continued in office) Appendix H, 1551

FACULTY OF ARTS

Deans

1451	William Elphinstone, senior
1452, 28 Jul.	William Elphinstone, senior continued
1453, 26 Jun.	William Semple
1454, 26 Jun.	William Semple
1455, 25 Jun.	William Semple
1456, 25 Jun.	John Crichton
1457, 25 Jun.	Alexander Kersane
1458	Duncan Bunch
1459, 25 Jun.	William Semple

1460	Blank
1461, 25 Jun.	John Montgomery
1462, 28 Jun.	William Arthurlie
1463, 25 Jun.	Martin Wan ·
1464, 25 Jun.	(John) Montgomery
1465, 26 Jun.	William Arthurlie
1466, 25 Jun.	John Maxwell
1467, 25 Jun.	Duncan Bunch
1468, 25 Jun.	John Crichton
1469, *c.* 25 Jun.	William Elphinstone, senior
1470, 25 Jun.	Vedastus Muirhead
1471, 25 Jun.	William Semple
1472, 25 Jun.	William Elphinstone, junior
1473, 25 Jun.	William Elphinstone, junior
1474, 25 Jun.	William Arthurlie
1475, *c.* 25 Jun.	William Carmichael
1476, 26 Jun.	David Gray
1477, 25 Jun.	William Arthurlie
1478, 25 Jun.	John Maxwell
1479, 25 Jun.	David Gray
1480, *c.* 25 Jun.	William Semple
1481, 25 Jun.	Andrew Stewart
1482, 25 Jun.	Patrick Elphinstone
1483, 25 Jun.	David Gray
1484, 26 Jun.	Robert Houston Deputed Walter Leslie vice-Dean
1485, 25 Jun.	Robert Houston Died in office
1485, *c.* 19 Oct.	John Goldsmith
1486, 25 Jun.	John Goldsmith
1487, 25 Jun.	John Goldsmith
1488, 25 Jun.	John Goldsmith
1489, 25 Jun.	Patrick Elphinstone
1490, 25 Jun.	William Stewart Deputed John Doby vice-Dean
3 Jul.	William Stewart
1491, 25 Jun.	Patrick Elphinstone
1492, 25 Jun.	Thomas Forsyth
1493, 25 Jun.	Ninian Dalgleish
1494, 25 Jun.	John Hutchinson (Hugonis)
1495, 25 Jun.	John Hutchinson (Hugonis)
1496, 25 Jun.	Thomas Forsyth
1497, 25 Jun.	Thomas Forsyth
1498	Thomas Forsyth
1499, 25 Jun.	Thomas Forsyth
1500, 25 Jun.	Thomas Forsyth

1501, 25 Jun.	Archibald Crawford	
1502, 25 Jun.	Archibald Crawford	
1503, 26 Jun.	Archibald Crawford	
1504	Blank	
1505	Blank	
1506, 26 Jun.	Robert Hamilton	
1507, 25 Jun.	Robert Hamilton	
1508, 10 Aug.	Robert Hamilton	
1509, 19 Jun.	Robert Hamilton	
25 Oct.		27 Nov.
1510	Blank	
1511	Blank	
1512, 25 Oct.	James Neilson	
1513	Blank	
1514, 25 Oct.	James Neilson	
1515	Blank	
1516	Blank	
1517, 25 Oct.	Thomas Lees	
1518, 3 Nov.	John Doby	
1519, 23 Nov.	James Neilson	
1520	Blank	
1521, 25 Oct.	Matthew Stewart	
1522, 20 Jun.	John Reid	
1523	Blank	
1524	Blank	
1525	Blank	
1526	Blank	
1527	Blank	
1528, 26 Oct.	James Neilson, dean 'of university'	
1529, 25 Oct.	James Neilson	
1530, 25 Oct.	James Neilson	
1531	Blank	
1532, 25 Oct.	James Neilson, dean 'of university'	
1533, 6 Nov.	James Neilson	
1534	Blank	
1535	Blank	
1536, 8 Feb.	William Hamilton	
1536, 26 Jun.	William Hamilton	
1537, 25 Jun.	William Hamilton	
1538, 22 Nov.	William Hamilton	
1539	Blank	
1540, 25 Jun.	Robert Colquhoun	
1541, 25 Jun.	Robert Colquhoun	

1542, 2 Oct.	Robert Colquhoun
1543, 25 Jun.	Archibald Crawford
1544, 25 Jun.	Archibald Dunbar
1545, 25 Jun.	Archibald Dunbar
1546, 25 Jun.	John Stewart
1547, 25 Jun.	John Stewart
1548	John Stewart
1549	John Stewart
1550	John Stewart
1551, 25 Jun.	John Stewart
1552, 25 Jun.	John Laing
1553, 25 Jun.	John Laing
1554, 25 Jun.	John Laing
1555, 25 Jun.	John Laing
1556, 15 Jun.	John Laing
1556/7, 14 Mar.	John Houston
1559	John Laing
Blank for several years	
1573	Andrew Hay
1576	David Cunningham
1578	Thomas Smeaton
1580	David Wemyss
1581	Andrew Polwarth
1586	Andrew Polwarth
1592	John Blackburn
1594	John Blackburn
1595	John Blackburn
1597	John Blackburn
1599	John Blackburn
1600	John Blackburn

Principals

Before the foundation of the College of Arts, 1460, there appear for a time to have been two Pedagogies, but no Principals are named.

1451	Alexander Geddes, S.T.L., Cistercian, senior regent
1460, 6 Jan.	Duncan Bunch, M.A., S.T.B.
1475	Walter Bunch, S.T.B., Cistercian
1478, 25 Jun.	John Goldsmith, M.A., B.Dec. ⎱ Joint Principals John Doby ⎰
1480, 7 Oct.	John Brown, M.A., D.Dec.
1483	Walter Leslie, M.A.
1485, *c.* Jul.	John Goldsmith, M.A., B.Dec.
1485, 19 Oct.	George Crichton, M.A.

1490, 25 Jun.	John Doby, M.A.
1498, 25 Oct.	Patrick Coventry, M.A., B.Dec., S.T.B.
1510, 7 Oct.	Thomas Coutts, M.A.
1514, 25 Oct.	David Melville, M.A.
1517, 18 Jun.	David Abercrombie, M.A.
1518, 25 Oct.	John Mair, M.A., S.T.D.
1526, 25 Oct.	James Lindsay, M.A. (mentioned 1529, Liber Rectoris, 108)
1536, 8 Feb.	*Alexander Logan, M.A., senior regent*
1540, 3 Feb.	*Alexander Hamilton, M.A., senior regent*
1547	*John Hamilton, M.A., senior regent*
1555, 3 Oct.	*John Houston, M.A., senior regent* (described once as Principal, in rubric of 1556)
1556, 24 Oct.	(probably) John Davidson, M.A. (had some qualification in theology)
1560	John Davidson
1574	Andrew Melville
1581, Jan.	Thomas Smeaton
1585	Patrick Sharp
1615	Robert Boyd

Regents

Generally Principals acted also as regents and would be required to be added to these lists.

The absence of faculty records for certain years makes it difficult to compile a complete roll of all arts regents.

1451	Alexander Geddes, Cistercian 1453
	Duncan Bunch 1458 (see Principal)
	William Arthurlie 1468
1458	Nicholas Graham
1463	William Elphinstone, junior
1464	John Bargane (?)
	John Maxwell (?)
1466	Robert (Houston?)
	James Knox (ceased by 1468)
1467	David Gray (Liber Decani, f. 30) 1474
1468	Alexander Wemyss 1472
1472	James Ogilvie
1473	Humphrey Stirling (?)
1474	John Brown 1477 (see Principal)
1477	John Goldsmith (see Principal)
	Patrick Leitch
	John Doby (see Principal), Regent 1489

1480	Richard Douglas 1483
1482	John Glen (?)
1484	George Crichton (see Principal), Regent again 1488
1485	William Young 1486
1487	Archibald Crawford 1488
	Patrick Coventry 1498 (see Principal)
1493	James Twedy (?)
1498	David Dunn
1499	John Spreull 1508
1518	David Abercrombie 1519 (see Principal)
1519	James Lindsay (see Principal)
1526	Alexander Logan (see Principal)
1528	Alexander Hamilton (see Principal)
1540	John Houston 1555 (see Principal)
1548	John Hamilton 1551 (see Principal)
1554	Robert Cunningham (Liber Decani, f. 148) 1555
1562	Robert Hamilton (*Glasgow Protocols*, iii, no. 683)
1574	Peter Blackburn
1575	James Melville
1577	Blaise Lawrie
1580	Patrick Melville
1581	John Bell
1582(?)	Patrick Sharp
1586	John Millar (SRO, Register of Presentations to Benefices)
1588	John Forbes
1590	John Gibson
1592	Archibald Glen
1594	William Dunlop
1596	David Sharp
1599	John Cameron
1600	Archibald Hamilton

Faculty Bursars

1451	Faculty Receiver mentioned (Dean, it seems, kept purse)
1453–5	Patrick Leitch, senior
1455–6	Martin Wan
1456	William Semple
1457–71	Duncan Bunch
1475	John Brown
1477	John Brown, David Gray
1477–80	David Gray

1481–2	John Brown
1483	William Stewart
1484	Walter Leslie
1485	David Gray
1486–7	George Crichton
1487–9	Richard Hutchinson (Hugonis)
1490–3	John Doby
1493–4	Patrick Elphinstone
1495–9	Archibald Crawford
1500	John Spreull
1501–7	James Neilson
1536–7	Nicholas Wotherspoon
1547–51	John Houston, 'bursar of the university' (Post had coalesced with university bursar)
1577	Thomas Jack (*quaestor*)

Faculty Promotors

1490	Archibald Crawford
1492	Archibald Crawford
1498	John Hutchinson (Hugonis)
1499	Laurence Wallace
1500	John Bigholm
1502	John Bigholm

Quodlibetarii

1463	Duncan Bunch
1464	Duncan Bunch
1468	Duncan Bunch
1490	Patrick Coventry

Wardrobe Officers

1464	James Hynd
1467	David Gray
1469	David Gray
1479	David Gray, John Doby
1481	John Doby, John Brown
1484	John Doby

Faculty Scribes

| 1490 | David Gray |
| 1492 | David Gray |

Stewards ('*Provisors*')

1476	John Cook (Coci)
1490	John Shaw 1502
1502	William Lang
1547	Robert Lang (will of Alexander Hamilton, Regent)

Faculty Beadles

1453	Unnamed
1482	Unnamed

Appendix H

SUMMONS TO APPEAR BEFORE RECTOR'S COURT, 1551

This summons by Walter Beaton, Rector, dated 27 October 1551, is the sole surviving document directly connected with the Rectorial jurisdiction that seems to have survived. It authorises the beadle or any other member of the university to cite John Houston, vicar of Dunlop, to compear before himself or his vice-Rector and assessors on the following Thursday to answer the charges of Sir John Maxwell or his procurators under threat of excommunication for non-compliance. David Kirkland, beadle, notes on the paper that he had duly notified the offender. His endorsement is dated on the following day.

Strathclyde Regional Archives, Glasgow, Pollok Maxwell Writs (TPM 111/12).

Valterus betoun archidiaconus sanctiandree infra partes Laudonie Canonicusque glasguensis ac alme uniuersitatis eiusdem Rector bidello seu cuiuscumque alteri supposito Salutem

Cites legitime primo secundo tertio et peremptorie venerabilem virum Magistrum Johannem houstoun vicarium de dunlop quem nos etiam tenore presencium citamus quod compareat coram nobis seu nostris vice rectore et deputatis die Iouis proxime futuro nobili Iohanni maxwell de nethirpollok vel suis procuratoribus responsurum sub pena excommunicationis Et presentes debita executione earundem redditure latori Datum glasgw die xxvii mensis octobris anno domini Mcv quingentesimo (*sic*) primo

Endorsed: xxviii octobris

executa erat hec litera super prescripto magistro Jhoanne personaliter apprehenso per me dominum dauid kyrkland bidalum teste manu propria D K

Appendix I

SOME BOOKS IN ANDREW MELVILLE'S POSSESSION*

BEZE, Theodore de: *T. Bezae Vezelli, volumen tractationum theologicarum* fol., Genevae, apud I. Crispinum, 1570. (Inscribed on flyleaf 'Emptus ab heredibus Andreae Melvini 1626'. 'Georgius Hamiltoun Martii 30, 1636 dedicavit Bibliothecae Andreanae . . .'.) StAUL†

BIBLIA: *Biblia interprete Sebastiano Castalione* (Basle, 1556). GUL

BIBLIANDER, T.: *Christiana et catholica doctrina* (Basileae, 1550). (Contains MS epitaph on Thomas Smeaton.) EUL

BIEL, Gabriel: *Sacri canonis missae expositio* (Tubingen, 1499). (Inscribed 'Andreas Melvinus' on t.p.) GUL

BOUELLES, Charles de: *Aetatum mundi septem supputatio.* 2 pts. (Paris), venundantur I. Badio Ascensio, 1520–1. (Inscribed on t.p. (1) 'Alexandri gallouay canonici aberdonensis', (2) 'A. Melvinus'.) StAUL

BUCHANAN, George: *Rerum Scoticarum historia* (Edinburgh, 1582). StAUL

BUCHANAN, George: *Rerum Scoticarum historia* with *De jure Regni apud Scotos.* Ad exemplar Arbuthneti, Edin., 1583. (Inscribed 'Andreas Melvinus' on t.p. with notes in his hand.) NLS. MS 5170.

BUCHOLZER, Abraham: *Isagoge chronologica.* In officina Sanctandreana (False imprint), 1596. (Inscribed 'And. Melvinus' on t.p. with notes in his hand, some autobiographical.) NLS

CALVIN, John: *Commentaria in Evangelia et Acta Apostolorum* (Geneva, 1564). StAUL

CENSORINUS: *De die natali liber* (Lyons, 1593). (Inscribed 'And. Melvinus' on t.p.) GUL

CICERO: *De Natura Deorum ; Somnium Scipionis* (Venice, 1494). (Inscribed on last leaf 'Sum Mri Andreae Melvini'.) NLS

DRIEDO, Johannes: *Opera theologica,* tom. 1 et 2 (Louvain, 1550). (Inscribed 'Andreas Melvin' on t.p.) Glasgow, People's Palace Museum.

---

* I am grateful to Messrs J. Baldwin, J. Durkan, C. P. Finlayson, D. MacArthur, J. Morris and J. Russell for assistance in compiling this list—J. K. Other works owned by Melville are to be found in James Melville's *Diary,* 46–7, 49, 55, 75, 84.

† StAUL—St Andrews University Library; EUL—Edinburgh University Library.

DRUSIUS, Joannes: *Miscellanea Locutionum Sacrarum* (Franeker, 1586). Dunblane, Leighton Library.

GRZEBSKI, Stanislaw: *De multiplici siclo et talento Hebraico* (Antverpiae, 1568). (Inscribed 'An. Melvinus' on t.p.; one note in Melville's hand.) NLS

GRYNAEUS, J. J.: *Epitomes Sacrorum Bibliorum pars prima* (Basle, 1577). (Inscribed 'Andreas Melvinus' on t.p.) EUL

GUIDACERIUS, A.: *Peculium* (Paris 1537). (Inscribed 'Andreas Melvinus' on t.p.), bound with KIMCHI, David: *Liber Michlol* (Paris, 1546). GUL

KALENDARIUM: *Kalendarium Hebraicum* (Basle, 1527). (Inscribed 'And. Melvinus' on t.p.) GUL

MUNSTER, Sebastian: *Dictionarium Chaldaicum* (Basle, 1527). GUL

PAGNINUS, Santes: *Euchiridion expositionis vocabulorum Haruch*. Fol., Romae, impensis T. Strozii, 1523. (Initials in form of monogram 'AM' on t.p.) St AUL

PEREZ, Jacobus, de Valentia: *Cantica Canticorum Salomonis* (Paris, 1507). GUL

PINDAR: *Olympia, Pythia, Nemea, Isthmia* (Basle, 1535). Montrose Academy.

PONTIFICALE: *Pontificale secundum ritum Romanae ecclesiae* (Lyons, 1542). GUL

RHODOMANNUS, Laurentius: *Poiesis Christiana* . . . (Francofurdi, apud Andreae Wecheli heredes Claudium Marnium & Ioan Aubrium, 1589). (Inscribed 'Andreas Melvinus' on t.p.) StAUL

STURM, J.: *Institutionis literatae*, tomus primus (Torunii Borussorum, 1586). EUL

THEOCRITUS: *Commentaria vetera in Theocriti eglogas* (Venetiis, 1539). EUL

TRAVERS, Walter, *De Disciplina Explicatio*. (Inscribed 'AM dd 1575 *id Decemb*.) St AUL

VERRIUS FLACCUS, Marius: *M. Verrii Flacci quae extant* . . . (Lutetiae, . . . in off. Rob. Stephani, 1576). (Inscribed 'And. Melvinus' on t.p.) StAUL

Appendix J

THE COLLEGE FOUNDATIONS OF 1573 AND 1577

In the course of preparing the second section of the book, a search was made for any relevant university material in Strathclyde Regional Archives incorporating Glasgow City Archives, but none was known to exist. As the book was due to go to press, an uncatalogued document entitled 'Controverseis betuix the fundationes of Glasgow college' was discovered engrossed among the Pollok Maxwell Estate Papers in Strathclyde Regional Archives, the text of which is offered below.

The document, which is undated, begins by comparing the provisions of the foundation granted by the town in January 1573 with the king's foundation or *nova erectio* of 1577, and of the discrepancies or inconsistencies between the two charters. In a series of recommendations for resolving controverted matters, appeal is made to the crown for a new college foundation of 19 persons to replace the 15 foundationers of 1573 and the 12 foundationers of 1577; and new regulations for governing the college were also drafted for discussion.

It was envisaged that the principal should demit the ministry of Govan, a proposal which did not take effect until 1621, but the terms of service of the principal and four regents were reviewed; and, as a subject for study, astrology made its reappearance in the proposed curriculum. Of the twelve bursars mentioned, four were to be presented by the king and eight by the town council. Only the genuinely poverty-stricken were eligible for appointment to a bursary. In return, it was expected that each of the bursars should undertake certain menial tasks in college: by acting as porter, by ringing the college bell, by wakening the staff and students and lighting their candles, by carrying the regents' books or by reading passages at meal times and serving at table. The duties of the provisor or steward are also outlined; and the document ends by recommending the appointment of a professor of law.

From internal evidence, it is clear that the document could not have been drawn up before the 1580s, for mention is made not only of the king's minority and the regency of Morton, of four college regents, not three, but also of Glasgow presbytery, one of the thirteen model presbyteries which came into being only after 1581. At the same time, the document still envisages the appointment of a provisor and a cook, which suggests that it was composed earlier than 1608 when college catering was transferred to an outside contractor. From external evidence, the document, which seems to have been drawn up in the interests of the college rather than the town, can be dated more accurately to 1601 or 1602; a dispute between the college and town council over college revenues was settled only by the intervention of the privy council which appointed commissioners in 1602 to visit the college and to make recommendations for the future management of college affairs.

Controverseis betuix the fundationes of Glasgow college

	Tounes fundatioune	*Kingis fundatione*
Persones fundatoris and tyme of fundatioune	Foundit be Jhone Stewart off Minto, provest, Mr Adam Wallace, Archibald Lyoune, George Elphinstoun, bailzeis, counsellouris and communitie off Glasgou, 8 Januar anno 1572.	Foundit be James Erle off Mortoun in the minoretie off King James the sext, 3 July anno 1577.
Rent	Chapellis, chapell landis, freir land, alterageis and annuell rentis of howsis within the burghe, with divers utheris annexis extending communibus annis to the summ off aucht hundrethe lib. or thairby.	The personage and vicarage of Govan extending to twentie four chalders victuall and sumquhat better.
Numer of persones	Fyftene persones, viz. ane principall, twa regentis, twolf bursaris.	Twolff persones, ane principall, thrie regentis, four bursaris, provisor, principallis servand, cuik, portar.
Principallis electioune	The electioune and depositioune off the principall in the power off fyve persones chanceller, rectour, deane off facultie, the grit deane off Glasgou and persone off Glasgow.	The electioune and depositioune off the principall in the powar off aucht persones, bischope, rector, deane off facultie, ministers off Glasgou, Hamiltoune, Cadder, Munkland, Renfrowe.
Principallis office	Ilk day in the owlk to be exercisit in reiding the holy scripture in the colledge pulpit.	Fyve dayis in the owlk to teiche vicissim theologie, and the Hebrewe and Syriak toung.
Principalis stipend	The vicarage off Calmanell extending to fourtie markis, and twentie markis to the provisor.	Twa hundrethe markis owt off awld donatiounis dotit befoir to the college.
Regents office	Regentis to reid prayers in the blak freir kirk.	Na apoyntment off reiding.
Regents stipend	Ilk regent twentie lib. off stipend.	Ane off the regentis fyftie lib., ilk ane off uther two fyftie markis.
Bursaris admissioune	Bursaris admissioune be the principall and regentis.	Bursaris admissioune be the principall onlie.

	Tounes fundatioune	*Kingis fundatione*
Bursars office	Ilk bursar vicissim be owlkis to be portar to ring the freir bell, karie in the reideris buik, gwyd the freir knok.	Na sik injunctioune givein unto thame.
Studentis	Studentis to give aneis confessioune off faithe befoir thay be admittit in the colledge.	Studentis ilk yeir to give confessioune off faithe
Visitatioune	Visitatioune off the colledge be the rector, deane off faculteis and bailzeis twyse in the yeir, the first off Marche and September for tryell off lyff, diligence and bestowing off the rent.	Visitatioune off the colledge be rectour, deane off facultie, and minister off the toune four tymes in the yeir, the first dayis off October, Februar, May, August, for taking up off comptis.

Inrespect off thir contraverseis in the fundatiouneis, quhairby the ane, pairtlie alteris, pairtlie impairis, pairtlie nullis the libertie off the uther: for remeid heiroff and for farder weill to the universitie thir thingis falloweing wald be prosequut.

First that the toune off Glasgou resigne thair fundatioune in the kingis majesteis handis with conditioune that thair twa priviledgeis concerning presentatioune off bursareis and tryell off comptis only be reservat.

Nixt that the kingis majestie mak newe fundatioune nawayis mentioning nor making relatioune thairto ether to the fundatioune off the toune or erle off Mortoune: for it is aequitie that his majestie suld tak to him self that honour, seing baithe the gritest pairt off the first rent, dotit to the toune, was gevein be his majesteis derest mother, and the haill rest be his regent as curatour to his minoritie.

Thirdlie that thair be in the fundatioune nynteine persones, viz., ane principall, four regentis, twoll bursairis, ane provisor, ane cuik.

Principall

1. The principall wald be burdenit allanerlie withe the simple chairge off the principalitie quhilk will be to him (quhowe lernit and wyse sa ever) baithe be instructioune and governement ane full and daylie occupatione being richtlie discharget. Nather can he be pastor to ony flok speciallie off Govan, being distant from the citie, for the pastorall charge requeiris the indevoire off the haill mynd and inwart sensis off man, with quotidian owtwart residence off body, as the conscience off everilk well disposit pastour beris him record, famous laweis hes apoyntit and lovable consuetud alloweis. Farder seing the rent off the kirk off Govan is mortifeit to the colledge, ressoune wald that a

portione off that rent sustenit the minister theroff, heirfor it is expedient that the presentatioune off the minister off Govan be the fundatioune be devolveit in the handis off the rector, deane off facultie and principall, and that the provisor off the colledge give yeirlie unto him in name off stipend off the first and reddiest four chalderis victuall ex libere importatis, besyd mans and gleib.

2. The principallis presentatioune be the kingis majestie, his tryell, admissioune and depositioune be the chancellar, rectour, deane off facultie, and ane off the ordinar ministeris off Glasgou quhom thay or ony twa off thame will chuise to that effect with sa mony uther lernit and profund scholleris as sall pleis his majestie delegat. The vaking off the place, quhither be transportatioune, dethe or dispositioune to be dewle signifeit be the regentis.

3. The principall sall teiche ilk uther day during the space off ane hour theologie the ane day and the Hebrew and Syriak toung the uther, bot upon the sext day off the owlk he with the regentis from ten houris unto twoll sall give attendence in the commoune schuil to the philosophie disputis off all the discipillis haveing ony way taistit the art off dialectik and upon the said day he and thay, from fyve houris to sax at evin, try and punische the offensis committit in that owlk bot upon the sevint day to use his awin privat and godlie meditatiounes at his plesour, alwayis convoying the scholleris to divine service that be his and the regentis presence thay may be movit to give better attendence therto.

4. The principall sall have ordinar jurisdictioune speciallie be admonitioune and thretning above all the inferiour memberis off the universitie. The principall sall have in custodie all the evidentis and commone buikis off the colledge giving his memoriall off particular notis off ilk ane off thame to the visitouris, the said buikis furthcoming to the use off the masteris and evidentis to the provisor as thay sall requeir.

5. The principallis residence and nichtlie rest into the inwart precinct off the colledge being ane single man, being mareit may have his ludgeing in the owtmest bordour off the colledge howsis nameit Arthourlie.

6. The principall sall not divert from the toune to be absent the space off thrie dayis unless first he communicat the necessitie off his erand with the rector, deeane off facultie and regentis.

7. The principalls stipend fyve hundrethe markis yeirlie payit be the provisor, besyd his honest sustentatioune in meit and drink at the commoune table.

8. Give the principall dois not his dewtie in all poyntis according the prescript off the fundatioune bot declynes in slowthe, brekis owt

in intemperance or ony uther vyce in that case to be depryveit be the same quhombe he was admittit.

Regentis

1. Regentis electioune, admissioune, depositioune in the handis off the rectour, deane off facultie and principall.
2. The lawest to teiche and profess the Latin and Greik toung, the nixt the art off dialectik, the thrid mathematik, aithik, the fourt and supreme phisik, geographie, astrologie, chronographie.
3. Ilk regent his Saboth abowt in the morning give exhortatioune upon sum pairt off the scripture to the discipulis and sik weill affectit peple as sall cum thairto in the blak freir kirk, and the rest off the owlk reid morning prayeris thair except quhen the place is occupeit be teiching (*i.e.* preaching) off the ordinar pastor.
4. Ilk regent at his entrie to bind him self to remane in the charge sevin yeiris.
5. Na regent to marie during his remaneing in the colledge.
6. The suprem regentis stipend twa hundrethe markis, the nixt ane hundrethe pundis, the thrid and fourt ilk off thame ane hundrethe markis.

Bursaris

1. Twolf bursares, four off thame presentit be the kingis majestie, aucht be the counsall off the toune off Glasgou, all admittit be the rector, deane off facultie and principall, provyding ether thay be parentles haveing na thing for their awin sustentatioune or give thay have parentis that thair povertie be cleirlie notifeit to the admitteris be quhom also thay may be ejectit incace thay declyne from virtewe or ony portioune off thair dewte.
2. All thir twolf be the command off the principall and maisters to be occupeit in sik service to the colledge as sall not mekle prejudge thair lerning, thrie off thame owlklie abowt, ane to be porter quha also may ring the morning and evening bell in the colledge and immediatlie efter the morning bell wakin the maisteris and discipillis and licht thair candellis give thay requeir him, the uther to ring the freir bell to the morning prayeris and kary in the regentis buikis quha sall fall to be reidet and the same befoir and efter meit and in tyme thairoff to reid scripture or historie as sall be in[j]oynet to him. The thrid to cover and discover the table, minister water to the maisters handis, fill the cuppis to thame and the rest quha sall sit at the table.
3. All the twoll to ludge within the colledge and be intertenit at the commoune table during the space off thrie yeiris and ane half.
4. That the bursaris be discernit be thair habit from the rest off the

studentis and discipillis and that thay be guid exemples to the rest off all humilitie, sobrietie and diligence, and that nane be admittit till thay pass thair cours in grammar.

Provisor

1. Provisor off the colledge to be chosin be the principall and regentis be advys off rector and deane off facultie, and incase off misgyding or infidelitie be thame to be depryvet.

2. He sall ingadder the haill rentis off the colledge.

3. He sall travell in the haill effairis off the college in and about the toune upon the commone chargeis.

4. He sall provyd the haill hows with meit, drink and uther necessaris.

5. He sall give to everie office beirer his stipend.

6. He sall ilk owlk give compt off his bestoweing unto the principall and regentis and he and thay all thryse in the yeir, the first off Januar, Apryl and July to mak compt to the ordinar visitouris, the rectour, deane off facultie, ane off the ministeris off the toune and thrie bailzeis thairoff that the residew (give ony beis) may be bestoweit be thair sicht upon the godlie and necessar usis off the colledge, reparatioune off the edifice theroff and kirk off Govan.

8. [*Sic*] He sall have for his hyre fourtie markis yeirlie besyd his meit and drink at the table.

Cuik

Cuik to be chosin be the provisor; hir wadge ten markis yeirlie.

Thir foundit persones na wayis to dilipidat thair rent, except setting off takis to kyndlie taksmen onlie and that be sicht and allowence off the rectour and deane off facultie, the commoditie thareoff to the weill off the colledge.

All the foundit persones to give better honour and reverence to the chanceller, rector and deane off facultie, and to behave thame selfis discreitlie and modest[l]ie towald all men.

The college to be frie off all thridis and taxatiounis haveing all uther immunities as ony universite within this natione.

All the foundit persones to recommend the maist worthie and memorable fundator King James the sext withe daylie prayeris to the maist highe God for his majesties lang and prosperous regne, for the continuance off his princelie race to sit upon his throne till all arthlie kingdomes be finischit and thairefter for his and thair coronatioune withe the incorruptible croune off blissit immortalitie designit for thame be the powerfull dominator off hevin and erthe, Jesus Chryst cui gloria in saculum.

It war expedient that in the colledge war ane professour off the lawes seing in the toune off Glasgou ar divers judicatoreis, viz., synodall assemblie, presbitrie, sessioune, haldin be ministeris; consistorie be commissaris; burghe and baroune courtis be bailzeis; quhais proceidingis aught all to be terminit be the boundis off lawe, the ignorance quhairoff breidis and fosteris mony confusiones. This micht be helpit without grit lois to ony ea man be the guid will off the bischope and canones off Glasgou, with advyse off counsell and interpositioune off his majesteis authoritie in this maner. The bischope haveing thrie millis Partik auchteine chalder, Clydis mill sevinteine chalder, Badermanok mill nyne chalder or thairby off ilk ane off the first twa to be dedicat and mortifeit ane chalder, off the uther, half a chalder. The grit deane, subdeane and persone off Glasgou, the leist off quhais beneficeis extendis to fourtie fyve chalderis victuall to dedicat ilk off thame ane chalder. All the rest off the chanonis mortifie four chalder and ane half, quhilk in the haill mounting to ten chalderis victuall will be ane ressonable provisioune.

Appendix K

Charter by King James VI granting the parsonage and vicarage of the parish church of Govan to the college or pedagogy of Glasgow, and new confirming all lands, houses and revenues granted to it in time past, to be applied in the manner set forth in the king's new erection and foundation engrossed in the charter for the maintenance of a principal, three regents, a steward, four poor students, the principal's servant, a cook and a janitor. Dalkeith, 13 July 1577.

JACOBUS Dei gracia rex Scotorum, omnibus probis hominibus totius terre sue clericis et laicis, salutem. Sciatis quia nos ac fidelissimus noster consanguineus Jacobus comes de Mortoun dominus de Dalkeith nostri ac regni et liegiorum nostrorum regens, intelligentes quod annua proficua et redditus collegii seu pedagogii Glasguensis tam exigua sunt ut hac nostra etate minime sufficientia sint ad sustentandum principalem magistros regentes bursarios et officiarios necessarios in quovis collegio, nec adminiculandum sustentationi et reparationi eiusdem, ac itaque volentes exiguitatem dictorum parvorum reddituum iuvare et ad faciendum ac erigendum illic quandam faciem collegii pro zelo et bona voluntate quam ad propagationem et incrementum bonarum literarum et iuventutis instructionem gerimus ut membra utilia ad serviendum ecclesie Dei et reipublice intra hoc nostrum regnum alantur instruantur et educentur, cum avisamento et consensu dicti nostri fidelissimi consanguinei et regentis dedimus concessimus disposuimus incorporavimus et per mortificationem pro perpetuo confirmavimus, tenoreque presentis carte nostre damus concedimus disponimus incorporamus et per mortificationem pro perpetuo confirmamus dicto collegio seu pedagogio Glasguensi principali magistris regentibus bursariis servis et officiariis per nos specificandis in nostra erectione et fundatione subsequenti desuper confecta et eorum successoribus, totam et integram rectoriam et vicariam ecclesie parochialis de Govane cum omnibus decimis fructibus redditibus proficuis emolumentis devoriis mansis gleba terris ecclesiasticis eiusdem et suis pertinentiis iacentis infra diocesim Glasguensem et vicecomitatum nostrum de Ranfrew, nunc per decessum quondam Magistri Stephani Betoun ultimi rectoris et possessoris eiusdem vacantis, idque liberas et exemptas a solutione tertie taxationis seu aliarum impositionum quarumcunque, tenendam et habendam totam et integram predictam rectoriam et vicariam ecclesie parochialis de Govane cum omnibus fructibus redditibus proficuis emolumentis devoriis mansis gleba terris ecclesiasticis eiusdem ac omnibus suis pertinentiis predicto collegio et pedogogio principali magistris regentibus bursariis servis et officiariis eiusdem ac successoribus suis pro perpetuo mortificatam in futurum, cum potestate ipsis per se suos factores et servitores ipsorum nominibus dictis rectoria et vicaria utendi gaudendi et possidendi ac decimas fructus redditus proficua emolumenta devoria earundem ac mansorum glebarum et terrarum ecclesiasticarum eisdem spectantium cum suis pertinentiis percipiendi levandi et intromittendi ac desuper ad usum et effectum suprascriptum disponendi, pro reductione et annullatione infeofamentorum feudifirme earundem mansorum seu glebarum vel assedationum de eisdem seu aliqua earundem parte vocandi et prosequendi, eadem de novo locandi et assedandi, simili modo ac adeo libere et legitime sicuti rectores vel vicarii dicte ecclesie parochialis potuerunt seu in usu facere consueverunt aliquibus temporibus retroactis, sine aliqua revocatione contradictione aut obstaculo aliquali. Acetiam de novo dedimus concessimus ac pro nobis et successoribus nostris pro perpetuo confirmavimus, tenoreque presentis carte nostre damus concedimus ac pro nobis et successoribus nostris pro perpetuo confirmamus dictis collegio magistris regentibus studentibus servis ac aliis officiariis subscriptis in eodem servientibus, omnes et singulos alios annuos redditus fructus proficua devoria et emolumenta predicto collegio antea per quemcunque ordinem seu quovismodo fundata dotata et concessa, ac presertim omnes et singulas terras tenementa domus edificia capellanias hortos pomaria croftas annuos redditus fructus devoria proficua et emolumenta firmas *lie obit silver* ac annuos redditus quoscunque que quovismodo pertinuerunt seu pertinere dinoscuntur ad aliquas capellanias altaragia prebendas in quacunque ecclesia seu collegio intra civitatem Glasguensem fundatas vel de locis omnium fratrum eiusdem civitatis, unacum omnibus et singulis terris domibus tenementis et annuis redditibus quarumcunque terrarum domorum et tenementorum intra dictam civitatem Glasguensem seu extra eandem eisdem pertinentibus et spectantibus ac dicto collegio antea concessis et fundatis. Quosquidem fructus et proficua annuorum reddituum et capellaniarum cum fratrum terris domibus redditibus et emolumentis antedictis, nos et successores nostri tenore presentis carte nostre volumus et concedimus pacifice levari et disponi ad usum dicti collegii sine aliqua tertia impositione aut aliqua alia taxatione quacunque, non obstantibus quibusvis legibus consuetudinibus parliamentorum actis seu ordinationibus in contrarium, acetiam cum potestate

432 APPENDIX K

ipsis ad usum dicti collegii colligendi tertiam fructuum omnium
illarum prebendarum et capellaniarum quarum presentes possessores
nunc vivunt. Reddendo inde annuatim dicti principalis magistri
regentes bursarii servi et officiarii dicti collegii seu pedagogii Glasguensis et eorum successores servitium communium precum et supplicationum omnipotenti Deo pro statu prospero nostro et successorum
nostrorum ac doctrinam bonarum literarum et linguarum aliarumque
professionum necessariarum ac utendo bonis disciplina et ordine in
dicto collegio disponentes redditus in educationem iuventutis iuxta
erectionem et fundationem per nos desuper confectam cuius tenor
sequitur: Jacobus sextus Dei gratia Scotorum rex, omnibus et singulis
Christiani nominis cultoribus, salutem. Cum divina providentia nos iis
temporibus ad regni gubernacula perduxerit in quibus Evangelii lucem,
expulsis papismi tenebris, Scotie nostre prelucere voluit, nosque in
primis sollicitos esse oporteat ut tantum Dei beneficium ad posteros
nostros propagetur, neque id ratione commodius fieri possit quam
proba educatione et iuventutis recta informatione in bonis literis, que
nisi honoribus et premiis alantur prorsus sunt interiture. Hinc est quod
nos dum rem literariam passim per regnum nostrum in Dei gloriam
promovere studeremus animum etiam nostrum adiecerimus ad colli-
gendas relliquias academie Glasguensis quam pre inopia languescentem
ac iam pene confectam reperimus. Et cum concilio et consensu dilecti
nostri consanguinei Jacobi comitis a Mortoun domini Dalkeith
tutoris nostri et proregis charissimi, ei malo prospicere volentes ad tela
paupertatis delenda que bonarum arcium studiosis maximopere infesta
esse solent, dederimus et concesserimus prout per presentes damus et
concedimus et pro nobis ac successoribus nostris perpetuo confirmamus
et ad mortuam manum perpetuo unimus ac confirmamus collegio
nostro Glasguensi totam et integram rectoriam de Govane cum
vicaria eiusdem, iacentem in diocesi Glasguensi et vicecomitatu nostro
de Ranfrew vacantem per decessum Magistri Stephani Betoun rectoris
eiusdem non ita pridem vita functi, cum omnibus decimis emolumentis
et fructibus gleba et mansionibus omnibusque aliis commodis que de
iure aut consuetudine regni quomodolibet pertinere queant. Volumus
autem in dicto nostro collegio duodecem personas ordinarias residere
ad gymnasii commoda procuranda et iuventutem bonis literis infor-
mandam que ex impensis et fructibus eiusdem alantur et sustententur
pro modo ac facultate reddituum dicto collegio assignatorum secundum
discretionem gymnasiarche et regentium subscriptorum, nimirum
gymnasiarcham, tres regentes, oeconomum, quatuor pauperes studentes, servum gymnasiarche, coquum, et ianitorem, quorum singulos
in suis muneribus obeundis sedulos esse volumus et pro laboribus
honoraria ac stipendia percipere quo maiore alacritate suis officiis

invigilent. Ac primum quidem omnes has duodecim personas collegialiter vivere volumus, quibus pro victu quotidiano assignamus ex prefato beneficio et rectoria de Govane, extendente insolidum in suo rentali ad viginti quatuor celdras, viginti et unam celdras ad esculenta et poculenta dictis fundatis personis sufficienter sine luxu et profusione sustentandis ut frugali victus racione ad seriorem studiorum curam incitentur. Quod si subductis racionibus et calculo initio quid fuerit residui, id in pios usus collegii et sarta tecta collegii impendatur eorum arbitratu quos postea in eadem hac fundatione collegio invisendo prefecimus. Gymnasiarcham autem pium et probum hominem inprimis esse oporteat, cui totum collegium et singula eius membra subesse oporteat cui in singulas collegii nostri personas jurisdictionem committimus ordinariam. Is in sacris literis probe institutus ad aperienda fidei misteria et reconditos divini verbi thesauros explicandos idoneus linguarum etiam gnarus et peritus sit oportet inprimis vero Hebraice et Syriace cuius professorem esse instituimus, linguam enim sanctam ut par est promoveri inter subditos nostros cupimus ut scripturarum fontes et misteria rectius aperiantur. Itaque dicto nostro gymnasiarche committimus quo sedulitatis exemplum toti collegio diligentia sua subministret ut indies singulos horam saltem unam prelegendo impendat quo tempore maxime erit oportunum, alternis autem diebus prelectionem theologicam selegat ad explicandos scripturarum recessus alternis linguam ipsam sanctam auditoribus explicaturus, die autem Sabbatino immunem esse a prelectionibus concedimus, quoniam totius septimane ratio ei ab auditoribus exigenda est et opera danda formande ad Goveanum populum concionis, nam cum collegium nostrum ex decimis et proventibus eius ecclesie sustentetur equum esse duximus ut qui temporalia ministrant spiritualia percipiant, nec pane vite quod est Dei verbum defraudentur. Curam itaque quo ad poterit diligentissimam adhibebit gymnasiarcha ut eum populum pascat et in recta morum et vite disciplina contineat, singulisque diebus Dominicis adhortetur ad pietatem et probitatem. Resideat vero in dicto collegio neque inde pedem moveat ad longinquiorem aliquam profectionem nisi re cum rectore academie, decano facultatis, et ceteris suis collegis regentibus cummunicata et venia impetrata graviore aliqua de causa aut evidenti collegii commodo. Quod si gymnasiarcha sine licentia legitime petita et obtenta per triduum extra gymnasii septa pernoctaverit volumus ut muneri eius quod eo casu vacare pronunciamus alius idoneus modo infrascripto sufficiatur. Quoties vero dictum gymnasiarche munus quovismodo vacare contigerit regentes qui pro tempore fuerint nobis et successoribus nostris eiusdem vacationis denunciationem ilico facere tenebuntur ut nos certiores facti alium virum gravem et idoneum qui id muneris obeat presentare possumus cuius etiam presentatio omnibus etiam futuris temporibus ad nos et successores nostros pertinebit. Legitimum autem presentandi tempus nobis et successoribus nostris erit intra triginta dies a denunciatione vacationis dicti muneris, quod nisi fecerimus licebit personis electoribus subscriptis ad electionem idonee persone modo quo sequitur legitime procedere. Examinatio autem et electio dicti gymnasiarche ad Glasguensem archiepiscopum, qui est universitatis cancellarius, rectorem academie facultatis decanum ecclesiarum Glasguensis, Hammiltonensis, Cadder, Monkland et Ranfrew ministros et pastores qui ministerio verbi Dei tum fungentur ac alios viros graves et doctos quos nos et successores nostri dicte examinationi electioni et admissioni adesse curabimus. Quamquidem examinationem electionem et admissionem procedere volumus precedente edicto publico valuis collegii et ecclesie Glasguensis per regentes affixo super premonitione triginta dierum ad minus. Admoneant insuper dicti regentes suo edicto Sanctiandreanos, Abirdonenses et si que alie sint nostre academie ut si qui sint idonei ad id munus capescendum presto adsint ad diem condictum quo neque favore neque partium gratia sed virtute et eruditionis prestantia electio consummabitur, prefinito ad dictam electionem spatio quadraginta dierum duntaxat a die vacationis, quod si infra indictum tempus prefinitum vir gravis doctus et idoneus ex eiusdem electionis prescripta formula minime in dictum gymnasiarcham eligetur ea vice antedicte persone quibus examinandi eligendi et admittendi gymnasiarche ius fecimus idem ius amittent, et eo casu nobis et successoribus nostris licebit providere de remedio oportuno nisi per nos et successores nostros steterit si forte personam que facto examine minus idonea comperietur presentaverimus. Quoniam vero eruditum hominem querimus cuius humeris totius collegii onus incumbat eique insuper ecclesie de Govane curam demandamus, isque neque labores sustinere neque sumptibus sufficere posset nisi honestis premiis invitetur, idcirco pro honorario ei constituimus ducentas marcas annuatim levandas et percipiendas ex proventibus et annuis redditibus dicti nostri collegii que ad idem ante presentem nostram erectionem pertinebant et que in suo rentali perveniunt ad tercentum libras monete Scotie ex quibus ducentas ut dictum est marcas dicto preposito attribuimus et assignamus pro suis in collegio laboribus et pro ecclesie de Govane administratione tres celdras frumenti quas supra ex eiusdem ecclesie proventibus a communi tabula ad usus ministerii reservavimus. Et sic quidem prefectum nostri collegii vitam suam instituere volumus qui si negligentior fuerit in suo munere et que sunt ei per specialem erectionem iniuncta non impleverit neque resipiscere velit cum ter admonitus fuerit per academie rectorem, decanum facultatis, collegii regentes vel eorum maiorem partem sed in malos mores proclivis fuerit iisdem auctoribus exauctorabitur quos prius in electione locum habere decrevimus. Tres insuper regentes putavimus e re et commodo gymnasii fore qui iuventuti instituende presint et preposito auxilientur. Primus precepta eloquentie ex probatissimis auctoribus et Grece lingue institutionem profitebitur, adolescentesque tum scribendo tum declamando exercebit ut in utriusque lingue facultate pares et ad philosophie precepta capescenda magis idonei evadere possint. Proximus dialectice et logice explicande operam dabit earumque precepta in usum et exercitationem proferet idque ex probatissimis auctoribus ut Cicerone, Platone, Aristotile de vita et moribus et policia administratione que studia huic secundo regenti degustanda prebemus. Et pro adolescentulorum captu enarranda adiunget insuper elementa arithmetice et geometrie in quarum principiis non parum momenti ad eruditionem parandam situm est et ingenii acumen excitandum. His duobus salarii nomine quinquaginta marcas in singulos assignamus levandas et percipiendas quotannis ex redditibus et proventibus ad dictum collegium ante presentem erectionem pertinentibus. Porro tertius regens phisielogiam omnem eamque que de natura est auscultationem utpote in primis necessariam quam diligentissime enarrabit, geographiam etiam et astrologiam profitebitur nec non generalem etiam chronographiam et temporum a condito mundo supputationem que res ad alias disciplinas et historiarum cognitionem non parum lucis adferet. Quoniam vero huius tertii regentis opera ac laboribus colophonem philosophico stadio imponi volumus ac pileo donatos adolescentes ad graviora studia alacrius contendere quia etiam procuratio gymnasii eiusque cura ad eum precipue pertinebit in preposti qualicunque absentia aut distractione propter ecclesie Goveane administrationem et curam eidem pro salario concedimus libras monete nostre quinquaginta annuatim levandas et percipiendas ex redditibus et proventibus dicti collegii qui ante hanc nostram erectionem prius ad dictum collegium spectabant. Tres autem hos regentes nolumus prout in reliquis regni nostri academiis consuetudo est novas professiones quotannis immutare, quo fit ut dum multa profiteantur in paucis periti inveniantur verum in eadem professione se exerceant ut adolescentes qui gradatim ascendunt dignum suis studiis et ingeniis preceptorem reperire queant. Quod si e re gymnasii fuerit idque gymnasiarcha decreverit mutare inter se provincias poterunt. Eorum electio presentatio et admissio penes rectorem, decanum facultatis et gymnasiarcham esto, qui bona fide nostram institutionem sequuti de quam optimis et doctissimis preceptoribus collegio providebunt qui adolescentes docendo scribendo declamando disputando quam diligentissime in palestra literaria exerceant. Potestas autem emendandi et corrigendi dictos regentes erit penes dictum gymnasiarcham, cui etiam potestas erit eosdem collegio

P

eiiciendi, si postpositis eorum officiis ter ut dictum est admoniti resipiscere noluerint cognita tamen causa et adhibito consilio rectoris et decani facultatis. Porro paupertatis cura habita et quod multi pre inopia a bonis literis deterreantur adiunximus quatuor pauperes studentes, quos bursarios vocant, eisque assignamus victum ex communibus fructibus dicte ecclesie de Govane et communi tabula dicti collegii, eos et paupertatis nomine commendatos esse volumus quibus amici pre inopia suppeditare victum non queant et ingenii prestantia et grammatice facultatis peritia valere. Eorum presentationem penes comitem a Mortoun consanguineum nostrum et tutorem charissimum eiusque heredes masculos succedentibus temporibus esse volumus quibus deficientibus penes legitimos quosque heredes suos secundum tenorem novi infeofamenti dilecto nostro consanguineo et tutori predicto desuper concesso prout in eodem latius continetur. Admissionem vero et collationem dictorum bursariorum penes gymnasiarcham cuius erit cure providere ne divites pauperum loco admittantur, neve fuci alvearia depascant, sed eos in gymnasium recipere qui patrie ornamento et ecclesie usui esse poterunt. Hos autem pauperes nostros humilitatis et obedientie exemplar esse volumus et per omnia preceptoribus morem gerere, quod nisi fecerint potestatem facimus dicto gymnasiarche et preceptoribus eos puniendi et pro ratione delicti usque ad eorundem eiectionem de dicto collegio inclusive si propter eorum contumaciam id promeriti fuerint. Eorum in collegium ingressus calendis Octobris sit, permaneantque in stadio literario et gymnasii sumptibus alantur totos tres annos cum dimedio, quod tempus idoneum iudicamus pro ceterarum academiarum regni nostri consuetudine ad stadium philosophicum consummandum et lauream adipiscendam, quibus exactis novi bursarii provideantur donec iterum ad metam decurrerint. Economum autem et provisorem hominem bonum et industrium requirimus cui salus collegii sua ipsius longe sit potior. Is initio sue administrationis cautionem prestabit res collegii salvas fore seque bona fide administraturum. Penes eum erit proventus et redditus collegii qualescunque colligere, dicere diem debitoribus convenire in iudicio nomine collegii et cetera legitima peragere. Eius erit tempestive ex preceptorum arbitrio collegio providere in iis que ad victum pertinent et fori quotidie curam agere in iis emendis que ad collegii sustentationem pertinent. Is autem tenebitur in singulos dies rationem reddere emptorum et importatorum gymnasiarche et reliquis preceptoribus presentibus ne qua in re minima fraus fiat collegio, quotidiane enim rationes in adversaria redacte magno erunt familie usui. Porro preceptores ipsi unacum oeconomo tenebuntur rationem reddere administrationis quater in anno rectori, decano facultatis et ministro urbis Glasguensis qui operam dabunt calendis Octobris, calendis Februarii, calendis

Maii, calendis Augusti, ut quam exactissimo calculo omnia subducantur, quorum etiam conscientias appellamus ut omnia recte et secundum nostram intentionem in dicto collegio administrata esse videant et in ordinem sua authoritate redigant et quater in annos singulos dictis rationibus subscribant, que tum solummodo auctentice habebuntur. Eorumque consilio quicquid fuerit residui sive ex veteri erectione sive ex hac nostra fundatione id omne rentalibus probe examinatis et discussis in necessarios collegii usus et sarta tecta tum collegii tum chori Goveani aliosque usus gymnasii non pretermittendos impendatur et distribuatur. Quoniam autem variis curis et occupationibus distrahi provisorem nostrum oportebit, ei salarii nomine viginti libras monete nostre persolvi iubemus, preter ea que necessario ad recipiendos collegii proventus ab eodem impenduntur que illi in rationibus deduci equum est. Victum preterea honeste ex communi nostra tabula et ecclesie de Govane proventibus assignamus ut rectius liberalitate nostra invitatus munere suo fungi queat. Ad hec gymnasiarche sive prefecti servum sine cuius opera commode et honeste in collegio degere non potest volumus ex communi tabula et ecclesie de Govane proventu ali ac sustentari. Coquo etiam et ianitori victum et sex marcas annuatim in singulos attribuimus, eosque (quorum eligendi et deprivandi ius apud primarium esto) et omnes fundatas personas hortamur et monemus ut pie Christiane magnaque cum diligentia et fide suis officiis invigilent nostreque expectationi ea in re satisfaciant. Studentes autem quos magno numero speramus passim ex toto hoc regno ad gymnasium nostrum confluxuros, volumus quiete et pacifice degere neminem civium verbo vel facto ledere rectori gymnasiarche et regentibus morem gerere sedulos esse in bonarum literarum studiis ut parentibus honori ecclesie usui et reipublice ornamento esse queant. Insuper cum Sathane astum percipiamus nullibi non dantis operam ut iuventutem ab Evangelii professione ad plusquam cymmerias papismi tenebras abducat, districte mandamus ut singuli qui in hanc nostram academiam fuerint coaptati fidei professionem edant, eadem nimirum que e Dei verbo petita et transcripta a nobis in regni nostri conventibus edita atque publicata est. Idque faciant semel ad minimum quotannis ut profligato humani generis hoste collegium nostrum virtute eruditione et piis moribus efflorescat in Dei sempiternam gloriam quam nostra hac fundatione solummodo ob oculos nostros proposuimus utpote unicam nostrarum omnium actionum metam. Volumus autem nostrum hoc collegium et academiam Glasguensem iis omnibus immunitatibus et privilegiis gaudere que a maioribus nostris aut nobis aut aliis quovismodo concessa sunt ulli aliarum in regno nostro academiarum tam libere pacifice et quiete acsi eedem ab antiquis retro temporibus ultra hominum memoriam illi obvenissent. Sit autem Deo patri Christo Jesu

filio et Spiritui Sancto omnis honor et gloria in omne euum, Amen.
Quare mandamus et precipimus archiepiscopo Glasguensi vel in eius
absentia cuicunque ministro intra diocesim Glasguensem ad tradendum
institutionem et possessionem rectorie et vicarie de Govane ante-
dictarum prefato collegio principali magistris regentibus bursariis
servis et fundatis officiariis eiusdem, apud parochialem ecclesiam de
Govane ut remaneant mortificate omnibus temporibus affuturis sine
ulla alia institutione aut possessione earundem aliquo tempore futuro
suscipienda. In cuius rei testimonium huic presenti carte nostre magnum
sigillum nostrum apponi precepimus. Testibus reverendo in Christo
patre Adamo episcopo Orcadensi commendatario monasterii nostri
Sancte Crucis prope Edinburgh, dilectis nostris consanguineis Willelmo
comite Mariscalli domino Keith, Joanne domino Glammis, cancellario
nostro, venerabili in Christo patre Roberto, commendatario monasterii
nostri de Dunfermeling, nostro secretario, dilectis nostris familiaribus
consiliariis Magistris Georgio Buquhannane pensionario de Corsrag-
well, nostri secreti sigilli custode, Jacobo Makgill de Rankelour Nethir,
nostrorum rotulorum registri ac consilii clerico, Lodovico Bellendene
de Auchnoull, milite nostre justiciarie clerico, et Alexandro Hay nostre
cancellarie directore. Apud Dalkeith decimo tertio die mensis Julii
anno Domini millesimo quingentesimo septuagesimo septimo, et regni
nostri decimo.

[*Endorsed*] Die sexto mensis Septembris anno Domini millesimo
quingentesimo septuagesimo septimo.

Quo die mense et anno prescriptis personaliter accessit reverendissi-
mus in Christo pater Jacobus miseratione divina archiepiscopus
Glasguensis vigore et virtute unius precepti et mandati in retroscripta
fundatione contenti ad ecclesiam parochialem de Govane ex requestu
Magistri Petri Blakburne unius regentium collegii Glasguensis. Et
ibidem secundum tenorem vim formam et tenorum, [*recte* effectum]
eiusdem dictum Magistrum Petrum nomine principali, regentibus,
bursariis, servis, et aliis fundatis officiariis in dicta erectione et fundatione specificatis presentibus et successoribus suis omnibus temporibus
affuturis, in tota et integra rectoria et vicaria infrascripta de Govane
cum omnibus decimis, fructibus, redditibus, proficuis, emolumentis,
devoriis, mansis, gleba, terris ecclesiasticis cum pertinentiis iacentibus
infra diocesim Glasguensem et vicecomitatum de Renfrew per delibera-
cionem Bibliae instituit ac in realem actualem et corporalem possessionem investivit nullo protenus opponente seu contradicente. Super
quibus premissis petiit dictus Magister Petrus nomine quo supra a me
notario publico subscripto sibi fieri instrumentum seu instrumenta.
Acta erant hec apud dictam ecclesiam de Govane hora duodecima

meridiei aut circiter, presentibus ibidem Magistro Davide Wemys, ministro Glasguensi, Magistro Patricio Scharp, preceptore schole grammaticalis eiusdem, Andrea Chalmeris, Davide Chalmeris, fratribus, Magistro Roberto Fullertoune, Jacobo Gibsoune, vicario pensionario de Govane, Joanne McKnair, scriba, testibus ad premissa vocatis, etc.

> Ita est ut premittitur Archibaldus Eglyngtoune, notarius publicus, in premissis requisitus testantibus hec mea manuali subscriptione et signo subsequenti.

[*Text*: From the original, GUA MS 16612 *Nova Erectio* Charter, collated with MS 16612a (a contemporary copy).]

Translation

JAMES by the grace of God King of Scots to all good men of his whole land, clerics and laics, greeting. Know ye that we and our most faithful cousin, James, earl of Morton, lord of Dalkeith, Regent to us and our kingdom and lieges, understanding that the annual profits and rents of the college or pedagogy of Glasgow are so small that they are not sufficient in this our time for the maintenance of the principal, masters, regents, bursars, and officers necessary in any college, nor to assist in the upholding and repairing thereof, and therefore desiring to aid the slenderness of the said scanty rents, and for making and erecting therein some appearance of a college, of the zeal and good-will which we bear to the spread and growth of learning and the instruction of youth to the end that useful members may be reared, instructed, and educated for serving the church of God and the commonwealth within this our kingdom, with advice and consent of our said most faithful cousin and Regent, have given, granted, disponed, incorporated, and in mortmain for ever confirmed, and by the tenor of our present charter, give, grant, dispone, incorporate, and in mortmain for ever confirm to the said college or pedagogy of Glasgow, the principal, masters, regents, bursars, servants and officers, to be specified by us in our erection and foundation following made thereupon, and their successors, all and whole the parsonage and vicarage of the parish church of Govan, with all teinds, fruits, rents, profits, emoluments, dues, manses, glebe, kirklands of the same and their pertinents lying within the diocese of Glasgow and our sheriffdom of Renfrew, now vacant by decease of the late Master Stephen Betoun, last parson and possessor thereof; and that free and exempt from payment of third, taxation, or other impost whatsoever: to have and to hold all and whole the foresaid parsonage and vicarage of the parish church of Govan, with all fruits, rents, profits, emoluments, dues, manses, glebe, kirkland thereof, and all their pertinents to the foresaid college and pedagogy, to the principal, masters, regents, bursars, servants and officers thereof, and their successors, in mortmain for ever in time to come: with power to them, by themselves, their factors and servants in their names, to use, enjoy, and possess the said parsonage and vicarage, and to receive, uplift, and intromit with the teinds, fruits, rents, profits, emoluments, dues of the same, and of the manses, glebes, and kirklands belonging to the same, with their pertinents, and to dispone upon the same to the use and effect above written, to call and pursue for reducing and annulling of infeftments in feu-farm thereof, of the manses or glebes, or of tacks of the same, or any part thereof, to set in tack and let the same of new, in like manner and as freely and lawfully as the parsons or vicars of the said parish church could have done, or were in use to do, at any time bygone, without any revocation, gainsaying, or hindrance whatsoever. And also of new we have given, granted, and for us and our successors for ever confirmed, and by the tenor of our present charter give, grant, and for us and our successors for ever confirm to the said college, masters, regents, students, servants, and other officers underwritten serving therein, all and sundry other annual rents, fruits, profits, dues, and emoluments before founded, gifted and granted to the foresaid college by any order or in any manner: and particularly all and sundry the lands, tenements, houses, buildings, chaplainries, gardens, orchards, crofts, annual rents, fruits, dues, profits, and emoluments, maills, obit silver, and annual rents whatsoever, that in any way belonged or are known to belong to any chaplainries, altarages, prebends, founded in any church of college within the city of Glasgow, or of the places of all the friars of the said city: together with all and sundry lands, houses, tenements and annual rents of whatsoever lands, houses, and tenements within the said city of Glasgow, or outwith the same pertaining and belonging to them, and formerly granted and founded in favour of the said college. Which fruits and profits of annual rents and chaplainries, with the friars' lands, houses, rents, and emoluments aforesaid, we and our successors, by the tenor of our present charter, will and grant to be peaceably uplifted and disponed to the use of the said college, without any third, impost, or any other taxation whatsoever; notwithstanding any laws, customs, acts of parliament, or ordinances to the contrary; and also with power to them to ingather for the use of the said college the third of the fruits of all those prebends and chaplainries, the present possessors of which are now in life. Paying therefore yearly the said principal, masters, regents, bursars, servants and officers of the said college or pedagogy of Glasgow and their successors, the service of common prayers and supplications to Almighty God, for the pros- perity of us and our successors, and instruction in letters and languages, and other necessary studies, and the exercise of good discipline and order in said college, applying the rents for the education of youth according to the erection and foundation made by us thereupon, whereof the tenor follows:

James the Sixth, by the grace of God, King of Scots, to all and sundry who bear the Christian name, greeting. Since divine providence has brought us to the government of the kingdom, in these times in which it ordained the light of the gospel to illumine our country of Scotland, and the darkness of popery to be dispelled, and it behoves us to be specially concerned that so great a blessing of God should be transmitted to our posterity, and since by no other means can that be so conveniently done, as by a sound education and right training of youth in learning which will soon wholly perish unless it be fostered by honours and rewards. Therefore it is that we, while striving to advance learning everywhere throughout our realm to the glory of God, turned our attention also to gather together the remains of our university of Glasgow, which we found to be pining in poverty and now well nigh ruined. And we, with advice and consent of our well beloved cousin James, earl of Morton, lord Dalkeith our dearest guardian and Regent, wishing both to provide against that calamity and to obviate the sting of poverty which is wont to be most adverse to persons studious of the liberal arts, have given and granted, as by these presents we give and grant, and for us and our successors for ever confirm and in mortmain for ever unite and confirm, to our said college of Glasgow, all and whole the parsonage of Govan, with the vicarage thereof, lying in the diocese of Glasgow and sheriffdom of Renfrew vacant by decease of Master Stephen Betoun, parson thereof, lately deceased, with all teinds, emoluments and fruits, glebe and manses, and all other advantages which by right or custom of our kingdom may in any way belong thereto. And we will that twelve persons in ordinary reside in our said college, for attending to the welfare of the college, and instructing the youth in letters, who shall be maintained and supported from the charges and fruits thereof, according to the measure and ability of the rents assigned to the said college, at the discretion of the principal and regents underwritten: to wit, the principal, three regents, a steward, four poor students, a servant of the principal, a cook, and a janitor, every one of whom we desire to be attentive in discharging of their duties, and to receive fees and stipends for their work, that they may attend to their duties with the greater alacrity. And in the first place it is our will that all these twelve persons live in community; and we assign to them for their daily provision, out of the foresaid benefice and parsonage of Govan, extending in all in its rental to twenty four chalders, twenty one chalders for food and drink for sustaining the said foundationers sufficiently, without extravagance and waste, that by means of frugal fare they may be incited to more earnest application to their studies. And if on casting up and balancing of the accounts any residue remain over, it shall be spent on pious uses of the college and repairing the buildings of the college, at the will of those whom we have hereafter appointed in this our foundation to make a visitation of the college. And especially must the principal be a good and upright man, to whom the whole college and every one of its members must be subject; and to him we commit ordinary jurisdiction over every one of the persons of our college. It behoves him to be well versed in holy writ, to open up the mysteries of the faith, and fitted to unfold the hidden treasures of the word of God, and knowing and skilled in languages, and particularly in Hebrew and Syriac, of which we appoint him to be professor. For, as is reasonable, we wish to promote the knowledge of the sacred tongue among our subjects, that the springs and mysteries of the Scriptures may be the more rightly laid open. Wherefore we charge our said principal that he, by his diligence, exhibit a pattern of assiduity to the whole college, that he spend an hour at least every day in prelecting at whatever time is most convenient, and on alternate days he shall choose a theological lecture to unfold the mysteries of the Scriptures, and on the intermediate days shall explain the said sacred language to his hearers. And we grant that he be exempt from prelecting on the Saturday, since an account of the whole week should be required by him from his hearers and attention given to prepare a discourse for the people of Govan, for since our college is upheld out of the teinds and revenues of that church we deem it right that they who furnish the temporal things should receive of the spiritual and not be defrauded of the bread of life which is the word of God. Wherefore the principal shall bestow the most diligent care to feed that people, and keep them in right discipline of life and manners and on every Lord's day shall exhort them to godliness and integrity. And he shall reside in the said college, and not move thence on any considerable journey, unless he have communicated his business to the rector of the university, the dean of faculty, and his other colleagues the regents, and have got leave, for some very weighty reason, or the obvious advantage of the college. But if the principal without leave lawfully sought and obtained shall have spent the night for the space of three days outside the bounds of the college, it is our will that in manner underwritten another fit person be elected to his office which in that case we declare to be vacant. And as often as the office of the said principal shall happen to fall vacant in any manner, the regents for the time shall be bound instantly to make intimation to us and our successors of the said vacancy that we, on being so informed, may present another grave and fit person to undertake that office which presentation moreover in all times to come shall belong to us and our successors. And the lawful time for us and our successors to present shall be within thirty days from intimation of the vacancy of the said office, and if we do not it shall be lawful to the persons electors underwritten lawfully to proceed to the election of a fit person in manner as follows. And the examination and election of the said principal [shall belong] to the archbishop of Glasgow, who is the chancellor of the university, the rector of the university, the dean of faculty, the ministers and pastors of the churches of Glasgow, Hamilton, Cadder, Monkland, and Renfrew, who are at the time engaged in the ministry of the word of God, and other grave and learned men whom we and our successors shall procure to be present at the said examination, election, and admission. Which examination, election, and admission, we ordain to take place, a public intimation having been previously affixed by the regents on the doors of the college and of the church of Glasgow, on a warning of thirty days at least. Further the said regents shall warn those of St Andrews, Aberdeen, and any others of our university that if there be any who are fit to undertake that office, they be present on the day appointed on which the election shall be completed neither for favour nor influence of party but for worth and superiority in learning; the space of forty days only from the day of vacance being prescribed for the said election. But if within the appointed time prescribed a grave, learned, and fit man shall not be chosen for the said principal, after the form of the said election above described, the foresaid persons, to whom we have given the right of examining, electing, and admitting the principal, shall lose the said right for that occasion; and in that case it shall be lawful to us and our successors to provide a suitable remedy, unless the default be chargeable on us and our successors from happening to present a person who on trial made shall be found unfit. And seeing that we seek a man of erudition on whose shoulders the burden of the whole college may lie, and we further commit to him the charge of the church of Govan; and that he could neither undergo the labour, nor bear the charges, unless he were encouraged by suitable recompense; therefore we appoint to him for salary two hundred merks yearly, to be uplifted and taken out of the revenue and annual rents of our said college which belonged to it before our present erection and which in the rental thereof come to three hundred pounds Scots money, out of which, as said is, we give and assign to the said principal two hundred merks for his labours in the college and for serving the church of Govan three chalders of corn which we have reserved above out of the revenue of the said church from the common table for the use of the ministry. And it is our will that the principal of our college so order his life, and if he prove negligent in his office and do not fulfil the duties enjoined on him by special erection and refuse to amend when he shall have been thrice warned by the rector of the university, the dean of faculty, the regents of the college, or the greater part of them, but shall persist in ill behaviour, he shall be deprived of office by the same authorities whom we have above appointed to have share in his election. Farther, we have thought it fitting and advantageous to the college that there should be three regents to preside over the education of the youth, and assist the principal. The first shall be professor of the principles of rhetoric, out of the most approved authors, and shall give instruction in the Greek language; and shall practise the young men both in writing and declaiming, that they may become equally ready in the use of either tongue, and more fit to receive the principles of philosophy. The next shall give his endeavour to explain dialectics and logic, and set forth the principles of the same for use and practice, and that out of the best authors such as Cicero, Plato, Aristotle on life, morals and policy, government, which studies we assign to be treated of by the second regent. And according to the capacity of the boys he shall further teach the elements of arithmetic and geometry, the principles of which are of no small importance for the acquisition of learning, and sharpening the intellect. To these two we assign in name of salary fifty merks apiece to be uplifted and taken yearly out of the rents and profits which belonged to the said college before the present erection. Further the third regent shall teach with his utmost diligence the whole of physiology, and the observation of nature, as especially necessary; he shall also profess geography and astronomy, and likewise general chronology, and computation of time from the creation of the world, a thing which sheds not a little light on other branches of learning and the knowledge of history. And since it is our will to set a period to the work and labours of this third regent in the philosophic course, and that young men, being released from it, apply themselves with greater alacrity to their graver studies; whereas also the superintendence of the college and charge thereof shall devolve specially on him in case of absence of the principal, or his preoccupation with the management and charge of the church of Govan, we grant to him for salary fifty pounds of our money yearly, to be uplifted and taken out of the rents and profits of the said college that formerly belonged to the said college before this our erection. And it is not our will that these three regents change every year into new courses, as is the custom in the other colleges of our kingdom, whereby it comes to pass that while they profess many branches of learning they are found skilled in few; but they shall exercise themselves in the same course that young men who ascend step by step may find their preceptor worthy of their studies and gifts.

But if the condition of the college require it, and the principal so determine, they shall have power to change their departments with each other. And their election, presentation, and admission shall lie in the hands of the rector, the dean of faculty, and the principal; and they carrying out our erection in good faith, shall provide for the college the best and most learned preceptors they can find to train the young men in teaching, writing, declaiming, debating, with the utmost diligence in the palaestra of letters. And the power of correcting and reproving the said regents shall lie in the hands of the said principal, who shall also have the power of expelling them from the college, if they neglect their duties and, on being thrice warned as said is, refuse to amend; only, however, after examination of the cause and deliberation had by the rector and dean of faculty. Farther taking account of poverty and how many are held back from learning through lack of means, we have added four poor students called bursars, and we assign to them their provision out of the common fruits of the said church of Govan and common table of the said college, and it is our will that they be recommended thereto on the ground of poverty, being persons whom their friends, being needy, cannot maintain, and who are gifted with excellent parts and knowledge in the faculty of grammar. We will that their presentation be vested in the earl of Morton our dearest cousin and guardian, and his heirs male in time to come, whom failing his lawful heirs, whomsoever according to the tenor of the new infeftment made thereupon to our well-beloved cousin and guardian foresaid, as is at greater length contained in the same. And the admission and collation of the said bursars shall be in the power of the principal, whose care it shall be to take heed that rich men are not admitted instead of poor, nor drones feed upon the hive, but to receive into the college those who may prove an ornament to their country, and useful to the church. And we will that these our poor students be a pattern of humility and obedience and do the will of their preceptors to punish them, according to the character of their fault, even to their expulsion from the college, if they have merited it by their contumacy. Their entry to the college shall be on the first of October; and they shall continue in literary study and be supported at the charge of the college three whole years and a half; which time we deem sufficient, according to the usage of the other universities of our kingdom, for finishing a philosophical course, and taking a degree; on the expiry whereof, new bursars shall be provided, till they again shall have run their course. And we require the steward and provisor to be a good and industrious man to whom the weal of the college shall be more dear than his own. At entering on his charge he shall give caution that the goods of the college shall be safe, and that he will administer them faithfully. It shall be his duty to gather in the profits and rents of the college whatsoever, to set a day for debtors to appear in court, in the name of the college, and to transact other lawful business. He shall be bound timeously to provide the college, at the will of the teachers, in whatever belongs to their victuals, and to attend to marketing daily in buying of those things that belong to the sustenance of the college. He shall also be bound to render an account every day to the principal and other teachers present of what things have been bought and brought in, lest in anything the least fraud be practised upon the college; for the entering of the accounts daily in a day-book will be of great advantage to the household. Further the said teachers, together with the steward, shall be bound to give in an account of their management, four times a year, to the rector, the dean of faculty, and the minister of the city of Glasgow, who shall give heed on the first day of October, first of February, first of May, first of August, that all be reckoned up as exactly as possible, to whose consciences also we appeal that they see that all things in the said college be administered rightly and according to our intent and that they reduce them to order by their authority and four times in the year subscribe the said accounts which then only shall be held as authentic; and by their advice whatever residue shall remain over, whether from the ancient erection or from this our foundation, shall all, after the rentals have been thoroughly examined and investigated, be spent and disbursed on the necessary requirements of the college, and repair of the buildings, both of the college, and of the choir of Govan, and other needs of the university that may not be passed over. And since our provisor cannot fail to be fully occupied with variety of cares and duties, we command twenty pounds of our money to be paid to him, in name of salary, besides what is necessarily spent by him in collecting the revenues of the college, which it is right should be allowed to him in his accounts. Further we assign him sufficient provision out of our common table and revenues of the church of Govan that he may be the better able to do his duty when encouraged by our liberality. In addition, it is our will that the servant of the principal or president, without whose attendance he cannot live comfortably and respectably in the college, be kept and upheld out of the common table and revenue of the church of Govan. We also assign to the cook and porter their food and six merks yearly apiece, and we exhort and warn them (the right of election and dismissal of whom shall be with the principal), and all the foundationers, that they apply themselves to their duties in a pious and Christian way with great diligence, and fulfil our expectation in this respect. And it is our will that the students, whom we expect to flock in great numbers from every part of our whole realm to our university, live quietly and peaceably, injure none of the citizens by word or deed, be obedient to the rector, principal, and regents, be sedulous in their pursuit of learning, that so they may be a credit to their parents, useful to the church, and an ornament to the common-wealth. Moreover, since we perceive the craftiness of Satan everywhere endeavouring to withdraw youth from the profession of the gospel to the more than Cimmerian darkness of popery, we strictly command that every one who shall be admitted to this our university shall make a profession of his faith, to wit, that which derived and transcribed from the word of God, has been given forth and prescribed by us in the parliaments of our realm. And this shall they do once every year, at least, that discomfiting the enemy of mankind, our college may flourish in virtue, learning, and godly behaviour, to the everlasting glory of God, which alone we have had in view in this our foundation, as the only goal of all our proceedings. We will also that this college and university of Glasgow enjoy all those immunities and privileges which have been granted by our ancestors or us or formerly in any manner of way to any of the other universities in our kingdom, as freely, peaceably, and quietly as if the same had come into their possession from ancient times beyond the memory of man. To God the Father, Christ Jesus his Son, and the Holy Ghost be all honour and glory, world without end, Amen. Wherefore we charge and command the archbishop of Glasgow, or in his absence any minister within the diocese of Glasgow, to give institu-tion and possession of the foresaid parsonage and vicarage of Govan to the foresaid college, principal, masters, regents, bursars, servants, and founded officers thereof, at the parish church of Govan, to remain mortified in all times to come, without any other institution or posses-sion thereof to be taken at any time to come. In witness whereof we have commanded our great seal to be affixed to this our present charter. Witnesses, the reverend father in Christ, Adam, bishop of Orkney, commendator of our monastery of Holyrood, near Edinburgh; our well beloved cousins, William, earl Marischal, lord Keith; John, lord Glamis, our chancellor; the venerable father in Christ, Robert, com-mendator of our monastery of Dunfermline, our secretary; our well beloved familiar counsellors, Masters George Buchanan, pensioner of Crossraguel, keeper of our privy seal, James McGill of Rankelour Nether, clerk of our rolls, register, and council, Ludovic Bellenden of Auchnoull, knight, clerk of our justiciary, and Alexander Hay, director of our chancery. At Dalkeith, the thirteenth day of the month of July, the year of God, one thousand five hundred and seventy seventh, and of our reign the tenth year.

[*Endorsed*] 6 September 1577

On the abovewritten day, month and year, the most reverend father in Christ James by divine mercy archbishop of Glasgow by the force and virtue of a precept and mandate contained in the aforewritten foundation proceeded to the parish church of Govan at the request of Master Peter Blackburn, one of the regents of the college of Glasgow. And there in accordance with the tenor, force, form and effect of the same by delivery of a Bible instituted and invested in real, actual and corporal possession, none opposing or contradicting, forthwith the said Master Peter in name of the present principal, regents, bursars, servants and other founded officers specified in the said erection and foundation, and their successors in all times to come in the whole and entire aforesaid parsonage and vicarage of Govan, with all teinds, fruits, returns, profits, emoluments, duties, manses, glebe, and kirklands with their pertinents lying within the diocese of Glasgow and sheriffdom of Renfrew. Upon which premisses, the said Master Peter, in name of the above, requested from me, the notary public underwritten, an instrument or instruments to be made for himself. This was done at the said church of Govan at twelve noon or thereabouts, there being present Master David Wemyss, minister of Glasgow, Master Patrick Sharp, preceptor of the grammar school of the same, Andrew Chalmers, David Chalmers, brothers, Master Robert Fullerton, James Gibson, vicar pensionary of Govan, John McNair, scribe, witnesses called to the premisses, etc.

I, Archibald Eglinton, notary public, requested for the aforesaid [certify that] it is as aforesaid as these my signature and sign following bear witness.

Bibliography

I **Manuscript Sources**

Aberdeen

Aberdeen University Library
   MS 239. Gul. Hay, Quaestiones
   MS 264
   J. Ireland. In Libros 3 et 4 Sententiarum

Dublin

Trinity College
   MS 416. Andreae Melvini, Scoti. Dan. 9
   MS 510. Glasguensis Academiae Jura
   MS 533. Second Book of Discipline
   MUN/P/1. Papers, General and Miscellaneous
   MUN/P/32. Papers relating to College estates
   MUN/P/1/201. Early University Statutes
   Library Muniments: MS Catalogue No. 1 (dated 1604), MS Catalogue
      No. 2 (dated 1610)

Edinburgh

National Library of Scotland
   Advocates MS 18.3.10
   Advocates MS 25.9.4 (Riddell Collection 44)
   Advocates MS 29.2.7–8 Balcarres Papers, vols. 7–8
   Advocates MS 34.7.2
   Advocates MS 29.4.2 Hutton (Shires), ix
   Wodrow MSS. Folio vol. xlii
Scottish Record Office
   E45/14–24. Accounts of the Collector-General of Thirds of Benefices
      (1580–1595)
   CC10/1/1. Act Book of the Commissary Court Records of Hamilton
      and Campsie
   RH11/32/1. Archbishopric of Glasgow: Charters, depositions of wit-
      nesses and productions relative to the claim of the archbishops to
      appoint the provost and bailies of the city of Glasgow, 1543–1557
   B6/12/1. Ayr Burgh Court Book, vol. 1
   GD10. Cally and Broughton Writs
   GD27. Dalquharran Writs
   GD97. Duntreath Muniments
   CH2/121/1. Edinburgh Presbytery Records

GD32/21/14. Elibank Writs
E4/1. Exchequer Act Book or Register. Feb. 1584–Jan. 1587
RH6. General Register House Calendar of Charters
CH2/550/1–2. Glasgow Kirk Session Records
RH11/32/1. Glasgow Regality Papers
CH6/5/1. Glasgow Registrum (Liber Ruber)
GD85. Nasmith Writs
GD248/548. Cullen Writs
GD237/202/4. Duke of Hamilton, nos. 1–4, Estate and Legal Papers, 1521–1698
GD1/12/42. Inventory of Titles pertaining to the Edinburgh Incorporated Craft of Tailors
GD151/13/13. Letter Book of Sir David Graham of Fintry
CH2/294/2. Paisley Presbytery Records
PA10/1. Papers relating to the Visitation of St Andrews University, 1574–76
NP1/195. Protocol Book of Cuthbert Simson
CH2/252/1. Records of the Synod of Lothian and Tweeddale
C57/15–61. Register of Acts and Decreets, vols. 15–61 (1557–1575)
NP2/1–2. Register of Admissions of Notaries, 2 vols., 1563–1579
E47. Register of Assignations and Modifications of Ministers' Stipends
CH4/1/1–4. Register of Presentations to Benefices
PS1. Register of the Privy Seal
CC8/8/34. Register of Testaments, Edinburgh
CC9/7/11. Register of Testaments, Glasgow
GD30. Shairp of Houstoun Muniments
GD135/Box 121. Stair Muniments
GD1/371/1. Warrender Papers
Edinburgh University Library
MS La.III.321. Collection of copies of various instruments and letters by the Queen Regent and other persons relating chiefly to the see of Glasgow, written by George Makeson, notary, 1554, etc.
La.III.322. Formulary book
MS Dc.7.63. John Law's Chronicle
MS Dc.6.45. Melvini Epistolae

Geneva

Bibliothèque Publique et Universitaire Genève
MS Fr. 410

Glasgow

Mitchell Library
MS 'Cartularium Glasguense', 2 vols.
Glasgow Presbytery Office
Porteous Manuscript
Strathclyde Regional Archives incorporating Glasgow City Archives
Glasgow Presbytery Records

TPM111/12. Pollok Maxwell Writs
TPM131. Pollok Maxwell Estate Papers
Glasgow University Archives
  Box F5. Discharges. Bundle of 10 vouchers
  Drawer A9 c6. Presentation to the Vicarage of Maybole, 1569
  Drawer C6b. Presentation to the Vicarage of Maybole, 1590
  Drawer E3b. Tacks of College property, 1575, 1578
  MS 11615–6
  MS 12412
  MS 12425
  MS 14235
  MS 16299
  MS 16375
  MS 16391
  MS 16571–4
  MS 16612. *Nova Erectio* Charter
  MS 16612a. Copy of *Nova Erectio* Charter
  MS 22003
  MS 26613. 'Annales Universitatis Glasguensis, 1451–1558' (Clerk's Press
    No. 1) Liber Rectoris
  MS 26614. 'Annales Collegii Facultatis Artium in Universitate Glasguensi,
    1451–1555' (Clerk's Press No. 2) Liber Decani
  MS 26615. 'Liber Statutorum Facultatis Artium Studii Glasguensis'
    (Clerk's Press No. 3)
  MS 26619. 'Jura, Leges Instituta' (Clerk's Press No. 7)
  MS 26620. (Clerk's Press No. 8)
  MS 26623
  MS 26624. Library Accounts, 1630–1745
  MS 26730. Schedule of Boarders in the College and Accounts relative
    to them, 1626–1633
  MSS 28800–28805
Glasgow University Library
  MS 199. Cartulary of Glasgow, Paris transcripts
  Murray MSS 643, 645
  Wodrow's MS Biographies
  MS Principium on the Sentences (in printed book, W. Manderston,
    Bipartitum, 1518)

London
  British Library
    Additional MS 32446
  Public Record Office
    SP52/8. State Papers, Scotland

Oxford
  Bodleian Library
    MS Cherry 5
    MS Cherry 37

MS Fairfax 30
MS Smith 77

Paris

Archives Nationales
H2588(3)
Bibliothèque Nationale
MS Lat. 7812 (Ludovicus Lassere, Oratio)
MS Lat. 14947
MS français 22861
Sorbonne Archives de l'Université
Registres 15, 91

Rome

Vatican Archives
Registrum Supplicationum, vols. 364–1442, 2855, 2875–6, 2930, 2963
Resignationes, Series A, vols. 171, 208
Vatican Library
Vat. Lat. MS 200

St Andrews

Holy Trinity Parish Church
St Andrews Presbytery Records, vol. 1
St Andrews University Archives
MS Acta Rectorum, 2 vols.
MS Liber Computorum Divi Leonardi, 1549–1591
SS 110. AP2 Testament of William Skeyne
MS University Statutes
Registrum Evidentiarum et Privilegiorum Universitatis Sanctiandree

Zurich

Staatsarchiv Zurich
MS E.II. 382

II Primary Printed Sources

Abstracts of Protocols of the Town Clerks of Glasgow, ed. R. Renwick, 10 vols.
(Glasgow 1894–1900)
Accounts of the Collectors of Thirds of Benefices, 1561–1572, ed. G. Donaldson
(SHS, Edinburgh, 1949)
Accounts of the Lord High Treasurer, edd. T. Dickson and J. Balfour Paul
(Edinburgh, 1877–1916)
Acta Capitulorum Generalium Ordinis Praedicatorum, vol. 5, ed. B. M.
Reichert (Rome, Stuttgart, 1901)
Acta Capitulorum Provinciae Germaniae Inferioris, 1515–1569, ed. S. P. Wolfs
(The Hague, 1964)
Acta Dominorum Concilii: Acts of the Lords of Council in Civil Causes, edd.
T. Thomson *et al.* (Edinburgh, 1839, 1918–)

Acta Facultatis Artium Universitatis Sanctiandree, 1413–1588, ed. A. I. Dunlop, (SHS and St Andrews University Publication No. 56, Edinburgh, 1964)

Acts of the Lords of the Council in Public Affairs, 1501–1554, ed. R. K. Hannay (Edinburgh, 1932)

Acts of the Parliaments of Scotland, edd. T. Thomson and C. Innes, 12 vols. (Edinburgh, 1814–75)

Album Studiosorum Academiae Lausannensis, 1537–1837, ed. L. Junod (Lausanne, 1937)

Album Studiosorum Academiae Lugduno Batavae MDLXXV–MDCCCLXXV, ed. G. du Rieu (Hagae Comitum, 1875)

ALEANDRO, G., *Gnomologia* (Paris, 1512)

Analecta Hibernica, vol. 12, Irish Historical Manuscripts Commission (Dublin, 1943)

The Apostolic Camera and Scottish Benefices, 1418–1488, ed. A. I. Cameron, (Oxford, 1934)

Archives Départmentales, Calvados, series D, ed. E. Chatel, ii (Caen, 1894)

Archivum Franciscanum Historicum, vol. 54 (Rome, 1960)

Asloan Manuscript, ed. W. A. Craigie, 2 vols. (STS, Edinburgh, 1923–24)

Auctarium Chartularii Universitatis Parisiensis, vols. 1–2, edd. H. Denifle and E. Chatelain; vols. 3–5, edd. C. Samaran and E. van Moé; vol. 6, edd. A. L. Gabriel and G. C. Boyce (Paris, 1894–1964)

The Autobiography and Diary of Mr. James Melvill, ed. Robert Pitcairn (Wodrow Society, Edinburgh, 1842)

The Basic Works of Aristotle, ed. R. McKeon (New York, 1941)

Bibliothèque de la Compagnie de Jesus, ed. C. Sommervogel, vol. vii (Paris, 1896)

The Black Book of Taymouth (Bannatyne Club, Edinburgh, 1885)

BOECE, H. *Hectoris Boetii Murthlacensium et Aberdonensium Episcoporum Vitae* (New Spalding Club, Aberdeen, 1894)

The Book of Pluscarden (Historians of Scotland), ed. F. J. H. Skene, vol. 1 (Edinburgh, 1877)

The Booke of the Universall Kirk of Scotland: Acts and Proceedings of the General Assemblies of the Kirk of Scotland, 3 vols. and appendix vol. (Maitland Club, Edinburgh, 1839–45)

DU BOULAY (BULAEUS), C. E. *Historia Universitatis Parisiensis*, 6 vols. (Paris, 1665–73)

British Museum General Catologue of Printed Books (London, 1965–72)

BUCHANAN, G., *Opera Omnia*, ed. T. Ruddiman (Edinburgh, 1715)

Burgh Records of the City of Glasgow, 1573–1581, ed. J. Smith (Maitland Club, Glasgow, 1832)

CALDERWOOD, DAVID, *The History of the Kirk of Scotland*, ed. T. Thomson, 8 vols. (Wodrow Society, Edinburgh, 1842–49)

Calendar of Entries in the Papal Registers: Papal Letters, edd. W. H. Bliss et al. (London, 1893–)

Calendar of Entries in the Papal Registers: Petitions, vol. 1, ed. W. H. Bliss (London, 1896)

Calendar of Patent Rolls, Philip and Mary, vol. 3 (London, 1938)

Calendar of Scottish Supplications to Rome, vol. 1, edd. E. R. Lindsay and A. I. Cameron (SHS, Edinburgh, 1934), vol. 2, ed. A. I. Dunlop (1956); vol. 3, edd. I. B. Cowan and A. I. Dunlop (1970)

Calendar of State Papers relating to Ireland: Henry VIII, Edward VI, Mary and Elizabeth, edd. H. C. Hamilton *et al.*, iv (1588–1592); v (1592–1596); viii (1599–1600) (London, 1885, 1890, 1900)

Calendar of the State Papers relating to Scotland and Mary, Queen of Scots, 1547–1603, edd. J. Bain *et al.*, 13 vols. (Edinburgh, 1898–1969)

Calendar of Writs preserved at Yester House, 1166–1625, edd. C. C. Harvey and J. Macleod (SRS, Edinburgh, 1930)

CALVIN, JOHN, *Commentaries on the Book of the Prophet Daniel*, ed. T. Myres, 2 vols. (Edinburgh, 1852, 1853)

CAMERARIUS, D., *De Scotorum Fortitudine* (Paris, 1631)

CANIVEZ, J. M., *Statuta Capitulorum Generalium Ordinis Cisterciensis*, vol. 5 (Louvain, 1937)

Cartularium Ecclesiae Sancti Nicholai Aberdonensis, 2 vols. (New Spalding Club, 1888–92)

A Catalogue of the Graduates in the Faculties of Art, Divinity and Law of the University of Edinburgh since its foundation (Edinburgh, 1858)

CHALMERS, GEORGE, *Caledonia*, vol. 3 (London, 1824)

Charters and Documents relating to the Burgh of Peebles (Scottish Burgh Records Society, Edinburgh, 1872)

Charters of the Abbey of Coupar Angus, ed. D. E. Easson, 2 vols. (SHS, Edinburgh, 1947)

Charters and Other Documents relating to the City of Glasgow, AD 1175–1649, vol. i, ed. J. D. Marwick (pts. i and ii) (Glasgow, 1894–1897); vol. 2, 1649–1707 (with appendix 1434–1648), edd. James D. Marwick and Robert Renwick (Glasgow, 1906)

Charters of the Abbey of Crosraguel, ed. F. C. Hunter Blair, 2 vols. (Edinburgh, 1886)

Charters of the Hospital of Soltre, of Trinity College, Edinburgh, and other Collegiate Churches in Midlothian (Bannatyne Club, Edinburgh, 1861)

Charters, Statutes and Acts of the Town Council and the Senatus, 1583–1858, ed. A. Morgan (Edinburgh, 1937)

Chartularium Universitatis Parisiensis, edd. H. Denifle and E. Chatelain, 4 vols. (Paris, 1889–97)

Clan Campbell Papers, vol. 8, ed. H. Paton (Edinburgh, 1922)

CLERVAL, A., *Registre des Procès Verbaux de la Faculté de Théologie de Paris*, Archives de l'histoire religieuse de la France, vol. 1 (Paris, 1917)

Codice Diplomatico dell'Università di Pavia, ed. R. Maiocchi (Società Pavese di Storia Patria), vol. 2 (Pavia, 1915)

Concilia Scotiae, ed. J. Robertson (Bannatyne Club, Edinburgh, 1846)

Copiale Prioratus Sanctiandree: The Letter Book of James Haldenstone, ed. J. H. Baxter (St Andrews University Publications, no. xxxi, London, 1930)

COWAN, I. B. and EASSON, D. E., *Medieval Religious Houses: Scotland*, 2nd ed. (London, 1976)

COWAN, I. B., *The Parishes of Medieval Scotland* (SRS, Edinburgh, 1967)

CRANSTON, D., *Quaestiones in Posteriorum Lectura* (Paris, 1506)
DALLARI, U., *I Rotuli dei Lettori Legisti e Artisti dello Studio Bolognese dal 1384 al 1789*, vol. 1 (Bologna, 1888)
Deeds instituting Bursaries, Scholarships and other foundations in the College and University of Glasgow (Maitland Club, Glasgow, 1850)
DEMPSTER, T., *Historia Ecclesiastica*, 2 vols. (Bannatyne Club, Edinburgh, 1829)
Devotional Pieces in Verse and Prose, ed. J. A. Bennett (STS, 3rd series, vol. 23, 1949, Edinburgh, London)
DIAZ, J. D., *Impresos Del Siglo XVII* (Madrid, 1972)
Dictionary of National Biography, ed. L. Stephen (London, 1885–1912)
Dictionary of Scientific Biography, vol. 9 (New York, 1974)
Dictionnaire de Droit Canonique, ed. R. Naz, 7 vols. (Paris, 1935–65)
A Diurnal of Occurrents (Bannatyne Club, Edinburgh, 1833)
Documents relatifs à l'histoire de l'Université de Louvain, 5 vols., ed. E. H. J. Reusens (Louvain, 1881–1903)
DOWDEN, J., *The Bishops of Scotland* (Glasgow, 1912)
DURKAN, J., *William Turnbull, Bishop of Glasgow* (Glasgow, 1951)
DURKAN, J. and ROSS, A., *Early Scottish Libraries* (Glasgow, 1961)
Early Records of the University of St. Andrews, ed. J. M. Anderson (SHS, Edinburgh, 1926)
Early Travellers in Scotland, ed. P. H. Brown (Edinburgh, 1891)
EHRLE, F., *Statuta facultatis theologiae Bononiensis* (Bologna, 1932)
EMDEN, A. B., *A Biographical Register of the University of Cambridge to 1500* (Cambridge, 1963)
—— *A Biographical Register of the University of Oxford*, 3 vols. (Oxford, 1957–59)
ENGLISH, E. D., *Rare Books in the McKissick Library* (New York, 1952)
Evidence, oral and documentary, taken by the Commissioners appointed by King George IV, for visiting the Universities of Scotland, 4 vols. (London, 1837)
Extracts from the Records of the Burgh of Edinburgh, 1573–1589, ed. J. D. Marwick (Edinburgh, 1882)
Extracts from the Records of the Burgh of Glasgow, vol. i, 1573–1642, ed. J. D. Marwick (Glasgow, 1914)
Extracts from the Records of the Burgh of Peebles (Scottish Burgh Records Society, 1872)
Fasti Aberdonenses, Selections from the Records of the University and King's College of Aberdeen, ed. C. Innes (Spalding Club, Aberdeen, 1854)
Fasti Academiae Mariscallanae Aberdonensis, vol. 1 (New Spalding Club, Aberdeen, 1889)
Fasti Ecclesiae Hibernicae, 4 vols., ed. H. Cotton (Dublin, 1847–50)
Fasti Ecclesiae Scoticanae, ed. H. Scott, revised edition, 8 vols. (Edinburgh, 1915–50)
FEENSTRA, R., *Fata Iuris Romani* (Leiden, 1974)
FERME, CHARLES, *A Logical Analysis of the Epistle of Paul to the Romans . . . and a Commentary on the same Epistle by Andrew Melville*, ed. W. L. Alexander (Wodrow Society, Edinburgh, 1850)

Festschrift zur Erinnerung an die Gründung der alten Universität Köln im Jahre 1388, ed. H. Graven (Cologne, 1938)

The First Book of Discipline, ed. J. K. Cameron (Edinburgh, 1972)

FULLER, T., *The Church History of Britain*, ed. J. S. Brewer (London, 1845)

GANOCZY, ALEXANDRE, *La Bibliothèque de l'Académie de Calvin* (Geneva, 1969)

GOLDAST, P., *Epistolicae Quaestiones et Responsiones Variae* (Frankfurt, 1614)

HACKETT, M. B., *The Original Statutes of Cambridge University* (London, 1970)

The Hamilton Manuscripts, ed. T. K. Lowrie (Belfast, 1867)

HAWS, C. H., *Scottish Parish Clergy at the Reformation, 1540–1574* (SRS, Edinburgh, 1972)

HAY, ARCHIBALD, *Ad Reverendissimum in Christo patrem D. Iacobum Betoun . . . pro Collegii Erectione Archibaldi Hayi Oratio* (Paris, 1538)

HAYE, G., *Gilbert of the Haye's Prose Manuscript*, 2 vols (STS, Edinburgh, 1901, 1914)

HERKLESS, J. and HANNAY, R. K., *Archbishops of St. Andrews*, vol. 3 (Edinburgh, 1910)

Historical Manuscripts Commission, Hamilton, i, 11th Report, Appendix, part 6 (London, 1887)

Historical Manuscripts Commission, Hope Johnstone, 15th Report, Appendix, part 9 (London, 1897)

Historical Manuscripts Commission. Salisbury (Cecil) MSS at Hatfield, vol. vii (London, 1899)

HUTTEN, U. VON, *Operum Supplementum*, ed. E. Bocking (Leipzig, 1867)

Inventaire Sommaire des Archives Départementales antérieures a 1790, ed. M. Bligny-Bondurand. *Gard-Archives Civiles—Série E*, vol. 2. *Notaires* (Nîmes, 1900)

IRLANDIA, J. DE., *The Meroure of Wyssdome*, vol. 1, ed. C. Macpherson; vol. 2, ed. F. Quinn (STS, Edinburgh, 2 series, n. 19, 4 series, no. 2, 1926, 1965)

KEITH, R., *An Historical Catalogue of the Scottish Bishops*, ed. M. Russell (Edinburgh, 1824)

—— *History of the Affairs of Church and State in Scotland*, 3 vols. (Spottiswoode Society, Edinburgh, 1844–50)

KNOX, J., *History of the Reformation*, ed. W. C. Dickinson, 2 vols. (Edinburgh, 1949)

—— *Works*, ed. D. Laing, 6 vols. (Wodrow Society, 1846–64)

LEFEVRE, J., *Rithmimachia* (Paris, 1514)

LESLIE, J., *The Historie of Scotland* (STS, 1895, and Bannatyne Club, 1830)

The Letters and Journals of Robert Baillie, ed. D. Laing, 3 vols. (Bannatyne Club, Edinburgh, 1841–2)

Letters and Papers, Foreign and Domestic of the Reign of Henry VIII, ed. J. Gairdner, vol. x (London, 1887)

Letters of James IV, 1505–1513, calendared by R. K. Hannay (SHS, Edinburgh, 1953)

Letters of James V, edd. R. K. Hannay and D. Hay (Edinburgh, 1954)

Letters of John Johnston and Robert Howie, ed. J. K. Cameron (Edinburgh, 1963)

Liber Collegii Nostre Domine: accedunt Munimenta Fratrum Predicatorum de Glasgu, ed. with appendix of documents by J. Robertson (Maitland Club, Glasgow, 1846)

Liber Protocollorum M. Cuthberti Simonis Notarii Publici et Scribae Capituli Glasguensis, 1499–1513 (Grampian Club, London, 1875)

Liber S. Marie de Calchou (Bannatyne Club, Edinburgh, 1846)

Liber Sancte Marie de Melros, 2 vols. (Bannatyne Club, Edinburgh, 1837)

The Life of Mr. Robert Blair, ed. T. McCrie (Wodrow Society, Edinburgh, 1848)

Le Livre du Recteur de l'Académie de Genève, 1559–1878, ed. S. Stelling-Michaud, 2 vols. (Geneva, 1959)

Livy, ed. T. A. Dorey (London/Toronto, 1971)

A Logical Analysis of the Epistle of Paul to the Romans by Charles Ferme . . . and a Commentary on the same Epistle by Andrew Melville, ed. William L. Alexander (Wodrow Society, Edinburgh, 1850)

The Logike of the Moste Excellent Philosopher P. Ramus Martyr. Translated by Roland MacIlmaine (1574), ed. by C. M. Dunn (Northridge, California, 1969)

Luther's Works, ed. H. T. Lehmann, vol. 44 (Philadelphia, 1966)

MAIR (MAJOR), J., *Acutissimi artium interpretis magistri Johannis maioris in Petri Hyspani summulas commentarii* (Lyons, 1505)

—— *Ethica Aristotelis* (Paris, 1530)

—— *A History of Greater Britain*, translated by Archibald Constable, with author's life by Aeneas J. A. Mackay (SHS, Edinburgh, 1892)

—— *In Primum Sententiarum* (Paris, 1516)

—— *In Quartum Sententiarum* (Paris, 1519)

—— *In Quartum Sententiarum* (Paris, 1521)

—— *Octo Libri Physicorum* (Paris, 1526)

—— *Quaestiones Logicales* (Paris, 1528)

Maitland Folio Manuscript, ed. W. A. Craigie, vol. 1 (STS, Edinburgh, 1919)

Matricule de l'Université de Louvain, vol. 1, ed. E. J. H. Reusens; vol. 2, ed. H. Wils; vols. 3–4, ed. A. Schillings, with tables (Brussels, 1903–58)

Die Matrikel der Hohen Schule und des Paedagogiums zu Herborn, edd. G. Zedler and H. Sommer (Wiesbaden, 1908)

Die Matrikel der Universität Basel, ed. H. G. Wackernagel (Basel, 1956)

Die Matrikel der Universität Heidelberg von 1386 bis 1662, ed. G. Toepke (Heidelberg, 1884)

Die Matrikel der Universität Köln, ed. H. Keussen, 3 vols, (Publikationen der Gesellschaft für Rheinische Geschichtskunde Bd. 8) (Cologne, 1892; vol. 1, 2nd edn., revised, 1928)

Die Matrikel der Universität Rostock, ed. A. Hofmeister (Rostock, 1889)

Die Matrikel der Universität Wien, vol. 1. (Publikationen des Instituts für Oesterreichsche Geschichtforschung: VI Reihe) (Graz/Cologne, 1954)

Melrose Regality Records, ed. C. S. Romanes, vol. 3 (SHS, Edinburgh, 1917)

Memoirs of Sir Ewen Cameron of Locheill (Maitland Club, Edinburgh, 1842)
Memorials of Montrose and his Times, ed. M. Napier, 2 vols (Maitland Club, Edinburgh, 1848–50)
Miscellanea Mediaevalia: Kölner Mediävistentagung, ed. A. Zimmermann, vol. ix: *Antiqui und Moderni* (Berlin/New York, 1974)
Miscellany of the Maitland Club, vols. i-ii (Edinburgh, 1833–40)
Miscellany of the Scottish History Society, vol. i (Edinburgh, 1893); vol. 2 (1904); vol. 5 (1933)
Miscellany of the Spottiswoode Society, vol. i (Edinburgh, 1844)
The Miscellany of the Wodrow Society, vol. i, ed. D. Laing (Wodrow Society, Edinburgh, 1844)
The Montgomery Manuscripts, ed. G. Hill (Belfast, 1869)
Monumenta Historica Universitatis Carolo—Ferdinandeae Pragensis (Liber Decanorum Facultatis Philosophicae), i, edd. A. Dittrich and A. Spirk (Prague, 1830)
MORE, SIR T., *More's English Works*, edd. W. E. Campbell and A. W. Reed, vol. 2 (London/New York, 1931)
Munimenta Alme Universitatis Glasguensis, ed. C. Innes, 3 vols. and appendix vol. iv (Maitland Club, Glasgow, 1854)
NANCELIUS, N., *Petri Rami Vita*, ed. P. Sharratt, *Humanistica Lovaniensia*, xxiv (1975), 161–277
Narratives of Scottish Catholics under Mary Stuart and James VI, ed. W. Forbes-Leith (London, 1889)
North of England and Scotland in MDCCIV (Edinburgh, 1818)
Officers and Graduates of the University and King's College, Aberdeen, ed. P. J. Anderson (New Spalding Club, Aberdeen, 1893)
Origines Parochiales Scotiae (Bannatyne Club, Edinburgh, 1851–5)
Protocol Book of Gavin Ros (SRS, Edinburgh, 1908)
Protocol Book of Mr. Gilbert Grote, ed. W. Angus (SRS, Edinburgh, 1914)
Protocol Book of James Young, 1485–1515 (SRS, Edinburgh, 1952)
Protocol Book of Sir John Cristisone, ed. R. H. Lindsay (SRS, Edinburgh, 1930)
Questiones Johannis Galli, ed. Marguerite Boulet. *Bibliothèque des Ecoles françaises d'Athènes et de Rome*, vol. 156 (Paris, 1944)
QUICK, J., *Synodicon in Gallia Reformata*, 2 vols. (London, 1692)
Ratis Raving, ed. R. Girvan (STS, Edinburgh, 1937)
Records and Charters of the Burgh of Glasgow, ed. R. Renwick, vol. 7 (Glasgow, 1902)
Records of the Monastery of Kinloss, ed. J. Stuart (Society of Antiquaries of Scotland, Edinburgh, 1872)
Register of the Minister, Elders and Deacons of the Christian Congregation of St. Andrews, 1559–1600, ed. D. H. Fleming, 2 vols. (SHS, Edinburgh, 1889–90)
Register of the Privy Council of Scotland, edd. J. H. Burton and D. Masson, 14 vols. (Edinburgh, 1877–98)
Register of the University of Oxford, vol. i, ed. C. W. Boase; vol. ii, ed. A. Clark (Oxford, 1885, 1887)

Registres de la Compagnie des Pasteurs de Genève, edd. O. Fatio and O. Labarthe, iii (Geneva, 1969)

Registrum Episcopatus Aberdonensis, 2 vols. (Spalding Club, Aberdeen, 1845)

Registrum Episcopatus Brechinensis, 2 vols. (Bannatyne Club, Edinburgh, 1856)

Registrum Episcopatus Glasguensis, ed. C. Innes, 2 vols. (Bannatyne and Maitland Clubs, Edinburgh, 1843)

Registrum Magni Sigilli Regum Scotorum: Register of the Great Seal of Scotland, edd. J. M. Thomson *et al*. vols. i–vii (Edinburgh, 1882–1912)

Registrum Monasterii de Passelet (New Club, Paisley, 1877)

Registrum Secreti Sigilli Regum Scotorum. Register of the Privy Seal of Scotland, edd. M. Livingstone *et al*., 7 vols. (Edinburgh, 1908–1966)

REICHERT, B. M., *Registrum Litterarum Salvi Cassettae et Barnabi Saxoni* (Quellen und Forschungen zur Geschichte des Dominikanerordens in Deutschland, vol. 7) (Leipzig, 1912)

Rentale Dunkeldense (SHS, Edinburgh, 1915)

ROLLAND, J., *The Seuin Seages*, ed. G. F. Black (STS, 3rd series, 3, Edinburgh/London, 1931)

ROLLOCK, R., *Select Works*, ed. William M. Gunn, 2 vols. (Wodrow Society, Edinburgh, 1844, 1849)

Rotuli Scaccarii Regum Scotorum. The Exchequer Rolls of Scotland, edd. J. Stuart *et al*. (Edinburgh, 1878–1908)

ROW, J., *The History of the Kirk of Scotland* (Wodrow Society, Edinburgh, 1842)

St. Andrews Formulare, 1514–46, edd. G. Donaldson and C. Macrae, 2 vols. (Stair Society, Edinburgh, 1942–44)

St. Andrews Kirk Session Records: Register of the Minister, Elders and Deacons of the Christian Congregation of St. Andrews, ed. D. Hay Fleming, 2 vols. (SHS, Edinburgh, 1889, 1890)

Scots Peerage, ed. J. B. Paul, 9 vols. (Edinburgh, 1914)

Scottish Alliterative Poems, ed. F. J. Amours (STS, ser. 1, vols. 27, 38, Edinburgh, 1892, 1897)

Select Biographies, ed. W. K. Tweedie, 2 vols. (Wodrow Society, Edinburgh, 1845, 1847)

Selections from the Records of the Regality of Melrose, ed. Charles S. Romanes, 3 vols. (SHS, Edinburgh, 1914–17)

Sermons and Life of Mr. Robert Bruce, ed. W. Cunningham (Wodrow Society, Edinburgh, 1843)

SLEZER, J., *Theatrum Scotiae* (London, 1693)

SPOTTISWOODE, JOHN, *History of the Church of Scotland*, 3 vols., ed. M. Russell (Spottiswoode Society, Edinburgh, 1851–65)

Statuta Antiqua Universitatis Oxoniensis, ed. S. Gibson (Oxford, 1931)

Statuta et Liber Promotionum Philosophorum Ordinis in Universitate Jagellonica ed. J. Muczkowski (Cracow, 1849)

Statutes of the Faculty of Arts and the Faculty of Theology at the Period of the Reformation, ed. R. K. Hannay (St Andrews University Publications no. 7, St Andrews, 1910)

Statutes of the Realm, iv, pt. i (London, 1819)

Statutes of the Scottish Church, ed. D. Patrick (SHS, Edinburgh, 1907)

Statuti delle Università e dei Collegi dello Studio Bolognese, ed. C. Malagola (Bologna, 1888)

'Statuts de l'Université de Louvain antérieurs a l'an 1459', ed. A. van Hove, *Bulletin de la Commission Royale d'histoire de Belgique*, vol. 76 (1907)

Statuts et Privilèges des Universités Françaises, ed. M. Fournier (Paris, 1890–94)

'Statuts primitifs de la Faculté des Arts de Louvain', ed. E. H. J. Reusens, *Compte Rendu des Séances de la Commission Royale d'Histoire*, ser. 3, vol. 9 (Brussels, 1867)

'Statuts primitifs de la Faculté de Theologie de l'ancienne Université de Louvain', ed. E. H. Reusens, *Annuaire de l'université de Louvain*, vol. 46 (1882)

STEVENSON, J. H. and WOOD, M., *Scottish Heraldic Seals*, 3 vols. (Glasgow, 1940)

Stirlings of Craigbernard and Glorat, ed. J. Bain (Edinburgh, 1883)

University of Cambridge: The Book of Matriculations and Degrees, 1544–1659, edd. J. Venn and A. Venn (Cambridge, 1913)

Vernacular Writings of George Buchanan, ed. P. H. Brown (STS, Edinburgh, 1892)

Warrender Papers, 2 vols., ed. A. I. Cameron (SHS, Edinburgh, 1931–32)

WATT, D. E. R., *Fasti Ecclesiae Scoticanae Medii Aevi ad annum 1638* (SRS, Edinburgh, 1969)

Wigtownshire Charters, ed. R. C. Reid (SHS, Edinburgh, 1960)

WODROW, R., *Collections upon the Lives of the Reformers and most eminent Ministers of the Church of Scotland*, 2 vols. (Maitland Club, 1834–35)

III Secondary Works

AITKEN, J. M., *The Trial of George Buchanan before the Lisbon Inquisition* (Edinburgh, 1939)

The Alba Amicorum of George Strachan, George Craig, Thomas Cumming, ed. J. F. K. Johnstone (Aberdeen, 1924)

ALEXANDER, W. M., *The Four Nations of Aberdeen University and their European Background*. Aberdeen University Studies, no. 108 (Aberdeen, 1934).

ALLEN, J. W., *A History of Political Thought in the Sixteenth Century* (London, 1961)

ALLEN, P. S., *Erasmus: Lectures and Wayfaring Sketches* (Oxford, 1934)

ARMSTRONG, BRIAN G., *Calvinism and the Amyraut Heresy* (London, 1969)

BARROW, G. W. S., *Robert Bruce* (London, 1965)

BATAILLON, M., *Erasme et l'Espagne* (Paris, 1937)

BIANCO, F. J. VON, *Die alte Universität Köln* (Cologne, 1855)

BLACK, A., *Monarchy and Community: Political Ideas in the Later Conciliar Controversy, 1430–1450* (Cambridge, 1970)

BOEHNER, P., *Medieval Logic* (Manchester, 1952)

BOISSONNADE, P., *Histoire de l'Université de Poitiers passé et présent (1432–1932)* (Poitiers, 1932)

BORGEAUD, C., *Histoire de l'Université de Genève: L'Académie de Calvin, 1559–1798* (Geneva, 1900)

BOURCHENIN, P., *Etude sur les Académies Protestantes en France au XVIᵉ et au XVIIᵉ siècle* (Paris, 1882)

BRANDMULLER, W., *Das Konzil von Pavia-Siena 1423–4*, ii, Quellen (Munster, 1974)

BROWN, P. H., *George Buchanan, humanist and reformer* (Edinburgh, 1890)

BRYCE, W. M., *The Scottish Grey Friars*, 2 vols. (Edinburgh, 1909)

BURNS, J. H., *Scottish Churchmen and the Council of Basle* (Glasgow, 1962)

BUXTON, L. H. D. and GIBSON, S., *Oxford University Ceremonies* (Oxford, 1935)

CAMPBELL, W., *History of the Incorporation of Cordiners in Glasgow* (Glasgow, 1883)

CANT, R. G., *The College of St. Salvator* (Edinburgh, 1950)

—— *The University of St. Andrews*, revised edition (Edinburgh, 1970)

CARRO, V. D., *La Teología y los Teológos-Juristas Españoles ante la Conquista de América*, 2 vols. (Madrid, 1944; 2nd ed., Salamanca, 1951)

CATHERINOT, N., *Annales Académiques de Bourges* (n.p., 1684)

CHARLTON, K., *Education in Renaissance England* (London, 1965)

CLELAND, J., *Statistical Tables* (Glasgow, 1823)

COBBAN, A. B., *The Medieval Universities* (London, 1975)

COHN, NORMAN, *The Pursuit of the Millennium* (London, 1957)

The College of Glasgow v. Muirhead, 1808

COLLINSON, P., *The Elizabethan Puritan Movement* (London, 1967)

COSTELLO, WILLIAM T., *The Scholastic Curriculum at Early Seventeenth Century Cambridge* (Cambridge, Massachusetts, 1958)

COULTRE, J. LE, *Maturin Cordier et les Origines de la pédagogie protestante dans les pays de langue française* (Neuchâtel, 1926)

COUTTS, JAMES, *A History of the University of Glasgow* (Glasgow, 1909)

CRAMOND, W., *The Church and Churchyard of Cullen* (Cullen, 1883)

CRESSY, D., *Education in Tudor and Stuart England* (London, 1975)

CURTIS, MARK H., *Oxford and Cambridge in Transition* (Oxford, 1959)

DICKINSON, W. C., *Two Students at St. Andrews* (St Andrews University Publications, no. 50, London, 1952)

DOHERTY, D., *The Sexual Doctrine of Cardinal Cajetan* (Regensburg, 1966)

DONALDSON, G., *Scotland: James V to James VII* (Edinburgh, 1965)

—— *The Scottish Reformation* (Cambridge, 1960)

DUNCAN, A., *Memorials of the Faculty of Physicians and Surgeons of Glasgow, 1599–1850* (Glasgow, 1896)

DUNLOP, A. I., *The Life and Times of James Kennedy, bishop of St. Andrews* (St Andrews University Publications no. 46, Edinburgh/London, 1950)

—— *The Royal Burgh of Ayr* (Edinburgh, 1953)

—— *Scots abroad in the Fifteenth Century*, Historical Association Pamphlet, no. 124 (London, 1942)

DURKAN, J., 'The Scottish Universities in the Middle Ages, 1413–1560' (unpublished Edinburgh Ph.D. thesis, 1959)

EASSON, D. E., *Gavin Dunbar* (Edinburgh, 1947)

EELES, F. C., *King's College Chapel, Aberdeen: its fittings, ornaments and ceremonial in the sixteenth century* (Aberdeen University Studies, no. 136, Aberdeen, 1956)

EHRLE, F., *Der Sentenzenkommentar Peters von Candia* (Munster, 1925)

ELIE, H., *Le Complexe Significabile* (Paris, 1937)

—— *Le Traité 'De l'Infini' de Jean Mair* (Paris, 1938)

EMDEN, A. B., *A Survey of Dominicans in England based on the Ordination and Episcopal Registers 1268–1538* (Rome, 1967)

Essays on the Scottish Reformation, ed. D. McRoberts (Glasgow, 1962)

FINLAYSON, J., *Account of the Life and Works of Maister Peter Lowe* (Glasgow, 1889)

FISCHER, Th. A., *The Scots in Germany* (Edinburgh, 1902)

Florilegium Historiale: Essays presented to Wallace K. Ferguson, edd. J. A. Rowe and W. H. Stockdale (Toronto, 1971)

FORBES, A. P., *Lives of St. Ninian and St. Kentigern* (Edinburgh, 1874)

Fortuna Domus: A Series of Lectures delivered in the University of Glasgow in commemoration of the fifth centenary of its foundation, (various contributors) (Glasgow, 1952)

FRANCISQUE-MICHEL, *Les Ecossais en France, les Français en Ecosse*, 2 vols. (London, 1862)

FRASER, A., *The Frasers of Philorth*, 3 vols. (Edinburgh, 1879)

FRASER, W., *The Lennox*, 2 vols. (Edinburgh, 1874)

—— *Memorials of the Montgomeries, Earls of Eglinton*, 2 vols. (Edinburgh, 1859)

—— *The Sutherland Book*, vol. 2 (Edinburgh, 1892)

French Renaissance Studies, 1540–70: Humanism and the Encyclopedia, ed. P. Sharratt (Edinburgh, 1976)

FRIEDE, J., and KEEN, B., *Bartolomé de las Casas in History* (De Kalb, Illinois, 1971)

GAUFRÈS, M.-J., *Claude Baduel et la Réforme des Etudes au XVIᵉ siècle* (Paris, 1880; repr. Geneva, 1969)

GAUTHIER, R. A. and JOLIF, J. Y., *L'Ethique à Nicomaque*, vols. 1 (2 parts), 2 (2 parts) (Louvain/Paris, 1970)

Eine Geschichte der Alten Fuggerbibliotheken, ed. P. Lehmann, 2 vols. (Tubingen, 1956 and 1960)

GIBSON, J. C., *Diary of Sir Michael Connal* (Glasgow, 1895)

GLORIEUX, P., *La Littérature Quodlibétique* (Bibliothèque Thomiste, ed. P. Mandonnet, vol. 21; Paris, 1935)

GRANT, A., *Story of the University of Edinburgh during its first three hundred years*, 2 vols (London, 1884)

GRAVES, F. P., *Peter Ramus and the Educational Reformation of the Sixteenth Century* (New York, 1912)

HAMILTON, G., *A History of the House of Hamilton* (Edinburgh, 1933)

HANNAY, R. K., *The College of Justice* (Edinburgh, 1933)

HARGREAVES-MAWDSLEY, W. N., *A History of Academic Dress in Europe* (Oxford, 1963)

HAY, D., *Europe: The Emergence of an Idea*, revised edition (Edinburgh, 1968)

HENDERSON, G. D., *The Founding of Marischal College, Aberdeen* (Aberdeen, 1946)

HERKLESS, J. and HANNAY, R. K., *The College of St. Leonard* (Edinburgh, 1905)

HILL, C., *Antichrist in Seventeenth Century England* (Oxford, 1971)

—— *The Intellectual Origins of the English Revolution* (Oxford, 1965)

HOOYKAAS, R., *Humanisme, Science et Réforme: Pierre de la Ramée (1515–1572)* (Leyden, 1958)

—— *Religion and the Rise of Modern Science* (Edinburgh, 1972)

HORN, D. B., *A Short History of the University of Edinburgh* (Edinburgh, 1967)

HOWELL, W. S., *Logic and Rhetoric in England, 1500–1700* (Princeton, 1956)

Humanism in France, ed. A. H. T. Levi (Manchester, 1970)

JARDINE, L., *Francis Bacon: Discovery and the Art of Discourse* (Cambridge, 1974)

KEARNEY, H., *Scholars and Gentlemen: Universities and Society in Pre-Industrial Britain, 1500–1700* (London, 1970)

KIBRE, P., *The Nations in the Medieval Universities* (Cambridge, Mass., 1948)

—— *Scholarly Privileges in the Middle Ages* (London, 1961)

KNEALE, W., and KNEALE, M., *The Development of Logic* (Oxford, 1962)

KNOX, S. J., *Walter Travers: Paragon of Elizabethan Puritanism* (London 1962)

LE COULTRE, J., *Maturin Cordier et les Origines de la pédagogie protestante dans les pays de langue française* (Neuchâtel, 1926)

LEE, M., *James Stewart, Earl of Moray, A Political Study of the Reformation in Scotland* (New York, 1953)

LEFF, G., *Paris and Oxford Universities in the Thirteenth and Fourteenth Centuries: An Institutional and Intellectual History* (New York, 1968)

LEFRANC, A., *Histoire du Collège de France* (Paris, 1893; Genève, 1970)

—— *et al., Le Collège de France, 1530–1930* (Paris, 1932)

LIEVRE, A., *Histoire des Protestants et des Eglises Réformées du Poitou*, 3 vols. (Paris, 1856–60)

LINDER, R. D., *The Political Ideas of Pierre Viret*, Travaux d'Humanisme et Renaissance no. 64 (Geneva, 1964)

LINDSAY, LORD, *Lives of the Lindsays*, 3 vols., vol. i (London, 1849)

LOHR, G. M., *Die theologischen Disputationen und Promotionen an der Universität Köln in ausgehenden 15 Jahrhundert*, Quellen und Forschungen zur Geschichte des Dominikanerordens in Deutschland, xxi (Leipzig, 1926)

LUPTON, J. H., *A Life of John Colet, D.D.* (London, 1887)

MCCRIE, T., *Life of Andrew Melville* (Edinburgh, 1899)

MACKIE, J. D., *The University of Glasgow, 1451–1951* (Glasgow, 1954)

MCLYSAGHT, E., *Irish Families: Their Names and Origins* (Dublin, 1972)

—— *More Irish Families* (Galway/Dublin, 1960)

McMillan, W., *The Worship of the Scottish Reformed Church, 1550–1638* (London, 1931)

Marchant, R. A., *The Puritans and the Church Courts in the Diocese of York, 1560–1642* (London, 1960)

Maxwell, C., *A History of Trinity College, Dublin, 1591–1892* (Dublin, 1946)

Mellon, P., *L'Académie de Sedan* (Paris, 1913)

Michalski, K., *La Philosophie au XIVe Siècle: Six Etudes*, ed. K. Flasch (Frankfurt, 1969)

Miller, P., *The New England Mind* (New York, 1939)

Milne, R., *The Blackfriars of Perth* (Edinburgh, 1893)

Morgan, A., *Scottish University Studies* (Oxford, 1933)

Moorman, J., *A History of the Franciscan Order* (Oxford, 1968)

Muirhead, J. S., *The Old Minute Book of the Faculty of Procurators, 1668–1758* (Glasgow, 1948)

Mullinger, J. B., *The University of Cambridge*, vol. 2 (Cambridge, 1884)

Murray, D., *Memories of the Old College of Glasgow* (Glasgow, 1927)

Naiden, J. R., *The Sphera of George Buchanan* (n.p. 1952)

Napier, M., *Memoirs of John Napier of Merchiston* (Edinburgh, 1834)

Nicholson, R., *Scotland: the later Middle Ages* (Edinburgh, 1974)

Nicolas, M., *Histoire de l'ancienne Académie protestante de Montauban (1598–1659) et de Puylaurens (1660–1685)* (Montauban, 1885)

Ong, W. J., *Ramus Method and the Decay of Dialogue* (Harvard, 1958)

Paatz, W., *Sceptrum Universitatis. Die europäischen Universitätsszepter*, Heidelberger Kunstgeschichtliche Abhandlungen Neue Folge (Heidelberg, 1953)

Parent, A., *Les Métiers du Livre à Paris au XVIe siècle (1535–1560)* (Paris, 1974)

Patry, R., *Philippe du Plessis-Mornay* (Paris, 1933)

Peacock, G., *Observations on the Statutes of the University of Cambridge* (Cambridge, 1841)

Pearson, A. F. S., *Thomas Cartwright and Elizabethan Puritanism, 1535–1603* (Cambridge, 1925)

Perceval-Maxwell, M., *The Scottish Migration to Ulster in the Reign of James I* (London, 1973)

Piana, C. and Cenci, C., *Promozioni agli ordini sacri a Bologna e alle dignità ecclesiastiche nel Veneto nei secoli XIV–XV*, Spicilegium Bonaventurianum, iii (Quaracchi/Florence, 1968)

Piana, C., *Ricerche su le Università di Bologna e di Parma nel secolo XV*, Spicilegium Bonaventurianum, vol. 1 (Quaracchi/Florence, 1963)

Porter, H. C., *Reformation and Reaction in Tudor Cambridge* (Cambridge, 1958)

Post, R. R., *The Modern Devotion: Confrontation with Reformation and Humanism.* Studies in Medieval Life and Thought (Leiden, 1968)

Quistorp, H., *Calvin's Doctrine of the Last Things*, translated by H. Knight (London, 1955)

Rait, R. S., *The Universities of Aberdeen* (Aberdeen, 1895)

RASHDALL, H., *The Universities of Europe in the Middle Ages*, 2nd edn., edd. by F. M. Powicke and A. B. Emden, 3 vols. (Oxford, 1936)

Reformation and Revolution, ed. D. Shaw (Edinburgh, 1967)

REID, H. M. B., *The Divinity Principals in the University of Glasgow, 1545–1654* (Glasgow, 1917)

RENAUDET, A., *Préréforme et Humanisme à Paris pendant les premières guerres d'Italie (1494–1517)*, 2nd ed. (Paris, 1953)

RENWICK, R., *Glasgow Memorials* (Glasgow, 1908)

RENWICK, R., LINDSAY, J., and EYRE-TODD, G., *History of Glasgow*, 2 vols. (Glasgow, 1921, 1931)

RICHARD, L. J., *The Spirituality of John Calvin* (Atlanta, Ga., 1974)

ROBERTS, F., *The Grammar School of Dumbarton* (Dumbarton, 1948)

RONDEAU, J., *Les Calvinistes Chatelleraudais (1559–1789)* (Châtellerault, 1907)

SCOTT, J., *A History of the Life and Death of John, Earl of Gowrie* (Edinburgh, 1818)

The Scottish Tradition: Essays in honour of Ronald Gordon Cant, ed. G. W. S. Barrow (Edinburgh, 1974)

SNOW, W. G. S., *The Times, Life and Thought of Patrick Forbes, Bishop of Aberdeen, 1618–1635* (London, 1952)

SORBELLI, A., *Storia dell'Università di Bologna* (Bologna, 1944)

SPINKA, M., *Advocates of Reform* (London, 1953)

STUBBS, J. W., *The History of the University of Dublin* (Dublin, 1889)

TIERNEY, B., *Foundations of the Conciliar Theory*, Cambridge Studies in Medieval Life and Thought, new series, 4 (Cambridge, 1955))

Tudor School Boy Life, ed. F. Watson (London, 1908)

TUVESON, E., *Millennium and Utopia—A Study in the Background of the Ideas of Progress* (Gloucester, Mass. 1972)

ULLMANN, W., *Law and Politics in the Middle Ages*, The Sources of History: Studies in the Uses of Historical Evidence, ed. G. R. Elton (London, 1975)

Universities in Politics, ed. J. W. Baldwin and R. A. Goldthwaite (Baltimore and London, 1972)

The University in Society, ed. Lawrence Stone, 2 vols. (London, 1975)

URWICK, W., *The Early History of Trinity College, Dublin, 1591–1660* (London, 1892)

VACCARI, R., *Storia della Università di Pavia* (Pavia, 1948)

VASOLI, C., *La Dialettica e la Retorica dell'Umanesimo* (Milan, 1968)

VERGER, J., *Les Universités au Moyen Age* (Paris, 1973)

Veterum Laudes, St Andrews University Publications no. 48 (Edinburgh, 1950)

VILLOSLADA, R. G., *La Universidad de Paris durante los Estudios de Francisco de Vitoria O.P. (1507–1522)*. Analecta Gregoriana XIV, Series Facultatis Historiae Ecclesiasticae Sectio B(2) (Rome, 1938)

WALLACE, W. A., *Causality and Scientific Explanation* (Ann Arbor, Michigan, 1972)

WARRACK, J., *Domestic Life in Scotland, 1488–1688* (London, 1920)

YATES, FRANCIS A., *The Art of Memory* (London, 1966)

IV Articles and Periodicals

AMATO, A. d', 'Gli atti dei capitoli generali del 1474^e del 1485', *Archivum Fratrum Praedicatorum*, xvii (Rome, 1947)

ANDERSON, J. M., 'James I of Scotland and the University of St. Andrews', *SHR*, vol. 3 (1906)

ANDERSON, P. J., *Aberdeen Friars, Red, Black, White and Grey*, Aberdeen University Studies (1909)

BAKER, D., 'Heresy and Learning in early Cistercianism', *Schism, Heresy and Religious Protest: Studies in Church History, ix*. ed. D. Baker (Cambridge, 1972)

BAXTER, J. H., 'The Philosopher Laurence of Lindores', *The Philosophical Quarterly*, v (1955)

BLACK, A., 'Heimericus de Campo: The Council and History', *Annuarium Historiae Conciliorum*, vol. 2 (Amsterdam, 1970)

BORGEAUD, C., 'Cartwright and Melville at the University of Geneva, 1569–1574', *American Historical Review*, v (1900), 284–90

BROOK, A. J. S., 'An Account of the Maces of the Universities of St. Andrews, Glasgow, Aberdeen and Edinburgh', *Proceedings of the Society of Antiquaries of Scotland*, xxvi (1891–92), 440ff.

BROTHER BONAVENTURE, 'The Popular Theology of John Ireland', *IR*, xiii (1962)

—— 'John Ireland and the Immaculate Conception', *IR*, xvii (1966)

BURRELL, S. A., 'The Apocalyptic Vision of the Early Covenanters', *SHR*, xliii (1964), 1–24

BURNS, J. H., 'The Scotland of John Major', *IR*, ii (1951)

—— 'New Light on John Major', *IR*, v (1954)

—— 'John Ireland and *The Meroure of Wyssdome*', *IR*, vi (1955)

—— 'The Conciliar Tradition in Scotland', *SHR*, vol. 42 (1963)

CAMERON, J. K. and SMART, R. N., 'A Scottish Form of the Emblème de la Religion Reformée: the post-Reformation seal of St Mary's College in the University of St. Andrews', *Proceedings of the Society of Antiquaries of Scotland*, vol. 105 (1972–74), 248–54

CAMPBELL, G. W., 'The Seals of the University of Glasgow', *Transactions of the Glasgow Archaeological Society*, new series, vol. 4 (1903)

CAMPBELL, W. M., 'The First Archbishop of Glasgow', *Records of the Scottish Church History Society*, vol. 8 (1944)

CANT, R. G., 'The St. Andrews University Thesis, 1579–1747. A Bibliographical Introduction' and 'Supplement to the St. Andrews University Theses', *Transactions of the Edinburgh Bibliographical Society*, ii (1938–45), 105–50, 265–72

CHADWICK, H., 'A Memoir of Fr. Edmund Hay, S. I.', *Archivum Historicum Societatis Jesu*, viii (1939), 66–85

CLANCHY, M. T., '*Moderni* in Education and Government in England', *Speculum*, 1 (1975)

CLOUSE, R. G., 'Johann Heinrich Alsted and English Millenarianism', *Harvard Theological Review*, vol. 62 (1969), 189–207

COOPER, J., 'The Principals of the University of Glasgow before the Reformation', *SHR*, xi (1914)

COWAN, I. B., 'The Vatican Archives', *Glasgow University Gazette*, no 74 (1974)

DASSONVILLE, M. M., 'La genèse et les principes de la dialectique de Pierre de La Ramée', *Rev. Univ. Ottawa* (1953), 322–55

DELGADO, V. M., 'La Logica en Salamanca durante la Primera Mitad del Siglo XVI', *Salmanticensis*, vol. 14 (1967)

—— 'La Logica en la Universidad de Alcalá durante la Primera Mitad del Siglo XVI', *Salmanticensis*, vol. 15 (1968)

'Diaire de Jacques Merlin ou Recueil des choses [les] plus mémorables qui se sont passées en ceste ville [de la Rochelle] de 1589 à 1620', ed. C. Dangibeaud, *Archives historiques de la Saintonge et de l'Aunis*, v (1878)

DONALDSON, GORDON, 'Aberdeen University and the Reformation', *Northern Scotland*, i, 129–42

—— 'Scottish Presbyterian Exiles in England, 1584–1588', *Records of the Scottish Church History Society*, xiv (1963), 67–80

DURKAN, J., 'Alexander Dickson and S.T.C. 6823', *The Bibliotheck*, iii, 183–90 (1962)

—— 'George Buchanan: Some French Connections', *The Bibliotheck*, iv, 66–72 (1963)

—— 'An Arbroath book inventory of 1473', *The Bibliotheck*, vol. iv (1963)

—— 'Some Local Heretics', *Transactions of the Dumfriesshire and Galloway Natural History and Antiquarian Society*, vol. 36 (Dumfries, 1959) .

—— Review of *Acta Facultatis Artium Universitatis Sanctiandree 1413–1588*, by A. I. Dunlop, in *English Historical Review*, vol. 81 (1966)

—— 'John Major: After 400 Years', *IR*, vol. 1 (1950)

—— 'Robert Cockburn, Bishop of Ross and French Humanism', *IR*, vol. 4 (1953)

—— 'St. Andrews University Medieval Theological Statutes: Revised Dating Suggested', *IR*, vol. 13 (1962)

—— 'Scots National Feeling at Constance and Siena', *IR*, vol. 17 (1966)

—— 'Notes on Glasgow Cathedral', *IR*, vol. 21, 46–76 (1970)

—— 'Archbishop Robert Blackadder's Will', *IR*, vol. 23 (1972)

—— 'St. Andrews in the John Law Chronicle', *IR*, vol. 25 (1974)

—— 'The Great Fire at Glasgow Cathedral', *IR*, vol. 26 (1975), 89–92

EASSON, D. E., 'The Lollards of Kyle', *Juridical Review*, vol. 48 (1936)

ELIE, H., 'Quelques Maîtres de l'université de Paris vers l'an 1500', *Archives d'histoire doctrinale et littéraire du Moyen Age*, vol. 18 (1951)

FLETCHER, J. M., 'The Teaching of Arts at Oxford', *Paedagogica Historica*, vol. 7 (Ghent, 1967)

GAGNE, J., 'Du Quadrivium zux Scientiae Mediae', *Actes du Quatrième Congrès Internationale de Philosophie Médiévale* (Montreal/Paris, 1969)

GANOCZY, A., 'Jean Major, exegete gallican', *Recherches de Science religieuse*, vol. 56 (Paris, 1968)

GESCHER, F., 'Die Statuten der theologischen Fakultat an der alten Universität

Q

Köln, *Festschrift zur Erinnerung an die Grundung der alten Universität Köln im Jahre 1388* (Cologne, 1938)

GLORIEUX, P., 'L'Enseignement au Moyen Age', *Archives d'histoire doctrinale et littéraire du Moyen Age*, vol. 43 (1968)

HAY, G. and MCROBERTS, D., 'The Rossdhu Book of Hours', *IR*, vol. 16 (1965)

HRABAR, V. E., 'Le droit politique et le droit international dans les Questions de Jean Mair sur les Sentences de Pierre Lombard', *Académie des Sciences Oukrainienne* (Kiev, 1927)

KIBRE, P., 'Academic Oaths at the university of Paris in the Middle Ages', *Essays in Medieval Life and Thought presented in honour of Austin Patterson Evans*, edd. by J. H. Mundy, R. W. Emery and B. N. Nelson (New York, 1955)

KIRK, J., 'The Influence of Calvinism on the Scottish Reformation', *Records of the Scottish Church History Society*, xviii (1974), 157–79

KIRKPATRICK, J., 'The Scottish Nation at the University of Orleans', *Miscellany of the Scottish History Society*, ii (Edinburgh, 1904)

KOEPPLER, H., 'Frederick Barbarossa and the Schools of Bologna', *English Historical Review*, vol. 54 (1939)

KRISTELLER, P. O., 'L'Etat présent des études sur Marsile Ficin,' in *Platon et Aristote à la Renaissance, XVIᵉ Colloque international de Tours* (Paris, 1976)

LITTLE, A. G., 'Introduction of the Observant Friars into England', *Proceedings of the British Academy*, vol. 10 (1924); vol. 27 (1941)

LOHR, C. H., 'Medieval Latin Aristotle commentaries', *Traditio*, vol. 27 (1971)

LYALL, R. J., 'Alexander Barclay and the Edwardian Reformation 1548–52', *Review of English Studies*, New ser., vol. 20 (1969)

MCFARLANE, I. D., 'Notes on the Composition and Reception of George Buchanan's Psalm Paraphrases', *Forum for Modern Language Studies: Renaissance Studies*, vii, no. 4 (1971), 319–60

—— 'George Buchanan and French Humanism', *Humanism in France at the end of the Middle Ages and in the early Renaissance*, ed. A. H. T. Levi, 295–319 (Manchester, 1970)

MACFARLANE, L. J., 'William Elphinstone's Library', *Aberdeen University Review*, vol. 37 (1957–58)

—— 'William Elphinstone, founder of the university of Aberdeen', *Aberdeen University Review*, vol. 39 (1961–62), 1–18

—— 'The Primacy of the Scottish Church', *IR*, vol. 20 (1969)

MCNEILL, W. A., 'Scottish Entries in the *Acta Rectoria Universitatis Parisiensis* 1519 to *c.* 1633', *Scottish Historical Review*, vol. 43 (1964), 66–86

MCRAE, K. D., 'Ramist Tendencies in the Thought of Jean Bodin', *Journal of the History of Ideas*, xvi (1955), 306–23

—— 'A Postscript on Bodin's Connections with Ramism', *Journal of the History of Ideas*, xxiv (1963), 569–71

MCROBERTS, D., 'The Manse of Stobo in 1542, Part 2', *IR* vol. 22 (1971)

MAGOUN, F. P., 'Football in Medieval England', *American Historical Review*, vol. 35 (1929)

MARKOWSKI, M., 'Studien zu den Krakauer mittelalterlichen Physikkommentaren: die Impetustheorie', *Archives d'histoire doctrinale et littéraire du Moyen Age*, xxxv (1969)

MEEK, D. E. and KIRK, J., 'John Carswell, Superintendent of Argyll: a reassessment', *Records of the Scottish Church History Society*, xix (1975), 1–22

MEERSSEMAN, G., 'Les origines parisiennes de l'albertisme colonais', *Archives d'histoire doctrinale et littéraire du Moyen Age*, vii (1932)

MICHAUD-QUANTIN, P., 'La conscience d'être membre d'une universitas', *Miscellanea Mediaevalia: Beiträge zum Berufsbewusstein des mittelalterlichen Menschen*, ed. P. Wilpert, vol. 3 (Berlin, 1964)

MOONAN, L., 'Lawrence of Lindores on Life in the Living Being', *Classica et Mediaevalia*, xxvii (1966)

OAKLEY, F., 'Almain and Major: Conciliar Theory on the Eve of the Reformation', *American Historical Review*, vol. 70 (1965)

—— 'From Constance to 1688: The Political Thought of John Major and George Buchanan', *Journal of British Studies*, vol. i (1962)

POST, G., 'Alexander III, the *Licentia docendi* and the rise of universities', *Anniversary Essays in Medieval History by Students of Charles Homer Haskins* (Boston/New York, 1929)

—— 'Parisian Masters as a Corporation', *Speculum*, vol. 9 (1934)

—— *et al.*, 'The Medieval Heritage of a Humanistic Ideal: "Scientia Donum Dei est, unde vendi non potest" ', *Traditio*, vol. 11 (New York, 1955)

QUYNN, D. M., 'The Early Career of John Gordon, Dean of Salisbury', *Bibliothèque d'Humanisme et Renaissance: Travaux et Documents*, vii (Paris, 1945), 118–38

RANKIN, R., 'A Missing Manuscript of Robert Boyd', *The College Courant: The Journal of Glasgow University Graduates Association*, vol. 25, (no. 50) (1973), 10–17

RAIT, R. S., 'Andrew Melville and the Revolt against Aristotle in Scotland', *English Historical Review*, xiv (1899), 250–60

ROOVER, R. de, 'La Pensée économique de Jean Mair', *Journal des Savants*, vol. 109 (1970)

ROSS, A., 'Notes on the Religious Orders in Pre-Reformation Scotland', *Essays on the Scottish Reformation*, ed. D. McRoberts (Glasgow, 1962)

SHARRATT, P. (ed), 'Nicolaus Nancelius, *Petri Rami Vita*', *Humanistica Lovaniensia*, xxiv (1975) 161–277

—— 'The Present State of Studies on Ramus', *Studi Francesi*, 47–8 (1972), 201–13

SHAW, D., 'Laurence of Lindores', *Records of the Scottish Church History Society*, xii (1954–56)

SPRUNGER, K. L., 'Ames, Ramus and the method of puritan theology', *Harvard Theological Review*, vol. 59 (1966), 133–51

STEIN, P., 'Roman Law in Scotland', *Ius Romanum Medii Aevi*, part 5 (13b) (Milan, 1968)

SWANSON, R., 'The University of St. Andrews and the Great Schism', *Journal of Ecclesiastical History*, vol. 26 (Cambridge, 1975)

Swiezawski, S., 'Le problème de la "via antiqua" et de la "via moderna" au XVe siècle et ses fondements idéologiques', *Miscellanea Mediaevalia*, vol. 9. *Antiqui et Moderni*, ed. A. Zimmermann (Berlin/New York, 1974)

Thomson, J. A. F., 'Innocent VIII and the Scottish Church', *IR*, vol. 20 (1969)

—— 'Papalism and Conciliarism in Antonio Rosselli's *Monarchia*', *Mediaeval Studies*, vol. 37 (Toronto, 1975)

Torrance, T. F., 'La Philosophie et la Théologie de Jean Mair ou Major', *Archives de la Philosophie*, vols., 32–3 (1969–70)

Vereecke, L., 'Jean Mair: Un acte permis mais scabreux', *Mariage et Sexualité au declin du Moyen Age*, Supplément de *La Vie Spirituelle*, vol. 14, (Paris, 1961)

—— 'La licéité du *cambium bursae* chez Jean Mair', *Revue historique de droit français et étranger*, ser. 4, vol. 30 (1952)

Wallace, W. A., 'The "Calculatores" in Early Sixteenth Century Physics', *British Journal for the History of Science*, vol. 4 (1969)

—— 'The Enigma of Domingo de Soto', *Isis*, vol. 59 (Berkeley, Cal., 1968)

Watt, D. E. R., 'Scottish Masters and Students at Paris in the 14th Century', *Aberdeen University Review*, vol. 36 (1955)

—— 'University Clerks and Rolls of Petitions for Benefices', *Speculum*, vol. 34 (1959)

Weisheipl, J. A., 'The Structure of the Arts Faculty in the Medieval Universities', *British Journal of Educational Studies*, vol. 19 (1971)

—— 'Curriculum of the Faculty of Arts at Oxford in the early Fourteenth Century', *Mediaeval Studies*, vol. 26 (1964)

—— 'Classification of the Sciences in Mediaeval Thought', *Mediaeval Studies*, vol. 27 (1965)

Index

Personal names composed of a forename, immediately followed by 'de' or 'of' and a place-name, are inverted, e.g. Essy, Robert de; those composed of a surname, followed by 'de' or 'of' and a place-name, are not inverted, e.g. Ross of Hawkhead.

Saints' names are assembled alphabetically under 'St'.

Abbreviations: Aber—Aberdeen; App.—Appendix; G—Glasgow; St A—St Andrews; U *or* u.—University; UG—University of Glasgow.

Important references are given in **bold** type.

474 INDEX